History of the

Town of Exeter

New Hampshire

Charles H. Bell

HERITAGE BOOKS
2015

HERITAGE BOOKS
AN IMPRINT OF HERITAGE BOOKS, INC.

Books, CDs, and more—Worldwide

For our listing of thousands of titles see our website
at
www.HeritageBooks.com

A Facsimile Reprint
Published 2015 by
HERITAGE BOOKS, INC.
Publishing Division
5810 Ruatan Street
Berwyn Heights, Md. 20740

Originally published:
Press of J. E. Farwell & Co.
Boston
1888

— Publisher's Notice —
In reprints such as this, it is often not possible to remove blemishes from the original. We feel the contents of this book warrant its reissue despite these blemishes and hope you will agree and read it with pleasure.

International Standard Book Numbers
Paperbound: 978-1-55613-304-6
Clothbound: 978-0-917-89014-7

PREFACE.

My chief aim in preparing this history has been to make it useful. I have quoted largely from the manuscript records of the town, because they are liable to be destroyed, and what is in print is safe. For the same reason, and for the benefit of genealogists, I have given many lists of early names.

A town history is valuable almost in proportion to the accessibility of its contents. For the sake of ease of reference I have made a general classification of subjects in the present work; have introduced numerous sub-titles; have arranged all considerable lists of names in alphabetical order; have given a full table of contents at the beginning and a sufficient index at the end. Classification necessitates some repetition, but that is of small consequence in comparison with the advantages of the method.

A complete genealogical history of Exeter is a desideratum. But it would be a work of years. In this volume will be found all the information deemed most valuable to the investigator of family history, which is contained in the records of the town; to wit: all the " family registers " in any books; all the marriages and births in the first (oldest) book, and all the deaths in the same, before the year 1800.

In addition to these I have added, from other sources, the following: excerpts from the records of old Norfolk county, Massachusetts; a list of all the baptisms of children in Exeter, by the Rev. Woodbridge Odlin, between 1743 and 1763; a list of all the publishments of intentions of marriage in the town between 1783 and 1800. These lists may properly be termed *new*, as they are taken from manuscripts which have not been open to public inspection.

The orthography of proper names has been a source of perplexity. A uniform rule is hard to fix and harder to follow. In spite of the best intentions variations have crept in. My only consolation is that I have probably not spelt names in half so many ways as their owners did.

My thanks are especially due to Professor Bradbury L. Cilley for the unlimited use of the manuscripts of his grandfather, the Hon. John Kelly, and of the late William Smith, Esq., each of whom planned a history of the town; also to John Ward Dean, Esq., of Boston, and to my townsmen Messrs. George W. Dearborn, John T. Perry, William H. Belknap, Edward Giddings and many others who have most obligingly aided me in obtaining information.

It would be idle to suppose that this work is free from mistakes. In writing the history of a town the difficulties may be said to be in a direct ratio to the remoteness of the period treated of. Exeter being two hundred and fifty years old, the information respecting it has had to be gleaned from a multitude of sources, and the liabilities to errors of all kinds are correspondingly increased. The greatest care and pains have been bestowed, however, to insure accuracy, and it is hoped that mistakes will not be found to be numerous or important.

My townsmen will of course note many omissions, due for the most part to limited time and space. It is not believed that they will seriously detract from the value of the work to others.

CHARLES H. BELL.

CONTENTS.

MUNICIPAL.

CHAPTER I.

EXETER AS AN INDEPENDENT REPUBLIC. — The Rev. John Wheelwright; the deeds from the Indians; the disputed Indian deed of 1629; trials of the opening year; the first church; another Indian deed; the Combination; the first criminal proceeding; the Elders' oath; the oath of the people; first allotment of lands; notices of early settlers; early enactments. . . . . 3 — 43

CHAPTER II.

EXETER UNDER THE MASSACHUSETTS GOVERNMENT. — The conditions of annexation; the fishery; the care of the cattle; the staple commodity; project for a change of government; number and names of inhabitants. . . . . 44 — 61

CHAPTER III.

EXETER UNDER THE NEW HAMPSHIRE PROVINCIAL GOVERNMENT. — Gove's rebellion against Cranfield; Robert Tufton Mason's land suits; resistance to illegal taxation; the province without a government; specimens of early town accounts; the mast-tree riot of 1734; a disorderly election; demonstration against the stamp act; patriotic action of the town in 1770; another patriotic expression of the town; help for the suffering poor of Boston; the census of 1775; the earliest written Constitution. . . . . 62 — 89

CHAPTER IV.

EXETER UNDER THE STATE GOVERNMENT. — The Association test of 1776; first reading of the Declaration of Independence; the evils of a paper currency; the paper money mob of 1786; the Convention for the adoption of the Federal Constitution; the visit of Washington; court-house, fire engine, library, etc.; honors to the memory of Washington; temperance; War of 1812; prayer in town meetings; support of the poor; celebration of bi-centennial anniversary; re-naming streets; new court-house; lighting streets; sidewalks; steam fire engine; water works. . . . . 90 — 111

CHAPTER V.

BOUNDARIES AND DIVISIONS; ROADS AND BRIDGES. — The Hampton bound of 1653; the Dover bound of 1653; Captain Thomas Wiggin's deed of gift; enlargement of Exeter bounds; Squamscót Patent under Exeter government; townships carved from Exeter territory; highways, their location, laying out and repairs; bridges; the village streets.
112 — 128

CHAPTER VI.

THE COMMON LANDS. — Lands of Edward and William Hilton; grants of town lands; list of distributees of land as reported in 1725; proceedings to hasten a distribution; final distribution. . . . 129 — 146

CHAPTER VII.

OFFICERS OF THE TOWN. — List of town officers: rulers; assistant rulers; town clerks; selectmen; moderators; representatives. 147 — 152

ECCLESIASTICAL.

CHAPTER VIII.

THE FIRST RELIGIOUS SOCIETY. — Attempts to get a pastor, after Mr. Wheelwright's departure; Mr. Dudley engaged; new house of worship; difficulty of paying salary; fears of losing Mr. Dudley; death of Mr. Dudley; Elder Wentworth temporarily employed. . . 155 — 170

CHAPTER IX.

THE FIRST SOCIETY AND ITS OFFSHOOTS. — A new meeting-house; re-organization of the church; death of Mr. Clark; engagement of Mr. John Odlin; parish of Newmarket set off; a new meeting-house; Epping parish set off; Brentwood parish set off; Rev. Woodbridge Odlin, colleague; second parish incorporated; succession of pastors, Isaac Mansfield, William F. Rowland, John Smith, William Williams, Joy H. Fairchild, Roswell D. Hitchcock, William D. Hitchcock, Nathaniel Lasell, Elias Nason, John O. Barrows, Swift Byington. 171 — 193

CHAPTER X.

THE SECOND PARISH; OTHER RELIGIOUS SOCIETIES. — Rev. Daniel Rogers; his epitaph; Joseph Brown; Isaac Hurd; Asa Mann; Orpheus T. Lanphear; John W. Chickering, Jr.; George E. Street; Quakers; the Baptist society; the Universalist society; the Christian society; the Methodist society; the Advent society; the Roman Catholic society; the Unitarian society; the Episcopal society. 194 — 211

MILITARY.

CHAPTER XI.

THE INDIAN AND FRENCH WARS. — Philip's war; King William's war; services of Exeter men; a fortunate escape; Queen Anne's war; Colonel Winthrop Hilton's expeditions; his death; occurrences of 1712; assault upon the Rollins family; the Louisburg expedition; roll of Captain Light's company; occurrences of 1746; the Crown Point expeditions; Captain Nathaniel Folsom at Lake George; capitulation of Fort William Henry; inventory of Major John Gilman's losses; later expeditions against French posts; the Exeter Cadets. . . . 215 — 239

CHAPTER XII.

THE REVOLUTION AND THE WAR OF 1812. — The powder from Fort William and Mary; the Exeter volunteers march to Cambridge; Exeter soldiers in 1775; in 1776; in 1777; in 1778; in 1779; in 1780; in 1781; supplies furnished by the town to soldiers' families; the War of 1812; roll of Captain Nathaniel Gilman's company; roll of Captain James Thom's company. . . . . 240 — 259

CHAPTER XIII.

THE WAR FOR THE UNION. — Exeter soldiers in the several New Hampshire regiments; in the military or naval service. Notices of officers, Gen. Gilman Marston; Lieutenant Colonel Henry H. Pearson; Lieutenant Colonel Moses N. Collins; Captain Albert M. Perkins. . 260 — 282

EDUCATIONAL.

CHAPTER XIV.

THE SCHOOLS AND ACADEMIES. — Law of Massachusetts and New Hampshire; list of early instructors; town orders concerning schools; formation of school districts; the Robinson Female Seminary; the Phillips Exeter Academy; the Female Academy. . . . 285 — 300

CHAPTER XV.

THE PRESS. — The earliest newspaper; first New Testament printed in the State; samples of early journalism; the News-Letter; the Gazette and present publications; contributors to the press. . . 301 — 314

INDUSTRIAL.

CHAPTER XVI.

MILLS AND MANUFACTURES. — The first saw-mill; Pickpocket falls granted; Crawley's falls; Pickpocket; paper-mills; powder-mills; "falls of the Squamscot;" Exeter Manufacturing Company; other water-mills. 317 — 334

CONTENTS.

CHAPTER XVII.

BUSINESS AND TRADE. — Lumbering; ship-building; pottery; duck manufactory; saddlery and carriages; hats; wool; leather; the earlier merchants; banks; insurance companies. . . . . 335—348

BIOGRAPHICAL.

CHAPTER XVIII.

JUDGES AND LAWYERS. — John Gilman; Robert Wadleigh; Kinsley Hall; Peter Coffin; Richard Hilton; Nicholas Gilman; Samuel Gilman; Nicholas Perryman; Noah Emery; William Parker; John Pickering; Oliver Peabody; Nathaniel Parker; George Sullivan; Moses Hodgdon; Solon Stevens; Jeremiah Smith; James Thom; Joseph Tilton; Jotham Lawrence; Stephen Peabody; Jeremiah Fellowes; George Lamson; William Smith; Oliver W. B. Peabody; John Sullivan; Samuel T. Gilman; James Bell; John Kelly; Timothy Farrar; Amos Tuck; Henry F. French; John S. Wells; William W. Stickney; Alva Wood; George C. Peavey; other lawyers. . . . . 349—377

CHAPTER XIX.

MEDICAL MEN. — Thomas Deane; Josiah Gilman; Dudley Odlin; Robert Gilman; Eliphalet Hale; John Giddinge; John Odlin; Nathaniel Gilman; Caleb G. Adams; Joseph Tilton; Samuel Tenney; Nathaniel Peabody; William Parker, Jr., Nathan North; William Perry; David W. Gorham; Samuel B. Swett; other physicians. . . 378—389

CHAPTER XX.

FAMILIES AND INDIVIDUALS. — Dudley family; Folsom family; Leavitt family; Thing family; Conner family; Lyford family; Robinson family; Smith families; Odlin family; Barker, Colcord, Dolloff, Kimball, Shute and others. Jonathan Cass; Enoch Poor; John Rogers; James Burley; Samuel Hatch; Seth Walker; Joseph Pearson; Waddy V. Cobbs; John C. Long. The colored population. . . . 390—399

MISCELLANEOUS.

CHAPTER XXI.

HOMICIDES; BURIAL-PLACES; THE "WHITE CAPS."— Mrs. Willix; Johnson; John Wadleigh; Mrs. Ferguson; first four public burial-places; the cemetery; other burial-places. The "White caps;" their search for hidden treasure. . . . . . . 403—414

CONTENTS.

CHAPTER XXII.

THINGS NEW AND OLD.—Trees; the oldest elm; early houses; the Clifford house; Dean house; Ladd house; Rowland house; Odiorne house; Hildreth house; Peabody house; Gilman house; Tilton house; other old houses; statistics; societies; localities. . . 415—428

APPENDIX.

I. The Indian deed of 1629 to Wheelwright and others. II. Transcripts of the Exeter Records, 1639 to 1644. III. Extracts from Hon. Jeremiah Smith's bi-centennial address, 1838. . . . . 431—469

GENEALOGICAL.

FAMILY REGISTERS, from the Exeter Records. MARRIAGES, from the Exeter Records. BIRTHS, from the town Records. DEATHS, prior to the year 1800, from the town Records. BIRTHS, DEATHS AND MARRIAGES from the earliest town Records. MARRIAGES, BIRTHS AND DEATHS from the Records of old Norfolk county, in Massachusetts. BAPTISMS of children in the First society, from 1743 to 1763. PUBLISHMENTS of intentions of marriage, from 1783 to 1800. . . . 3—82

CORRECTIONS.

Page 149, Thomas Deane, Nathaniel Webster and Josiah Gilman were selectmen in 1741.
" 151, John Gilman was representative in 1697 as well as in 1693.
" 219, line 38, for Huntson, read Huntoon.
" 220, note, for Edward, read Nathaniel, Swasey.
" 239, line 13, for lieutenant, Colonel, read lieutenant colonel.

ILLUSTRATIONS.

Fac-simile of Exeter "Combination" drawn July 4, 1639; re-subscribed April 2, 1640 . . . . . Frontis.
Plan of the village of Exeter in 1802 . . . . Page 103
Plan of the township of Exeter in 1802 . . . . .
Exeter with its sub-divisions . . . . . " 121

MUNICIPAL.

HISTORY OF EXETER.

CHAPTER I.

EXETER AS AN INDEPENDENT REPUBLIC.

THE river Pascataqua which forms the bound, next the sea, between New Hampshire and Maine, may, with its tributaries, be rudely represented by a man's left hand and wrist laid upon a table, back upwards and fingers wide apart. The thumb would stand for the Salmon Falls or Newichwannock river, the forefinger for Bellamy river, the second finger for Oyster river, the third for Lamprey river and the fourth for Exeter or Squamscot river; while the palm of the hand would represent the Great Bay, into which most of those streams pour their waters, and the wrist the Pascataqua proper.

Before the foundation of Exeter there were but two organized settlements within the limits of New Hampshire, the one at the mouth of the Pascataqua about Strawberry Bank, now Portsmouth; the other about Dover at the confluence of the Salmon Falls and the Pascataqua. Both settlements were straggling, small and weak, being wholly self-ruled, for as yet there was no general government in New Hampshire. The Europeans who composed the population had most of them come thither to better their worldly condition by fishery and trade, and with no purpose of a religious character. The greater number of them were bred in the English church, and had little sympathy with the Puritans of the Massachusetts Bay.

Besides the inhabitants of these two settlements there were a few scattered dwellers along the Pascataqua and its affluents. Two of the most prominent of these, Edward Hilton and Thomas Wiggin, belong to Exeter history. Hilton was originally a fishmonger in the city of London, and emigrated to this country in 1623, doubtless with the expectation of engaging in the fishery here. He settled in Dover at what is now styled the Point, and after seven years obtained from the Council of Plymouth, under the authority of the British Crown, a grant of lands on the upper

Pascataqua, known as the Hilton or Squamscot Patent. It embraced Dover Point and a belt of territory south of the Pascataqua and east of the Squamscot, three miles in breadth, and extending to the falls of the latter river, at what is now Exeter. This grant afterwards passed into the hands of a company who appointed Captain Thomas Wiggin their agent.

Hilton and Wiggin had before 1640 both quitted Dover, and planted themselves on opposite sides of the Squamscot, and within three or four miles of the falls. There they were found by the company who settled Exeter, on their arrival, or soon afterward, Hilton domiciled in what is now South Newmarket, and Wiggin in what is now Stratham. Both were men of enterprise and natural leaders, and each, no doubt, had his retainers about him. Hilton was attached, in a quiet way, to the observances of the English church, and, consequently, was held in small consideration by the Puritan authorities of the Massachusetts Bay, when they came subsequently to rule over the New Hampshire settlements. Wiggin's religious professions harmonized more nearly with their own, and he consequently enjoyed a much greater share of their approbation and confidence.

If we are to credit tradition there were three other persons dwelling at the falls of the Squamscot before the arrival of the company of Wheelwright in 1638. These were Ralph Hall, Thomas Leavitt and Thomas Wilson, all of whom were located on the eastern side of the river, while most of the other early comers chose the western side. Hall and Leavitt were young men, and may, for aught we know, have been the pioneers of the settlement; but the antecedents of Wilson leave little room to doubt that he was of Wheelwright's company.

The falls of the Squamscot, round which the village of Exeter has clustered from the beginning, are formed by the passage of a beautiful inland stream over a succession of ledges into a broad basin below, where its waters mingle with the tides from the sea. This was a well known fishing place of the Indians. The country around was covered, for the most part, with dense forests, broken here and there by tracts of natural meadow, and by marshes bordering upon the tide-water.

On the third day of April, 1638, the Rev. John Wheelwright purchased by a deed from the local sagamore and his son, a release of the right of the Indian occupants to this locality and to a tract of the surrounding country, thirty miles in extent, reaching from the northern boundary of the Massachusetts Bay on the south, to the Pascataqua patents on the east, and on the north to Oyster river. His purpose in making the purchase was to begin a settlement, to which he gave the name of Exeter.*

THE REV. JOHN WHEELWRIGHT.

Mr. Wheelwright, who is justly styled the founder of Exeter, deserves a more extended notice. He was born in or near the hamlet of Saleby in Lincolnshire, England, probably in the early part of the year 1592. His father was a man of sufficient means to afford him a university education, and to leave him heir to some freehold property. At Sidney College, Cambridge, he gained his bachelor's degree in 1614, and that of M. A. four years later. One of his fellow collegians was the famous Oliver Cromwell, who afterwards bore testimony to his athletic vigor and pluck, "that he was more afraid of meeting Wheelwright at football than he had been since of meeting an army in the field, for he was infallibly sure of being tripped up by him." Mr. Wheelwright was married on the eighth of November, 1621, to Marie, daughter of the Rev. Thomas Storre, vicar of Bilsby, in the county of Lincoln; and on the ninth of April, 1623, having taken holy orders, on the death of his father-in-law, succeeded him in the vicarage. He is described as a faithful and zealous minister; but like many able and conscientious men of his time, he was led to question the authority of certain dogmas and observances of the English church, until he found himself at length arrayed in the ranks of the Puritans, so that after about ten years he was silenced by the ecclesiastical powers, for non-conformity. He continued to reside in England for two or three years afterwards and then emigrated to the new world. He took with him his wife by a second marriage, Mary, daughter of Edward Hutchinson of Alford, and his five children, and landed in Boston on the twenty-sixth of May, 1636.

There he soon became highly esteemed, insomuch that after about six months, it was proposed by some of the members of the Boston church that he should be settled over them as a second teacher, in conjunction with the Rev. John Wilson and the Rev.

---

*Of course this name was borrowed from Exeter in England. The cause of its selection is unknown. There is no evidence that Wheelwright ever had any acquaintance with the English Exeter, and the only one of his companions who is known to have come from that place, or its vicinity, was Godfrey Dearborn.

John Cotton, two of the most eminent divines of the colony. But upon some objection being made to this, Mr. Wheelwright was placed in charge of a new church gathered at Mount Wollaston, afterwards Braintree and now Quincy; and received a grant of two hundred acres of land there.

About this time Anne Hutchinson, a woman of keen wit and dominant disposition, the wife of William Hutchinson, a brother of Wheelwright's second wife, rendered herself a conspicuous figure in the religious circles of Boston. With the fondness for theological speculations which was characteristic of that age, she had adopted some opinions not in unison with those of the majority of the ministers and elders of the Massachusetts Bay, and was in the habit of enunciating them in the shape of criticisms on their sermons and doctrines, at weekly meetings of the sisterhood held at her house in Boston. These heterodox opinions were the merest theoretic abstractions imaginable, such as that "the person of the Holy Ghost dwells in a justified person," and that " no sanctification can help to evidence to us our justification," and the like, and had no possible relation to the practical concerns of life. Their opponents, however, gave them the bad name of "Antinomian." But Wheelwright also professed the same views in the main, and Cotton timidly indorsed them, while a large proportion of the members of the Boston church approved them. All this was bitterly unpalatable to the authorities of church and state (who were substantially the same) in the Massachusetts Bay, and they took counsel together how to suppress the rising heresy. Excommunication of the offenders was the obvious remedy; but as by far the greater part of the Boston church were in sympathy with them, there was danger that in the attempt to apply that remedy the movers might find themselves victims instead of victors. They therefore resolved on other and safer measures.

Apparently every utterance of Wheelwright was strictly watched, to find cause of accusation against him. At length the desired pretext was obtained, in a sermon which he preached on a Fast day in Boston, on the nineteenth of January, 1636-7. It is impossible for any unprejudiced person of our time to discover in this production, which is still extant, anything to cause alarm to the most timorous heart, but to the jaundiced eyes of the Massachusetts rulers of that day, it seemed to be filled with threatenings of ruin and destruction. And they determined that out of his discourse they would find matter for his condemnation. It would require too much space to follow in detail the various proceedings which they instituted against Wheelwright. First, the great and General Court, backed by an advisory counsel of the clergy, pronounced him guilty of "sedition and contempt of the civil authority." Wheelwright was not daunted by this. The next application was a synod of the clergy of the colony, who, after a laborious session of twenty-four days, condemned no less than eighty-two erroneous opinions, which they alleged had been brought to New England and "spread underhand there." Wheelwright attended the meetings of the synod, and, of course, understood very well that its conclusions were in effect, if not by name, a condemnation of his position and course; but he did not swerve a hair's breadth for that. Then his prosecutors determined to oust him by force. The General Court was to be the instrument; and in order to make sure of a majority of deputies who would perform their behests, the authorities resorted to the extraordinary course of a special election. Before this tribunal, thus organized to convict, Wheelwright appeared and pleaded not guilty. To such a trial there could be but one ending. For the offences of which he had previously been found guilty, " and for now justifying himself and his former practice, being to the disturbance of the civil peace," he was by the court disfranchised and banished.

Wheelwright was not the only victim. Mrs. Hutchinson also was banished from the colony, and several of their adherents were "disarmed"— deprived of all weapons — an ignominious and harsh punishment at that time when the means of protection and defence were so essential. Thus one of the earliest acts of those who emigrated hither to obtain their religious freedom, was to establish a religious despotism. The poor pretence that the act was necessary for the maintenance of "the civil peace," finds no justification in any fact which the most prejudiced apologist has been able to urge in its favor.

The sentence against Wheelwright was pronounced early in November, 1637, and he was allowed two weeks to depart out of the jurisdiction. Much to the surprise of many, instead of accompanying his sister-in-law to Rhode Island, where he would have been welcomed to an asylum of religious freedom, he turned his face towards the far less inviting solitude of the falls of the Squamscot. It is probable that he sailed from Boston to the mouth of the Pascataqua in a coaster belonging to John Clark, afterwards of Rhode Island, one of his sympathizers; and then made his difficult way overland to his destination. The succeeding inclement season he must have passed in the rude cabin of some neighboring settler, perhaps that of Edward Hilton. It was a bitter winter, and the snow covered the ground to the depth of three feet, from the fourth of November to the fifth of the following March.

But no sooner were the icy chains of winter loosed, than the resolute and indefatigable Wheelwright began to bestir himself in making preparations for his new settlement.

THE DEEDS FROM THE INDIANS.

The release of the Indians' right to the lands in and about Exeter was contained in two deeds which are still preserved, and are here given, with the original orthography and contractions.

Know all men by these presents that I Wehanownowit Sagamore of piskatoquake for good considerations me therevnto mouing & for certen comodys which I have received have graunted & sould vnto John Whelewright of piscatoquake, Samuel Hutchinson & Augustine Stor of Boston Edward Calcord & Darby Field of piscatoquake & John Compton of Roxbury and Nicholas Needome of Mount Walliston all the right title & interest in all such lands, woods, meadows, riuers, brookes springs as of right belong vnto me from Merimack riuer to the patents of piscatoquake bounded wch the South East side of piscatoquake patents & so to goe into the Country north West thirty miles as far as oyster riuer to haue & to hold the same to them & their heires forever, onely the ground w^h is broken up excepted. & that it shall be lawfull for the said Sagamore to hunt & fish & foul in the said limits. In Witness whereof I haue hereunto set my hand the 3^d day of April 1638.

  Signed & possession giuen. These being present

    James Wall.
    James, his m'ke   Wehanownowit his m'ke.
     his W. C. m'ke.
    William Cole
     his M m'ke.
    Lawrence Cowpland

Know all men by these p'sents y^t I Wehanownowitt Sagamore of Puschataquake for a certajne some of money to mee in hand payd & other m'chandable comodities wch I haue recd as likewise for other good causes & considerations mee y^r unto spetially mouing

haue granted barganed alienated & sould vnto John Wheelewright of Pischataqua & Augustine Storr of Bostone all those Lands woods Medowes Marshes rivers brookes springs with all the app^{r}tenances emoluments pfitts comoditys there unto belonging lying and situate within three miles of the Northerne side of ye river Meremake extending thirty miles along by the river from the sea side & from the sayd river side to Pischataqua Patents thirty Miles vp into the countrey North West & soe from the ffalls of Pischataqua to Oyster river thirty Miles square ev^{r}y way, to haue & to hould the same to them & y^r heyres for euer only the ground wch is broaken vp is excepted & it shall bee lawfull for ye sayd Sagamore to hunt fish & foule in the sayd lymitts. In witnesse w^{r}of I have hereunto sett my hand & seale the third day of Aprill 1638.
  Signed sealed & deliv^{r}ed &
possession given in the p^{r}sence of
  James his m'ke   Aspamabough
                    his m'ke
  Edward Calcord   Wehanownowit his m'ke.
  Nicholas Needham   Pummadockyon* his m'ke.
  William Furbar   the Sagamore's son

It will be observed that in the description of the premises released, the main difference between these two instruments was in regard to the southern boundary; in the former deed it was a line three miles north of the Merrimac river; in the latter it was the river itself. The occasion of this duplication of the title-deeds was, in all likelihood, the want of knowledge of the exact location of the northern limit of Massachusetts; and the intention was to claim to that limit, and to rely on whichever of the deeds the better sustained that claim.

The change of grantees named in the deeds indicates that there could have been no intention of vesting the title in them personally; and, accordingly, it will be found that they never assumed the ownership in themselves, but allowed the conveyances to enure to the benefit of the great body of the settlers, and the lands to be at their disposal and control. This fact, taken in connection with the prompt appearance upon the ground of no less than nine of Wheelwright's friends and supporters, in the character of grantees

---

* The original deeds bear the totems or distinctive marks of the Indians, being rude sketches, as follows: those of James and of Wehanownowit a man holding a tomahawk; that of Pummadockyon a man holding a bow and arrow; and that of Aspamabough a bow and arrow.

and witnesses, and the speedy arrival of numerous others, leaves little question that the project of the Exeter settlement had been fully organized and understood beforehand.

THE DISPUTED INDIAN DEED OF 1629.

In the trial of the action at law of Allen against Waldron in 1707, which involved the title to substantially all the lands in New Hampshire, the defendant introduced in evidence a deed purporting to have been executed by Passaconaway, sagamore of Penacook, Runawit of Pentucket, Wahanownawit of Squamscot and Rowls of Newichwannock, to the Rev. John Wheelwright and others, on the seventeenth day of May, 1629, nearly nine years prior to the date of the deeds already mentioned. It assumed to convey the rights of the grantors' tribesmen to the same territory described in those deeds, and even more. The instrument underwent the ordeal of the courts unscathed, and passed into the history of the time as a genuine document, and was universally so regarded for a hundred years. In 1820 Mr. James Savage, while editing an edition of Winthrop's Journal, was led, by a comparison of dates, to inquire into the authenticity of the deed, and with characteristic positiveness, to pronounce it spurious. His view was adopted by several of the historians of New Hampshire, including Mr. John Farmer and the Rev. Dr. Nathaniel Bouton. It has, however, been queried by some others whether the reasons given for discrediting the instrument are conclusive.

But it seems quite unnecessary to go, in this work, into any inquiry on the subject. Whether the deed of 1629 was true or false, it is certain that Wheelwright in making his settlement did not rely upon it, but upon the conveyances of the later date. The question respecting the authenticity of the earlier deed, therefore, however interesting it may be to antiquaries, can affect no one's title or claim, and is of no practical importance.

The instrument, however, as a historical curiosity, is worthy of preservation. Being of considerable length it will be placed in the appendix (I).

TRIALS OF THE OPENING YEAR.

The opening year of Exeter's settlement must have tested to the utmost the courage and endurance of the colonists. Everything needed to render the place habitable had to be created; for the lack of means of transport in the wilderness precluded the conveyance thither of anything beyond the absolute essentials of existence. The trees of the primeval forest had to be felled, and from their trunks rude dwellings constructed, to shelter the tender ones. The absence of household furniture compelled the fashioning of substitutes from wood or bark. Planting-land must be cleared, and seed sown, to provide against the danger of starvation. Numerous other wants, the products of civilization, clamored also to be at once supplied; so that every hour of the first season must have been devoted to providing the means for rendering life secure and tolerable. Nothing short of extraordinary firmness of character, the consciousness of right in their religious trials, and their confidence in their leader and pastor, would have enabled the early settlers of the town to bear up under the difficulties and hardships of their position.

From the best information that can now be obtained, the population of Exeter did not advance during the first year much, if at all, beyond a score of families. These consisted in about equal proportions of Wheelwright's parishioners and adherents from Mount Wollaston and its vicinity in Massachusetts, and of his connections and friends lately arrived from Lincolnshire in England. In July, 1637, in the midst of the Antinomian excitement, a ship had reached Boston, from England, bringing as passengers a brother of Mrs. Anne Hutchinson, and a number of other transatlantic friends of Wheelwright. The General Court of Massachusetts had recently enacted a law forbidding new comers to tarry in the colony for a longer time than three weeks, without the written permission of a member of the council or of two other magistrates. That friends of Wheelwright should be suffered to make their permanent homes in Massachusetts was out of the question. Governor Winthrop gave them leave to remain for four months, but no longer. In November, 1637, therefore, they had to seek an abiding place elsewhere. They, doubtless, chose to go where Wheelwright went, and found winter quarters somewhere on the Pascataqua; and in the following spring sat down with him at Exeter. Of these we can reckon about ten heads of families, and of those who came from the neighborhood of Boston, about the same number.

The wives and little ones did not stay long behind. Wheelwright's family left Massachusetts in March, 1638, to follow him to Exeter by water. The difficulties of travelling thither by land were too great for women and children, even at the most favorable season. But it was quite practicable to navigate a vessel of fair size along the coast and up the river to the very foot of the falls of the Squamscot; and it is altogether likely that most of the families adopted that mode of conveyance for themselves and their more portable household effects.

THE FIRST CHURCH.

This was essentially a religious colonization, and there can be no doubt that at an early stage, a church was gathered, though its records have long since disappeared. We assume that this was done before December 13, 1638, because the fact is recorded in the past tense in Winthrop's contemporaneous History of New England, under that date. The time of the formation of the church is not there given, but the facts recited would imply that it must have been in existence for some weeks, if not months before that date. It probably included in its membership all, or nearly all, the adult persons in the settlement. The members of the newly gathered church wrote to the church in Boston, no doubt, in the autumn of 1638, asking for the dismission of Wheelwright therefrom, in order that he might be their minister; but as Wheelwright himself, for obvious reasons, did not join in the petition, the elders of the Boston church declined to lay the proposal before the members. Upon this being made known to Wheelwright he sent his own request to the same effect, which reached the elders early in December; and thereupon on the sixth of the following January the Boston church dismissed Wheelwright, Richard Morris, Richard Bulgar, Philemon Pormort, Isaac Gross, Christopher Marshall, George Bates, Thomas Wardell and William Wardell "unto the church of Christ at the falls of the Pascataqua, if they be rightly gathered and ordered." And two months afterwards, on March 3, 1639, they dismissed to the same church, also, Susanna Hutchinson, widow, Mary, the wife of Wheelwright, Leonora, the wife of Richard Morris, Henry Elkins and his wife, this time without conditions, being apparently satisfied that the church of Exeter *was* "rightly gathered and ordered."

It was a circumstance none too creditable to the temper of the authorities of Massachusetts, that after they had relieved themselves from all, even imaginary danger from their heterodox brethren by banishing them from their territory, they must needs grudge them a friendly reception among their new neighbors. In September, 1638, the General Court of that colony directed the governor to write to the Rev. George Burdett at Dover, Thomas Wiggin at Squamscot, and others, of the vicinity, reproaching them for having aided Wheelwright in founding the plantation at Exeter. This gratuitous act of unfriendliness must naturally have reached the ears of the parties at whom it was aimed, and could not fail to embitter them still more against their persistent persecutors.

Shortly afterwards the settlement of Winicowet, now Hampton, was begun under the authority of Massachusetts. Prior to this time that colony had made no claim nor attempt to exercise jurisdiction over any territory lying more than three miles north of the Merrimac river—the line to which the obvious construction of her charter would appear to restrict her. But Winicowet was above that distance north of the Merrimac, and, moreover, was embraced in Wheelwright's purchase from the Indians. He, therefore, gave notice to the settlers of Hampton and to the General Court of Massachusetts that the lands of Hampton had been bought by Exeter from the Indian sagamores, and would be lotted out in farms, unless Massachusetts could show a better title. The General Court replied that they looked upon this as against good neighborhood, religion and common honesty, as Exeter knew that Massachusetts claimed Hampton as within her patent, or as vacant land, and had taken possession thereof by building a house there above two years before. The Exeter proprietors made reply, that they claimed nothing which was within the patent of Massachusetts. But, before that, the authorities of Massachusetts had sent men to explore the course of the Merrimac, and had discovered that its source was far to the northward of the Pascataqua plantations, and thereupon resolved upon that construction of their charter which they promulgated by a solemn order in 1652, claiming that the northern bound of their patent was an east and west line drawn through a point three miles northerly of the northernmost extremity of the Merrimac. This new interpretation must be admitted to be highly artificial; but Massachusetts had a strong government, while the New Hampshire settlements were feeble, and England was hopelessly far away. Massachusetts was thus in a condition to enforce her claims, and they were submitted to for the time. But when they were subsequently brought before the English tribunals they were unhesitatingly rejected.

Thus passed the first year of the life of the new town, if town it can be called which was without municipal regulations or any kind of civil government. Thus far the inhabitants had been so fully engrossed in providing for their prime necessities, their interests were so little conflicting, and the influence of their leader was so complete, that no disorder or serious differences had occurred. But the second year was to bring accessions to their numbers, of those who could not be expected to yield equal obedience to Wheelwright's wishes. The existence of the new plantation had been bruited about, and another set of inhabitants, of different antecedents and purposes, began to come in. And before the end of the second year the population had at least doubled.

ANOTHER INDIAN DEED.

On the tenth of April, 1639, Wheelwright succeeded in strengthening the town's title to the territory purchased from Wehanownawit and Pummadockyon the year before, by the confirmatory grant of another Indian of authority, indorsed upon their deed, in the following terms:

Know all men by these p'sents that I Watohantowet doe fully consent to the grant within written, & do yeild up all my right in the said purchased lands to the ptys wth in written. In witnesse whereof I haue herevnto set my hand the tenth day of April 1639.

I doe likewise grant vnto them for goode consideration all the meadows & grounds extending for the space of one english mile on the East side of Oyster river. April 10. 1639.

These being p'sent
Jo: Underhill
    his ꓷ m'ke
Darby Field

Watohantowet * his m'ke.

From the last clause in the foregoing grant it appears that Watahantowet claimed the proprietorship of lands beyond Oyster river, afterwards appropriated by Dover, and now included in Durham. So far as those lands were concerned, Exeter benefited little by the conveyance.

---

* The totem of Watahantowet delineated upon the deed was an armless man.

THE COMBINATION.

As the second season advanced the need of some form of civil government became apparent. There were no constituted authorities over the patent of New Hampshire, and the Exeter settlers were driven to the expedient adopted nineteen years before by the Pilgrim Fathers, and perhaps employed by one at least of the other plantations upon the Pascataqua. They agreed upon a voluntary association for governmental purposes, which was drawn up by their pastor and subscribed by him and probably by the greater number of the adult males of the settlement. It bore date the fourth day of July, 1639; just one hundred and thirty-seven years before the adoption of the memorable declaration of American Independence.

The following is the language of this compact:

Whereas it has pleased the lord to moue the heart of our Dread Soveraigne Charles, by the grace of god King of England, Scotland France & Ireland, to grant licence & liberty to sundry of his subjects to plant them selves in the Westerne partes of America; Wee his loyall subjects, brethren of the church of Exeter, situate & lying upon the river of Piscataquacke wth other inhabitants there considering wth our selves the holy will of god and our owne necessity that we should not live wthout wholsome lawes & civil government amongst us, of w^h we are altogether destitute, doe in the name of Christ & in the sight of god combine our selves together, to erect & set up amongst us such government as shall be to our best discerning, agreeable to the will of god, professing our selves subjects to our Soveraigne Lord King Charles according to the libertys of our English Colony of the Massachusets & binding our selves solemnely by the grace & helpe of Christ & in his name & feare to submit our selves to such godly & christian laws as are established in the Realme of England to our best knowledge, & to all other such lawes w^h shall upon good grounds be made & inacted amongst us according to god y^t we may live quietly & peaceablely together in all godlyness and honesty.

Mon. 5th, d. 4th 1639.

This instrument was soon found to be unsatisfactory to some of the brethren, because of its too lavish expressions of loyalty to the king, who was of course in their minds identified with prelacy. Like their neighbors of Massachusetts they were willing to acknowledge, in a general way, that he was their lawful sovereign, and that they were his subjects, but they had no disposition to make any unnecessary or exuberant professions of allegiance. It might have been at this time and on this account that some of the inhabitants made overtures to the Massachusetts authorities to be received under their government, as the people of Dover had just done. The Exeter people, however, soon "repented themselves" and withdrew the proposal. The objectionable feature of the Combination had been cancelled, and a new compact drawn, of the same purport, except that it simply acknowledged the king to be their sovereign, and themselves to be his subjects. This second compact was executed in due form, was apparently satisfactory to the former dissentients, and went into effect, as the basis of government. But, quite curiously, it seems to have led to trouble in the opposite direction — because it did not contain loyalty enough.

THE FIRST CRIMINAL PROCEEDING.

One Gabriel Fish, a member of the Exeter church, who perhaps understood by the change in the compact for government, that royalty was at a discount, was guilty of "speaking against" his majesty; possibly of uttering speeches which might be construed as treasonable. This by no means suited the views of the leading men of Exeter. They at once caused Fish to be arrested, and some of them proceeded to Massachusetts to take advice what to do with him.

This occurrence brought a new and singular figure into the history of the town. Captain John Underhill was a military adventurer who after having lived for seven years in Massachusetts and distinguished himself in the Pequot war, and otherwise, was disarmed for his adherence to the opinions of Wheelwright and Mrs. Hutchinson, and came to Dover, where he was chosen chief magistrate, under the style of governor. He was fond of brave apparel, addicted to the use of "the good creature tobacco," and possibly not averse to a stoup of strong waters, a little too partial to the other sex, and wore his political and religious principles rather loosely; in short, he showed a singularly incongruous outline against the prim background of New England Puritanism. He, hearing of the detention of Fish, and perhaps to ingratiate himself with the prelatical party who were strong at the mouth of the Pascataqua, and would be glad to see a maligner of the king soundly punished, sent thirteen armed men from Dover to Exeter, who took Fish from custody there, and conveyed him to Dover. This and other instances of misconduct occasioned a change of opinion in Dover respecting Underhill, which resulted in deposing him and electing Thomas Roberts in his place, who at once restored Fish to the authorities of Exeter. It is not improbable that his return was a source of embarrassment. The change in the Exeter Combination would hardly justify his punishment for speaking against the king, and the authorities of Massachusetts were by no means anxious to claim jurisdiction of the case ; so we may imagine that the charge against Fish was not pressed.

But the result of this fiasco appears to have been to make yet another change in the Exeter compact for government. On the second of April, 1640, the original Combination, as already given in these pages, was re-executed, with the following explanatory preamble :

Whereas a certen combination was made by us the brethren of the church of Exeter wth the rest of the Inhabitants bearing date Mon. 5th, d. 4, 1639 w^h afterwards upon the instant request of some of the brethren, was altered & put into such a form of wordes, wherein howsoever we doe acknowledge the King's Majesty our dread Soveraigne & our selves his subjects, yet some expressions are contained therein w^h may seeme to admit of such a sence as somewhat derogates from that due Allegiance w^h we owe ûto his Highnesse quite contrary to our true intents and meanings : Wee therefore doe revoke, disanull make voŷd and frustrate the said latter combination, as if it never had been done & doe ratify, confirme & establish the former, w^h wee only stand unto, as being in force & vertue, the w^h for substance is here set down in manner and form following.

Mon. 2^d, d. 2, 1640.

Here follows the combination substantially as it was originally drawn, and appended to it are the following signatures :

John Whelewright	Richard Bullgar
Augustine Storre	Christopher Lawson
Thomas Wight	George Barlow *
William Wantworth	Richard Moris
Henry Elkins	Nicholas Needham
George Walton *	Thomas Willson *
Samuell Walker	George Ruobone *

Thomas Pettit	William Coole *
Henry Roby	James Walles *
Willia Wenbourne	Thomas Levitt *
Thomas Crawley *	Edmond Littlefield
Chr: Helme	John Crame *
Darby Field *	Godfrye Deareborne *
Robert Read *	Philemon Pormort
Edward Rishworth	Thomas Wardell
Francis Mathews *	Willia Wardell *
Ralph Hall	Robert Smith *
Robert Soward *	

We have advanced a little beyond the chronological order of our narrative, for the purpose of giving a continuous history of the formation and changes of the Combination. We will now return to the original date of it, July 4, 1639.

At the same time when that Combination was formed, a regular scheme of government was apparently established. The executive and judicial functions were vested in a board of three magistrates, or elders, of whom the chief was styled Ruler. They were chosen by the whole body of the freemen, who were the electors and legislators, their enactments, however, requiring the approval of the Ruler. An inhabitant had to be admitted a freeman, before he could enjoy the privileges of an elector; and there is one instance of a freeman being deprived of his privileges as such, by reason of misconduct.

Both the Elders and the People were required to take certain prescribed oaths, which are here given.

THE ELDERS OATH, Y° 4TH DAY, 5TH M°. 1639.

You shall sweare by the great and dreadfull name of the high God maker & Govr of heaven and earth, and by the Lord Jesus Christ ye Prince of the Kings and Rulers of the earth that in his name and feare you will Rule and Governe this his people according to the righteous will of God's Ministeringe Justice and Judgm^t upon the workers of iniquity and Ministering due incurridgm^t and Countinance to well doers — protecting of people so farre as in you by the helpe of [God] lyeth, from forren Annoyance and inward disturbance that they may live a quiett and peacable life in all godlyness and honesty. Soe God bee helpful and gratious to you and yo^{rs} in Christ Jesus.

---

* These made their marks; although at least one of them James Wall (here written Walles) was capable of writing a neat signature.

THE OATH OF THE PEOPLE.

Wee doe here sweare by the Great and dreadfull name of ye high God, maker & Gouern^r of Heaven & earth and by the Lord Jesus X^t ye King & Savio^r of his people that in his name & fear we will submitt o^r selves to be ruld & gouerned by, according to ye will & word of God and such holsome Laws & ordinances as shall be derived theire from by o^r honr^d Rulers and ye Lawfull assistance with the consent of ye people and y^t wee will be ready to assist them by the helpe of God in the administracon of Justice and p'servacon of peace with o^r bodys and goods and best endeauo^{rs} according to God, so God protect & saue us and o^{rs} in Christ Jesus.

Isaac Gross was chosen the first Ruler, and undoubtedly qualified himself by taking the Elder's oath. It is not unlikely that he was also a ruling elder in the church. On the eighteenth of January, 1640, Augustine Storre and Anthony Stanyan were joined with him, and the three were to have "the ordering of all town affairs according to God." These officers corresponded closely to our modern selectmen, in respect to their duties, and under their administration the affairs of the little town went on satisfactorily.

A glimpse of the customs of the time is afforded us by a transaction recorded in the Note Book of Thomas Lechford, Esq., an English lawyer, who practised his profession in Boston in Massachusetts from 1638 to 1641. Under date of July 5, 1639, he records the drawing of a covenant between Elizabeth Evans of Bridgend in the county of Glamorgan in Wales and John Wheelwright, minister, by which she engaged to become his servant for three years from June 25 then last past, for three pounds per annum as wages, and in consideration that her passage to this country was paid by Wheelwright. The instrument appears not to have been executed in Boston, and we know that Wheelwright's sentence of banishment was still in force. No doubt it was completed in Exeter, having been brought thither by Richard Bulgar or Richard Morris, both of whom had business with the lawyer about that time.

FIRST ALLOTMENT OF LANDS.

It was near the close of the second season before any general distribution of land appears to have been made, from the ample domain at the disposal of the town. On Wednesday of the first week in December, 1639, the town made a beginning, by first defining the extensive uplands and meadows which belonged to Edward Hilton, whose claim was treated as antedating that of the Exeter proprietors.

They then provided that all the meadows belonging to the town between the village and Mr. Hilton's house, and from Lamprey river to the head of the Little Bay should be equally apportioned into four parts; of which one part should be divided by lot among those inhabitants who had no cattle, or a less number of goats than four; the hay growing thereon, however, to be distributed among the others, until such time as they should have cattle of their own, or sell the meadows to those having cattle. The other three parts of the meadows were to be divided by lot among the inhabitants having cattle, according to the number thereof; and the division was to be made before the next court or town meeting.

The town also provided that upland lots for planting should be laid out by lot to all the inhabitants, by the river between Stony creek and the creek on this (the south) side of Mr. Hilton's, according to the number of persons and cattle belonging to each, except such persons as lived on the eastern side of the river, and William Hilton and John Smart, who were to have lots on that side of the river, where the town should think most convenient, [acting] by Ruler Needham and Augustine Storre.

The division of lands thus ordered was duly made, doubtless in the course of the same month.*

The marshes and meadows, bearing spontaneously a species of grass on which when dried the cattle could well subsist, were at this early period, when no considerable clearing away of the forest had been effected, of great value to the settlers. The whole extent of them was but one hundred and ten acres, but they were apportioned with particularity among the thirty-seven heads of families then belonging to Exeter, excluding Edward Hilton, whose lands had already been secured to him. These marshes were situated partly in the vicinity of Lamprey river, and partly between the Hilton place in what is now South Newmarket, and the present village of Exeter.

The uplands for planting-lots, which were also divided, amounted to about four hundred and thirty-three acres, and were allotted to thirty-two inhabitants, not including Edward Hilton, nor those who lived on the eastern side of the river. The shares varied from

---

* A complete record of the allotments may be found in the appendix (II).

four acres and twenty rods, per man, to eighty acres. Ten of the inhabitants received each no more than the smaller amount; and only Wheelwright received the larger. The uplands here distributed lay on the western bank of the salt river, beginning at the brook on the southerly side of the Hilton place in South Newmarket and extending towards Exeter village about one mile and three-quarters, if the measurements are correct.

The inhabitants began early to exercise their new privileges as legislators, and before the second year of the settlement had passed by, had enacted a small body of orders, made necessary by the circumstances of a frontier life. Setting fire to the woods and thus destroying the feed of the cattle was forbidden. So was digging a saw-pit and leaving it open, and the offender was made liable to pay the damage caused thereby to man or beast. Every man was required to cut down such trees *on his own lot*, as were offensive to any other, under the penalty of half a crown for each refusal. This last requirement is a refinement of legislation, the like of which is probably not to be found in any other code in Christendom.

NOTICES OF EARLY SETTLERS.

The close of the second year of the new settlement found the inhabitants increased in numbers, with an organized government founded on a voluntary association, and constituting a complete autonomy; with rights of property secured, and apparently nothing wanting but greater population and strength to insure their perpetuity.

This seems a convenient time to take an inventory of the material of which the original settlement of Exeter was composed. The following is a list of the adult males, almost without exception of English birth, and mostly heads of families, who are known to have been inhabitants of the place within the first two years after its foundation in the spring of 1638.

1. George Barlow, of whom, prior to his appearance in Exeter, nothing has been learned. He had no assignment in the uplands or marshes in 1639, but was a subscriber of the restored Combination, April 2, 1640; so it seems probable that he came in the early spring of that year. In 1641 he received from the town a grant of forty acres of upland, and in 1650 four acres more. In 1649–50 leave was given him and others to set up a saw-mill at

the falls on Lamprey river a "a little above the wigwams." He is said to have been a preacher while in Exeter, and he certainly was so in Saco in 1652; but his style was so little relished by the powers of Massachusetts that in 1653 they forbade him to preach or prophesy under a penalty of ten pounds for each offence. About 1660 he removed to Plymouth and there essayed to be a lawyer. He is referred to in Bishop's *New England Judged* for his severity against the Quakers.

2. George Bates, a thatcher, was an inhabitant of Boston as early as December, 1635, and, two years later, received a grant of fifteen acres of land there. He had been admitted to the Boston church in January, 1636, but having taken his departure to Exeter he was on the sixth of January, 1639, in company with several others, dismissed to the church newly gathered in that place. His stay in Exeter, however, proved brief, and he was received back again into the Boston church May 31, 1640. From his associations he was probably a sympathizer with Wheelwright, but though his handicraft must naturally have been in request in a new place, it is very likely that the hardships and privations of a frontier life were too much for his strength or his resolution, and he abandoned it.

3. Jeremiah Blackwell came to this country in the ship Truelove in 1635, being then eighteen years old. Where he passed the succeeding three or four years is not ascertained. At the end of that time he appeared in Exeter. In the division of the uplands in 1639 he received four acres and twenty poles, being, no doubt, the share of a single or childless man. After that his name is not mentioned. It is clear that he made no long stay in Exeter.

4. Richard Bulgar, born in 1608, probably came over in the fleet with Winthrop, and in 1637 had an allotment of twenty acres of land in Boston. He was admitted to the church there in 1634, and had a child baptized the same year. His residence was in Roxbury, and he is described as a bricklayer. His handwriting would indicate that his education was good. Being disarmed in 1637 on account of his sympathy with the Antinomian party, he departed the next year to Rhode Island, but in 1639 received his dismission to the church in Exeter. There he was allotted four acres and twenty poles of upland, and subscribed the Combination. In 1641 he was chosen lieutenant of "the band of soldiers," and in 1644 lot layer. Soon afterwards he left Exeter, and in 1646 was described as of Boston. Later he returned to Rhode Island,

where his intelligence and business capacity were rewarded with the office of Solicitor General, which he held in 1656, and two or three subsequent years.

5. Edward Colcord was born in 1616 or 1617 and came to this country in 1631. For the next seven years he probably lived somewhere on the Pascataqua, and being an active man and acquainted with the Indians he rendered assistance to Wheelwright in obtaining his land grants from the sagamores, and was a party to one of the deeds.

A religious colony could not have been greatly to his taste, and in 1640 he had removed to Dover, where he was a magistrate to end small causes. But in 1645 he was a resident of Hampton, and the following year saw him back again at Exeter, where he obtained a grant of lands from the town, and the right of an inhabitant. It is doubtful if he availed himself of this, for in 1652 the town again voted to receive him, together with two others, as inhabitants, and invited them to take up their residence in Exeter. Colcord received more than one grant from the town, and was appointed to some minor offices. But he was incorrigibly litigious and something of a rolling stone, and after a brief sojourn in the town he made himself a home in Hampton, where he died February 10, 1681-2. He and his wife Ann had ten children, several of whom were married. Their descendants still live in Exeter and the vicinity.

6. William Cole was of Boston February 20, 1637, when he received an allotment of two acres of land "only for his present planting," at Mount Wollaston. No doubt he was a parishioner there of Wheelwright, and certainly was one of his earliest companions at Exeter, for he witnessed one of the Indian deeds of April 3, 1638. In the first division of lands he received a share both in the marshes and the uplands, and he was a signer of the Combination. He was appointed an overseer of fences in 1643, but probably soon followed Wheelwright to Wells. He afterwards removed to Hampton, where his wife Eunice became " vehemently suspected " of being a witch. He died in Hampton May 26, 1662, aged eighty-one years. His descendants are still found in the vicinity.

7. John Compton was of Roxbury in 1634, and was disarmed in 1637 for his adhesion to the Wheelwright party. The circumstance that a summons was issued March 12, 1638, to him and others who "had licence to depart" out of Massachusetts, to

appear at the next court if they were not gone before, was not likely to have prolonged his stay there, and it is safe to infer that he was at the falls of the Squamscot with Wheelwright on April 3, 1638, as he was a grantee in one of the Indian deeds then executed. In the first division of lands he received a considerable share both of marsh and upland. He did not subscribe the Combination, but probably soon returned to Boston, where the Book of Possessions shows that he owned a house and garden, about 1652.

8. Lawrence Copeland was of Braintree and presumably a parishioner of Wheelwright. He was in Exeter April 3, 1638, and witnessed one of the Indian deeds of that date. It is not probable that he remained long in the town. He returned to Braintree to reside, where he attained the extraordinary age of one hundred years.

9. John Cram probably began to live in Boston as early as 1635, and in 1637 was assigned sixteen acres of land at Muddy River (Brookline). At the first division of lands in Exeter he was no doubt settled there, as he was allotted eight acres and forty poles of upland; he was also a signer of the Combination. He had a wife and two or more children when he came to Exeter. His son Joseph, supposed to be the oldest, was drowned June 24, 1648, aged fifteen years; and his daughter Lydia was born July 27 of the same year. He served as townsman in 1648 and 1649 and soon after removed to Hampton and there died March 5, 1681–2. The town record commemorates him as "good old John Cram, one just in his generation." He was twice married, his first wife being named Lydia; his second Esther. His descendants are still found in the vicinity.

10. Thomas Crawley, of whom nothing is learned, prior to his appearance in Exeter. His name does not occur in the first apportionment of lands, but as he subscribed the Combination, it is very likely that he came to Exeter between January and April, 1640. In 1644–5 he had a grant of a house lot of four acres on condition of building upon it and fencing it within a twelvemonth. Other grants were subsequently made him by the town, the most important of which was that of a saw-mill privilege, in the present Brentwood, in 1652, which has been known as "Crawley's falls," to this day. He had children, one of whom was named Phebe, a minor in 1660. Crawley probably went to Maine, where his name was afterwards found.

11. Godfrey Dearborn was from Devonshire in England, perhaps from the city of Exeter, and brought to the new Exeter a wife and two or three children. An assignment of ten acres and fifty poles of upland was made him, and his name is affixed to the Combination. Later he received other grants of land, and in 1648 was one of the selectmen. It has been supposed that he lived in what is now Stratham, near the Scammon place. About 1650 he removed to Hampton. His wife having died he married November 25, 1662, Dorothy, the widow of Philemon Dalton, and himself died February 4, 1686. His posterity is numerous.

12. Henry Elkins, a tailor, was of Boston in 1634, and there had an assignment of eight acres of land in 1637. Siding with Wheelwright in the theological controversy of that year, he was disarmed, and came in 1638 to Exeter. He, with his wife Mary, was dismissed from the Boston church to that of Exeter March 3, 1639. They had a daughter, Maria, baptized in Boston, April 8, 1638. In the first division of lands in Exeter he received one of the smaller shares of upland; and he set his name to the Combination. He continued in Exeter till 1645, but some time afterwards removed to Hampton and died there November 19, 1668.

13. Darby Field is described by Winthrop as an Irishman, though some slight evidence has been discovered to connect his patronymic with the Hutchinson family. He appeared in Exeter as one of the grantees of the Indian deed of April 3, 1638, and witnessed the deed of confirmation of Watohantowet April 10, 1639. He had no share in the first division of lands, but was a subscriber of the Combination. He is noted as the first European who visited the White mountains, which he did in 1642. In 1645 he was living at Oyster river, now Durham, and died in 1649, leaving children.

14. Gabriel Fish, fisherman, was an early inhabitant of Boston and moved to Exeter in 1638. On the third of August, 1639, he gave Edward Rishworth a letter of attorney to receive ten pounds from James Carrington of Thorsthorpe in Lincolnshire, England; whence we may infer that he, perhaps, came from that great hive of the friends of Wheelwright. After Fish was arrested for speaking against the king, as has already been mentioned, he probably thought it wise to return to Boston, where apparently his offence was easily condoned. The records show the birth and baptism of several of his children there in 1642 and subsequently. Fish was a householder in Boston, according to the Book of Possessions,

15. Isaac Gross, of Boston in 1635, was termed husbandman, and received a "great" allotment of fifty acres of land at Muddy River in 1637. Being a friend of Cotton and Wheelwright he was disarmed, and followed the latter to Exeter. There in the first division of lands he had, under the honorary title of "Mr.," an assignment of twenty-eight acres and one hundred and forty poles of upland, and of marsh land six acres and fifty poles "on this side of Mr. Hilton's" and two acres at Lamprey river. From this liberal allowance, it is to be inferred that he had a considerable family, and also an unusual number of cattle. He was dismissed January 6, 1639, from the Boston to the Exeter church, and was chosen the first Ruler of the plantation of Exeter, in which capacity he served about a year, probably. He returned to Boston "in a few years," according to Savage, and there died in 1649, leaving a good estate to be divided among his widow, children and grandchildren.

16. Ralph Hall, said to be a son of John Hall, senior, and a brother of Deacon John Hall of Dover, was born in 1618. If, therefore, as tradition asserts, he was located in Exeter before the arrival of Wheelwright's company, he could not have been above twenty years of age. It is understood that he lived on the eastern side of the salt river, down nearly to the mouth of Wheelwright's creek. It might have been for that reason that he had no share in the first division of lands, but his name appears to the Combination. He may have lived in Charlestown about 1647 with his wife Mary, as has been alleged. The Exeter records show the death of his daughter Mercy in July, 1648, aged about one year and a half, and the birth of his daughter Hildea, April 16, 1649. He is said to have gone to Dover in 1650. But he returned to Exeter fourteen years afterward, when he was admitted an inhabitant, October 10, 1664, and received a grant of fifty acres of land. He was a lieutenant, then an officer of responsibility, and held various positions of trust in the town, the most important being that of delegate to the first provincial assembly in 1680. His death took place in March, 1701. Some of his descendants have been men of note, and the name has always been kept alive in the town.

17. Christopher Helme, a Lincolnshire man, connected by blood with others of the Exeter pioneers, arrived in Boston in July, 1637, no doubt, and was suffered to remain there not above four months, so that he probably reached Exeter among the foremost. He received no share in the first allotment of lands, for

what reason it is not known, but he set his hand to the Combination. Upon the departure of Wheelwright in 1643, Helme returned for a little time to Boston, and thence migrated with the Gortonists to Warwick, Rhode Island. There he died before December, 1650, leaving a widow Margaret and a son William. Some of his name, presumably descendants, have been prominent in Rhode Island.

18. Edward Hilton has already been mentioned. The records of Exeter show that he was settled and had a house in the part of Exeter which is now South Newmarket, at least at early as December, 1639. He became a leading man in the place, serving as townsman or selectman from 1645 nearly every year up to 1652. In 1646 he was one of the purchasers of Wheelwright's house, in order that it might be used as the residence of the Rev. Nathaniel Norcross, afterwards of Lancaster, who had been invited to settle in Exeter; and after the declination of Mr. Norcross he was in 1650 one of the inhabitants who, in behalf of the town, entered into the engagement with the Rev. Samuel Dudley to become their minister. Mr. Hilton was repeatedly chosen by the inhabitants on important committees to look after their interests, and was in all respects a useful and valuable citizen. He died early in the year 1671.

19. William Hilton, a brother of Edward, and a member of the Fishmongers' Guild of London, came over to Plymouth in the ship Fortune, November 11, 1621. There he remained till the arrival of his wife and two children in the Anne, in July or August, 1623. In a little time afterwards they settled themselves on the Pascataqua with Edward Hilton at or near Dover. In the first division of lands in Exeter, he was assigned three acres of marsh, and it was voted that he and John Smart were to have lots on the other (eastern) side of the river, where it should be thought most convenient; and on the third of February, 1641, it was agreed by the town that he might enjoy certain marshes and uplands at Oyster river. He seems to have occupied some part of the debatable ground between Exeter and Dover, but was perhaps accounted a citizen of the latter place. This was certainly the case in 1644 when he was chosen a deputy to the Massachusetts General Court from Dover. But shortly afterwards he went further to the eastward, and maintained much the same divided citizenship between Kittery and York. His death occurred in the latter place in 1665 or 1666.

20. Samuel Hutchinson was an unmarried brother of Mrs. Wheelwright, and no doubt landed in Boston with other Lincolnshire friends July 12, 1637, and was upon his special request licensed to remain there until the first month after winter. Then he proceeded to Exeter, and was made a grantee in one of the Indian deeds of April, 1638. Little more than a month afterwards a grant of land appears to have been made him in Rhode Island, where his brother William had gone. Though Samuel resided there at a later period, he probably did not go at once, but staid for a year or two in and about Exeter. His mother, Mrs. Susanna Hutchinson, was there, an inmate of Wheelwright's family, as probably he was also. He, with Needham and others, negotiated with Thomas Gorges, September 27, 1641, for the tract of land at Wells, which was the second place of refuge of Wheelwright and his followers. He died in Boston, it is believed, in 1677.

21. Christopher Lawson, a connection of Helme and others of the Combination, without much question arrived with them from Lincolnshire at Boston in New England, in July, 1637, and probably proceeded to Exeter the next year. His name appears on the Combination, but not in the division of lands. He was a cooper by trade, and a trader by nature. Some of his dealings in Exeter appeared rather too sharp for the primitive fashions of the place, and on the fifth of September, 1643, he was bound over in the sum of ten pounds to answer to the charge of extortion brought against him by five of his neighbors. Apparently his character was not seriously affected by this circumstance; for the town bestowed upon him, the next year, a right of fishery in the river, which would now be regarded as an indefensible monopoly. Lawson vibrated for some years between Exeter and Boston, two of his children being baptized in the latter place, one in 1643 and the other in 1645. In 1648 he was a member of a committee to invite the Rev. Mr. Tompson of Braintree to settle over the church in Exeter, and the same year the town made him a grant of one hundred acres of land. After buying and selling lots in Dover and in Boston, and dabbling to a considerable extent in shares of the "Squamscot Patent," Lawson went, before 1665, to Maine, where he became a considerable man. There he suffered some domestic infelicities, which resulted in bringing mutual complaints between his wife Elizabeth and himself before the General Court in 1669. And there, for want of further knowledge, we leave him.

22. Thomas Leavitt was very probably a connection of Wheelwright's wife, and another of those "friends" who reached Boston in July, 1637. It is possible that he proceeded at once to Exeter, and thus antedated the organized settlement, as the tradition is. He took upland on the eastern side of the fresh river just above the falls, and the same long remained in the possession of his descendants. In the first division of lands he received one of the smaller shares, four acres and twenty poles of the uplands; being then a young man, for he lived till November 28, 1696. His name was also appended to the Combination. He became an inhabitant of Hampton about 1643. His wife was Isabel, daughter of John Bland of Martha's Vineyard, who came from Colchester, England. They had eight children, and numerous descendants. Three of the sons were probably residents of Exeter.

23. Edmund Littlefield not improbably came to Boston with Wheelwright's other friends in July, 1637, accompanied by his son Anthony. His wife Ann and six of their other children did not accompany him, but sailed later, and reached Boston in the ship Bevis in May, 1638. Littlefield was a warm partisan of Wheelwright, and probably was early at Exeter. He had assigned him in the first division of lands, twenty-one acres of upland; and was a subscriber of the Combination. The circumstance that he had no share of the meadows implies that he owned no cattle, which is likely to have been the case, as he was a new comer in the country. Littlefield remained in Exeter no longer than Wheelwright, but accompanied him to Wells, where he was a leading man, and is spoken of in handsome terms by Judge Bourne in his history of that town. He died December 11, 1661.

24. Francis Littlefield was the eldest son of Edmund, and was born in 1619. Tradition, fortified by some known facts, asserts that he had at an early age quitted his parents, who, believing him to be dead, gave the name Francis to another son born in 1631; but that the older Francis, who was really living, crossed the Atlantic and rejoined his father, probably at Exeter, and before the division of the uplands in 1639. In that division he received one of the smaller shares, four acres and twenty poles. It is probable that he was already married, or he would hardly have had an assignment separate from his father's. He probably left Exeter as early as his father did, and went to Woburn, Massachusetts, where his wife Jane died December 20, 1646, leaving a daughter six days old. Shortly afterwards he went to

Dover. In 1648 he was again married, and after two or three years removed to Wells, and there passed the rest of his long life. He died in 1712, leaving several children.

25. Christopher Marshall was of Boston in 1634, and joined the church in August of that year. He was admitted freeman May 6, 1635; in 1637 belonged to the party of Cotton and Wheelwright. He was married between August, 1634, and May 13, 1638, and was dismissed to the church at Exeter, January 6, 1639, but did not remain long in the place. Savage thinks he returned to England in 1640 or 1641, and nothing more is learned of him.

26. Francis Mathews was one of the company sent over by John Mason in 1631. He was a signer of the Combination, but probably soon afterwards removed to the part of Dover which is now Durham, with his wife Thomasine and three children. There he died about 1648, and his descendants in Strafford county have been numerous. They more commonly spell the name Mathes.

27. Griffin Montague was of Brookline in 1635. He received in December, 1639, ten acres and fifty poles in the division of uplands in Exeter, and one acre and thirty-six poles in the division of the marsh "next the town." From this we infer that he had a family and some cattle. His name appears several times upon the Exeter records within the ensuing twelve years. He belonged to Cape Porpoise, Maine, in 1653, and died before April 1, 1672, leaving his property to his wife Margaret.

28. William Moore (spelled Mauer or Mawer) was probably the same person to whom it appeared to the selectmen of Boston, on the twenty-sixth of September, 1636, that William Hudson had "sold a house plot and garden without the consent of the appointed allotters, contrary to a former order, said Mawer being a stranger." On February 19, 1638, there was granted to him "a great lot at the Mount (Wollaston) for nine heads." On February 7, 1640, he was described as "late of Boston," in a conveyance which he made to Captain Edward Gibbon, for fifteen pounds, of one house and garden plot with the building thereon and appurtenances. William Moore received in Exeter in December, 1639, twenty-two acres and one hundred and ten poles, in the division of the uplands, two acres and forty poles in the marsh "on this side of Mr. Hilton's," and one hundred and twenty poles of that at Lamprey river; the amount of the former corresponding well with the "nine heads" of his family, and the latter showing that he was possessed of cattle. He did not subscribe the Combination,

for what reason is unknown. He remained a lifelong inhabitant of the town, and bore his share of its burdens, as well as enjoyed its rewards and honors. He received grants of lands, and held various offices of responsibility. He was a captain in the militia; and the last appearance of his name upon the records is as moderator of a town meeting in 1699. He must have been then an old man, and probably died soon afterwards. He left numerous descendants.

29. Richard Morris was of Boston, having probably immigrated thither in the fleet with Winthrop in 1630; and in 1631 was, with his wife Leonora, admitted to the church. At that time he was styled sergeant; in 1633 he was made ensign, and later lieutenant. He was deputy to the General Court in 1635 and 1636, and the next year was in command of the fort at Castle Island. Apparently something had occurred to weaken his standing with the authorities before 1637, but in that year he forfeited all their good will by signing a remonstrance in favor of Wheelwright; so that he was disarmed, and retired to Exeter, the next year, probably. In the first division of lands he received thirty-three acres of upland, and seven acres and forty poles of marsh; so he probably had a considerable household and cattle. His name appears on the records with the honorable prefix of "Mr." He was a signer of the Combination, and was dismissed to the church at Exeter in January, 1639. It is probable that Mr. Morris did not care to remain in Exeter after Wheelwright's departure, and the extension of the jurisdiction of Massachusetts over the New Hampshire settlement; and it seems likely that he was the person of that name who went to Portsmouth, Rhode Island, in 1643, and was living there in 1655.

30. Nicholas Needham was of Boston in 1636, and received on the twentieth of February of that year an allotment of two acres of land at Mount Wollaston, "only for his present planting." No doubt a parishioner and sympathizer of Wheelwright, he probably came with him to Exeter, as he was made a grantee in one of the Indian deeds of 1638. In the apportionment of the lands, he received twelve acres and sixty poles of upland, and four acres of marsh. He also set his signature to the Combination. Being elected the second Ruler of the settlement, he held the office about two years, when he resigned it October 20, 1642. His residence in Exeter did not outlast that of Wheelwright. Foreseeing the hour of need, he, with others, negotiated with Thomas Gorges in

1641 for a tract of land in Wells, to which Wheelwright and his immediate friends retired, when the long arm of Massachusetts power was extended over the New Hampshire plantations. The historian of Wells is not certain whether Needham settled in that place. If he did not his subsequent history is unascertained. Savage thinks he was living in 1652.

31. Thomas Pettit was of Boston in 1634, from which time he served for three years and a half with Oliver Mellows, and thereupon January 8, 1638, received from the town a grant of a house plot "towards the new mylne." Mellows was in sympathy with Wheelwright, and was disarmed in 1637, and it would be very natural that his journeyman should be led by the same feeling to migrate to the new settlement which Wheelwright was founding. Pettit received six acres and thirty poles as his share of the Exeter uplands, and also affixed his name to the Combination. He was for a while a man of some prominence in the town and served as selectman in 1652 and 1655, after which his name disappears from the records. His wife was named Christian; they had a daughter Hannah, born in Exeter in the beginning of February, 1647-8. His son, Thomas Pettit, Jr., had a grant of thirty acres of land in 1649.

32. Philemon Pormort was married in Alford, Lincolnshire, England, October 11, 1627, to Susanna, daughter of William Bellingham. They emigrated to New England, probably with one child or more, and were admitted to the Boston church in August, 1634. He was chosen schoolmaster April 13, 1635, and in 1637 had a grant of thirty acres of land. Pormort was an adherent of Wheelwright, having quite likely known him in England, and was, on Wheelwright's expulsion from Massachusetts Bay, advised to depart himself, on pain of imprisonment; therefore he came to Exeter. He was a subscriber of the Combination, was dismissed in January, 1639, to the Exeter church, and received fourteen acres and seventy poles in the division of the uplands. He had three children, at least, born in this country, one or two of them at Exeter. He went with Wheelwright to Wells, and, according to the historian of that town, remained there some years, taking an active part in the affairs of the church, but at length was denied the privilege of communion for the reason that his theological views did not agree with those of the ruling powers in Massachusetts. He was in Boston in 1653, and is supposed to have removed thence to Great Island or Portsmouth. Descendants

33. Robert Read was of Boston as early as 1635, and in Exeter early enough to be entitled to an allotment of nine acres and fifty poles in the division of the uplands, and to set his name to the Combination. He removed to Hampton after 1645, according to Kelly, and afterwards to Boston, and finally to Hampton again, according to Quint. To him and his wife Hannah were born three children: Rebecca, September 29, 1646; Deborah, January 25, 1649; and Samuel, who was baptized April 3, 1653, and died March 31, 1654. Read's wife died June 24, 1655, and he himself was drowned October 20, 1657, with six others by the upsetting of a boat sailing out of Hampton river; a catastrophe on which was founded Whittier's poem of the *Wreck of Rivermouth*.

34. Edward Rishworth was baptized at Saleby in Lincolnshire, England, May 5, 1617. In all probability he came to this country with others of Wheelwright's friends in July, 1637, and became one of the earliest settlers of Exeter. He appears to have been nearly connected, by his marriage, with the family of Wheelwright's wife. In the division of the uplands he was awarded one of the smaller shares, and he was a signer of the Combination. In 1640 he was chosen by the court of the town to be "Secretary, to look to the book, and to enter all actions that are brought." This undoubtedly included the functions of Town Clerk. When Wheelwright left Exeter, Rishworth departed with him to Wells, where he became a man of consequence. He was a magistrate and a representative of York, to which place he removed from Wells, for thirteen years. He lived to be nearly seventy, and a son of his, bearing the same name, was the husband of Wheelwright's daughter Susanna.

35. Henry Roby was of the Combination, but had no share in the first division of the uplands or meadows; so very likely he did not come to Exeter till the spring of 1640. He was granted liberty in 1649, with others, to set up a saw-mill, and in 1650 was chosen selectman. Soon afterwards he removed to Hampton where he died in the spring of 1688. After the erection of New Hampshire into a royal province, Roby was appointed a judge of the Court of Sessions, before which the Rev. Joshua Moody was tried in 1684 for refusing to administer the Lord's Supper in the form set forth in the book of common prayer, to Governor Cranfield. Roby was at first for acquitting Moody, but Cranfield "found means" to gain him over, and he concurred with other justices in the judgment of condemnation. In his later years Roby is said

by Kelly to have become intemperate and embarrassed, so that at his death he was buried hastily to avoid arrest of his body. His wife was named Ruth, and they had several children. His descendants are still found in this region.

36. George Ruobone or Rabone was assigned one of the smaller shares in the division of the uplands; and was a subscriber of the Combination. He appears to have remained in Exeter but a short time, as he is represented by Judge Bourne in his history of Wells, to have been one of the earliest settlers of that place "before Wheelwright and his fellow refugees came from Exeter." He seems afterwards to have changed his rather unusual name to Haborne, and under that designation is described in a deed as of Hampton in 1650.

37. Robert Seward subscribed the Combination, but had no share of the uplands, having probably not arrived in Exeter before the spring of 1640. He staid but a brief time, and was living in Portsmouth in 1649, after which nothing has been ascertained respecting him.

38. John Smart came from the county of Norfolk, England, to Hingham, Massachusetts, in 1635, with his wife and two sons, and in September of that year drew his house lot there. He came to Exeter in time to receive an assignment of one acre and twenty-six poles of the meadows "next the town," which implies that he had cattle or goats. The lands he first took up appear to have been situated on the eastern or Stratham side of the river, and he did not subscribe the Combination. But he was a public-spirited citizen, and joined with others in the agreement to purchase Wheelwright's house, to be used as a parsonage. He lived in the northerly part of the town, now Newmarket, and his descendants live there still.

39. Robert Smith is thought to have been of Boston in 1638. In the division of the Exeter uplands he had six acres and thirty poles, a share one-half larger than the smallest; and his name was affixed to the Combination. When the town came under the Massachusetts government, on the seventh of September, 1643, he was appointed one of the magistrates "to end small business at Exeter." After a residence of some years in the place he removed to Hampton. Hon. Joseph Smith, a judge of the Superior Court, and a man useful and prominent in his day, was his son.

40. Anthony Stanyan, described as glover, was a passenger from England to Boston in 1635, and in February, 1637–8, had

assigned to him "a great lot for eleven heads" at Mount Wollaston. In Exeter, in December, 1639, there were awarded to him, under the honorary designation of "Mr.," twenty-seven acres and one hundred and thirty-five poles of upland, and ten and one-half acres of the marshes. These large grants imply that he had a considerable family, and a good number of cattle. He was a member of the Exeter church, and though a resident of the town prior to the execution of the Combination, did not set his hand to it. Possibly he was in doubt whether to fix his residence in the new settlement, as in July, 1641, he was "granted to be a townsman" of Boston, and on the twenty-fourth of July, 1642, his son John was baptized there, at the age of six days. But if he meditated abandoning Exeter he soon changed his mind, for he was back again in May, 1643, and held the office of magistrate to end small causes in 1645, and that of town clerk in 1647. Subsequently he removed to Hampton from which he was representative to the General Court of Massachusetts in 1654. He was living in 1683. His first wife was named Mary, and after her decease he married, January 1, 1656, Ann, widow of William Partridge of Salisbury, Massachusetts. He left children by whom his name has been handed down to our time.

41. Augustine Storre was doubly a brother-in-law of Wheelwright, being a brother of his first wife, and the husband of a sister of his second. He undoubtedly came over from England in July, 1637, and probably left Boston in the autumn following, and was in Exeter in the spring of 1638. When the first division of lands was made, he was allotted, with the title of respect of "Mr.," twenty acres and one hundred poles of upland, and two and three-quarters acres of the marshes. His name appears on the Combination, the next in order to Wheelwright's, and he was chosen an assistant to the first Ruler. It is evident that he was held in high esteem by the inhabitants. When Wheelwright's residence in Exeter came to an end, Storre, as might be expected from their connection, quitted the place also, and is understood to have gone to Wells, after which nothing is learned of him.

42. Samuel Walker had one of the smaller assignments of land in Exeter, and was a signer of the Combination. Of his former history nothing has been discovered. In 1643, in a time of scarcity, he was one of those appointed by the town to appropriate and dispose of to the needy, any corn not required by the owners before harvest. This appointment speaks well for his character

for discretion and fairness. It is supposed that he left the town soon afterwards, probably for the eastward.

43. James Wall was a carpenter, and was sent over from England, with two others, by John Mason, the patentee of New Hampshire. They came in the Pied Cow, under a written contract dated March 14, 1634, to run five years, by which they were employed to build saw-mills and houses for him at Newichwannock. They arrived there the thirteenth of July of the same year, and there Wall remained till some time after the death of Mason in 1635. He was in Exeter April 3, 1638, and witnessed one of the Indian deeds to Wheelwright of that date, and no doubt remained there during the formation of the settlement, when his services as a carpenter would be most important. On the assignment of the lands, ten acres and ninety poles of uplands and something less than two acres of the marshes fell to his share. His name also appears upon the Combination. He must have lived in Exeter about twelve years, and was a useful citizen, repeatedly intrusted with town offices. In 1650 he changed his residence to Hampton, and died there October 3, 1659, leaving a widow, Mary, and two children.

44. George Walton, born about 1615, became an inhabitant of New Hampshire about 1635, and so remained till his death, half a century later. He had no assignment in the first division of lands in Exeter, but joined in establishing the Combination a few months later; so it is not unlikely that he came to Exeter between those events. He did not remain very long, for in 1648 he was in Dover, where he was licensed to keep an "ordinary," and in 1662 was a vintner in Portsmouth. His later years were passed at Great Island, where he suffered from the persecutions of a "stone-throwing demon," an account of which may be found in Mather's *Magnalia* and elsewhere. Less superstitious persons, however, attributed his tribulations to mischievous human agency. His wife was named Alice, and they had several children, one of whom was Shadrach Walton, well known in the military, civil and judicial service of the province.

45. Thomas Wardell, a shoemaker, and an inhabitant of Lincolnshire, England, came to this country, and was admitted to the Boston church November 9, 1634. By his wife Elizabeth he had two children, baptized in Boston; Eliakim, November 23, 1634, and Martha, September 3, 1637, and two others, born probably in Exeter; Benjamin, in February, 1640, and Samuel, May 16, 1643.

In January, 1637, he was allotted twenty acres of land in Boston, but being an outspoken supporter of Wheelwright he was disarmed; and thereupon proceeded, in 1638, no doubt, to Exeter. In January, 1639, he was recommended by the Boston church to membership in that formed at Exeter. He received twelve acres and sixty poles in the division of the Exeter uplands, and was a signer of the Combination. Evidently he was a man in whom his townsmen reposed confidence; for in 1641 he was chosen sergeant of the band of soldiers in Exeter, and approved as such by Nicholas Needham, Ruler; in 1642 he was chosen one of the committee to collect and distribute to the poor the surplus corn, in a time of scarcity; and in 1643 he was appointed by the General Court of Massachusetts a magistrate to end small causes in Exeter. But he did not continue there very long afterwards. It is uncertain whether he removed to Ipswich or to Boston, where the death of a person bearing his name is recorded December 10, 1646.

46. William Wardell, supposed to be a brother of Thomas, probably came to this country in 1633 with Edmund Quincy, whose servant he is described as being, and joined the Boston church February 9, 1634. By his wife Alice he had a daughter Meribah, born May 14, 1637, and a son Uzell, April 7, 1639; the latter born in Exeter. He received in Boston February 20, 1636, two acres of land laid out at the Mount (Wollaston) only for his present planting; and February 19, 1637, a great lot at the same place "for three heads." But the next year he migrated to Exeter, on being disarmed as a friend of the Antinomian party. He took with him some cattle, or goats, as it appears that he had in the first division of lands one hundred and twenty poles of meadow "on this side of Mr. Hilton's," and the same quantity at Lamprey river. He also had ten acres and fifty poles of upland; and set his hand to the Combination. He left Exeter with Wheelwright, and his name is subscribed as a witness to the deed of Sagamore Thomas Chabinocke to John Wadleigh at Wells October 18, 1649, and attested by said Wardell's oath March 25, 1657. He also swore allegiance to Massachusetts at Wells July 5, 1653. Another person of the same name was living in Boston at the same time, but whether a relative is not known.

47. William Wenbourne was of Boston in 1635, in which year there was born to him and Elizabeth his wife, a son John, on the twenty-second of November. A second son was born September 21, 1638, bearing the same name, the former one having doubtless

died. The latter-part of the next year Wenbourne was in Exeter, where he was allotted seven acres and thirty poles of upland, and a few months later signed the Combination. Upon the town being received under the jurisdiction of Massachusetts, he was appointed clerk of the writs and one of the three inferior magistrates. He probably returned to Boston before 1648, where he was chosen constable in 1653, and was living in 1662. The name of Winborn has been preserved in Durham up to recent times, so it is not unlikely that his descendants are still to be found in the vicinity.

48. William Wentworth was a native of Lincolnshire, England, and was born in March, 1615-16. He was a family connection and parishioner of Wheelwright, and probably came to this country in July, 1637, in the vessel with others of Wheelwright's "friends." No doubt he made little stay in Boston, but pushed on speedily to the Pascataqua country, and was one of the earliest at the settlement of Exeter. He had in the division of the uplands one of the small shares, and set his signature, in excellent chirography, to the Combination. When Massachusetts began to stretch out her hand over the New Hampshire towns, he joined Wheelwright in departing into Maine, and resided in Wells until 1649, when he removed to Dover, where, with the exception of temporary absences, he spent the residue of his life. He was a ruling elder in the church, and as such was a preacher and expounder, though not technically a clergyman. At some time after the decease of the Rev. Samuel Dudley, which occurred in 1683, he was employed to preach at Exeter, and continued to do so until 1693, when by reason of age and infirmity he was compelled to desist. He lived, however, till March 15, 1696-7, when he had completed his eighty-first year. His physical vigor was remarkable, as is evidenced by his successful resistance to the attempts of the Indians to enter the house where he was at the Dover massacre in 1689; and no one of the little company of Exeter pioneers, save Wheelwright, was of a more sturdy manhood than Wentworth. He was the progenitor of a long line of descendants, able and stalwart, mentally and physically; three of whom held the highest executive offices in the province of New Hampshire; others have sat in the councils of the nation, and many more have manifested the hereditary capacity and force in various callings. The history of the family has been laboriously compiled by one, by no means the least distinguished of Elder Wentworth's descendants.

49. John Wheelwright deserves here a brief sketch of his

subsequent career. He retreated before the advance of Massachusetts to Wells in the spring of 1643, and while he was there the General Court, in not the most gracious manner, annulled his sentence of banishment, and re-enfranchised him. After ministering to the little community at Wells for four years, he accepted the invitation of the church at Hampton to settle over them as the pastoral colleague of the Rev. Timothy Dalton, their religious teacher. In Hampton he continued, to the entire acceptance of his flock, until 1655 or 1656 when he made a voyage to England. There he was received with high favor by Oliver Cromwell, his fellow collegian, now the highest personage in the land; and also by Sir Henry Vane, a friend and fellow sufferer in the Antinomian struggle in Massachusetts. After Cromwell's death Wheelwright returned to New England, in company with several other ministers, in the summer of 1662. He accepted the invitation of the church at Salisbury, Massachusetts, to become their spiritual guide, and, though then arrived at the age of threescore and ten, enjoyed among them the longest pastorate of his checkered life. He had his trials there, indeed, for he was not one to yield his opinions because another opposed them, but on the whole his ministrations were useful and his motives and independence were respected. It was a pleasant episode in his later life that he preached a sermon in 1671-2 in behalf of Harvard College, soliciting contributions for the rebuilding of Harvard Hall which had been destroyed by fire,—thus showing that he harbored no malice against the dignitaries of Massachusetts for the harsh treatment that he had formerly received at their hands. His death took place at Salisbury November 15, 1679.

50. Thomas Wight, of whom nothing is learned prior to his appearance in Exeter, had six acres and thirty poles allotted him as his share of the uplands; and was a subscriber of the Combination. In the five subsequent years that he spent in the town, his name appears seldom on the records. He had a house, and perhaps two, as his "old house" is referred to; and he was censured and fined in 1642 by the town court for "contemptuous carriage and speeches against the court and magistrates." He lived in the town at least two years and a half, afterwards, and then went away, we know not whither. Mr. Savage thinks Thomas Wight was the same person elsewhere called Thomas Wright, but he gives no authority for the belief. The name is uniformly written Weight in the town records; but is subscribed Wight, apparently in his own hand, to the Combination.

51. Balthazar Willix, whose name would indicate that he was of foreign origin, was undoubtedly in Exeter as early as the beginning of 1640, as he was then awarded one of the smaller shares of the uplands. He was not a signer of the Combination. His name appears, however, repeatedly in the records, at a later date, in his own bold and handsome chirography. In May, 1643, he was one of the petitioners to the General Court of Massachusetts to receive Exeter under their government. His name is not found in the records after 1650. In the month of May or June, 1648, Willix's wife was robbed and brutally murdered on her way from Dover to Exeter. Whether the perpetrator of the outrage was ever brought to justice is not known. Willix did not remain in Exeter long afterwards, but took up his residence in Salisbury, where he was taxed in 1650, and died March 23, 1651.

52. Thomas Wilson came to this country in June, 1633, with his wife and three sons; Humphrey, Samuel and Joshua. He also had children born here: Deborah in August, 1634, and Lydia in November, 1636. His home was in Roxbury, and he had the misfortune to lose his house and goods by fire. Being in sympathy with Wheelwright he came with him to Exeter to reside, but subsequently made peace with the church which he had left. He was a signer of the Combination, and occupied the island at the falls and some lands on the eastern side of the river. In the first division of lands he received four acres and twenty-eight rods of marsh. He built the first grist-mill in the town. On the twentieth of October, 1642, on the resignation of Nicholas Needham as Ruler, he was elected his successor. He died in the summer of 1643, leaving a will in which he made provision for his widow and children. The former was married the next year to John Legat. A difference arose about the estate between her and her oldest son, Humphrey, which was by the General Court referred to the County Court at Ipswich. Humphrey Wilson continued an inhabitant of the town through life, probably, and his descendants, though none bearing his name, are still living in Exeter.

The foregoing are the names of all the men who are known to have been inhabitants of Exeter in the first two years of its existence. William Furber and John Underhill, though temporarily in the place at the times of the execution of the Indian deeds, which they respectively witnessed, were residents of Dover, and never of Exeter.

EARLY ENACTMENTS.

The third year opened upon Exeter, in the spring of 1640, with a population of from one hundred and fifty to two hundred souls, including women and children, living under a practicable and regular system of government. The municipal regulations adopted by the inhabitants from time to time, as long as they ruled themselves, were generally marked by equity and good sense. A few examples are given :

It was enacted that any inhabitant might sell to the Indians such merchandise as he pleased, except weapons, ammunition and strong waters. The charges of the town were to be ratably proportioned among the inhabitants, owners of land, and cattle, and privileges. In conformity with the professions of the Combination, treason, "reviling his majesty the Lord's anointed" and the like, were made punishable capitally. Judicious regulations were prescribed in regard to the purchase of lots, the felling of timber, and the attendance of the inhabitants at town meetings. The miller's toll was limited; all creeks were declared free for fishing; fences were ordered to be erected, and highways of three rods in width to be made. Rules were laid down to prevent injury to growing crops by swine. The control of the lands by the town was jealously preserved; and no inhabitant was permitted to buy for his own use from the Indians any of the planting ground reserved for their cultivation; but must tender it first to the town.

It would appear that even in this early stage of the settlement, slander was not wholly unknown, and an order was passed that any persons spreading abroad any accusation which could not be proved by the mouth of two or three witnesses, should be liable to the court's censure. Thus early too was enacted the law that no foreigners should be employed to work in the town, if inhabitants would do the work as cheaply and as well. Of course it was not natives of foreign countries that were here referred to, but any persons not citizens of Exeter. This disinclination to encourage "foreigners" to come into the town, was exhibited repeatedly by similar orders, at later dates; and, indeed, is thought by some not to have entirely died out yet !

These regulations appear to have been scrupulously carried into effect, without distinction of persons.

The first clerk of the town and court was Edward Rishworth. The second was John Legat, who had been a resident and schoolmaster of Hampton in 1640, and afterwards filled the same important station in Exeter. He wrote a handsome hand, and was well informed and business-like, and for several years took a somewhat prominent part in the affairs of the town. He received repeated grants of lands and privileges, and was one of the townsmen from 1647 to 1649. It was probably in the latter year that he removed back to Hampton. There he was living in 1664. His name is not extinct in the vicinity.

By the spring of 1641 a " band of soldiers " had been organized in Exeter, and the freemen elected Richard Bulgar lieutenant and Thomas Wardell sergeant; and their choice was approved by Ruler Needham.

On the twenty-sixth of October, 1642, Nicholas Needham resigned his office of Ruler, and Thomas Wilson, being chosen in his place, gave his approbation to all the laws and orders which had been made during Ruler Needham's administration.

The grain crop of the season of 1642 was for some reason a very scanty one, and by the succeeding spring the poorer class of inhabitants began to suffer from scarcity of food. The majority of the town made no scruple in applying the doctrine of " eminent domain " to the case. On May 6, 1643, they appointed a committee of discreet and judicious citizens, and authorized them to search the houses, and take therefrom any corn not needed by the owners, and dispose of the same to such poor people as stood most in need of it, for such pay as they could make; the owners, however, to be compensated at market rates; an arbitrary measure, but one entirely justifiable under the peculiar circumstances.

Meadow or marsh lands were considered specially desirable by the owners of cattle, as no other mowing ground had yet been rescued from the forest. Patches of this natural grass land were found by explorers here and there, on the margins of streams; and it was ordered, August 21, 1643, that any inhabitant who should discover any piece of marsh land of less than twenty acres, should be at liberty to enjoy it as his own; if above twenty acres, it was to be at the disposal of the town, except that the finder was to be entitled to a double proportion of it.

At a town court held September 5, 1643, Christopher Lawson was put under recognizance to answer to the charge of extortion " at the next Court to be holden for Exeter either here or elsewhere." This language indicates an understanding that the town government was about to be merged in an authority of a wider sweep, which we shall see was soon accomplished. One of the last acts of the town court was to fill up the measure of justice to Thomas Biggs, who was found guilty of sundry petty larcenies, by adjudging him to make ample restitution to the sufferers, and also to be whipped six stripes. It is satisfactory to know that this punishment was very likely the making of the young culprit, for he became a useful citizen, and was repeatedly elected to posts of responsibility in the town, in after years.

The records of the town, during the period of its self-government, contain many particulars of interest that could not well be included in this chapter; and for the satisfaction of the curious, it has been thought expedient to print them entire in the original language and orthography, in the appendix (II).

CHAPTER II.

EXETER UNDER THE MASSACHUSETTS GOVERNMENT.

By the spring of 1643 all the New Hampshire plantations, except Exeter, were under the sway of Massachusetts. Hampton had orignally been settled from that colony; Dover and Portsmouth had been induced to submit themselves to her rule, partly by her claim that they fell within her patent, but more, perhaps, by the favorable terms which she held out to them. That church-membership was a prerequisite to the privilege of voting in civil affairs, was a cardinal doctrine in Massachusetts. This was now surrendered, and the citizens of the New Hampshire towns were to be allowed the elective franchise without reference to that qualification; a proof of the price which the Bay Puritans were ready to pay, to purchase an extension of their jurisdiction.

Exeter was the last to yield. A large part of her inhabitants felt that they had been treated with harshness and injustice by the authorities of Massachusetts, and some of them utterly refused to submit again to her dominion but quitted the place to avoid it. A petition, however, was forwarded in May, 1643, to the Massachusetts General Court, that Exeter might be received within their jurisdiction. It was subscribed by Thomas Rashleigh, Richard Bulgar, William Wenborne, Thomas Wardell, Samuel Walker, Christopher Lawson, John Legat, Henry Roby, Thomas Biggs, William Cole, Thomas Pettit, Robert Smith, John Cram, Nathaniel Boulter, Robert Seward, Abraham Drake and William Moore. Eleven of these were signers of the Combination. The petition itself has been destroyed, and we can only infer its contents from the reception it met with. It could not have been an unconditional surrender to Massachusetts, but must have stipulated for some terms which her rulers were unwilling to grant. The General Court answered curtly, that "as Exeter fell within the Massachusetts patent, they took it ill that the petitioners should capitulate with them." In other words the Exeter people must accept such conditions as Massachusetts chose to impose.

Immediately afterwards a second petition was forwarded, couched in language sufficiently humble, as follows:

To the Right Worshipful the Governor, the Deputie Governor and the Magistrates, with the assistance and deputyes of this honored Courte at present assembled in Boston.

The humble petition of the inhabitants of Exeter, who do humbly request that this honored Court would be pleased to appoint the bounds of our Towne to be layed out to us, both towards Hampton & also downe the River on that side which Capt. Wiggons his farm is on, for he doth Clame all the land from the towne downwards, on the one side, & Hampton on the other side doth clame to be neere us, that we shall not be able to subsist to be a Towne except this honored Court be pleased to releave us. And we suppose that Capt. Wiggens his farme and a good way below it, may well be laid within our Township if this honored Court so please.

Also we do humbly crave that the Court would be pleased to grant that we may still peaceably enjoy thouse small quantitie of meddows, which are at Lamperell river that Dover men now seeme to lay clame to, notwithstanding they know we long since purchased them & allso quietly possest them with their consent.

Likewise we do humbly request that this honored Court would be pleased to establish three men among us to put an Ishew to small differences amongst us, & one to be a Clarke of the writes, that so we might not be so troblesom to the Courts for every small matter. The three men which we desire the ending of Controversies are Anthony Stanean, Samuel Greenffield & James Wall & we do desire that John Legat may be the Clarke of the writes. Thus leaving our Petition to your Judicious Consideration & yourselves to the Lord, we rest and remaine ever ready to do you our best service.

Samuel Greenfield *	Henry Roby
Anthony Stanyan	Richard Carter
Thomas Wight	William M[oore]
Nathaniel Boulter	James Wall
John Tedd *	Humphrey Willson
Robert Hethersay	Ralph Hall
John Legat	John Bursley *
Abraham Drake	Francis Swain
Thomas Jones *	John Davis
Nicholas Swain	Balthazer Willix
Thomas King *	John Smart

Of these twenty-two subscribers only four had set their hands to the Combination, and not one of them was in any way connected with the Antinomian dissensions of 1637.

This petition bore date May 12 [1643], and apparently was presented near the close of the current session of the General Court. The printed records make no mention of it then; but an indorsement upon the petition shows that both branches of the Legislature acceded to it.

On the seventh of the following September the General Court formally received Exeter within the Massachusetts government and assigned it to the newly formed county of Norfolk. But it is a curious fact that in the appointment of permanent town officers the nominees of the accepted petition were rejected, and signers of the rejected petition and of the Combination were preferred. William Wenborne was appointed clerk of the writs, and William Wenborne, Robert Smith and Thomas Wardell were made magistrates to decide small causes. Massachusetts knew how to conciliate as well as to coerce.

THE CONDITIONS OF ANNEXATION.

The terms on which Exeter was admitted were substantially those accorded to the other New Hampshire towns: namely, "the same order, and way of administration of justice and way of keeping courts, as is established at Ipswich and Salem;" exemption from "all public charges other than those that shall arise for or from among [the people] themselves, or from any occasion or course that may be taken to procure their own proper good or benefit;" and the enjoyment of "all such lawful liberties of fishing, planting, felling timber as formerly they have enjoyed in the said [Pascataqua] river." The town was to send no delegate to the General Court, but this was no hardship, as the inhabitants could ill afford the expense which would thereby fall upon them, and their apparent need of a representative in the Legislature was small.

At first it was ordered that Exeter causes at law should be tried at Ipswich; afterwards at the courts held in one of three or four towns (not including Exeter) in the county of Norfolk. There ample opportunities were afforded to the inhabitants for settling all litigated questions above the jurisdiction of the town magistrates; and towns were compelled by presentments of the grand jury to keep their meeting-houses, watch-houses, stocks, roads and bridges in good and serviceable order; while the General Court exercised a watchful and paternal care over their ecclesiastical and municipal concerns.

The government of Exeter was of course modified, to conform to the usages of Massachusetts. Three townsmen were chosen, Richard Bulgar, Samuel Greenfield and Christopher Lawson, whose duties approximated those of selectmen of the present day. By a vote of the town, April 8, 1644, they were empowered to "make town rates; to distrain for all town debts; to pay the town's debts out of the town's treasury, or to make rates for it; to look to the execution of all town orders; to grant and lay out lots, provided they be not above twenty acres; to receive into the town as inhabitants, or to keep out, such as they in their wisdom think meet."

THE FISHERY.

The fishery furnished a very important article of subsistence to the early inhabitants; indeed, for the first few seasons, before the land had been brought fairly under cultivation, it must have been well nigh indispensable. The river, above and below the falls, abounded in fish of various kinds, and the salmon, we learn from tradition, were especially plentiful. Still we can hardly give credence to the often repeated tale that the ancient indentures of apprenticeship in Exeter used to contain a proviso that the apprentices should not be compelled to eat salmon more than twice a week! No instrument containing such a clause has ever been found; and the story has been told of half a score of towns in England, and was, undoubtedly, an importation from that country.

The salmon, for the excellent reason that they can no longer pass the dams to breed their young in the fresh water above, have long deserted the Squamscot; but the alewives still frequent the river, though probably not in such profusion as formerly. At first the latter were chiefly used as manure for the cultivated lands; and thus rendered necessary the stringent regulations that were adopted to prevent swine and dogs from feeding upon them.

As early as the second of November, 1640, it was ordered by the town that "all creeks are free; only he that makes a weir therein is to have in the first place the benefit of it in fishing time; and so others may set a weir either above or below, and enjoy the same liberty."

On the twenty-eighth of June, 1644, the town granted to Christopher Lawson and his heirs " the right to set a weir in the river of Exeter " upon certain conditions, one of which was that the inhabitants should be supplied with alewives to *fish* their land, at three shillings a thousand, in such pay as the town afforded; and another that he should make flood gates " so that barks, boats and canoes may come to the town." The inhabitants reserved to themselves liberty to fish in the falls and elsewhere in the river, but not to set any other weir so as to forestall Lawson's. This monopoly, though formidable in sound, being extended to Lawson's " heirs forever," enjoyed but a brief span of life; for the very next year, April 26, 1645, the town resumed the control of the fishery by passing the following vote:

All the creeks for fishing this year are divided into three divisions by lot, eleven or twelve persons to a division according as the lots lie, as follow: the first division of lots, from the mill downward, are to have Rawbone's creek and the creek above it; the second division from the mill downward, are to have all the creeks on the mill side of the river; and the third division are to have all the creeks on the town side of the river, except Mr. Needham's creek and the great cove creek, which two creeks lie common.

This vote casts a little light upon the topography of the town at that early date. *The* mill (there was then but one) was Wilson's, on the eastern side of the island at the falls. The " mill side " of the river was the opposite from the " town side " which was, of course, the western. This indicates that, from the very beginning, the main settlement was on the western side of the river; though tradition asserts that two or three settlers planted their houses on the opposite bank, between what is now styled Powderhouse point and Wheelwright's creek; and depressions in the soil, which may have been cellars, go to confirm the tale.

The people of Exeter were not long in discovering that the Massachusetts control was to be no sinecure, but was to extend sometimes to their pettiest concerns. When, in 1644, they chose Samuel Greenfield to " keep a sufficient ordinary, and draw wine and strong waters, and trade with the Indians," the General Court " denied him to draw wine until they had a more full and satisfactory information of him." And when the town " took the minds of the trained bands for the re-establishing Richard Bullgar in his former office of lieutenant," the General Court " thought it not meet that he should be their lieutenant until further information be given to this Court of said Bullgar; in the meantime he to exercise the trainband as their sergeant."

The first three or four years after Exeter submitted to Massachusetts appear to have formed a critical period in the history of the town. The departure of Wheelwright and other leading inhabitants was a heavy draft upon the little colony, not to be counterbalanced by the ordinary recruits of a frontier settlement. Religious differences had crept in among the inhabitants to such an extent that the aid of the General Court was evoked to compose them. A committee of ministers was accordingly appointed to examine the ground of the complaints, and to do their best to bring about harmony. At the same time the town prayed to be excused from the payment of taxes — " rate and head money,"— no doubt upon the plea of their poverty and unsettled condition. The General Court, willing as they were to afford relief in spiritual matters, were not inclined, however, to remit their pecuniary obligations, but " conceived meet that they forthwith send in their rates to the Treasurer."

Two events concurred, however, within the next three years, to give renewed strength to the town, and tide it over the threatening period, to stability and prosperity. The first was the settlement in Exeter of Edward Gilman in 1647, and his relatives shortly afterwards, men of property and energy, who set up saw-mills and gave an impulse to the business of the place. The second was the engagement in 1650 of the Rev. Samuel Dudley as the minister of the town, who united the previously discordant religious elements, and became in every respect one of the most useful citizens.

THE CARE OF THE CATTLE.

On the first of May, 1649, the selectmen, in behalf of the town, entered into a written agreement with Gowen Wilson to drive, and take the oversight of the cows and other cattle of the inhabitants, for the season. As the transaction illustrates the customs of the times, the instrument is here given in full:

It is covenanted and agreed upon between Gowen Wilson and the town of Exeter that the said Gowen is to keep all the neat herd of the town of Exeter from one-year-old and upward (working cattle excepted) from the day of the date hereof until three weeks after Michaelmas, to go every morning through the town at the usual time that cow-herds go forth, and so to have the cattle turned into the town street and the said Gowen to drive them into the woods, and all the day to keep them in such convenient places as may be best for their feeding, on both sides of the river, and at night to bring them home again, at the like usual time of herds coming home; in like manner to bring them through the street from the first house to the last who have cattle in that street, and to seek up or cause to be sought any that shall be lost from before him, and in like manner to keep them every third Sabbath day.

And in consideration hereof the inhabitants of the town who have cattle are to pay or cause to be paid unto the said Gowen Wilson the sum of eleven pound, to be paid by every man's equal proportion according to the number of their cattle in manner as followeth, viz.: at the first entry to have a peck of corn a head for all and every the milch cows, and a pound of butter a cow, suddenly, after his entry upon the said work, as he shall have occasion to use it. And the rest of the aforesaid (11 l.) is half of it to be paid in good English commodities at price current, about the beginning of August next, and the other half of the pay to be paid in corn at harvest at 3 ˢ a bushel.

Witness to this agreement the hands of us,

> GOWEN WILSON,
> JOHN LEGAT,
> JAMES WALL,
> HENRY ROBY.

This writing discloses to us some facts of interest about the condition of the settlement and its people at that period. The cattle were compelled to gather their subsistence "in the woods," because so little of the surrounding country was as yet cleared from the forest growth. A cow-herd was necessary to keep them from straying; therefore it is clear that there was an absence of enclosures. "*The* town street" implies that as yet there was but a single thoroughfare, doubtless along the line of the present Water street. The fact that the herd was to be driven to pasture only "every third Sabbath," shows the respect entertained by the people for the Lord's day. And the mode in which compensation was to be made, in corn, butter and English commodities, without a particle of cash, reveals the extreme scarcity of money among the people. Indeed, for long years afterwards, much of the business of the place was carried on by barter, or "country pay," as it was termed, and would have been practicable in no other method.

Up to the year 1650 the General Court had at intervals made appointments of local magistrates to end small causes in the town. In 1645 they were Anthony Stanyan, Robert Smith and John Legat; in 1646 Anthony Stanyan, Samuel Greenfield and James Wall. But when in May, 1650, the inhabitants made application for another similar appointment, it was refused by the General Court upon the ground that there was no need of such commissioners, as Captain Thomas Wiggin, an Associate, lived so near. But the town were allowed the privilege of choosing a constable, provided the person of their choice should be approved by the county court " as fit for the place."

The fathers of Exeter early learned the need of a system of supervision of the conduct of their public servants. As early as August 26, 1650, a vote was passed that one of the duties of the townsmen should be to "call to account" their predecessors in office. And this, or some equivalent mode of auditing the accounts of the receiving and disbursing officers of the town, was maintained with great regularity afterwards, from that time to the present.

THE STAPLE COMMODITY.

The manufacture of lumber was, for more than a century, the chief source of revenue to the inhabitants. There was everywhere an abundance of the fittest oaks and pines that had survived their weaker brethren, and were truly monarchs of the forest. The land was owned in common, and a long period elapsed before much of it was divided. The lumber, therefore, cost the inhabitants nothing but the necessary labor in getting it out. Naturally, some secured much more than others; there was a great deal of waste; and non-residents did not hesitate to help themselves from the bounteous supply. To remedy these troubles, and to insure something like equality or equity among the inhabitants in the enjoyment of the products of their common domain, as well as to prevent strangers from encroaching thereon, the town from time to time adopted regulations; a brief summary of which will be presented.

On the first of October, 1640, the felling of timber within half a mile of the town, except on one's own particular lot, or for building or fencing, was prohibited under a penalty of five shillings per tree; and it was provided that none but inhabitants or town dwellers should have liberty to fell or saw any pine, oak or other timber under a like penalty to the offender.

On the fourteenth of January, 1642, " upon the great complaint of the great destruction and spoil of timber about the town," it was ordered that the inhabitants who had felled timber for pipe staves or bolts, should have a year's time to work it up, except that those who had timber lying for a year unwrought, should have but six months more; after which if still unwrought, it should be forfeited.

On the sixteenth of February, 1647, it was required that every inhabitant should cease felling timber for the present till further order. Such as had timber felled had liberty to work up so much of it as would complete their proportions formerly granted or legally purchased; and what they had felled more than their shares, they were to leave to the town's use. Every inhabitant should give an account to the townsmen what shares he had purchased and what timber he had already used. They who had not made up their proportional shares might fell timber and work it up, to the amount of their said shares. A penalty of five shillings was imposed " for every tree that any man shall transgress in." John Legat and Thomas Pettit were appointed cullers of pipe staves for the town, and sworn according to the order of the court.

On the twenty-second of April, 1650, it was ordered " by the freemen and some others, chosen for the ordering of the sole affairs of the town," that every inhabitant should pay for every thousand of pipe staves made by him, two shillings, for the maintenance of the ministry; for every thousand of hogshead staves one shilling and six pence; and for every thousand of bolts, sold before made into staves, four shillings.

On the twenty-sixth of August, 1650, it was voted by the town that none but settled inhabitants should have the privilege upon the Common to fell or use timber, and not future comers into town until they should be accepted for inhabitants; all others were prohibited. Only one person to each house lot was to enjoy the privilege, and he must build a good, habitable house thereon within six months.

On the first day of May, 1657, it was voted that "for the preservation of pipe-stave timber, and that there might be some proportion [fixed], that some might not have great [share] of timber and some none," it was ordered that from that time forward there should not be above one person in a family at one time employed in making of pipe staves, hogshead staves or bolts, or in any other work concerning white oak timber, except it be for saw-mills or building of houses or fencing stuff, on pain of forfeiture of ten shillings for each transgression, one-half to him who should give notice, and the other half to the use of the town. This order applied to work upon the Common, and on all ground not laid out.

It was voted June 28, 1654, that the order theretofore made, debarring strangers from coming into town to fell timber and make staves, should be still in force; and that for time to come no man living in another town, should, under any pretence whatsoever, fell timber or make staves or bolts or any timber work, unless he became a settled inhabitant, approved of by the town, and resident three months in the town before he should make any improvement of timber.

On the first day of December, 1664, "the town having taken into consideration the worth of masts, and that every year they may be still of greater consequence, and that his majesty for his own shipping may cause some to be transported from hence; for the preservation of such timber as may make masts," ordered that John Folsom be authorized to mark such trees as he thought fit for masts; to impose a penalty of twenty shillings upon any one felling a tree so marked; and to sell such trees for the benefit of the town, at the following prices: "for those of thirty inches [diameter] and upwards, thirty shillings each; between thirty and twenty-four inches, twenty shillings; between twenty-four and twenty inches, ten shillings."

At a town meeting March 3, 1673-4, it was ordered that thenceforth every single person who was legally admitted into the town should have liberty to make one thousand white oak pipe staves within one year, or the value of them in hogshead or barrel staves, red or white, and no more; and every family of less than four, servants excepted, three thousand; provided, that neither single persons nor families should sell their privilege to any other, but might hire men to work out their proper proportions.

Samuel Leavitt and John Wedgewood were empowered to "seize upon" any transgressor of the order, and to have for their pains, one-half the overplus of his proper share; the other half to go to the town.

On the twentieth of April, 1652, the town agreed to pay to the Rev. Samuel Dudley twenty shillings for the use of his two bulls. Mr. Dudley, in addition to his qualifications as a religious teacher, was a notable man of affairs. He acquired numerous tracts of land, was interested in mills and in agriculture, was employed to keep the town books, was the general conveyancer and attorney of the place, and now seems to have added to his other cares the desire to improve the breed of the cattle of the town.

The early records of Exeter are made up pretty largely of the elections of officers and of grants of land, but an occasional entry is met with which apparently must have had in its time a special significance. Such a one is a vote passed November 9, 1652, that the town book should be kept in Thomas King's house, and should not go therefrom unless there should be special occasion, and that by consent of the major part of the town; and that any person warned to be at a town meeting who should not be there at half an hour after the time appointed, should pay for the use of the town two shillings; and John Robinson was appointed to " gather up " any fines incurred for violation of this order. Curiosity is naturally excited to learn the occasion of such action. Had any unscrupulous hand attempted to tamper with the records? Had some obnoxious vote been prematurely sprung upon a town meeting? We ask these questions in vain. Interesting as the information might be, no clue to it has reached to our time.

In the lumber business many transient persons were employed. If disabled by sickness or accident, there was danger that the town would be made liable for their support. To guard against pauperism from this source, the following vote was passed April 3, 1665:

Ordered that what person soever shall hire any servant for more or less time, if it happen that he that is hired shall be lamed or any ways unserviceable made in work during that time [he] shall be kept by the charge of him that hires him, if he be not able to keep himself, that so the town may be freed from such charges.

This vote was supplemented by a rule promulgated by the selectmen, August 30, 1671, as follows:

Ordered that no man shall receive any person or persons into town without the consent of the selectmen, or security to free the town from any charge that may ensue thereby, upon twenty shillings a month forfeiture; and that no man shall come to inhabit, by purchase or otherwise, without the consent of the selectmen, upon the same penalty.

PROJECT FOR A CHANGE OF GOVERNMENT.

For nearly a quarter of a century after the death of John Mason, the patentee of New Hampshire, in 1635, little had occurred to remind the inhabitants that his representatives still claimed the title to the soil. They lived in England, and Robert Tufton Mason, to whom his grandfather's American estates descended, did not become of age till 1650. He was attached to the established church and the royal government; therefore it would have been idle for him, during the protectorate of Cromwell, to expect any aid from the ruling powers in regaining the lands of which he alleged that Massachusetts had dispossessed him. But upon the restoration of Charles II. to the English throne, in 1660, he petitioned his majesty for the restoration of the lands. The king's attorney general, to whom the subject was referred, reported that Mason had a good and legal title to the province of New Hampshire. Though no immediate action resulted therefrom, yet we shall see that this movement of Mason was destined ere long to produce momentous consequences.

Until 1664, the king did nothing; but on April 25, of that year, in consequence of other complaints and petitions, respecting matters of dispute in New England, he commissioned Colonel Richard Nicholls, Sir Robert Carr, George Cartwright and Samuel Maverick to visit the several colonies of New England; to determine all complaints; to provide for the peace and security of the country according to their discretion and to such instructions as they should receive from the king; and to report to him their doings.

This commission was exceedingly obnoxious to the rulers of Massachusetts, who were conscious that it was especially aimed at themselves and their conduct, and who claimed that it was an interference with rights vested in the colonists by their charter. The commissioners, however, pursuant to their instructions, visited the several colonies of New England, and their inquiries caused little friction, except in Massachusetts and her dependencies. They determined that the assumption of that colony to include within her charter limits and jurisdiction the New Hampshire settlements, was an act of usurpation; and gave the people of those settlements to understand that they would release them from the

Accordingly a petition was drawn, addressed to the King of England, purporting to represent the wishes of the towns of Portsmouth, Dover, Exeter and Hampton, expressing their great joy that his majesty had sent over the Commissioners, and sorrow at their ill treatment by the Bay government; and praying that the king would take the petitioners (towns) into his immediate protection, that they might be governed by the known laws of England; and that they might enjoy the sacraments they had been so long deprived of. This petition, so far as known, contained but nine signatures, two of them of Exeter men, Edward Hilton and John Folsom. The former was a moderate church of England man, the latter, who apparently was concerned in circulating the paper, was of a high and somewhat turbulent temper. There is no doubt that there was a party in New Hampshire disaffected to the government of Massachusetts, and had there been a reasonable probability that they would have bettered themselves by a demonstration against it, a considerable number of names might have been obtained for that end. But the reflecting part of them had little confidence in the present movement, and prudently kept clear of it.

The General Court of Massachusetts in their turn appointed a committee to inquire into the disposition of the New Hampshire towns towards their government. Respecting that of Exeter they interrogated the Rev. Samuel Dudley, who replied as follows:

Concerning the question that is in hand, whether the town of Exeter hath subscribed to that petition to his majesty for the taking of Portsmouth, Dover, Hampton and Exeter under his immediate government, I do affirm to my best apprehension, that the town of Exeter hath no hand in that petition directly or indirectly.

It is sufficient for our purpose to know that the action of the royal commissioners led to no change of government, but rather to a demonstration in favor of Massachusetts. The several New Hampshire towns united in a general collection to aid in building a new hall for Harvard College, to replace that which had been recently destroyed by fire. For this laudable purpose the town of Exeter contributed ten pounds.

In connection with this subject it is worthy of mention that Samuel Maverick, one of the king's commissioners, had about the year 1660, made a brief report to his majesty, Charles II., respecting the several settlements in the New England colonies, which he was, by his early and long residence in this country, well qualified to do. This paper, after lying unknown to historians for more than two hundred years, has recently come to light. Every scrap of information of that early date, is of interest. Maverick's notice of Exeter, therefore, meagre though it is, is entitled to a place here:

Exeter. Above this (the saw-mill on Lamperell creek), at the fall of the river Pascataqua, is the town of Exeter, where are more saw-mills; down the south side of this river are farms and other straggling families.

Taxation was probably no more agreeable to property holders in former times than it is at present. In February, 1672, the selectmen gave notice to the inhabitants to bring in a list of their estates, both of outlands and all else, to one of the selectmen, together with an account of all debts due them from the town, on or before the next sixth day of March; under the penalty of forfeiting what was due them from the town, upon their neglect to bring in an account thereof, and of the payment of two shillings by every one who should not bring in a list of his estate to make a true rate by. We can imagine that this rule would cause the exhibition of all claims against the town; but whether it would bring to light all taxable property, might depend much on the amount which the rate payer would be liable to be assessed.

The year 1675 was made memorable by the fierce outbreak of Indian hostilities known as King Philip's War. The loss of life with which Exeter was visited, is related in detail in another chapter. To defray the growing charges of the Indian war the General Court of Massachusetts on the thirteenth of October levied upon the New Hampshire towns seven single country rates. The proportion of Exeter was eight pounds, eight shillings for a single rate, and the entire tax required of the town was twenty-five pounds, four shillings in November, 1675, and thirty-three pounds, twelve shillings in March, 1676. Happily, the war was of brief duration.

On the eleventh of March, 1679, Edward Smith, Edward Gilman and Peter Folsom were appointed by the town a committee to ascertain the town debts and the legality of the same. It thus appears that we have an early precedent for incurring a town debt; and the report of the committee having fortunately been preserved, is given here, as an example of the formal manner in which agents of the town performed their functions two hundred years ago.

Theis may certifie all whome it may concerne that whereas wee underwritten, at a Towne meeting ye 11th of March 1678 [9] were appointed a comittee to examine ye Towne Debts & ye legallity thereof, and ye Towne standing to ye same as wee should bring in o^r Judgm^{ts}, doe declare & informe as followeth; that wee underwritten as aforesd haveing tryed & examined ye accounts, charges and disbursments of Captn. John Gillman, doe find for & allow unto him, Errors excepted, — 77^l. 19^s. 00^d.

The last Barr^{ll} of powder wch Captn. Gillman bought for ye Towne stock is not included in ye Sume aboue written.

Edw^D Smith.
Edward Gilman
Peter × Follsham.

Exeter continued under the laws of Massachusetts between thirty-six and thirty-seven years, until New Hampshire, in 1680, was erected into a royal province. The rule of the sister colony was on the whole equitable and beneficial; and the little town exhibited marked improvement, both in respect to material advantages, and in the temper and harmony of the people.

NUMBER AND NAMES OF INHABITANTS.

The population made but a very gradual increase, as was to be expected, for there was little in the frontier settlement to attract new comers. It was those who were content to endure hard work and hard fare, in the faith of securing better things in the future, who were the bone and sinew of Exeter. Yet there was a gain in numbers. On the twelfth of October, 1669, the General Court appointed John Gilman lieutenant of the military company, at the same time declaring that there were "about sixty soldiers in Exeter." This, if the usual ratio holds good, would imply that there were about three hundred inhabitants of all classes. A fair proportion of the early settlers had passed their lives in the town, and were succeeded by their children. Others had come in, some for a temporary, others for a permanent residence. The new names that appear upon the town records between 1640 and 1680 will be given here, together with others derived from other sources. No complete list is to be found, on the books of the town, or elsewhere, and it is probable that the fullest that can now be gathered, is quite imperfect.

NAMES FIRST ON THE TOWN BOOKS BETWEEN 1640 AND 1680.

John Barber,	April 1, 1678
John Bean,	January 21, 1660-1
Thomas Biggs,	September 5, 1643
Nathaniel Bolter,	May 6, 1645
Robert Booth,	February 10, 1647-8
Richard Bray,	October 10, 1664
William Bromfield,	December 1, 1664
John Bursley,	September 5, 1643
Philip Cartee,	March 29, 1668
Philip Chesley,	January 21, 1664-5
John Clark,	August 29, 1661
Jeremy Connor,	October 10, 1664
Thomas Cornish,	January 12, 1648-9
Christian Dolloff,	March 30, 1668
Abraham Drake,	June 10, 1644
Nathaniel Drake,	April 22, 1649
Teague Drisco,	October 10, 1664
Biley Dudley,	April 1, 1678
Samuel Dudley,	May 13, 1650
Theophilus Dudley,	December 1, 1664
Eleazer Elkins,	March 3, 1673-4
Ephraim Folsom,	April 1, 1678
Israel Folsom,	October 10, 1664
John Folsom,	November 4, 1647
John Folsom, Jr.,	September 28, 1668
Nathaniel Folsom,	October 10, 1664
Peter Folsom,	March 30, 1670
Samuel Folsom,	October 10, 1664
John Garland,	August 26, 1650
Charles Gilman,	September 28, 1668
Edward Gilman, Sr.,	May 10, 1652
Edward Gilman (Jr.),	November 4, 1647
John Gilman,	January 12, 1648-9
John Gilman, Jr.,	April 1, 1678
Moses Gilman,	February 10, 1647-8
Charles Glidden,	March 30, 1674
James Godfrey,	March 16, 1660-1
Alexander Gordon,	October 10, 1664
Samuel Greenfield,	May 19, 1644
William Hacket,	October 10, 1664

Joseph Hall,	October	10, 1664
Samuel Hall,	March	11, 1678–9
Robert Hathersay (Hersey),	August	5, 1644
William Huntington,	February	27, 1644–5
Edmond Johnson,	August	26, 1650
Thomas Jones,	August	5, 1644
Joel Judkins,	April	2, 1675
Duny (?) Kelley,	October	10, 1664
James Kidd,	March	11, 1678–9
John Kimming,	October	10, 1664
Thomas King,	January	16, 1644–5
Nathaniel Ladd,	February	18, 1678–9
Cornelius Lary,	October	10, 1664
David Lawrence,	March	30, 1674
Jeremy Leavitt,	March	30, 1670
Moses Leavitt,	October	10, 1664
Samuel Leavitt,	September	28, 1668
John Legat,	October	20, 1642
Nicholas Liston,	January	12, 1648–9
Henry Magoon,	April	2, 1664
Thomas Marston,*	January	16, 1644–5
Richard Morgan,	March	29, 1668
Nicholas Norris,	August	30, 1671
George Person (Pearson),	March 18 (about), 1679	
Thomas Pettit, Jr.,	May	20, 1652
Robert Powell,	October	10, 1664
Thomas Rashleigh,	May	6, 1643
John Robinson,	April	20, 1652
Jonathan Robinson,	March	3, 1673–4
Jonathan Rollins,	October	10, 1664
Thomas Rollins,	March	30, 1670
John Saunders,	January	16, 1644–5
Edward Sewall,	April	2, 1675
Jonathan Sewall,	April	1, 1678
Robert Seward,	April	1, 1678
John Sinclair,	October	10, 1664
John Smart,	January	16, 1644–5
John Smart, Jr.,	April	22, 1649
Robert Smart,	April	22, 1649
Edward Smith,	March	30, 1670
Nicholas Smith,	March	4, 1658–9
Francis Swain,	March	31, 1645
Nicholas Swain,	December	16, 1646
Richard Swain,	November	4, 1647

* Probably never came to live in Exeter.

Joseph Taylor,	March	4, 1658-9
William Taylor,	June	26, 1650
John Tedd,	November	4, 1647
Jonathan Thing,	January	22, 1659-60
Jonathan Thing, Jr.,	March	30, 1670
Thomas Tyler,	May	20, 1652
Robert Wadleigh,	March	15, 1667-8
John Warren,	April	22, 1649
Thomas Warren,	October	10, 1664
John Wedgewood,	March	3, 1673-4
William Whitridge,	April	3, 1649
Gowen Wilson,	November	24, 1650
Humphrey Wilson,	June	17, 1644
John Young,	March	30, 1670

In addition to the foregoing, the following names of persons belonging to Exeter within the period referred to, appear on the records of old Norfolk county, to wit:

John Barsham, 1669
Isaac Cole, 1671
Isaac Cross, 1651
David Cushing, 1655

John Goddard (?) 1678
Thomas Hithersea, 1650
Henry Lamprey, 1666
Edward Littlefield, 1651

And the following additional names are extracted from a list of those who took the oath of allegiance and fidelity to the country, November 30, 1677, at Exeter; all, with a few possible exceptions, inhabitants of the town.

John Clark, Jr.
James Daniel
Stephen Dudley
Mr. Michael French
Daniel Gilman
Jeremy Gilman
Moses Gilman, Jr.
Kinsley Hall
Armstrong Horn
William Morgan
James Perkins

David Robinson
George Roberts
Edward Roe
James Sinclair
Mr. Richard Smart
Robert Smart, Jr.
Jonathan Smith
Mr. John Thomas
John Wadleigh
Joseph Wadleigh

CHAPTER III.

EXETER UNDER THE NEW HAMPSHIRE PROVINCIAL GOVERNMENT.

The new government of the province of New Hampshire went into operation in January, 1680. A governor and six councillors were appointed by the Crown. One of the councillors was an Exeter man, John Gilman, who, under the Massachusetts *régime*, had been a magistrate and an Assistant. The members of the lower house of Assembly were elected by the people of the several towns, Exeter being entitled to choose two. Her deputies in 1680 were Captain Bartholomew Tippen and Lieutenant Ralph Hall. The latter had been a resident of the town for a number of years; but Tippen was a new comer, and apparently did not remain long. He had been a man of some prominence under the Massachusetts government, which was probably the reason that he was so speedily elected to office here.

Though the population of the town must have been about three hundred, the number of qualified voters at the first election was but twenty; there being in the entire province only two hundred and nine. There was no uniform rule determining the qualifications of voters, but they were selected arbitrarily; one consequence of which was that Exeter had a less number, in proportion to her population, than some of the other towns. Exeter had nearly seventy tax-payers.

For the first two years after New Hampshire had become a distinct province, and so long as the principal offices of government were filled by her own citizens, affairs went on smoothly. But Robert Mason, who, as the heir of John Mason, the patentee, claimed the soil of New Hampshire as his property, and at whose solicitation, and for whose benefit, in a great measure, a separate government had been provided for the province, found that he was yet no nearer the fruition of his hopes of securing the title and emoluments of the lands, than he was under the rule of Massachusetts. He therefore made application to the king for the appointment of a new governor, a stranger to New Hampshire, Edward Cranfield, a needy, arbitrary and unscrupulous man. Mason's request was complied with, and he at once took effectual means to attach the appointee to his interest.

The people speedily read the character and purposes of their new governor. He took his seat in October, 1683, and summoned an assembly in November, with whose concurrence a fresh body of laws was enacted, one of the most important of which provided for a change in the manner of selecting jurors. They had before been chosen by the inhabitants of the several towns; thenceforth they were to be appointed by the sheriff, after the English custom. This piece of legislation was a fatal mistake for the people, for it put the entire *personnel* of the judicial courts into the control of the governor; who, having the right to suspend refractory councillors, could thus appoint such judges and sheriffs, and through them, such jurors as he pleased.

The governor, however, kept up a show of fairness, until the assembly had voted him a present of two hundred and fifty pounds, by which they vainly hoped to detach him from the interest of Mason. Immediately afterwards he came out in his true colors; and because he could not make the popular branch consent to a bill which he approved, and because he refused to approve certain bills which they presented, he resorted to the extreme and unprecedented step of dissolving the assembly.

GOVE'S REBELLION AGAINST CRANFIELD.

Then, for the first time, the full extent of their utter powerlessness against the tyranny of a mercenary governor dawned upon the understanding of the mass of the people. It is not strange that it suggested to some unbalanced minds the idea of forcible resistance. Edward Gove of Hampton, who had been a member of the dissolved assembly, distracted by indignation and heated by strong drink, attempted to raise the standard of revolt. He succeeded, however, in enlisting only eight or ten young fellows in his own town and Exeter, who joined him probably in a spirit of adventure, fortified, perhaps, with the idea that they were thus championing the cause of the people. Gove, with his little following, armed with sword and pistol, appeared on horseback in the streets of Exeter, and rode to the sound of the trumpet, into

Hampton, where they were soon arrested and committed to prison for trial.

The hare-brained project never could have endangered the government for a moment, but Cranfield chose to regard it in the most serious light, and without delay issued a commission for a court to try the culprits. Through his attorney general he caused an indictment to be presented to the grand jury against them, for treason, the highest crime known to the law. For this offence the prisoners, nine in number, were tried, with indecent haste, little more than a week after the acts complained of were committed; and, apparently undefended, were found guilty; Gove of the entire offence of treason, and the others of lesser offences. Gove was sent to England and imprisoned in the Tower of London about three years, and then was pardoned and returned home.

The Exeter men concerned in this escapade were Robert, John and Joseph Wadleigh, sons of Robert Wadleigh who was a member of the dissolved assembly, Thomas Rollins and John Sleeper, and perhaps Mark Baker. They were all permitted by the governor to be set at liberty on giving security to keep the peace, except one of the Wadleighs, who was detained in prison for more than a year afterwards by the governor, apparently out of ill will to his father. Edward Smith and John Young, both of Exeter, had also been complained of as associated with Gove, but were not indicted. Nathaniel Ladd, likewise of Exeter, acted as the trumpeter to Gove's train, but when the others were captured, made his escape. It is probable that he remained *perdu* until after the trial. He put his mettle to a better use a few years later when he fought at Maquoit against the hostile Indians, though he received his death-wound there.

Governor Cranfield finding his selfish projects impeded by the presence in his council of men identified in feeling with the people, suspended, by virtue of the power conferred by his commission, three of his councillors, among them John Gilman of Exeter; and filled their places with others more subservient to his will. Then, all things being prepared to his mind, Mason entered upon his legal campaign against the landholders of the province.

ROBERT TUFTON MASON'S LAND SUITS.

In order to understand the feelings of the people it is necessary to look at Mason's claim from their point of view. They were aware that, half a century before, the soil had been granted to Captain John Mason by the Council of Plymouth, by virtue of a royal patent. But they believed that though he maintained a settlement upon it for a few years, his heirs after his death had abandoned it. During the more than forty years that had elapsed since that time, the territory had been regarded and dealt with as if it had never been granted. A title had been purchased from the Indian occupants, and the lands had thenceforward been bought and sold, and transmitted by inheritance, in all respects as if they were allodial. They had been improved by the sweat of the settlers' brows, and defended by their blood against the incursions of savage enemies. These claims outweighed a thousand-fold in their minds the stale paper title of Mason. His demands they regarded as unjust and inequitable in the highest degree, and they were prepared to resist them to the bitter end.

But as the courts were now constituted, and the jurors selected, they knew that they were helpless. Mason brought a great number of suits, in the different towns of the province, to recover the lands from their occupants. In Exeter the following persons were sued: Nathaniel Folsom, Richard Morgan, Kinsley Hall, Ralph Hall, Christian Dolloff, Ephraim Folsom, Philip Cartee, Moses Leavitt, John Folsom, Eleazer Elkins, Jonathan Robinson, Jonathan Thing, Humphrey Wilson, Peter Folsom, John Gilman, Jr. and Ephraim Folsom; — in the adjoining precinct of Squamscot, Andrew Wiggin and William Moore, Jr.

Pliable juries were empanelled by the sheriff, a creature of Cranfield's, and the tenants knew it to be idle to make defence; so verdicts were returned against them "at the rate of from nine to twelve in a day." So far as the courts were concerned the governor and Mason had everything their own way.

But when the attempt was made to put the judgments in force, the tenants had their innings. The sheriff could indeed formally deliver to the claimant the possession of the lands he had recovered; but the formality amounted to nothing, and the tenants continued to enjoy the premises as before. Attempts were made to sell the lands that had been thus levied on, but nobody would buy them. After a few experiments of this kind Mason recognized the futility of the proceedings, and for the time desisted. But it was fully a quarter of a century before the verdict of an independent jury put a quietus on the Masonian claims, and relieved the land-owners from apprehension.

RESISTANCE TO ILLEGAL TAXATION.

But the irrepressible Cranfield, in the language of one of his contemporaries, "had come here after money, and money he would have." After vainly trying several devices to induce the General Assembly to pass a bill to raise money, he determined in 1684 to levy taxes on the people with the assent of the council only, and without the concurrence of the popular branch of the assembly. This was clearly a usurpation of power; and even his accommodating council at first remonstrated against it. But the apprehension of an outbreak among the Indians at the eastward induced them to comply. The taxes were ordered by the governor and council, and warrants were issued to the constables of the several towns for their collection. But they met everywhere the same reception as in Exeter, where John Folsom, the constable, returned his warrant with the statement "that he had demanded the taxes, but was answered by almost all of them that the [governor's] commission directed the taxes should be raised by the General Assembly, but these being done by the governor and council, they would not pay."

Thereupon the Exeter warrant was committed for collection to Thomas Thurton, provost marshal of the province, together with an order of the Court of Sessions for a fine of fifty shillings against John Folsom, for neglect of duty as constable. Thurton was a coarse, brutal man, and his errand was not calculated to win him a very hearty welcome. He came to Exeter by way of Hampton, attended by his deputy, both on horseback, with swords by their sides. Half a score of Hampton men, armed with clubs, followed them on horseback to see and share the anticipated sport. They proceeded first to the house of Edward Gilman, situated nearly opposite the site of the present First church. Such a cavalcade naturally attracted attention, and it took little time for the whole village to learn the business that had brought it. A crowd gathered. John Folsom, the delinquent constable, appeared, and Thurton demanded of him the fine imposed by the Quarter Sessions. Folsom replied that if the marshal "came to levy execution at his house, he should meet with a red-hot spit and scalding water; and that he did not value any warrant from the governor, council or justice of the peace, and that the marshal might go, like a rogue as he was."

Two of Mr. Gilman's aunts were at his house, the wife of John Gilman, the suspended councillor, and of Moses Gilman, his brother; and they likewise gave Thurton to understand that they had kettles of boiling water ready for him, if he came to their houses to demand rates. The marshal now began to realize that he had come on a bootless errand. The crowd, reinforced by the addition among others of the Rev. John Cotton, the temporary minister of the town, then began to hustle the marshal and his deputy up and down the house, asking them tauntingly what they wore at their sides,— meaning their swords, which were, to be sure, rather ridiculous appendages, when their wearers dared not use them. There was nothing worse than horse play, but the marshal understood very well that if he were to attempt any serious resistance, he was liable to be roughly treated. From Edward Gilman's he and his deputy went next to the house of the widow of Henry Sewall, to obtain refreshment for themselves and their horses. The crowd followed them thither, and still kept up the same system of annoyance. Then the officers and their unwelcome retinue proceeded to the house of Jonathan Thing, to serve an attachment upon him; but the crowd would not suffer them to do so, but plainly declared to the marshal that he " should do no business relating to the execution of his office." In the end, the officers were glad to get off with whole skins, and without making the least progress in the business they had come for.

We obtain our only knowledge of this transaction from the testimony of Thurton himself, a bitterly prejudiced and unscrupulous witness; but it is evident that though the whole community were indignant at the illegal attempt at taxation, and determined that the marshal should not be permitted to execute his warrant, yet they scrupulously refrained from acts of violence. The glimpse, too, that we get of the Exeter women of two hundred years ago proves that they possessed a spirit worthy of the mothers of men who had to endure the hardships of a frontier life, and to meet the onslaughts of a savage foe, with no defence save their own right arms and trusty weapons.

THE PROVINCE WITHOUT A GOVERNMENT.

The records of Exeter tell nothing of the transactions of a period of several years between 1680 and 1690. There were probably reasons in the condition of the times for this reticence. Robert Mason sought to support his land-claims by searching the books of records of the several towns, whereupon the books were abstracted, and for a time disappeared. Meantime Governor Cranfield became discouraged in his attempt to gather wealth from his position in New Hampshire, and abandoned his office. Walter Barefoote succeeded him, and was in his turn succeeded by Joseph Dudley. Then in 1686 the province passed under the rule of Edmund Andros, governor of New England. As the appointee and representative of a Catholic sovereign, James II., he made few friends in Puritan Massachusetts where was his official residence. His downfall approached on this side of the water, with equal steps with that of his royal master, on the other side. Almost simultaneously with the deposition and imprisonment of Andros by the Massachusetts colonists, in the spring of 1689, came the news of the Revolution in England, and the accession of William III. The New England colonies were thus left without a representative of royalty to rule over them. Massachusetts, with her charter and long experience, easily set up a temporary government which answered all her wants; but New Hampshire had no facilities for the purpose, and simply went on for nearly a year without an executive; and, thanks to the orderly disposition and good sense of the people, without serious difficulties; and this notwithstanding the situation was further complicated by the fact that an Indian war was raging in the province at the time, and Dover and Oyster river were the scenes of savage incursions and atrocities.

More than one attempt was made to induce the people of the province to unite in choosing delegates to establish a government *ad interim*, but for a time without avail. They did, indeed, go so far as to elect William Vaughan of Portsmouth, a member of the board of commissioners of the United Colonies of New England, for defence against the Indians; though there is no entry upon the records of Exeter that she took part in the election. And it was not until December, 1689, that the New Hampshire towns reached the point of choosing delegates to meet for the purpose of devising some method of protection against the common enemy. Delegates were then elected by Portsmouth, Dover, Exeter and Hampton, who assembled in convention at Portsmouth on the twenty-fourth of January, 1690. The whole number was twenty-two, of whom four were from Exeter: Robert Wadleigh, Samuel Leavitt, William Hilton and Jonathan Thing; the last two taking the place of William Moore, who was originally chosen. The convention agreed upon a brief plan for the present government of the province, and submitted it to the people; and in pursuance thereof in Dover, if nowhere else, an election was held and officers were voted for. But the unreasonable jealousy manifested by Hampton towards the other towns, prevented the proposed government from going into effect.

By this time the need of a recognized head of authority in the province was so apparent and so pressing, that some of the principal men of Portsmouth who were kindly affected towards Massachusetts, drew up a petition, addressed to the authorities of that colony, to be received under their government and protection, as formerly, until their majesties' pleasure should be known. The petition was speedily circulated in the several towns, and received the signatures of three hundred and seventy-two persons, a very large proportion of the adult males in the province. Of these, sixty or seventy, at least, were residents of Exeter. Agreeably to the prayer of the petition the old union with Massachusetts was renewed on the nineteenth of March, 1690, and lasted until the commission of Governor Samuel Allen was published in New Hampshire on the thirteenth of August, 1692.

During the second union Massachusetts made a call upon the New Hampshire towns to choose each "two meet persons" to assemble together with the Justices of the Peace of the province, to adjust the charges of the Indian war, and to assess the amount thereof upon the inhabitants. Exeter chose Peter Coffin and John Gilman as her representatives for this duty.

The records of the town do not show any important action for several years after this, save what properly belongs to other departments of this history. At the annual meeting in April, 1705, John Light was received an inhabitant, and had a conditional grant of land; perhaps the last instance of this formal investiture with the privileges of citizenship. It was not many years later that the final division of the town's lands was made, after which there was no reason, and no attempt, to keep up the old theory of a close corporation of the inhabitants.

Shortly afterwards the town began to improve their system of records. It was voted in 1707 that "all rates made by the selectmen shall be committed to the town clerk to be entered upon record, before they be delivered to the constable;" in 1713 that "the town clerk buy a book at the town's charge and enter all the votes needed by the selectmen, at large, and all accounts of the town's disbursements, debt and credit;" and in 1721 that "a book shall be bought for the selectmen to keep a fair record of what money they raise, and how they dispose of it." These acts speak well for the care and prudence of the people, and merit the warmest gratitude of the antiquary and historian in later times.

From the selectmen's accounts we learn that in the year 1714 they paid bounties to Captain Hill and Samuel Dudley, Jr., on "five wolves' heads." These animals were so great a source of annoyance that the bounty paid for their destruction was raised by the town, two years afterwards, to two pounds a head.

In the year 1717 the selectmen paid to Peter Folsom, Jr., for work on the stocks, fifteen shillings and eight pence; and to Samuel Goodhue for mending the glass in the meeting-house, one pound and eleven pence. Later payments for the same objects, especially the latter, appear on the selectmen's account books, with some frequency. The meeting-house windows must have been a burden on the rate-payers.

In the same year the province authorized an issue of paper money to the amount of fifteen thousand pounds, which was to be lent to inhabitants in small sums on approved landed security. The town chose Samuel Thing, Nicholas Gilman, Nicholas Gordon, Moses Leavitt and Jonathan Thing a committee to act with the representatives, in letting a portion of the money, in Exeter, and empowered a majority of them to appraise upon oath the value of the lands offered as security for such loans.

At the same meeting it was voted that Samuel Thing and Henry Dyer request Colonel John Bridger, his majesty's surveyor general, to mark the trees in the town which were fit for the king's service, "so that his majesty's subjects may go to work to get their livelihood." The law which reserved for masts for the royal navy the largest and finest growth of the forest, was a standing grievance to the colonists, as the language of the above vote implies, and led, as we shall see, to later trouble. In the same year the town for the first time voted compensation to their officers; twenty shillings to each of the selectmen and five shillings to each of the assessors, and committee. The presumption is that before that time these officers had performed their duties gratuitously, regarding the honor of their positions as a sufficient recompense. It is, perhaps, needless to add that the fashion of payment, once set, has been pretty faithfully followed, from that time to this.

On March 22, 1722, the town voted to make the minister's rate by itself, to be paid in money; and all other town charges to be paid in "peichers;" an ineffectual attempt, probably, to write "specie." But specie at that time meant something quite different from gold and silver coin. It must have referred to articles of produce or merchandise at certain specified prices, for the vote proceeds to define the "specishers" (as the word is spelled this time) in which the town charges may be paid, as being "merchantable boards and joist at 40/- per M.; Indian corn at 3/- per bushel; Barley 3/ 6; Rye 4/-; wheat 5/ 6; Red oak hhd. staves 30/- per M.; White oak 40/-; White oak bbl. 30/-; good pork 4 d a lb; beef at 3 d."

The accounts of the selectmen for the year 1721 show that they paid four shillings and sixpence for "a brazen head put on the black staff;" and those of 1728 a like sum for "a black staff." In our days of republican simplicity it requires a moment's thought to realize that these entries refer to the official badge of the constable, which was then a black rod surmounted by a royal crown of brass. Though we may smile at such insignia now, there was a deal of dignity and of authority too, in them, a hundred and fifty years ago.

At a meeting of the town, held September 28, 1731, a new meeting-house having been built, it was voted that the old one be taken down as soon as it could be with convenience, and that a court-house be built of the stuff of said old house. Theophilus Smith, Benjamin Thing and Jeremiah Conner were appointed a committee to "discourse with workmen" about taking down the old meeting-house and building a court-house, and to make report.

It was also voted that the town-house should be built forty feet long and twenty-five feet wide, and be set on the south side of the highway over against the meeting-house, as nigh the school-house as might be with conveniency to the town land; and that the court-house be finished, so far as it could be done, by the first of March next, so that the court might sit in it.

This provision for a court-house, which in all probability was designed to be fitted up in the town-house building, was made in consequence of an act passed by the General Assembly in 1730, which provided for one term of the Inferior Court to be held in each year in Exeter, and gave the like privilege to Dover and to Hampton. Prior to this, all the courts in the province were held in Portsmouth, to the manifest inconvenience of parties who resided in the interior. Great efforts were made before and after this time, to give the inland towns a small share, at least, of the courts; but the people of Portsmouth, aided by the influence of the provincial government, constantly resisted and obstructed the just legislation for the purpose, up to the time of the Revolution, when Exeter became in effect the capital of the State. It is not known whether under the law of 1730 even a single term of the Inferior Court was held outside of Portsmouth; for the provincial officials had the address to induce the king in council either to refuse his assent to the law, or to order the repeal of it. The tradition is that this was done by the influence of the lieutenant governor and surveyor general, in revenge for the insult to his authority committed by the "mast-tree mob" in Exeter, hereafter to be mentioned.

The town-house was finished in 1732 and stood nearly opposite the meeting-house. It was flanked by the stocks and whipping-post, erected in the most public position as a terror to evil-doers. The "town-house rates" amounted to two hundred and forty pounds, four shillings and eight pence.*

THE MAST-TREE RIOT OF 1734.

The lumbermen of the New Hampshire frontiers were not men troubled with nice scruples. They regarded the legal claim of the king to the most valuable trees on their lands, as one which it was not morally wrong for them to evade or to transgress. And this feeling was intensified by the domineering conduct towards them of the surveyor general and his agents. Consequently there were not a few of them who had no hesitation in taking the risk incurred by despoiling the royal navy of its timber, and the surveyor general of his perquisites. If they were detected *and convicted*, they were willing to pay the penalty; if they escaped discovery they slept none the less soundly.

Complaints had been repeatedly made in regard to some of the people of Exeter that they paid small regard to the laws on this subject. As early as 1708 John Bridger, then surveyor general, addressed a letter to Peter Coffin and Theophilus Dudley, justices of the peace in Exeter, charging that several mast trees which were reserved for her majesty's navy, had been felled, cut and destroyed by Jeremiah Gilman, James Gilman, David Gilman, Samuel Piper, John Downer, Moses Pike and Jonathan Smith; and requiring said Coffin and Dudley to do them justice according

---

*On March 26, 1733, the town excused the tax-payers of the new parish of Newmarket from an assessment of twenty-five pounds for this object, "in consideration that they had lately been at great expense in building a meeting-house and settling a minister there."

to law. What came of the application is not known, but it is questionable whether the surveyor general got much satisfaction.

His successor in office, David Dunbar, who had been a soldier and was arbitrary, needy and litigious, learning or suspecting that mast trees had been cut in Exeter, in the early part of the year 1734, visited a saw-mill at the Copyhold, as it was and still is called, in that part of Exeter which is now Brentwood, to see if he could discover any lumber there, from trees of the size reserved for the navy. The people employed in the woods around were of course at once apprised of his presence, and divined his purpose; but having very little respect for dignitaries of his sort, made the welkin ring with their shouts and cries and with the discharges of small arms. The surveyor general, fearing that if he persisted in his investigations, they would proceed to acts of violence, concluded that discretion was the better part of valor, and retreated. But he was satisfied that the law had been violated, and that an inspection of the piles of lumber about the mill would prove it. On his return to Portsmouth, therefore, he employed ten men to proceed in a sail boat to Exeter, and thence to go to the Copyhold mill, to set the king's broad arrow on any lumber they might find there, which gave evidence of being cut from mast trees.

These men landed at the village of Exeter in the evening of April 23, 1634, and proceeded to the public house of Samuel Gilman on Water street, the same house afterwards occupied by Oliver Peabody, and still standing, though much altered. There they passed the evening, in the fashion of the time. Meanwhile the fact of their arrival and the nature of their errand spread rapidly through the town. A number of the persons who were most aggrieved by the operations of the surveyor general, assembled at the public house kept by Zebulon Giddinge,* afterwards occupied by the family of the Rev. William F. Rowland, and also still standing, and there disguising themselves so as to resemble Indians, sallied forth, about thirty in number, to head off Dunbar's expedition.

What they did, we learn chiefly from the testimony of those whom they assailed, men neither by character nor by feeling likely to give a perfectly impartial account. But there seems little doubt that the quasi Indians seized upon several of Dunbar's party as they were about going to bed, and handled them pretty roughly,

---

* The orthography of this name has been modernized into Giddings.

hauling them down stairs and hustling them out of the door, at the same time uttering dire threats against them. They certainly frightened and dispersed the party, and scuttled their boat and destroyed the sails. The unlucky wights, who little expected such treatment, were fain to retrace their way to Portsmouth as best they could, bearing the marks of their adventure in the shape of torn clothes and bloody noses, if nothing worse.

The actors in this illegal proceeding were probably well known in Exeter, and included men who were by no means habitual lawbreakers. Dunbar was furious at their demonstration. Holding the office of lieutenant governor as well as of surveyor general, he instantly summoned a meeting of the council, Belcher, the governor, being at the time absent from the province. To them he represented that he believed the justices of the peace in Exeter had some knowledge of the affair, and proposed that they should be sent for and examined before the council, and that a proclamation should be issued, offering a reward for detecting the persons that were guilty of the offence. The council, however, were not prepared to sanction these proposals of the testy lieutenant governor, but replied that in their opinion the examination of the matter appertained to the justices of the peace, and not to the council, and the issuing of a proclamation appertained to the governor; and therefore they did not advise it without his order.

The governor did, indeed, issue a proclamation, but offered no reward, except the vague promise that "whosoever shall detect the offenders above mentioned, or any of them, shall receive all proper marks of the countenance and favor of this government." The governor and his lieutenant were not friends.

The baffled lieutenant governor subsequently addressed a letter to Nicholas Gilman, John Gilman and Bartholomew Thing, justices of the peace at Exeter, in which he demanded that some of them should go with Charles Gorwood, his assistant, to Copyhold mill, Black rock mill, upper and lower Tuckaway mills, Wadleigh's mill, the Book mill, Gilman's mill and Piscassic mill, all in Exeter, and the last two near Newmarket, and there oblige men to separate and mark for his majesty's use such white pine boards as they found sawn from mast trees. And in case of the non-compliance of said justices with the above order, he required them to hire or impress a man to go with said Gorwood for the purpose aforesaid.

The justices, after nearly a month's delay, replied that they had employed a man to go with Gorwood as desired; but as to his demand that some of *them* should go, they could not, upon the most deliberate consideration, find any authority to support them in so doing. Thus Dunbar had to submit to a snubbing in every quarter.

The ludicrous phase of the affair is to be found in the testimony of Peter Greeley, who was Dunbar's particular assistant and henchman. He deposed that Simon Gilman of Exeter revealed to him in confidence that the people of Exeter had hired three Natick Indians to kill Dunbar, Theodore Atkinson, and himself (Greeley), and had supplied the Indians with a quart of rum each every day, "that they should not fail of their work;" and that the Indians, as soon as they had accomplished the deed, were to go at once to Natick, where they would not be discovered. Apparently it never dawned on Peter Greeley or his headstrong employer that Simon was "chaffing" them, and that the whole demonstrations, from Dunbar's visit at Copyhold mill to the riotous proceedings at Exeter, were simply intended to prevent the further interference of the surveyor general with the lumbermen, however they failed to respect the trees reserved for the use of his majesty's navy.

At the annual town meeting in March, 1738, Elisha Odlin was chosen town clerk in the place of Bartholomew Thing, who had held the office for several years before. So far as we can now discover, the change was made in consequence of the feeling that had arisen on the then engrossing question of the division of the town's common lands. For some cause, now unknown, Thing declined to deliver up the town books and records to his successor. It may be that he had some show of right for withholding the records. Concealment of the public archives was no new thing in the history of the province, and it had taken place probably with very general approval. But in the present case the majority of the inhabitants were indignant at the late town clerk's conduct. A meeting of the town was called, and voted that the books should be removed out of Thing's hands and put into Odlin's; that Jonathan Wadleigh, Edward Hall, John Robinson, John Odlin, Jr. and Zebulon Giddinge, should be a committee to prosecute Thing if he refused to deliver them, and that the selectmen should raise money to defray the charges of such prosecution. Nothing further is heard of the recalcitrant town clerk's scruples.

The town meeting of June 15, 1738, was held in the town-house, the first information which the record affords, of its completion.

It appears that the town was somewhat infested with wolves,

even as late as 1742, for at the March meeting in that year a bounty of five pounds was voted "to any person of the first parish who should kill a grown wolf within said parish limits." At the first glance it does not appear why this offer should be confined to a single *parish*, unless indeed it referred to a "wolf in sheep's clothing." But when it is remembered that the inhabitants of the southwesterly part of the town had recently been set off into a separate parish, it is easy to see that the intention was to bind Exeter to pay the bounty, and to leave the new precinct of Brentwood to act for itself. The reason of making the bounty so large, undoubtedly, was the depreciation of the paper money of the period.

In looking over the records of the town meetings we are often met by entries of adjournments for fifteen minutes, or for other brief periods. The cause of these little intermissions of business was ostensibly to allow the voters time for consultation, or the committees the opportunity to prepare their reports. But when we remember the habits of the times, and that there were comparatively few men who did not indulge in strong potations pretty regularly every day, we can see that another consideration was, perhaps, not without its weight. It was manifestly only fair that men should be allowed time to take their customary refreshment, without apprehension that some objectionable vote might be carried in their absence. An adjournment put all upon an equal footing,— in one sense, at least. It is proper to say, however, that in the matter of dram-drinking, Exeter was no worse, and probably no better, than all other places. Indeed, in after years, when the temperance reform arose, the town early took advanced ground in its favor. As indicative, however, of the universal use of strong liquors on all occasions, we find among the town accounts for 1722 these entries: "Expenses of town, rum and shuger 5/6; rum, raising the bell 1/–; rum and shuger 2/6; same 10/–; same 1/6." In the accounts for 1736 are found the following: "paid Capt. Samuel Gilman for drink given to those men that signed a deed for land in the way that led to *drinkwater* road 17/4," and "for 1 gall. rum and 2 lb. sugar and allspice for William Gay's (a town pauper's) funeral, 1 l. 5 s. 2 d." and in 1743, these: "for rum and sugar in proving the bounds of Kensington 17/9;" and "Benjamin Thing for rum to move the pound 10/–."

In the year 1746 the people of Newmarket and others presented a petition to the General Assembly for leave to erect a drawbridge over the Squamscot river between Newmarket and Stratham. As early as the year 1700, a right of ferry had been granted there to Richard Hilton, which had been in use up to that time. The convenience of a bridge to the people of the towns which had in the meantime grown up on the northwestern side of the river, who had to pass it in order to go to Portsmouth the seat of government, furnished a powerful argument to the petitioners. But Exeter feared that a bridge would cause injury to its business, and appointed Ezekiel Gilman, Daniel Gilman and Nicholas Perryman a committee to oppose the petition. They set out, in a lengthy remonstrance to the assembly, various reasons against the erection of a bridge; the likelihood that it would prevent the ascent of the fish, especially the bass, which were represented as abundant; the obstruction to the free passage up and down the river, of mast trees, rafts, gundalows and vessels, and the consequent injury to the navigation and ship-building interest of Exeter; and, in fact, made the best of a rather weak case. But the Legislature passed a bill permitting the bridge to be built, under some restrictions. Various difficulties postponed the erection of it, and more legislation was found needful; among other things a lottery was legalized in aid of the enterprise; and it was not till a quarter of a century had elapsed that the bridge was fairly completed.

A DISORDERLY ELECTION.

The demeanor of the people of Exeter at town meetings in the earlier part of the present century, is said to have been in general a pattern of decorum. Every voter, for example, respectfully doffed his hat in passing the moderator to deposit his ballot. But it was not always so. At a meeting of the town held on the twenty-fifth of October, 1755, for the choice of representatives in the assembly, things were not conducted in this orderly fashion. The long contest over the question of incorporating a second parish had just ended in the triumph of the seceding members, who had procured an act of the assembly freeing them from all liability to the old parish; and it is more than likely that some bitterness of feeling was the result. Peter Gilman and John Phillips, two prominent partisans of the new parish, were declared elected representatives. A remonstrance was presented to the assembly, against their being allowed to take seats, upon the ground of unfair practices in their election. A hearing was had thereon, at which Ephraim Robinson, a prominent member of the old parish, testified that "when the votes were numbered and the person declared to be chosen, the moderator was told the votes were not all brought in; to which he answered it was too late to bring in, then, for the person was chosen. Then there was a poll desired by seven persons or more, and it was denied. In voting for the second person, a number of persons declared they would not vote till the first vote was decided; and in voting for the last person there was one vote changed after it was put into the hat, and some more was asked to be changed. And when the second person was declared to be chosen, there was a poll again demanded by seven persons or more, but not granted. The whole of the meeting was carried on with the greatest irregularity and confusion, after the moderator was chosen, that ever I see in any town meeting before."

The Legislature ordered the return to be set aside and a precept to be sent to the town for a new election; at which Peter Gilman and Zebulon Giddinge were chosen.

For several succeeding years the attention of the people was much occupied with the French and Indian wars, which, though carried on at a distance, yet demanded new military organizations at home, every season. Exeter sent forth her annual quota of combatants, and was substantially the headquarters of one or more battalions, as will appear in the chapter devoted to military history.

The year 1758 was memorable for the prevalence in the town of that most dreaded scourge, the small-pox, a legacy, not improbably, of the camp. It made such inroads among the inhabitants that a town meeting was found needful, to give authority to the selectmen to take effectual measures for its eradication.

DEMONSTRATION AGAINST THE STAMP ACT.

Scarcely had the welcome news of peace with France and her savage allies been proclaimed, before the determination of England to exact tribute from her American colonies was manifested, by the passage of the Stamp Act; which was rendered no more agreeable to the people of New Hampshire by the knowledge that it originated from the suggestion of one of her own sons, Mr. John Huske. There is no need to repeat here the oft told tale of the mingled sorrow and indignation with which this injudicious piece of legislation was universally received on this side of the water. The feeling of the citizens of Exeter was well expressed by the Rev. Daniel Rogers, pastor of the Second church, who wrote in his diary under date of November 1, 1765, the day when the law went into effect: "The infamous Stamp Act, abhorred by all the British Colonies, took place."

The fifth of the same month used in many places in New England to be observed as "pope's day," in commemoration of the discovery of Guy Fawkes's gunpowder plot. This year it was made the occasion of a display of popular feeling in Exeter against the Stamp Act. Three effigies, representing, according to the Rev. Mr. Rogers, the pope, the devil and a stamp master, but according to another eye witness, Lords North and Bute as two of the characters, were carried about the streets of the town, and finally taken across the river, to the front of where the jail afterwards stood, and there set fire to and burnt to ashes. We may safely assume that the exhibition was witnessed by the citizens with abundant tokens of approbation.

The person appointed stamp-distributor for New Hampshire was constrained by the expressions of popular feeling to resign his office, and consequently no stamps ever got into use. This led to the opinion on the part of some persons, that proceedings in the courts of law could possess no validity, and to fears that universal license was to rule. But the substantial citizens of Exeter did not hesitate to array themselves against disorder. They entered into a written engagement for mutual protection and defence, which they subscribed and published, in the following terms:

Whereas many evil minded persons have, on account of the Stamp Act, concluded that all the laws of this province, and the execution of the same, are at an end; and that crimes against the public peace and private property may be committed with impunity, which opinion will render it unsafe for the peace officers to exert themselves in the execution of their offices:

Therefore we the subscribers, inhabitants of the town of Exeter, to prevent, as much as in us lies, the evils naturally consequent upon such an opinion, and for preserving the peace and good order of the community and of our own properties, do hereby combine, promise and engage to assemble ourselves together when and where need requires, in aid of the peace officers, and to stand by and defend them in the execution of their respective offices, and each other in our respective properties and persons, to the utmost, against all disturbers of the public peace and invaders of private property.

Witness our hands at Exeter this 15th day of November A. D. 1765.

John Bellamy	John Ward Gilman	Thomas Parsons
Theodore Carleton	Josiah Gilman	Benjamin Philbrick
Eliphalet Coffin	Josiah Gilman ter.	John Phillips
Peter Coffin	Nicholas Gilman	Enoch Poor
John Dudley	Peter Gilman	John Rice
Noah Emery	Samuel Gilman	Charles Rundlet
Nathaniel Folsom	Samuel Gilman 4th	Theophilus Smith
Samuel Folsom	John Hall	Joseph Swasey
Trueworthy Folsom	John Lamson	Daniel Tilton
John Giddinge	John Nelson	Jacob Tilton *
Bartholomew Gilman	Thomas Odiorne	
Daniel Gilman	Winthrop Odlin	

PATRIOTIC ACTION OF THE TOWN IN 1770.

The following year the Stamp Act was repealed, to the great joy and gratitude of the colonists. But England insisted on her claim of right to tax the Americans without their consent, and imposed a duty on the importation of tea and a few other articles into the provinces. This renewed the irritation among the colonists, which, however, did not fairly break forth into open expression until the intelligence of the "Boston massacre," March 5, 1770. Twelve days after that tragical occurrence a meeting of the town of Exeter was called, upon a petition of a number of the inhabitants, to act upon the following articles:

1. To see whether the town will pass any vote for the encouragement of the produce and manufactures of this country.
2. To see whether they will pass any vote or votes to discountenance the importation and consumption of unnecessary and superfluous foreign articles; and very particularly, as the duty on TEA furnishes so enormous a sum towards the support of a set of miscreants who devour the fruits of our honest industry, and [are] justly deemed the bane of this country, to see if the town will pass a vote not to make use of any foreign tea, and use their influence to prevent the consumption of it in their respective families, till the duty is taken off.

---

* Two copies of this agreement have been found, differing slightly in the names of the subscribers. All the names upon each are here retained.

3. To see if the town will inquire, or choose a committee to inquire, of the representatives of this town, what legal and constitutional measures have been taken by the General Assembly of this province for the redress of our grievances, in order to know what, or whether any measures may now be advisable to be promoted by them, and if any measures be advisable, to give their Representatives [instructions] to be by them observed, at their next session.

At the meeting of the town, held on the twenty-fifth of March, 1770, the vote for the encouragement of the produce and manufactures of this country passed in the affirmative, as did also that to discountenance the importation and consumption of unnecessary and superfluous articles. The town also resolved not to make use of any foreign tea, but to exert their influence to prevent the consumption of it in their respective families, till the duty should be taken off. Upon the article relative to the inquiry and instruction of the representatives, a committee was appointed, consisting of Nathaniel Folsom, John Phillips, Nicholas Gilman, Samuel Folsom, Joseph Gilman and Enoch Poor.

The meeting was then adjourned to the succeeding second of April, on which day the committee made their report, at considerable length. The substance of it was, that the General Assembly of this province had authorized a letter to be prepared and signed by their Speaker, addressed to their agent at the Court of Great Britain, to be presented to the king, expressing their hearty concurrence with the patriotic sentiments contained in a communication received from the house of Burgesses of Virginia; that the proposed letter was drafted and sent to the Speaker (Peter Gilman) at Exeter, for his signature, but as it did not express his personal views, he failed to subscribe it, wherefore it was not transmitted to England seasonably to co-operate with the petitions from the other colonies; and "that our American brethren may not construe it as deserting their interest upon any ungenerous separate views, we therefore give it as our instruction to the representatives of this town to use their influence in the House to promote a more public demonstration of their being governed by those noble, patriotic and loyal principles in which they have so happily harmonized with the other provinces, and, particularly, that an address to his majesty for redress of grievances, may (though late) be forthwith transmitted without further loss of time."

The representatives were also instructed to expedite the act for dividing the province into counties.

The report of the committee was adopted by the town.

The facts of the case were that Peter Gilman, who was then, perhaps, the foremost citizen of the town, and had occupied the Speaker's chair in the General Assembly for a number of years, was opposed to measures looking to resistance to the Crown of England. He had received honors and emoluments from the royal governors, had repeatedly taken the oath of allegiance in his official capacity, had nothing to gain, but much that might be lost by a change of government, and had arrived at a period of life when a man becomes conservative and averse to radical measures. It is only fair to say, however, that in compliance with the evident will of his constituents he soon after set his signature to the letter referred to; and though it was well known that he disapproved of the measures of the Revolution, yet he remained at his home, unmolested, throughout the war that followed, and apparently retained the respect of his townsmen, though they, with scarce an exception, were whigs of the most determined character. In 1771, when he ceased to be a member of the assembly, the town gave him a vote of thanks for his past services as their representative.

The law for dividing the province into counties, a long delayed act of justice to the people, went into effect in 1771. By its provisions certain terms of the courts were to be held in Exeter, and it was proposed that the town should furnish a suitable site for a county court-house. The open space in front of the present town-house, was then disfigured by a pound and several small buildings, erected in the midst of it. At a meeting of the town held July 8, 1771, it was voted "to grant liberty for a county court-house to be built on the land on which the pound and the shops belonging to Dr. Josiah Gilman, John Ward Gilman, Samuel Gilman and Samuel Folsom now stand," and that the land should be cleared of all incumbrances whatsoever. It was some years, however, before the court-house was erected, and in the meantime the courts were held in the town-house, which stood nearly opposite the First church. The earliest session of the Superior Court in the town was held on the first Tuesday of September, 1771.

In the year 1771 was built, at the expense of the town, the brick powder-house, near the first point on the eastern side of the salt river. Whether this was done in anticipation of the armed struggle that was soon to follow, we cannot tell. It is probable, however, that it became the storehouse in that war, and perhaps in subsequent wars, of "the town's stock of powder." The quaint little structure is one of the links that connect us with the past, and should not be suffered to go to decay.

ANOTHER PATRIOTIC EXPRESSION OF THE TOWN.

Political affairs were now gradually but surely tending towards a wider separation of the colonies from the mother country. The British Parliament, with a perverse misunderstanding of the temper of our people, persisted in retaining the duty on tea imported into the colonies, as a token of their right to impose taxes on them without their consent. It was the fly in the ointment. The Americans, who had previously been liberal consumers of tea, would have no more of it. And when the attempt was made to force it upon them, the sons of liberty of Boston boarded the vessels laden with the detested herb, and flung their cargoes into the sea.

Thereupon, on the twenty-fifth of the same December a meeting of the citizens of Exeter was called for an expression of opinion in the premises; and was held on the third of January, 1774. Nathaniel Folsom was chosen moderator. The action of the voters is thus described:

The meeting proceeded to take into consideration the rise of the present general uneasiness through the continent, which appears to them to be fairly, as well as briefly, stated by the honorable his majesty's council of the province of Massachusetts Bay, in their late advice to their governor. It was then moved [and] ruled that a number present draw up what they conceive to be the general sense of the meeting upon the matter under consideration, who, having consulted together, report that they apprehend the sense of this town cannot be better expressed than by adopting the resolves of the patriotic citizens of Philadelphia, which are as follows, viz.:

Resolved, That the disposal of their own property is the inherent right of freemen; that there can be no property in that which another can, of right, take from us without our consent; that the claim of Parliament to tax America is, in other words, a claim of right to levy contributions on us at pleasure.

2. That the duty imposed by Parliament upon tea landed in America, is a tax on the Americans, or levying contribution on them without their consent.

3. That the express purpose for which the tax is levied on the Americans, namely, for the support of government, the adminis-

America, has a direct tendency to render assemblies useless, and to introduce arbitrary government and slavery.

4. That a virtuous and steady opposition to this ministerial plan of governing America, is absolutely necessary to preserve even the shadow of liberty, and is a duty which every freeman in America owes to his country, to himself and to his posterity.

5. That the resolution lately come into by the East India Company to send out their tea to America subject to the payment of duties on its being landed here, is an open attempt to enforce the ministerial plan, and a violent attack upon the liberties of America.

6. That it is the duty of every American to oppose this attempt.

7. That whoever shall directly or indirectly countenance this attempt or in any wise aid or abet in unloading, receiving or vending the tea sent or to be sent out by the East India Company while it remains subject to the payment of a duty here, is an enemy to America.

The foregoing resolves, after having been repeatedly read, passed almost unanimously.

Further Resolved, That we are ready on all necessary occasions to risk our lives and fortunes in defence of our rights and liberties, professing to have as great a veneration for freedom as any people on earth.

Voted, That this town do return their sincere thanks to all the cities, towns and persons in America who have at any time nobly exerted themselves in the cause of liberty.

Voted, That John Phillips, Esq., John Giddinge, Esq., Col. Nicholas Gilman, Mr. Samuel Brooks and Mr. Joseph Gilman, they or any three of them, be a committee to correspond with the committee of Portsmouth, and any and all other committees, in this or the neighboring governments, as they may see occasion; and that they cause the proceedings of this meeting to be published in the New Hampshire *Gazette* as soon as may be.

Voted, That the Committee of Correspondence wait on the dealers in teas in this town, and desire them to desist from purchasing any more teas, until the duty thereon is taken off.

Upon the eighteenth of July the town chose as deputies to the first Provincial Congress, John Giddinge, Theophilus Gilman, Nathaniel Folsom, John Phillips and Samuel Gilman, with power to them or any three of them to join in choosing delegates to the Continental Congress; and voted that ten pounds, lawful money, should be paid by the selectmen towards defraying the expenses of such delegates. The Provincial Congress met on the twenty-first of July at Exeter, and chose Nathaniel Folsom of Exeter, and John Sullivan delegates to the Continental Congress.

HELP FOR THE SUFFERING POOR OF BOSTON.

The next step taken by Great Britain towards effectually alienating her American subjects, was the passage of the Boston port bill. This measure put an end to all commerce and nearly all business in the principal town of New England, and as a matter of course, caused great distress to the laboring class there, whom it threw out of employment. The warmest sympathy was expressed from all quarters with the oppressed inhabitants of Boston.

In Exeter a town meeting was called to take into consideration "the distressing circumstances of the town of Boston, occasioned by a cruel and arbitrary act of the British Parliament in blocking up their harbor," and to pass a vote to raise money for the relief of the industrious suffering poor of said town.

At the meeting held October 31, 1774, it was resolved to raise by taxation one hundred pounds, lawful money, for the suffering poor of Boston; with the proviso that "if any person or persons shall be against paying their proportion of the tax, if they enter their names with the clerk within ten days, they shall be exempted from paying anything of said tax."

The assessment of this sum is set forth on the town books, and to the credit of our fathers it may be said that few, if any, appear to have taken advantage of the clause of exemption. The full amount was promptly collected and paid over to the authorities of the town of Boston.

The following correspondence respecting the gift, is worthy of preservation.

LETTER FROM EXETER TO THE COMMITTEE OF BOSTON.

Gentlemen,

It gives us peculiar satisfaction that we are the happy instruments of conveying relief to the distressed. We send you by the bearer hereof Mr. Carlton, one hundred pounds, which sum was unanimously and cheerfully voted by this town for our suffering brethren in Boston. The cause for which you now suffer we esteem the common cause of all America; your prudence and fortitude we admire. That you may be assisted by all the colonies in the present glorious struggle for liberty, and endued with wisdom and patience to persevere to the end is the desire and hearty prayer of your sincere friends.

I have the honor, Gentlemen, in behalf of the selectmen of Exeter, to subscribe myself your most humble servant,

SAMUEL BROOKS.

New Hampshire, Exeter, 6th February, 1775.

REPLY TO EXETER.

BOSTON, February 8, 1775.

Sir,

Our worthy friend Mr. Carlton has just now called in and left with me one hundred pounds, lawful money, a generous donation from the patriotic inhabitants of Exeter for their suffering brethren in Boston. You will please to tender the thanks of the Committee of Donations to our kind benefactors for this mark of their Christian sympathy and affection. The approbation of the past conduct of this greatly oppressed and distressed metropolis affords us great satisfaction, but especially the tender and benevolent sentiments expressed in your letter. Prudence and fortitude have doubtless been exhibited, but humility becomes us, and our thankful acknowledgements are due to God, from whom alone every good gift and every perfect gift is derived, and on Him alone we must constantly depend for all that wisdom, patience and fortitude, we need in this day of sore trial. By his help and favor we shall persevere, and in the end see the happy accomplishment of all our desires. We hope for the continuance of the prayers, countenance and assistance of our friends. We cannot doubt it since they unitedly consider the cause as common.

Yours and others', our friends' donations will be applied agreeable to the intent of the charitable donors. Printed accounts of the conduct of the Committee are now inclosed, and I trust will give satisfaction to all the friends of truth and righteousness.

I am, sir, your obliged friend and humble servant,

DAVID JEFFRIES.
Per order of the Committee of Donations.

To SAMUEL BROOKS, ESQ.

At a meeting of the town December 26, 1774, it was voted to adopt the association agreement determined upon by the Continental Congress, and by them recommended to the British colonies, commonly known as the non-importation agreement; and the following persons were chosen to see that the agreement be strictly adhered to, viz.: Daniel Tilton, Thomas Odiorne, Theophilus Gilman, William Parker, John Emery, Nicholas Gilman, Nathaniel Folsom, Theodore Carleton, Enoch Poor, Theophilus Smith, Thomas Folsom, Peter Coffin, Samuel Folsom, Joseph Gilman, James Hackett, John Giddinge, Josiah Gilman, Eliphalet Hale, Josiah Robinson, Josiah Barker, Nathaniel Gordon, Ephraim Robinson and Samuel Brooks.

We have information (though the record fails to show it), that at the same meeting a resolution was adopted against the intrusion of pedlers, hawkers and petty chapmen, who obviously could deal in the forbidden commodities with little danger of detection. The popular sentiment against violations of the non-importation agreement was plainly expressed in a published letter of the time written from Exeter, that if this vote of the town and the law of the province should be ineffectual to prevent them, "it is the opinion of many that an experiment ought to be made of Tar and Feathers!"

At the same meeting the following persons were chosen deputies to represent the town in the (second) Provincial Congress held in Exeter on the twenty-fifth of January, 1775: Nathaniel Folsom, Theophilus Gilman, Nicholas Gilman, William Parker and John Giddinge. By that congress John Sullivan and John Langdon were elected delegates to the Continental Congress.

Throughout the year events were hurrying on to a crisis. Three other congresses of the province assembled in Exeter in 1775. The first of these met on the twenty-first of April. Exeter was represented in it by Nathaniel Folsom, Nicholas Gilman, John Giddinge, Theophilus Gilman and Enoch Poor. On the seventeenth of May another like convention of deputies of the people opened its session. The delegates of the town were Nathaniel Folsom, Nicholas Gilman and Enoch Poor; but when the first and last of these were summoned into the military service, a new election was held June 26, to supply their places. John Giddinge and Theophilus Gilman were chosen. The latter desired to be excused, because he was elected "against his consent," and Noah Emery, and afterwards Samuel Brooks were selected "to serve six months, if necessary."

This body was kept alive, by repeated adjournments, till the fifteenth of November, and in its recesses the provincial committee of safety was in continual session, in Exeter.

It was from this Congress, it is alleged, that the earliest official suggestion of national independence emanated. Matthew Thornton, its president, in a "noble letter" to the Continental Congress at Philadelphia, bearing date May 23, 1775, held this language:

We will not conceal that many among us are disposed to conclude, that the voice of God and Nature to us, since the late hostile design and conduct of Great Britain, is, that *we are bound to look to our whole political affairs.*

THE CENSUS OF 1775.

On the twenty-fifth of August, 1775, the Provincial Congress the colony, to take the exact number of all the inhabitants therein, and make return of the same in several columns as specified; and also to report the number of fire-arms and the stock of powder in each place.

The return made by the selectmen of Exeter was as follows:

Males under 16 years of age	401
Males from 16 years to 50 not in the army	273
All males above 50 years of age	86
Persons gone in the army	51
All females	892
Negroes and slaves for life	38
Fire arms	193
Fire arms wanting	150
Powder	80¾ lbs.
Town stock of powder	50 lbs.

SAMUEL BROOKS
THEODORE CARLETON } Selectmen
PETER COFFIN JUN. } of
EPH^M ROBINSON } Exeter.

6 October 1775, Sworn to before Zaccheus Clough, Just. Peace.

THE EARLIEST WRITTEN CONSTITUTION.

The authority of the king's officers having come to an end, the need of a regular and stable system of government in New Hampshire had now become so urgent, that in October the province made application to the Continental Congress for advice and direction what course they ought to adopt. The answer of the Congress, given in November, was a recommendation in substance that a full and free representation of the people should be called, to establish, if thought necessary, a form of government such as should best promote the welfare of the province, during the continuance of the dispute with Great Britain.

In pursuance of this advice a fifth Provincial Congress was summoned, to be composed of persons having real estate in the province to the value of five hundred pounds each, to meet at Exeter on the twenty-first day of December, and to serve for one year, to transact such business and pursue such measures as they might judge necessary for the public good; and in case there should be a recommendation from the Continental Congress that the colony assume government in any particular form, which would require a House of Representatives, to resolve themselves into such a House as the Continental Congress should recommend.

John Giddinge and Noah Emery were selected as delegates of Exeter, without specific instructions.

This last provincial representation of New Hampshire came together on the day appointed, and spent the first two weeks of their session in disposing of preliminary matters, in order that time might be allowed for deliberate consideration before acting upon the momentous question of "taking up government," as the phrase of the day was.

Then, everything being made ready, on the fifth day of January, 1776, the delegates, in pursuance of the powers committed to them by their constituents, resolved themselves into a House of Representatives; adopted a WRITTEN CONSTITUTION, THE FIRST OF EITHER OF THE UNITED STATES; elected under it the needful legislative, judicial and executive officers; and thus New Hampshire became, in effect, free and independent of the British Crown.

CHAPTER IV.

EXETER UNDER THE STATE GOVERNMENT.

The Constitution adopted by New Hampshire in the early part of 1776, though in some respects imperfect, as might naturally have been expected, being the first of its kind, yet served the purposes of the people sufficiently well until it was superseded by a more complete instrument, framed about the close of the Revolution.

Exeter, by the census of 1775, containing seventeen hundred and forty-one inhabitants, had become practically the capital of the State, the seat of government, and the centre of all civil and military activity in New Hampshire.

There is little upon the records of the town to show that the people had become sovereign, except that new safeguards were set up against the selection of unsuitable persons for public office. The members of the council, for example, were required to be respectable freeholders, and no man could sit in either house of the Legislature who had treated electors with liquor to gain their votes. The people evidently valued at its true worth the privilege of governing themselves, which they were paying so heavy a price to secure.

THE ASSOCIATION TEST OF 1776.

The Continental Congress resolved on the fourteenth of March, 1776, to recommend to the several Assemblies or Committees of Safety of the United Colonies immediately to cause to be disarmed all persons within their respective colonies who were notoriously disaffected to the cause of America, or who refused to associate to defend by arms the United Colonies against the hostile attempts of the British fleets and armies.

The Committee of Safety of New Hampshire in order to carry this resolve into execution, on the twelfth of April, 1776, sent circulars to the selectmen of the several towns and places in the colony, requesting them to desire all males above twenty-one years of age (lunatics, idiots and negroes excepted) to sign the following declaration, and, when that should be done, to make return thereof together with the names of all who should refuse to sign the same, to the General Assembly or Committee of Safety of the colony. The declaration was in these words:

We the subscribers do hereby solemnly engage and promise that we will, to the utmost of our power, at the risk of our lives and fortunes, with arms oppose the hostile proceedings of the British fleets and armies against the United American Colonies.

It is a matter of deep regret that the complete return from Exeter has not been preserved. At least three hundred names, and probably more, must have been reported, for or against the patriotic declaration, but all except those upon a single sheet, forty-eight only, are lost. The names preserved are here given. From what is known of the sentiments of the voters of the town it is believed that the number of those refusing to sign might be counted on the fingers of one hand, with some to spare.

Josiah Beal	Samuel Folsom Gilman	William Odlin
John Bond	Zebulon Gilman	John Patten
John Cartee	Nathaniel Gordon	Samuel Quimby
Benjamin Cram	Daniel Grant	Jos. Rollins
Stephen [Creighton?]	Samuel Harris	David Smith
Thomas Dolloff	Jonathan Hopkinson	Theophilus Smith
Noah Emery	Kinsley H. James	Joseph Stacey
Gerould Fitz Gerould.	Benjamin Kimball	Benjamin Swasey
Josiah Folsom	Robert Kimball	Joseph Swasey
Bartholomew Gale	Edward Ladd	Joseph Thing
Eliphalet Giddinge	Joseph Lamson	Stephen Thing
John Giddinge	Samuel Lamson	Winthrop Thing
John Giddinge, Jr.	Robert Lord	Thomas Tyler
David Gilman	Thomas Lyford	Dudley Watson
Joseph Gilman	Benjamin Morse	Josiah Weeks
Josiah Gilman, Jr.	Habertus Neale	Josiah Wyatt

FIRST READING OF THE DECLARATION OF INDEPENDENCE.

A little more than seven months after New Hampshire had "taken up government," a scene was witnessed in Exeter which is worthy of a brief description.

Hostilities had been waged between Great Britain and the United Colonies for more than a year, and the foolish obstinacy of the king forbade all hopes of reconciliation on terms that Americans could submit to without disgrace. Even the conservative and the timid had begun to think of "independency" as something within the range of possibility, while the ardent sons of liberty chafed at the delay in shaking off the yoke of allegiance to the mother country. We have already seen that the subject had been mooted long before in the Provincial Congress of New Hampshire.

The leading men of Exeter and of the State government were fully prepared, and even anxious, for the final step of separation. Both houses of the Legislature had united in instructions "to our delegates in the Continental Congress to join with the other colonies in declaring the thirteen United Colonies free and independent States; solemnly pledging our faith and honor that we will on our parts support the measure with our lives and fortunes."

From this time forward all was impatience in Exeter to learn the action of the Continental Congress on the momentous question. At length, on the eighteenth day of July, 1776, the wished for news arrived. A courier rode into the village, bringing with him a packet addressed to the chief executive of New Hampshire, containing the immortal Declaration of American Independence, under the authentication of John Hancock, president of Congress.

As soon as its contents were ascertained, it was determined that the paper should be publicly read to the citizens, forthwith. The Legislature had adjourned, but the Committee of Safety were in session. The tidings circulated through the town with lightning rapidity. Men, women and children dropped their employments, and gathered about the court-house, to listen to the words that made them free.

John Taylor Gilman was chosen for the signal honor of reading for the first time in the capital of the State, the charter of American freedom. Prominent among his hearers were Meshech Weare, the President of the State, Matthew Thornton, who was himself a few months later to set his hand to the Declaration, General Nathaniel Folsom, Colonel Pierse Long and Dr. Ebenezer Thompson, all sterling patriots and members of the Committee of Safety. There too was Colonel Nicholas Gilman, the New Hampshire financier of the Revolution and the right hand of the executive. He had ardently longed for the time when independence should be proclaimed, and now he was to hear, from the lips of his son, that the hour had struck.

As soon as his hastily gathered audience had assembled, the youthful reader began his grateful task. We can imagine with what bated breath all listened for the first time to that impressive statement of the causes which led America to take up arms. The clear tones in which the eloquent periods were enunciated never faltered, until the masterly climax was reached, when the rush of patriotic feeling became too great for speech, and for a moment the reader was compelled to pause, to regain the power of utterance.

Often as the charter of our liberties has been since repeated in Exeter, in times of national trial and of national prosperity, it was never listened to with more devout thankfulness, greater faith, or more honest pride than on this, its first reading.

THE EVILS OF A PAPER CURRENCY.

The colonies committed the often repeated mistake of attempting to carry on a war by means of bills of credit. The result was a rapid inflation of the prices of all the necessaries of life, which the people vainly attempted to control, by legislation.

On May 5, 1777, a meeting of the town was called "to regulate and affix the prices of goods and other articles, for said town, and to do and act in all affairs agreeable to the directions of an act of this State passed the tenth day of April last." The following persons were chosen a committee to make report upon said matters: Eliphalet Hale, Josiah Barker, David Fogg, Samuel Folsom, Joseph Lamson, Josiah Gilman, Peter Coffin and Samuel Brooks. No report of their doings is upon record, but it is safe to say that any plan they could have devised, short of a complete change of the circulating medium, would have been inadequate to relieve the financial troubles of the time.

On May 11, 1778, the town chose Nathaniel Folsom, Samuel Hobart and John Pickering delegates to the convention to be held at Concord on the tenth of June following, to form a permanent plan of government for the State.

Another fruitless attempt to stay the constantly waning value of the paper currency was made by the town, a year later. On July 19, 1779, Josiah Robinson, Nathaniel Gordon, Eliphalet Giddinge, Eliphalet Hale, Eliphalet Ladd, Gideon Lamson and John T. Gilman, a committee appointed by the town to consider the subjects of a reduction of the price of the necessaries of life, and the support of the credit of the currency, reported the following scale of prices, to hold good until the succeeding first of September, viz.:

West India rum	8l. 8s.	per gallon	Salt made in New England,	7l. 4s.	per bushel
New England rum	5l. 8s.	" "			
Molasses	4l. 16s.	" "	Indian corn 5l. 8s.		per bushel
Brown sugar	16s. to 18s.	" lb.	Rye	6l.	" "
Chocolate	26s.	" "	Wheat	9l. 12s.	" "
Coffee	22s.	" "	Lamb	5s.	" lb.
Tea	8l. 8s.	" "	Beef	4s. 6d.	" "
Cottonwool	40s.	" "	Veal	4s. 6d.	" "
No W. I. or other foreign salt to exceed 9l. 12s. per bushel			Salt pork	12s.	" "
			Butter	12s.	" "
			Best English hay 30l. per ton		
			Other hay in proportion thereto.		

The committee also reported the following resolutions:

Resolved, That wool, flax, cloth and other articles of the produce of this country not herein particularly mentioned, shall not exceed the price of twenty shillings for what was commonly sold for one shilling in the year 1774, and in that rule of proportion to any sum or sums.

Resolved, That we will sell no articles of merchandise not particularly above mentioned, at a higher price than they are now sold.

Resolved, That the tradesmen and laborers of this town will not exceed the above rate of twenty for one for their labor and manufactures, including those articles they may have of the produce of this country, and excluding those of foreign import, and that they will reduce the same in proportion as the prices of merchandise and the produce of the country are from time to time lowered.

Resolved, Upon condition the other towns in this State adopt similar measures respecting their merchandise and produce, that from and after the first day of September next, we will continue to lower the prices month by month, unless some other general plan shall be adopted by the people of this State.

Resolved, That all those who shall hereafter dare to refuse continental currency, or require hard money for rent or any other article whatever, or shall in any way endeavor to evade the salutary measures proposed by this body, shall be deemed enemies to the interest and independence of this United States, and shall be treated in such manner as the town shall hereafter order.

Resolved, That the foregoing be offered for signing, to every male inhabitant of this town, paying taxes.

The report of the committee was unanimously adopted. Stephen Thing, David Fogg and Simeon Ladd were chosen a committee to offer the resolves to the inhabitants, for their signatures. At an adjourned meeting the committee reported that some persons had declined to sign the resolves. The town instructed them to present them to such persons a second time, and upon their refusal, to return their names to the selectmen, who were directed to publish the same in the New Hampshire *Gazette*. So far as can be learned from the imperfect files of the *Gazette* known to be in existence, no such publication of names was found to be necessary. But resolutions, however patriotic, could not annul the laws of finance and trade.

On the twenty-sixth of March, 1781, the credit of the paper currency had sunk so low that a day's work on the highway was by order of the town estimated at forty dollars. On the thirty-first of March, 1783, after the bills of credit had gone out of circulation, and accounts were kept in metallic currency, the same was reckoned at no more than three shillings.

The constitution agreed upon by the convention of 1778 for the government of the State, having been rejected on reference to the people; and another convention having been ordered, to be held in Concord on the second Tuesday of June, 1781, the town on the fourth of that month appointed Nathaniel Folsom and John T. Gilman delegates thereto.

The fourth of July, 1778, according to the recollection of a gentleman who witnessed it, was suitably observed in Exeter, although it is not known with what ceremonials. The first printed account of a celebration of the anniversary which has been met with, was that of 1781. A contemporary journal describes the day as "ushered in by a display of colors and the most lively tokens of joy. At noon the principal gentlemen assembled at the Raleigh tavern, kept by Colonel Samuel Folsom, where they were honored by the company of the honorable council, and speaker of the Assembly, at a genteel collation, after which a number of suitable toasts were drank and thirteen cannon discharged."

The people of Exeter endured their full proportion of the hardships that were caused by the War of the Revolution. A large share of the business from which the town had derived its support, was arrested, and had it not been that the public offices and State administration were transferred to the town, there would have been much more suffering. But the Legislature was in session much of the time, and during its adjournments the Committee of Safety, with equal powers, sat in its stead. Exeter was also the headquarters for most of the military operations; so that, altogether, there was no small amount of activity and remunerative employment in the town.

What Exeter did to furnish soldiers for the war, will be told in another chapter. Her citizens were loyal to their own country, with scarce an exception. A few were lukewarm, but the only downright tory that is known was Robert Luist Fowle, the printer, who was committed to prison on the charge of counterfeiting the provincial paper currency, but made his escape, and took refuge within the British lines.

But after the war was over, there came a time of peculiar stress. The Utopia that so many had looked forward to, as the natural result of independence, was not realized. Times were hard and cash was scarce. Ignorant and unreflecting people fancied that the panacea for these ills, was for the government to issue fresh bills of credit. But, fortunately, there were those in authority in the State with sufficient knowledge of political economy to prevent the Legislature from resorting to that deceptive remedy for financial troubles. But they could not convince the "green-backers" of those days; and at length matters came to such a pass that the infatuated clamorers for paper currency determined to make an attempt to dragoon the Legislature into sanctioning it.

THE PAPER MONEY MOB OF 1786.

A body of men from the towns in the western part of Rockingham county by a concerted movement assembled September 20, 1786, at Kingston, thence to march to Exeter, where the State Legislature was in session. They were mustered in a sort of military array under leaders, some of whom had served in the revolutionary army. Joseph French of Hampstead, James Cochran of Pembroke and John McKean of Londonderry were the principal officers. In the afternoon they made their entry into the village of Exeter, by way of Front street. They numbered about two hundred, one-half of them marching on foot and armed with guns or swords, and the remainder following on horseback, and carrying clubs or whips. The General Court was sitting in the First church, and the Superior (judicial) Court in the town-house on the opposite side of the street. The insurgents marched into the centre of the village, and by mistake surrounded the latter building. If their object had been to overawe the legal tribunal within it, they would have signally failed, for Judge Samuel Livermore was presiding, and so far was he from being daunted, that he ordered the business of the court to proceed, and sternly forbade every one to look out of the windows.

But it was the General Court that the insurgents meant to intimidate, and they attempted to stretch a cordon of men around the meeting-house where the legislators were. But there was by this time a great body of spectators on the ground, partly citizens of the town, and partly inhabitants of neighboring places who had come in to witness the proceedings. They were generally opposed to the lawless intruders, so that when the latter endeavored to draw near the meeting-house, they found it no easy matter to overcome the inertia of the unfriendly crowd. Little by little, however, they forced their way to the building, and stationed sentinels at the doors and windows. They then, after ostentatiously loading their fire-arms, announced their purpose to compel the Legislature to enact a law for the emission of abundant paper money which should be made a legal tender for debts and taxes, and their determination to hold the law-makers in durance until the demand was complied with. One or two representatives who attempted to make their escape were driven back with insult. It fortunately happened that the chief executive of the State was a man of courage and resolution, and not unacquainted with arms, John Sullivan, who had gained the rank of major general in the Revolution. He appeared at the entrance of the building and listened to the requirements of the assemblage. In a temperate and reasonable reply he gave them to understand that they need not expect to frighten him, for he had smelt powder before. "You ask for justice," he continued, "and justice you shall have." But he did not order them to disperse; he perhaps thought it was wiser to let them keep together, in order the more effectually to stamp out the tendency to insurrection against the constituted authorities.

The afternoon wore away; the General Court were still prisoners, and no progress had been made towards an adjustment. By this time many of the better class of citizens of Exeter were filled with shame and indignation at the unchecked riotous demonstration, and one of them, Colonel Nathaniel Gilman, with the assistance of others, successfully practised a *ruse de guerre*, in order to raise the siege. It had then become dusk, and a high and close fence around the church-yard prevented the rioters from seeing distinctly what was going on outside. He caused a drum to be beaten briskly at a little distance while a body of citizens approached with a measured military step, and then cried out in his stentorian voice, "Hurra for government! Here comes Hackett's artillery!" The cry was echoed by others, and the insurgents did not wait for more. Their valor was not up to the fighting point, and they rapidly retreated, standing not on the order of their going. They afterward made their rendezvous on the western side of the Little river, on the road to Kingston, and there a great part of them spent the night.

No sooner had they retired than steps were taken to crush this revolt in the bud. Messengers were sent into the neighboring towns bearing orders to the officers of the militia to muster their commands, and march at once to the scene of action; and in Exeter a company of the first citizens enrolled themselves under the command of Captain Nicholas Gilman, who had served as an officer through the war. The next morning saw nearly two thousand men under arms in Exeter. President Sullivan assumed the direction of the column, which at once moved against the insurrectionary force, the volunteers of Exeter claiming the post of honor in the van. Arrived within about an eighth of a mile from their antagonists, they were halted by order, when a small troop of horsemen * under Colonel Joseph Cilley, a revolutionary officer of distinction, galloped forward, forded the river, and made prisoners of the principal leaders of the insurgents; after which their followers surrendered at discretion.

Thus terminated the most formidable demonstration against the government which was ever made on the soil of New Hampshire. The happy result of it was in no small degree due to the loyal feeling and prudence and pluck of the people of Exeter. The attempt to dictate legislation by force having proved so ignominious a failure, it was not deemed necessary to inflict serious punishment upon the offenders.

But the Legislature, in order that the opinion of the people of the State should be fairly tested on the expediency of issuing a paper currency, passed a bill to authorize its emission, to be sub-

---

* Tradition says that Major Jonathan Cass, the father of the statesman Lewis Cass, distinguished himself on this occasion, and in the charge leaped his horse completely over a well.

mitted to the voters of the several towns for their approval or rejection. And on the twenty-third of October, 1786, a meeting of the citizens of Exeter was held for the expression of their opinion. A committee of leading men consisting of John T. Gilman, Oliver Peabody, Samuel Tenney, John Phillips, Nicholas Gilman, Thomas Folsom and Noah Emery was appointed, to make a report upon the subject, who prepared full and elaborate reasons in writing against the measure, which were read in the meeting; and when the vote was taken it was found that there were but six in favor of the plan, and seventy-nine against it.

THE CONVENTION FOR THE ADOPTION OF THE UNITED STATES CONSTITUTION.

On the thirteenth of February, 1788, assembled in convention at the court-house in Exeter the delegates chosen by the several towns in the State, to consider and pass upon the constitution framed for the government of the United States, under which we now live. It was an anxious period. The proposed constitution contained a provision that it was to go into effect upon its ratification by nine of the thirteen States. Eight had already voted their approval of it, and the interest of the country centred upon New Hampshire, the ninth to act upon it. The session of the convention in Exeter lasted ten days. So great was the opposition developed to the adoption of the new instrument, that its friends thought it wiser to postpone final action upon the question for a season; and the convention was adjourned to meet again at Concord in the following June. The public sentiment had by that time so distinctly manifested itself that after a session of four days the convention was ready by a fair majority to ratify the constitution, and thus to put the new government into operation. The delegate of Exeter, who was one of the most influential in bringing about this result, was John Taylor Gilman.

THE VISIT OF WASHINGTON.

The year 1789 is one to be remembered in Exeter, by a visit from the Father of his country. George Washington, having been inaugurated the first President of the Republic, was then making a tour through the Northern States. He had passed two or three days in Portsmouth, and left that place in the morning of the fourth day of November. His habits of extreme punctuality are well known, and he probably set out from Portsmouth exactly as the hands of the clock pointed to the half hour after seven. The people of Exeter had made arrangements to receive him with a handsome cavalcade. But some of the party were a little dilatory, and before they were in the saddle Washington made his appearance, it not yet being ten o'clock. He was mounted on horseback, as was his practice when entering a town, and was attended by his two secretaries, Colonel Tobias Lear and Major William Jackson, who rode in an open carriage, and by a single servant. He wore a drab surtout and a military hat. The streets were thronged with people waiting to welcome the distinguished visitor, and Captain Simon Wiggin in command of the artillery company of Exeter, had his men promptly in line, and received his Commander-in-Chief with a salute of thirteen guns.

The party alighted at the public house kept by Colonel Samuel Folsom, where they were waited upon by Colonel Nicholas Gilman, who had been a staff officer under Washington at Yorktown, and other revolutionary soldiers and citizens, proud to do the honors of the town to the President. They invited him to tarry for a night and partake of a public dinner. But his engagements, previously made, compelled him, with reluctance as he informs us in his diary, to decline. They, however, gave him a collation, which he graciously accepted. Among those who had the honor of waiting on him at the table was a young lady relative of Colonel Folsom, who had solicited the privilege. Washington saw at once that she was no menial servant, and calling her to him, addressed her a few pleasant words and kissed her. She lived to attain a good old age, and was the friend of some of the most distinguished men of a subsequent generation, but probably no incident of her life made so lasting an impression upon her memory as the kiss of Washington.

The few hours of Washington's stay in Exeter were soon ended, and he resumed his journey. A cavalcade of gentlemen escorted him outside the village. He took the road to Kingston, on his way to Haverhill, Massachusetts. When he reached the top of Great hill, he directed the driver of his carriage to halt, that he might look back upon the wide view of Exeter and its vicinity. He gazed a few moments at the fair landscape that lay at his feet and stretched away to the ocean, and remarked admiringly upon its beauty; and with this pleasant farewell to Exeter he went on his way.

COURT-HOUSE, FIRE ENGINE, LIBRARY, ETC.

The town, on October 13, 1788, had instructed the selectmen to put up a chimney in the town-house, and to make such repairs on the building as to render it suitable for the sessions of the General Court and county courts. But three years afterwards the need of a new court-house became apparent, and on the twelfth of September, 1791, the town voted to raise, to be assessed the next year, two hundred and fifty pounds for the purpose of building one, to be placed on the land between the house of the late General Folsom and that of Ward Clark Dean; and that so much of said land as should be necessary, be appropriated for the purpose. This location was in the middle of the present Court square, just in front of the town-house. The building was completed, there, in season for the town to hold its annual meeting in it, in March, 1793.

The State constitution which was adopted by the people in 1783 was found on trial to require amendment, and on August 8, 1791, the town, at a meeting held for the purpose, appointed Samuel Tenney a delegate to the convention to be held at Concord on the succeeding first Wednesday of September, to revise the constitution.

At the March town meeting in 1794, it was voted to raise a sum not exceeding seventy pounds, for the purchase of a new fire engine, hooks, etc., for the use of the town; and that Gideon Lamson be empowered to bargain for the same, and to sell the engine then belonging to the town, and account for the proceeds thereof. The former engine here referred to was procured in 1774 at the cost, including transportation, of fifty-two pounds.

It was also voted that any persons who might be unwilling to pay their taxes assessed for the new engine, could have them abated upon application to the selectmen, by the first Monday of May following. This, and one or two other similar cases of consideration, exhibited by the majority, for the inability or opposition of a minority of the tax-payers, are worthy of being recorded, to the credit of the town. They are in sharp contrast to the ideas and practice of some communities, in later times.

At the adjourned annual meeting in March, 1797, it was voted by the town that Benjamin Clark Gilman and his associates should have the privilege of sinking an aqueduct in Fore street, and such other streets as they might find convenient, for supplying water to customers; and of breaking ground to repair the same; on condition that they should put the streets in as good a state as they found them in, within a reasonable time, and should indemnify the town against prosecutions on that account.

In 1797 the Legislature incorporated several of the principal citizens of the town as the "Exeter Social Library." They at once completed an organization, and adopted rules and regulations. From a little pamphlet printed for their use by Henry Ranlet in the same year, it appears that they began with thirty-eight proprietors and one hundred and sixty-eight volumes. The number of the latter was subsequently much increased, and the society continued in existence for a considerable period, until the books having probably become pretty familiar, the interest in the library so far abated, that its contents were divided among the proprietors.

In the year 1798 a number of citizens, for the better protection of their property from loss by fire, entered into a voluntary association called the "Fire Society of Exeter." Their constitution provided that the number of members should not exceed twenty-five, and that no person should be admitted, except at a meeting where three-fourths of the society were present; and if more than a single ballot were cast against him. Each member was to keep always in readiness two leather buckets, and two bags a yard and a half in length and three-quarters of a yard in breadth, with strings at the mouth; and at every alarm of fire was instantly to repair with his buckets and bags to the house or other building of the member whose danger should appear greatest, and make every exertion for the preservation of his building and personal property. Various fines were prescribed for delinquencies, which went, if this society was conducted like similar associations elsewhere, to pay for an occasional dinner and jollification for the members. The society, having this happy commingling of the *utile* with the *dulci*, was kept up for many years, and was the precursor of other combinations for the same object. The "Junior Fire Society" was in successful operation in 1817, and the "Phœnix Fire Society" in 1832.

HONORS TO THE MEMORY OF WASHINGTON.

Nearly all the sessions of the State Legislature were held in Exeter from the beginning of the year 1776 to 1784; but for the succeeding fifteen years they were distributed among three or four towns, Exeter receiving but a small share of them. The

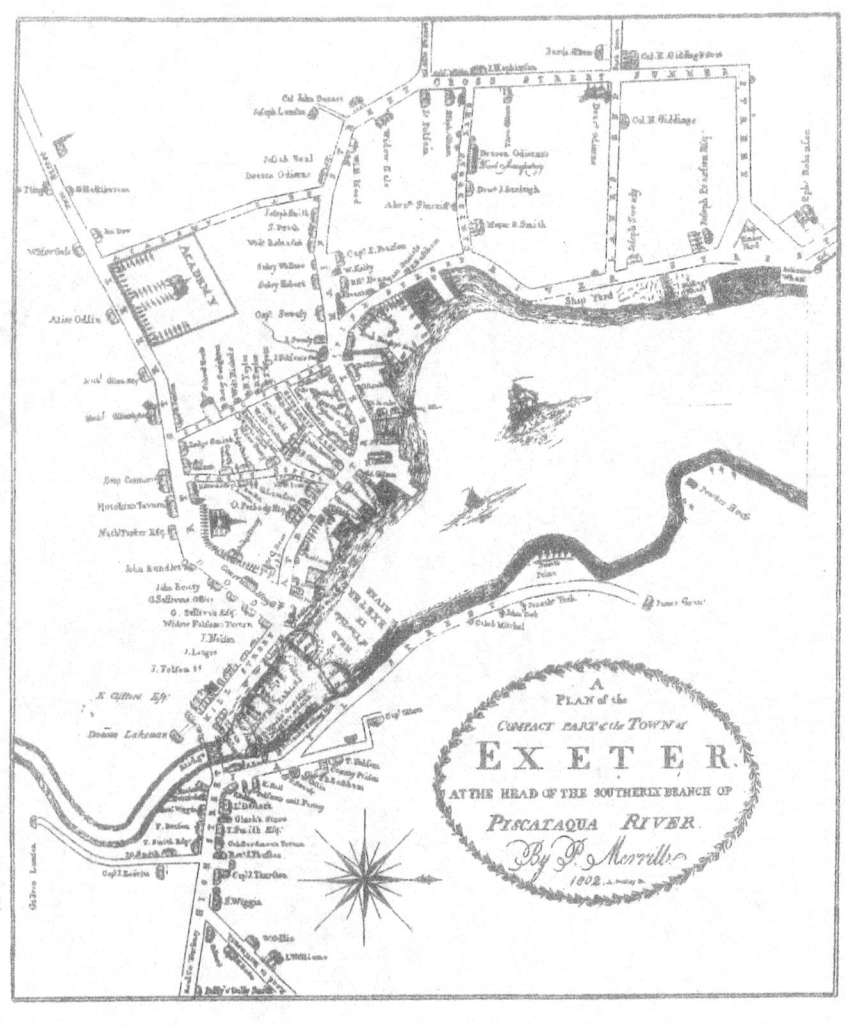

last meeting there was in December, 1799. Near the close of the session intelligence was received of the death of Washington, which occurred on the fourteenth day of the month. The General Court immediately suspended business and resolved, in respect to the memory of the deceased patriot, to go into mourning for the term of three months. And on the day following, the executive and legislative officers of the State, with the selectmen and citizens of the town, escorted by a military company of students of the academy in uniform with proper badges of mourning, marched in procession to the First meeting-house, where religious exercises were performed, appropriate to the sad event. The citizens of the town resolved to take further and more formal notice of the national bereavement. They accordingly invited the Hon. Jeremiah Smith to deliver a eulogy on the late President. On the succeeding twenty-second of February, which was generally observed as a day of mourning throughout the land, they gathered, with all the insignia of respect and grief, in the meeting-house of the First parish, and there listened to an eloquent oration in honor of the deceased First Citizen of America, pronounced by one who was fully capable of appreciating his greatness and his virtues, and who had known him in public and in private life, in his official position at the national capital and as his visitor at Mount Vernon.

In 1799 the streets of the town for the first time received authoritative names, recommended by a committee of citizens, and adopted by the town, as they are given upon the plan drawn by Phineas Merrill in 1802, a copy of which is contained in this volume.

In 1801 the "Exeter Aqueduct" received incorporation from the Legislature of the State, and brought into the village water drawn from springs not far from the present station of the Boston and Maine Railroad. It was conveyed through perforated logs, and, of course, the supply was quite limited. Benjamin Clark Gilman was the projector of the enterprise in 1797; and in later time the management of the aqueduct fell into the hands of Nathaniel S. Adams, and finally of John Bellows. It was abandoned a number of years ago.

At the annual town meeting in 1804 it was voted that the selectmen, in case of blocking snows, should employ proper persons to open the roads, at the expense of the town.

In 1811 the town voted that the selectmen purchase for the use of the town a new fire engine and appurtenances at a cost not exceeding three hundred dollars; the engine of 1794 being deemed insufficient.

TEMPERANCE; WAR OF 1812; PRAYER IN TOWN MEETINGS.

As early as 1812 germs of the temperance reform began to show themselves in the action of the town. A vote was passed at the annual meeting to request the selectmen to prevent the selling or having of any liquors at the court-house on town-meeting days, and to make it the duty of a constable to see that the vote should be carried into full effect. The following preamble and resolution were also adopted:

Retailers of ardent spirits duly observing the laws are a necessary class of men. But when they so grossly abuse the trust and confidence reposed in them as to sell ardent spirits in less quantities than the laws permit, harbor citizens of the town in their stores and shops day after day and night after night, spending the money which ought to be expended in the support of their families in corrupting the morals and setting a destructive example before others, it is time for the town to arouse from their slumbers, place the axe at the root of the tree of vice and idle habits by rigidly executing the laws amply sufficient to effect it. This is an increasing evil, and for which a remedy is immediately wanted.

Resolved, therefore, That the selectmen and overseers inspect all disorderly licensed houses, etc., and prosecute such offenders with the utmost severity of the law.

The war against England, which was declared in 1812, was regarded by the majority of the people of New England as unnecessary and wrong. Exeter partook of that feeling, and when a meeting of the town was called in August, 1812, to see what pay and bounty should be offered to the militia called into the service of the United States, appointed a committee, consisting of John T. Gilman, Oliver Peabody, Samuel Tenney, Gideon Lamson and Joseph Tilton, Jr., to take the subject into consideration. At an adjourned meeting the committee submitted a written report, setting out that for reasons therein given, the town ought not to pay bounties or add to the compensation provided by law for men employed in the military service in that war. The report was accepted.

On the second of November following, the meeting of the citizens for the choice of representatives in Congress and presidential electors, was opened by "a well adapted prayer by the Rev. Mr.

Rowland." This appears to have been the inauguration or possibly the revival of a practice which afterwards continued for more than a quarter of a century.

SUPPORT OF THE POOR.

In 1817 the town passed a vote that the selectmen and overseers be authorized to purchase a farm or house for the use of the town where they might place the poor, and that they hire for that purpose a sum not exceeding four thousand dollars. A purchase was accordingly made of a house and land near Beech hill; and in 1821 the town voted to enlarge the town farm by the addition of the "Cuba" land adjoining it, and to establish an almshouse and house of correction. Prior to that time the mode of providing for those who needed support was by letting them out by auction, or rather by diminution, to the lowest bidder. Their number was comparatively small, and their several capacities and incapacities were well known. The responsible citizens who were willing to board, clothe and care for them at the least cost to the town, were allowed to take them to their homes, and have the charge of them. It is believed that under this system the paupers usually received good treatment; and they certainly were not sent far away from their acquaintances and familiar surroundings, to pine among strangers in a strange place.

In 1823 the town adopted an act of the Legislature for the establishment of police in towns.

In 1826 the town appropriated four hundred dollars to procure a lot of land for the use of the county, to erect a fire-proof building upon, for public offices and the preservation of public records. The building was constructed of brick with stone vaults to contain the books and files of the county, and was located on Front street, just easterly of the Phillips Exeter Academy. It answered its purpose satisfactorily for half a century, but the increase of the records, and the demand for greater care for their preservation, will soon render necessary enlarged and better constructed accommodations.

At the annual meeting in March, 1832, the town appropriated three hundred dollars for the purchase of a hay scale. It was placed nearly opposite the First church and in front of the lot on which the Squamscot House was afterwards erected, in 1837.

The situation of the court-house was felt to be inconvenient on many accounts, and in 1834 the town gave the selectmen authority to purchase a lot of land, and remove the court-house thereon, and fit up the same at the expense of the town, upon condition that one hundred and fifty dollars of the cost should be contributed by individuals. The condition was complied with, and the building was removed to the southerly corner of Court and River streets, where its immediate successor still stands. Petitions were subsequently presented for the sale or lease of the lot where it had stood, but the town wisely declined to part with the control of the land, and it has since constituted what is known as Court square, and now has a very useful drinking fountain in the centre.

In 1838, at the annual meeting, the town again put upon record its sentiments in relation to the mischiefs of the habit of strong drink, as follows:

Resolved, That as much of the pauperism, disease and misery existing among us may be attributed to intemperance, it is desirable that all suitable means should be used for the promotion of the temperance cause, and we, the citizens of this town, in town meeting assembled, authorize our selectmen to take all lawful and equitable measures for the removal of this evil from among us.

CELEBRATION OF BI-CENTENNIAL ANNIVERSARY.

The year 1838 being the two hundredth anniversary of the foundation of the town, was recognized as a proper occasion for public exercises in commemoration of that event. The necessary preparations were seasonably made, and the Hon. Jeremiah Smith was designated to prepare a historical address to be pronounced on the occasion. The fourth of July was chosen as a suitable day, and the citizens of the neighboring towns which had once formed parts of Exeter, were invited to join in the celebration.

The day was favorable. A procession, composed of a large body of citizens, the children of the Sunday schools and of the town schools, and the students of the Phillips Exeter Academy, escorted by the company of Exeter Artillery, all under the direction of Captain Nathaniel Gilman, 3d, chief marshal, marched through the principal streets of the village to the meeting-house of the First parish, which was filled to overflowing. After music by the band, and the singing of appropriate pieces by the choir, the Rev. Isaac Hurd offered an impressive prayer. Then the venerable Judge Smith delivered his interesting and valuable address, extracts from which will be found in the appendix to this volume (III).

After the close of the exercises at the meeting-house a procession was again formed, of the invited guests and subscribers to the public dinner, and moved to the court-house, in the lower story of which the tables had been arranged. The Hon. Timothy Farrar presided at the dinner, assisted by the Hon. William Plumer, Jr., of Epping, Captain Nathaniel Gilman, 3d and William W. Stickney, Esq., of Newmarket. After the cloth was removed the presiding officer made an address of welcome and congratulation. A series of sentiments were then read, which were severally responded to, by the Hon. William Plumer, Jr., the Hon. Prentiss Mellen, and other gentlemen of note present.

In the evening there was a levee at Howard hall, and the day was closed with a brilliant display of fireworks. The entire celebration was most satisfactory, and was highly enjoyed by the numerous assemblage which had gathered from far and near. The chairman of the committee of citizens, to whom much credit was due, was Joseph Tilton, Esq.

RE-NAMING STREETS; NEW COURT-HOUSE.

In 1840 the selectmen received authority to name the streets anew, and performed that duty as follows:

The street leading from Great bridge towards Hampton is to be called High street.
From Mary Jones's corner towards Stratham, Portsmouth avenue.
" Great bridge to James Grant's, Pleasant street.
"   "   " to Joseph Furnald's, Water street.
"   "   " to Christian chapel, Franklin street.
" Franklin street to Court street, South street.
" Joseph Tilton's to John Gordon's, Front street.
" Kinings's brook to James Bell's, Main street.
" James Bell's to Jeremiah Smith's, Middle street.
" Squamscot house to Little river bridge, Court street.
" Widow Odiorne's to Exeter bank, Centre street.
" Margaret Emery's to Colonel Chadwick's, Ladd street.
" Sherburne Blake's to William Lane's, Spring street.
" J. Robinson, Jr.'s to Main street, Academy street.
" Isaac Leavitt's to Samuel Philbrick's, Winter street.
" Samuel Philbrick's to Water street, Back street.
" Rev. Mr. Rowland's to Joseph Furnald's, Summer street.
" Samuel Moses's to Back street, Cross street.
" Cross street to Water street, Green street.

Most of the streets still retain the names here given them, but a few have taken others, more in accordance with the fitness of things. Cross street, for example, has given place with great propriety to Cass street, as it contains the house where the Hon. Lewis Cass was born. And therein is a hint that ought to be taken and improved. The town is noted for the number of distinguished men who have resided in it. What more appropriate nomenclature for its streets could be adopted than the names of its principal inhabitants and families? Wheelwright, Hilton, Dudley, Gilman, Folsom, Phillips, Sullivan and other historic names are far preferable for this purpose, in every point of view, to such unmeaning appellations as Front, Back, Middle, Centre, and the like. This would be a graceful method of keeping green the memory of the Exeter worthies of the past, and the quarter millennial anniversary of the town is a peculiarly suitable occasion to make the change.

In the spring of 1841 the court-house, that had been moved seven years before into Court street, was destroyed by fire. An exhibition called the "Burning of Moscow" had just been held in it, and was the cause of this less extensive conflagration. The town held a meeting on the sixth of April of the same year, and appropriated the sum of three thousand five hundred dollars for a town-house, to contain a town hall and court rooms. The building committee were James Burley, Nathaniel Gilman, Jr., William Conner, James Bell and Ira B. Hoitt. The building was promptly erected, of wood, and is still standing on the lot where the former court-house was situated, but is now occupied by the Town Library, the Natural History Society, the Grand Army of the Republic, etc. It was used for the purposes for which it was originally designed, only about fifteen years.

At the March town meeting in 1842 a resolution was passed, to license one apothecary to sell spirituous liquors, for medicinal purposes and the arts only, and to grant no further license therefor. And the next year it was resolved, with but a single dissenting voice, to license one town agent and no more, and to prosecute offenders against the license law.

In 1844 the useful practice was begun of printing the annual accounts of the selectmen and overseers, for distribution among the tax-payers. The practice has been kept up each year since, and has been extended to the reports and accounts of all the officers of the town.

The selectmen had been empowered in 1840 to procure to be made a survey and plan of the town. This was accomplished in 1845. Joseph Dow of Hampton was the surveyor employed, and from his draft two plans were published, the one of the village and the other of the entire township. Similar plans had been issued forty-three years previously, by Phinehas Merrill of Stratham; and a plot of the village on a larger scale has been since published from a survey made in 1874.

In 1844, at the annual meeting, an appropriation of four hundred dollars was made for the purchase of a town clock, which was set up in the tower of the First church.

On October 8, 1850, the town appointed Gilman Marston, John Kelly and Joseph G. Hoyt delegates to the convention to be held at Concord on the sixth of November following, to revise the constitution of the State.

In 1852 the town, taking warning from a disastrous conflagration which had recently occurred, by which the two principal hotels had been laid in ashes, caused the purchase of another fire engine at the cost of six hundred and fifty dollars, and laid out a further considerable sum in the improvement of the reservoirs.

The wooden town-house which was erected in 1841 was found to be ill located, and insufficient, and a movement was made in 1853 to build another, better suited to the public needs. For that purpose the town authorized an appropriation of thirty thousand dollars. The measure was not carried without strenuous and bitter opposition. Some of the older and more conservative citizens contended that the building then in use answered its end sufficiently, particularly as it had been erected only twelve years before, and were especially aggrieved by the exorbitant sum purposed to be expended. The question of the location of the proposed building, too, caused a difference of opinion, which was not settled until March, 1855. The Dean lot, at the northwestern corner of Court square and Water street, received the majority of suffrages, and there the new building, which is of brick, and of fine architectural proportions, and has from that time to the present been equally ornamental and useful to the town, was placed.

It was in 1853 that the first appropriation was made by the town for the establishment of the Public Library. The project originated with some public spirited citizens, who laid the foundations for its success by contributing to the infant Library, from their own collections, a considerable number of useful books. The town was quite ready to adopt the enterprise, and appropriated for the care and increase of the Library for the first few years three hundred, and since then five hundred dollars annually, besides providing suitable rooms for its accommodation in the old town-house. As the expense of library service is small, the chief part of the annual appropriations has been laid out in books, and from that source, and by donations from various quarters, the shelves have been gradually filled.

A fund of five thousand dollars for the enlargement of the Library was given by the late Dr. Charles A. Merrill; the income of which is to be applied to the purchase of works of sterling value.

The number of volumes now in the Library amounts to more than six thousand. They are, with few exceptions, well selected, and are very generally circulated in the households of the town, and diligently perused.

LIGHTING STREETS; SIDEWALKS; STEAM FIRE ENGINE; WATER WORKS.

The streets of the town were first lighted in 1868, although gas works had been in operation several years previously. The lights at first were rather few and far between, and some persons complained that they only served to make the darkness more visible; but the number has since been so much increased that there is no longer any question of their utility.

In the same year it was voted to fund thirty thousand dollars of the debt of the town, which had been incurred in building the town-house, and in bounties and aid to soldiers' families in the War of the Rebellion.

About the year 1871 the sidewalks of the village underwent a very general renovation. Before then they were mostly made of gravel, except in the business part of Water street. It was felt that they were hardly up to the requirement of the times, and an order was adopted to encourage the citizens to reconstruct them in an improved fashion. The town agreed to repay to all landowners in the village one-half the expense of sidewalks of concrete, brick or other durable materials, which they should cause to be laid in front of their respective lots. The offer was quite generally taken advantage of, and the village has since afforded better facilities for pedestrians than are to be found in most places

Notwithstanding Exeter had for a century been quite in the fore front of country towns in providing against the danger of fires, and had made very considerable annual payments for that purpose, yet, up to the year 1873, nothing more efficient than hand engines had been procured. It was then determined that a steam fire engine was a necessity. Though the expense of it and of all the needful accompaniments, including a substantial house of brick on Water street, was somewhat onerous, yet the service rendered by the acquisition, on one or two occasions, fully outweighed the cost. The fire department of the town is highly efficient, and its members have shown their pluck and endurance on many a hard fought field. And now that abundant hydrants have been added to all other safeguards, the risk of any wide conflagration seems reduced to a minimum.

A new convention to revise the constitution of the State was ordered, to be held at Concord on the sixth of December, 1876, and the town elected as delegates thereto, William W. Stickney, Gilman Marston, William B. Morrill and John J. Bell.

The "Exeter Water Works" went into operation in 1886. This is the title of an incorporated company, which has established its reservoirs and pumping apparatus on a little stream which leads to the historic "Wheelwright's creek." Thence the water is driven to a stand pipe on the summit of Prospect hill, which gives it a sufficient head to reach the top of the highest building in the village. A contract has been executed between the corporation and the town, by which the former, in consideration of an annual subsidy of two thousand dollars, engaged to furnish to the town for the term of twenty years, all the water needed for the extinguishment of fires and for other municipal purposes; and also, on certain conditions, to turn over to the town, its works, plant and property, upon being reimbursed the cost thereof.

CHAPTER V.

BOUNDARIES AND DIVISIONS; ROADS AND BRIDGES.

The original township of Exeter, as described in the deeds of the Indian sagamores to John Wheelwright and his associates, embraced all the territory between the Merrimac river (or three miles north of it) on the south; the sea on the east; the Pascataqua patents on the eastern north, and a line one mile beyond the Oyster river on the western north; and extended from the sea thirty miles into the country. This was a goodly domain, and must have contained, at the lowest estimate four or five hundred square miles. But only a fraction of it was ever occupied by the people of Exeter. It was soon curtailed on nearly every side.

Winicowet, or Hampton, was settled shortly after Exeter. Its entire original territory, including the present townships of Hampton, North Hampton, Seabrook, South Hampton, Hampton Falls and Kensington, and containing not less than seventy square miles, was carved from the Indians' grant to Wheelwright. Dover, on the north, pushed her occupancy, under the claim of a purchase from the Indians, not only to Oyster river, but southerly across the intervening space to Lamprey river, excepting a small triangle of land bordering on the Great Bay. Of the western north part of the Wheelwright Indian purchase, not less than thirty square miles were held to belong to Dover; the greater part of it in the present township of Durham.

The western bound of Exeter was fixed by a committee of the General Court of Massachusetts at about twenty miles distance from the sea, instead of thirty miles, the limit of the Indian grant; so the area of the town was thus further shorn of about one-half its original dimensions.

A single addition to the town's territory is also to be recorded. In 1656, or earlier, Thomas Wiggin, agent of the owners of the southern division of the Squamscot patent, by his deed of gift conveyed to the town a belt of land from the southerly end thereof, about a mile in breadth and between two and three miles in length.

When all these subtractions and this addition were made, Exeter, in place of its original ample precincts was reduced in territory to about seventy square miles. This is occupied by the present townships of Exeter, Newmarket, South Newmarket, Epping, Brentwood and Fremont.

These various alterations of boundary were not accomplished without objection. Towns are as averse as land-owners to any diminution of their possessions, and there are few more fruitful subjects of contention than conterminous boundaries.

There is scarcely a doubt that the bounds of Dover and of Hampton were laid out by committees of the General Court of Massachusetts, before Exeter acknowledged the jurisdiction of that colony. It was claimed by Dover that Lamprey river was thus fixed as the line between that township and Exeter in 1641 or 1642; and the western bound of Hampton, where it adjoined the eastern extremity of Exeter, was early assumed to be distant two miles from the meeting-house of the latter town, and, without much question, had been so defined under the authority of the Massachusetts colony.

When the petition of Exeter to be received within the government of Massachusetts was presented, May 12, 1643, the consent of the deputies and of the magistrates was indorsed thereon, and Samuel Dudley, Edward Rawson and Edward Carleton were appointed a committee for laying out the bounds. It is not known what, if anything, was done by the committee. On the seventh of the following September, when the petition was *formally* granted, William Payne, Matthew Boyes and John Saunders were appointed to settle the bounds between Exeter and Hampton, within two months. If they performed that duty, it was not very satisfactorily, for the General Court on the sixth day of May, 1646, in response to the petition of several inhabitants of Exeter, appointed Samuel Dudley, Edward Rawson and Edward Carleton to "lay out Exeter bounds next to Hampton, and so round about them, provided there be no entrenching on the bounds of the patent of the lords and gentlemen mentioned in the patent of Squamscot, or in any grant formerly made to Dover by this court." This resulted, no doubt, in fixing the location of the line between the eastern extremity of Exeter and Hampton, but not of that dividing the two towns farther to the westward.

8

THE HAMPTON BOUND OF 1653.

On the fourteenth of October, 1651, Hampton petitioned the General Court for a committee to lay out the west end of the bounds of their township, and Samuel Winslow, Thomas Bradbury and Robert Pike were appointed for the purpose. Thereupon, the people of Exeter, wishing to adjust all matters of boundary which were in dispute with their neighbors, on the twenty-ninth day of December following, gave authority to Samuel Dudley, Edward Hilton, Edward Gilman, John Legat and Humphrey Wilson, to "make an agreement with Hampton and Dover about the bounds of the town, or to petition to the General Court about it if they cannot agree with the other towns." And on May 10, 1652, having then probably received notice of the appointment of the commissioners by the General Court in the preceding October, the town chose Samuel Dudley, Edward Hilton, Edward Gilman and Thomas King, to meet with those commissioners "to lay out the bounds between us and Hampton, to agitate and conclude with them, or to make their objections according to the court order, if they cannot agree."

On the same day the town requested Samuel Dudley and Edward Gilman to "go to the next General Court as messengers for the town, to treat with the Court about the liberties and bounds of our town, that we be not infringed upon either by Dover or Hampton." Ten days later, the town excused Mr. Gilman from the duty and appointed Edward Hilton in his stead; and Mr. Dudley and John Legat were desired to compose the petition to send to the said General Court. Samuel Dudley, Edward Hilton, Thomas Pettit, John Legat, Edward Gilman, James Wall, Humphrey Wilson, Nicholas Listen and Thomas Cornish, or any six of them, were authorized to set their hands to the petition in behalf of the rest of the town.

The report of the commissioners appointed by the General Court in October, 1651, was returned on the thirtieth of September, 1653, in the following terms:

Mr. Samuel Winslow, Mr. Thomas Bradbury and Mr. Robert Pike, being chosen by the General Court to lay out the west line of Hampton bounds, upon their best information have concluded that their west line shall run from the extent of the line formerly agreed on, to come within two miles of Exeter meeting-house upon a direct line to that part of Ass brook where the highway goes over, and from thence upon a direct line so as to leave Exeter falls at the town bridge, a mile and a half due north of the same, and from thence upon a west and by north line as far as the utmost extent of Salisbury bounds that way.

THE DOVER BOUND OF 1653.

While the questions with Hampton were pending, Dover, on the twentieth of October, 1652, petitioned the General Court to have " their limits confirmed to them;" and thereupon, and on the said petition of Exeter, the General Court, on the twenty-sixth of October, of the same year, appointed William Payne, Samuel Winslow and Matthew Boyes, or the major part of them, to lay out the bounds between the two townships, and certify the court and the towns what they should determine.

Their report bore date March 9, 1653, and was in these words :

We have determined and agreed that the line formerly laid out shall stand, they taking a point from the middle of the bridge on the first fall on Lamprey river, and so to run six miles west and by north, but the land betwixt the line and the river shall belong to Exeter, they not having liberty to set up any mill except the right specified on the first fall, but the timber betwixt the line and the river shall belong to Dover in such time as they shall see meet to make use of the same to their best advantage; provided that both the towns shall have full liberty to make use of the river upon all occasions [as ?] before. Exeter hath liberty to make use of all the timber half a mile between the line and Lamprey river towards the bridge, and one mile between the line and the said river towards the second fall, and for these Mr. Edward Hilton is to have belonging to his mill all the timber within compass of one mile and a half square, if it be to be had betwixt the line and the river Lamprey.

WILLIAM PAYNE,
SAMUEL WINSLOW,
MATTHEW BOYES.

Such remained the dividing line, in substance, between Dover and Exeter for the next fourteen years. In 1657 representatives of the two towns, Valentine Hill, John Bickford, Sr. and William Furber for the former, and Edward Hilton and John Gilman for the latter, " settled the bounds" by marking the line ; and agreed upon the enjoyment that each should have, of the border land. Nothing further was done so far as is known, till Exeter asked for the enlargement of her territory in 1667.

CAPTAIN THOMAS WIGGIN'S DEED OF GIFT.

In the order of time the next change of bounds of Exeter was occasioned by the gift to the town by Thomas Wiggin in or before 1656, of a tract of land one mile in breadth, from the southern end of the Squamscot patent. The occasion of this gift is now unknown. Wiggin is described in connection with it, as agent of the proprietors of the southern division of the patent, so that the act may have been performed in their behalf. Or, as Wiggin was apparently dilatory in paying to Exeter his minister's tax, it is possible that the gift had some relation to that. The land was bounded as follows: beginning at the falls of the Squamscot, thence running northerly by the salt river to the mouth of Wheelwright's creek; thence southeasterly to the line of Hampton; thence by the line of Hampton and of Exeter to the bound begun at. The town of Exeter, in order that there might be no uncertainty about the title or jurisdiction of their new acquisition, on the twenty-eighth of April, 1656, ordered that a petition be presented to the next General Court that Captain Wiggin's deed of gift to the town, of land and meadow, might be confirmed to them; and that Mr. Bartholomew of Ipswich be employed to present the petition. It happened by a fortunate coincidence that Mr. Bartholomew was a member of the committee appointed by the General Court to make partition among the several proprietors of the Squamscot patent, of which the land in question was a part; and in the return of the committee, May 22, 1656, the gift was recited and confirmed.

On the thirtieth of March, 1668, the town deputed John Gilman, John Folsom, Sr., Jonathan Thing, Ralph Hall and John Warren, to lay out the line between the Shrewsbury (division of the Squamscot) patent then held by Richard Scammon and the territory of Exeter adjoining the same, with the consent of the said Scammon. It appears that Hampton laid some claim to the land given by Captain Wiggin, as above mentioned, for when, on the thirtieth of March, 1670, a portion of it was granted to Edward Gilman, Peter Folsom, John Young, Edward Smith, Thomas Rollins, Jeremy Leavitt, Jonathan Thing, Jr. and John Clark, the grantees were required to bind themselves in the sum of ten pounds each to the town, to try the title of their lands with the town of Hampton, if need should require.

ENLARGEMENT OF EXETER BOUNDS.

No further controversy in regard to the extent of the town appears to have arisen until March 15, 1667, when John Gilman was empowered " to petition the General Court for an enlargement of the bounds of the town, and to prosecute the business ; and to procure Captain Hubbard or Josiah Hubbard to assist him if he sees it needful." The petition was duly presented, and on May 15, 1667, the court ordered that Richard Waldron, Robert Pike and Samuel Dalton, as a committee, should view the land desired by the petitioners, and make return at the next session. The report of the committee bore date the eighth of October, 1667, and was in these words :

We whose names are hereunto subscribed being appointed by the honored General Court to view and consider of the bounds of the township of Exeter and to make return to the next session of the court, two of us having taken a survey of the lands about their town and the bounds of other towns adjacent,

We whose names are underwritten do judge that the bounds of the town of Exeter shall extend northward to Lamprey river, and from the first fall in Lamprey river six miles upon a west and by north line adjoining to Dover bounds as they are laid out and confirmed, and then two miles further upon the same point of the compass, that to be their north bounds ; and from the foot of Exeter falls by the present grist-mill a mile and a half due south to Hampton bounds, and from that south point to run upon a west and by north line ten miles into the woods adjoining to Hampton bounds, that to be their south bounds ; and so from the end of that line upon a straight line over the land to meet with the other line on the north that extendeth from Dover bounds, that to be their head line, westward, and Squamscot patent to be their east bounds.

SAMUEL DALTON,
RICHARD WALDERNE.

Though I could not by reason of straitness of time make a full view of all the lands above mentioned, yet from what I do know of it, together with that information that I have had of those that do well know of the quality of the rest of the land, do judge that the bounds above mentioned may be just and reasonable, and do concur in subscription.

ROBERT PIKE.

The substantial change made by this report was to give to Dover the tract of land south of Lamprey river and between that river and the west and by north line prescribed by the commission of 1653, being an area of some eight or ten square miles, and to add to Exeter a belt of about two miles in width along the whole western end of the township, making, perhaps, fifteen square miles of territory. The report of the committee was confirmed by the General Court, with the proviso " that all pine trees fit for masts, which are twenty-four inches diameter and upwards, within three foot of the ground, that grow above three miles from the meeting-house where it now stands, in any place within the bounds of said town (Exeter), are hereby reserved for the public; and if any person or persons shall presume to fell down any such pine tree fit for masts, he or they shall forfeit ten pounds for every tree; the one-half to the informer, and the other half to the public treasury of the country."

It remained only to mark upon the ground the lines thus described, and the town on the twenty-ninth of March, 1668, chose John Gilman, Jonathan Thing, John Folsom, Sr. and Moses Gilman to run the line between the two meeting-houses of Hampton and Exeter; Jonathan Thing, Robert Smart, Ralph Hall, John Folsom, Sr. and Nicholas Listen to run the line between Dover and Exeter; and John Folsom, Sr., John Folsom, Jr., Jonathan Thing, William Moore and Moses Gilman to run the west and by north line between Hampton and Exeter.

For some cause a good deal of delay occurred in performing the work, and on the twenty-second of February, 1670-1, the town added to the last committee Ralph Hall, Nicholas Listen and John Gilman, who were empowered to run the line between Hampton and Exeter " according to the court order, that is, to begin at the bound tree at Ass brook and so upon a direct line so as to leave Exeter falls a mile and a half due north of the same, and from thence upon a west and by north line to the extent of ten miles; and what these men or a major part of them shall do, shall stand in as good force as if the whole town were present."

But the work went on at a snail's pace, if it went on at all. The duty was perhaps not an agreeable one, and the committee were reluctant to act, and on the tenth of July, 1671, the town took up the subject anew. Philip Cartee, Christian Dolloff and John Folsom, Sr. were chosen "to make an end of measuring" the line between Hampton and Exeter; Nicholas Smith, John Bean, John Young and John Folsom, Sr. were designated to run the line between Exeter falls and Lamprey river falls. "If any of these men refuse to go, he is to pay ten shillings." John Gilman, Jonathan Thing, William Moore, Ralph Hall, Moses Gilman, Nicholas Listen, Samuel Leavitt, Peter Folsom, Robert Smart and John Folsom, Sr. were chosen to run the line between Dover and Exeter, with power to a major part of them to determine the same.

But the end was not yet. On the twenty-ninth of April, 1672, the town gave to Samuel Dudley, Ralph Hall and John Gilman, "full power to agree with Hampton men about all differences that may be between the inhabitants of Hampton and Exeter concerning lands." Under this authority it is probable that the long pending questions of town lines were finally adjusted, and to the substantial satisfaction of the parties concerned.

It took a little longer to put a quietus on the difference with the people of Dover. On the twenty-fifth of March, 1672, the selectmen of that town and the selectmen of Exeter agreed, in behalf of their respective towns, to refer "the difference between them about Lamprey [river point]" to the arbitrament of Robert Pike, Samuel Dalton and John Wincol. This probably related to the gore of land northerly of Lamprey river and between the first fall thereon and the Great Bay, claimed by Exeter, and still retained by Newmarket as successor to Exeter. The report of the arbitrators has not been found, but there can be little doubt that it sustained the claim of Exeter.

No question of boundary appears to have arisen again between the towns until 1679, when on March 11 the town resolved that "in answer to Major Waldron's request of some of our town to come and meet with some of their town (Dover) in reference to the running of the line between us, and for a final agreement of the same, it is agreed by the town that they will not any otherwise run the line or agree with the town of Dover, but as the line is already run by the town of Exeter." A rebuff so pointed as this seems to have silenced the worthy Major, for nothing further is heard of the subject for a long period. At length, on the sixteenth of January, 1710-11, the town of Exeter took final action upon it by appointing Nicholas Gilman, Jonathan Wadleigh and Jonathan Thing, a committee "to procure the settlement of the line between Dover and Exeter out of any office, and to new run the line if occasion be."

As this boundary line was settled in 1667 so it has substantially remained to this day. If it has been the subject of later contention, the original parties have long ceased to be interested in it, for the northern section of Exeter became Newmarket in 1727, and the southern section of Dover became Durham in 1738.

SQUAMSCOT PATENT UNDER EXETER GOVERNMENT.

The Squamscot patent, situated mostly on the eastern side of the Squamscot river and Great Bay, was, in 1656, divided under the authority of Massachusetts into three shares. With the first (northern) division, Exeter history has nothing to do. The second (middle) division was assigned to Thomas Wiggin and his partners. The third (southern) division was awarded to a company known, from the place of their residence in England, as "the Shrewsbury men." Of this company Wiggin was then the agent, and from the southern part of this division he gave a strip of land a mile in width to the town of Exeter. The second and the third division thus curtailed compose substantially the present town of Stratham.

Wiggin had been living at Sandy point near the northern extremity of the middle division, probably from the very foundation of the Exeter settlement. His name occurs frequently in the Exeter records, as if he were regarded in the light of an inhabitant. It is evident that he was rated in the town for the support of the ministry, though he was somewhat dilatory in payment. Possibly he may have thought that the Exeter assessments were onerous, and that he would fare better if assigned to another place. However, on the sixth of May, 1657, the Massachusetts General Court, in an order which recited that "his land and property had not as yet been brought within the limits of any town, nor been liable to pay taxes and assessments as others of our honored magistrates have done," required that "his dwelling house, with all the lands and proprieties thereto appertaining, shall belong to the town of Hampton, and by the selectmen of the said town to be assessed in all rates according to law, any law or usage to the contrary notwithstanding."

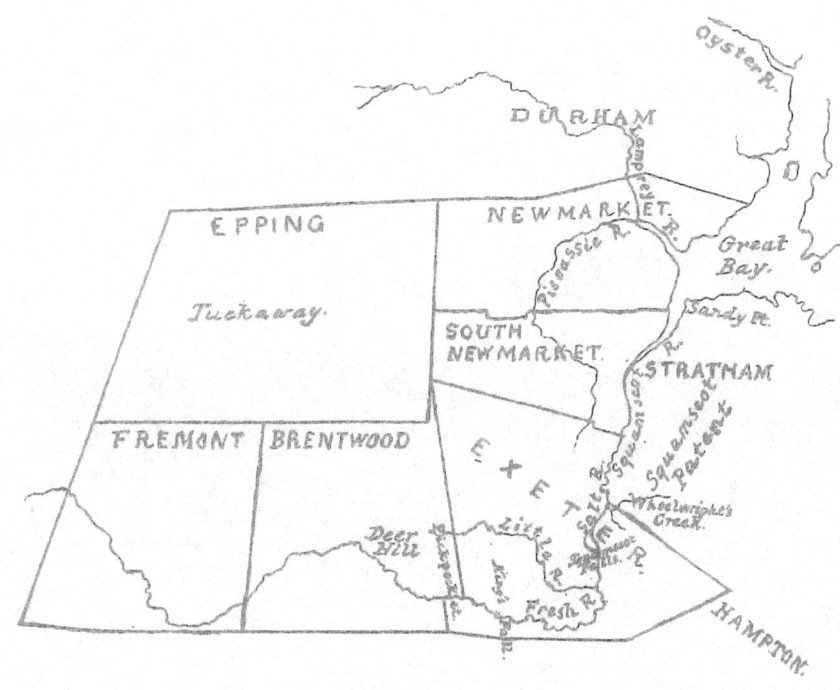

EXETER, WITH ITS SUBDIVISIONS

Thereafter, not only Wiggin's estate, but presumably all the taxable estates in that portion of the Squamscot patent, were assessed in Hampton until November 28, 1692, when it was ordered by the president and council of the province of New Hampshire that "the inhabitants of Squamscot, within this province, beginning from Mr. Thomas Wiggin's at Sandy point and upwards, shall be rated by the selectmen of Exeter to all public assessments; also that they be under the command of the militia of Exeter until further orders."

This enactment continued in force for more than twenty-three years. Its effect was to unite the inhabitants of the two contiguous precincts under the same town government. The citizens of each were vested with the same rights, and subject to the same liabilities. They all took part in town meetings and were equally eligible to town offices. A fair proportion of the municipal officers were selected from each territory. But as the population of Squamscot patent increased, the desire naturally grew up among the inhabitants to be incorporated into a town by themselves. Their remoteness from church and school, to which they had to contribute their share of the cost, was an unanswerable argument in favor of their wish, and after some disagreement among themselves on the subject, they were incorporated with town privileges under the name of Stratham by a charter dated March 20, 1716. This, of course, terminated their connection with Exeter.

TOWNSHIPS CARVED FROM EXETER TERRITORY.

Since that time Exeter has lost about three-fourths of its area by new townships successively set off from it. The history of the several earlier partitions will be found in the ecclesiastical portion of this work, as the towns were originally detached in the form of parishes.

Newmarket was taken from Exeter December 15, 1727. South Newmarket was set off from Newmarket June 27, 1849.

Epping was taken from Exeter February 23, 1741.

Brentwood was taken from Exeter June 26, 1742; Poplin was severed from Brentwood June 22, 1764, and its name was changed to Fremont July 8, 1854.

Exeter now contains a little short of seventeen square miles of land, not a twentieth part of the quantity which the deed of the Indian sagamores purported to grant.

HIGHWAYS, THEIR LOCATION, LAYING OUT AND REPAIRS.

It would be interesting, if it were practicable, to trace the origin and history of the various roads in and about Exeter. But for the first century most of them were opened without any public authority that can now be discovered, and many were as unceremoniously discontinued when they ceased to be needed. Only the fittest survived.

The river was the first great highway, so far as it would serve as such. Each dweller on its banks had his canoe, and boats of burden were abundant. Every road terminated or connected with its landings. Where there was no water way, but there was frequent need of communication, as with the neighboring village of Hampton, a land way had to be provided. But as the travel for several generations was chiefly on horseback, the roads were little more than bridle paths. They are referred to as such in the earlier records, as "the path towards Hampton," "the Salisbury path," and the like.

In the opposite direction wider thoroughfares were needed for the convenience of hauling lumber to the landing places on the river. We find early mention, for example, of "the mast-way," leading in the direction of Epping, a chief use of which was indicated by its name; and there is no doubt that wood-paths, passable by sleds and wheels, were rudely constructed to the northern and western sections of the township. The great importance and value of the lumber business demanded them.

The need of maintaining suitable roads in the town was fully recognized from the beginning. A vote of February 1, 1640–1, referred to a former order (not preserved) that highways were to be at least three poles in width; and required that since they had become narrowed in various places, they should be rectified and made of full breadth betwixt that time and the middle of April, 1642.

On June 17, 1644, it was agreed at a town meeting that four days should be set apart to mend the highways, "to begin on the fourth day of the week come a sevennight;" that the inhabitants should be at their labors at six and leave at twelve, then rest till two, and work till six o'clock; and such as might be absent should be fined five shillings for every day; and they that had teams should work them, upon the penalty of twenty shillings for every day's neglect, until the four days should be expired. When the scarcity and relatively greater value of money at that period are considered, the penalty for non-appearance which the people imposed upon themselves, seems enormous, and shows the sacrifices they were willing to undergo in order to provide their town with suitable thoroughfares.

The earliest record of the appointment of officers to superintend the highways is dated November 24, 1650. Abraham Drake and John Legat were chosen to view the highway, and to give Henry Roby liberty to enlarge his garden out of it, but to restore the highway to its usual breadth out of his lot; and so Edward Gilman and others, provided that the highways be not made worse than they then were.

On the first of September, 1651, Edward Gilman was chosen surveyor of the highways for the year, "to call forth laborers for the work and give directions." In 1652, April 20, James Wall, John Legat and Thomas King were appointed to view the highways, to see that they were not reduced in width, and were authorized to pull up fences that encroached on them, or that stopped up any common places of access to the river side.

At a town meeting January 21, 1660-1, Thomas King and John Warren were appointed to call upon Hampton for laying out of a county way between Exeter and Hampton.

At the time of the election of selectmen in 1660, their powers were very fully defined, but they were forbidden, among other things, to lay out new highways. In 1664, October 10, the town gave authority to Thomas King, John Folsom, Sr. and John Robinson to lay out highways where they should judge convenient.

On the third of April, 1671, Moses Gilman and Samuel Leavitt were elected surveyors of the highways, and it was ordered that whoever of the inhabitants should fail to come into the highways to work at such time as they should appoint, should forfeit five shillings for every day's neglect, to be distrained upon by the constable forthwith.

It was ordered by the town August 30, 1671, that there should be sufficient room for "a loaden cart to pass in all highways, and whosoever shall block up the highways so as a cart cannot conveniently pass, or what timber shall be dangerous, shall be forfeited to the town, and the constable forthwith to take it away by distress." There seems a little confusion of ideas in the order; it could hardly have been intended that the person blocking the highways should be forfeited to the town and taken by distress.

In 1675 a surveyor of highways for each side of the river was chosen, and for several years that method was annually pursued.

BRIDGES.

The earliest mention of a bridge in the records of the town is upon May 19, 1644, when it was determined that the townsmen should procure a bridge over Lamprey river. This was while that river was understood by the inhabitants to be wholly within the limits of Exeter. Before the resolution was carried into effect, however, the town became apprised of the claim of Dover that Lamprey river had been authoritatively fixed upon as the general boundary between that township and Exeter; and then the inhabitants of the latter ordered, January 27, 1644-5, that Anthony Stanyan and James Wall should go to Lamprey river to meet with "the men of Dover to consult, conclude and bargain with them concerning the making of a bridge over the said river." If Dover were to have the land to the river, then it was just that she should pay her share for bridging it. In 1647 both towns were fined for neglect to keep a bridge there, Dover five pounds, but Exeter only thirty shillings. It is not known whether the court assumed to adapt the penalties to their respective degrees of delinquency.

In all probability the first bridge erected in the town was that across the fresh river, just above the falls, where the "great bridge" now is. That was most immediately necessary to accommodate the residents on either side of the river, and for the communication between Exeter and Hampton, which was not inconsiderable. At first the bridge was only suitable for passengers on foot or on horseback, and it was not until it had become a part of the "county way," that it was widened sufficiently to accommodate carts. In 1675, the County Court ordered that the town of Exeter should make "their 'boom' six foot wide within the rail, and raise it on both sides sufficiently; to be finished by the next Hampton Court upon the penalty of ten pounds." It is rather mortifying to add that the required improvements were not made, and the penalty was incurred. The court, however, was lenient, and allowed further time, being well aware that such public exactions were heavy burdens upon the struggling frontier settlements.

As early as 1693, this had acquired the designation of "great" bridge, by which it has been ever since known. This name indicated that there was then at least one other bridge, and of less dimensions. In 1708, May 30, the town resolved that the great bridge be made a horse bridge, wide enough for two horses to pass "on breast." The other bridge, which by contrast, gave the former its distinctive name, was, without much doubt, the predecessor of the present "string bridge." It was not built all at one time, nor by a single person. The earliest mill was situated on the island at the lower falls. The proprietor of it was Thomas Wilson, and after his death his son, Humphrey Wilson. They also owned land on the eastern side of the river, near the mill, and that part of the river which formed the channel between the mill and that shore was called "Wilson's creek." No doubt a "stringer" was at an early day laid across the creek to connect the island with the nearest shore. Thus the inhabitants would be enabled to take their grists to the mill without the aid of a boat. At a later date, Captain John Gilman became the owner of another grist-mill on the western side of the island. He naturally desired it to be connected with the western shore by a bridge of his own; his mill and the Wilson mill being rival establishments. At a town meeting on the first Monday of April, 1709, the town gave him all their right to the stream and the island where his mill was, "with the privilege for a bridge to go on the island." This led to the completion of the second bridge across the river. It consisted for above a century of nothing more than one or two timbers laid across each of the channels of the river, with hand rails at the side, so that a man could safely pass with a bag of meal on his shoulder. It obtained the name of "string bridge" from the manner of its original construction, and still retains it, though for many years past it has been rebuilt in a substantial shape, with space for carriages to pass each other upon it, and a sidewalk.

There can be little doubt that the first highway was made along the western bank of the river, nearly in the line of the present Water street, leading from the great bridge on the one hand, to the earliest meeting-house on the other. This was doubtless what is spoken of as the "village street" in the contract between Gowen Wilson and the town, May 1, 1649. The road which led from that street near its northern extremity, westerly into the interior, is mentioned by the name of "lane's end" in the town records as early as 1650. This was for a hundred and fifty years one of the main avenues to the water side; and over it was transported a large proportion of the original growth of the forests which covered many square miles of the old township. In later times its importance has dwindled, and it has assumed the picturesque aspect of one of the old English country lanes, its roadway being worn deeply below the surface level on each side, and lined by pollard trees and bushes. Its name, too, has undergone transformations. It appears on the town plan of 1846 as "Back street," and on that of 1874 as "Park street," but it is popularly known as "Katy's lane" from the residence there of a colored woman whose Christian name adhered to it by natural affinity.

Roads to Hampton, to Stratham and to Salisbury, to those parts of the township which were afterwards set off as Newmarket, Epping and Brentwood, and to Kingston, were undoubtedly in use long before the year 1700.

On the fourth of March, 1658-9, it was ordered by the town that Thomas King and his partners in the mill set up about three miles up the river, should have liberty to build a bridge and make a highway, over which others might pass on foot, or on horseback, or drive cattle; but in case others made use of it in the way of carting, they should make a proportionate allowance to the said partners, according to their use. This was probably the authority for building what were called the "neck road" and "King's bridge." That territory which was included between the Exeter fresh river and Little river was known by the name of "the neck." It was crossed by this road in a southwesterly direction. The original names of the road and of the bridge are still familiar to old residents, but to the present generation the way is better known as the road to East Kingston.

THE VILLAGE STREETS.

The thoroughfare now termed "Front street" received in the original nomenclature of the town ways, ninety years ago, the name of "Fore street," afterwards that of "Court street," and finally the present designation. It probably had nothing that could be properly called sidewalks before the year 1807. A paper is still extant bearing date in that year containing subscriptions for "defraying the expense of making a gravel walk with posts, rails, etc., in Court street," the amount of which was eighty dollars and twenty cents. The names of the public spirited subscribers deserve to be preserved. They were Phillips Exeter Academy, John T. Gilman, Oliver Peabody, Nathaniel Gilman, Nicholas Gilman, George Sullivan, Jeremiah Smith and Samuel Tenney.

The avenues which connect Front and Water streets are of later date. Spring street was laid out in 1730, Centre street in 1734, and Academy street, which, by reason of its manufactories of leather, long bore the euphonious title of "Tan lane," was not opened till still later. The road along the eastern shore of the river was not formally laid out till 1739, though there can be little doubt that it had been used by the public as a way to the mills and to the water side for three-fourths of a century before at least. In fact, as already intimated, the early roads appear to have been made and unmade, just according to the varying needs of the people, without the aid of engineers, and irrespective of direction or grades. The consequence is that in the older parts of the town there is scarcely a furlong of highway built on a straight line. This circumstance undoubtedly contributes greatly to the picturesqueness of the place. Rectangular streets are convenient, but they are anything but beautiful.

None of the streets in the village southerly of Front street and of that part of Water street between the two bridges are much above half a century old. Court, Franklin and Pine streets, and their connections, were laid out across fields, but Elm street had its germ in Moulton's lane, and Elliott street in Whitefield's lane. Those lanes led to the dwellings of persons bearing those names respectively. Lincoln and Garfield streets, as their names would indicate, are still more recent.

The records of the town and of the courts show that in the earlier times, the highways were sometimes suffered to fall into sad disrepair, and to become inconvenient or unsafe for travel by reason of incumbrances. For example, "meeting-house hill," whose sloping side formed an easy chute for logs into the river, was used from early times as a convenient place of deposit for timber. No doubt travellers were often incommoded by it, and at length, August 30, 1671, the town passed an order that "whereas there is likely to be great damage by laying logs on meeting-house hill, by beating down the banks of it, there shall be no more logs laid between Nicholas Norris his house and the southeast side of the hill, upon forfeiture of what timber shall be laid there, to be forthwith seized on by the constable for the use of the town."

The open space in front of the present town hall, now bearing the name of Court square, was another locality tempting to cumberers of the ground. Near the middle of the last century a pound, which was doubtless more useful than ornamental, and several small shops had been huddled there, so that not only was the eye offended by the sorry group, but the highway must have been reduced to the narrowest dimensions. The need of a site for a court-house

But of all parts of the town, Water street has been the heaviest burden upon the patience of travellers and highway surveyors. As late as 1768, the eastern part of it, between the great and the string bridge, was so narrow that the selectmen were authorized, by a purchase of land or otherwise, to make it sufficient and wide enough for safe passing. The street was originally much nearer the level of the river than it now is, and has been raised by continually repeated layers of earth and gravel, until its present grade is in some parts several feet higher. The sub-cellars of some of the business blocks are little, if at all, below the natural surface of the ground. About the point where the street turns to the north, it was within the century past so depressed that in very high tides the water flowed over it to a depth that admitted of the passage of boats above the roadway for a considerable distance.

CHAPTER VI.

THE COMMON LANDS.

The inhabitants of Exeter having the absolute disposal of the lands within the township, it was to be expected that numerous applications would be made to them for allotments therefrom. This was in fact done to such an extent that a great part of the early records are filled with grants of lands, and descriptions thereof by the lot layers chosen by the town. The descriptions are unfortunately so vague, and refer to so few permanent landmarks, that it is impossible, without a degree of labor far out of proportion with the value of the result, to fix the present location of most of the earlier lots. No equality or rule of proportion, so far as can be perceived, was observed in making the allotments, except in the division of lands in December, 1639, and in the final distribution; but each inhabitant received as much as the town saw fit to give him. No doubt the assignments were intended to be equitable, in view of the circumstances of each case, which were of course well known to the voters. But it is not remarkable that in process of time this method of doling out the lands created dissatisfaction, especially to those who fancied that they were not treated so well as others, which led at length to a general division of the residue of the public domain, and almost literally gave "every man a farm." This conclusion, however, was not reached until nearly a century had expired. An account of the disposal of the common lands, as brief as is consistent with clearness, is a necessary part of this history.

When the town was first settled in 1638, each person probably chose such a site for his dwelling as best suited his convenience, with due reference to the rights of others. If any record was made of their several holdings it has disappeared. We only know that the main settlement was near the falls of the Squamscot, and on the western side of the river.

At the close of the second season, in December, 1639, a systematic distribution of certain uplands, perhaps all that were free from the forest growth, and of all the meadows and marshes lying on the salt river, was made, among all, with few exceptions, of the inhabitants. The details of this transaction appear elsewhere.*

LANDS OF EDWARD AND WILLIAM HILTON.

Before doing this, however, the town designated the bounds of Edward Hilton's lands, which lay in the present township of South Newmarket, as follows: "his upland ground is bounded in breadth from the creek next from his house towards Exeter on the one side and a certain point of land over against Captain Wiggins his house, between the marsh and the upland, that his bounds on the other side, and it is to extend into the main the same distance in length as it is in breadth; and that he shall have all the meadows which he formerly occupied from his house to the mouth of Lamprey river."

To these lands the town laid no claim of proprietorship. At a later period they were alluded to in the records as a grant made to Hilton "by composition." It is evident that he held them by virtue of some prior claim; whether by actual possession, or as appurtenant to the "Hilton patent," is not known.

The town also agreed, on May 3, 1640, that Willam Hilton should continue to enjoy those two marshes on Oyster river which he then, and had formerly, possessed, and "which Mr. Gibbies (Gibbons?) doth wrongfully detain from him, with the rest of those marshes which formerly he hath made use of, so far forth as they may be for the public good of this plantation; and so much of the upland [adjacent] to them as shall be thought convenient by the neighbors of Oyster river which are belonging to this body."

GRANTS OF TOWN LANDS.

Depositions on the files of the old county of Norfolk show that the town at a very early date bestowed upon Thomas Wilson the island in the river at the falls, on which his house and grain-mill were situated, reserving to the inhabitants only the right to land their canoes, and lay their fish there.

---
* See Appendix (I).

On May 6, 1643, the town granted to Thomas Rashleigh 14 or 16 acres of land, with the expectation probably that he was to make a permanent settlement there as their minister. He remained about a year, and on his departure the land reverted to the town, and was subsequently regranted to the Rev. Samuel Dudley. On August 21, of the same year, a vote was passed that any inhabitant who should find a marsh of less than twenty acres, might enjoy it as his own forever; if of more than twenty acres, it was to be at the town's disposal, but the finder was to have a double portion out of it.

From the earliest surviving book of the town is taken the following record of such marshes:

Found, by Samuel Greenfield and Nathaniel Boulter, two parcels lying westward from the town, by estimation nineteen acres apiece; found the first of May, 1644. Granted at a town meeting the 16th of 11th month to Nathaniel Boulter and Samuel Greenfield.

Found, by Robert Booth, one parcel westward from the town, by estimation thirty acres, which is in the town's hands to be lotted out, if Mr. Wheelwright doth not come to live in Exeter again.

Found, by James Wall and Ralph Hall, two parcels, both of them by estimation three acres.

Found, by Robert Hathersay, Thomas Jones and Richard Bullgar, two pieces of meadow, the fifth of August, 1644, which lieth half way up the fresh river, and on both sides of it, being the same brook which goodman . . . Said meadow lieth westward from Exeter some two miles, be it more or less, which is by estimation ten acres, be they more or less, provided that they do not exceed twenty acres.

Richard Bullgar doth assign his part of the aforesaid meadows to Robert Hathersay; witness his hand.

RICHARD BULLGAR.

On June 10, 1644, the town made a grant to Samuel Greenfield of 20 acres; and on June 17, following, voted that a tract of marsh should be given to the Rev. John Wheelwright, on condition that "he doth come amongst us again."

On January 16, 1644-5, the town made grants as follows to these persons: Thomas Biggs; Thomas Crawley 4 acres, conditionally;* Thomas King; John Legat, conditionally; Thomas Marston 80 acres, "if he come to live among us;" William Moore; Henry Roby; John Saunders; John Smart, Sr. 10 acres; Anthony Stanyan 30 acres.

---

* The condition usually was that the grantee should improve the land by building upon it, fencing it, or the like, within a limited time. The number of acres is stated in all cases where it is given in the record.

On the same day it was ordered that "there shall be 500 acres of land on the back side of the common field, and 500 acres beyond Humphrey Wilson's great lot towards Hampton, divided by lot to all the inhabitants of the town according to their ratements."

It was also ordered that "the flats between James Wall's point and Thomas Wight's old house shall be divided out equally to the inhabitants against whose lots it lies, and the flats on the other side of the channel to be divided to the rest of the inhabitants whose lots do not but against the flats on this (the western) side, yet all to lie in common for fishing, till it be improved."

The following grants were made by the town in the year 1645:

January 27, John Cram; Thomas Crawley; Godfrey Dearborn; Robert Hersey: William Huntington; Thomas Jones; John Legat; Thomas Pettit; Robert Smith; James Wall; Balthasar Willix. April 26, Edward Colcord 100 acres. December 31, John Legat, ½ acre.

The following grants were made in 1646:

February 5, Thomas Biggs 13 acres; Nathaniel Boulter. May 25, Francis Swain 6 acres; Goodman [John] Smart. June 8, Goodman [John] Smart 300 acres.

The planting grounds of the Indians were excepted and reserved to them in the grant of the Indian sagamores to Wheelwright. They were probably small and not numerous. Inhabitants were forbidden by the town to buy them, except with the approval of the townsmen.

One such purchase is noted upon the records. John Legat and Humphrey Wilson on the eighth of June, 1646, bought of the sagamore a tract of land containing, by estimation, six or seven acres, lying on the eastern side of the river by the lower falls, where said Legat's and Wilson's house lots were. The bargain probably being a fair one, the townsmen gave their written approval of it.

The following grants were made in 1647:

February 16, Mr. [Anthony] Stanyan 20 acres. November 4, George Barlow 40; Nathaniel Boulter 50; Edward Gilman [Jr.]; Samuel Greenfield 50; William Moore 10; Francis Swain and Nicholas Swain 100; Richard Swain 30. December 15, Thomas Jones 20; William Moore 30; James Wall, 138; Humphrey Wilson 30.

The following grants were made in 1648:

February 10, John Cram 40 acres; Ralph Hall 20; Thomas Jones 40; John Legat 140; Thomas Pettit 40; Anthony Stanyan 300; Balthasar Willix 20. March 4, Thomas Biggs, Godfrey Dearborn, Thomas Jones, 50 each; Henry Roby 20. November 16, George Barlow 4; Mr. Edward Gilman [Jr.] 100; Christopher Lawson 100.

At the last named date is the first record of the appointment of lot layers: John Cram and John Legat.

On the same day "it was agreed that 500 acres of land next the two great lots above mentioned shall be laid for a common field, to be fenced by the town, planting ground for every man to have his equal share, that are householders."

It was also agreed "that the remainder of that [plain] before mentioned to the corner of John Cram's lot or Bell Willix's, and so unto the fresh river, shall be [laid] out for an ox common, for working cattle and steers and horses, for every man to have his equal share, provided he do his portional share of fencing by the last day of May next, and those who do not fence are to have no right in said common."

The following grants were made in 1649:

January 12, Thomas Biggs and John Bursley 10 acres each, "to cut firewood and timber;" Thomas Cornish 10, "to cut firewood;" John Cram 10; Thomas King 100; Nicholas Listen 10, "to cut firewood;" James Wall.

The following grants were made in 1650:

March 21, John Legat ½ acre. June 26, Samuel Dudley; Gowen Wilson conditionally. August 26, Abraham Drake and Nathaniel Drake 30 each; Thomas King 8; John Legat 10. November 24, Thomas Biggs 20; Thomas Cornish 10; Thomas Crawley 5; Ralph Hall; Nicholas Listen 20; Henry Roby 10; Francis Swain 20; Nicholas Swain 5; Gowen Wilson 10. December 5, John Warren 5.

COMMON PLANTING FIELD.

On January 2, 1650–1, it was ordered by the town "that there shall be a common field laid out for planting ground beyond the second river from the town, westward about two miles and a half, for every man that is an inhabitant of the town to have his part laid out by lot, and in quantity according to his rate to the ministry bearing date the 1 of the 11 month, 1650, viz., for every ten shillings which he pays to have 15 acres of land, laid out together by lot, beginning at the head of the fall and so to but upon the river downward, and every acre to be one rod in breadth, provided that if any man that now is an inhabitant shall leave the town before one whole year after the date hereof be expired, then he is to leave his lot to the town again."

The following grants were made in 1651:

January 2, Henry Roby 60 acres. February 19, Samuel Dudley 80. December 29, Samuel Dudley, for grazing, etc.

The following grants were made in 1652:

April 20, Samuel Dudley 100 acres; Edward Gilman [Jr.]; John Legat 100; John Robinson, conditionally; Robert Smart. May 10, Thomas Cornish 40; Samuel Dudley 100; John Garland, conditionally; John Legat 100; Nicholas Listen 40; Thomas Pettit 40; Francis Swain 40 and 20; Thomas Taylor 20; John Warren 40 and 20. May 20, Thomas King 100; Thomas Pettit, Jr. 30. July 8, Edward Gilman, Sr., John Leavitt,[*] John Gilman and Moses Gilman 200, "those of them that come not to live with us by the next summer to forfeit their shares again to the town."

On May 20, 1652, it was ordered by the town "that all the land within a mile and a half of [or about] that northeast end of the town that is not already granted out, shall continually lie common for feeding and firewood and the like use."

On November 6, 1652, "it was ordered and also granted to Mr. Edward Hilton, in regard that he hath been at charge in setting up of a saw-mill, that he shall enjoy for himself and his heirs forever, a quarter of a mile below his mill, with the land and timber belonging thereunto, and also above his mill a mile and a quarter with the land and timber belonging thereunto. This land and timber is to lie square, only on this side of Piscassock river to come about a stone's cast."

---
[*] It is believed that John Leavitt, who was a son-in-law of Edward Gilman, Sr., never lived in Exeter. He was of Hingham, Massachusetts.

The following grants were made from 1654 to 1661, inclusive:

1654, February 15, Nicholas Listen 20 acres, conditionally.
1655, September 30, Ralph Hall 10 acres.
1657, January 21, John Robinson, conditionally. May 11, Edward Hilton, Jr. 50 acres, conditionally.
1659, March 4, Samuel Dudley, "upon consideration of drawing out all the grants in the town book," etc.; Joseph, son of William Taylor, 40 acres.
1660, January 21, John Bean and Nicholas Listen 10 acres. January 22, Goodman [John] Folsom; Thomas King and Jonathan Thing 40; Goodman [John] Robinson 10. June 11, Goodman [John] Folsom 20; Gowen Wilson 10.
1660-1, March 16, John Hilton 30 acres.

At the town meeting held on the day last named, it was ordered "that though there may be a proposition for the giving of land, yet from this time forward there shall none be granted till the next meeting following that on which it was propounded."

This excellent rule appears to have checked the bestowal of lands for a brief season, but it broke forth again, three years afterwards, more profusely than ever before.

The following grants were made in 1664:

January 21, Philip Chesley 30 acres, conditionally.[*] October 10, John Bean 30; Richard Bray 30; William Bromfield 30; Arthur Cham [or Cane] 15; Biley Dudley 50; Samuel Dudley; Theophilus Dudley 50; Israel Folsom 10; John Folsom, Sr. 60 and 20; John Folsom, Jr. 20; Nathaniel Folsom 10; Peter Folsom 10; Samuel Folsom 15; John Gilman, Jr. 20; Moses Gilman 50; Alexander Gordon 20; William Hacket 30; Joseph Hall 15; Ralph Hall 50; Dany (?) Kelley 10; James Kidd 20; Thomas King 40 and 3; John Kiming 30; Cornelius Lary 15; Samuel Leavitt 15; Nicholas Listen 40; William Moore 30 and 6; Richard Morgan 20; Robert Powell 20; John Robinson 15; Jonathan Robinson 15; John Sinclair 15; Robert Smart 80 and 20; William Taylor 20; Jonathan Thing 60; John Warren 40; Thomas Warren, Jr., son of John, 10. December 1, John Gilman, Sr.; Henry Magoon 10.

---

[*] The condition not being complied with, the land was regranted, October 10, 1664, to William Bromfield.

The following grants were made from 1665 to 1669 inclusive:

1665, April 3, John Gilman, Jr. 20 acres; James Kidd 20.
1666, April 4, James Godfrey 10 acres. July 3, Charles Gilman 30, conditionally.
1668, March 15, Nicholas Listen and Robert Wadleigh 10 acres. March 29, Philip Cartee (often written Carter) 16 or 17. September 28, John Folsom, Jr. 20; John Gilman 30; Samuel Leavitt 20; Jonathan Thing.
1669, May 3, John Folsom, Sr. 20 acres.

The following grants were made from 1670 to 1672 inclusive:

1670, March 30, Samuel Dudley 10 acres; John Robinson 30; Goodman [John] Clark 30; Peter Folsom 30; Edward Gilman 100; Jeremy Leavitt, Thomas Rollins, Edward Smith, Jonathan Thing, Jr. and John Young 30 each. These last eight grants were of land given to the town by Thomas Wiggin, and the grantees bound themselves to try the title, if contested by Hampton. October 25, Samuel Folsom 2; Lieut. [Ralph] Hall 30.
1671, April 3, John Bean 6 acres; Henry Magoon 20.
1672, April 29, Samuel Leavitt 50 acres.

The following grants were made from 1674 to 1678 inclusive:

1674, February 9, Moses Gilman; Kinsley Hall 10 acres. March 3, John Clark; William Moore 12. March 30, Christian Dolloff 10; Samuel Dudley 600; Edward Gilman 200; Lieut. [John] Gilman 600; Moses Gilman 600; Lieut. [Ralph] Hall 400; David Lawrence 10; John Robinson 200; Thomas Rollins 12; Humphrey Wilson 400.
1675, April 2, John Folsom, Sr. 200 acres; John Folsom, Jr. 200; Daniel Gilman 30; John Gilman, Jr. 30; Joel Judkins 10; Samuel Leavitt 300; Goodman [Nicholas] Listen 300; William Moore 300; Edward Sewall 4; Robert Smart, Sr. 300; Edward Smith 100.
1676-7, March 19, Samuel Leavitt 6 acres.
1677, August 27, Kinsley Hall.
1678 (about) March 18, George Pearson.
On March 11, 1678-9, Jonathan Thing was put in the place of Ensign [William] Moore with Mr. [Samuel] Dudley and Lieut. [Ralph] Hall, for the equal distribution of lands to such as had none when the great lots were granted (March 30, 1674).

HISTORY OF EXETER.   137

The following grants were made in 1681 and 1682:

1681, January 31, Philip Cartee 20 acres; John Clark 50; Jeremy Connor 20; Biley Dudley 50; Theophilus Dudley 100; Teague Drisco 20; Eleazer Elkins 50; Peter Folsom 100; Joseph Hall 50; Kinsley Hall 100; Samuel Hall 50; John Kiming 50; Moses Leavitt 50; Henry Magoon 20; Nicholas Norris 50 and 50; James Sinclair 50; John Sinclair 20; Edward Smith 100; Mr. [Robert] Wadleigh; John Wadleigh 50. February 7, Mr. [Samuel] Dudley 20. March 30, Ephraim Folsom 100; Cornelius Lary 40; Richard Morgan 60; David Robinson 100; Joseph Wadleigh 100; John Young 100.

1682, March 14, Samuel Dudley, Jr. 100 acres; Stephen Dudley 100; Jeremy Gilman 100; Nathaniel Ladd 100; Moses Gilman, Jr. 100; Robert Wadleigh 200.

On March 14, 1681-2, these orders were adopted by the town:

That all the inhabitants of this town have free liberty to clear any swamp land within this township for the producing of meadow, not exceeding ten acres for each inhabitant, provided they entrench not upon former proprieties. And it is further ordered that what heretofore hath been done and hereafter may be done in pursuance of this act and order shall be as good a title as any other town grant.

Whereas it was formerly enacted by this town that the neck of land on the southwest side of the little river was to lie for a perpetual common, but being not found upon record, it is now ratified and confirmed at this meeting, and the selectmen are to set the bounds; which said neck of land is intended to be all the land between the great river and the little river, and towards Pickpocket near about King's falls, and on the northwest side as far as a place called King's meadow.

On March 30, 1682, it was "enacted by general consent that that piece of land between Edward Sewall's fence, Christian Dolloff's fence or land, John Bean's fence, Henry Magoon's fence or land and the way that goes from Henry Magoon's land to Pickpocket mill, which said piece of land now lying common, shall lie perpetually common for the use of the town, either for a common field or for what else shall be thought convenient for the town."

The following grants were made from 1690 to 1697 inclusive:

1690, October 6, Peter Coffin.
1693, October 10, Captain Peter Coffin, two parcels, one of 60

138   HISTORY OF EXETER.

1697, March 29, Samuel Leavitt 20 acres. November 4, Mr. [Rev.] John Clark, 100 acres, "provided he live in the town ten years."

The following grants were made in 1698:

February 3, Samuel Bean 40 acres; Edward Gilman; James Gilman 40; Jeremy Gilman 40; Nicholas Gilman 40; Richard Hilton 100; Winthrop Hilton 100; Thomas Lyford 30; Samuel Piper 20; William Taylor 20; Samuel Thing 50; Henry Wadleigh 10. February 21, William Ardell 100; Robert Barber 50; James Bean 30; John Bean, Sr. 100; Jonathan Clark 20; Peter Coffin 200; Robert Coffin 60; Jeremy Conner 30; Christian Dolloff 10; Richard Dolloff 100; Samuel Dolloff 100; Philip Dudy 50; Abraham Folsom 50; Ephraim Folsom, Jr. 20; John Folsom, Sr. 100; John Folsom 40; Peter Folsom, Jr. 30; David Gilman and James Gilman 80; John Gilman 50; John Gilman, son of Capt. John, 40; Moses Gilman, Jr. 30; Stephen Gilman 50; Charles Glidden 100; John Glidden 50; Richard Glidden 50 and 50; Alexander Gordon 60; James Gordon 60; John Gordon 20; Nicholas Gordon 30; William Grafs (Graves) 30; Richard Hilton 20; Philip Huntoon 30; Job Judkins 30; Benjamin Leavitt 50; Daniel Leavitt 70; John Leavitt 100; Moses Leavitt 6; Lieut. Samuel Leavitt 100; Samuel Leavitt, Jr. 70; Samuel Lawrey 20; Thomas Lyford 30; Richard Mattoon 50; Clement Moody 30 +; William Moore, Jr. 60; Richard Morgan, Sr. 100; Richard Morgan, Jr. 50; Samuel Pease 50; Robert Powell 50; Benjamin Rollins 50; Joseph Rollins 50; Moses Rollins 50; Thomas Rollins, Sr. 100; Thomas Rollins, Jr. 20; Charles Rundlet, Jr. 30; John Scribner 40; James Sinclair 50; Theophilus Smith 30; Thomas Speed 50; Philip Spenlow 40; Francis Steel 20; Nathaniel Stevens 20; Benjamin Taylor 20; Nathan Taylor 30; Jonathan and John Thing 60; Henry Wadleigh 20 and 20; Jonathan Wadleigh 50; Robert Wadleigh 50, 20 and 50; Thomas Wilson 50; Israel Young 30; James Young 30; John Young 30 and 20; Robert Young 30; Sarah Young 50. March 28, John Bean, Jr. 60 acres; Biley Dudley 30; Theophilus Dudley 50; Moses Gilman, Sr. 50; Richard Glidden 40; Dudley Hilton 50; Philip (?) Huntoon 10; Benjamin Jones, Sr. 50; Moses Leavitt; Francis Lyford 200; Alexander Magoon 50; Richard Mattoon 20; James Norris 40; Moses Norris 30; Nicholas Norris 3; George Pearson 50; William Powell 20; Thomas Rollins 20;

Charles Rundlet, Jr. 50; James Rundlet, 50; John Scribner 10; Jonathan Smith 20; Nicholas Smith 20; Theophilus Smith 30; Francis Steel; Haines (?) Woolford 30. April 29, Peter Coffin 100; Joel Judkins 60; Jonathan Norris 50. August 26, Richard Bounds (?).

At the town meeting on March 28, 1698, the very sensible vote was passed, "that those who had land given them at the last meeting shall have no more given them at this meeting."

The following grants were made from 1699 to 1709 inclusive:

1699, September 5, Samuel Elkins 20 acres; Thomas Gordon 40; Moses Leavitt.

1700, April 17, Cornelius Conner 30 acres; Ephraim Folsom, Sr. 20; Peter Folsom, Sr. 100; Joshua Gilman 50; Stephen Gilman 30; Dudley and Richard Hilton 20; Jonathan Hilton 50; Joseph Young 40. May 10, Jeremiah Gilman 100. September 9, Ephraim Folsom, Jr. 20; James Leavitt 100; Jonathan Robinson, Sr. 100.

1701, April 1, Jeremiah Conner 15 acres; Thomas Rollins, Sr. 100; Jonathan Thing 30; Thomas Webster 50. September 9, Robert Coffin, mill privilege and flats.

1702, first Monday of April, Capt. Peter Coffin 200 acres; Robert Coffin 100; Cornelius Conner 30; Capt. John Gilman, Sr. 100; Ens. John Gilman 100; John Gilman, son of Moses; Nicholas Gilman 100; Capt. Kinsley Hall 100; Dudley Hilton 50; Benjamin Jones, Sr. 40; Job Judkins 40; Mr. Moses Leavitt, Sr. 100; Israel Smith 100; Ithiel Smith 50; Jacob Smith 50; Jonathan Smith 100; Joseph Smith 50; John Thing 30; Jonathan Thing 100.

1703, first Monday of April, Richard Dolloff 20 acres; Thomas Dolloff 40; Daniel Gordon 50; Bartholemew Thing 50.

1705, first Monday of April, John Glidden 50 acres; Nathaniel Ladd 50; Nehemiah Leavitt 50; John Light 60, "provided he shall live 7 years in the town;" Nicholas Norris 20; Jethro Pearson 50; John Sinclair, son of James, 100; George Veasey 100; Thomas Veasey 100; Jonathan Wiggin 100.

1706, first Monday of April, Daniel Bean, Jr. 100 acres; Samuel Dudley, Jr. 100; Stephen Dudley, Jr. 50; Francis Durgin 20; Cartee Gilman 100; Col. Winthrop Hilton 400; Moses Norris 50; Aaron Rollins 100; John Rollins 100; Charles Rundlet, Jr. 50; James Rundlet 50; Thomas Seawell 100; John Sinclair

50; Theophilus Smith 30; Samuel Stevens 60; John Thing 100; Joseph Thing 100; Thomas Webster 50.

1707, first Monday of April, Lieut. John Gilman 100 acres; Daniel Ladd 100; Satchell Rundlet 100.

1709, first Monday of April, Daniel Bean 80 acres.

For the next five years it does not appear that any land grants were made, nor that any action was taken by the town in regard to the common lands.

On April 5, 1714, the town resolved "that two miles of the west end of the township be laid out by men appointed, for a perpetual commonage for the use of the town."

This decision was not to the liking of many of the inhabitants, and, as will be seen, attempts were soon made to revoke it, which were never abandoned until that object was effected.

On March 13, 1717, it was voted "that Nicholas Gilman, Thomas Webster and Samuel Thing be a committee to make diligent search in the town records that whereas there is complaint by several persons that they have not had their proportion in lands given them by the town, in order that they may have their share; the committee to make report of their doings therein to this meeting."

The meeting was accordingly adjourned to the first Monday in November, 1717. There is no record of the adjourned meeting, nor that any proceedings were had under the vote.

For the five years ensuing, the only action taken by the town in relation to its lands, was the appointment of a committee in 1720 to report whether any inhabitants' land grants had been encroached upon by the late lines run between town and town. The committee reported that certain lands laid out to Jonathan Gilman and Nathaniel Webster were included within the bounds of Kingston; and in consequence thereof there were laid out to them in 1725 by the lot layers of Kingston four acres of the common land in Exeter, to make good their loss. Exeter at that time was without lot layers, having failed to choose any.

On March 30, 1724, the town resolved as follows:

Whereas sundry persons desire to have a town meeting to grant out land, who have not had their share of land as they ought to have, and desire a committee to be chosen to hear what those persons have to say, and to draw up what they conclude of, and to present it to the selectmen, who are to call a town meeting to effect what the committee conclude of. Mr. Justice [Samuel] Thing, Bartholomew Thing, Joseph Hall, Josiah Hall and Edward Gilman to be a committee to search the town book to find who ought to have land and who ought not

At an adjournment of the town meeting called for the purpose aforesaid, held April 12, 1725, it was voted :

That the grant of the two miles common at the western end of the township be wholly null and void, and that the said two miles with all the other common land in the township not heretofore granted, be divided in proportion according to the return of Samuel Thing, Esq., Joseph Hall, Bartholomew Thing, Edward Gilman, Josiah Hall, committee chosen by the town for that end, as per list under the said committee's hands of every person's name who had land allowed him with the number of acres annexed thereto,— the said land not to be divided till the expiration of ten years from the date hereof.

The following is the list reported by the committee :

LIST OF DISTRIBUTEES OF LAND AS REPORTED IN 1725.

NAMES.	ACRES.	NAMES.	ACRES.
Samuel Akers,	20	Capt. Eliphalet Coffin,	100
Daniel Ames,	30	Edward Colcord,	20
John Barber, Senr.,	50	Jonathan Colcord,	40
John Barber, Jr.,	30	Cornelius Conner,	100
Robert Barber,	30	Jeremy Conner, Senr.,	100
Nathaniel Bartlett,	20	Jonathan Conner,	50
Edward Bean,	30	Moses Conner,	40
Jeremiah Bean, Senr.,	100	Philip Conner,	40
Jeremiah Bean, Jr.,	40	Samuel Conner,	30
John Bean, Senr.,	40	Dr. Thomas Dean,	30
John Bean, Jr.,	30	Sampson Doe,	20
Samuel Bean, Senr.,	50	Samuel Doe,	20
William Bean,	30	Richard Dolloff,	80
John Brown,	20	Samuel Dolloff,	80
Giles Burleigh,	30	Samuel Dolloff, Jr.,	30
James Burley,	20	Cornelius Drisco,	50
Josiah Burleigh,	30	Mr. Biley Dudley,	100
Joseph Burleigh,	20	James Dudley,	70
Jeremiah Calef,	20	Jonathan Dudley,	50
Jonathan Clark,	40	Joseph Dudley,	40
Richard Clark,	40	Nicholas Dudley,	100
Solomon Clark,	30	Samuel Dudley, Senr.,	100
Mr. Ward Clark,	50	Samuel Dudley, Jr.,	50

HISTORY OF EXETER.

NAMES.	ACRES.	NAMES.	ACRES.
Stephen Dudley, Senr.,	100	Nehemiah Gilman,	50
Stephen Dudley, Jr.,	30	Maj. Nicholas Gilman,	250
Trueworthy Dudley,	50	Nicholas Gilman, Jr.,	50
Francis Durgin,	30	Peter Gilman,	70
Samuel Edgerly,	20	Samuel Gilman,	60
Thomas Edgerly,	20	Simon Gilman,	50
Samuel Elkins,	100	Thomas Gilman,	30
Seth Fogg,	20	Andrew Glidden,	100
Abraham Folsom,	100	Benjamin Glidden,	30
Benjamin Folsom,	100	Joseph Glidden,	30
Edward Folsom,	30	Nathaniel Glidden,	30
Ephraim Folsom, Senr.,	100	Richard Glidden, Senr.,	50
Ephraim Folsom, Jr.,	30	Richard Glidden, Jr.,	30
Jeremiah Folsom,	100	Alexander Gordon,	100
John Folsom, Senr.,	80	Daniel Gordon,	30
John Folsom, Jr.,	100	James Gordon,	30
Jonathan Folsom,	100	John Gordon, Jr.,	30
Estate of Peter Folsom, Jr.,		Jonathan Gordon,	50
deceased,	50	Nicholas Gordon,	100
William Folsom, Senr.,	30	Thomas Gordon,	50
William Folsom, Jr.,	30	Thomas Gordon, Jr.,	30
Daniel Giles,	30	John Graves,	30
Andrew Gilman,	100	William Graves, Senr.,	50
Benjamin Gilman,	80	William Graves, Jr.,	30
Caleb Gilman,	150	Thomas Haley,	20
Carty Gilman,	50	Edward Hall,	150
Daniel Gilman,	50	Joseph Hall,	150
David Gilman,	70	Josiah Hall,	120
Edward Gilman, Senr.,	150	Capt. Kinsley Hall,	200
Edward Gilman, Jr.,	50	Paul Hall,	80
Ezekiel Gilman,	30	Theophilus Hardy,	80
Israel Gilman,	50	Benjamin Hilton,	30
Lieut. James Gilman,	100	Edward Hilton,	40
James Gilman, Jr.,	50	Jonathan Hilton, Senr.,	50
Capt. Jeremiah Gilman,	100	Jonathan Hilton, Jr.,	30
Maj. John Gilman,	250	Joseph Hilton,	70
Capt. John Gilman,	200	Capt. Richard Hilton,	150
Lieut. John Gilman,	100	Samuel Hilton,	60
Jonathan Gilman,	50	William Hilton,	50
Joseph Gilman,	50	Winthrop Hilton,	50
Joshua Gilman,	30	Job Judkins, Senr.,	70
Maverick Gilman,	30	Job Judkins, Jr.,	30
Moses Gilman, Senr.,	120	Joseph Judkins,	40
Moses Gilman, Jr.,	50	Caleb Kimball,	20
Nathaniel Gilman,	50	John Kimball,	20

HISTORY OF EXETER. 143

NAMES.	ACRES.	NAMES.	ACRES.
Moses Kimming,	30	Robert Pike,	20
Capt. Nathaniel Ladd,	60	Richard Preston,	20
Nathaniel Ladd, Jr.,	40	John Quimby,	20
Daniel Leary,	40	John Robinson,	130
Samuel Leary,	40	Jonathan Robinson, Senr.,	50
Dudley Leavitt,	30	Jonathan Robinson, Jr.,	100
Lieut. James Leavitt,	200	Joseph Robinson,	70
John Leavitt,	50	Thomas Robinson,	20
Joseph Leavitt,	30	Benjamin Rollins,	40
Dea. Moses Leavitt,	200	John Rollins, Jr.,	30
Selah Leavitt,	50	Samuel Rollins,	50
Stephen Leavitt,	40	Edward Scribner,	30
Timothy Leavitt,	50	John Scribner, Senr.,	50
John Lord,	20	John Scribner, Jr.,	50
John Lougee,	30	Joseph Scribner,	30
Stephen Lyford,	100	Samuel Scribner,	40
Thomas Lyford,	100	Edward Sewall,	40
Alexander Magoon,	100	Stephen Sewall,	30
Benjamin Magoon,	30	James Sinclair,	100
Samuel Magoon,	50	John Sinclair, Senr.,	100
John Marsh,	30	John Sinclair, Jr.,	30
Richard Mattoon,	30	Joseph Sinclair,	40
Samuel Mighill,	30	Richard Sinclair,	40
Clement Moody, Senr.,	50	Samuel Sinclair,	40
Clement Moody, Jr.,	50	John Smart,	40
John Moody,	40	Joseph Smart,	30
Jonathan Moody,	30	Robert Smart,	50
Walter Neal,	30	Benjamin Smith,	30
James Norris,	30	Benjamin Smith, Jr.,	30
John Norris,	30	David Smith,	30
Jonathan Norris,	30	Edward Smith,	30
Moses Norris, Senr.,	60	Jacob Smith,	70
Moses Norris, Jr.,	40	Jonathan Smith,	50
Nicholas Norris, Senr.,	30	Nathaniel Smith,	30
Samuel Norris,	30	Nicholas Smith,	30
Rev. John Odlin,	100	Oliver Smith,	70
Jethro Pearson, Senr.,	70	Richard Smith,	50
Jethro Pearson, Jr.,	30	Capt. Theophilus Smith,	150
Nathaniel Pease,	50	Theophilus Smith, Jr.,	50
John Perkins, Senr.,	100	Benjamin Taylor,	30
John Perkins, Jr.,	40	Joseph Taylor,	50
William Perkins, Senr.,	30	Nathan Taylor,	30
William Perkins, Jr.,	40	William Taylor,	80
Nicholas Perryman,	20	Lieut. Bartholomew Thing,	150
Ephraim Philbrick,	20	Benjamin Thing,	100

NAMES.	ACRES.	NAMES.	ACRES.
Daniel Thing,	80	Philip Wadleigh,	50
Jonathan Thing,	50	Robert Wadleigh, Senr.,	100
Heirs of Capt. Jonathan Thing, Jr., dec^d.,	100	Nathaniel Webster,	50
		Thomas Webster,	100
Joseph Thing,	100	Humphrey Wilson,	50
Josiah Thing, Jr. (son of Samuel),	50	Dea. Thos. Wilson,	200
		Benjamin York,	50
Nathaniel Thing,	50	Richard York,	40
Samuel Thing, Esq.,	300	Charles Young,	30
Abner Thurston,	20	Daniel Young,	80
Ensign Henry Wadleigh,	100	James Young,	30
Capt. Jonathan Wadleigh,	200	Jonathan Young,	50
Jonathan Wadleigh, Jr.,	30	Robert Young,	50

The aforenamed 249 persons are they to whom the committee has proportioned the common land of this town.

PROCEEDINGS TO HASTEN A DISTRIBUTION.

It is not surprising that a majority of the inhabitants were unwilling to wait ten years in accordance with the report of the committee, for the actual division of the lands. Such a prospect was particularly tantalizing to those who were then without real estate, when it lay with the majority of their own number to say how soon they might come into possession of very substantial homestead lots.

Accordingly, in something less than four years, the subject was resumed; this time by the inhabitants as "Proprietors of the Common Lands." The first proprietors' meeting was called by the selectmen of the town, upon an application stating that the common lands were being trespassed upon. It was held January 6, 1729, and adjourned to the twentieth of the same month. A vote was passed that the clause in the return of the committee forbidding the division of the lands for ten years, be null and void, and that a division be made forthwith; and Edward Gilman, Edward Hall, Jeremiah Conner, John Folsom and Andrew Gilman were chosen a committee to make partition of the lands according to the return of the committee who proportioned them, and "go about the work as soon as may be."

This committee failed to do the "work" for which they were appointed; apparently for the reason that some of their number were opposed to the plan of immediate division. So nearly two years more went by before the matter was again moved. Another meeting of the proprietors was then called, and held November 9, 1730, at which Captain John Gilman, Edward Gilman, Joseph Hall, Peter Gilman and Israel Gilman were chosen a committee to lay out the common lands agreeably to the proportion made by the committee in 1725; and Edward Hall and Jeremiah Conner were subsequently added to the new committee.

After nearly two years' consideration, the last-named committee reported a plan for the separation of the common la ds, at the west end of the township, into sixteen ranges, containing in the aggregate 1485 lots of ten acres each, to be distributed among the inhabitants, agreeably to the apportionment made by the committee appointed in 1725. This report was accepted by the town October 19, 1732; and it was voted that Mr. Maylem should draw all the lots for the proprietors, according to the division made by the last appointed committee. The resolution was at once carried into effect; and a full list of the drawing appears in the Proprietors' Records.

FINAL DISTRIBUTION.

But there was still some dissatisfaction with the allotments. Complaint was made that some of the inhabitants had never received their "ten acre lots," to which they considered themselves entitled, under the vote of the town of March 14, 1681-2, and that certain inequalities existed in the former divisions, which ought to be corrected. Another meeting of the town was therefore held June 15, 1738, which was continued by adjournments to August 28, at which it was resolved (for the third time?) that the vote passed by the town April 5, 1714, that two miles of the western end of the township should be for a perpetual commonage, be null and void, and that the said two miles be laid out and divided with the rest of the commons among the inhabitants.

A committee of seven were appointed, consisting of Captain Samuel Gilman, Lieutenant John Robinson, Captain Peter Gilman, Mr. Trueworthy Dudley, Cornet Ezekiel Gilman, Ensign Richard Mattoon and Captain John Gilman, Sr., who received specific instructions as to their duties in dividing the lands; were to be allowed compensation at the rate of eleven shillings each per day; were empowered to hire a surveyor at the cost of fourteen shillings per day, and were given twelve months in which to make their report. The time was subsequently enlarged to two years. The committee attended to the duty assigned them and filed their return on August 18, 1740. In it they provided ten acre lots for several persons who had not hitherto received them, and added twenty names to the list reported by the committee of 1725, as follows:

NAMES.	ACRES.	NAMES.	ACRES.
John Burley's heirs,	20	John Light's heirs,	20
Thomas Dolloff's heirs,	40	Ebenezer Martin,	10
Samuel Fogg,	10	John Mudget,	10
Israel Folsom,	10	Thomas Mudget,	10
John Fox,	10	John Roberts,	13
Joel Judkins,	12	Samuel Smith, son of Jacob,	15
Christopher Kenniston,	10	Francis Steel's heirs,	50
Daniel Ladd,	40	Edward Stevens's heirs,	40
Thomas Lary,	30	Samuel Stevens's heirs,	10
Nehemiah Leavitt's heirs,	15	Thomas Young,	20

The committee were empowered to make changes in the lots as drawn in 1732, in certain cases when found needful, and a few such changes were made; but in general those lots were allowed to remain without alteration.

The adoption of the last report completed the disposal of the public lands of the town, with the exception of a few fragments chiefly by the side of the river. The titles granted by the town have never been questioned.

The meetings of the proprietors were kept up a few years after the division of 1740, and then abandoned; and the Proprietors' Records were ordered to be delivered to the town clerk.

CHAPTER VII.

OFFICERS OF THE TOWN.

In this chapter is given a list of the principal officers of Exeter from its foundation to the present time. It is generally taken from the town books, but in the few cases where they fail to afford information, it has been sought for elsewhere. With the exception of some of the earlier years, the list is almost complete.

For a long time the elections were held at irregular intervals, and the terms of service varied correspondingly. The general rule must have been that incumbents of offices held over until their successors were elected. This is especially the case with reference to the office of town clerk, which was never treated as an annual one before 1720. The number of selectmen was variable; from 1644 to 1690 it was three; then it was raised to five, and so continued till 1817, when it was reduced to three again.

It may interest those who are curious about "first things," to know that the earliest election of lot layers in the town which is on record was in 1648; the earliest (and only) election of clerk of the market was in the same year; the earliest surveyor of highways, in 1651; of tithing men, in 1678; of pound-keeper, in 1680, and of moderator, not until 1686. This may be the fault of the records, for very probably such officers were chosen earlier, and the fact failed to be recorded. We can hardly suppose, for example, that town meetings were held for near half a century without a moderator.

Apparently a good deal of interest used to be taken in the choice of constables. Attached to this office was the irksome duty of collecting the rates. The person chosen could decline the office, but only on the payment of the then heavy fine of five pounds. This a great many did rather than accept the disagreeable position. At length the practice grew up of allowing the constable-elect to excuse himself from performing the duties, on his furnishing a substitute acceptable to the town.

HISTORY OF EXETER.

LIST OF TOWN OFFICERS.

RULERS.

Isaac Gross, 1630. Nicholas Needham, 1639 to 1642. Thomas Wilson 1642 to 1643.

ASSISTANT RULERS.

Augustine Storre and Anthony Stanyan, 1639–

TOWN CLERKS.

John Legat,	1649	John S. Sleeper,	1832, 3
Edward Smith,	1684 (?)	Daniel Melcher,	1834–1837
Jonathan Thing,	1689	Charles Conner,	1838–1842
Samuel Thing,	1700–1719	Joseph T. Porter,	1843–1846
Kinsley Hall,	1720–1725	James M. Lovering,	1847–1849
Josiah Hall,	1726–1729	John Tyrrell,	1850
Bartholomew Thing,	1729–1737	Franklin Lane,	1851–1854
Elisha Odlin,	1738–1743	Samuel D. Wingate,	1855
Zebulon Giddinge,	1744–1782	Augustus H. Weeks,	1856, 7
Josiah Gilman, Jr.,	1783–1800	Charles Grant,	1858–1860
Ephraim Robinson,	1801–1809	William H. Belknap,	1861–1865,
Joseph Tilton,	1809–1811		1875–1888
John J. Parker,	1812–1831	Joseph S. Parsons,	1866–1869
George Smith,	1831, 3	George E. Lane,	1870–1874

SELECTMEN.

Richard Bulgar,	1644	Humphrey Wilson,	1653, 8
Samuel Greenfield,	1644–1646	Moses Gilman,	1653, 60, 73, 4, 7, 93
Christopher Lawson,	1644	Nicholas Listen,	1654, 5, 7, 62, 6
Edward Hilton,	1645, 6, 1651	John Warren,	1655, 7
Anthony Stanyan,	1645, 6	Jonathan Thing,	1658, 61, 8, 71, 2,
William Moore,	1647, 54, 8, 71, 2,		6, 82, 3
	91, 4, 9	Nicholas Smith,	1658
James Wall,	1647, 9	John Tedd,	1658, 62
John Legat,	1647–1650	John Folsom,	1660, 8, 91
Godfrey Dearborn,	1648	Thomas Biggs,	1660
John Cram,	1648, 9	Ralph Hall, 1666, 73, 4, 5, 6, 7, 8, 80
Henry Roby,	1650	Samuel Leavitt,	1675, 91, 6
Thomas King,	1650, 2, 8, 62	Edward Smith,	1679, 80
Nathaniel Drake,	1651	Edward Gilman,	1680, 1, 2, 3, 90
John Gilman, 1652, 4, 5, 7, 61, 8, 71,		Kinsley Hall,	1681, 90, 3
	2, 4, 5, 6, 7, 8, 87	John Folsom, Jr.,	1681, 96
Thomas Pettit,	1652	Moses Leavitt,	1682, 3, 91, 6
John Robinson,	1653, 61, 6, 73	Biley Dudley, 1687, 90, 4, 5, 9, 1700

John Wadleigh,	1687	Thomas Wilson,	1720, 3, 4
William Hilton,	1690	Cornelius Conner,	1720
Francis Lyford,	1690	James Leavitt,	1721, 2, 3, 4, 8, 9, 32
Ephraim Folsom,	1691	Bartholomew Thing,	1721, 6, 7, 8, 9, 33, 6, 7
Theophilus Dudley,	1693, 4, 5, 9		
Richard Hilton,	1693, 1701, 2, 3, 7, 8, 15	Samuel Thing,	1722
		Eliphalet Coffin,	1725, 33
John Wilson,	1693	Caleb Gilman,	1725, 30, 1, 6, 7
Robert Smart, Sr.,	1694	Theophilus Gilman,	1726
Moses Gilman, Jr.,	1694	Joseph Thing,	1728, 30, 1, 2, 3, 4, 6, 7, 9
Jonathan Robinson,	1695	Thomas Webster,	1730, 1, 2
Henry Wadleigh,	1695	Samuel Gilman,	1733, 6, 7, 8
James Sinclair,	1695, 1700, 6, 21	Edward Gilman,	1734, 40
Winthrop Hilton,	1696	Stephen Lyford,	1734
James Gilman,	1696	Jonathan Gilman,	1734, 55, 60
Andrew Wiggin,	1699, 1712, 4	Peter Gilman,	1738
William Scammon,	1699, 1700	Ezekiel Gilman,	1738
Nicholas Gilman,	1699, 1700, 1, 9, 18, 21, 5, 6, 7, 9	Trueworthy Dudley,	1738
		Daniel Thing,	1739
Theophilus Smith,	1699, 1706, 11, 12, 7, 8, 27, 33, 4, 6, 7, 9, 40 *	James Gilman,	1739, 40, 3–1750
		Josiah Gilman,	1739, 55, 6
Theophilus Dudley,	1700–1709, 11	Thomas Dean,	1740
Simon Wiggin,	1701–1705	Elisha Odlin,	1740
Jonathan Thing,	1701–1705, 14, 5, 6	Jonathan Conner,	1743–1748
John Gilman (son of Moses),	1701–1705, 8	Josiah Sanborn,	1743, 4, 5, 6, 50, 1, 2, 3, 4, 7, 8
Samuel Leavitt,	1704, 7	John Odlin, Jr.,	1743–54, 6, 7, 8, 9
Robert Coffin,	1705, 7, 8	John Rice,	1743, 52, 6, 7, 8, 9, 61, 2, 3, 4, 6, 7, 8, 9, 70
Jonathan Wadleigh,	1705, 7, 8, 12, 4, 5, 6, 23, 4, 6, 7, 8, 29, 32		
John Robinson,	1706, 20, 5, 38	Zebulon Giddinge,	1744–1748
Bradstreet Wiggin,	1706	Samuel Fogg,	1747–1749
William Moore,	1709, 11, 2	Ephraim Robinson,	1749, 50, 2, 3, 4, 60, 72, 5, 7, 8, 80–1785
William French,	1709	Nathaniel Bartlett, Jr.,	1749–1754
Jeremiah Conner,	1709, 22, 30, 1		
Capt. John Gilman,	1711, 4, 5, 6, 8, 20, 3, 4, 8, 9, 30	Samuel Gilman, Jr.,	1751, 3, 4, 60
		Robert Light,	1751, 5
		James Leavitt,	1755
Lieut. John Gilman,	1711, 2, 4, 7, 31, 2	Charles Rundlett,	1755, 66, 7, 8, 9
		John Phillips,	1756
Joseph Hall,	1715, 6, 7, 21, 3, 4	Peter Folsom,	1756
Nicholas Gordon,	1716, 7, 8, 22, 5	John Kimball,	1757
Moses Leavitt,	1717	Joseph Leavitt,	1757
Edward Hall,	1718, 20, 2, 6	John Giddinge,	1758, 9, 61, 2, 3, 4

---

*This is one of several instances where the same name was handed down through two or more generations, and it is difficult to ascertain where the father's term of office terminated, and the son's began. The same is true of other names, John Gil-

Nicholas Gilman,	1758, 9, 61, 2, 3, 4, 6, 7, 8, 70, 1	Edmund Pearson,	1808–1813
		Thomas Kimball,	1808
Josiah Robinson,	1759, 66, 7, 8, 9, 70, 1	Josiah Folsom, Jr.,	1808, 9
		Harvey Colcord,	1809–1814
Theophilus Gilman,	1760, 1	Enoch Rowe,	1810–1816
John Dudley,	1760–1764	John Gordon,	1814–1816
Daniel Tilton,	1762, 3, 4, 6, 7, 8, 9, 70, 1, 80, 1	Joseph Osborne,	1815, 6
		John Rogers,	1817–1829
Joseph Gilman,	1769, 70, 1	Freese Dearborn,	1825–1829
Peter Coffin,	1771–1775	Josiah Robinson,	1830–1835
Nathaniel Gordon,	1772, 6, 93	John Smith,	1830
Samuel Brooks,	1772–1775	Theodore Moses,	1830
Theophilus Smith,	1772, 6	George Smith,	1831–36, 8, 9
Ephraim Folsom,	1773, 4	James Burley,	1831–37, 40, 1, 2
Theodore Carleton,	1773–1775	Josiah R. Norris,	1836–1839
Thomas Folsom,	1773, 4, 5, 7, 9	John Dodge,	1837, 40
Joseph Cram,	1776, 80–90	Jeremiah Robinson, Jr.,	1838–41, 3, 4, 5
Eliphalet Giddinge,	1776–1778, 1788–94, 1802, 3	William Conner,	1841–46, 50, 1
Trueworthy Gilman,	1776, 7, 8, 80–87	William Philbrick,	1842
		John T. Gordon,	1843–1848
John T. Gilman,	1777, 8	Retire H. Parker,	1846–1848
Benjamin Boardman,	1778, 9	Nathaniel Swasey,	1847, 8
Eliphalet Ladd,	1779, 84, 5, 6	Jewett Conner,	1852–54, 63–67, 1879–85, 7
Jedediah Jewett,	1779, 82, 3, 4		
Samuel Folsom,	1779	Benjamin Lang,	1849–1851
James Thurston,	1780–1783	William P. Moulton,	1849
Nathaniel Gilman,	1785, 91, 2	John Foss,	1849, 50
Ephraim Robinson,	1786–93, 95–1805, 7	Lewis W. Perkins,	1851–1853
		George W. Furnald,	1852–1854, 1868–70
Gideon Lamson,	1786, 1794–1805, 9		
Oliver Peabody,	1787–1791	Edwin O. Lovering,	1854
Dudley Odlin,	1787–1790	William H. Robinson,	1855, 6
Jeremiah Robinson,	1792, 3, 1810–16	Asa Jewell,	1855–1857
Samuel Tenney,	1792–1800	Ammi R. Wiggin,	1855, 6
Jeremiah Leavitt,	1794–1807	Alfred Conner,	1857, 8, 72
George Odiorne,	1794–1796	John W. Elliott,	1857, 8
Benjamin C. Gilman,	1797–1801, 14, 5, 6	James W. Odlin,	1858, 9
		John Clement,	1859, 60
Samuel Gilman,	1801, 2	Nathaniel G. Giddings,	1859, 60
Trueworthy Robinson,	1803–1806	Nathaniel Shute,	1860, 1
Daniel Conner,	1804–1807	Joseph D. Wadleigh,	1861, 2
Nathaniel Parker,	1806	Josiah J. Folsom,	1861–63, 1879–86
Jeremiah Dow,	1806	Adoniram J. Towle,	1862
Nehemiah Folsom,	'1807, 17–24	Solomon J. Perkins,	1863–1867
John Kimball,	1807–13, 17–29	Joseph T. Porter,	1864–1867

HISTORY OF EXETER. 151

Jacob Carlisle,	1868, 9	Nathaniel G. Gilman,	1874–1876
John H. Kimball,	1868, 9	Oliver L. Giddings,	1874–1876
Daniel F. Hayes,	1870, 1	Charles H. Downing,	1877, 8
Joseph Perkins,	1870, 1	John M. Wadleigh,	1877, 8
William B. Morrill,	1871–84, 6	Andrew J. Fogg,	1885, 6
Joshua Getchell,	1872, 3	George W. Green,	1887
Lyford Conner,	1873	Charles H. Towle,	1887

MODERATORS.

Peter Coffin,	1696, 1705	Nathaniel Folsom,	1774, 5, 7, 9, 85–90
William Moore,	1698	John Phillips.	1778
Kinsley Hall,	1700, 4	Nicholas Gilman,	1780–84
Theophilus Dudley,	1706, 9	John T. Gilman,	1791–1794, 1806, 7,
Moses Leavitt, 1707, 8, 13, 4, 5, 23, 6			9, 10, 1, 7, 8, 20–25
John Gilman,	1711	Oliver Peabody,	1795, 7, 1801, 5, 12
Nicholas Gilman,	1716, 7, 8, 30–35,	Samuel Tenney,	1796, 8, 9, 1800, 8
	7, 9, 43–48	Jeremiah Smith,	1802, 3, 4, 13–16
Captain John Gilman,	1720, 4, 5, 7,	Nathaniel Gilman,	1819
	9, 36, 8	James Burley,	1826–1842
Samuel Thing,	1721, 2, 8	James Bell,	1843–1846
Ezekiel Gilman,	1740	Woodbridge Odlin,	1847–1849
Zebulon Giddinge,	1741	Nathaniel Gilman,	1850–1853
Peter Gilman,	1742, 54, 5, 60–68,	William B. Morrill,	1854, 5, 9, 60–66
	70–73, 6	James M. Lovering,	1856, 7
James Gilman,	1749, 50, 3	Joseph G. Hoyt,	1858
Samuel Gilman,	1751, 2, 9	Charles G. Conner,	1867–1886
John Odlin,	1756–1759	John J. Bell,	1887

REPRESENTATIVES.

Bartholomew Tippen,	1680	Samuel Thing,	1703, 13, 4, 5, 27, 8
Ralph Hall,	1680	Nicholas Gilman,	1709, 11–15, 1732
William Moore,	1681, 92	Capt. John Gilman,	1716–1722
Robert Wadleigh,	1681	Lieut. John Gilman,	1716–1722
Robert Smart,	1684	Bartholomew Thing,	1727, 8, 31–35
Thomas Wiggin,	1684	Benjamin Thing,	1730, 1
Samuel Leavitt,	1685, 92, 6, 1703	Peter Gilman,	1733, 4, 5, 7, 9, 40–42
John Folsom,	1685, 94, 5		5, 9, 52, 5, 8, 62, 5, 8
John Gilman,	1693	Edward Hall,	1736
Jonathan Thing,	1693	Samuel Hall,	1736
Moses Leavitt,	1693, 5, 8, 1702	Nathaniel Gilman,	1737, 9, 40
Theophilus Dudley,	1693, 5, 8, 1702,	Zebulon Giddinge,	1741, 5, 9, 52, 5,
	9, 11, 2		8, 62, 5, 8
Kinsley Hall,	1694, 5	Samuel Gilman,	1742
David Lawrence,	1696, 1703	John Phillips,	1755, 71

John Giddinge,	1771, 4, 5, 6		Oren Head,	1852, 3
Nathaniel Folsom,	1774, 5, 8, 82, 3		Nathaniel G. Perry,	1852, 3
Noah Emery,	1776		William Conner,	1853, 4
Thomas Odiorne,	1777		William W. Stickney,	1854
Samuel Hobart,	1777, 8		Retire H. Parker,	1854
John T. Gilman,	1779, 81, 1810, 1		James M. Lovering,	1855–1857
Ephraim Robinson,	1779, 81, 6		George F. Waters,	1855
Jedediah Jewett,	1782–1784		Jeremiah W. March,	1855, 6
Joseph Cram,	1782		Henry Shute,	1856, 7
Josiah Gilman, Jr.,	1785		Isaiah S. Brown,	1857, 8
Dudley Odlin,	1787–1790		William B. Morrill,	1858, 9
Benjamin Conner, Jr.,	1791–1803		Charles H. Bell,	1858–1860, 72, 3
Nathaniel Gilman,	1804		Nathaniel K. Leavitt,	1859, 60
George Sullivan,	1805, 13		Jewett Conner,	1860, 1
Nathaniel Parker,	1806–1809		Moses N. Collins,	1861, 2
Oliver Peabody,	1812		Charles Burley,	1861
Joseph Tilton, Jr.,	1814–1822		Abraham P. Blake,	1862, 3
John Kimball,	1820, 1		Joseph C. Hilliard,	1862, 3
William Smith, Jr.,	1822–1824		Samuel D. Wingate,	1863, 4
Oliver W. B. Peabody,	1823–1830		Nathaniel G. Giddings,	1864, 5
Jeremiah Dow,	1825–1828, 31, 2, 3		Henry C. Moses,	1864, 5
Samuel T. Gilman,	1829		Charles G. Conner,	1865, 6
Nathaniel Conner,	1829, 30		Joseph W. Merrill,	1866, 7
Jotham Lawrence,	1831		James W. Odlin,	1866, 7
John Rogers,	1832–1834		William H. Robinson,	1867, 8
John Sullivan,	1834–1837		Andrew J. Hoyt,	1868, 9
William Odlin,	1835–1837		Sebastian A. Brown,	1868, 9
William Perry,	1838		Eben Folsom,	1869, 70
Daniel Conner,	1838, 9		John G. Gilman,	1870, 1
Nathaniel Gilman, 3d,	1839, 40		John H. Kimball,	1870, 1
Samuel Hatch,	1840		George W. Furnald, .	1871
Woodbridge Odlin,	1841		Jacob Carlisle,	1872, 3
Josiah Robinson,	1841, 2		Asa Jewell,	1874, 5
Amos Tuck,	1842		John D. Lyman,	1874, 5
Theophilus Goodwin,	1843, 4		Thomas Leavitt,	1874, 5
Charles Conner,	1843, 4		Josiah J. Folsom,	1876
Gilman Marston,	1845–48, 72, 3, 76, 8, 80, 2, 4, 6		Joseph T. Porter,	1876, 7
			Horace S. Cummings,	1876
John Kelly,	1845		William Burlingame,	1877, 8
James Bell,	1846		Alfred Conner,	1877, 8
William Wadleigh,	1846–1848		Daniel Sanborn, 2d,	1878
George Gardner,	1847, 8		Winthrop N. Dow,	1878, 80
John F. Moses,	1849, 50, 1		Charles O. Moses,	1880
Nathaniel G. Gilman,	1849, 50		Andrew J. Fogg,	1882
Nathaniel Gordon,	1849, 50		John J. Bell,	1882, 4, 6
Charles J. Gilman,	1851		Edward H. Gilman,	1884
Isaac Flagg,	1851, 2		John Templeton,	1886

ECCLESIASTICAL.

CHAPTER VIII.

THE FIRST SOCIETY.

THE formation of the First church in Exeter, and the events of the pastorate of the Rev. John Wheelwright, have already been narrated. Mr. Wheelwright was not inclined to stay to witness the extension of the authority of Massachusetts over the settlement that he had founded, but removed with his family, probably in the early spring of 1643, to the almost unbroken forests of Wells, in Maine. But it would not have been like him to leave his flock without a shepherd, and accordingly we find that the people were provided with another religious teacher, Mr. Thomas Rashleigh.

Mr. Rashleigh had been admitted to the Boston church three years before, being then a student of divinity. In 1641 he had ministered "as chaplain" to the people of Cape Ann, afterwards Gloucester, in Massachusetts, where there was then no organized church. He came to Exeter in the spring of 1643, no doubt, by the desire of Mr. Wheelwright, and with some intention of making a permanent settlement there. On the sixth of May, in that year, the town granted him a house lot, and he undoubtedly continued to act as their minister during the remainder of his stay in the place, which was something less than a twelvemonth. His house lot, of which the grant must have been conditional only, was re-granted by the town, five years after he went away, to the Rev. Samuel Dudley. Why Mr. Rashleigh remained no longer is not known; though the subsequent existence of two parties in the church or town, may furnish the clue to his early departure.

In the spring of 1644 some of the inhabitants made an attempt to gather a new church in Exeter, and to call the aged Rev. Stephen Bachiler of Hampton to the ministry thereof. They went so far as to appoint a day of humiliation, on which to carry both these purposes into effect, but intelligence of their design having reached the ears of the Massachusetts General Court, that body summarily overruled it, by adopting, on the twenty-ninth of May, 1644, the following resolution :

Whereas it appears to this court that some of the inhabitants of Exeter do intend shortly to gather a church and call Mr. Bachiler to be their minister, and forasmuch as the divisions and contentions which are among the inhabitants are judged by this court to be such as for the present they cannot comfortably and with approbation proceed in so weighty and sacred affairs ; it is therefore ordered that direction should be forthwith sent to the said inhabitants to defer the gathering of any church, or other such proceeding, until this court or the court at Ipswich, upon further satisfaction of their reconciliation and fitness, shall give allowance thereunto.

On the same day the General Court passed this further order :

That Mr. Wheelwright (upon a particular, solemn and serious acknowledgment and confession by letters of his evil carriages and of the court's justice upon him for them*) hath his banishment taken off, and is received as a member of the Commonwealth.

The adoption of both the foregoing orders on the same day leaves little doubt of the willingness of the government of Massachusetts that Mr. Wheelwright should return to his charge in Exeter, if he desired. The people evidently so understood it, for immediately after learning the court's decision, they made a grant to Mr. Wheelwright, his heirs and successors forever, of certain marshland, " with these conditions, that he doth come amongst us again." The major part of the inhabitants having thus evidenced their desire for their former pastor's return, it seems unquestionable that he might have resumed his position there, to the general acceptance.

But Mr. Wheelwright, for reasons satisfactory to himself, did not choose to go back. And the project of gathering another church and of settling Mr. Bachiler over it, was very wisely abandoned. Still it is not probable that the people, a large proportion of whom were members of the church, went on without some religious ministrations. Mr. Hatevil Nutter was an " exhorting elder " of the church of Dover, and the following facts, gleaned from the records of Exeter, establish a strong probability that he was employed to minister to the spiritual wants of the

* A careful perusal of Wheelwright's second letter will show how unjust to him this statement is.

people of the latter place. Mr. Nutter was the owner of a tract of land at Lamprey river, and at least as early as the beginning of the year 1645 the town "covenanted" to inclose it with fence; and more than once betwixt that time and 1650 called upon all the inhabitants to do their shares of fencing, under the penalty of paying the wages of others, who should be hired in their stead. The town continued to render this service for the Elder for five years; and until they had provided themselves with a regular minister, the Rev. Samuel Dudley. Then, on June 11, 1650, Mr. Nutter, by his receipt upon the town book, acknowledged that the fence which the town "was engaged by covenant" to set up for him at Lamprey river, was accepted; and he was heard of no more in Exeter.

In view of Mr. Nutter's gifts as an exhorter, and in the absence of any other known or imaginable consideration for which the inhabitants could have so bound themselves to keep his land inclosed, it seems reasonable to infer that it was done in return for his services as a religious teacher among them, during that interval of five years or more, while they were without a regular minister.

ATTEMPTS TO GET A PASTOR.

But the town in the meantime did not abate their efforts to secure a resident minister. In the spring of 1646 an invitation was given to Mr. Nathaniel Norcross, a young clergyman and "an university scholar," to settle over the church; and on May 25, of that year, it was agreed that Edward Hilton and Thomas King should purchase Mr. Wheelwright's house and land, in the town's behalf, for Mr. Norcross. Sixteen of the principal citizens entered into a written agreement to be responsible to the purchasers for the price paid, in case the town should fail to fully reimburse them. But Mr. Norcross did not accept the proposal. Possibly he may have been deterred by the divisions which still continued among the people.

Those divisions were the subject of a petition presented the succeeding year to the Massachusetts General Court, the great tribunal for the redress of all grievances, civil and ecclesiastical; and the following order was passed in response thereto:

In answer to the petition of some of Exeter the court think meet that Mr. Ezekiel Rogers, Mr. Nathaniel Rogers and Mr. Norton be requested by this court and authorized to examine the grounds of the complaint, and, if it may be, to compose things amongst them; which if they cannot do, then to certify to this court what they find, and also think best to be done, which may conduce to peace and the continuance of the ordinances amongst them.

No record is found of the doings of the committee under this order, but the people of Exeter were sufficiently united, November 16, 1648, to join in a call to the Rev. William Tompson of Braintree, "a worthy servant of Christ," to become their minister. And it was voted that "in case he could be attained to come," he should be allowed by the town thirty pounds a year, and the profits that should accrue to the town from the saw-mill, and the use of the house and land which were purchased of Mr. Wheelwright, so long as he continued with them as a minister. Christopher Lawson, Edward Gilman and John Legat were appointed to present the offer to him; and if he declined it, to invite some other person, with the counsel and advice of the elders of Boston, Charlestown and Roxbury.

Mr. Tompson did not see fit to accept the call, and the town voted April 22, 1649, to invite Mr. Joseph Emerson of Rowley, to come to Exeter and be the minister there; but they met with no better success in this, than in their preceding applications.

MR. DUDLEY ENGAGED.

But at length their persistent efforts to obtain a settled pastor were rewarded by a fortunate issue, in the engagement of the Rev. Samuel Dudley. In anticipation of his coming and to provide means for his support, the town by its officers and leading citizens, on the twenty-second of April, 1650, established this order:

Every inhabitant of the town shall pay for every thousand of pipe staves he makes, two shillings, which shall be for the maintenance of the ministry; and for every thousand of hogshead staves, one shilling sixpence; and for every thousand of bolts sold before they be made into staves, four shillings; and what is due from the saw-mills shall also be for the maintenance of the ministry.

It is ordered that after the publication hereof any man that shall deliver any staves or bolts before they have satisfied the town orders, they shall pay ten shillings for every thousand staves, and twenty shillings for every thousand bolts.

And on the thirteenth of May, 1650, the following agreement was executed between a committee of the town and Mr. Dudley,

It is unanimously agreed upon by Mr. Samuel Dudley and the town of Exeter that Mr. Dudley is forthwith so soon as comfortable subsistence can be made by the town for him and his family in the house which was purchased of Mr. Wheelwright, that then the said Mr. Dudley is to come to inhabit at Exeter and to be a minister of God's word unto us, until such time as God shall be pleased to make way for the gathering of a church, and then he to be ordained our pastor or teacher according to the ordinance of God. And in consideration of this promise of Mr. Dudley, the town doth mutually agree to fit up the aforesaid house and to fence in a yard and garden for the said Mr. Dudley, and to allow forty pounds a year towards the maintenance of the said Mr. Dudley and his family; and that the use and sole improvement of the aforesaid house bought of Mr. Wheelwright, and all the lands and meadows thereunto belonging, shall be to the proper use of him the said Mr. Dudley, during the time that he shall continue to be a minister of the word amongst us. And what cost the said Mr. Dudley shall bestow about the said house and lands in the time of his improvement, the town is to allow unto him or his, so much as the said house or lands are bettered by it, at the time of the said Mr. Dudley's leaving of it either by death or by some more than ordinary call of God otherwise. And it is further agreed upon that the old cow-house, which was Mr. Wheelwright's, shall by the town be fixed up fit for the setting of cattle in, and that the aforesaid pay of £40 a year is to be made in good pay every half year, in corn and English commodities at a price current, as they go generally in the country at the time or times of payment.

To the premises which concern myself I consent unto. Witness my hand.

SAM: DUDLEY.

And for the town's performance of this part of this aforesaid agreement we whose names are hereunder written do jointly and severally engage ourselves to Mr. Dudley. Witness our hands.

EDWARD HILTON,
EDWARD GILMAN,
JOHN LEGATE,
HENRY ROBY,
JAMES WALL,
HUMPHREY WILSON.

The people of Exeter were fortunate in inducing Mr. Dudley to son-in-law of Governor John Winthrop, he had acquaintance and influence with the principal characters of the Massachusetts Bay. He was born in England about the year 1610, and passed the first twenty years of his life there, in the society of people of intelligence and position. Though not bred at the university, his education had not been neglected, and as early as 1637 he was spoken of as qualified for the clerical office, and in 1649 is said to have preached at Portsmouth, though it is not known that he was settled in the ministry before he came to Exeter. For the preceding twelve years he had resided in Salisbury, Massachusetts, where he had repeatedly served as a delegate to the General Court, and for two years had held the office of Assistant. It is evident that such a man was a great acquisition to the little community of Exeter.

The language of Mr. Dudley's contract implies that the church which was formed in Wheelwright's time had, in the seven years when it was destitute of a regular pastor, lost its organization. Whether the wished for opportunity for gathering a new church occurred during Mr. Dudley's ministry, the books of the town afford us no information.

On the twenty-sixth of June, 1650, it was ordered by the town that Francis Swain have twenty shillings for his pains and time "in going into the Bay to receive Mr. Dudley his pay." This undoubtedly refers to that clause of Mr. Dudley's contract which provided that his salary might be paid in "English commodities." Those were only to be procured from some trader in "the Bay," as Massachusetts was commonly called; and, no doubt, Mr. Swain had been employed by the town to make inquiry there for some person who was willing to exchange those commodities for lumber or such other products as the town could furnish.

It tells well for the zeal and energy of the new minister of Exeter that in six weeks from the time of his settlement, he induced the people to pass a vote to build a new meeting-house. It was on the same twenty-sixth of June, 1650, and was in these terms:

Its agreed that a meeting-house shall be built, of twenty foot square, so soon as workmen can conveniently be procured to do it, and the place appointed for it is at the corner of William Taylor's lot next the street, and William Taylor is to have of the town 20 s. for five rods square of his land in that place.

This location was undoubtedly upon the elevation on the western side of the salt river afterwards known as "meeting-house hill."

It is in the northerly skirt of the present village, near where Summer street unites with the road to Newmarket. There is little question, too, that an earlier place of worship had been situated near the same spot, probably a little northwesterly of it, surrounded, in the English fashion of the time, by a yard for the burial of the dead. On December 29, 1651, the town gave Mr. Dudley liberty to fence "the piece of ground where the graves are, and to have the use of it for grazing or feeding of cattle whilst he stays in Exeter, but not to break up the said land." Uniform tradition points out this spot as the earliest churchyard. The surface of the ground is covered with clay, and is now utilized for the manufacture of drain tiles. There was formerly a brick-yard there. From time to time the decayed remains of human bones have been exhumed from the soil, which gave occasion for the remark, respecting a certain brick house erected in the town a couple of generations ago, that it was "built from the dust of our ancestors!"

No doubt even the light burden which the town had assumed in their contract with their minister weighed somewhat heavily upon some of the poor parishioners, for an order was agreed upon, December 5, 1650, that the townsmen should have power to "make a rate upon all such of the inhabitants of the town as do not voluntarily bring in according to their abilities, for the satisfying of the town's engagement unto Mr. Dudley for his maintenance."

On the same day the town authorized Francis Swain or Henry Roby, if they could, to bargain with some able merchant in the Bay, to furnish Mr. Dudley, in exchange for hogshead and pipe staves, forty pounds' worth of good English commodities, in the following May, for his year's maintenance.

Before Mr. Dudley had lived a year in the town he had so won the favor and confidence of his people, that they volunteered to defend his reputation when it was assailed by the tongue of slander. On the nineteenth of February, 1651, they authorized "the present townsmen, Henry Roby, Thomas King and John Legate, to vindicate the credit and reputation of Mr. Dudley against the reproachful speeches and calumniation of John Garland, by proceeding against him in law, according to the demerit of his [offence]." This John Garland had, a few months before, been accused of taking the town's timber as an inhabitant, without sufficient warrant. It is not at all unlikely that Mr. Dudley, who stood up manfully for the rights of his parishioners, was forward in making the accusation, and thus incurred the ill-will and "reproachful speeches" of his defamer. It is not known that a suit was brought; but is more probable that the slanders were retracted and apologies made.

On the first of September, 1651, it was determined that John Warren should "go into the Bay to receive the town's pay of Mr. Kimball for Mr. Dudley." The repeated negotiations for the forty pounds' worth of English commodities had, therefore, been brought to a successful termination.

NEW HOUSE OF WORSHIP.

The meeting-house, which was resolved upon more than a year previously, was not yet built, but it was now voted to complete it, by the primitive expedient of requiring all the inhabitants to contribute their personal labor for the purpose. The order was passed September 1, 1651, as follows:

That the meeting-house shall begin to be built upon the next second day [Monday], and a rate to be made how much work every man shall do towards it, and so be called forth to work upon it by Thomas King and John Legate, as need shall require; that the work be not neglected till it be finished; and that every man that neglects to come to work upon a day's warning shall pay 5 shillings the day, to be forthwith seized by the constable.

In spite of this peremptory vote, however, the meeting-house was not erected, nor apparently even begun, for more than three-fourths of a year afterwards.

The following order was therefore passed, July 8, 1652:

It is ordered that a meeting-house shall forthwith be built, and that every man, both servants as well as others, shall come forth to work upon it, as they are called out by the surveyors of the work, upon the penalty of 5 s. a day for their neglect; and teams are to be brought forth to the work by the owners, as they are called for by the said surveyors, upon the penalty of 10 s. a day for their neglect. And the surveyors or overseers appointed for the said work are Mr. Edward Gilman, Thomas King and Edward Hilton, Jr., and they are to see the work finished and not to have it neglected.

There is little doubt that this attempt proved successful, and that the meeting-house was substantially completed within the year. On the twenty-third of October, 1652, John Robinson and John Gilman were chosen as overseers of work on the meeting-house in place of Edward Gilman and Edward Hilton, the former of whom was about to sail for England, and the latter was immersed in his private business; and in August of the year following, a return of commissioners appointed by the General Court of Massachusetts to lay out the western bounds of Hampton, refers to the "Exeter meeting-house" as an accomplished fact. It is, however, a pathetic illustration of the narrow resources and poverty of the early settlers, that though their purpose was to build merely the most primitive structure, only twenty feet in extent, probably of squared logs, and furnished with rude benches of boards as they came from the saw-mill, yet in order to accomplish it, they were obliged to impress the services of every inhabitant and servant, and to occupy more than two years of time. The poor building, however, with some additions, had to serve them as a place of worship for over forty years.

DIFFICULTY OF PAYING SALARY.

The task of raising Mr. Dudley's stipend was found no easy one. Not every person who had the means, had also the disposition to contribute. Captain Thomas Wiggin, as has been elsewhere stated, resided in what was known as the Squamscot patent, which was not within any township. He was, however, presumably a member of Mr. Dudley's congregation, being rated as such. But he was not prompt in paying his rates, and on the fifteenth of December, 1653, the town voted that "the selectmen have power to take some course with Captain Wiggin about Mr. Dudley's rate, as they shall see meet." How the captain adjusted the matter at the time is unknown;* but a few years afterwards, on May 6, 1657, he induced the General Court of Massachusetts to pass an act making his house and property taxable in the town of Hampton. This gave him such vantage ground over the people of Exeter that they could not take any legal "course" with him, however delinquent he might prove; and they were fain to resort to negotiation. On March 4, 1658, they empowered Mr. Dudley and Mr. [Edward] Hilton "to treat with Captain Wiggin, and to agree with him what annual payment he is to make to the town

---

* As the captain was a large holder of land, it is possible that he turned over to the town some tracts of it, to balance the account. The town certainly received from him certain "land and meadow," for which no other consideration is known.

towards bearing the charges of the public ministry." Thereafter, of course, the captain paid no more than he chose to pay. But this episode has carried us a little in advance of our main story.

After the expiration of five years the charge of maintaining a minister was found almost too onerous for the town, which had lost some of its inhabitants, and was otherwise incapacitated, and on June 13, 1655, a new agreement was made with Mr. Dudley to this effect:

By reason of the town's decreasing and other disabilities, the town cannot well bear the burden of paying him forty pounds a year as their minister, and he is not willing to urge from them what they could not comfortably discharge, therefore, the contract between them, recorded on the town books, is annulled, and he lays down his place as a minister; and what exercises he shall perform on the Sabbath day he does as a private person; for the present summer he promises to perform them constantly; afterwards he is to be at liberty. But so long as he continues at Exeter he promises to be helpful, what he may with convenience, either in his own house or some other which may be appointed for the Sabbath exercises.

The inhabitants of the town have sold Mr. Dudley that dwelling house wherein he lives, cow-house, house lot and meadow with the commonage and the appurtenances for which he pays fifty pounds, twenty of which being half of the rate due him the present year; fifteen for which the town is behindhand for former rates; and fifteen pounds "in respect of what labor shall be performed this present summer."

And should said Dudley remove his family from the town he promises to offer the said premises to the town for the same price of fifty pounds to be paid in corn, and English goods, or in neat cattle at an appraisal; and in case of his decease his family may occupy the premises for a year and then the town shall have the said offer.

Said Dudley will require nothing of the town for what pains he shall take in performing Sabbath exercises after this summer.

Any cost or charge laid out upon the house by said Dudley after he pays for it, shall be reimbursed to him to the extent of the additional value thereof, in case of purchase by the town.

The contract signed by   SAMUEL DUDLEY,
                          JOHN GILMAN,
                          THOMAS PETTIT,   } for the

In the following spring the people made a new attempt to insure a suitable support to their minister. On the twenty-eighth of April, 1656, it was agreed that for the maintenance of the public ordinances, all the saw-mills belonging to the town should be rated, as follows : the old mill upon the fall, seven pounds ; Humphrey Wilson's mill, seven pounds ; the new mill of John Gilman, six pounds ; Mr. Hilton's mill, five pounds. Those who made pipe staves should pay three shillings a thousand, and those who made barrel staves two shillings a thousand therefor ; all for the maintenance of the ministry. And in case any maker should send away any staves without acquainting the town therewith, he should forfeit to the town ten shillings for every thousand so sent away. In consideration of the saw-mills being so rated, they were to be freed from the rate which they formerly were to pay the town ; " but when the ministry faileth, the old covenant to be of force."

FEARS OF LOSING MR. DUDLEY.

In the autumn of the same year the people of Portsmouth made an attempt, in which they were nearly successful, to induce Mr. Dudley to quit Exeter and settle in that place. They voted, on the twenty-seventh of October, to give him an invitation to be their minister, and to pay him a salary of eighty pounds a year. Their selectmen were appointed a committee to present him the vote, and to close a contract with him. On November 10 they waited upon him and acquainted him with the proposal.

He is said to have acceded to it, and agreed to visit them the next spring. But the prospect of losing their minister stimulated the people of Exeter to renewed exertions to retain him. This is the record of their action :

At a full town meeting in this place legally warned the 8 day of June 1657, it was ordered and agreed that so long as Mr. Dudley shall be a minister in the town, the town is to pay him fifty pounds yearly in merchantable pine boards and in merchantable pipe staves at the current price ; if the boards and staves do not reach the said sum, the remainder to be paid in merchantable corn. Furthermore the dwelling house, house lots and other lots and the meadow on the west side of the Exeter river, all formerly Mr. Wheelwright's, shall be confirmed unto Mr. Dudley, his heirs and assigns from this time forever, notwithstanding any promise or engagement to the contrary.

The selectmen of the town shall yearly, as aforesaid, gather up the said sum, and in case they be defective herein, to be answerable to the town for their default, and to pay themselves what is not gathered up by them.

This last provision certainly indicates that the office of selectman, in the olden time, was no sinecure! The action of the town, however, induced Mr. Dudley to forego any design he may have had of leaving Exeter, and he was content to accept the smaller stipend and continue among his old parishioners. The people were not ungrateful, as the numerous grants of lands and privileges from time to time made him by the town bear testimony. And that they had implicit confidence in his integrity may be gathered from the final proviso in the following resolution, passed in town meeting March 4, 1658:

It was granted to Samuel Dudley that tract of land between Griffin Mountague's house lot and Mr. Stanyan's creek, lying all on the right hand of the path next to the river, upon consideration of drawing out all the grants in the town book or any other necessary orders contained in the same, which grants or orders are to be fairly written; provided that if there be any grant or order recorded formerly in any town book to hinder this grant, then this grant to Samuel Dudley to be of no effect, otherwise to stand in force.

From time to time, afterwards, orders were adopted by the town for the purpose of facilitating the collection of Mr. Dudley's salary.

On the twenty-eighth of March, 1662, it was ordered that for every thousand of heading and barrel staves that were got out, there should be eighteen pence allowed to the town's use, "that is, to the ministry."

On the twenty-fifth of April, 1664, it was voted that Captain John Clark's mill should pay five pounds annually to the public ministry.

And on the same day it was determined that "a lean-to" should be added to the meeting-house, with a chimney, which should serve as a watch-house.

A lean-to, in the parlance of the time, was an addition, usually of one room, with a single sloping roof, like a shed, such as used to be often attached to the rear of old-fashioned houses.

On the fifteenth of March, 1668, it was voted that Lieutenant Ralph Hall have full power given him to arrest and sue any inhabitants who refused to pay to the rate of the ministry, which he was authorized to gather up or to collect by distraint.

On the tenth of July, 1671, it was ordered that "instead of the selectmen gathering up the minister's rate, Mr. Dudley is from this time forward to gather up his rate himself, and instead of £40 yearly as heretofore, there is now granted to him £60 in such kind of pay as hath been formerly agreed of." The selectmen were to make the rate yearly, and in case any inhabitant should refuse to pay his rate, the selectmen were to empower Mr. Dudley to "get it by the constable."

Matters were now so well arranged between parson and people that no further action of the town appears to have been necessary for a considerable period. But only five years after the last entry, a most surprising and unaccountable thing was done at the Hampton court; the town of Exeter was presented for "letting their meeting-house lie open and common for cattle to go into," and the selectmen were ordered under a penalty of five pounds to cleanse the house, and have the doors hung, and shut tight, etc. This accusation has a formidable sound, and on the face of it would convey the impression that the town was guilty of gross negligence, nearly approaching to sacrilege. But that cannot be believed of a people who were maintaining at no small cost, a minister of high character and much energy and influence. It would rather seem to be the result of an accident of a day, exaggerated to the court by some malicious mischief-maker. Those were days of few door fastenings, and of many indictments. Nothing further being heard of the present case, it is to be presumed that all suitable amends were made for the misadventure, whatever it might have been.

Two years after this, on the first of April, 1678, Jonathan Thing, John Folsom, Jr., Jonathan Robinson and Theophilus Dudley were chosen tithing men; the first instance of the election of such officers in the town, so far as the records show.

On the eighteenth of February, 1679, the following order was made by the selectmen, for the better accommodation of the church-goers:

At the request of Jonathan Thing, Edward Gilman, Edward Smith, Peter Folsom, Nathaniel Ladd, Moses Leavitt, for the erecting of a gallery at the end of the men's gallery, for their wives, it is granted unto them the privilege thereof, provided they build the same upon their own charge, leaving also room to build another end gallery if the same be required. Also, the gallery wherein Edward Smith, Biley Dudley, Edward Gilman and the rest do sit in, and have upon their own proper charges built, we do further confirm and allow of.

The "other end gallery" was soon required. On the second of July, 1680, the north end of the meeting-house was granted to Mrs. Sarah Wadleigh, Sarah Young, Alice Gilman, Abigail Wadleigh, Ephraim Marston's wife, Grace Gilman and Mary Lawrence, "there to erect and set up another gallery adjoining the other women's."

Thus it appears that the little meeting-house of twenty feet square, which had been outwardly enlarged by the addition of a lean-to with a chimney, had had its interior capacity increased by two galleries, and was now about to receive a third. This denotes not only a larger population, but surely no diminution of religious interest.

In the year 1680 the town passed out of the jurisdiction of Massachusetts, under the newly established royal provincial government of New Hampshire. The most notable effect which the change produced in parochial affairs, was to make the minister's rate payable on the twentieth of March, instead of one month later, as before.

DEATH OF MR. DUDLEY.

There was no visible sign of failure of the powers, physical or mental, of Mr. Dudley, as he drew on to old age. When he was sixty-nine, he was appointed upon a committee for the equal distribution of the town lands, a duty which no feeble man would have been selected to perform. And during the four years of life which still remained to him, we do not learn that his natural force had abated, or that he failed to minister acceptably to the wants of his people. He died in Exeter on the tenth of February, 1683, at the age of seventy-three years.

In his death the people of the town suffered a serious loss. He had become to them, in his thirty-three years of service, much more than a religious teacher. He was an important member of the civil community, an intelligent farmer, a considerable mill owner, a sound man of business, and the legal adviser and scrivener of the entire people. The town intrusted him with its important affairs, and he in return was the stanch defender of its interests. It is true that he always had a sharp eye to his own advantage, but he had a large family to provide for, and he was never accused of wrong or dishonesty. He was a gentleman of "good capacity and learning" in his profession, and a sincere and useful minister. Fortunate was it for Exeter that in its feeble stage it was favored with the counsel and example of a man of such goodness, and wisdom and practical sagacity.

Mr. Dudley's remains rest in the neglected burying-ground just south of the gas-house, on Water street, and, no doubt, beneath a stone slab from which the inscription-plate has disappeared.

He was thrice married, first in 1632 or '33, to Mary, the daughter of Governor John Winthrop of Massachusetts, who died in about ten years; second, to Mary Byley of Salisbury, who died in Exeter about a year after her husband was settled there; and third, to Elizabeth, whose family name is not known. He had children by each marriage, and in all ten sons and eight daughters, five or six of whom died before reaching maturity. But several of each were married, and lived in Exeter, and their descendants are still numerous in the vicinity.

For several years after the decease of Mr. Dudley, the town was without a settled pastor. The records are wanting between 1682 and the latter part of 1689, and no tradition has survived to tell us what religious privileges were within the reach of the inhabitants during that period. But it is not to be supposed that a people who had recently provided increased accommodations in their meeting-house would long permit them to go unimproved. It is altogether probable that temporary engagements were made with such clergymen as could be procured, to perform clerical duty. From outside sources we learn that in the latter part of 1684 the Rev. John Cotton, son of the Rev. Seaborn Cotton of Hampton, was living, and officiating, in a ministerial capacity, in Exeter, but how long he continued there, we cannot ascertain. From that time forward we have no definite information, until October 6, 1690, when the town

Voted, That Elder William Wentworth is to be treated with for his continuance with us in the work of the ministry in this town for one complete year ensuing. The men chosen to treat with him are Biley Dudley, Kinsley Hall and Moses Leavitt.

William Wentworth, when just arrived at man's estate, was one of the original settlers of Exeter. After a residence there of five years, he quitted the place, in company with Mr. Wheelwright, and tarried a while in Wells, and then established his permanent home in Dover. There he had become a leading elder in the church. And now, after near half a century's absence, he was called back to the scene of his earliest American experience, to occupy the honorable and responsible post of religious teacher. How long he had already so officiated in Exeter we have not the data to determine, but as he was to be employed to "continue" his work there, it is clear that this was not the beginning of it. Nor was it the end; for on October 6, 1691, William Moore and Peter Coffin were chosen to treat with Elder Wentworth to supply and carry on the work of the ministry in the town the ensuing year; and on March 30, 1693, after having voted that the salary payable to the minister shall be accounted a necessary town charge, the town agreed with Mr. William Wentworth "to supply and perform the office of a minister one whole year, if he be able; and if performed, the town do promise to pay him the sum of forty pounds in current pay, or proportionable to any part of the year."

But Mr. Wentworth had reached the age of seventy-eight years, and, though his life was still somewhat further prolonged, he had probably become unable, by reason of natural infirmities, to comply with their proposal. It soon became necessary, therefore, to look elsewhere for a minister.

CHAPTER IX.

THE FIRST SOCIETY AND ITS OFFSHOOTS.

The first step which the town took for the purpose of finding a suitable minister was highly characteristic of the simplicity of the times and of the deference then paid to the judgment of the clergy. On the twenty-third of June, 1693, John Gilman and Biley Dudley were selected in behalf of the town "to go to the neighboring ministers and take their advice for a meet person to supply the office of the ministry in the town of Exeter."

In less than three months the desired person was found, and on the eighteenth of September, John Gilman, Peter Coffin and Robert Wadleigh were appointed to "treat with Mr. John Clark, and procure him to come to this town to be our minister." A month later, it was voted to empower the same committee to "agree with Rev. John Clark to be our minister, and what salary they do agree with him for the first half year, the town do engage to pay."

There is every reason to believe that Mr. Clark was at once engaged, and that he performed satisfactorily his clerical functions in Exeter during the stipulated six months; for at the end of that period, on the twentieth of April, 1694, the town began to take measures for securing a parsonage.

Peter Coffin, Robert Wadleigh and Richard Hilton were chosen in behalf of the town to treat with and buy from Captain John Gilman, Moses Gilman, Sr., Humphrey Wilson, Samuel Leavitt, John Folsom, Peter Folsom, Jonathan Thing and John Wadleigh, "a certain house and land lying and being near unto the present meeting-house, and to be improved by the town for the use and benefit of the ministry of the town for the time being; and what they agree therefor, the town will pay by way of rate upon the inhabitants, as the law directs; and the committee is empowered to finish the house and make it habitable for the minister forthwith, and to repair the fences about the land, and to inquire the expense of redeeming the marsh at Wheelwright's creek, commonly called the town marsh; and whatever the committee judge to be due for the premises to report to the selectmen, and they to make rate for the same upon the inhabitants."

A later record, however, renders it unlikely that the authorized purchase was ever made. The house referred to was situated near "the present meeting-house;" but it was soon after determined to build a new place of worship, which the town located at quite a distance from the former; and in view of that contingency the committee very probably thought the selection of a parsonage were better postponed.

On the twenty-fifth of April, 1695, the town gave authority to the selectmen to make a "Ratt (rate) for the use of the ministry according to the province law."

A NEW MEETING-HOUSE.

In the following January the important question of erecting a new house of worship was mooted; and at a town meeting held on the twentieth day of that month, after debate in the matter, the major part of the freeholders of the town voted that there was great need to build a meeting-house, "where the worship and service of God may be performed, and that the same should be erected on the hill between the great fort and Nat. Folsom's barn." Peter Coffin, Samuel Leavitt and Moses Leavitt were appointed building committee.

This location was upon the little elevation on which the First church now stands. Old residents remember that there was formerly more of an ascent than now from the street to the church, which has been diminished, perhaps, by the continual raising of the grade of the road-bed and the sidewalk.

It was afterwards ordered that Captain Coffin should keep the account of the inhabitants' labor upon the meeting-house, and that men should have but three shillings a day for their work, and lads what the committee should order.

The meeting-house was completed in due time, and was, of course, much more spacious than the little building which it superseded. It stood, perhaps, a little nearer to the street than the present First church, and had doors at the east and west ends, the pulpit on the north side, and stairs leading to a women's gallery on the south side. Round the walls were erected the pews, the privilege of which was purchased by the well-to-do worshippers, and the middle space was probably occupied with benches. These latter seats were public property, and were assigned to the members of the congregation who had no pews, according to seniority and social position, probably, by a committee chosen for the purpose.

On the seventh of December, 1696, the new structure was so far completed that the first assemblage of the town for business purposes was held in it; when Joseph Smith of Hampton and John March of Greenland (?) were chosen to decide the controversy among the inhabitants about "seating" the meeting-house, that is, designating the seats to be occupied by the several families and individuals of the congregation who had not pews. It was a difficult and delicate task to give to every one just the place to which he considered himself entitled, and the referees were authorized to select an umpire in case they could not agree. And in order that they might have the assistance of persons acquainted with the standing and claims of all the parties interested, the town appointed Peter Coffin, Moses Leavitt, Theophilus Dudley and William Moore, to meet the referees and "lay the case before them," within sixteen days.

But seating the meeting-house was apparently no easy matter, for it was not until more than a year had passed that the business was finally settled. At a town meeting held February 3, 1698, it was voted that "the new meeting-house should be seated by the committee now chosen, William Moore, John Smart, Biley Dudley, Kinsley Hall, Samuel Leavitt and Moses Leavitt, and they have full power to seat the people in their places, and to grant places for pews to whom they seem meet; and those men that have places for pews shall sit in them with their families, and 'not be seated nowhere else.'"

And on the same day the committee assigned places for pews to the following persons:

To Kinsley Hall, his wife and five children, at the west door.
To Moses Leavitt and his family, at the left hand of said Hall's pew.
To Edward Hilton, for himself and wife, and son Winthrop, and his wife and two daughters, Mary and Sobriety, on the north side of the meeting-house joining to the pulpit and Moses Leavitt's pew.
To Richard Hilton, for himself, and wife and four children, his mother and sister Rebecca, on the north side of the meeting-house joining to the parsonage pew.

To Mr. [Humphrey] Wilson and his wife, and his son Thomas, and two daughters, Martha Wilson and Mary, and Elizabeth Gilman, joining to Richard Hilton's pew on the east side of the meeting-house.

To Nicholas Gilman and his wife, and John Gilman, and Alice and Catharine Gilman, joining to Mr. Wilson's pew and the east door.

To Captain Robert Wadleigh and his wife, and his son Jonathan Wadleigh, at the south side of the meeting-house joining to the women's stairs.

To Robert Coffin and his wife, and Elizabeth Coffin, and the widow Coffin and her children, joining to Captain Wadleigh's pew.

To Jeremiah Gilman and his family, joining to the south door.

To Simon Wiggin and his family, joining to Jeremiah Gilman's pew.

In the meantime the new minister appears to have conducted in his office in a most discreet and satisfactory fashion, so that on November 4, 1697, the town gave him "one hundred acres of land upon the neck, provided he lives in the town ten years after this, and if he should die before the end of ten years, the land to fall to his heirs." It was also voted to add ten pounds to his salary "if he take care of the parsonage [lands] and provide himself with wood." And on March 28, 1698, the town voted that Mr. Clark "be considered for what charge he be out upon the hundred acres of land, provided he be drowf (drove?) away out of town within seven years after the grant."

On the twenty-sixth of August, 1698, this definite arrangement was made with Mr. Clark for his stipend:

Whereas it was agreed with Rev. Mr. Clark that he should have 60 l. salary, but now voted that he shall have 10 l. more to find him in firewood and keep the fences in repair, being 70 l. in all, together with use of parsonage lands and meadows.

And at the same time:

Voted, That a church be gathered, and Mr. Clark ordained September 21, and a day of humiliation be held the 7 day of same month, and Captain Peter Coffin, Captain [Kinsley] Hall and Theophilus Dudley were chosen to make provision for same.

RE-ORGANIZATION OF THE CHURCH.

Accordingly, on the day fixed, the young minister duly received ordination at the hands of several neighboring clergymen, and was placed in charge of the church, which had been re-organized on the Sunday preceding, when a covenant and confession of faith were subscribed by the following members:

John Clark, pastor	Peter Coffin
John Gilman	William Moore
Thomas Wiggin	Kinsley Hall.
Nicholas Gilman	Richard Glidden
Theophilus Dudley	Elizabeth Gilman
Samuel Leavitt	Elizabeth Clark
Byley Dudley	Judith Wilson
Moses Leavitt	Margaret Bean
John Folsom	Sarah Dudley
Henry Wadleigh	Deborah Sinkler
Jonathan Robinson	Deborah Coffin
Thomas Dudley	Sarah Sewell
John Scrivener	Mehitabel Smith

There must have been an understanding that the town was also to furnish a habitation for the minister, which had not been complied with, since on the first of May, 1699, it was voted to pay Mr. Clark one hundred pounds, in consideration that he relinquished his claim for a parsonage house during his life.

The new church was not considered quite complete without some means of calling the congregation together, and on the fifth of September, 1699, it was voted that a bell should be bought of Mr. Coffin for the use of the town, and Henry Wadleigh and Samuel Thing were appointed to agree with him for it, and get it hung. From that time to the present, now nearly two hundred years, the summons to the inhabitants to assemble for public worship on Sundays, and the proclamation of mid-day and of nine o'clock at night on every day of the year, have been rung out from the towers of the successive meeting-houses of the First church.

The estimation in which Mr. Clark continued to be held by his people, is shown by a vote of the town, passed the first Monday of April, 1704, that his rate be made distinct by itself, and that a contribution be forthwith set up for him. The "contribution" is understood to mean a box for the offerings of casual attendants at church. Such gifts were termed "strangers' money," and the purpose of the town was to appropriate them to the benefit of the pastor.

At the annual meeting of the town, on the first Monday of April, 1705, it was decided that the old meeting-house should be sold by the selectmen, and a school-house built at the town's charge, and set below Jonathan Thing's house next the river.

DEATH OF MR. CLARK.

But on July 25, 1705, the connection so happily formed between the town and its minister was dissolved by his death, at the early age of thirty-five. Mr. Clark was a son of Nathaniel and Elizabeth (Somersby) Clark of Newbury, Massachusetts, and was born January 24, 1670. He graduated from Harvard College at the age of twenty, and married Elizabeth, daughter of the Rev. Benjamin Woodbridge of Medford, Massachusetts. Mrs. Clark's grandmother was a sister of the Rev. Samuel Dudley, and Mr. Clark's widow married the Rev. John Odlin, and was the mother of the Rev. Woodbridge Odlin, both of Exeter; so that the settled clergymen of the town from 1650 to 1776, more than a century and a quarter, were connected by the ties of blood or marriage.

Mr. Clark left four children, and an estate appraised at about a thousand pounds, of which his "library of books" was valued at twenty pounds. He was a man of piety and much usefulness, and had evidently attached his people to him in an extraordinary degree. They paid to his widow the full amount of his salary, and erected a tomb over his remains at the expense of the town, and made repairs upon it, twenty years afterwards. His body reposes in the yard of the First church, and over it were inscribed these lines :

> A prophet lies under this stone,
> His words shall live, tho' he be gone,
> When preachers die what rules the pulpit gave
> Of living, are still preached from the grave.
> The faith and life which your dear Pastor taught
> Now in the grave with him, sirs, bury not.

On the first of August, 1705, the town took the primary steps for finding a successor to the Rev. Mr. Clark, by appointing Peter Coffin, Samuel Leavitt and Moses Leavitt to "take care of the ministers who come to preach, till a day of humiliation, which was fixed for the last day of August, and to take advice of said ministers or of any whom they see good, where the town may be supplied with a minister suitable for the town."

On the third of September, Samuel Leavitt, Moses Leavitt, Theophilus Dudley, Simon Wiggin, Richard Hilton and Jonathan

Thing were chosen a committee to provide preaching for three months; and Nicholas Gilman and Jonathan Thing, to "give Mr. Adams, Mr. Whiting or Mr. Curwin (?) a call to carry on the work of the ministry among us;" their time and expenses to be paid by the town.

On the twelfth of November, 1705, Peter Coffin, Samuel Leavitt and Moses Leavitt were appointed a committee to call a minister, in order to a full settlement, if the town and said minister agree; and at a town meeting on the first Monday of April, 1706, it was voted to give Mr. [John] Odlin a call "to carry on the work of the ministry in this town, and that the following persons be empowered to make full agreement with Mr. Odlin about salary and other things needful, viz.: Peter Coffin, Winthrop Hilton, Theophilus Dudley, Richard Hilton, Samuel Leavitt, Moses Leavitt, Simon Wiggin, David Lawrence, Theophilus Smith and Samuel Thing."

ENGAGEMENT OF MR. JOHN ODLIN.

The committee agreed with Mr. Odlin that he should receive seventy pounds a year salary, with the use of the parsonage lands and meadow, and the "strangers' contribution money," and two hundred acres of land on the commons, and one hundred pounds besides, in three payments within one year; also five pounds yearly for wood, "if the town see it convenient." And on the next annual meeting on the first Monday of April, 1707, it was voted that "the contribution be set up, and begin next Sabbath, and the inhabitants to paper their moneys with their names upon the paper; and they that don't paper, it shall be accounted strangers' money."

The Rev. Mr. Odlin was ordained over the society on the twelfth of November, 1706, being then in the twenty-fourth year of his age. As he had on the twenty-first of the preceding October married Mrs. Elizabeth Clark, the widow of his predecessor, it is probable that he had preached in Exeter for some time before. For some years after his settlement, very little appears upon the records in relation to parochial affairs; evidence that minister and people were well satisfied with one another.

At the annual town meeting in 1711, it was determined that the minister's rate be made single by itself, for time to come; and in 1713 ten pounds were added to Mr. Odlin's salary, making it eighty pounds a year. Again in 1718 the town voted another increase of ten pounds to Mr. Odlin's salary, and the selectmen were empowered to make a rate for the same. There were two very good reasons for these increments of salary; first, the enlargement of the minister's family by the birth of four or five children, and second, the introduction of paper currency, which raised the prices of the necessaries of life. The latter cause went on increasing, as we shall see later, for a generation and more.

In 1720 the town voted to add still another ten pounds to Mr. Odlin's salary; in 1722 to make the minister's rate by itself, to be paid in cash, and that the selectmen raise money to repair the meeting-house, what is necessary; and in 1725 voted another increase of twenty pounds to the salary.

PARISH OF NEWMARKET SET OFF.

Up to the year 1727 the whole township of Exeter was a single parish. Its dimensions, if it had been a perfect square, would have been more than nine miles on every side. The labors of the minister, in performing his pastoral duties throughout such an extent of territory, must have been extremely arduous; while the scattered inhabitants in the more distant parts of the town were often deprived of the privilege of attending religious worship. It is not strange, therefore, that the little communities of outlying inhabitants, as soon as they were strong enough to maintain ministers for themselves, desired to be cut loose from the mother parish. But as the law then stood, all residents in a town were liable to taxation to support the established ministry in it, unless they were released from the obligation by the consent of a majority of the inhabitants, or by a legislative enactment.

The first part of old Exeter to ask a separation for parochial purposes, was the northeastern quarter, the territory which now constitutes in the main, the towns of Newmarket and South Newmarket. A petition for that object, subscribed by upwards of thirty of the residents of that section, was in the early part of the year 1727 presented to the selectmen; and at a meeting of the town held on the ninth of October, 1727, it was

Voted, That the petitioners of the north part of the town (being more than 30 in number) shall be set off to be a parish by themselves, and bounded as follows: beginning at the south side of Major Nicholas Gilman's farm, next to the town, beginning at the salt river and from thence to run a cross northwest line 4 miles into the woods, and from thence to run a north and by east line while it comes to Dover line, and so bounding upon Dover line east and by north to the extent of the town's bounds, and so bounding upon the salt water to the bounds first mentioned; *provided* that the above said parish do settle an orthodox minister and do pay the minister themselves at their own charge, that then the said new parish shall be excused from paying to the ministry of the old parish.

The new parish, which received the name of Newmarket, was incorporated December 15, 1727. But apparently it was not till more than five years afterwards, that it was fully emancipated from its obligations to pay taxes to Exeter for municipal purposes.

A NEW MEETING-HOUSE.

In 1728, November 16, at a meeting of the "First parish in Exeter," a vote was passed that a new meeting-house should be built and set on "some part of that land which the present meeting-house standeth on, which land the town purchased of Captain Peter Coffin for that use."

This resolution was probably rendered necessary by the increase of population consequent on the termination of the Indian wars. Men had now ceased to carry their guns with them to church, and the tide of immigration into the frontier settlements had resumed its normal flow.

But the early meeting-houses were of slow growth, and it was nearly a year later before the next step was taken. On the eighth of October, 1729, it was voted that the proposed meeting-house should be sixty feet long and forty-five feet wide, and have two tiers of galleries. And at an adjourned meeting,

Voted, That the meeting-house to be built shall stand near our present meeting-house where our committee shall order; shall be built and finished as soon as may be with economy within two years; that there be as many pews built therein as may be with conveniency, and sold by the committee to those that will pay down the money for them for paying for the building of the house; that the committee shall be allowed nothing for their trouble and charge until the house be finished, and then no more than what shall be allowed them by a committee of three men chosen by the inhabitants to examine their accounts. Major John Gilman, Jonathan Wadleigh, Nicholas Gordon, Bartholomew Thing and John Robinson were chosen committee to carry on the work.

On the next annual meeting of the town March 30, 1730, it was

Voted, That those inhabitants of the First parish who are desirous of having a steeple to the meeting-house now a-building, shall have liberty to build and join a steeple to the said house, provided it be built wholly by subscription and no charge to the town.

The meeting-house was raised July 7 and 8, 1730, and completed, with due economy no doubt, within the stipulated period of two years, so that it was occupied on Thanksgiving day, August 28, 1731. John Folsom is said to have been the master workman. The dimensions of the building were fixed by vote of the town. It had two galleries and a broad aisle running up to the pulpit, on each side of which were benches for those of the congregation who did not own pews. They were assigned seats by a committee, who took into consideration their several ages, infirmities and social standing. The pews were generally situated around the sides of the house, and appear to have been thirty-two in number, besides ten in the lower gallery. In March and April, 1731, the pews on the main floor were sold, and were purchased at the prices and by the persons named below:

No.			
14	to Maj. Nicholas Gilman for	£21.	
24	Capt. Theophilus Smith	16.	
15	Lieut. Bartholomew Thing	21.	
20	Dr. Thomas Dean	15.	
30	Capt. Eliphalet Coffin	18.10	
19	Capt. Peter Gilman	13.10	
31	Dea. Thomas Wilson	13.	
13	Jonathan Gilman	23.	
10	Nathaniel Webster	11.	
21	Francis Bowden	12.	
12	Samuel Conner	20.	
32	Edward Ladd	17.	
22	Capt. Jonathan Wadleigh	15.	
25	Capt. James Leavitt	16.	
23	Lieut. John Robinson	20.	
5	Benjamin Thing	12.10	
4	Nathaniel Bartlett	16.10	
9	Samuel Gilman	13.	
18	Daniel Gilman	13.5	
6	Dea. John Lord	12.15	
16	Nathaniel Gilman	17.	
8	Mrs. Hannah Hall	13.5	

No.			
3	to Ezekiel Gilman for	£20.	
29	Caleb Gilman	17.	
27	Thomas Webster	17.	
11	Capt. John Gilman, Jr.	21.	
28	Jeremiah Conner	20.10	
7	Col. John Gilman	13.5	
2	Jonathan Conner	21.15	
1	Mr. John Odlin	15.	
17	Col. John Gilman	12.13	

And on the seventh of November, 1731, the following sales were made of pews in the lower gallery:

No.			
9	to Col. John Gilman for	£10.	
1	Nicholas Gordon	12.5	
5	Bartholomew Thing	10.5	
6	Jeremiah Conner	10.5	
7	Richard Smith	13.	
8	Daniel Thing	11.	
4	Philip Conner	11.	
10	Joseph Thing	10.	
3	Nathaniel Webster	12.	
2	William Doran	12.	

Agreeably to permission given by the town a high steeple was erected upon the structure at the west end thereof, at the charge of a number of public-spirited citizens, who afterwards, on April 4, 1639, transferred the ownership thereof to the town on the re-payment of the cost, about one hundred and fifteen pounds. Peter Gilman and Nathaniel Gilman were the building committee of the steeple, and the contributors thereto were

John Gilman	Daniel Gilman
Nicholas Gilman	William Lampson
Nicholas Gilman, Jr.	Abraham Folsom
Peter Coffin	Ephraim Philbrick
Samuel Gilman	Jonathan Gilman, Jr.
Francis James	Jonathan Folsom
Dudley James	Robert Light
Cartee Gilman	Thomas Webster
Joseph Thing	Moses Swett
Nicholas Gordon	John Lord
John Leavitt	Benjamin Thing
Theophilus Smith	Daniel Thing
Thomas Dean	Josiah Gilman
Nathaniel Ladd	Henry Marshall

John Folsom	Josiah Ladd
Oliver Smith	Joshua Gilman
Benjamin Folsom	Abner Thurston
Jeremiah Calfe, Jr.	Peter Gilman
Kinsley James	Nathaniel Gilman
John Baird	

This steeple stood till 1775, when it was blown down in a heavy gale, and afterwards was rebuilt at the expense of the town.

On the twenty-eighth of September, 1731, the town voted to take down the old meeting-house, which had been left standing while the new one was built beside it, as soon as it could be done with convenience, and to construct a court-house with the materials thereof, and appointed Theophilus Smith, Benjamin Thing and Jeremiah Conner a committee to " discourse with workmen " about taking down the one and putting up the other, and make report.

The expected occasion for a court-house proving illusory, the materials taken from the old meeting-house were used in building a town-house, which was located on the opposite side of the street, near the site of the present Gorham Hall.

Those who are conversant with the construction of the early churches in this country, are aware in what a high box of a pulpit the minister used to be perched. It must have been hard for him to establish any link of sympathy with hearers so far away. And it seems that some of the people of Exeter realized this truth, and wished to diminish the distance between people and pastor. On March 26, 1733, the town voted that "any particular person or persons that are desirous of having the pulpit lowered, have liberty to lower it eighteen inches, provided they do it at their own charge, and leave it in as good order as it now is."

As early as 1735, the dwellers in the western part of the town, who were now becoming somewhat numerous, and were at an inconvenient distance from the meeting-house, made petition to the town for help to support a minister among themselves. But the town declined the request, probably on the ground that the inhabitants of that section were not yet strong enough to set up a religious establishment of their own. It will appear, however, that the petitioners were persistent, and eventually succeeded in creating not only one, but two new parishes in that territory.

The value of the paper currency had declined in 1736 to such an extent that, on the twenty-ninth of March of that year, the town voted an addition of fifty pounds a year, for five years next ensuing, to Mr. Odlin's salary of one hundred and fifty pounds, payable in good public bills of credit on either of the provinces, "he acquitting all further claims for the time past."

In 1737 the town books show that an hour-glass was purchased, at the cost of four shillings and six pence. This, undoubtedly, was to be placed upon the pulpit, not as an admonition of brevity to the preacher, but simply to serve the purpose of a clock.

In 1737 forty-two of the inhabitants of the southwestern part of the town petitioned the selectmen to call a town meeting, to consider their request to be set off as a separate parish, with the following bounds, viz.: "Beginning at old Pickpocket upper sawmill, and from thence running south to Kingston line, thence west and by north by Kingston line four miles; thence north four miles; thence easterly to Newmarket, southwest corner bounds; and so bounding by Newmarket south bounds so far till a south line will strike Pickpocket mill, and then to run from Newmarket line south to said mill, the bound first mentioned." These bounds are very nearly those of Brentwood, as it was afterwards incorporated.

But the town was not yet prepared to consent to the separation, and at the meeting held on November 14, 1738, voted not to grant the request of the inhabitants of the west end of the town for a new parish.

At the annual town meeting, the twenty-sixth of March, 1739, a vote was passed to pay the cost of the steeple to the contributors to the erection thereof, as has already been stated, and the selectmen were instructed to hang the bell therein. This was probably a new bell, bought by individual subscriptions. For two or three years previously the subject of the purchase of a new bell, to be placed in the steeple of the church, had been pending, and the town repeatedly refused to make the order. In the meanwhile, however, the people were not without the means to call them to public worship, and to give them the hour for retiring at night. The bell which had been purchased of Peter Coffin in 1699 was still in the steeple of the old church, and, after the demolition of that building, was hung upon the town-house, no doubt, as the old account books show that it continued to be regularly rung. Very likely the reason for the refusal to procure a bell for the new meeting-house was, that the steeple was not the town's property; for, as soon as it became so, all objection seems to have ended. It is said that the old bell of 1699 was afterwards removed to Pickpocket, and long did duty upon the factory there in calling the

EPPING PARISH SET OFF.

At the annual meeting of the town, on the thirtieth of March, 1741, the petition of a number of the inhabitants "living at Tuckaway or thereabouts," praying that the town would set them off as a parish by themselves, was presented, and by vote of the town was denied.

These were residents of the northwestern part of the town; and they did not sit down contented with the refusal, but within the succeeding year presented their petition to the General Assembly of the province, by which, after a notice to Exeter and a hearing thereon, it was granted, February 3, 1742. The bounds of this parish, which received the name of Epping, and was soon afterwards, on the twenty-third day of the same month, incorporated as a town under the same designation, were as follows, viz.: "Beginning at Durham line at the northwest corner of the parish of Newmarket, and from thence bounding on the head line of said Newmarket to the southwest corner of the same, and from thence to run south about twenty-nine degrees west parallel with the head line of the town of Exeter, extending to half the breadth of the township of Exeter from Durham line aforesaid, and from thence to run west and by north to the middle of the head line of the town of Exeter, and from thence to bound upon Chester and Nottingham to the northwest corner of Exeter, and from thence bounding east and by south on Nottingham and Durham to the first bounds."

BRENTWOOD PARISH SET OFF.

A petition of some of the inhabitants of the southwestern part of the town, that they should be set off as a separate parish, was presented about the same time, and the town, at a special meeting, on the twenty-second of February, 1742, voted to grant the petition, and that "the petitioners have set off to them and their successors one-half the breadth of the land in said town lying at the westerly end thereof, for a parish, bounded as follows, viz.: beginning at the head of Newmarket line, thence running on a south line to Exeter great fresh river, and then one-half mile by said river, and then south to Kingston line, and so to the head of the township; provided that the abovesaid parish do settle an orthodox minister of Christ, and maintain and support the same, and all other parish charges within the same, of themselves."

This vote received the sanction of the General Assembly, and the parish of Brentwood was incorporated June 26, 1742.

Thus the original territory of the town was now divided into four distinct parishes: the northeastern quarter being Newmarket; the northwestern, Epping; the southwestern, Brentwood, and the southeastern retaining the primary designation of Exeter. These were of nearly equal areas, except Brentwood, which was somewhat larger than the others.*

Scarcely had these difficulties with the outlying sections of the town been adjusted, when a more serious trouble arose in the very heart of the place. This was about the time of the great religious awakening in New England, when the influence of Whitefield, preaching a new gospel of enthusiasm, was felt more or less in all the churches. His followers were the "new lights," but the more conservative religionists set their faces like a flint against his methods. The members of the First parish in Exeter were divided in their preferences. Mr. Odlin, their minister, was a conservative, as were a majority of his congregation. But a considerable minority of them held different views. Mr. Odlin was getting in years, and somewhat infirm, and was desirous of having his son Woodbridge settled with him, as his colleague. Nearly two-thirds of his parish were of the same mind.

At the annual meeting of the town, on the twenty-eighth of March, 1743, upon an article in the warrant, inserted on the petition of seventy-one of the inhabitants, it was voted that Nicholas Gilman, Thomas Wilson, Benjamin Thing, James Leavitt, Stephen Lyford, James Gilman and Nicholas Perryman be a committee to treat and agree with the Rev. Woodbridge Odlin, relating to settling as a colleague with his father, with power to complete an arrangement with him.

From this vote forty-four of the inhabitants entered their written dissent. It is not understood that there was any personal exception to the younger Mr. Odlin; the sole objection was to his religious views and position. The dissentients seceded from the church and society, and established a religious organization of their own, the history of which will be found under its appropriate head.

REV. WOODBRIDGE ODLIN, COLLEAGUE.

On June 21, 1743, the committee communicated to the Rev. Woodbridge Odlin the invitation of the majority of the town to

* The town of Poplin (now called Fremont) was set off from Brentwood June 22,

settle over them as colleague with his father, upon the salary of £37 10 s., lawful money, also £50 yearly for the first four years of his settlement; and after his father's death, £65 annually, and the use of the parsonage. He on the same day accepted the invitation; and the committee at once made an agreement with the Rev. John Odlin that his salary should be reduced to £50 a year, with the improvement of the parsonage.

The Rev. Woodbridge Odlin was, on the twenty-eighth of September, 1743, ordained as colleague, accordingly.

The seceders from the congregation maintained separate religious worship at their own expense; but according to the law of the time, they were not exonerated thereby from paying taxes to support the Messrs. Odlin. They made repeated attempts, as will be seen, by petition to the town and to the provincial government, to be relieved from this burden, but for near twelve years in vain. The bitter feeling that had been aroused by their opposition to the party of the Messrs. Odlin, and their rather unceremonious departure, forbade all hopes of harmony between the antagonistic elements.

On the twenty-sixth of March, 1744, the town voted not to grant the petition of Samuel Gilman and others, to be exempted from paying to the stated ministry, or having a reasonable sum allowed them annually by the town toward the support of a gospel minister among themselves.

Thereupon the petitioners made application on the eighteenth of July following, to the General Assembly of the province, for relief from taxation, for the support of the ministry of the town, provided they should maintain a minister themselves. On July 24, the town appointed Nicholas Perryman, James Gilman and Zebulon Giddinge a committee to oppose the petition. After repeated written statements and counter-statements by the parties, the General Assembly thought proper to do nothing in the premises.

It was during this year that the Rev. John Odlin, learning that the Rev. George Whitefield was coming to Exeter, with the intention of preaching there, met him on the border of the town, and solemnly adjured him not to trespass upon his parochial charge.

On the ninth of April, 1748, the mischievous effects of paper currency were again shown, by the necessity of an addition of £200 old tenor to the Rev. Mr. Odlin's salary for the year, and on the twenty-seventh of March, 1749, by a further increase of £100 old tenor, for that year, provided he would give an acquittance for all arrearages.

The seceding society had again preferred their petition to be exempted from taxation for religious services, by which they did not profit, but the town again voted to "do nothing about the petition of a number of the society of the new meeting-house."

On the eighteenth of June, 1750, the town voted to pay the Rev. John Odlin £600 old tenor for the year, provided he would, at the end thereof, give a receipt for all arrearages; and to add to the Rev. Woodbridge Odlin's salary £350 old tenor for the year, on like conditions. And the town again refused "to allow the petition of those in the new meeting-house."

On the thirtieth of March, 1752, the petition of "those worshipping in the new meeting-house" was again brought before the town, and again denied.

The Rev. John Odlin died November 20, 1754. He was born in Boston, Massachusetts, November 18, 1681; graduated from Harvard College in 1702, and ministered to the people of Exeter for forty-eight years. He was twice married; first to Mrs. Elizabeth (Woodbridge) Clark October 21, 1706, by whom he had five children, and who died December 6, 1729; and second, to Mrs. Elizabeth (Leavitt) Briscoe, widow of Captain Robert Briscoe. Mr. Odlin, though somewhat unyielding in his opinions, was a faithful and zealous pastor, and he lived in a time of strong religious excitement and division. He chose the conservative rather than the progressive side, and was supported by the majority of his people. But it must have been a bitter trial to him to see so large a portion of his church and parish alienated from him. He was persevering and conscientious, however, and retained the affection and respect of his followers to the last, as is evidenced by their vote on the twenty-first of November, 1754, to raise £100 new tenor, for defraying his funeral charges.

He is represented as a man of excellent powers of mind. He presided over the convention of ministers which assembled in 1747, and was made chairman of one of its most important committees. A sermon which he preached in 1742 was printed by the agency of the Rev. Mather Byles of Boston, who wrote a preface to it which contained this commendatory allusion to the author:

It is with no small pleasure that in this precarious season I see such a harmony among the ministers of superior reputation among us, and especially that our living fathers in the ministry are so united, who saw our temple so much in its first glory.

At length, the continual efforts of the members of the new society accomplished their purpose of independent existence. On the eighth of April, 1755, sixty-two members of that society presented their petition to the General Assembly, that they and their associates might be freed from paying taxes for the support of the ministry in the old meeting-house, for the future, and be incorporated as a parish. The town appointed Peter Gilman and Zebulon Giddinge agents to resist the petition. Peter Gilman was a leading member of the assembly, and also the principal petitioner. It would appear, therefore, that the majority of the town had extraordinary confidence in his obedience, in expecting him to oppose his own petition, or that their feelings had become mollified towards the petitioners, and they no longer expected to compel them to contribute to the support of Mr. Odlin. At all events, the petition was successful, and the petitioners were, on the ninth day of September, 1755, incorporated as the Second parish in Exeter; and for the future, any new comer in the town, or any person arriving at full age, was to "have the liberty of three months to determine to which parish such person will belong."

Thereafter, the warrants for the annual meetings of the supporters of the First church in Exeter were for many years addressed to "all the inhabitants of the town exclusive of all the parishes;" meaning all the inhabitants who were not included in Newmarket, Epping, Brentwood and the Second parish in Exeter.

On the twenty-ninth of March, 1762, at a meeting of the society so warned, it was voted that a new bell be purchased, of eight hundred pounds weight; and on the thirteenth of December, following, that "the meeting-house be repaired, the repairs to be new glazing with sash glass, shingling, and clapboarding on the fore side and east end, and that it be painted according to custom;* and that the bell be for the town's use." On the twentieth of March, 1764, it was voted "to use the part of the money divided to this parish by the town from the sale of wharf lots, to pay for the bell."

The succeeding years were a transition period from the most inflated paper currency to hard money. In April, 1765, Mr. Odlin's salary received an addition of £700 old tenor; in April,

---

* The custom at that time was to paint only the doors and window-frames, and the finish around them. It is doubtful if there was then a house in the town which was completely painted.

1766, an addition of £400 old tenor; and in 1767 his entire salary was fixed at £100 lawful money. Old tenor had become a thing of the past, and a specie basis had been reached.

Mr. Odlin continued to minister to his people through the troublous period which preceded the Revolution, and was a warm supporter of the rights of his countrymen. The pulpit at that day was a chief advocate of American liberty, and in both the religious societies of Exeter its utterances were of no uncertain sound. Mr. Odlin died the tenth of March, 1776. His parish manifested their regard for his memory by the payment of the expenses of his funeral and a gift of twenty-five pounds to his widow.

He was born April 28, 1718, and graduated from Harvard College at the age of twenty. He married, October 23, 1755, Abigail, the widow of the Rev. Job Strong of Portsmouth, and the daughter of Colonel Peter Gilman of Exeter, by whom he had eight children.

He is described as a very pious man; his preaching was practical; his manners were plain and modest. There was an unaffected simplicity in all he said or did. He has also been termed a "perfect gentleman," no doubt rather in reference to his qualities of character than to his external appearance or manners.

In July following the decease of Mr. Odlin, the society gave a call to the Rev. Isaac Mansfield to become their pastor, who was accordingly ordained over them October 9, 1776.

In the year 1778, Mr. John Rice, a member of the society, died, giving to the parish, by his will, the house on Centre street, which is now the parsonage, and certain lands on the little river, "to be appropriated to the support of a minister so long as the parish shall continue, and constantly support a regular learned minister or ministers," but in case of failure thereof, to be appropriated for the benefit of a grammar school in Exeter forever. The devise was to take effect upon the decease of his wife. She died five years afterward, and by her will gave certain house lots and a wharf to the parish, on the same conditions specified in the will of her husband.

After Mr. Mansfield had been in Exeter about ten years, there was a disposition manifested by both parishes to reunite. Resolutions were adopted by each, expressing such a desire. But it was found that they could not come together under the ministry of Mr. Mansfield, who had, by some imprudent speeches and actions, lost, to some extent, the attachment of his people. An arrangement was therefore made between him and his society the following year, that if a majority of the parish were in favor of his dismissal, he would request it at the hands of a council. That course was taken, and his connection with the society was dissolved September 18, 1787.

Mr. Mansfield was born in Marblehead, Massachusetts, in the year 1750, and graduated from Harvard College in 1767. He had served as a chaplain in the continental army about Boston, before he came to Exeter. He remained in the town awhile, after his dismissal, and taught a school. Afterwards, he returned to his native place, where he became a magistrate. He died in Boston, at the age of seventy-six years.

After Mr. Mansfield surrendered the pastoral charge, the two societies, for two years and more, united in supporting public worship, and in 1788, jointly invited the Rev. David Tappan of Newbury, Massachusetts, to settle over them. It happened, unfortunately, that the call was not unanimous and on that account was not accepted. The two societies did not agree in another choice, and the first society, in 1790, invited the Rev. William F. Rowland to the pastoral office, and he was ordained over them the second of June in that year. Eight years afterwards, a new church building was erected, which is still in use by the society, though its interior was altered and modernized in 1838. The exterior was fortunately unchanged. Its style and proportions have been much admired, and it is undoubtedly a fine specimen of the architecture of the period. Ebenezer Clifford of Exeter is understood to have designed it.

For thirty-eight years Mr. Rowland continued to minister to the people, during which time he witnessed the substantial extinction of the church of the other society, and the growth of a new church rising from its ashes; and a very considerable increase in the population and wealth of the town. He was dismissed at his own request December 5, 1828, and continued to live in Exeter until his death, June 10, 1843.

Mr. Rowland was born in Plainfield, Connecticut, May 26, 1761. He was a graduate of Dartmouth College in the class of 1784. He was twice married; first, to Sally, daughter of Colonel Eliphalet Ladd of Portsmouth, July 30, 1793; and second, to Ann, daughter of Colonel Eliphalet Giddinge of Exeter, August 29, 1802. He left one son and two daughters, who all died unmarried. Mr. Rowland was honored in a way that no other New Hampshire clergyman has been, — he was twice appointed to deliver election sermons, in 1796 and in 1809, both of which were published.

His successor in the pastorate was the Rev. John Smith, installed March 12, 1829, and dismissed at his own request February 14, 1838. He was a native of Weathersfield, Connecticut, and a graduate of Yale College in 1821.

Shortly after Mr. Smith was settled, the need of a vestry was urgently felt, for evening religious meetings and the like, and, with the concurrence of the parish, a few gentlemen, Dr. William Perry, Captain Nathaniel Gilman, Jr. and others, took upon themselves the immediate expense of erecting such a building on the northern part of the parsonage land, on Centre street. It was of two stories, the upper of which was used for singing schools and other purposes not necessarily religious. This building subsequently became the property of the parish, and in the year 1843, after the construction of a vestry in the meeting-house rendered it no longer necessary, was sold to a number of gentlemen for the purpose of a Female Academy; and later, when that use had terminated, was altered into a dwelling house. It is now occupied as such by Mrs. Joseph W. Gale.

The Rev. William Williams was the next minister of the society, installed May 31, 1838. The first year of his stay was signalized by extensive alterations made in the interior of the church building. Up to that time the entire space within the walls was included in the audience room; the high pulpit, surmounted by a sounding-board,* was on the north wall, and galleries ran around the other three sides. A great part of the pews were of the old square pattern, with seats facing in all directions.

The changes in the building consisted in flooring over the lower story, and finishing rooms in it for a vestry, lecture room, etc., and in adapting the upper story for an auditorium. Of course, the old galleries were removed, and a smaller one erected for the choir; a pulpit of modern and moderate dimensions was placed at the west side, the pews were altered into "slips," and the walls were frescoed. Excepting that the change involved the ascent of a flight of stairs, it was an undoubted improvement.

Mr. Williams was dismissed October 1, 1842, by reason of the failure of his health and some difficulties that arose. He after-

---

* The ladies of the society, unwilling that so interesting a relic of the old times should go to destruction, have caused the sounding-board to be rehabilitated and suspended in the lower hall of the church.

wards entered the medical profession. He was a graduate of Yale College in the class of 1816.

The society next chose for their minister the Rev. Joy H. Fairchild, who was installed September 20, 1843, and resigned July 30, 1844. A charge of incontinence at the place of his former settlement preferred against him, gave rise to protracted controversies that forbade all hope of his future usefulness in Exeter. He was a native of Guilford, Connecticut, and a graduate of Yale College in 1813.

The Rev. Roswell D. Hitchcock was the next regular occupant of the pulpit. He was ordained November 19, 1845, and dismissed July 7, 1852. He was a native of East Machias, Maine, born August 15, 1817, and an alumnus of Amherst College of the class of 1836. While settled in Exeter, he spent one year in Germany, in the universities of Halle and Berlin. After leaving Exeter he was a professor in Bowdoin College for three years, and then was appointed to a like position in the Union Theological Seminary, New York. Of this institution he was afterwards made president, and held the office up to the time of his death June 17, 1887.

He was succeeded in Exeter by the Rev. William D. Hitchcock, who was installed October 5, 1853, and began his ministrations with every prospect of permanence and usefulness, but his career was cut short in a single year by his death November 23, 1854.

More than a year and a half expired before the pulpit was again permanently filled. The Rev. Nathaniel Lasell was installed June 19, 1856, and asked his dismission, after three years of service, June 12, 1859. He was subsequently engaged in the profession of teaching.

The Rev. Elias Nason was the next incumbent, installed November 22, 1860, and dismissed May 30, 1865. He was a native of Billerica, Massachusetts, and a graduate of Brown University. He had been a teacher and an editor before he was ordained, and through life held the pen of a ready writer, on literary and historical subjects. He published several works of history and biography, and delivered numerous lectures. He died in Billerica, Massachusetts, June 17, 1887, the same day as his predecessor in the Exeter ministry, the Rev. Dr. R. D. Hitchcock.

The next on the list of pastors was the Rev. John O. Barrows, a graduate of Amherst College in 1860, who was installed December 5, 1866, and received his dismission October 6, 1869, which he had requested in order that he might enter upon mission work in Asia.

The Rev. Swift Byington, the present minister of the society and the sixteenth in order, was installed June 2, 1871. He is a graduate of Yale College in the class of 1847, and a native of Bristol, Connecticut.

CHAPTER X.

THE SECOND PARISH. OTHER RELIGIOUS SOCIETIES.

The circumstances under which the secession from the original parish took place, in the year 1743, have been related. The seceders, who numbered about one-third of the tax-payers, and comprised some of the principal and wealthiest citizens, set up separate religious services, and proceeded without loss of time to erect a house of worship and organize a church.

Their meeting-house was finished in 1744, on land given them by Colonel Peter Gilman and Samuel Gilman, situated on the northerly side of what is now Front street, between the houses of Dr. Josiah Gilman and John Dean, on the lot now owned by Colonel W. N. Dow. It was of two stories and of good dimensions, standing parallel with the street, with a steeple in which a bell was hung, on the western end. The pulpit was in the side farthest from the street; a gallery ran round the other three sides, and the main entrance was opposite the pulpit.

The attempts made from time to time by the worshippers in the new meeting-house to obtain exemption from the payment of minister's rates for the support of the old parish have already been detailed. In these days of wider religious tolerance we may think that the adherents of the Messrs. Odlin should have been more liberal, and ought to have exonerated their withdrawing brethren from the forced contribution which the law enabled them to exact; but it is not quite safe to say what would have been our own conduct if we had lived in their time, and had felt the same provocation which they did. It is too late now to attempt to decide upon the merits of the respective parties.

The new society for some years had no settled pastor. In 1746 they made an unsuccessful attempt to engage the services of the Rev. Samuel Buel; and in 1747 they invited Mr. John Phillips, one of their own number, and afterwards the founder of the Phillips Exeter Academy, to assume the pastoral office, but he modestly declined, upon the ground of his incapacity, partly by reason of the delicacy of his lungs, to perform all the duties of the position. They were more successful with the Rev. Daniel Rogers, who preached for them early after their separation, and again in the latter part of 1747, and pleased them so well that he remained with them during the rest of his life. They gave him a formal call, and on the thirty-first of August, 1748, he was, by consent of a council of churches, installed over the society as their minister. This was not done, however, without a remonstrance from the old church, backed by the opinion of six ministers from neighboring towns, that the proceeding was irregular.

The interest felt by the members of the new society in its welfare may be inferred from the disposal which one of their number, Nicholas Gilman, Jr., made of his property. At his death in 1746, he devised to his brother Peter Gilman, Samuel Gilman and Daniel Thing, his dwelling house, barn, orchard, and about twenty-two acres of land, to be improved by them for and towards the support of the minister of the church or for any other pious use. The house was pleasantly situated by the side of the river near the great bridge, just at the entrance of the present Franklin street, and facing towards Water street. It was occupied as the parsonage by the Rev. Mr. Rogers during his life; and in 1786 after his death, the trustees were incorporated by act of the Legislature, and let the property for various terms until the year 1826, when they disposed of it by leases for the period of nine hundred and ninety-nine years. The income of the proceeds has been employed towards the support of the minister of the society, in repairs upon the meeting-house, and in other " pious uses," such as the distribution of Testaments, the support of young men designed for the ministry and the like.

In July, 1755, while the last petition for the incorporation of the new parish was pending in the Provincial Assembly, the two churches mutually agreed upon an ecclesiastical council, to which were referred the differences between them, in order to a reconciliation, though apparently without any expectation of effecting a reunion. The council censured the course of the separatists in certain particulars, but advised the old church to receive them into fellowship again, whenever they should accept the report and manifest their readiness to practise agreeably thereto. This the new church voted to do, but the old church required some further acknowledgment, which the former refused to make. After the incorporation of the new parish, however, on the ninth of September, 1755, there was no collision between the two societies, and for many years no fellowship, but each went its way, in peace.

Mr. Rogers's connection with the Second parish terminated only with his life. It extended over the stormy political period of the American Revolution, but the relations between him and his people were always pacific. He died in Exeter in 1785, at the age of seventy-eight. He was born in Ipswich, Massachusetts, August 8, 1707, graduated from Harvard College in 1725, and was tutor there from 1732 to 1741. He was married November 3, 1748, to Anne, daughter of the Rev. Thomas Foxcroft of Boston, on which occasion his church presented him with the sum of two hundred and fifty pounds. From middle life, when he came to Exeter, to his death at an advanced age, he labored assiduously for the welfare of his people, and to the entire satisfaction of church and congregation. For more than half a century he kept in interleaved almanacs a brief record of his daily life and employments, which show him to have been an amiable, faithful and devoted religious teacher. He was a warm friend and admirer of the Rev. George Whitefield to whom he attributed his own conversion, and had that eloquent divine twice to preach to his Exeter charge, first on the twenty-sixth of October, 1754, and again on the twenty-ninth of September, 1770, when Whitefield delivered his last discourse the day before his death.

In token of their esteem for their late pastor, his parishioners voted to bear the expense of his funeral. His body lies in the old burying-ground on Front street, west of the railroad, and upon the massy tablet above it is the following inscription:

Here lie the remains of
the Reverend Daniel Rogers,
Pastor of a church gathered in this place 1748,
who died December 9th 1785 aged 78 years.
He had been many years a Tutor in Harvard College,
was a faithful pious minister of Jesus Christ,
and a worthy son of the Reverend John Rogers,
pastor of the first church in Ipswich,
who died December 28th 1745 in his 80th year;
who was a son of John Rogers of the same place
Physician and Preacher of God's Word,
And President of Harvard College,
who died July 2d 1684 aged 54 years;
who was eldest son of the Revd Nathaniel Rogers,

who came over from England in 1636, settled at Ipswich
colleague pastor with the Revᵈ Nathaniel Ward,
and died July 2ᵈ 1655 aged 57 years;
who was son of the Reverend John Rogers
a famous minister of God's word at Dedham, England,
who died October 18ᵗʰ 1639 aged 67 years;
who was a grandson of John Rogers of London
Prebendary of St. Paul's, Vicar of St. Sepulchre's
and Reader of Divinity,
who was burned at Smithfield February 14, 1555,
first martyr in Queen Mary's reign.*

Thou martyred saint and all ye holy train
O be your honor'd Names ne'er read in vain,
May each descendant catch your hallow'd fire
And all your virtues all their breasts inspire.
Prophets like you in long succession rise
Burning and shining, faithful firm and wise,
And millions be their crown beyond the skies.

For nearly seven years after the death of Mr. Rogers the new parish was destitute of a settled minister. During that time there was a strong feeling in favor of a permanent reunion of the two parishes. In 1786 resolutions were passed by both expressing their desire for a restoration of their former relations, and in the latter part of 1787 when both were without pastors, they apparently united in hiring a temporary supply until the next annual meeting. On March 29, 1788, the members of the new church partook of the communion with those of the old, at the invitation of Deacon Samuel Brooks of the latter, and during that and the succeeding year both parishes joined in attendance upon public worship, which was maintained at their joint charge. In 1788 both societies united in a call to the Rev. David Tappan of Newbury, Massachusetts, to settle over them, but because the call was not unanimous, he declined it. Attempts were made to agree upon another candidate, but without success.

In 1790 the new parish invited the Rev. Samuel Austin of New Haven, Connecticut, to their pulpit for two months, and on the twelfth of July in the same year, gave him a unanimous call to a permanent settlement, at an annual salary of one hundred pounds. Mr. Austin did not accept, and on September 24, 1792, the parish

---

*The claim that this family was descended from the Smithfield martyr has of late years been disallowed, as based upon a mistaken belief.

voted to concur with the church in giving a call to the Rev. Joseph Brown, who accordingly was installed over them on the succeeding twentieth of November. After a service of five years he was dismissed at his own request, the twenty-eighth of August, 1797, the parish making him a gift of fifty dollars upon his departure. Mr. Brown was a native of Chester, in England, and was educated at the seminary of the pious Lady Huntingdon, whose chaplain was the Rev. George Whitefield. His ministration in Exeter was quite successful, and he was afterwards settled at Deer Isle, in Maine, and died there in 1804.

After the removal of Mr. Brown, the society not being readily disposed to provide themselves with a successor, its numbers gradually began to decline. Religious services, however, were kept up with more or less frequency, and the organization of the parish was regularly preserved. Every year a certain sum was voted to sustain public worship, and various clergymen were temporarily employed to conduct the Sunday services. Thus matters went on until about the year 1812, the church having dwindled until it became practically extinct, though the parish received accessions from time to time.

In 1811 the Rev. Hosea Hildreth came to Exeter as an instructor in the Academy, and was employed to fill the pulpit of the society. This he continued to do most of the time for about five years, and until the society was provided with a settled pastor. On the twenty-fourth of December, 1812, the church was re-organized, with a creed drawn up by Mr. Hildreth, which would admit those who questioned the doctrine of the trinity, of whom there were several in the society.

On December 2, 1816, the parish gave a unanimous call to the Rev. Isaac Hurd to become their minister at a salary of six hundred and fifty dollars, and he was installed over them September 11, 1817. At the same time he was appointed theological instructor in the Academy.

On the thirty-first of March, 1823, the society appointed a committee to report a plan for a new meeting-house, to replace the old one which had been in use nearly eighty years, and on the eighteenth of May following, Nathaniel Gilman, Joseph Tilton, Jeremiah Dow, Jotham Lawrence and Peter Chadwick were chosen to superintend the erection thereof. It was placed on land furnished by the trustees of the Academy for the purpose, and the master builder was Nathaniel Conner. It was completed in season for the next annual meeting of the parish in March, 1824, to be held therein, and has well answered the needs of the parish to the present time, with an addition to its length of about fifteen feet, which was made in 1863.

After a harmonious and successful ministry of nearly thirty years Mr. Hurd proposed to the society to settle a colleague with him, generously relinquishing all claim to pecuniary compensation thereafter. To this proposal the society, assuring their pastor of their undiminished affection and regard, assented, and in April, 1846, called the Rev. Robert S. Hitchcock of Randolph, Massachusetts, to the associate pastorate, but by reason of the state of his health he declined the invitation. The Rev. Samuel D. Dexter was subsequently invited, and, giving a favorable response, was ordained as colleague pastor with the Rev. Mr. Hurd December 2, 1847. His ministry was cut short, however, by his death April 20, 1857. He was a native of Boston, and a graduate of Harvard College. During his residence in Exeter his personal and religious character was such as to gain him a strong hold upon the people, and his premature decease, at the early age of twenty-four years, closed a career of bright promise.

The Rev. Asa Mann was installed as colleague, in the place of Mr. Dexter, November 19, 1851. During his term of service, the Rev. Dr. Hurd, on the fourth of October, 1856, at a ripe old age, beloved and honored for his amiable character, his Christian virtues and his faithful labors, went to his rest. Mr. Mann continued in Exeter less than a year afterwards, being dismissed from his charge July 8, 1857. He was a native of Randolph, Massachusetts, and a graduate of Amherst College, and had been settled at Hardwick, Massachusetts, before he came to Exeter.

His successor in the pulpit of the Second parish, the Rev. Orpheus T. Lanphear, was installed February 2, 1858, and after a successful service of six years, on being called to a church in New Haven, Connecticut, was dismissed by council February 21, 1864. He was a native of West Fairlee, Vermont, and a graduate of Middlebury College, and had previously been the pastor of the High street church in Lowell, Massachusetts.

The Rev. John W. Chickering, Jr., began to preach for the society on the first Sunday of July, 1865, was invited to become their permanent minister, and was installed the fifth of the succeeding September. He remained for five years, and was dismissed July 18, 1870. During latter part of his pastorate the society purchased, enlarged and remodelled the dwelling house on Court street, which has since been occupied as the parsonage. Mr. Chickering left Exeter to accept a professorship in the Deaf Mute College in Washington, D.C. He was a native of Portland, Maine, and a graduate of Bowdoin College, and had served as pastor of the church in Springfield, Vermont, prior to his coming to Exeter.

The eighth and present pastor of this society, is the Rev. George E. Street, who was installed March 30, 1871. He is a native of Cheshire, Connecticut, and a graduate of Yale College, and was the minister of the First church in Wiscasset, Maine, when invited to Exeter. Since his installation, the society have provided themselves with a chapel for evening meetings and the like, situated on Elm street.

QUAKERS.

About the middle of the last century there were a few Quakers in Exeter, who held meetings for a time in a barn which stood on the southerly side of what is now Front street, just opposite the head of Centre street. Among them were Samuel and John Dudley, grandsons, it is presumed, of the Rev. Samuel Dudley. The Rev. Daniel Rogers's diary for the year 1753 shows that on the twenty-fifth of January, "the Quakers, Samuel Dudley, etc., came into our meeting and spoke;" that on March 7, "the Friends were carried to court this week," and on March 10, "Lord's day, John Dudley spake after the first singing, A.M."

The Friends who were carried to court were undoubtedly Elizabeth, wife of Joseph Norris, and Joanna, wife of James Norris. The records of the Court of General Sessions show that at the March term, 1753, these two women were indicted for a breach of the peace and violation of the act for the better observance of the Lord's day. It is probable that their offence was the disturbance of the Sunday service in one of the meeting-houses. They were arraigned, and pleaded not guilty. When inquired of whether they would be tried by the court or the jury they resolutely refused to answer, probably having little expectation of an acquittal by either.

The court, upon hearing the testimony of witnesses, and the answers of the respondents themselves, found them both guilty, and they were ordered to pay a fine of five shillings each, and to find sureties for their future good behavior.

The fine and costs were at once paid, and no further account is found of Quakers in the town.

THE BAPTIST SOCIETY.

A Baptist church was organized in Exeter, October 17, 1800, consisting of ten members. The elders and brethren forming the council on the occasion, were from the churches in Haverhill and New Rowley in Massachusetts, and in Newton and Brentwood in New Hampshire. The Rev. Hezekiah Smith, D.D., was president of the council, and the Rev. Shubael Lovell, clerk. In the spring of 1801 a society was formed, in connection with the church, by voluntary subscription. The members were few in number and of means somewhat limited, so that for several years they were able to have preaching but a third or a half of the time; but having those in their own church whose gifts of exhortation were acceptable to the congregation, and edifying to the brethren, meetings were regularly held on Sundays when no minister could be procured; a practice which they found to be attended with the best results. Their first place of meeting was at the dwelling house of Harvey Colcord, and afterwards at the Centre schoolhouse. In the year 1805, they built and dedicated their first meeting-house, situated on Spring street.

In 1806 Mr. Barnabas Bates, afterwards distinguished as the advocate of cheap postage and otherwise, preached for the society for several months. In the spring of 1809 the Rev. Ebenezer L. Boyd became their preacher, and labored with them for two years with encouraging results. In 1814, and the two succeeding years, the Rev. Charles O. Kimball and the Rev. James McGregore supplied their pulpit a part of the time. In the winter and spring of 1817 the services were conducted by students from the theological school at Danvers, Massachusetts, then under the care of the Rev. Jeremiah Chaplin. To one of those students, the Rev. James Coleman, they gave an invitation to become their pastor, but, having determined to devote his life to missionary work, he declined.

In the year 1817 a Sunday-school was first commenced in connection with the society, which has ever since been continued. The first teacher was Deacon John F. Moses, who, for half a century, with little interruption, held the office of superintendent, and was, during his life, one of the principal pillars of the church and society.

The society was incorporated by the Legislature of the State in 1818, and the same year had their first settled minister, the Rev. Ferdinand Ellis, who served them from June, 1818, to September, 1828. After the close of his pastoral connection he continued to reside in Exeter, and was, for a number of years, a successful school teacher. In the autumn of 1828, the Rev. John Newton Brown was settled over the society and remained until February, 1833. He resumed the pastorate again in 1834, and retained it until he was dismissed in April, 1838. It was during this period, in the years 1833 and 1834, that the society built their second meeting-house on Water street,* dedicated November 19, 1834, in which they held public worship until the erection of their present church on Front street. In the interim between the two settlements of Mr. Brown, from May 29, 1833, to February 16, 1834, the Rev. John Cannan, from Yorkshire, England, ministered to the society. After Mr. Brown's final departure, it was more than two years before another minister was settled, but for about half that period the Rev. J. G. Naylor regularly supplied the pulpit.

In November, 1840, the church gave an invitation to the Rev. Noah Hooper, Jr., to become their minister, which he accepted, and continued with them from December 1, of that year, until July 20, 1845. For nearly three years after this the church was without a regular pastor, though for about one-third of that period Mr. T. H. Archibald, licentiate, preached to them. Their next settled minister was the Rev. Elijah J. Harris, who remained from the spring of 1848 to April 7, 1850. Then the Rev. James French became their minister from January, 1851, to January 1, 1853. After his dismission, the Rev. Mr. Russell was employed as preacher for a time. The Rev. Franklin Merriam was the next settled minister, installed in September, 1854, and dismissed in November, 1856. His successor was the Rev. James J. Peck, whose pastorate continued from February, 1857, to April, 1861.

On the first of July, 1861, the Rev. Noah Hooper was solicited to assume the pastoral charge of the society a second time, to which he assented, and filled the position until the autumn of 1871, when, at his repeated request, he was dismissed. He is still residing in Exeter, at a good old age, in the enjoyment of much bodily and mental vigor.

---

* The Water street building is still standing; and after serving the purpose of a military armory for some years, has now been transformed into an opera house.

The Rev. John N. Chase was next invited to the pastorate of the society, and was received into that connection January 16, 1882, and still remains therein, having already served a longer time than any of his predecessors.

In December, 1854, twenty-two members withdrew from the Water street church, and formed themselves into a new society. They held their meetings at first in a hall on Water street, until they built themselves a house of worship on Elm street, which was dedicated October 1, 1856. Up to this time the Rev. J. B. Lane supplied them with preaching. Soon after their removal to their new house, the Rev. T. H. Archibald was settled over them. His term of ministerial service continued about two years. For some time after his dismissal their pulpit was supplied by students from the Theological Institution of Newton, Massachusetts, and afterwards by the Rev. Mr. Mayhew. About the year 1862 the Rev. Charles Newhall was installed as the pastor, and continued in the office some eight years. In 1871 the two Baptist societies resolved to reunite; the Elm street organization was given up, and its members were merged again in the Water street society. Their meeting-house on Elm street afterwards passed into the possession of the Second Congregational parish, and is used by them as a chapel.

In 1874 the reunited Baptist society purchased a lot on the corner of Spring and Front streets, on which, in that and the following year, they erected their present handsome brick church. Notwithstanding the liberality of the members of the society, it left upon them a heavy load of debt, which, however, by the strenuous, continued efforts of the people, supplementing the generous gifts of Deacon John F. Moses and his son, Henry C. Moses, Esq., has since been fully discharged, and the seats of the church are made free.

THE UNIVERSALIST SOCIETY.

It is said that a society of Universalists was formed in Exeter as early as 1810, who supported public worship for ten years or more, when their organization was abandoned and the members were dispersed among the other religious societies. They had been incorporated by an act of the Legislature in the year 1819. Some years later their interest revived, and Sunday services were maintained in the old court-house, by the Rev. Hosea Ballou and other able preachers of the denomination. On the twenty-sixth of May,

1831, several of the leading men of the sect formed themselves anew into a society, erected a house of worship on the east side of Centre street, and soon supplied themselves with regular ministers. Among the earliest were the Rev. Theophilus K. Taylor and the Rev. William C. Hanscom, the latter of whom appears to have preached at Newmarket also. The Rev. James Shrigley of Baltimore, Maryland, was installed over the society June 16, 1837, and remained three years or more. He was a man of much ability, and became subsequently an officer of the Maryland Historical Society. The Rev. H. P. Stevens was the next minister, but continued only a year or two. Then the Rev. Henry Jewell assumed the pastoral charge, and under his administration the congregation increased to such an extent as to warrant the erection of a new and larger church. Accordingly, the lot on the eastern corner of Front and Centre streets was purchased, and upon it was built the structure which has served as a place of worship, successively for the Universalists and the Unitarians, and now is occupied by the Methodist society. It was dedicated December 18, 1845, Mr Jewell preaching the discourse on the occasion.

The next minister settled over the society was the Rev. R. O. Williams. He was a practitioner of the medical, as well as of the clerical profession. His stay was not very long, and his successor is believed to have been the Rev. John L. Stevens, who ministered to the society with ability for some years. He has since been distinguished as the editor of an influential political journal in the State of Maine, as a diplomatist and author. After his departure, the Rev. Silas S. Fletcher was the occupant of the pulpit, and the last of the preachers of Universalism settled in the town. In 1854 the society disposed of their church to the newly formed Unitarian society, and abandoned their separate organization. Mr. Fletcher continued to reside in Exeter until his death several years later.

THE CHRISTIAN SOCIETY.

The members of the Christian society were in the habit of holding meetings for religious worship in private houses, for some time prior to the year 1830. They aimed to free themselves from the constraint of theological dogmas, and so professed no creed but the Bible. Elder Abner Jones is said to have been the founder of the sect, and at one time lived in Exeter, and occasionally preached to the people. Their first permanent minister appears to have been Elder John Flanders, who remained five or six years. In the meantime, the congregation grew, a church was formed, and a chapel was built at the foot of Franklin street. Elder Elijah Shaw became subsequently the minister of the society, and published, in a little pamphlet, a sketch of the doctrines of his people, entitled "Sentiments of the Christians." About the year 1840 Elder Edwin Burnham had the pastoral charge, and this was apparently the culminating point of the society. The chapel had to be enlarged to accommodate the hearers. But soon after this, the noted William Miller, who predicted the destruction of the world in 1843, preached in Exeter, and many of the Christian Society became believers in his theory, and deserted their former associates.

This succession weakened the Christian society, but it still went on for nearly twenty years longer. Elder Simeon Swett, who was the compounder of several medical preparations which acquired popularity, Elder Julius C. Blodgett and, finally, Elder John W. Tilton, successively ministered to the society, but it never recovered fully from the loss of members which it sustained in 1842, and at length, toward the year 1860, came to an end. Its house was closed, and its records and papers are said to have been destroyed.

THE METHODIST SOCIETY.

The first steps towards the formation of a Methodist society were taken by five ladies in 1830. Upon their invitation, the Rev. D. I. Robinson, then stationed in Newmarket, came to Exeter and arranged for religious meetings to be held on every alternate Sunday. The next year the Rev. Amos H. Worthing of Newmarket, continued to hold occasional services in Exeter; and in 1832 Exeter became a regular station, to which the Rev. Azel P. Brigham was appointed by the Conference. The meetings of the society were at that time held in the old court-house, and the number of attendants was much increased. In November, of the same year, John Clement, Samuel Tilton and Moses P. Lowell organized the First Episcopal Methodist Society in Exeter, by publication in a newspaper, according to law.

In 1833 the Rev. A. H. Worthing was stationed in Exeter, and in 1834 the Rev. Samuel Hoyt, the society, by invitation, occupying the old Universalist church on Centre street. In the latter year, however, they erected a brick church of their own, on the east side of the river, upon Portsmouth avenue. The dedicatory sermon was preached, February 10, 1835, by the Rev. George Storrs. In 1835 the Rev. W. H. Hatch was appointed minister of the society; in 1836 the Rev. Alfred Medcalf, on account of whose illness the Rev. O. Hinds, and afterwards the Rev. Jacob Sanborn took his place. Mr. Sanborn remained for the succeeding three years, and under his charge the church was highly prosperous.

It was in 1836, on the evening of the tenth of August, that the town was disgraced by a scene of public disorder at the meeting-house of the Methodist society. The Rev. George Storrs, a noted advocate of the abolition of slavery, attempted to deliver a lecture there on that subject. A crowd of pro-slavery men, idlers and boys gathered, and determined that he should not. As he persisted in his attempt, he was interrupted by hooting, by the flinging of stones at the windows and blinds, and by streams of water from the fire engines; so that, finding it impossible to go on, he at length desisted, and his audience dispersed. No serious damage was done to persons or property; the worst injury was to the good fame of the town. All that can be said in mitigation of the offence is that it was not an unexampled one in New England at that time.

The Rev. E. D. Trickey was the pastor in 1840 and 1841, at which time the church numbered about one hundred and eighty members. In 1842 the Rev. D. I. Robinson was stationed at Exeter. The divisions on the slavery question, and the "Miller excitement," seriously interfered with the harmony of the society, and a majority of the members with their pastor seceded, and a Wesleyan Methodist church was organized. This was never very prosperous. For some years after 1842, Exeter was united with Amesbury, Massachusetts, and had no separate minister. In 1847 the Rev. Isaac W. Huntley was the pastor, and in the two years following, the Rev. Ebenezer Peaslee.

In 1858 the Rev. James M. Buckley, then just from college, supplied the pulpit. He was earnest, able and eloquent, and drew a large congregation. He has become distinguished in later years, and is now a doctor of divinity and editor of the New York *Christian Advocate*, the leading Methodist journal of the country. The next year the Rev. Mr. Stokes had charge of the society, but the interest awakened by Mr. Buckley died away after his departure, and the society declined, and soon came to a full stop.

In 1861 and 1862 the brick meeting-house was occasionally opened, but it was not till 1867 that the Methodists, including some new comers, re-organized their society. In that year the Rev. C. W. Millen supplied them with preaching for a few weeks, holding services in a hall on Water street. After he left, the Rev. J. D. Folsom began his labors with them, and the congregation increased. The Rev. H. B. Copp succeeded Mr. Folsom in 1868, and remained three years. During his stay the society purchased from the Unitarian society the church on the corner of Front and Centre streets, where they still worship. The Rev. S. E. Quimby was the next pastor, for the term of three years. The society had now grown in strength and numbers. In 1874 and 1875 the stationed minister was the Rev. S. C. Farnham; and in the three following years the Rev. J. H. Haines. The church and congregation were largely increased during his administration. The Rev. M. Howard was the next minister, for the years 1879 and 1880; and the Rev. J. W. Walker succeeded him in 1881 and part of 1882; and the Rev. C. H. Hannaford filled out the latter year. In 1883 the Rev. C. J. Fowler was the pastor, and in 1884 the Rev. John W. Adams was assigned to the place.

The society had long struggled with a considerable debt, incurred when they purchased their house of worship in 1868, and Mr. Adams resolved to make a determined effort to pay it off. By the concurrent action of his church and society he was enabled to accomplish the desirable result, and on December 28, 1884, announced it to his society, on which occasion he delivered a discourse on the Centenary of Methodism.

In 1886 Mr. Adams was transferred to another scene of labor, and the Rev. C. N. Nutter succeeded to the Exeter charge.

THE ADVENT SOCIETY.

This society probably took its rise from the doctrine of the immediate second coming of Christ, preached by William Miller in the year 1842. It was chiefly made up of members of the Christian and the Methodist churches, who left their old communions in the full faith that the end of the world was at hand. Of course when the time fixed for the final catastrophe came and went without the expected event, the faith of many was shaken, but a considerable part of the believers decided that a mistake in the time was no reason for rejecting any other tenet of their religion, and so have continued their regular worship in their chapel on Clifford street. Their views as to doctrines are much the same as those which were held by the "Christians," but of course the expected second advent of Christ is the prominent subject of interest with them, and their aim is to be constantly ready to welcome it.

THE ROMAN CATHOLIC SOCIETY.

The Catholic society of Exeter was organized in 1853 by the Rev. John McDonnell of Haverhill, Massachusetts. For some years it was small in numbers, and lacked the means to build a house of worship. There was no resident priest, and services were held only occasionally. But as the numbers increased a regular pastor was found necessary, and the Rev. J. Ph. Perrache was appointed in July, 1859. Meetings were held in the building on Centre street which had formerly served as the Universalist church. Father Perrache remained in Exeter something less than three years, when he was succeeded by the Rev. Bernard O'Hara, in the month of April, 1862.

The Rev. Canon Walsh assumed charge of the society in December, 1865, and retained it about three years and a half, until the appointment of the Rev. M. C. O'Brien in June, 1869. His stay was very brief, and the Rev. Charles Egan followed him in November of the same year. Father Egan's residence was longer than that of either of his predecessors, and he did not give place to his successor, the Rev. Michael Lucy, until December, 1875. The next incumbent was the Rev. John Power, who was placed in charge of the society in October, 1878, and was succeeded in January, 1883, by the present pastor, the Rev. John Canning.

The society in 1868 erected their brick church in Centre street, and purchased the house adjoining, on the corner of Water street, for the residence of the pastor.

THE UNITARIAN SOCIETY.

The Unitarian society was formed in June, 1854. It was chiefly composed of members of the Second parish who entertained Unitarian opinions, and were not satisfied with the style of preaching there, and of the Universalists, whose society had declined in numbers and means. The new organization purchased the Universalist church at the corner of Front and Centre streets, and there maintained their worship for the succeeding fourteen years. For nearly two years they had no settled minister, but were temporarily supplied; though a considerable part of that time the Rev. Joseph Angier, a graduate of Harvard College in 1829, was their preacher.

On the twenty-fourth of April, 1856, the Rev. Jonathan Cole was installed as their pastor. After remaining about four years he asked his dismission, but was prevailed upon at the request of the society to remain for a year or two longer, until they could decide upon his successor. Mr. Cole was a graduate of Harvard College of the class of 1825, and after he left Exeter removed to Newburyport, Massachusetts, where he died in 1877.

In September, 1862, the society invited the Rev. John C. Learned, who had then just completed his course of study in Divinity School at Cambridge, to become their minister. He accepted the invitation and, after completing a tour in Europe, was ordained over them May 6, 1863. He retained the connection nearly six years and a half, when it was dissolved upon his application on account of the impaired condition of his health. After quitting Exeter he took up his residence in St. Louis, Missouri, where he still remains. During his pastorate the society acquired the strength and means to provide themselves with a new place of worship, and erected their present church on the corner of Maple and Elm streets.

His successor was the Rev. Edward Crowninshield (Harvard Divinity School, 1870), who was ordained over the society about the first of August of the same year. His health was found to be insufficient for the position, and he resigned it after a single year's labor.

Another year had nearly expired before his place was supplied by the Rev. Benjamin F. McDaniel, who received his theological education at the same school, in the class of 1869. His pastorate extended over a period of ten years and a half, but during that time he was twice compelled to ask for temporary leave of absence, to recruit his health by foreign travel. At length he was dismissed by his own desire, and after a short settlement in Salem, Massachusetts, he removed to the milder climate of San Diego, California. It was while Mr. McDaniel was in Exeter that the society built upon the lot adjoining the church their present parsonage house.

Mr. McDaniel was followed by the Rev. John E. Mande, a graduate of Harvard College, who was ordained October 9, 1883. His term of service lasted only one year, when he fell a victim to disease.

The Rev. Alfred C. Nickerson, a graduate from the Harvard Divinity School in 1871, is the present pastor, and assumed the office in the month of April, 1886.

THE EPISCOPAL SOCIETY.

The Episcopal society in Exeter dates from the year 1865. It originated with students of the Academy who had been brought up in that church, and wished to enjoy its services while pursuing their education. The Rev. Dr. (now Bishop) F. D. Huntington cordially seconded the movement and conducted the first service in the town hall, in July, 1865. In September following the parish of Christ Church was organized.

The next month the Rev. Dr. George F. Cushman, a graduate of Amherst College in 1840, took charge of the parish, and remained six months. Services were at first held in the town hall, and afterwards in the building on Centre street, originally used by the First Congregational society as a vestry.

The Rev. James Haughton, a native of Boston, and a graduate of Harvard College in the class of 1860, succeeded Dr. Cushman, and under his rectorship the present church on Elliott street was built. The means for it, $12,500, were raised by the exertions of the indefatigable treasurer of the parish, Miss Caroline E. Harris, and of the rector. The church was ready for occupation at Christmas, 1867, and consecrated September 30, 1868, with no debt, and with free sittings.

After the resignation of Mr. Haughton, to take the charge of the new society in Hanover, New Hampshire, the Rev. Dr. Samuel P. Parker, an alumnus of Harvard College, succeeded to the rectorship. He remained two years, during which the society prospered and increased in strength. For some time after his departure there was no settled clergyman over the parish, but in July, 1872, the Rev. Henry Ferguson, a native of Connecticut, and a graduate of Trinity College, Hartford, assumed the charge. In 1875 he obtained a year's leave of absence, and travelled abroad. During his absence the Rev. J. H. George had the charge of the parish. Mr. Ferguson resumed his duties, upon his return, and remained about two years longer. Afterwards he was for a time rector of the church in Claremont, and then received an appointment to the professorship of history, in his alma mater, which he still holds.

The Rev. George B. Morgan, also a native of Connecticut and an alumnus of Trinity College, was the successor of Mr. Ferguson. His ministry extended over the period of eight years, when he resigned it, to take the rectorship of a church in New Haven.

The present rector is the Rev. Edward Goodridge, like his two immediate predecessors, born in Connecticut and educated at Trinity College. He began his labors in Exeter February 26, 1887. He had previously been stationed in Geneva, Switzerland in charge of the American church there.

MILITARY.

CHAPTER XI.

THE INDIAN AND FRENCH WARS.

ALTHOUGH under the laws of Massachusetts the people of Exeter had to maintain a watch-house and some show of an organized militia, yet until the year 1675 the place had never been made the object of any Indian hostilities. There must have been frequent intercourse between the whites and the aborigines, but their relations were pacific and friendly. Possibly the precautions taken by the former contributed to maintain this tranquillity.

But in the year named an Indian war broke out, brief, but in some sections active and bloody. Philip, chief sachem of the Wampanoags, has the credit, or discredit, of being the instigator of the movement. His own people belonged in the southern part of New England, but he had the power and address to enlist some of the eastern tribes to make common cause with him. This was the less difficult, because some of them had grievances of their own to revenge.

Exeter was a frontier town, and necessarily suffered to some extent from the raids of the barbarous enemy. In the month of September, 1675, a party of savages made a descent upon the settlement of Oyster river, adjoining Exeter on the north, and burned two houses and killed four persons. They also made captives of two others, one of them " a young man from about Exeter " according to the historian, Hubbard, but whose name is unknown. By the aid of an Indian " better minded than the rest " he succeeded in giving them the slip, and returned to the garrison at Salmon Falls, after about a month's absence.

Four of the same party of Indians, probably, proceeded to Exeter, and made a prisoner of Charles Rundlet, an inhabitant of the town. He was left in the custody of one of their number, named James, whom he induced to connive at his escape. Rundlet was accidentally drowned at the mouth of Exeter river, nearly a quarter of a century later.

The other three Indians, whose names were John Sampson, Cromwell and John Linde, placed themselves in ambush in the woods near the road leading to Hampton. Soon afterwards John Robinson, a blacksmith who had removed from Haverhill, Massachusetts, to Exeter in 1657, made his appearance, with his son, on their way to Hampton. The father, according to tradition, was carrying a warming-pan. The Indians fired from their lurking place upon them, and shot the elder Robinson dead.* The bullet passed through his body from back to front, and lodged just under the skin. The son, upon hearing the report of the guns, ran into a swamp where the Indians pursued, but could not overtake him. He reached Hampton about midnight and gave information of what had occurred.

About the same time that Robinson was shot, another Exeter man, John Folsom, was riding on horseback along the same road, driving a pair of oxen before him. He heard the report of the guns which gave Robinson his death wound, and presently discovered the three Indians creeping on their bellies towards him. He abandoned his oxen, put his horse to speed and made his escape, though it is said that one of the savages sent an ineffectual shot after him.

In October following the occurrences just related, the Indians made another incursion to Exeter, and killed one man near Lamprey river. Several of them were seen about Exeter, and between Hampton and Exeter, where they killed one or two men in the woods as they were travelling homewards. The names of those slain have not been preserved. These outrages naturally terrified the people of the town and vicinity, and prevented them from attending to their daily business, or exposing themselves in any way to the rifle and the scalping-knife of the cruel and stealthy foe. Fortunately this outbreak of hostilities was of brief duration, and was ended in 1676 by the death of the chief fomenter of it, and Exeter experienced no further molestation at this time.

KING WILLIAM'S WAR.

Nearly fifteen years passed away before the Indians again took up the hatchet. They were then set on by the French in Canada, and the brunt of their attacks fell upon the border settlements of

---

*There seems to be an uncertainty exactly when this tragedy occurred. The record of the town gives the date as the twenty-first of *October*, 1675.

New Hampshire and Maine. A terrible massacre was committed upon the settlers of Cochecho in 1689; but it was not until the succeeding year that Exeter was invaded. On the fourth of July, 1690, eight or nine white men went out to work in the field near Lamprey river, when a party of Indians fell upon them and slew them all, and departed, carrying with them a lad into captivity. The next day the enemy beset Captain Hilton's garrison in Exeter. Lieutenant Bancroft being then stationed in the town with a small force, at the distance probably of three or four miles, relieved the garrison, at the loss, however, of eight or nine of his party. It was of one of his men, Simon Stone * by name, that the wonderful preservation from death, after numerous and seemingly mortal wounds received on this occasion, is related by Cotton Mather, in his *Magnalia*.

On the sixth day of the same July, a severe conflict took place between two scouting companies under the command of Captains Floyd and Wiswall, and a large body of savages at Wheelwright's pond in Lee, in which thirteen of the whites were killed. The enemy then pursued their way westward, and within the period of one single week added at least fifteen more victims, slain between Lamprey river and Amesbury, Massachusetts, to those already enumerated, in their bloody raid. How many of these belonged in Exeter we have unfortunately no present means of ascertaining.

About June 9, of the next year, 1691, the Indians killed two men at Exeter, whose names are unknown.

In the latter part of the succeeding month of July, an expedition was sent to the eastward against the Indian enemy, under the command of Captain March and others, and landed at a place called Maquoit, near Casco, on the coast of Maine. They were attacked by great numbers of the enemy, and Nathaniel Ladd, an inhabitant of Exeter, who was in the expedition, received a mortal wound, of which he died on the eleventh of August, following.

During the continuance of the Indian wars, Exeter, by reason of its exposed situation, needed to be garrisoned a large part of the time, not only for the protection of its own inhabitants, but as a bulwark against assaults upon the interior settlements. Sometimes the militia of other places were detailed for this duty, but most of the time, probably, the guard was composed of Exeter men. The records of their service are not now to be found, in

---

* Then or afterwards of Groton, Massachusetts.

most cases, but a few have fortunately escaped destruction, to give us an idea of the trying experiences of the time.

The earliest that we can discover bears date March 17, 1693, and is as follows:

The soldiers under my command, quartered by the inhabitants of Exeter from the 1 day of December, 1692, to the 17 of March, 1692-3, the number is twenty and two, and two quartered at Mr. Andrew Wiggins, one of them since the arrival of their majesty's government in this province, to the 17 March, 1692-3, the other quartered fifteen weeks in the aforesaid time.

per me, THOMAS THAXTER, Capt.

The above is a true account of the soldiers quartered by the inhabitants of Exeter.

JONATHAN THING, Capt.

In the year 1693 a truce was "patched up," as Belknap pithily expresses it, between the aborigines and the English, which was violated without scruple by the former in the following year.* But Exeter happily escaped any further attack until the month of July, 1695, when two men are recorded to have been slain there by the Indians. Like so many others who perished in the same manner, they are to us nameless.

The precept directed to the authorities of Exeter, November 2, 1695, for the election of assemblymen, contained also the order following:

You are required to give notice to the captain of your town that he stands upon his guard, the Indians being on the frontiers.

WILLIAM REDFORD, Dpt.

Kinsley Hall was the captain of the first company of militia in Exeter, and from his return we learn that he lost no time in providing for the emergency. He impressed men from time to time through the autumn and winter, and until April, 1696, requiring of each instalment about a month's service, as follows:

John Young, Sr., Jacob Smith, Alexander Gordon, Francis Steel and Job Judkins, from November 4 to December 2, 1695.
Thomas Rollins, John Sinclair, Joshua Gilman, Edward Masry (?) and John Judkins, from November 14 to December 12, 1695.

---

* By the massacre at Oyster river on July 18, 1794. On that occasion Exeter was ordered to furnish twenty men to range the woods in pursuit of the enemy, but no record of their service is to be found.

Edward Dwyer, Ebenezer Folsom, John Ficket, Jethro Pearson and Strong Horne, from December 2 to December 30, 1695.

Samuel Bean, Jeremy Conner, Edward Cloutman, Samuel Dolloff and James Randlet, from December 12, 1695, to January 9, 1696.

John Bean, James Bean, Israel Smith, James Leavitt and Stephen Gilman, from December 30, 1695, to January 20, 1696.

Samuel Piper, Nicholas Smith, Nicholas Gilman, Philip Spenlow and Moses Rollins, from January 9 to February 6, 1696.

William Graves, Clement Moody, Jonathan Smith and John Leavitt, from January 27 to February 24, 1696.

Francis Lyford, Biley Dudley, Alexander Magoon and Nathaniel Ladd, from February 6 to March 5, 1696.

Nicholas Gordon, James Young, Mark Stacy and William Powell, from February 24 to March 23, 1696.

Peter Folsom, from March 5 to April 2, 1696.

The whole account of the soldier's wages from November 5, 1695, to April 2, 1696, was £52, 16 s.

In addition to the above Exeter men whose tour of duty was in their own town, another, Jonathan Thing, served in the garrison at Oyster river, one month from April 2, 1696 ; and sixteen others were summoned to Oyster river for two days.

It appears, also, that Exeter furnished the garrison in the town through the spring and summer, and until November 9, 1696, as follows :

Job Judkins, Alexander Gordon, D—— Meserve, Charles Rundlet, Armstrong Horne, Ebenezer Folsom, Francis Steel, John Gordon, Nathan Taylor and Richard Dolloff, from April 13 to August 3, 1696.

David Lawrence, Thomas Wilson, John Gilman, Israel Young, Richard Morgan, Jonathan Clark, Ephraim Folsom, Samuel Dudley, Job Judkins and David Robinson, from August 3 to August 31, 1696.

Charles Glidden, George Pearson, William Taylor, William Jones, George Gorly (?), Nicholas Norris, Alexander Gordon, Sr., Jonathan Wadleigh, Daniel Bean and Roger Kelly, from August 31 to September 28, 1696.

James Gilman, Philip Huntson, Philip Dudy, Jacob Smith, Moses Kimming, Theophilus Smith, Jeremiah Gilman, Joseph Rollins, Benjamin Jones and Moses Norris, from September 28 to October 26, 1696.

Cornelius Leary, John Bean, Sr., James Gordon, Caleb Gilman, Jeremiah Bean, Abraham Folsom, William Scammon, Richard Morgan, Sr., Benjamin Taylor and Jonathan Robinson, from October 26 to November 9, 1696.

Moses Leavitt also served in the garrison at Exeter from July 28 to September 22, 1696.

No lists of the Exeter soldiers in "King William's War," except those above given, have been found; but these are enough to show that the daily life of the people was never wholly free from apprehension, and that there was no craven spirit in the Exeter men of two centuries ago.

A FORTUNATE ESCAPE.

A remarkable coincidence, which resulted in frustrating a plan formed by a party of savages for the destruction of the town, occurred June 9, 1697. On that day a party of women and children went into the woods, against advice and without a guard, for the purpose of picking strawberries. To frighten them, so as to render them more cautious in future, some one, without the least suspicion that an enemy was near, fired an alarm, upon which a great part of the men hurried together, with arms in their hands. In point of fact, a party of Indians were at that very time lying in ambush in another part of the town,* with the intention of making an assault the next morning, but hearing the alarm, they supposed they were discovered, and hurriedly decamped, killing, on their way, John Young, wounding his son, a child, and taking captive a third, Luke Wells, by name. Young was one of those who had been impressed into service in the Exeter garrison in the winter of 1695-6.

Peace was concluded in Europe between the English and French by the treaty of Ryswick in 1697. King William's war ended the next year, and for a brief period no hostile tribes committed depredations on the northern provinces in America. But in less than four years there were such indications that the Indians were again about to take the war path, that the governor and council of New Hampshire, in February, 1702, ordered Captain Peter Coffin of Exeter, and the captains of Oyster river and Dover, to keep scouts of two men daily from Kingston to Salmon Falls river till further orders; and in March, following, ordered Captain Coffin to send two men to scout from Exeter to Pickpocket mill, thence to Kingston, and so back to Exeter; also to send two men to Lamprey river, to the house of John Smith and so back to Exeter.

Queen Anne came to the English throne in 1702, and her name has been applied to the Indian war which broke out afresh in America the next year.

---

* The place of the ambush was what is now called Fort Rock, in a pasture in the rear of the present house of Mr. Edward Swasey.

QUEEN ANNE'S WAR.

In the winter of 1703-4 the government of New Hampshire resolved to send out a scouting expedition against the savage enemy. Captain John Gilman, Jr., a son of Councillor John Gilman, and Captain Winthrop Hilton, were the commanding officers of the two companies in Exeter, and were encouraged to raise volunteers for the expedition. The former reported, in a week, that he had enlisted twenty men, and expected twelve more, exclusive of officers; and that several gentlemen of Exeter had subscribed for the purchase of thirty pairs of snow-shoes, for their use, which were in preparation. Captain Hilton, a grandson of Edward Hilton and a nephew of Governor Joseph Dudley, reported that he had only received his notice the night before, and was of the opinion that if one company were to go from Exeter, it would weaken the place too much to take more men away from it. Captain Hilton, who was soon to become a successful and distinguished commander, was commissioned major, and took the command of the three companies composing this scouting party.

They ranged the woods on snow-shoes in quest of the savages, but did not succeed in meeting any. It was "an honorable service," the council declared, and ordered a handsome gratuity to each of the commanding officers.

In March, 1704, a force was raised to range the shores of Maine, and was put under the command of that veteran Indian fighter, Colonel Benjamin Church. Hilton was appointed his major, and rendered excellent service. He was allowed to have the militia of the New Hampshire towns mustered, from which to procure volunteers for the enterprise, and took with him, according to Belknap, "a body of men;" but, unfortunately, no means of knowledge exist how many were contributed by Exeter. The expedition occupied the summer of 1704.

On the twenty-sixth of April, in the same year, a party of Indians, who had committed depredations in Oyster river the day before, killed Edward Taylor near Lamprey river, and afterwards took his wife Rebecca and their son, and carried them into captivity. Mrs. Taylor was subsequently restored to her friends, but had been harshly treated. Her master, who was called Captain Sampson, was on one occasion so enraged with her (without provocation) that he determined to put an end to her life. He first attempted to hang her to the limb of a tree by his girdle, but it gave way under the weight of her body. The disappointment angered him to such a degree, that he resolved, if a second attempt failed, he would beat her brains out with his hatchet. Fortunately, before he could put his resolve into execution, Bomaseen, an Indian of authority, made his appearance and arrested the fatal blow.

The histories inform us in disappointing general terms, that about August 10, 1704, the savages did much mischief at Amesbury, Haverhill and Exeter. But no particulars are preserved, save that John Young was slain at Exeter while travelling between the town and Pickpocket. He was probably the son of the person of the same name who fell beneath the weapons of the savage foe seven years before.

COLONEL HILTON'S EXPEDITIONS.

In the winter of 1704–5, the indefatigable Colonel Winthrop Hilton with two hundred and seventy men, among whom were twenty friendly Indians, was sent to Norridgewock on snow-shoes, to harry the enemy. They found the village deserted, but burnt the wigwams and a chapel, erected by the French.

The summer of 1705 was spent in negotiations for exchanges of prisoners; but in July, 1706, notice was received that a large body of French Mohawks were on their way towards Pascataqua. Colonel Hilton with sixty-four men marched from Exeter to intercept them, but was obliged to return for want of provisions, without meeting them. The enemy committed depredations at Dunstable, Amesbury and Kingston, after which a party of them numbering about twenty remained lurking around the house of Colonel Hilton in Exeter, with the intent of destroying that brave and energetic officer. On the twenty-third of July they observed ten men go out to the field in the morning, with their scythes, to mow. The Indians crept cautiously between them and the weapons which they had laid aside, and then fell upon them. They killed four, Richard Mattoon, his son Hubertus, Robert Barber and Samuel Pease, and three others they carried captive, Edward Hall, Samuel Mighill and a mulatto. Three only escaped, Joseph Hall, John Taylor, who was sorely wounded but recovered, and another. Edward Hall (a nephew of Colonel Hilton) and Mighill were carried to Canada, where Hall obtained so much favor from the French and Indians by building them a saw-mill that they allowed him and Mighill to go out into the woods to hunt, and sometimes unattended. The two prisoners took advantage of one of these opportunities and made their escape. They were for three weeks traversing the forests on foot, with nothing to subsist on except lily roots and the rind of trees, till Mighill was so exhausted that he lay down to die. Hall made all possible provisions for his comfort and left him, to seek the nearest English settlement. He soon reached Deerfield, Massachusetts, and immediately sent a party to Mighill's relief. They found him alive, and brought him to the fort where he recovered his strength, and returned with his companion to their home. The names of Hall and Mighill are found upon the tax list of Exeter in 1714.

In the winter of 1706-7, Colonel Hilton, in command of two hundred and twenty men, made another excursion to the eastward, which resulted in the destruction of above twenty of the enemy.

In the month of July, 1707, two brothers, Stephen and Jacob Gilman, as they were riding from Exeter to Kingston, were ambushed and fired upon by a party of seven Indians. Stephen had his horse shot under him, and was in danger of being scalped before he could get clear. The other received several shot through his clothes, one of which grazed his body. His horse also was wounded, yet he defended himself on foot, and succeeded in getting into the garrison. One escaped to Kingston, the other to Exeter.

Later in the year, on the thirteenth of September, one man was killed near the meeting-house in Exeter, by the Indians; and two days afterward, another, John Dolloff, in the woods.

In the winter of 1708-9, Colonel Hilton made a long and tedious march with one hundred and seventy men to Pequawket in search of the enemy, but without success.

In 1709, on the sixth of May, William Moody, Samuel Stevens and two sons of Jeremiah Gilman, Jeremiah and Andrew, were surprised by the Indians at Pickpocket mill in Exeter, and carried away prisoners. Moody was taken to Canada, and while his captors were traversing French river with him in canoes, a few days afterward, they were attacked by a party of English under Captain Wright of Northampton, Massachusetts. Several of the Indians were killed, and Moody was left alone with one savage in a canoe. The English encouraged him to despatch the Indian, which he attempted, but in the struggle the canoe was overset, and Moody swam to the shore. Two or three of the English ran down to the bank and helped him to land, but a number of the enemy attacked them, and Moody unhappily yielded himself again to the savages, who afterwards put him to cruel torture, roasted him alive at the stake, and devoured his flesh.

The brothers Gilman, after their capture, were separated from each other. Andrew was told that Jeremiah was killed and eaten; and as the latter never returned to Exeter the story was for a long time believed to be true. But it is since alleged that after a tedious captivity Jeremiah escaped to the Connecticut river, followed it to its mouth, and there spent the residue of his life, and that his descendants are now to be found in the States of Connecticut and New York. Andrew returned to his friends, and lived in that part of Exeter which is now Brentwood, for almost half a century afterwards. Stevens, too, returned to Exeter, and was taxed there in 1718.

On the eleventh of June, 1709, as Ephraim Folsom was riding home about sunset, from the village of Exeter to his house in what is now South Newmarket, he was fired upon by an Indian and killed.

In 1710 the Indians were very menacing, and scouts were kept up continually on the frontier. A few rolls of their names have been preserved, which show that Exeter was not backward in furnishing men for this duty. Captain Nicholas Gilman led a scouting party from June 21 to 23, comprising the following persons:

John Barber, Thomas Dolloff, John Dudley, Jonathan Folsom, William French, Dudley Hilton, Jonathan Hilton, John Lougee, Thomas McKeen, Richard Smith, Robert Woolford and Richard York.

And from June 23 to 25, the following:

Daniel Bean, Jeremiah Conner, John Drisco, James Dudley, Samuel Dudley, Stephen Dudley, Daniel Eames, Ephraim Folsom, John Folsom, Jonathan Folsom, Cartee Gilman, David Gilman, Edward Gilman, Jeremiah Gilman, Benjamin Jones, Daniel Ladd, John Ladd, Nathaniel Ladd, Joseph Lawrence, Daniel Leary, Samuel Mitchell, James Sinclair, Nicholas Smith, Bartholomew Thing, John Thing, Daniel Young, Jonathan Young.

Captain Nicholas Gilman was also in command of a detachment at Hilton's garrison of Exeter, of which the following persons had, on the third of July, served seven days: Jeremiah Arringdine, Samuel Bean, Daniel Eames, Cornelius Leary, Thomas Lowell, Bartholomew Thing, John York and John Young; and the following, fourteen days: Armstrong Horn, Thomas Leary and Samuel

HISTORY OF EXETER. 225

Lovering. And on the fifth of July he went again on a scout of two days in command of the following persons: Daniel Bean, John Bean, Jeremiah Conner, Philip Duda, James Dudley, Samuel Dudley, Abraham Folsom, John Folsom, Cartee Gilman, Daniel Gilman, Jeremiah Gilman, Jonathan Hilton, John Ladd, Nathaniel Ladd, Daniel Leary, John Nash, John Perkins, John Scribner, James Sinclair and Daniel Young.

DEATH OF COLONEL HILTON.

Scarcely two weeks after the return of this scout, the enemy, who had long been on the watch for an opportunity to take their daring and dreaded enemy, Colonel Winthrop Hilton, at a disadvantage, succeeded in their purpose. He went out on the twenty-second of July with a party of seventeen men, to peel some large hemlock logs which he had cut for masts the previous season, and which were liable to be injured by worms unless stripped of their bark. They were lying at the distance of about fourteen miles to the westward of his house. The day had been stormy. While the party were employed in doing the work, a body of Indians fired upon them from an ambush and killed three, Colonel Hilton and two others. The remainder of the whites, intimidated by their loss, and finding their guns unserviceable by the wet, fled, except two who were taken captive. These were Dudley Hilton, a brother of the colonel, and John Lougee, both of Exeter. The next day one hundred men marched in pursuit of the Indians, but discovered only the bodies of the fallen. The enemy in their triumph had struck their hatchets into the brain of Colonel Hilton, and left a lance sticking in his heart. His body was brought to his home, and buried with every mark of respect and honor.

Dudley Hilton was never more heard from, and probably perished in captivity. Lougee was taken to Canada and thence to England. He returned to Exeter as early as 1716, and was married and left descendants there.

The enemy were so much emboldened by their success that they appeared in Exeter in the open road, and carried away prisoners four children who were there at play. Three of them were undoubtedly daughters of Richard Dolloff; and the next that we hear of them is from a petition of their father to the Assembly of the Province in May, 1717, in which he stated that in the preceding summer he went to Canada to redeem them, and succeeded in getting one, by paying to her Indian captor twelve pounds and seven shillings. For this money he gave a bond to Major Schuyler, a commissioner appointed by the province of New York; and he prayed that the province of New Hampshire would afford him aid, that he might go again to Canada to obtain the release of his other two children. The assembly voted him ten pounds in 1717, and a like amount, the year following. The printed records from which the foregoing account is gathered, are supplemented by tradition, to the effect that the children were on their way from school to the strong-house in what is known as the "garrison pasture," and were stopping to play, when they were captured, and that another child had just gone into the woods to gather an armful of hemlock, and seeing the fate of her companions was enabled to conceal herself in the bushes, and so escaped. Tradition further states that after peace was established, their father brought two of the girls back from Canada. The other one, who had married an Indian husband, also returned to Exeter with the intention of remaining, but, thinking she was slighted on account of the match she had made, went back to Canada.

The Indians, at the same time that they captured the Dolloff children, took John Wedgwood and carried him to Canada, and killed John Magoon. The fate of the latter was attended by a singular coincidence. Three nights before, he had dreamed that he should be slain by the Indians at a certain place near his brother's barn. He repeatedly visited the spot, and told the neighbors that he should, in a little while, be killed there; "and it fell out accordingly."

On the sixteenth of August, 1710, less than a month after the death of Colonel Hilton, a company of ninety-one men marched, under the command of Captain John Gilman, in pursuit of the enemy. They were out five days, but returned without meeting the invaders. The roll of the company is given in Potter's Military History of New Hampshire, and the commander and about half of the number appear to have been inhabitants of Exeter.

The following named persons, believed all to have belonged to Exeter, served at various times in 1710 in scouting parties in pursuit of the savages, under the command of Captain Nicholas Gilman or Captain John Gilman.

Jeremiah Arringdine
John Barber
Daniel Bean

John Bean
Samuel Bean, Jr.
Jeremiah Conner

Thomas Dolloff	Joseph Lawrence
John Drisco	James Leavitt
Philip Duda	John Light
James Dudley	John Lougee
John Dudley	Samuel Lovering
Samuel Dudley	Thomas Lowell
Stephen Dudley	Thomas McKeen
Daniel Eames	Alexander Magoon
Abraham Folsom	John Marsh
Ephraim Folsom	Samuel Mighill
John Folsom	John Perkins
Jonathan Folsom	Thomas Powell
Nathaniel Folsom, Jr.	Jonathan Robinson
William French	Thomas Robinson
Cartee Gilman	Benjamin Rollins
Daniel Gilman	John Scribner
David Gilman	James Sinclair
Edward Gilman	James Sinclair, Jr.
Jeremiah Gilman	John Sinclair
Andrew Glidden	John Sinclair, Jr.
Thomas Gordon	Israel Smith
Josiah Hall	Ithiel Smith
Dudley Hilton	Nicholas Smith
Jonathan Hilton	Richard Smith
Armstrong Horn	Benjamin Taylor
Benjamin Jones	Bartholomew Thing
Daniel Ladd	John Thing
John Ladd	Robert Woolford
Nathaniel Ladd	John York
Cornelius Lary	Richard York
Daniel Lary	Daniel Young
Thomas Lary	Jonathan Young

OCCURRENCES OF 1712.

No other loss of life at the hands of savages occurred in Exeter so far as can be ascertained, until the sixteenth of April, 1712. At about four o'clock in the afternoon of that day, Timothy Cunningham, as he was travelling from Hilton's garrison to the village of Exeter, was shot down by a party of Indians. He was a shop keeper in Boston,* and left a wife and four children, and a respectable property there. It is not known what errand it was that

---

* The writer is indebted to the papers of that distinguished antiquary, the late Charles W. Tuttle, Ph. D., for information as to the residence and circumstances of this stranger victim of savage hostility.

called him forth on the journey that terminated so tragically. His body was interred in the second burying-ground in Exeter, where his gravestone still remains, with the inscription: "Here lies buried y⁵ body of Timothy Cunningham, aged 46 years. Departed this life y⁵ 16 of April 1712."

In the year 1712 the following men were drawn from the Exeter companies of Captain Nicholas Gilman and Captain John Gilman for a scouting party under the command of Captain James Davis. Sixteen others from the same place served with these, but as their names are already given in the list of 1710, they are not repeated here.

Edward Bean	Nathaniel Mason
Jeremiah Bean	Clement Moody
John Bean	Abraham Morgan
John Bean, Jr.	Jonathan Norris
Samuel Bean	Jethro Pearson
Jabez Bradbury	Richard Preston
John Clark	Owen Reynolds
Ebenezer Clough	John Roberts
Tristram Coffin	Aaron Rollins
Samuel Dolloff	Joseph Rollins
Jonathan Dudley	William Scammon
Samuel Elkins	Samuel Scribner
Jeremiah Folsom	Samuel Sinclair
Joshua Gilman	Daniel Smith
Morris Gilman	David Smith
Alexander Gordon	Nathaniel Smith
Thomas Harris	Joseph Taylor
Peter Havey	Joseph Thing
John Leavitt	Matthew Thompson
Selah Leavitt	Robert Young
Samuel Magoon	

ASSAULT UPON THE ROLLINS FAMILY.

The last Indian raid upon Exeter territory that history relates, was during what is known as "Lovewell's war," on the twenty-ninth of August, 1723, at Lamprey river. Edward Taylor, who was killed by the Indians, as already stated, on April 26, 1704, left a daughter who was the wife of Aaron Rollins. Most of the inhabitants at that time retired to the garrison houses at night, for greater security, but this Rollins and his family, which consisted of his wife, a son and two daughters, had neglected to do; and on the night of the day mentioned, eighteen redskins assaulted his house. His wife, with two of the children, attempted to make their escape by flight, but were immediately seized. The husband secured the door before the assailants could enter and, with his eldest daughter of about twelve, stood on the defence, repeatedly firing upon the enemy whenever they attempted to force an entrance, and at the same time calling loudly to his neighbors for help, which none dared to render. Rollins was at length killed, and the savages broke open the door and slew his daughter. Him they scalped, and cut off the poor girl's head. Mrs. Rollins and her son and the remaining daughter were carried to Canada. The mother was redeemed after a few years, but the son was adopted by the Indians, and lived all his life with them. The daughter married a Frenchman, and when she had reached the age of sixty years, returned to her native place, with her husband, in the expectation of recovering the property which had belonged to her father; but finding that to be impracticable they returned after a year or two to Canada.

In the month of May, the next year, 1724, Captain Daniel Ladd of Exeter, was ordered with a company from the same place to march on a scouting expedition in search of the Indians, in the direction of Lake Winnipisaukee. They were most of them absent six days, and found no enemy. Their names are recorded as follows:

Daniel Ladd, Captain	Abraham Folsom
Andrew Gilman, Lieutenant	John Folsom
Ezekiel Gilman, Clerk	Patrick Greing (?)
Daniel Giles, Sergeant	Nathaniel Glidden
John Moody, Corporal	Joseph Leavitt
John Huntoon, Corporal	John Magoon
Abner Thurston, Corporal	Philip Moody
Nehemiah Leavitt, Pilot	John Mudget
Samuel Akers	James Norris
John Bean	Ephraim Philbrick
John Cartee	John Quimby
Joseph Coleman	Christopher Robinson
Jonathan Conner	Jacob Smith
Samuel Eastman	Jonathan Young

For a score of years after this there was peace with the Indians and their French abettors. During that time, two or three tiers of townships were partially settled on the Canada side of Exeter, so that that place was no longer an exposed frontier, and did not directly suffer from hostile inroads, during the French and Indian war which began in 1744. But the town was from time to time called upon to furnish men for scouting parties, and for the protection of the exterior settlements. The following troopers, from the company of Captain Dudley Odlin of Exeter, performed scout duty to Nottingham and on the frontier from July 29 to August 7, 1745, in pursuance of the governor's orders:

  Jethro Pearson, Q. Master Daniel Robinson
  John Dudley, Jr. Ephraim Robinson
  Jonathan Fogg John Rundlett
  Peter Hersey Richard Sanborn
  Ebenezer Light Joseph Wadleigh, Jr.

THE LOUISBURG EXPEDITION.

In 1745 occurred that seemingly quixotic campaign against the strong fortress of Louisburg on the island of Cape Breton, which was projected by a tanner, "planned by a lawyer, and executed by a merchant, at the head of a body of husbandmen and mechanics," but which, to the surprise of the world, resulted, by reason of a series of fortunate accidents, in a triumphant success. New Hampshire contributed five hundred men to the expedition in the first instance, and a reinforcement of one hundred and fifteen more. From Exeter, Ezekiel Gilman went as major of the New Hampshire regiment, Trueworthy Ladd and Daniel Ladd as captains, James Dudley, Samuel Conner and Jonathan Folsom as lieutenants, and Dr. Robert Gilman as surgeon; and John Light enlisted and commanded a company of the reinforcement. No complete rolls of the troops employed in this enterprise are found, but we have what purports to be a list of Captain Light's company, which numbered forty-seven men, nearly all of Exeter.

ROLL OF CAPTAIN LIGHT'S COMPANY.

  John Light, Captain Caleb Brown (sick)
  Joshua Winslow, Lieutenant John Brown
  Jeremiah Veasey, Ensign Jack Covey
  Jonas Addison George Creighton
  Joseph Akers Amos Dolloff (sick)
  Joseph Atkinson David Dolloff

Joseph Dudley	Moses Lougee
Joseph Dudley	James Marsh
John Edgerly	Clement Moody
Moses Ferrin	William Morey
William Fifield	Joseph Philbrick
Moses Flanders	William Prescott
Joseph Folsom	Eliphalet Quimby
John Forrest	Benjamin Robinson
John Gibson	Josiah Sanborn (sick)
Joseph Giles	Samuel Scribner
James Gilman	John Severance
James Glóyd (?)	Ebenezer Sinclair
James Gordon	Samuel Sinclair
Robert Gordon	Abram Stockbridge
Joseph Judkins	Jonas Ward
Daniel Kelley (sick)	Thomas Watson
Nathaniel Lamson	John Wells
Thomas Lary	

It is evident that the rolls of the New Hampshire troops engaged in this expedition are very imperfect. A petition addressed to the General Assembly in November, 1745, setting out the shameful defects of the commissary department, is subscribed by eight persons, all of whom describe themselves as "commissioned officers" of the New Hampshire forces who took part in the expedition. Of these eight, seven were inhabitants of Exeter; namely, Trueworthy Dudley, James Dudley, Jonathan Folsom, Andrew Downer, Daniel Gale, Peter Thing and Benjamin Kimming. But the names of the last four of them are not found in any roster of the troops that is known.

It is on this occasion that the town, for the first time, granted partial exemption from taxation to volunteer soldiers. On the third of February, 1745–6, it was

Voted, That all who went in the first embarkation against Cape Breton be exempted from their town poll-tax rate the present year, and that all who yet remain at Cape Breton be exempted from paying their province rate for their polls the present year.

Major Gilman distinguished himself by his ingenious device for transporting the artillery over the swamps, into which the wheels of the gun carriages sank so deeply that they could not be moved. He had been engaged in lumbering, and was used to drawing masts by teams of men over boggy ground upon sleds, and advised the same course with the artillery. It was adopted, and with complete success, and the expedient contributed greatly to the speedy reduction of the town.

Dr. Gilman was severely wounded near Louisburg by a piece of shell, and returned to his home.

OCCURRENCES OF 1746.

In 1746 a regiment of eight hundred men was raised in New Hampshire for an expedition against Canada, and placed under the command of Colonel Theodore Atkinson. One of the companies was raised by Captain Dudley Odlin of Exeter; but no further information in reference to it is to be found. The expedition accomplished nothing.

On the first of June, in the same year, Captain Daniel Ladd of Exeter commanded a company of about fifty men to perform scout duty at Canterbury and vicinity. His lieutenant, Jonathan Bradley, and a part of his men were from Exeter. They were on duty through June, August and September. On the tenth of August they were at Rumford, now Concord, and Lieutenant Bradley, with a party of seven, started for a garrison two miles distant, and fell into an ambush of a large party of savages, who killed the lieutenant, fighting valiantly till the last, and five of his companions, and carried two into captivity, one only escaping.

Two days after Captain Ladd's company set out, a squad of fourteen men, all from Exeter it is believed, marched under the command of Sergeant Joseph Rollins, from Portsmouth to Canterbury, to carry provisions to the soldiers there stationed. They took with them a train of sixteen horses. The roll comprises the names of Jeremiah Bean, Wadleigh Cram, Joshua Folsom, Josiah Folsom, Daniel Grant, Samuel Hall, Thomas Kimball, Joseph Leavitt, Samuel Norris, Jonathan Robinson, Josiah Robinson, Josiah Rollins, Josiah Sanborn and Benjamin Smith. They were absent three days.

On the twenty-first of August, 1746, John (or Nathaniel) Folsom of Exeter was shot dead by Indians at Nottingham, where he was stationed for the defence of the inhabitants. The tradition is that he volunteered to take the place of a neighbor who had been drafted for the service, but whose sweetheart was unwilling that he should go; and that he was left alone at Nottingham by his companion soldiers, before those drawn to succeed them had arrived there; also that two of the Indians in the party who killed him were Sabatis and Plausawa, who were, in the fall of 1753, slain by Peter Bowen and one Morrill at Contoocook.

THE CROWN POINT EXPEDITIONS.

In 1755, war having broken out again between the English and the French, and an expedition being projected against Crown Point, under the command of General William Johnson, New Hampshire raised a regiment of five hundred men for the purpose, and put it under the command of Colonel Joseph Blanchard. The Exeter company consisted of eighty-four men.

The following is a roll of the company, being the imperfect list given in Potter's Military History, completed from papers left by Captain Folsom, who, during the Revolution, was a major general in command of the State militia:

Nathaniel Folsom, Captain
Jeremiah Gilman, Lieutenant
Jonathan Folsom, Ensign
David Page, Ensign
John Cartee, Sergeant
Gilman Dudley, Sergeant
Jonathan Norris, Sergeant
Elias Smith, Sergeant
Jacob Smith, Sergeant
Moses Gilman, Corporal
William Gilman, Corporal
Dudley Hardy, Corporal
Solomon Smith, Corporal
Nathaniel Folsom, Jr., Clerk
William Moore, Drummer
Moses Baker
Benjamin Batchelder
William Batchelder
Ebenezer Bean
Dudley Becket
Jacob Bridgham
Daniel Cartee
Benjamin Cass
Francis Coombs
Robert Cram
Thomas Creighton
William Davis
David Dolloff
Joseph Dolloff

Nicholas Dolloff
Benjamin Dow
Samuel Dudley
Trueworthy Dudley
Benjamin Folsom
John Folsom
Benjamin Fox
Edward Fox
Caleb Gilman
Jeremiah Gilman, Jr.
Joseph Goodhue
Benjamin Green
Ambrose Hinds
Jacob Hobbs
John Holland
Ebenezer Hutchinson
John Kimball
Nathaniel Kimball
Benjamin Kimming
Joseph Leavitt
Nathaniel Leavitt
Green Longfellow
Nathaniel Meloon
Isaac Perkins
Thomas Perkins
Ephraim Pettingill
Joseph Pettit
Jacob Pike
James Piper

234   HISTORY OF EXETER.

Jeremiah Prescott	Jonathan Smith
Samuel Pulsifer	Solomon Smith, Jr.
Joseph Purington	Thomas Smith
Robert Rollins	William Smith
Daniel Sanborn	John Steel
Tristram Sanborn	Nathaniel Stevens
Joseph Scribner	John Taylor
Robert Seldon	John Thing
Abraham Sheriff	Caleb Thurston
Abraham Smart	John Thurston
Edward Smith	Matthias Towle
Israel Smith	Samuel Webb
Jacob Smith, Jr.	Josiah Wiggin
Jacob Smith, 3d.	Samuel Winslow
John Smith	John Whittum

CAPTAIN FOLSOM AT LAKE GEORGE.

On the eighth of September General Johnson was attacked in his camp at Lake George by Baron Dieskau at the head of the French troops and Indians, who met with a disastrous repulse. The New Hampshire regiment was stationed at Fort Edward, several miles away, but a scouting party having reported that there were indications of a conflict, Captain Folsom was ordered out with eighty men of the New Hampshire regiment (presumably the Exeter company) and forty men of New York under Captain McGinnis. They attacked and dispersed the guard placed over the baggage of the French army, and when the retreating troops of Dieskau appeared, Folsom stationed his men among the trees, and kept up a fire upon the enemy till night, inflicting much damage. This exploit, in which Folsom lost but six men, and deprived the enemy of their baggage and ammunition, gained great credit to that officer and his command.

After the engagement at Lake George it was deemed necessary to reinforce General Johnson, and New Hampshire put in the field a second regiment, of three hundred men, commanded by Colonel Peter Gilman of Exeter. The first company had for its officers two Exeter men, Jethro Pearson, captain, and Nicholas Gilman, lieutenant, and was composed of inhabitants of the town and vicinity.

A contribution by several of the citizens of the town in September, 1755, produced the sum of two hundred and seventy pounds, to be divided as bounty between six volunteer troopers in the Crown Point expedition. The names of five of the volunteers appear by a contemporaneous document to have been Nathaniel Thing, Eliphalet Giddinge, Samuel Conner, Jr., Joseph Smith and Robert Smith. It is not known who was the sixth.

About the same time a scout was led into the vicinity of Number Four (Charlestown), by Captain Summersbee Gilman. It is uncertain who or how many others of the citizens of Exeter were of the party, but tradition gives the names of Dr. Robert Gilman and Captain James Leavitt as among them.

The regiment contributed by New Hampshire in 1756 for the expedition against Crown Point, and commanded by Colonel Nathaniel Meserve, contained these three subaltern officers, Samuel Folsom, David Page and Trueworthy Ladd, and a number of men, belonging to Exeter, several of whom were attached to a company of carpenters, under the command of Captain John Giddinge. Toward the close of the campaign Captain John Gilman joined the regiment with a company of seventy-three men, recruited from Exeter and neighboring places. Little was accomplished by the expedition.

Another "Crown Point" expedition was organized in 1757, and a New Hampshire regiment under the same colonel took part in it. John Gilman was the major, and John Lamson the surgeon's mate, of the regiment, both of Exeter. A company under Captain Richard Emery was raised in Exeter and the adjacent towns. The greater part of the regiment with its lieutenant colonel and major, including this company, were surrendered at Fort William Henry on the ninth of August, by the English Colonel Monroe, to the French General Montcalm. The capitulation provided that the English and provincials should be allowed the honors of war and a safe escort with their baggage to Fort Edward. This stipulation was shamefully violated. The Indian allies of the French fell upon the defenceless prisoners, and plundered and butchered or made prisoners of a great portion of them. The New Hampshire regiment lost eighty of its two hundred men.

CAPITULATION OF FORT WILLIAM HENRY.

Of Exeter men, Dr. John Lamson, James Calfe, Antipas Gilman, Thomas Parker and Cæsar Nero (a slave of Major Gilman) are known to have been carried captive to Canada. It is believed that they all, excepting Calfe, eventually returned to their homes, though Cæsar Nero continued a prisoner for three years or more. As for Dr. Lamson, his adventures deserve especial mention. When the savages were let loose upon the prisoners he allowed himself to be stripped of his clothing, rather than lose his life, and was taken a captive to Canada. His Indian master there, when under the influence of strong drink, repeatedly threatened his life, and the doctor, upon application to the French governor at Montreal, was ransomed, and despatched to France in a cartel ship, whence he was exchanged and sent to England. There, by reason of his familiarity with the French language, he was suspected of being a spy, but a letter which he wrote in exoneration of himself attracted the attention of General Edward Wolfe, the father of the future captor of Quebec, and Lamson was appointed surgeon's mate in the king's regiment which the elder Wolfe commanded. But Lamson desired to return to his home, and the general procured him a position on the Norwich man-of-war bound to America. He thus returned to Exeter after an absence of less than two years. He was not deterred by his hard experience from subsequently serving as surgeon of another New Hampshire regiment, as will appear.

At the same massacre at Fort William Henry, Major John Gilman was fortunate enough to escape captivity, but at the cost of losing his clothing and of suffering great hardships. It is said that to avoid the savages he was obliged to swim the Hudson river three several times.

His statement of the loss of property which he sustained on the occasion, and for which he was reimbursed by the province, is here given, as evidence of the style in which an officer of rank, at that day, took the field.

An Inventory of Cloaths &c Taken by the Indians from Major John Gilman after the Capitulation at Fort William Henry in August, 1757.—Viz.

To 1 Great Coat £15,—three other Coats £40—	£55.	0. 0
3 Jackets £30–2 Waiste Coats £12—	42.	0. 0
1 Gown £9–2 pr breeches £14—	23.	0. 0
5 White Shirts £25–4 Striped Do £10—	35.	0. 0
1 pr boots 90s.–2 pr shoes 50s—	7.	0. 0
2 Worsted Caps 22s 6–3 Linnen Do 20s—	2.	2. 6
2 black ribbands 22s 6–2 Silk handk'fs 60s	4.	2. 6
1 Tea pot 15s–1 Coffe pot 9s–2 tin pint pots 7s 6– 1 Do ½ pint 2s 1 Do Jill 1s 6 1 Tunnel 2s–Grater 1s 6	2.	6. 6

4 lb. Chocolate 20s 1lb. Tea 35s–8 lb. Coffee 32s	4.	7. 0
3 pr worsted stockins 100s–3 pr Cotton Do. 75s– 3 pr yarn Do. 52s 6–	11.	7. 6
1 gold Laced Hatt £12 1 Ditto plain £4	16.	0. 0
1 Wigg 90s–2 tin Canisters 10s 1 lb Ginger 5s	5.	5. 0
Bible 2 Vols 60s Sermon book 10s Ivory book 15s	4.	5. 0
1 book of Military discipline	0.	15. 0
2 c Pump nails 2s 6 ¼c 10d Ditto 3s–1 brass Ink pot 10s–	0.	15. 6
1 Pocket knife & fork 7s–1 paper Ink powder 5s		12. 0
2 pr gloves 20s–1 bridle 20s–Saddle baggs 40s	4.	0. 0
1 Comb 1s 6 2 blankets £6–1 Chest Lock 20s–	7.	1. 6
1 gun £17. 10 1 Sword Silver hilted £20–1 Flask 30s	39.	0. 0
1 Watch £20 1 Tin paper Case 7s 6	20.	7. 6
1 Pocket book 5s Cash 50s–Table Cloth 15s } 1 glass bottle 2s–1 wooden Ditto 4s–	3.	16. 0
2 flat Irons 33s 9, 1 Punch bowl 13s 3d–	2.	7. 0
6½ lb Pewter 60s 9d–½ Doz Tea Cups & Sausers 15s–	3.	15. 9
½ Doz knives & forks 33s 9d ½ Doz wine glasses 33s 9	3.	7. 6
1 pepper box 2s–a Cuttoo 6s–¼ Pins 4s–	0.	12. 0
⅞ yd Quality for gunstring 3s– 1 hodd 12s 6	0.	15. 6
1 Sword belt 15s–6 lb Soap 18s	1.	13. 0
To my Negro boy's Gun & Cloathing } he being taken & carryd to Canada	30.	0. 0
New Tenor	330.	13. 3

Errors Excepted per   JOHN GILMAN

Sworn to in yᵉ house May 5, 1758–

MEMORANDUM

    The Great Coat within mentioned was of Drabb Kersey almost new — one of the other Three Coats & one pair of the Breeches were of blue broad Cloth Fine (lately made) such as is now sold for £27 old Tenor per yard — another of the said Three Coats was of Fine Duroy lined with the same — about one Quarter worn — The other of said Coats was of Light Coloured broad Cloth had been Turn'd & New lined — one of the Jackets was of Scarlet broad cloth fine and new lined with white Tammy — another of the Jackets was of Cutt Velvet Figured — The other Jacket was of Green Silk Camblet Trimmed with Silver Twist on Vellum — the other pair of the Breeches were of New Deer Skin — both of the waiste Coats was of broad cloth light coloured about half worn.

LATER EXPEDITIONS AGAINST FRENCH POSTS.

    Immediately after the capitulation of Fort William Henry, a battalion of two hundred and fifty men was recruited and placed under the command of Major Thomas Tash. One of the companies had for its captain, John Ladd of Exeter. A small part of the company, apparently, came from the same place. The battalion was stationed at Number Four in the western part of the province.

Yet another regiment for the Crown Point expedition under Colonel John Hart was contributed in 1758 by the province. Its surgeon's mate was Dr. John Odlin of Exeter, and from the same place went Captain Summersbee Gilman and Captain Trueworthy Ladd, and a considerable proportion of the members of their respective companies, as well as Ensign Trueworthy Dudley of Captain Ladd's company. The regiment was divided, a part joining the expedition against Louisburg, and the residue, under the lieutenant colonel, performing guard duty on the western frontier.

In the year 1759 New Hampshire sent a regiment of a thousand men, under the command of Colonel Zaccheus Lovewell, to serve under General Amherst against the French stations on Lake Champlain. Exeter was the headquarters of the regiment, and among its officers were Richard Emery, major, Dr. John Lamson, surgeon, and Winthrop Odlin and Samuel Folsom, captains, all of Exeter. The company of the last was undoubtedly composed in great measure of men from the same town. The regiment participated in the reduction of Ticonderoga, and in the capture of Quebec, under General James Wolfe.

The next year, another New Hampshire regiment was raised for an expedition against Canada. John Goffe was its colonel, and Richard Emery served again as major, and John Lamson as surgeon. A company from Exeter and vicinity was commanded by Captain Jacob Tilton, whose ensign was Eliphalet Hale. This campaign resulted in the capture of Montreal and the reduction of Canada, so that peace once more allowed the American colonies to turn their entire attention to the promotion of their material prosperity.

After every war there is a manifest improvement in the militia. Those who have served and returned from the field, are not satisfied until they impart some of the soldierly discipline and drill which they there acquired to the citizens' military organizations at home. There had always been a militia in New Hampshire from the earliest settlement. The officers prided themselves very much on their titles, but the exercise of their commands was not very regular or imposing. If a man could shoot, and was ready to perform his tour of duty, the absence of uniform and ignorance of facing and wheeling were excusable.

THE EXETER CADETS.

But after the French wars, more attention was paid to the niceties of the military art. Governor John Wentworth took pride in a fine display of soldiery, and in 1769, encouraged the people of Exeter to form a *corps d'élite* as a sort of exemplar to improve the character of the militia in general. It consisted of a battalion, termed the "Cadets," and was handsomely uniformed and equipped. Several gentlemen of the town, of age and position, joined it; among them George Odiorne, Christopher Rymes, James Hackett, John Emery, Ephraim Robinson, Caleb Robinson, Nathaniel Gookin and William Elliott. They were allowed to choose their officers, who were commissioned by the governor; John Phillips as colonel, Samuel Folsom as lieutenant, Colonel and Peter Coffin as major. In 1770 the governor came up from Portsmouth with his lady and suite, when the commissions were published, and dined with Colonel Phillips; and two years afterwards, paid another visit to his Cadets, as he termed them, and was much pleased with their military proficiency. The colonel paid great attention to the discipline and appearance of the battalion, and called them out often for exercise.

The governor furnished new bright muskets and equipments to the corps, and, perhaps, flattered himself that he could rely upon their support under any and all circumstances. How entirely he mistook his men, a few short years were to demonstrate.

CHAPTER XII.

THE REVOLUTION, AND THE WAR OF 1812.

In New Hampshire, the American Revolution may be fairly said to have begun with the armed raid upon Fort William and Mary, at Newcastle, in December, 1774. This was strictly an uprising of the people, at the bidding of no higher authority than an advisory committee; and as those engaged in it were liable to be visited with condign punishment if it led to no change of government, it well bespeaks the intensity of the popular feeling of resistance to the coercive measures of the mother country.

In this enterprise a considerable number of Exeter men were concerned, though the occasion did not require that they should contribute anything beyond their presence and moral support. The following account of the part they took was drawn in substance from the lips of Gideon Lamson of Exeter, about fifty years after the occurrence:

A private scheme was laid by a few, the last of November, to get the powder and cannon from Fort William and Mary. General Sullivan, Colonel Langdon and Major Gaines and a few that could be trusted in Portsmouth, went down the river in boats in the night, and were to be supported early in the morning from Exeter. General Folsom, Colonel Nicholas Gilman and Dr. John Giddinge, with about twenty-five, who carried their arms, set off in the night agreed on. We rode into Portsmouth after daybreak, and stopped at Major Stoodley's inn; no appearance of the design; nothing was said about Sullivan's party. We had coffee about sunrise. Major Stoodley looked queer on such guests, with guns and bayonets. Colonel Hackett, with fifty or sixty foot, soon after eight o'clock, stopped at the hay-market, and waited for information from General Folsom. The inhabitants, on Hackett's arrival, looked on with wonder. Little was said in answer to inquiries. At nine, Colonel Langdon came to Stoodley's and acquainted General Folsom and company with the success of the enterprise,— that General Sullivan was then passing up the river with the loaded boats of powder and cannon. The guard at the fort was small; no resistance was made. Governor Wentworth knew nothing of the affair till it was too late. The narrator was the youngest person in the company of horse, and the only survivor of the party.*

While this account, as might be expected from the lapse of time, and the age of the relater, is incorrect as to some of the details of the transaction, there is no doubt that it is true in the main. A large party of Exeter men, seventy-five or upwards in number, marched to Portsmouth under arms, in pursuance of a concerted plan to render any necessary aid in stripping the fort of its armament, and in the movement they were headed by some of the principal citizens of the town, whose names are given in the foregoing account. For this, as well as for other demonstrations of his sympathy with the patriotic party, Colonel Nathaniel Folsom, two months later, was, by order of the royal governor, John Wentworth, deprived of his commission as a justice of the peace.

THE POWDER FROM FORT WILLIAM AND MARY.

There were taken from Fort William and Mary, besides cannon and small arms, about one hundred barrels of gunpowder. This was conveyed up the river to places of safety. There is a popular tradition that it was deposited under the pulpit of the Rev. Mr. Adams's meeting-house in Durham. Quite likely some part of it was hidden there; but as it was important to put it out of the reach of any party that might be sent to recover it, prudence would dictate, instead of storing it all in one place, to distribute it, and at rather distant points. A letter of the time, which has fortunately been preserved, seems to indicate such a disposition of it, in Exeter and the neighboring towns.

The letter contains an application from the chairman of the Portsmouth Committee of Correspondence to the like committee of Exeter, for four barrels of powder, under the apprehension that Portsmouth was in danger of being attacked. This was on the twenty-first of April, 1775, two days after the opening of hostilities at Concord and Lexington. The request was duly honored, and on the blank leaf of the application is a statement made at the time, of the quantity of powder stored in Exeter and the vicinity, as follows:

---

* A corroboration of this statement is found in the account presented afterwards by the town to the State of New Hampshire, as follows:

To Capt. James Hackett's company to Portsmouth to take the cannon, etc.,	£27. 11. 4
To Capt. John Giddings' company to ditto, etc.,	10. 11. 2
To Capt. Eliphalet Ladd's account, do,	6. 0. 0

Kingston, in possession of	Eben[r] Long,	12 barrels.
Epping, do.	David Lawrence & others, per rect.	8
Poplin,	Zach. Clough,	4
Nottingham,	Maj. Jos. Cilley, Jr.	8
Brentwood,	Capt. Marshall & James Robinson,	6
Londonderry,	Messrs. Sam[l] Allison & John Bell,	1
Exeter,	Col. Sam[l] Folsom,	2
"	Col. Nath[l] Folsom,	1
"	Col. Poor,	2
"	Theophilus Gilman,	2
"	Thomas Odiorne,	2
"	Ephraim Robinson,	2
"	John Rice, Esq.	2
"	Samuel Brooks,	2
"	Nath[l] Gordon,	6
"	John Row,	4
"	James Pickering,	4
Portsmouth,	Jos. Ayers, del[d] by Col. Gilman & D[r]. Giddings,	4
		72

There can be little doubt, from all the circumstances, that this return indicates the depositaries of the greater portion of the spoils of Fort William and Mary.

THE EXETER VOLUNTEERS MARCH TO CAMBRIDGE.

Events now crowded fast upon one another. On the evening of the nineteenth of the same April, came a flying rumor to Exeter that the British regulars had marched forth from Boston, and had opened hostilities at Concord. Very soon afterward the news was confirmed from Haverhill, with the addition that the country was gathering, and a severe action was raging, when the messenger left to alarm the towns. The inhabitants of Exeter were put in great commotion. Men thronged the streets, discussing the momentous intelligence until a late hour of the night. About daybreak the next morning an express arrived summoning volunteers to march at once for Cambridge. The bells rang, and the drums beat to arms. There was no hesitation in the men of Exeter. Notwithstanding the absence of their trusted leaders, Nathaniel Folsom, Nicholas Gilman and Enoch Poor, who happened to be in Dover, they made haste to be ready. Some cast bullets, others made up cartridges, and every preparation was completed in the shortest time possible. At nine o'clock in the morning one hundred and eight men paraded near the court-house, armed and equipped. No time was wasted in preliminaries. Which road shall we take? The nearest, through Haverhill. Who shall command us? Captain Hackett. Are you ready? demanded the newly chosen officer. Yes. March! And they were off.

The mothers and wives and sisters of the volunteers had busied themselves in fitting them out for the march, and bade them adieu with tearful eyes, but no word of discouragement. The Exeter company spent the first night at Andover, having crossed the Merrimac by ferry at Haverhill. They found the latter town shrouded in gloom, for in addition to the prospect of a war, the best part of their village had just been laid in ruins by a destructive conflagration. The company reached Cambridge about two o'clock in the afternoon of the second day. They were assigned quarters in one of the college buildings, the floor of which, as one of the men quaintly remarked, they found as hard as any other floor!

The next day they elected permanent officers. James Hackett was chosen captain; a ship-builder by profession—resolute, peremptory and courageous. In his youth he is said to have served in Major Robert Rogers's famous Rangers. John Ward Gilman and Nathaniel Gookin were the lieutenants, and John Taylor Gilman, Gideon Lamson and Noah Emery, Jr. were the sergeants. Nearly all of these served in some military capacity later in the Revolution. John T. Gilman, then only twenty-one years of age, was one of the most active and energetic in getting the company so promptly in the field. He was afterwards a member of the Continental Congress and fourteen years Governor of the State.

The company was well armed and equipped for actual fighting. Twenty-five of their muskets were from the stock furnished to the Exeter Cadets by the royal Governor Wentworth, who little imagined that he was supplying arms to be turned against the authority of the mother country. They had also bayonets, belts and cartridge boxes well filled with ammunition, and a good drum and fife, but neither tents nor blankets. They attracted no little notice, by their soldierly bearing, and were handsomely complimented by General Heath. The company, as such, remained at Cambridge but little more than a week, when, the immediate exigency having passed, some of the members returned home, and the remainder probably joined some of the permanent military organizations then forming.

Of the one hundred and eight men who marched to Cambridge on the morning of April 20, 1775, no complete list is known. It is unfortunate that the names of all the patriots who were so ready to respond to their country's earliest call to arms, cannot be handed down to posterity. The few which are known with certainty, are here given:

James Hackett, Captain	Eleazer Ferguson
John Ward Gilman, Lieutenant	Ebenezer Light
Nathaniel Gookin, Lieutenant	Jonathan Lougee
John Taylor Gilman, Sergeant	John Light
Gideon Lamson, Sergeant	Caleb Mitchell
Noah Emery, Jr., Sergeant	

At a meeting of the town on the ensuing fifteenth of May it was

Voted, That the men that went to Cambridge on the late alarm be paid ten shillings each, and that Mr. Hackett be paid ten dollars for his service.

Voted, To refund the money expended by the committee on that occasion; and that the provisions which were purchased for the support of said men, and are now in the committee's hands, be taken care of; that the powder, ball and flints be returned to the selectmen.

Voted, The thanks of the town to the committee for their good service.

The accounts of the selectmen show what the town expended on the occasion:

1775		
April.	Cash paid Timothy Chamberlain for bread supplied to the men that went to the Lexington battle	£3. 10. 0
	Cash paid the committee for the money advanced to the men that went to Cambridge	22. 10. 0
	For purchasing lead for the town to make bullets	10. 0. 0
1776	By paid 74 men for their service at Cambridge in April, 1776(5) as per town note	30. 7. 9
1777	Paid Eleazer Ferguson, Ebenezer Light, Jonathan Lougee, John Light and Caleb Mitchell in full for their service at Cambridge in the year 1775	1. 17. 3

An account was afterwards presented to the State of New Hampshire by the town, containing these items:

> To Captain Hackett's pay for his company
> to Cambridge in 1775 £137. 13. 10
> To Ephraim Robinson account to Cambridge
> in 1775 3. 0. 0

EXETER SOLDIERS IN 1775.

Of the men who filled the New Hampshire regiments in April and May, 1775, the names of the volunteers from Exeter, so far as they can be now ascertained, are here given.

Of Captain Henry Dearborn's company, in Colonel Stark's regiment it is stated in the fourteenth volume of the New Hampshire Provincial Papers that a part were from Exeter. The tax lists of the town contain three of the names on the roll of that company, Jonathan Gilman, Jeremiah Conner and Zebulon Marsh; but these may not be all, as a considerable proportion of those in the army probably had not reached the taxable age.

In Captain Winthrop Rowe's company, in Colonel Poor's regiment, were the following persons, with their several occupations and ages:

Jonathan Flood, husbandman,	31	Thomas Creighton, shipwright,	38
Noah Robinson, blacksmith,	19	Spencer Wallace, "	30
Eliphalet Lord, hatter,	20	Asa Ireland, saddler,	22
Moses Clark, blacksmith,	19	William Mugridge, blacksmith,	17
Moses Rollins, "	19	William McKim, barber,	47
James Beal, cordwainer,	21	Cato Duce.	

In Captain Philip Tilton's company, Colonel Poor's regiment:

Joseph Marsh, blacksmith,	21	Benjamin Loud, barber,	20
Nathaniel Coffin, husbandman,	26	Joseph Leavitt, husbandman,	50

In Captain James Norris's company, Colonel Poor's regiment:
Eliphalet Norris, blacksmith, 18

In Captain Samuel Gilman's company, Colonel Poor's regiment:
Eliphalet Coffin.

In Captain Richard Shortridge's company, Colonel Poor's regiment:

William Bennett
Simon Gilman
John Hilton
Simeon Marshall

Thomas Speed
Elijah Vickery
Thomas Webster

Colonel Enoch Poor was himself of Exeter, as was the surgeon of his regiment, Dr. Caleb G. Adams.

Returns of the following companies in Massachusetts regiments show that they contained Exeter men as follows:

Captain Jeremiah Gilman's company, Nixon's regiment, September 30, 1775:
    Samuel Magoon.

Captain Hugh Maxwell's company, Prescott's regiment, September, 1775:
    Edward Brown.

Captain John Currier's company, James Frye's regiment, October 6, 1775:
    Michael Brown.

Captain Isaac Sherman's company, Baldwin's regiment, September 26, 1775:

Caleb Robinson, 1st Lieutenant
Ebenezer Light, Sergeant
Caleb Mitchell, Sergeant
Jonathan Cass, Corporal
Isaac Grow, Corporal

Samuel Lamson, Sergeant
Joseph Brooks, Sergeant
John Light, Corporal
Thomas Carlton, Corporal
Moses Lougee, Fifer

Daniel Barker
William Cushing
Joseph Dolloff
Simeon Farmer (Palmer?)
Eleazer Ferguson
Caleb Gilman
John Gilman
Josiah Gordon
Theophilus Hardie
Ebenezer Judkins

Daniel Leary
Benjamin Leavitt
William Leavitt
Jonathan Lougee
Joseph Lovering
Dudley Marsh
John Nichols
Benjamin Norris
Samuel Norris
Abraham Perry

Joseph Purmort
James Ross
Elisha Smith
Samuel Smith
Trueworthy Smith
Josiah Steel
Isaac Stubbs
Bradstreet Taylor
Nathaniel Thing

Captain Isaac Sherman was a native of Connecticut, and had been a school teacher in Exeter; so that his acquaintance there enabled him to enlist so large a number in his company. It is probable that many of the men had gone to Cambridge on the first alarm, April 20, 1775; and remained there after their comrades of the Exeter company returned home; and the fact that New Hampshire did not organize her regiments at once, would explain why they and others joined regiments credited to Massachusetts.

On the sixth of October, 1775, the selectmen of Exeter, in response to a mandate of the General Court for a census, returned fifty-one inhabitants "gone to the army."

In December, 1775, at the urgent request of General Washington, New Hampshire furnished thirty-one companies of militia for service in the army, for the term of six weeks. Two of these companies came in part, at least, from Exeter. No rolls of them have been preserved, but the officers were as follows:

Twenty-second company: Benjamin Boardman, captain, Porter Kimball, lieutenant, Winthrop Dudley, second lieutenant.

Thirtieth company: Peter Coffin, captain, John Hall, lieutenant, James Sinclair, second lieutenant.

Each of these companies contained, also, three sergeants, three corporals, two musicians and forty-seven privates.

After their six weeks' service expired, a regiment was organized from the members of the thirty-one companies who were willing to remain, and Captain Peter Coffin was commissioned major thereof. How many other Exeter men served in it, there is no means of learning, as no rolls are known to be extant. The regiment continued in service under Colonel John Waldron until after the evacuation of Boston in March, 1776.

The Exeter rates assessed in 1775 against the following persons, all of whom were in the military service, were abated: Jonathan Brown, Samuel Hardy, Thomas Lord, William McKim and Timothy Sanborn.

EXETER SOLDIERS IN 1776.

A return of Colonel Poor's regiment in 1776, shows that William Evans of Exeter, twenty-seven years old, enlisted January 1, and deserted March 29, and that John Gilman, Jr., aged twenty-two, was sick and absent July, 1776.

In June and July, 1776, Colonel Isaac Wyman's New Hampshire regiment was raised to reinforce the army in Canada.

Exeter was represented in it by Noah Emery, paymaster, and by several members of Captain William Harper's company, of whom we are able to specify only two: Jonathan Flood and John Steel, the latter of whom enlisted as a private, but is said to have

In July, 1776, a second regiment was organized from men obtained from the militia of the State, to reinforce the army in Canada, and placed under the command of Colonel Joshua Wingate. In Captain Simon Marston's company were the following Exeter men:

William Bennett, Ensign	James Creighton	Simon Gilman
James Rundlett, Drummer	Levi Robertson	Moses Leavitt
Simeon Marshall	David Fogg	Abraham Sheriff
Edward Eastham*	Seth Fogg	Elijah Vickery
John Wadleigh	Simon Drake	Kinsley H. James
Ebenezer Ferguson	Thomas Webster	Samuel Daniels
Simeon Palmer	Samuel Dutch	William Cushing

On the nineteenth of September, 1776, Colonel Pierse Long was commissioned commander of a battalion organized on the continental basis, which, in November of the same year, was ordered to reinforce the army at Ticonderoga, and was there stationed when that post was evacuated on the approach of General Burgoyne in the year following. Adjutant James McClure was of Exeter, as were also the following persons:

In Captain Mark Wiggin's company:

Richard Dolloff	Joel Loud	Joseph Dolloff
Benjamin Perkins	William Chelsea	Joseph Kennison

In Captain John Calfe's company:

William McKim.

In Captain Nathan Brown's company:

Benjamin Hoyt	William Hoyt	Paul Lambert

In September, 1776, the General Court of New Hampshire voted to reinforce the army at New York with two regiments, the first of which was placed under the command of Colonel Thomas Tash. Captain Daniel Gordon's company of this regiment contained the following officers and men belonging to Exeter:

Zebulon Gilman, Lieut.	Dole Pearson	Caleb Thurston
Jonathan Norris, Ensign	Josiah Rollins, Jr.	Benjamin Conner
Dudley Watson	Samuel Smith	Abraham Brown
David Jewett	Daniel Barker	Samuel Moody
James Gordon	Jonathan Woodman	John Nealey, Jr.

---

* This name, being uncommon, is frequently confounded with Eastman, and so written.

In the month of December, 1776, an order was made for the drafting of five hundred men from the several militia organizations of the State, into a regiment to be commanded by Colonel David Gilman. Peter Coffin was major and Samuel Brooks, Jr., quartermaster, both of Exeter. It is probable that some six or seven of the members of Captain Daniel Gordon's company were Exeter men, but it is not easy to identify them.

From a return of the men enlisted for the war in Colonel Cilley's regiment of the New Hampshire line, 1776, it appears that two of them were from Exeter, viz. :

 Samuel Locke   Abner Thurston

EXETER SOLDIERS IN 1777.

Upon a re-organization of the New Hampshire troops in the continental service, in 1777, the roster shows the following officers from Exeter :

In Colonel Hale's (second) regiment :

 William Elliott, Adjutant   Ebenezer Light, Second Lieut.
 William Parker, Surgeon   Noah Robinson, Second Lieut.
 Caleb Robinson, Captain

In Colonel Scammell's (third) regiment :

 Nicholas Gilman, Adjutant   Nathaniel Gilman, Lieutenant

Exeter men enlisted in the second regiment :

In Captain Carr's company :

 Thomas Webster   John Dolloff
 Samuel Norris   Robert Arnold

In Captain Titcomb's company :

 James Creighton.

The following is a list of Exeter men hired or enlisted between January and March, 1777, for three years or during the war, belonging to the fourth regiment of militia, to complete the continental battalions :

Henry Barter	Trueworthy Dudley	Joseph Gordon
James Beal	Jonathan Flood	William Gordon
William Bell	Jonathan Folsom	Isaac Grow
James Creighton	Michael George	Simeon Haines
Samuel Davis	Cartee Gilman	Jonathan Hill

John Hilton	Daniel Morse	James Rundlett
Benjamin Hoyt	Enoch Morse	William Sloan
William Hoyt	Benjamin Nealey	Thomas Speed
Jonathan Hopkinson	William Nealey	Daniel Sullivan
John Jepson	Eliphalet Norris	Bradstreet Taylor
James Kelley	James Norris	Abner Thurston
Ebenezer Light	Samuel Norris	John Wadleigh
Moses Lougee	Paul (a negro)	Thomas Webster
Samuel Magoon, Jr.	Noah Robinson	
Jacob Merrill (Morrill?)	Moses Rollins	

In addition to these we find on various rolls, of the three years' men in the continental regiments in the spring of 1777, these names, from Exeter:

Dennis Bickford	Edward Leavitt	Abraham Wadleigh
Edward Eastham	John Nichols	
Simon Gilman	James Sloan	

In the month of June, 1777, the State authorized a battalion to be raised for the defence of Rhode Island, to serve six months. The command of it was given to Lieutenant Colonel Joseph Senter. Joseph Leavitt and Enoch Rowe of Exeter were respectively sergeant major and quartermaster of the battalion. It is believed that there were other Exeter men in it; probably in Captain Robert Pike's company.

Later, in September of the same year, the alarm was spread of the incursion of Burgoyne, and orders were given to raise one-sixth part of the men of the several militia regiments for immediate service, to resist the invasion.

Among those drawn from the Exeter men in the fourth regiment were the following, most of whom served in Colonel Stephen Evans's regiment:

Benjamin Cass	Nathaniel Ladd	Abraham Sheriff
William Chelsea	Eliphalet Lord	John Swett
Zebulon Gilman, Capt.	Joseph Lovering	Ebenezer Swasey
James Gordon	Benjamin Morse	Nathaniel Thing
John Kimball	Jonathan Norris, 2d Lieut.	Daniel Tilton
Moses Kimball	Joseph Permort	

These names are all found upon the tax lists of Exeter, and it is probable that there were others below the taxable age, but liable to do military duty, among those drawn.

HISTORY OF EXETER. 251

In addition to the foregoing, there were several Exeter gentlemen of position and mature years who volunteered and marched to Saratoga, under the command of Captain John Langdon of Portsmouth. Of this number were:

Col. Nicholas Gilman, as lieutenant
Maj. James Hackett
Capt. Eliphalet Giddings
Capt. Nathaniel Giddings
Ephraim Robinson, Esq.
Samuel Gilman

The taxes of the following persons were abated in 1777, upon the ground that they were "in the army," and probably all in the New Hampshire line.

Henry Barter
Jonathan Cass, Lieut.
John Dean's boy
Ward C. Dean's boy
Trueworthy Dudley
Jonathan Flood
James Folsom's boy
Jonathan Folsom
Cartee Gilman
William Gordon, Sergt.
Isaac Grow, Sergt.
Benjamin Hoyt
William Hoyt
John Kimball, Jr.
Moses Kimball
Ebenezer Light, Lieut.
John Light
Moses Lougee
James McClure, Adjt.
William McKim
Joseph Marsh, Corp.
Caleb Mitchell
Benjamin Norris
Caleb Robinson, Capt.
Elisha Smith
Thomas Speed
Josiah Steel
Nathaniel Thing

These, of course, were exclusive of the younger men, below the taxable age.

EXETER SOLDIERS IN 1778.

In the list of absentees from Colonel Cilley's (first) continental regiment, January 10, 1778, were the following residents of Exeter:

William Nealey,	age 29,	wounded;		left at Albany.
Thomas Hammon,	32,	deserted;	"	" Exeter.
Enoch Morse,	16,	sick;	"	" Fishkill.
Abner Thurston,	20,	wounded;	"	" Albany.

Absentees from Colonel Hale's (second) continental regiment:

James Rundlett, Sergeant,	23,	missing;		left at Hubbardton.
James Beal,	22,	"		"
Thomas Creighton,	42,	"	"	" Ticonderoga.
John Nichols,	20,	"	"	" Hubbardton.
William Bell,	22,		" "	Albany.
Edward Wade,	23,	sick;	" "	"

William Gordon,	24,	missing;	left at	Hubbardton.
Samuel Smith,	24,	deserted;	" "	Fishkill.
Henry Barter,	25,	"	" "	"
William Leavitt,	25,	"	" "	"
Jonathan Hopkinson,	26,	"	" "	"
Dennis Bickford,	36,			Albany.
Noah Marsh,	22,			"
John Hilton,	20,			"
Jonathan Hill,	17,			Jerseys.
Cartee Gilman,	41,	missing;	" "	Hubbardton.
Simon Gilman,	28,	"	" "	"
James Creighton,	27,	wounded;	" "	Albany.

It is to be recollected that this regiment suffered greatly by casualties, and more by capture at the battle of Hubbardton, Vermont, after the evacuation of Ticonderoga; and those described as missing and left at Ticonderoga or Hubbardton, were probably prisoners. Those described as "deserters," were probably not such in the usual acceptation of the term, but simply missing, in the haste and confusion of retreat; and apparently had rejoined the colors before June, 1779.

When the invasion of Rhode Island, then held by the British, was projected in 1778, a number of Exeter gentlemen entered into a written engagement with General Sullivan, who was to lead the expedition, in the terms following:

HAMPTON FALLS, April 12th, 1778.

We severally engage, if called by the Hon. Major General Sullivan before the close of the ensuing campaign, we will immediately repair to the quarters properly equipped for battle, as volunteers from Exeter in New Hampshire.

Samuel Folsom	James McClure
James Hackett	Benjamin Lamson
Caleb Sanborn	I swear I will go or send a better man
Peter Coffin	Esq. (William) Parker
Nathaniel Giddinge	goes himself or send a hand
Thomas Odiorne	Ward C. Dean
Eliphalet Giddings	Samuel Gilman
James Thurston	

This paper is given as a proof of the patriotic feeling which animated the most responsible and respectable citizens of the town; though it is presumed that no call was made under it for the military service of the subscribers.

HISTORY OF EXETER.

EXETER SOLDIERS IN 1779.

The following Exeter soldiers were enlisted between April and August, 1779, to fill up the New Hampshire continental regiments, to serve during the war:

John Bartlett
Richard Cook
Samuel Lock

Alexander Patterson
George Patterson

It appears from the roll of absentees of the second New Hampshire regiment, June, 1779, that John Sanborn, a farmer, aged thirty-three, was a private, residing in Exeter.

Five Exeter men were enlisted for service in Rhode Island under General Gates, August 28, 1779, for the term of six months, viz.:

Jeremiah Folsom
Nathaniel Lovering
Jonathan Lyford

Jonathan Thing
Levi Thing

A return of the men enlisted for the war in the third New Hampshire regiment, dated December, 1779, shows the following Exeter soldiers, viz.:

Abraham Comings
Richard Cook
Jonathan Flood

Daniel Morse
John Wadleigh

EXETER SOLDIERS IN 1780.

In July, 1780, Exeter furnished the following recruits for the New Hampshire regiments in the continental army, to serve till the last day of the succeeding December. Their ages, when known, are given:

Prime Coffin,	30	Richard Loveren,	20
William Cushing,	20	Joseph Parsons,	20
Joseph Dolloff,	21	Dole Pearson,	
Ephraim Dudley,	21	William Robinson,	26
Trueworthy Dudley,	19	Daniel Taylor,	
Luke Libbey,	22	Stephen Watson,	18
Prince Light,	37		

In the same year Henry Dearborn paid bounties to the following Exeter recruits to fill up the continental army:

Michael George
Samuel Marsh
Benjamin Morse

Daniel Sullivan
John Weeks

In July, 1781, Exeter sent the following six months' men to serve in the continental army at West Point:

Daniel Bickford   Richard Loveren

EXETER SOLDIERS IN 1781.

From a return made by the selectmen of Exeter May 25, 1781, it appears that the following persons from the town had enlisted in the New Hampshire regiments before January, 1781, to serve during the war:

Henry Barter
Richard Cook
James Dockum
Zephaniah Downs
Jonathan Flood
Michael George
Cartee Gilman
Ezekiel Gilman
Joseph Gordon
William Gordon
Jonathan Hill
John Hilton
Samuel Lock
Moses Lougee

Samuel Marsh
Benjamin Morse
Daniel Morse
Enoch Morse
William Nealey
James Norris
Samuel Norris
Alexander Patterson
George Patterson
John Powell
Daniel Sullivan
John Wadleigh
Thomas Webster
John Weeks

And these enlisted since January, 1781, for three years:

Ephraim Dudley   John Edwards   Eliphalet Rollins

On September 18, 1781, the selectmen of Exeter paid travel money to the following soldiers in Captain Jacob Webster's company in Colonel Daniel Reynolds' regiment of militia:

William Cushing
Trueworthy Dudley
Josiah Gordon
Benjamin Loveren

Stephen Marsh
Phineas Richardson
Daniel Watson

The whole number of different men furnished by Exeter during the Revolution, for service in the army, was not less than two hundred; a pretty fair proportion from a town of less than eighteen hundred inhabitants. Most of them served for brief periods, to be sure, but many of them were out on two or more expeditions. A few were probably not inhabitants of the town, especially in the later stages of the war, when it became difficult to obtain recruits, but it is believed that their number was more than counterbalanced by that of the Exeter men who were hired to fill up the quotas of other places.

The town was not unmindful of those who went forth to fight its battles, but dealt generously with them and the families they left behind them.

At a meeting of the town held on July 8, 1776, to expedite the raising of men for the reinforcement of General Sullivan's army in Canada, a bounty of two pounds, two shillings, over and above the colonial bounty, was promised to each good and able man that should enlist and pass muster.

On the nineteenth of January, 1778, it was

Voted, That the selectmen be a committee to supply such families of the non-commissioned officers and private soldiers belonging to this town as now are or shall be engaged in the continental service, with such necessaries of life as their circumstances require.

A subsequent resolution provides similar assistance to the families of such as have died in the service, and to that of Captain Caleb Robinson, at the discretion of the selectmen.

On the thirtieth of March, 1778, it was voted that Captain Trueworthy Gilman, instead of the selectmen, be a committee to furnish aid to soldiers' families; and on the twenty-ninth of March, 1779, Captain Eliphalet Ladd was chosen to supply the families of soldiers, agreeably to the resolution of the General Court for the purpose.

On the twenty-seventh of March, 1780, it was voted that the selectmen supply the families of the soldiers with money, not exceeding one-half of their wages monthly.

On March 21, 1782, the town appointed the selectmen a committee to supply the families of the soldiers of the town now in the continental service.

The accounts of the selectmen show the following disbursements under the foregoing votes:

1778. Supplying soldiers' families   £ 570. 0. 0
1779. Cash paid committee to hire soldiers to go to Rhode

paid hire of 3 continental soldiers	£180. 0. 0
" continental and state bounty to 5 soldiers	675. 0. 0
supplying soldiers' families	2262. 18. 7
paid S. Folsom money paid to hire soldiers	24. 0. 0
1780. paid committee for hiring soldiers	513. 0. 0
cash paid wives of five soldiers	240. 0. 0
committee to hire soldiers	6000. 0. 0
" " " "	12,119. 14. 0
" " " "	18,510. 15. 0

These last enormous sums, fortunately, were equivalent to only a comparatively moderate amount in hard money.

Nor, after the war was over, did the town forget the veterans, who had followed the fortunes of Washington in the regular military service. On March 29, 1784, it was

Voted, That every soldier who has been in the New Hampshire line of the continental army from this town and who has received no town bounty, shall not be taxed in the town for his poll for so many years as he served in the line.

The list of officers belonging to Exeter was not a small nor insignificant one, especially if we reckon not only those who belonged to the continental line, but also the much greater number who took the field on various expeditions or emergencies. It included in the regular continental service alone, one brigadier general, one major, one captain and A. A. general, three surgeons, three commissaries, two captains and two lieutenants.

A considerable number of the men in service perished from casualty or disease. Many received wounds; and the names of two, whose injuries were of exceptional severity, were for years upon the State pension list. A few lived well into the present century, and, it is to be hoped, enjoyed, in the decline of life, substantial tokens of the gratitude of the country which they risked their lives to sustain.

The jail in Exeter, during the Revolution, was made a receptacle for foreign prisoners and for tories from this and other provinces, especially New York. It was not a very safe place of confinement, as was proved by the notorious Henry Tufts and others having made their escape from it. A guard had to be furnished in 1777 for two months, when it was filled with prisoners, to keep them secure, and the following Exeter men were employed in that capacity:

Samuel Gilman, 3d
Theophilus Folsom
Samuel Harris
William Odlin

Simeon Palmer
James Rundlett
Samuel Rust
John York

THE WAR OF 1812.

With the party which brought on the war with Great Britain in 1812, the people of Exeter, in common with the majority of those of New England, had little sympathy. It was not to be expected, therefore, that they would be ready to volunteer, to any extent, to serve in the army in that contest. The town early refused to add to the pay of the militia called into the military service of the United States, or to offer them a bounty.

In the year 1814, however, several bodies of the State militia, which were composed in part of residents of the town, were ordered out by the governor, for the defence of the towns on the seacoast.

Captain Jacob Dearborn's company, enlisted September 26, 1814, for sixty days' service, contained the following men credited to Exeter:

William Pearson, Ensign
Isaac Kendall, Sergt.
Albert Carleton
David Goodwin

James H. Hale
Jonathan Johnson
Walter Little

On the ninth of September, of the same year, Captain Nathaniel Gilman, 3d, was ordered to Portsmouth with his company of militia, the greater part of whom probably belonged in Exeter.

Their term of service was about three weeks. The roll of the company was as follows:

Nathaniel Gilman, 3d, Capt.
Nathaniel B. Gordon, Lieut.
William Odlin, Ensign
N. P. Poor, Sergt. and Clerk
William Channing, Sergt.
Oliver Brooks,   "
John Gordon, Jr.,   "
Samuel Somerby,   "
Thomas Tyler,   "
Edwin Channing, Corp.
William Robinson,   "
Phillips Gilman,   "

Henry O. Mellen, Corp.
John B. Hill,   "
Abram Prescott, Musician
Weare Prescott,   "
Samuel Eldridge,   "
Benjamin Bachelder
Moses Bickford
Nathaniel Bickford
Josiah Blake
Francis Becket
Benjamin P. Bachelder
Benjamin Barker

Elijah Bean
Jonathan Brickett
James Burley
James Clark
Daniel Colcord
John R. Caldwell
John Clark
James Clark, 2d
Daniel Clark
John Cook
Solomon Davis
William Dickey
Peter Elkins
Jeremiah Edgerly
Jeremiah Fuller
William Fuller
James Folsom, 4th
Josiah Folsom, 3d
Peter Folsom
David Fogg
Abba Gilman
John Gilman
Joshua C. Gates
Francis Grant
Joseph Greenleaf
William Hood, Jr.
John Haley
Joseph J. Hoyt
Theodore Hill
Noyes Hopkins
John Lougee
John Leavitt
John Marsh
Charles Marble
Benjamin Melcher
Eliphalet Marston
Meserve Meader
James Odlin
Joseph Odlin
Nathan Parker
Moses Pike, Jr.
Samuel Pottle
William Penney
John Peavey
Moses Perkins
Samuel Robinson
John Rowe
Nathaniel Robinson
John Roby
Lowell Rollins
Jacob Rowe
Meshach Rollins
Sargent Rowley
Eliphalet Sweet
Trueworthy Swasey
Benjamin R. Sanborn
William Sawyer
Henry Swasey
Isaac Shepard
Amos Stickney
George Smith
Gideon Scriggins
Josiah G. Smith
Joseph Safford, Jr.
William Smith
Abraham Towle
Ludovicus Towle
Simon Taylor
Lewis Wentworth
John Williams
Benjamin Wiggin, Jr.
William Wiggin
John Webber
Benjamin Webster
Joseph York

On the tenth of the same September, Captain James Thom's company was ordered to Portsmouth on the same service, and remained about the same length of time. It is believed that they were all, with a possible exception or two, Exeter men. Fortunately New Hampshire was not invaded, and therefore their campaign was a bloodless one. The following is the roll of the company:

James Thom, Capt.
Hollis C. Kidder, Lieut.
Simon Winslow, "
Jeremiah Palmer, Sergt.
Jonathan Dearborn, "
Edward Lawrence, "
John F. Moses, "
Jonathan Folsom, Corp.
Lawrence Brown, "
Nathaniel Rundlett, "
Stephen L. Gordon, "
Charles Parks, Drummer
Joseph Parks, Fifer
James Chase
David Clifford
Joseph R. Dearborn
Jesse Dolloff
Robert Dunn
Nathaniel Dutch
Orrin Edgerly

Isaac Flagg
Samuel Garland
Samuel R. Gilman
John T. Gordon
Samuel Haley
Alexander Hodgdon
David Keller
Nathaniel Kidder
Levi Morrill,
John S. Noble
Benjamin Paul
Henry Ranlet
Winthrop Robinson
John Rundlett
Charles F. Sleeper
Benjamin Swasey
Edward Thing
Mark Tilton
Daniel Veasey
Jeremiah F. Young

This constituted, so far as is known, the whole of the contribution to the military service rendered by the people of Exeter in the war of 1812.

CHAPTER XIII.

THE WAR FOR THE UNION.

The first gun that was fired against Fort Sumter by the Secessionists, April 12, 1861, aroused all the patriotic feeling of the people of New Hampshire, in common with that of the entire North. But the State was in no condition to contribute any immediate aid to the force that was demanded for the defence of the national capital. For years no regular militia organization had been maintained by New Hampshire; and though a few quasi-military companies in the larger towns existed for holiday parade, they were in most cases no more under the command of the executive, than any other associations of civilians.

But when the President issued his proclamation for seventy-five thousand volunteers, for three months' service, more than double the number needed to fill the one regiment required from New Hampshire, were enlisted in less than two weeks. In Exeter, fifty-three men, most of them belonging to the town, volunteered; but before the first regiment was fully organized, the call of the President for forty-two thousand three years' volunteers appeared. Those who had enlisted for three months were then given the option to volunteer for the longer term, and many of them accepted it. It thus happened that no Exeter men were included in the First Regiment of New Hampshire Volunteers, for three months' service.

In the meantime the work of raising and organizing regiments to serve for three years, went on in response to the repeated calls made by the President. In nearly every one of these Exeter was represented, by original members, or by recruits subsequently forwarded. In two or three of them the town furnished the greater part of a company each.

After the last of the three years' regiments was dispatched, there came a time of great stress. The government resorted to conscription to fill up the depleted ranks of the army. Those who were drawn from Exeter duly complied with the requirements of the law. But the subsequent calls for troops bore hardly upon the town. A small place, with a steady population, the departure of the large proportion of its young men left comparatively few of the class from whom armies are recruited. It was not like the case of a large city, from whose superabundant population men can always be found for any enterprise, "for a consideration." The consideration Exeter was ready and willing to pay, and furnished its officers with all the money that was needed, to fill up its quotas. But the class who were willing to become food for powder for hire merely, can hardly be expected to make patriotic soldiers. The men who enlisted for the town in the latest stages of the war were, to a great extent, strangers to Exeter, and although some of them rendered useful service in the field, others were mere "bounty jumpers," and never reached the front, but deserted on the way thither.

And on the whole, Exeter nobly performed her part in putting down the Rebellion and preserving the Union. The lists of names given in this chapter will show how large a proportion of her small population fought for their country on land and sea, how many rose to command, and how many proved their devotion with their blood. Every call for men was promptly met, and at the close of the war the town was credited with a surplus of twenty.

The following list of the officers and soldiers of Exeter who served in the several New Hampshire regiments, with a brief account of the military history of each, is taken from the Reports of the Adjutant General of the State. It is liable to be imperfect, however, as from various causes, those reports lack completeness, to say the least.

The regiments which contained Exeter men left the State for the seat of war, at the dates following: the Second, June 20, 1861; the Third, September 14, 1861; the Fourth, September 27, 1861; the Fifth, October 29, 1861; the Sixth, December 25, 1861; the Seventh, January 14, 1862; the Eighth, January 24, 1862; the Ninth, August 25, 1862; the Eleventh, September 11, 1862; the Twelfth, September 27, 1862; the Thirteenth, October 6, 1862; the Fifteenth, November 13, 1862. All these were three years' regiments except the Fifteenth which was for nine months only.

THE SECOND REGIMENT.

Gilman Marston, colonel, mustered June 4, 1861; resigned April 17, 1863. Brigadier general of volunteers; repeatedly severely wounded; resigned

William H. Smith, captain, mustered 1st lieutenant of Company E August 1, 1861; promoted to captain August 1, 1862; transferred to Company B; died of wounds June 7, 1864.

Albert M. Perkins, captain, mustered 1st sergeant of Company E June 3, 1861; promoted to 2d lieutenant August 16, 1861; promoted to adjutant September 1, 1862; promoted to captain of Company D June 18, 1863; severely wounded at Gettysburg, Pennsylvania, July 2, 1863; mustered out June 21, 1864; dead.

William H. Colcord, 1st lieutenant, mustered corporal of Company E June 3, 1861; promoted to 1st sergeant; promoted to 2d lieutenant May 18, 1863; promoted to 1st lieutenant July 2, 1863; wounded at Cold Harbor, Virginia, June 3, 1864; mustered out June 21, 1864.

Frank H. Hervey, 1st lieutenant, mustered private in Company E September 13, 1862; promoted to quartermaster sergeant September 12, 1864; promoted to 1st lieutenant May 20, 1865; not mustered; mustered out June 12, 1865.

John H. Bennett,	Co. E,*	must. June 3, '61; transf. to 4 U. S. Artillery Nov. 4, '62.
Charles E. Colcord,	" "	must. June 3, '61; disch. for disab. Aug. 2, '63.
Andrew J. Currier,	" "	must. June 3, '61; w. sl. July 2, '63; must. out June 21, '64.
Calvin L. Dearborn,	" "	must. June 3, '61; d. of disease in hospital Nov. 16, '61.
Frank Ellison,	" "	must. June 3, '61; unaccounted for.
Charles A. W. Flood,	" "	" " " " deserted Dec. 26, '62.
Samuel Flood,	" "	must. June 3, '61; disch. for disab. March 15, '62.
Peter W. Gardner,	" "	must. Dec. 8, '63; transf. from Co. A 12 N. H. V. June 21, '65; deserted Warsaw, Va., Aug. 18, '65.
John H. Hale,	" "	must. June 3, '61; disch. by order Aug. 30, '62.
Isaiah T. Haines,	" "	must. June 3, '61; pro. corp. Jan. 1, '63; must. out June 21, '64.
Oren M. Head,	" B,	disch.; pro. adjt. 8 N. H. V. Dec. 1, '61.
Elbridge A. Leavitt,	" E,	must. June 3, '61; disch. for disab. Oct. 16, '62; dead.

* The following contractions are used, in order to economize space, viz., must. for mustered; transf. for transferred; dis. or disch. for discharged; disab. for disability; captd. for captured; w. for wounded; sl. for slightly; sev for severely; d. for died; k. for killed; pro. for promoted; corp. for corporal; sergt. for sergeant. In giving the year, the centuries are omitted.

HISTORY OF EXETER. 263

James McIntee,	Co. E,	must. Dec. 8, '63; transf. from Co. A 12 N. H. V. June 21, '65; absent on detached service Dec. 19, '65.
Edward Marshall,	" B,	must. Aug. 8, '64; absent sick Dec. 19, '65.
John Mori,	" F,	must. Dec. 11, '63; transf. from Co. A 12 N. H. V. June 21, '65; must. out Dec. 19, '65.
William H. Morrill,	" E,	must. June 3, '61; k. Williamsburg, Va., May 5, '62.
Dennis Murphy,	" "	must. June 3, '61; re-enlisted Jan. 1, '64; deserted Fredericksburg, Va., Aug. 10, '65.
Daniel Nelligan,	" K,	must. Aug. 18, '64; w. sev. and missing in action Gettysburg, Pa., July 2, '63.
Patrick O'Neal,	" F,	must. Aug. 18, '64; must. out Dec. 19, '65.
Charles Page,	" E,	must. Aug. 30, '62; d. of disease Philadelphia, Pa., Nov. 12, '64.
Francis Pettigrew,	" "	must. Aug. 30, '62; must. out June 9, '65.
David Pike,	" "	must. Aug. 30, '62; pro. corp. July 1, '63; must. out June 21, '64.
William Robinson, Jr.,	" "	must. June 3, '61; pro. corp. March 1, '63; w. sl. July 2, '63; pro. sergt. July 1, '63; must. out June 21, '64.
James Rundlett,	Co. E,	must. Aug. 30, '62; transf. to Inv. Corps Feb. 4, '64; dis., Feb. 20, '65.
James H. Sanborn,	" I,	must. Aug. 30, '62; w. sl. July 2, '63; w. May 16, '64; dis. for disab. Concord May 20, '65.
John Shepard,	" E,	must. Aug. 30, '62; des'd Falmouth, Va., Dec. 17, '62.
Jeremiah Tanner,	" "	must. June 3, '61; re-enl. Jan. 1, '64; dis. for disab. June 24, '64.
George A. Taylor,	" "	must. June 3, '61; corp.; dis. for disab. Aug. 2, '61; dead.
George H. Thing,	" "	must. June 3, '61; w.; re-enl. Jan. 1, '64; d. of disease Oct. 28, '64.
John O. Thurston,	" "	must. June 3, '61; must. out June 21, '64.
William H. Twilight,	" K,	must. June 8, '61; disch. for disab. Aug. 1, '61.

HISTORY OF EXETER.

THE THIRD REGIMENT.

John E. Wilbur, captain of Company B, mustered August 22, 1861; dismissed May 11, 1863.

Andrew J. Fogg, 1st lieutenant, mustered August 22, 1861; 2d lieutenant; promoted to 1st lieutenant June 17, 1862; resigned May 9, 1863.

George H. Giddings, 1st lieutenant, mustered August 22, 1861; corporal of Company B; promoted to 1st sergeant; re-enlisted February 14, 1864; wounded slightly August 16, 1864; promoted to 1st lieutenant October 12, 1864.

John S. Bryant, 1st lieutenant, mustered August 22, 1861; corporal of Company B; promoted to sergeant; re-enlisted February 24, 1864; promoted to 1st lieutenant April 6, 1865; died of disease May 23, 1865.

Simon N. Lamprey, 2d lieutenant, mustered August 22, 1861; corporal of Company B; promoted to 1st sergeant; promoted to 2d lieutenant July 20, 1863; dead.

John M. Head, 2d lieutenant; mustered August 22, 1861; sergeant of Company B; promoted to 2d lieutenant August 22, 1862; dead.

Woodbury Berry,	Co. B,	must. Aug. 22, '61; must. out Aug. 23, '64.
John Broadbent,	" "	must. Aug. 22, '61; pro. corp.; dis. for disab. Dec. 4, '62.
Samuel Caban,	" "	must. Aug. 22, '61; w. June 16, '62; disch. on account of wds. Sept. 2, '62.
William Caban,	" "	must. Aug. 22, '61; w. sev. June 16, '62; d. of wds. June 30, '62.
James Carlisle,	" "	must. Aug. 22, '61; w. sl. May 13, '64; must. out Aug. 23, '64; dead.
Gideon Carter, Jr.,	" "	must. Aug. 22, '61; must. out Aug. 23, '64.
Edward F. Carver,	" "	must. Aug. 22, '61; must. out Aug. 23, '64; dead.
John W. Clement,	" "	must. Aug. 22, '61; pro. corp.; red. to ranks; pro. corp. Dec. 5, '62; must. out Aug. 23, '64.
Charles W. Colbath,	" "	must. Aug. 22, '61; w. sl. May 13, '64; must. out Aug. 23, '64.
Ezra G. Colcord,	" "	must. Aug. 22, '61; corp.; transf. to U. S. Sig. Corps Feb. 29, '64.
Warren S. Dearborn,	" "	must. Aug. 22, '61; w. July 10, '63, pro. corp.; re-enl. Feb. 22, '64; w. by disch. of own rifle May 13, '64;
Cornelius Donovan,	" "	must. Aug. 22, '61; transf. to V. R. Corps Sept. 16, '63.

HISTORY OF EXETER.   265

Daniel W. Dudley,	Co. B.	must. Aug. 22, '61; pro. corp. July 7, '63; w. sl. May 16, '64; must. out Aug. 23, '64.
Sereno G. Dudley,	" "	must. Aug. 22, '61; must. out Feb. 22, '64.
John Duffy,	" "	d. of disease, Hilton Head, S. C., Sept. 21, '62.
Daniel W. Elliott,	" "	must. Aug. 22, '61; w. June 16, '62. pro. corp. June 23, '63; must. out Aug. 23, '64.
Joshua Fieldsend,	" "	must. Aug. 22, '61; must. out Aug. 23, '64.
John Finn,	" C,	must. Aug. 22, '61; dis. for disab. Hilton Head, S. C., Dec. 26, '62.
Edward F. Hall,	" B,	must. Aug. 22, '61; lost rt. arm Aug. 16, '64; must. out Oct. 23, '64; dead.
Horace J. Hall,	" "	must. Aug. 22, '61; d. of disease July 19, '63.
Erskine W. Hebbard,	" "	must. Aug. 22, '61; dis. for disab. July 28, '62.
George R. James,	" D,	must. Aug. 23, '61; wagoner; re-enl. Feb. 27, '64.
Booth Kaye,	" B,	must. Aug. 22, '61; d. of disease Aug. 20, '63.
Joseph Ward Leavitt,	" "	must. Aug. 22, '61; pro. corp.; re-enl. Feb.1 3, '64; pro. 1 sergt.; July 7, '65; must. out July 20, '65.
William R. Leavitt,	" "	must. Aug. 22, '61; d. of disease Feb. 18, '62.
John M. Mallon,	" D,	must. Aug. 23, '61; pro. corp.; dis. for disab. March 16, '63.
William S. Marston,	" B,	must. Aug. 22, '61; w. June 16, '62; transf. to U. S. Sig. Corps Oct. 13, '63.
William J. Morrison,	" "	must. Aug. 22, '61; corp.; red. to ranks Sept. 24, '61; pro. corp. Oct. 11, '61; pro. sergt. Oct. 18, '62; must. out Aug. 23, '64.
Joseph E. Prescott,	" "	must. Aug. 22, '61; re-enl. Feb. 14, '64; pro. corp.; d. of dis. Portsmouth, R. I., Oct. 29, '64.
John Riley, Jr.,	" "	must. Aug. 22, '61; re-enl. Jan. 1, '64; dead.
Ambrose E. Rowell,	" "	must. Aug. 22, '61; corp.; suspended; reinstated; re-enl. Feb. 22, '64.

William Senior,	Co. B,	must. Aug. 22, '61; must. out Aug. 23, '64.
James Smith,	" I,	must. Jan. 6, '63; w. Aug. 16, '64; pro. corp. May 1, '65; must. out July 20, '65.
Jacob D. Stone,	" B,	must. Aug. 22, '61; dis. for disab. Dec. 13, '62.
Frederic F. Thing,	" "	must. Sept. 17, '62; destd.; sentenced to hard labor and forfeit. of pay; must. out Sept. 17, '65.
John H. Thing,	" "	must. Aug. 22, '61; sergt.; pro. 1st sergt.; red. to r.; pro. sergt.; pro. sergt. major April 5, '64; must. out Aug. 23, '64.
James H. Tuttle,	" "	must. Aug. 22, '61; re-enl. Feb. 14, '64; killed Deep Run, Va., Aug. 16, '64.
Irvin M. Watson,	" "	must. Aug. 22, '61; sergt.; must. out Aug. 23, '64.
Jeremiah S. Weeks,	" "	must. Aug. 22, '61; d. of disease March 23, '63.

THE FOURTH REGIMENT.

Abram Dearborn,	Co. B,	must. Sept. 18, '61; dis. for disab. Beaufort, S. C., Sept. 15, '62; dead.
Charles McDonald,	" "	must. Dec. 8, '63; desrtd. New York city, Nov. 12, '64.
Joseph Nichols,	" I,	must. Dec. 8, '63; must. out June 22, '65.
George E. Thing,	" B,	must. Sept. 18, '61; dis. for disab. Annapolis, Md., Oct. 19, '61.

THE FIFTH REGIMENT.

Thomas Warburton, 1st lieutenant, mustered August 11, 1863, private in Company I; wounded June 16, 1864; promoted to 1st lieutenant October 28, 1864; mustered out June 28, 1865.

Daniel Bennett,	Co. H,	must. Aug. 10, '64; must. out June 28, '65.
Benjamin F. Bowley,	" I,	must. Aug. 11, '63; w. June 3,' 64; pro. corp. Nov. 1, '64; must. out June 28, '65; dead.
William Brown,	" H,	must. Aug. 17, '64; must. out June 28, '65.

George H. Bussell,	Co. I,	must. Dec. 7, '63; transf. to U. S. Navy April 19, '64.
John Campbell,	" H,	must. Aug. 16, '64; w. April 7, '65; must. out June 15, '65.
John Clark,	" "	must. Aug. 8, '64; must. out June 28, '65.
Joseph Dailey,	" A,	must. Aug. 16, '64; missing April 7, '65; regained; must. out June 28, '65.
Abraham Dearborn,	" I,	must. Aug. 11, '63; transf. to Inv. Corps April 26, '64; dead.
Victor Dixon,	" B,	must. Aug. 18, '64; must. out June 28, '65.
John House,	" A,	must. Aug. 17, '64; pro. corp.; w. April 7, '65; absent sick since.
Robert Jackson,		must. Aug. 22, '64; sup. to have deserted *en route* to regiment.
Patrick Kelley,	" C,	must. Aug. 11, '63; must. out June 28, '65.
Edward Lafferty,	" H,	must. Dec. 28, '63; deserted from hospital Alexandria, Va., Nov. 15, '64.
Daniel Moore,		must. Aug. 22, '64; sup. to have deserted *en route* to regiment.
Patrick McMullen,		must. Aug. 16, '64; sup. to have deserted *en route* to regiment.
Francis Mullen,	" D,	must. Aug. 11, '63. w. June 3, '64; must. out June 28, '65.
Joseph Murray,	" K,	must. Dec. 7, '63; missing at Cold Harbor, Va., June 3, '64.
Joseph B. Sawyer,	" E,	must. Aug. 11, '63; absent sick since May 26, '64; dead.
John Scanlan,	" E,	must. Aug. 16, '64; pro. corp. June 11, '65; must. out June 28, '65.
William Smith,	" K,	must. Dec. 7, '63; deserted, Front Royal, Va., June 1, '64.
John White,	" G,	must. Aug. 16, '64; d. of disease July 5, '65.

THE SIXTH REGIMENT.

Henry H. Pearson, lieutenant colonel, mustered November 30, 1861; captain of Company C; promoted to lieutenant colonel October 15, 1862; killed in action May 26, 1864.

Matthew N. Greenleaf, captain, mustered November 2, 1861; sergeant of Company C; promoted to 2d lieutenant April 29, 1862; promoted to 1st lieutenant November 12, 1862; promoted to captain July 1, 1863; wounded July 30, 1864; honorably discharged November 28, 1864; restored to rank March 1, 1865; mustered out July 29, 1865.

Edward T. Bennett,	Co. C,	must. Nov. 27, '61; dis. for disab. Georgetown, D. C., June 6, '62.
Albert Bowley,	" "	must. Nov. 27, '61; dis. for disab. Concord, N. H., April 28, '63.
Albert A. Bowley,	" "	must. March 12, '64; must. out July 17, '65.
Benjamin F. Bowley,	" "	must. Nov. 27, '61; dis. for disab. New York city, Oct. 17, '62; dead.
Ezekiel Clough,	" "	must. Nov. 27, '61; dis. for disab. Dec. 30, '62.
Thomas H. Clough,	" "	must. Nov. 27, '61; dis. for disab. Newbern, N. C., June 2, '62.
Thomas Clough,	" I,	must. Feb. 4, '64; w. May 12, '64; w. July 3, '64; transf. to V. R. Corps; must. out Aug. 21, '65.
Lucius Cole,	" E,	must. Aug. 11, '63; must. out May 12, '65.
Frank Corcoran,	" I,	must. Dec. 3, '63; pro. corp.; captd. Poplar Grove Church, Va., Sept. 30, '64; paroled; must. out May 23, '65.
Andrew J. Davis,	" C,	must. Nov. 27, '61; w. July 30, '64; must. out Nov. 29, '64.
John Doody,	" "	must. Nov. 27, '61; missing at Bull Run, Va., Aug. 29, '62; regained; dis. for disab. Philadelphia, Pa., March 16, '63; dead.
William Doody,	" "	must. Nov. 27, '61; missing at Bull Run, Va., Aug. 29, '62; regained; deserted Annapolis, Md., Nov. 25, '62.
James Elkins,	" "	must. Nov. 27, '61; dis. for disab. Roanoke Isl., N. C., June 24, '62.
James M. Farnum,	" H,	must. Nov. 28, '61; d. of disease De Camp. gen. hospital, N. Y., Dec. 11, '62.
John G. C. Fuller,	" C,	must. March 20, '65; transf. from Co. C 9 N. H. V. June 1, '65; absent sick July 17, '65.
David F. Gilman,	" I,	must. March 12, '64; transf. to V. Res. Corps March 1, '65; must. out July 29, '65.

Thomas Hartnett, Co. C, must. Nov. 27, '61; deserted Lexington, Ky., April 7, '63.

Zephaniah Henninger, " F, must. Dec. 7, '63; transf. from Co. F 9 N. H. V. June 1, '65; must. out July 17, '65.

Samuel S. Hodgdon, " C, must. Nov. 27, '61; dis. for disab. Philadelphia, Pa., July 28, '63.

William Keefe, " " must. Nov. 27, '61; deserted Newport News, Va., Aug. 2, '62.

Joel A. Leighton, " " must. Nov. 27, '61; sergt.; dis. for disab. Fairfax Sem'y, Va., Oct. 14, '62; dead.

Edmund E. Lovering, " " must. Nov. 27, '61; transf. Inv. Corps May 1, '64.

Albert F. Marsh, " " must. Nov. 27, '61; d. Hatteras Isl., N. C., Jan. 31, '62.

Morris Reardon, " " must. Nov. 27, '61; dis. for disab. Washington, D. C., Jan. 11, '63; dead.

Josiah B. Robinson, " " must. Nov. 27, '61; d. Roanoke Isl., N. C., June 20, '62.

Pascal L. Robinson, " A, must. March 21, '65; transf. from Co. A 11 N. H. V. June 4, '65; pro. corp. July 1, '65; must. out July 17, '65.

Joseph Rock, " C, must. Nov. 27, '61; dis. for disab. Newbern, N. C., June 26, '62.

William Ryan, " " must. Nov. 27, '61; missing at Bull Run, Va., Aug. 29, '62; regained; deserted while on furlough Jan. 9, '63.

George H. Smith, " " must. Nov. 27, '61; re-enl. Jan 3, '64; corp.; pro. sergt.; captd. Poplar Grove Church, Va., Sept. 30, '64; paroled; must. out May 26, '65.

Jared P. Smith, " " must. Aug. 3, '64; must. out June 4, '65.

Merrick M. Smith, " " must. Nov. 27, '61; re-enl. Dec. 27, '63; w. July 30, '64; pro. sergt. July 1, '65; must. out July 17, '65.

George W. Stevens, " " must. Nov. 27, '61; d. Nicholasville, Ky., Sept. 4, '63.

Patrick W. Sullivan, " " must. Nov. 27, '61; dis. for disab. Washington, D. C., June 26, '62.

George W. Swain, " " must. Nov. 27, '61; dis. for disab. Newbern, N. C., June 24, '62;

Joshua W. Weeks, Jr.,	Co. C,	must. Nov. 27, '61; deserted Newport News, Va., July 12, '62.
Stephen White,	" "	must. Dec. 26, '63; deserted while on furlough in N. H. Feb. 10, '65.

THE SEVENTH REGIMENT.

John Morris,		must. Dec. 5, '63; sup. to have deserted *en route* for regiment.
Samuel P. Sargent,	Co. F,	must. Feb. 28, '64; pro. corp.; pro. sergt. Dec. 29, '64; must. out July 20, '65.

THE EIGHTH REGIMENT.

Oren M. Head, adjutant, mustered December 1, 1861; honorably discharged March 19, 1864.

George S. Cobbs, 2d lieutenant, mustered December 20, 1861; sergeant of Company B; promoted to 2d lieutenant December 16, 1863; killed in action near Alexandria, La., May 14, 1864.

Sewall A. Abbott,	Co. B,	must. Dec. 20, '61; dis. for disab. New Orleans, La., May 2, '63.
John H. Carpenter,	" D,	must. Dec. 20, '61; d. of disease Camp Parapet, La., Nov. 9, '62.
Timothy Coakley,	" B,	must. Dec. 20, '61; transf. Vet. Res. Corps July 2, '63; must. out Dec. 19, '64; dead.
Charles H. Davis,	" "	must. Dec. 26, '61; deserted Cheneyville, La., March 19, '64.
John Dyer, Jr.,	" "	must. Dec. 20, '61; must. out Jan. 18, '65.
George Gilman,	" D,	must. Dec. 31, '61; deserted New Orleans, La., Nov. 8, '62.
Charles E. Hale,	" A,	must. Oct. 20, '61; musician; re-enl. Jan. 4, '64.
Daniel P. Hartnett,	" B,	must. Dec. 20, '61; w. June 14, '63; pro. corp. Aug. 1, '63; re-enl. Jan. 4, '64; transf. Co. B Vet. Bat. 8 N. H. V. Jan. 1, '65.
Ira Healey,	" "	must. Dec. 20, '61; dis. for disab. New Orleans, La., Oct. 27, '64; dead.
Samuel H. Henderson,	" I,	must. Jan. 4, '64; captd. Sabine Cross Road, La., April 8, '64; released; transf. Co. C Vet. Bat. 8 N. H. V. Jan. 1, '65.

David G. Kelley,	Co. B,	must. Dec. 20, '61; pro. sergt.; re-enl. Jan. 4, '64; dead.
Michael Melvin,	" D,	must. Dec. 20, '61; re-enl. Jan. 4, '64; transf. Co. B Vet. Bat. 8 N. H. V. Jan. 1, '65.
Henry L. Ruggles,	" K,	must. Aug. 11, '64; transf. Co. B, Vet. Bat. 8 N. H. V. Jan. 1, '65.
Jonathan Tebbetts,	" B,	must. Dec. 20, '61; dis. for disab. Carrollton, La., July 5, '62; dead.
George E. Thyng,	" "	must. Dec. 20, '61; dis. for disab. Ft. Indep. Boston, Feb. 14, '62.
James G. Tilton,	" "	must. Dec. 20, '61; pro. corp. July 6, '62; re-enl. Jan. 4, '64; transf. Co. B Vet. Bat. 8 N. H. V. Jan. 1, '65.
Woodbury C. White,	" "	must. Dec. 20, '61; d. of disease Ship Island, Miss., May 2, '62.

THE NINTH REGIMENT.

Chester C. Stevens, captain of Company D, mustered August 10, 1862; resigned December 25, 1862.

Charles J. Simons, 1st lieutenant, mustered July 3, 1862; sergeant of Company A; wounded July 30, 1864; promoted to 2d lieutenant November 1, 1864; promoted to 1st lieutenant February 1, 1865; mustered out June 10, 1865.

Alfred A. Avery,	Co. D,	must. July 26, '62; d. Paris, Ky., Oct. 19, '63.
Charles W. Batchelder,	" "	must. July 26, '62; corp.; must. out June 10, '65.
Francis M. Caldwell,	" A,	must. July 3, '62; corp.; pro. sergt.; transf. to Vet. Res. Corps Feb. 28, '63; must. out July 1, '65.
Leonard H. Caldwell,	" "	must. July 3, '62; 1st sergt.; w. sev. Dec. 16, '62; dis. for disab. April 18, '63.
John K. Carswell,	" D,	must. July 26, '62; transf. to Vet. Res. Corps Feb. 28, '63; must. out July 5, '65; dead.
George D. Clay,	" A,	must. March 20, '65; must. out May 6, '65.
Patrick Crean,	" D,	must. July 26, '62; must. out June 10, '65.
Jeremiah F. Dearborn,	" "	must. July 26, '62; must. out June 10, '65.

John Edwards,	Co. H,	must. Dec. 10, '63; captd. Spottsylvania, Va., March 12, '64; d. of disease, Andersonville, Ga., Sept. 11, '64; grave 8426.
David Floyd,	" B,	must. Dec. 7, '63; deserted Harper's Ferry, Va., April 4, '64.
Franklin H. Foster,	" A,	must. July 3, '62; pro. sergt.; pro. sergt. major March 1, '63; captd. Petersburg, Va., July 30, '64; d. of disease Salisbury, N. C., Dec. 14, '61.
Moses D. French,	" D,	must. July 26, '62; dis. for disab. Oct. 17, '62.
John G. C. Fuller,	" C,	must. March 20, '65; transf. to 6 N. H. V. June 1, '65.
William Gleason,	" D,	must. Dec. 8, '63; supposed to have deserted *en route* to regiment.
Thomas Goodwin,	" "	must. July 26, '62; corp.; deserted Antietam, Md., Sept. 17, '62.
Paul Gordon,	" "	must. Dec. 8, '63; deserted Hall's Gap, Ky., June 28, '64.
Zephaniah Heninger,	" F,	must. Dec. 7, '63; captd. Poplar Grove Church, Va., Sept. 30, '64; ret. to duty May 5, '65; transf. to 6 N. H. V. June 1, '65.
James Hicks,	" H,	must. June 14, '64; deserted Petersburg, Va., July 14, '64.
James Hughes,	" B,	must. Dec. 7, '63; deserted Stone Bridge, Ky., Jan. 2, '64.
Philander Keyes,	" D,	must. July 26, '62; wagoner; d. Milldale, Miss., July 30, '63.
John Lord,	" A,	must. July 3, '62; dis. for disab. March 15, '63.
James J. Miller,	" H,	must. Dec. 5, '63; k. in action July 30, '64.
John Morris,		must. Dec. 5, '63; sup. to have deserted *en route* to regiment.
Ephriam McCusic,	" A,	must. July 3, '62; corp.; captd. Petersburg, Va., July 27, '64; d. of disease Danville, Va., Feb. 7, '65.
James O'Brien,	" "	must. July 12, '62; deserted Concord, N. H., Aug. 24, '64.
Patrick Reynolds,	" "	must. July 3, '62; missing in action May 12, '64.
Joseph S. Rowell,	" E,	must. May 15, '62; w. Dec. 13, '62; dis. for disab. Washington, D. C., Feb. 17, '63.

William Ryan,   must. Dec. 7, '63; sup. to have deserted en route to regiment.
Andrew J. Sanborn,   Co. D,   must. July 26, '62; sergt.; k. Spottsylvania, Va., May 12, '64.
Christopher Staples,   "   "   must. July 26, '62; must. out June 10, '65.
George W. Tanner,   " •A,   must. July 26, '62; must. out June 10, '65.
Seth Tanner,   "   "   must. July 26, '62; dis. for disab. Dec. 15, '62.
Eugene Thurston,   "   D,   must. July 26, '62; corp.; deserted Camp Denison, O., Dec. 7, '63.
Joseph B. Wadleigh,   "   A,   must. July 3, '62; pro. sergt.; d. of disease Feb. 2, '64.
John E. G. Weeks,   "   D,   must. July 26, '62; transf. to Vet. Res. Corps May 8, '64; dead.
Henry Wood,   "   "   must. July 26, '62; deserted Baltimore, Md., April 29, '63.

THE ELEVENTH REGIMENT.

Moses N. Collins, lieutenant colonel, mustered August 6, 1862; major; promoted to lieutenant colonel September 9, 1862; killed in action May 6, 1864.

John K. Cilley, 1st lieutenant, mustered September 1, 1862; 1st lieutenant Company I; mustered out April 30, 1864, to accept appointment of captain and A. Q. master in the regular army.

John J. D. Barker,   Co. I,   must. Sept. 2, '62; d. of disease June 28, '63.
John W. Gilman,   "   "   must. Sept. 2, '62; d. of disease Petersburg, Va., Sept. 27, '64.
Thomas Heritage,   "   K,   must. July 26, '64; d. of disease on transport Oct. 13, '64.
Henry Howard,   must. July 21, '64; sup. to have deserted en route to regiment.
James Keith,   must. July 27, '64; sup. to have deserted en route to regiment.
Charles H. Nealey,   Co. I,   must. Sept. 2, '62; must. out May 17, '65.
Richard D. Nealey,   "   "   must. Sept. 2, '62; sergt.; w. Dec. 13, '62; d. of wds. Washington, D. C., Jan. 5, '63.
George H. Reynolds,   "   "   must. Sept 2, '62; must. out June 4, '65.
Pascal L. Robinson,   "   A,   must. March 21, '65; transf. to 6 N. H. V. June 1. '65.

Moses H. Stickney,	Co. I,	must. Sept. 2, '62; k. in action Petersburg, Va., July 30, '64.
Josiah W. Taylor,	" "	must. Sept. 2, '62; pro. sergt. major Sept. 2, '62; w. sev. May 6, '64; d. of disease March 18, '65.
William P. Tilton,	" "	must. Sept. 2, '62; transf. to brig. band Nov. 1, '63; must. out June 4, '65.

THE TWELFTH REGIMENT.

Henry Allen,		must. Dec. 11, '63; sup. to have deserted *en route* to regiment.
John Anderson,	Co. D,	must. Dec. 11, '63; deserted Yorktown, Va., April 12, '64.
Alexander Brown,	" G,	must. Dec. 11, '63; transf. to U. S. Navy April 29, '64.
George Brown,	" D,	must. Dec. 11, '63; k. Cold Harbor, Va., June 3, '64.
Melvin Elwood,	" H,	must. Dec. 8, '63; deserted White House, Va., May 31, '64.
Charles Frederic,	" I,	must. Dec. 11, '63; k. Cold Harbor, Va., June 3, '64.
Peter W. Gardener,	" A,	must. Dec. 8, '63; transf. to 2 N. H. Vols. June 21, '65.
Samuel Grant,		must. Dec. 11, '63; sup. to have deserted *en route* to regiment.
William Green,		must. Dec. 11, '63; sup. to have deserted *en route* to regiment.
Louis Limbold,		must. Dec. 11, '63; sup. to have deserted *en route* to regiment.
James McIntee,	Co. A.	must. Dec. 8, '63; transf. to 2 N. H. Vols. June 21, '65.
Frank Malleck,	" I,	must. Dec. 11, '63; transf. to U. S. Navy April 29, '64.
Louis Miller,	" I,	must. Dec. 8, '63; k. Cold Harbor, Va., June 3, '64.
John Mori,		must. Dec. 11, '63; transf. to 2 N. H. Vols. June 21, '65.
Patrick Riley,		must. Dec. 8, '63; sup. to have deserted *en route* to regiment.
George Stuman,	Co. D,	must. Dec. 11, '63; w. June 3, '64; dis. for disab. May 17, '65.
Samuel F. Turner,	" E,	must. Dec. 12, '63; transf. to U. S. Navy April 29, '64.

HISTORY OF EXETER. 275

THE THIRTEENTH REGIMENT.

John Sullivan, Jr., assistant surgeon, mustered Sept. 16, 1862; assistant surgeon; honorably discharged August 16, 1864.

George N. Julian, captain, mustered September 27, 1862; captain of Company E; mustered out January 31, 1865.

Job C. Allard,	Co. E,	must. Sept. 19, '62; w. sl. June 1, '64; pro. corp. Feb. 13, '63; w. sl. Sept. 30, '64; must. out June 21, '65; dead.
Frederick Bearse,	" "	must. Sept. 19, '62; corp.; transf. to U. S. Navy April 26, '64; dead.
John C. Brown,	" "	must. Sept. 19, '62; wagoner; d. of disease Exeter Jan. 19, '65.
Alanson Cram,	" "	must. Sept. 19, '62; must. out June 10, '65.
Newton Cram,	" "	must. Sept. 19, '62; corp.; transf. to U. S. Navy April 26, '64.
Jesse L. Dolloff,	" "	must. Sept. 19, '62; pro. corp. Aug. 26, '62; pro. sergt. March 1, '65; must. out June 21, '65.
James W. Folsom,	" "	must. Sept. 19, '62; must. out June 21, '65.
George E. Garland,	" "	must. Sept. 19, '62; pro. corp. May 1, '65; must. out June 21, '65.
Alfred J. Gilman,	" "	must. Sept. 19, '62; must. out June 21, '65.
Rufus Lamson,	" "	must. Sept. 19, '62; must. out June 21, '65.
Howard M. Moses,	" "	must. Sept. 19, '62; must. out June 21, '65.
George H. Rollins,	" "	must. Sept. 19, '62; transf. to Vet. Res. Corps Sept. 30, '63.
Frederic W. Sawyer,	" "	must. Sept. 19, '62; dis. for disab. Philadelphia, Pa., Dec. 14, '63; dead.
George H. Vanduzee,	" "	must. Sept. 19, '62; sergt.; k. Cold Harbor, Va., June 1, '64.
John C. Vanduzee,	" "	must. Sept. 19, '62; pro. corp.; dis. for disab. Point of Rocks, Va., Jan. 27, '65; dead.
William West,	" "	must. Sept. 19, '62; corp.; must. out June 21, '65.
Lowell H. Young,	" "	must. Sept. 19, '62; w. sl. June 15, '64; must. out June 21, '65.

THE FIFTEENTH REGIMENT.

Joseph E. Janvrin, assistant surgeon, mustered October 28, 1862; assistant surgeon; mustered out August 13, 1863.

George W. Batchelder,	Co. I,	must. Oct. 22, '62; must. out Aug. 13, '63; dead.
William H. B. Brigham,	" "	must. Oct. 22, '62; must. out Aug. 13, '63.
Frederic W. Carter,	" "	must. Oct. 22, '62; must. out Aug. 13, '63.
Gideon Carter,	" "	must. Oct. 22, '62; d. of disease.
George W. Gadd,	" "	must. Oct. 22, '62; must. out Aug. 13, '63.
John W. Morse,	" "	must. Oct. 22, '62; must. out Aug. 13, '63; dead.
William Nudd,	" "	must. Oct. 22, '62; d. of disease Exeter Aug. 9, '63.
George A. Prescott,	" "	must. Oct. 28, '62; deserted Concord; retd. March 14, '63; must. out Aug. 13, '63.
John A. Sinclair,	" "	must. Oct. 22, '62; must. out Aug. 13, '63.
John T. Sinclair,	" "	must. Oct. 22, '62; discharged.
Jeremiah W. Smith,	" "	must. Oct. 22, '62; deserted Concord; retd. March 14, '63; w. May 27, '63; must. out Aug. 13, '63.
John A. Smith,	" "	must. Oct. 22, '62; must. out Aug. 13, '63.
George R. Thurston,	" "	must. Oct. 22, '62; must. out Aug. 13, '63.
James S. Tuttle,	" "	must. Oct. 28, '62; deserted Concord Oct. 21, '62.

THE FIRST REGIMENT OF N. H. CAVALRY.

John Harvey,	Troop H,	must. July 29, '64; deserted Camp Stoneman, D. C., Sept. 3, '64.
Harrison Jones,	" "	must. July 29, '64; deserted Camp Stoneman, D. C., Aug. 27, '64.
John P. Weston,	" "	must. July 29, '64; deserted Camp Stoneman, D. C., Sept. 5, '64.

In addition to the foregoing list, Exeter sent into the military and naval service almost an equal number of other men whose positions and history have not been accurately noted and preserved.

HISTORY OF EXETER.

The Rev. Mr. Nason, at the close of each of the years 1861, 1862 and 1863, published the names of all the Exeter men who had, at those dates respectively, gone into the service, and from those names the following list is chiefly taken. Its complete accuracy is not vouched for; indeed it is quite clear that it is erroneous in its assignments to New Hampshire regiments, if the Reports of the Adjutant General of the State are to be depended upon. But without doubt nearly every one of the men named entered the service of the country in some organization or capacity, though it may not be correctly given in this statement.

OTHER EXETER MEN IN THE MILITARY OR NAVAL SERVICE.*

Charles W. Batchelder,	9 A.	J. F. Dearborn,	9 A.
William Bean,	6 C.	J. S. Dearborn,	Cook's Mass. Bat.
Charles Bennett,	7 Maine.	A. P. DeRochemont,	2 Mass.
A. J. Bowley,	R. I. Cavalry.	G. W. Dewhurst, U. S. Navy acting	
Eben S. Bowley,	4.	master.	
Azel P. Brigham,	11 Mass.	G. W. Dewhurst, Jr.,	1 S. Carolina.
Bruce Brigham,	11 Mass.	Henry Dewhurst,	Clerk.
Ephraim Brigham,	11 Mass.	John E. Dodge,	22 Mass.
George H. Brigham,	11 Mass.	J. Donovan,	8 B.
William Broderick,	U. S. Navy.	Samuel Dow.	
George H. Brown,	14 Mass. C.	Daniel V. Durgin,	8.
G. W. Brown,	R. I. Cavalry.	William E. Durgin,	12 Maine B.
Freeman Caban,	U. S. Navy.	Ira E. Early,	8.
W. Edwin Carter,	15 I; dead.	Horace Ellison,	5 Mass.
James W. Chase,	Mass. Battery.	John Farnham,	5 Mass.
William Chase,	U. S. Navy.	C. E. Folsom,	17 Mass.
George W. Clark,	32 Mass.	Charles H. Folsom,	Clerk; U. S.
William A. Clark,	12 Mass. K.	Q. M.	
George Clough,	8 H.	James W. Folsom,	11.
H. C. Clough,	1 Mass. B.	Joseph Folsom,	13.
Charles W. Colcord,	8 B.	Charles H. Foss,	8 A.
Freeman Conner, 44 N. Y.; Colonel.		George W. Fuller,	13 E.
Edward J. Conner, 17 U. S. A.; Capt.		J. F. Furnald,	4.
John Conner,	U. S. Navy.	George W. Gale, Jr.,	U. S. Navy;
W. Conner,	15.	Asst. Surg.	
Maurice Cotter,	9 Mass.	James H. Garland,	14 Mass. F.
J. N. Crummett,	U. S. Navy.	George Gill,	R. I. Cavalry.
E. P. Cummings,	23 Mass. Asst.	Isaiah W. Gill, U. S. Navy acting	
Surgeon.		master.	
Albert O. Curtis,	13 Mass.	Nathaniel Gill,	11 Mass.
George Dearborn,	15 Mass. Bat.	Gardiner Gilman,	45 Mass.

*The figures refer to New Hampshire Regiments, unless a different State is indi-

Sewall Goodwin,	U. S. Navy.	Charles Sleeper,	U. S. Navy.
John Gordon,	55 Mass.; Captain.	William H. Sleeper,	3 B.
Charles Greenleaf,	15 Mass.	Charles Smith.	
Daniel D. Haines,	8 B.	J. R. Smith,	44 Mass.
J. H. Hartnett,	2 E.	—— Stacy,	U. S. Navy.
Michael Hartnett,	U. S. Navy.	C. H. Staples,	U. S. Navy.
D. C. Harris,	8.	Charles W. Stevens,	Ky. Pay. Dept.
S. C. Hervey,	14 Mass. B; Lieut.	David Stickney,	8 D.
William B. Hill,	17 Mass. F; Lieut.	Daniel W. Stone,	U. S. Navy.
J. H. Huse,	2 E.	W. C. Swasey,	12 Mass. K.
James Irving,	1 Mass. B.	William E. Swasey,	U. S. Navy.
George W. Kimball,	U. S. Navy.	James M. Tappan,	8 A.
James Kimball,	U. S. Navy.	L. F. Tebbetts,	2 B.
James Kincaid,	U. S. Navy.	J. I. Tebbetts,	U. S. Navy.
Augustus J. Leavitt,	29 Mass.	Warren V. B. Tebbetts,	17 Mass. F.
Charles H. Leavitt,	29 Mass. K.	Eugene Thurston,	9 A.
John Ward Leavitt,	5 Mass.	Charles J. Towle,	U. S. Navy.
John Leavitt,	9 E.	Henry Veasey.	
Joseph W. Leavitt,	5 Mass.	Wheelock G. Veasey,	16 Vt.; Colonel.
Patrick Little,	9 A.	G. A. W. Vinal,	6 Mass. K.
Thomas McEnery,	3.	George A. Wadleigh,	3 Mass. Cav.; Lieutenant.
Daniel McNary,	U. S. Navy.		
D. F. McNeal,	19 Mass.	James P. Wadleigh,	9 A.
A. Merrill,	12 Mass. E.	W. Wainwright,	U. S. Navy.
John Munjoy,	U. S. Navy.	Orin P. Waldo,	11.
James Murphy,	8 B.	Henry Walker,	8 G.
Paul F. Nason,	A. A. G. Artil. Brig. 5 Corps.	William H. Walton,	3.
		Edward Warren,	U. S. Navy.
C. P. H. Nason,	Clerk.	Freeman Wallace,	U. S. Navy.
Charles H. Nealey,	11 I.	H. Weeks,	6 E.
R. Nealey,	U. S. Navy.	Henry A. Weeks,	26 Mass. A.
—— Norris,	15.	J. E. G. Weeks,	9 A.
John O'Brien,	U. S. Navy.	Nathaniel Weeks, 2d,	U. S. Navy.
G. G. Odiorne,	16 Ind.; Asst. Surgeon.	John S. Weeks,	Inv. Corps.
J. C. Payson,	13 D.	W. Whitehouse,	
T. K. Payson,	U. S. Navy.	Alfred Willey,	17 U. S. A.
Asa E. Perkins,	40 N. Y.	Charles Willey.	
Valentine A. Pickering,	2 Mass. Bat.	Edwin Willey,	13 Mass. B.
George W. Robinson,	28 Mass. I.	George Willey,	U. S. Navy.
Henry S. P. Rollins,	U. S. Navy.	James Willey,	12 Mass.
Charles W. Rogers,	U. S. Navy.	Henry Wood,	9 A.
Charles Rowe,	3 D.	W. Wyman,	4.
Frank G. Rundlett,	U. S. Navy.	J. R. Young,	8 B.
A. J. Sanborn,	9 A.		

It is much to be regretted that no complete and authentic account dents of Exeter who perilled their lives in their country's cause, has been kept. This should no longer be. Late as it is, and difficult as it may now be to compile such an account, the town owes it to the memory of the heroic dead to ascertain the exact part taken by every one of its citizens in aiding to preserve the integrity of the Union, to be inscribed upon permanent record, for the information of present and future generations. Exeter has yet no memorial of her soldiers; such a history would be a tribute more appropriate than any monument of marble or bronze and equally enduring.

A few brief biographical notices of some of the more prominent officers will properly close this chapter of Exeter history.

General Gilman Marston was born in Orford, New Hampshire, of which town his grandfather, a captain in the old French war, was one of the earliest settlers from Hampton. His early life was passed on a farm, and he paid the expenses of his own education by school keeping, graduating from Dartmouth College in 1837. He studied law, and in 1841 came, an entire stranger, to Exeter. In a short time, his diligence, attention to business and personal interest in the affairs of his clients, secured him a valuable practice. In 1845 he took his first step in political life as a representative in the State Legislature, and was twice re-elected, and appointed a delegate to the Constitutional Convention in 1850. In 1859 he was chosen a representative in the Congress of the United States, and re-elected in 1861. Being in Washington in the anxious period that followed the inauguration of President Lincoln, he joined the battalion commanded by Cassius M. Clay for the defence of the national capital, and as soon as the exigency there had passed, returned to New Hampshire and tendered his services to the State Executive.

He was appointed colonel of the Second Regiment, originally enlisted for three months only, but its term of service then extended to three years. One month from its arrival in Washington it took part in the battle of Bull Run, where the colonel was severely wounded by a bullet which shattered his right arm near the shoulder. The surgeons would have amputated it, to save his life, but, by reason of the colonel's resolute refusal, it was saved, to become about as serviceable as the other. He soon returned to his regiment, and was in command of it at Williamsburg, at Fair Oaks, during the seven days' battles before Richmond, at

Malvern Hill, and at Fredericksburg. In the winter of 1862-3, while active operations were suspended, he returned to his seat in Congress.

He was appointed brigadier general in the fall of 1862, but did not accept the appointment till April, 1863, when he was put in charge of a large camp of confederate prisoners, in Maryland, in command of his own and two other New Hampshire regiments. A year later, the command of a brigade of New York troops in the Eighteenth Corps was given him, and he took part in the assault on Drury's Bluff. Thence his command was ordered to Cold Harbor, and in the memorable conflict there his brigade in one-half hour lost five hundred men. Subsequently, he participated in the assault on the works at Petersburg; and then was directed by General Grant to take charge of several posts on the James, where he remained until autumn, but, being attacked by chills and fever, from his long exposure in that miasmatic region, he was obliged to quit the army on sick leave. He was again elected to Congress in the succeeding March, and after the fall of Richmond resigned his commission of general.

General Marston's military services are matter of history. Perhaps no higher commendation could be given him than that paid by a field officer of his old command. The Second Regiment, as is well known, made a distinguished record in the war. Major Cooper, in his report to the adjutant general, wrote thus of its first commander: "Whatever name or fame the regiment may possess, it is indebted for almost wholly to the untiring zeal and effort of Colonel, now General Gilman Marston."

After the expiration of his third congressional term, General Marston returned to Exeter and resumed his law practice. Neither his political nor his military service had lessened his zeal or his industry in his profession, and he has ever since had all the business that he cared for. Few of the principal causes arising in his section have been tried without his assistance, and he has often been summoned to other parts of the State to conduct important suits.

The people of Exeter have manifested their confidence in his ability and usefulness as a law maker by continuing him for an unprecedented length of time as a representative in the State Legislature, where his position and experience have given him an influence second to that of no other member.

In 1882 Dartmouth College conferred upon General Marston the honorary degree of LL. D.

Lieutenant Colonel Henry H. Pearson was born in Newport, Illinois, February 26, 1840. By his own exertions he determined to obtain an education, and with that view came to Exeter and entered the Phillips Academy. He was a faithful student, and a great reader of books, especially of history and biography. Upon the breaking out of the Rebellion he was fired with military and patriotic ardor, and proceeded, a part of the way on foot, to Washington, where he joined a military company and took part in the battle of Bull Run. He then returned to Exeter, and was commissioned by the governor captain in the Sixth New Hampshire Regiment. In order to procure recruits, he appointed war meetings in the towns adjacent to Exeter, at which he addressed the people with great effect, and thus he enlisted his company. The people of Exeter, in recognition of his patriotic services, presented him with a handsome sword and other substantial tokens of their regard.

In April, 1862, he commanded his company in the action at Camden, North Carolina, and in August, at the second battle of Bull Run, and wrote accounts of both, which showed superior military capacity. The next year he distinguished himself in the engagements at Chantilly, South Mountain and Fredericksburg, and, later, at Vicksburg and Jackson, Mississippi. And when, in December, 1863, the regiment re-enlisted, he received the merited appointment of lieutenant colonel. In the great campaign of Grant in Virginia, he led his men in the battle of the Wilderness with judgment and ability. On the twenty-sixth of May, 1864, at North Anna river, while reconnoitring the enemy through his field glass, he received the bullet of a sharp-shooter in the forehead which deprived him of life, at the early age of twenty-three.

He was beloved by his men for his attention to their wants, and for his coolness and courage and ability. Few volunteer officers were better equipped than he with the knowledge and qualities required to make a successful commander. His brother officers respected and admired him, and his death was sincerely lamented by all who knew him.

Lieutenant Colonel Moses N. Collins was born in Brentwood, in April, 1820. He received a thorough academic education, and for several years was employed in teaching in the State of Maryland. He then returned to New Hampshire to prepare himself for the practice of the law, and completed his studies in Exeter in the office of General Gilman Marston, whose partner he became.

He was elected to the State Legislature from his native town in 1860, and from Exeter in 1861 and 1862. In the latter year he received the appointment of major, and subsequently, of lieutenant colonel of the Eleventh New Hampshire Regiment, then forming. After arriving at the seat of war, the regiment had not long to wait before receiving their "baptism of fire." At Fredericksburg they joined in the bloody, unavailing assault upon Marye's Heights, and were, for two hours, exposed to a tremendous cannonade, and lost heavily.

In 1863 the regiment was engaged in the siege of Vicksburg, and afterwards bore their part of the hardships and sufferings of Burnside's army in Knoxville. At this time Lieutenant Colonel Collins was in command, in the absence of the colonel. In the spring of 1864 the regiment was ordered to rejoin the army of the Potomac, and was engaged in the terrible conflicts of Grant's advance upon Richmond. In the battle of the Wilderness on May 6, 1864, the Eleventh was under fire nearly all the day. In an advance against the enemy, Lieutenant Colonel Collins received his death wound, being shot directly through the head.

He was a man of much resolution and force of character, and had established a high reputation as a lawyer of skill and ability. His death was a public loss.

Captain Albert M. Perkins was a native of Exeter, and at the time of the breaking out of the war was about eighteen years of age. He had received a good academic education and was bright, active and popular. He was of an adventurous spirit, and loyal to the core, and entered into the contest with enthusiasm. His first position was that of orderly sergeant, from which he was promoted through several grades to the office of captain, earning every step by his courage and good conduct. He not only never shrank from any exposure, but set an example to his men of boldness and enterprise on all critical occasions.

It was in the battle of Gettysburg, the turning point of the war, that he received the wound which occasioned the loss of his arm, and eventually was the cause of his untimely death. He lived to witness the triumphant close of the great conflict, but not long afterward. His life was short, but it comprised more daring and sacrifice than most lives of threescore years and ten.

EDUCATIONAL.

CHAPTER XIV.

THE SCHOOLS AND ACADEMIES.

The first settlers of Exeter were too intelligent not to realize the importance of furnishing proper instruction to their children, nor did they make their home in the remote region of the Squamscot without providing a suitable teacher for them. Philemon Pormort, one of their number, was an experienced schoolmaster. He had taught the youth of Boston acceptably, and, no doubt, as long as he remained in Exeter, exercised his calling there. His stay was about five years. Before he departed, another person well qualified to be his successor had come to settle in the town : John Legat. He had taught a school in Hampton, and presumably filled the same useful station in Exeter. He lived in the place up to the year 1652, at least. The records of the town contain no information in regard to the earliest schools, as they were probably maintained, not at the public charge, but by the parents of the children who attended them. Nor for many years after towns were made by law responsible for the maintenance of schools, do the records refer to the subject. We learn, however, that in 1669 John Barsham, who had been employed elsewhere as a teacher of the young, was living in Exeter, and it is natural to suppose that he was one of the line of schoolmasters.

About the middle of the seventeenth century the colony of Massachusetts passed a law that every town of fifty families should maintain a schoolmaster capable of teaching children to read and write, and every town of one hundred families should set up a grammar school, provided with a teacher qualified to prepare boys to enter the university, that is, Harvard College. And this law, in substance, was continued in force in the province of New Hampshire after its separation from Massachusetts.

For two generations or more, the limited population of Exeter required the maintenance of elementary schools only, and had not reached the number of families which obliged the town to support a grammar and classical teacher. But somewhere near the beginning of the last century the increase of inhabitants had probably made it necessary to provide facilities for the higher grade of instruction.

At the annual town meeting in April, 1703, a vote was passed that the selectmen should hire a schoolmaster for a year, "to keep school three months in the old meeting-house, and the rest of the year at their discretion."

The next year the town voted to sell the old meeting-house, and "to build a school-house at the town's charge, and set it below Jonathan Thing's house next the river."

In 1706 the rather indeterminate vote was passed, that "the town would have a schoolmaster hired."

No school-house had been built in the spring of 1707, for the town then resolved:

That the school-house be built on the land the town bought of Mr. Coffin by the new meeting-house, forthwith; to be thirty feet in length, twenty feet in breadth and eight feet stud.

There is no reason to doubt that this order was carried out; and we may therefore picture to ourselves this first building erected purposely for a school-house in Exeter, standing on the opposite side of the way from the meeting-house, in dimensions one-half larger than the earliest known house of worship in the town. It was intended for the grammar or Latin school, without doubt. The records show that schools of less pretensions were also kept for longer or shorter terms in the more distant parts of the town.

LIST OF EARLY INSTRUCTORS.

We do not learn who filled the important station of head of the grammar school before the year 1714, but from that date the account books of the selectmen give the names of the successive masters, with few interruptions, to the close of the century. It will be observed that they were generally college graduates. The following is the list, which includes also the names of such teachers of other schools as are given.

Jonathan Pierpont (Harvard College 1714), 1714 and 1715
Nicholas Perryman[*] and Enoch Coffin (H. C. 1714), 1716.

---

[*] Mr. Perryman was a native of England, and a man of excellent education. He became a lawyer and practised in Exeter.

Nicholas Perryman, 1717, 1718.
Joseph Parsons (H. C. 1720) and Robert Hale (H. C. 1721), 1720, 1721.
Robert Hale and John Graham, 1722.
Ward Clark (H. C. 1723), 1723, 1724.
Benjamin Choate (H. C. 1703 ?), 1729.
Elisha Odlin (H. C. 1731), 1730.
Nicholas Gilman, Jr. (H. C. 1724), 1731, 1732.
Cartee Gilman, 1732.
Peter Coffin (H. C. 1733) and William Graves, 1733.
Elisha Odlin, 1734.
Meshech Weare (H. C. 1735), 1735.
Cartee Gilman (on north side of river) and Edward Barnard (H. C. 1736), 1736.
Peter Coffin, 1736.
Maverick Gilman's wife (at Deer Hill), Cartee Gilman (on south side), 1737.
Nicholas Gilman, Jr., and Edward Barnard, 1737.
Elisha Odlin, 1738.
John Creighton (on Deer Hill road), Abigail Conner (at Mast swamp), 1739.
Woodbridge Odlin (H. C. 1738), 1739, 1740.
John Creighton (on Deer Hill road), 1740.
Joel Judkins's wife (on white pine plain), Elisha Odlin (at Deer Hill), 1741.
Woodbridge Odlin, 1741, 1742.
Jonathan Glidden (at Tuckaway), 1742.
Mr. (John) Phillips (H. C. 1735), 1742, 1743.
Elisha Odlin, 1743.
John Creighton, 1744.
John Chandler (H. C. 1743) and Nehemiah Porter (H. C. 1745), 1745.
Nathaniel Gilman (H. C. 1746), 1746.
Nathaniel Gilman and John Creighton, 1747.
Stephen Emery (H. C. 1730 ?) and Nathaniel Gilman, 1748, 1749.
Cartee Gilman, Samuel Brooks (H. C. 1749) and John Creighton, 1749, 1750.
Ebenezer Adams (H. C. 1747) and John White (H. C. 1751), 1751, 1752.
John Feveryear (H. C. 1751), John White and Samuel Brooks, 1753.
William Parker (H. C. 1751) and Samuel Brooks, 1755.
Samuel Brooks, 1756, 1757, 1758.
Joseph Pearson (H. C. 1758), 1760, 1761, 1762, 1763, 1764, 1765.
Tristram Gilman (H. C. 1757), 1761.
Moses Badger (H. C. 1761), Dr. Joseph Tilton, Theophilus Smith, Jr. (H. C. 1761), 1767, 1768, 1769, 1770.
Joseph Pearson, 1770, 1771.
Philip Babson, 1772.

Joseph Pearson, Abraham Perkins, Joseph Cummings (H. C. 1768), 1772, 1773.
John Frothingham (H. C. 1771), 1773.
Thomas Burnham (H. C. 1772), 1773, 1774.
Isaac Sherman (Y. C. 1770), 1774.
Joseph Pearson, William Fogg (H. C. 1774), 1778.
Dudley Odlin (H. C. 1777), 1779.
Nathaniel Healy (H. C. 1777), Dudley Odlin, William Fogg, 1780.
Dudley Odlin, 1781.
Dudley Odlin, William Fogg, Nathaniel Parker (H. C. 1779), 1782.
Joseph Lamson (H. C. 1741 ?), William Fogg, 1783.
Andrew Hinman, William Fogg, 1784.
Andrew Hinman, Joseph Lamson, John Morrison, 1785.
Leonard Whiting, John Morrison, 1786.
Rev. Isaac Mansfield (H. C. 1767), Jonathan Fifield Sleeper (D. C. 1786), Ephraim Robinson, Jr., William Peabody, 1789.
Isaac Mansfield, 1790.
Caleb Robinson, Jonathan F. Sleeper, 1792.

TOWN ORDERS CONCERNING SCHOOLS.

It may be of interest to give a brief synopsis of the action of the town, from time to time, in respect to their schools, in the last century.

In 1728 the town ordered that "the school shall be kept five months in the school-house, four months at Pickpocket and three months at Ass brook."

This yearly division of the instruction, so that the children of each section of the town might enjoy their equitable proportion of its advantages, was kept up for a considerable time.

In 1734 it was wisely determined that the school be kept the ensuing year in the school-house or in the town-house, "which the schoolmaster should think best."

In 1739 the following vote was adopted:

That there be £120 raised by the selectmen to be improved in schooling in manner following: the proportion of money raised within the limits hereafter mentioned be improved in keeping school in the town-house or school-house; that end of the town called Ass brook to belong to the town school and the road that leads to Newmarket, and Pickpocket road as far as Richard York's, and the road to Philip Wadleigh's, and all the people that live thereabout; all the people in those limits to be accounted to the town school, and the remaining part of the town to have their proportion of money to be improved in schooling.

In the year 1742 the appropriation for schools had been increased to one hundred and forty pounds, and the selectmen were instructed "to hire a standing school in the town for the year ensuing; and that the several branches of the town have their share of the money allowed to them in proportion to what they pay; and in case the £140 voted be not sufficient therefor, that they be empowered to raise a sufficiency."

In 1747 the arrangement for schools adopted by the town was as follows:

Voted, That the selectmen raise so much money for the school as that the part paid by the inhabitants between Capt. John Gilman's on Tuckaway road and the little river on Kingston road, and on the neck road and so farther as to take in Major Ezekiel Gilman on Newmarket road and Peter Folsom on Hampton road, shall be sufficient to keep a Latin school, and that the money that the other parts pay shall be for keeping school as they shall agree on.

On the twenty-eighth of April, 1755, at a meeting of the town it was voted that the selectmen "have liberty to part off a convenient part of the town-house and build a chimney in it so that the town be at no cost for the same, but at the cost of private persons, and be for the use of the school."

In 1768 the town gave the selectmen authority to get the old town bell recast into a bell for the use of the school; but as the people who lived outside its sound were to get no benefit from it, it was considerately added that the outskirts of the town were to be at no cost for it.

FORMATION OF SCHOOL DISTRICTS.

In the year 1805 a law was enacted by the Legislature of New Hampshire, providing for the separation of towns into districts for the purpose of maintaining schools. In conformity thereto the town appointed a committee to examine, and recommend a proper partition, and in 1807 voted to divide the town into six districts, as reported by the committee. From that time, for three-quarters of a century, the duty of providing instructors for the public schools was taken from the selectmen, and imposed upon the officers of the several districts. This law has since been changed, without disturbance to the school system of the town.

It would be impracticable to furnish a list of all the teachers, even if it were desirable. Among those, however, who have entitled themselves by long and faithful service to particular remembrance, may be mentioned the Rev. Ferdinand Ellis, and his two daughters, Charlotte and Rhoda, Benjamin B. Thompson, a veteran instructor, and Sperry French, who has for above a quarter of a century had the charge of a capital grammar school.

The superintending school committees appointed by the town have ordinarily been gentlemen of education, interested in the subject, and cheerfully giving much ill compensated labor to the object of improving the means of instruction. Their efforts and recommendations have contributed greatly to bring the system of schools up to its present state of efficiency. Several of their reports have been models of the art of enforcing sound sense by pleasantry. Those of the late Professor Joseph G. Hoyt were as full of wit as of wisdom.

The present school board consists of Messrs. John D. Lyman, John A. Brown and George W. Weston.

Of the various changes in the State laws which experience has dictated, for the promotion of popular education, that which provided for the grading of schools was one of the most important, and was adopted in the town in the year 1847. A High school was established, in district No. 1, to which pupils from the other districts were admissible, and the grammar and primary schools were kept distinct. A handsome house for the High school was erected near the old town-house, on Court street.

The High school has had for its principal teachers the following persons: Elbridge G. Dalton (A. M., Dart. Coll. 1855) from 1848 to 1853 inclusive; Joseph Eastman (Dart. Coll. 1850) for 1854; Nathan F. Carter (Dart. Coll. 1853) from 1855 to 1863; Orlando M. Fernald (Harv. Coll. 1864) for 1864; Lewis F. Dupee for 1866 and 1867; John T. Gibson (Dart. Coll. 1864) from 1867 to 1869, and for 1871 and 1872; Frederic A. Fogg (Bowd. Coll. 1869) and Martin H. Fisk (Dart. Coll. 1852) for 1870; Albion Burbank (Bowd. Coll. 1862) from 1872 to the present time.

The High and the grammar schools have always maintained an excellent standing, notwithstanding the fact that for the last twenty years their pupils have been exclusively boys. This was the result of the establishment of the Robinson Female Seminary, which was open to all the girls above the age of nine years, and qualified for admission to the grammar schools. The fears of some advocates of the co-education of the sexes, that this separation would work injury to both, have thus far not been realized.

In addition to the schools described, the town has also one sub-grammar school, two intermediate, five primary, and three ungraded schools. The whole number of pupils is four hundred and ninety-four. The school board highly commend the schools, but strongly recommend that some of them should be better housed.

THE ROBINSON FEMALE SEMINARY.

William Robinson, a native of Exeter, left the town after reaching his majority, to seek his fortune elsewhere. In this he was highly successful, and at his death in Augusta, Georgia, where he had resided for many years, he left a large property. After making, by his will, a handsome provision for his widow and relatives, he appointed the town of Exeter his residuary legatee, in trust, for the purpose of establishing a female seminary in which " the course of instruction should be such as would tend to make female scholars equal to all the practical duties of life; such a course of education as would enable them to compete, and successfully, too, with their brothers throughout the world, when they take their part in the actual duties of life." In admitting applicants to the advantages of the seminary he directed that, " all other things being equal, the preference should always be given to the poor and the orphan." There is little doubt that Mr. Robinson, in making this disposition, had in mind the academy in his native town founded by Dr. John Phillips, for the education of boys, and intended to make this a companion institution for the other sex.

His death occurred during the civil war, which delayed for a time the announcement to the town of the contents of his will, but in the spring of 1865 the tidings were received. The town voted to accept the bequest, and appointed agents to receive it. The amount realized was about a quarter of a million of dollars.

A plan for the establishment and regulation of the seminary was carefully elaborated by a committee, and adopted by the town, and received the sanction of the Legislature of the State. It provided for a board of trustees to whom the government of the institution was committed, to consist of seven citizens, to be elected by the town, one each year, and to serve for the term of seven years. Any girl resident in the town who had reached the age of nine years, and was qualified for the grammar school, was entitled to enter the seminary, and enjoy its instruction without the payment of tuition.

In order that there should be no delay in affording the benefits of the gift to all, a school was opened in 1867 in the old town hall for girls, answering the above requirement, and experienced teachers were employed. It was also determined to procure at once a suitable lot of land, and to erect a building for the seminary thereon. This was not accomplished without some difference of opinion which produced delay; but on the fourth day of July, 1868, the corner-stone of the seminary building was laid on a commanding part of the tract of land, of near sixteen acres, which had been purchased in the western part of the village. In 1869 the structure was completed, of brick, with a granite basement, and three stories in height.

The seminary went into operation in September of the same year. Eben Sperry Stearns, a native of Bedford, Massachusetts, and a graduate of Harvard College in 1841, was the first principal. He remained in charge of the institution until the year 1875, during which time the school was thoroughly organized, and proved to be a success. Mr. Stearns then accepted the offer of the presidency of a normal college at Nashville, Tennessee, and left Exeter. His successor in charge of the Robinson Seminary was Miss Harriet E. Paine, who discharged the duties for three years with acceptance, and was succeeded by Miss Annie M. Kilham in 1878. She resigned the position after five years of faithful service, and George N. Cross, A. M., was appointed principal, who has managed the school with much success to the present time.

The course of study is arranged to extend over a period of eight years, and there is also a course preparatory to admission to college of three years. As complete an education can be obtained at the seminary as at almost any other institution of the kind in the country. Of course, the great majority of the pupils do not complete the course; out of an attendance of from one hundred and fifty to one hundred and seventy-five, the number of graduates averages yearly about ten only. But far the larger number of the pupils remain long enough to acquire an education which renders them "equal to all the practical duties of life," and are undoubtedly great gainers by the means of instruction which the liberality of the founder of the seminary has placed within their reach.

Most of the students of the Robinson Seminary belong to Exeter, though non-residents may be admitted upon the payment of a small tuition, and a few such are always in the school.

The corps of instructors at the present time are these:

HISTORY OF EXETER.   293

George N. Cross, A. M., Principal, Natural Sciences and Elocution.
Adeline A. Knight, Latin and Greek.
Martha F. Rice, B. L., Higher Mathematics, English and Composition.
Lucy Bell, Drawing, Painting and Art Study.
Oscar Faulhaber, Ph. D., French and German.
Eliza C. Lufkin, Language, History, Physiology and Reading.
Georgie W. Shute, English Grammar, Geography and Natural History.
Maria L. Grouard, Arithmetic, Algebra and United States History.
Cecilia F. Gustine, Vocal Music.
Bessie P. Ordway, Assistant in the Laboratory.

The present board of trustees consists of the following residents:

Charles G. Conner, Henry C. Moses, George N. Proctor, William Burlingame, Edwin G. Eastman, George W. Furnald and Charles H. Gerrish.

THE PHILLIPS EXETER ACADEMY.

John Phillips was a son of the Rev. Samuel Phillips of Andover, Massachusetts, and was born there December 27, 1719. Under his father's tuition he prepared himself to enter Harvard College at the age of twelve years, and graduated in 1735. For a while afterwards he was employed in teaching, at the same time studying medicine and divinity. He was admitted to the ministry but was never settled over a parish. In 1741 he came to Exeter, and there made his permanent home, at first as teacher of a Latin school; but afterwards engaged in trade, which he found very profitable.

As he advanced in years and increased in wealth, he was more and more impressed with the desire of employing his property for benevolent and charitable uses. He contributed liberally to the funds of the infant Dartmouth College, and joined with his brother Samuel in founding the Phillips Academy in Andover, Massachusetts.

But his special project was to establish an educational institution in his own town of Exeter. This he wisely accomplished in his lifetime, and enjoyed the satisfaction of seeing it chartered, organized and in successful operation before his death. The Phillips Exeter Academy was formally opened on the first day of May, 1783. Dr. Phillips endowed it by gift and devise with property to the amount of about sixty thousand dollars; far the greatest sum that had at that time been devoted to such an enterprise in the country. He drew up with anxious care a constitution for the government of the institution, nominated a board of trustees of whom he was one, and naturally the president; appointed the instructors, and for twelve years until his death in 1795, virtually directed everything connected with the Academy.

For the first few years the principal instructor was William Woodbridge, one of a line of preachers and teachers; but by reason of ill health he gave up the position, and a singularly felicitous appointment was made for his successor, of Benjamin Abbot, a native of Andover, Massachusetts, and a graduate of Harvard College, in 1788. He possessed rare qualifications for the place, an amiable disposition, sound scholarship, the power of command, a high sense of responsibility and honor, and the combination of qualities that are implied in the expression "a complete gentleman." Under his efficient charge the academy soon acquired that pre-eminence which it still, after the lapse of a century, retains.

Dr. Abbot was most efficiently aided in his preceptorial duties by a succession of able men and accomplished scholars, not a few of whom became afterwards distinguished as presidents and professors of colleges or in the various walks of professional life. The names of Hosea Hildreth, Francis Bowen, Daniel Dana, Samuel D. Parker, Joseph S. Buckminster, Alexander H. Everett, Nathaniel A. Haven, Jr., Nathan Lord and Henry Ware, on the roll of instructors, are vouchers that no "journey-work" was allowed to pass, among the pupils.

To the first of these, Hosea Hildreth, the principal and the academy were especially indebted. He was educated for the ministry, and occupied the pulpit a considerable part of his life. But he had exceptionally valuable qualities as a teacher. He was not content to guide his pupils in the humdrum style of the old pedagogues. He possessed much originality and humor, and strove to rouse the pride and ambition of the students so as to bring out the best there was in them. The formation of the "Golden Branch" society, for the promotion of scholarship and literary training, was due to Professor Hildreth. For fourteen years he devoted his best powers to the work of instruction in the academy, and his influence was peculiarly stimulating and elevating.

Nor was the list of Dr. Abbot's pupils less remarkable, for the number of those who subsequently rose to the highest rank in scholarship and in literature, in political and professional position. Among them were Lewis Cass, Daniel Webster, Joseph G. Cogswell, John G. Palfrey, Jared Sparks, Edward Everett, John A.

Dix, George Bancroft, Richard Hildreth, and many others scarcely inferior to them in celebrity.

Dr. Abbot, after having rounded out his half century of useful labor, resigned the principalship in 1838, on which occasion there was a great assemblage of his pupils, to do him honor.

His successor was Dr. Gideon L. Soule, a native of Freeport, Maine, and a graduate of Bowdoin College in 1818. He had been a pupil of Dr. Abbot, and afterwards associated with him as a professor of ancient languages in the academy for a number of years. He was fully indoctrinated with the views and methods of his old preceptor, was a thorough classical scholar, and possessed rare natural qualities for the high post to which he was promoted. He was of commanding presence and dignified manners; and understood well how to appeal to the best instincts of his pupils. Like his predecessor he had the gift of command, and was a thorough gentleman in the best sense of the term, courteous, high minded, just and generous in his treatment of all. He also was ably supported by the professors and teachers associated with him in his work. One of the number, now no more, was Professor Joseph G. Hoyt, afterwards appointed Chancellor of the Washington University, St. Louis, Missouri. In some respects he was the counterpart of his predecessor, Professor Hosea Hildreth. He had much of the same impatience with outgrown methods, and much of the same power of impressing his own personality upon his associates and pupils. He was not only not afraid of novelties, but courted them. He never half supported a measure; he was for it or against it with his whole might. The scheme of allowing greater liberty to the students, and of trusting more to their own self-government, he supported with characteristic warmth. He was in the board of instruction for eighteen years, and few of those connected with the academy from the beginning have left a more marked impress upon its management and character than Professor Hoyt.

Although Dr. Soule was not one given to innovation, it was during his rule, and with his assent, that a radical change was inaugurated in discipline and methods in the academy. A wider liberty was allowed to the students; they were treated more like men, and less like children. They were taught that in their conduct they were to be governed by the unwritten code of propriety and honor which is recognized as the fundamental principle of every moral and enlightened community, and not by any set of written regulations. Instead of studying, as theretofore, under the eye of an instructor, they were permitted to prepare their lessons in their own rooms, and only required to assemble at the academy for recitations, usually thrice each day, and for prayers. This was a critical experiment to make, perhaps, and its success depended greatly upon the disposition of the pupils to wisely use, and not abuse, the greater freedom granted them. The reliance placed upon their good sense and self-control was not mistaken. The adoption of the new plan has never been regretted; and the good effects of it are visible in the increase of manliness and self-respect among the great majority of the students.

After Dr. Soule had completed his fiftieth year of duty, as a professor and as principal of the academy, he retired from active employment, bearing with him the respect and cordial affection of his associates and of the numerous body of pupils who had enjoyed the great advantage of his instruction and his example.

The next immediate head of the institution was Dr. Albert C. Perkins, a native of Byfield, Massachusetts, and a graduate of Dartmouth College. He occupied the post of principal for about ten years, when he resigned it to accept the presidency of the Adelphi Institute in Brooklyn, New York.

For two years after this the duties of the principalship were practically performed by the two senior professors, George A. Wentworth and Bradbury L. Cilley, each of whom had been connected with the academy as a member of the corps of instruction for about a quarter of a century. They were active coadjutors of Dr. Soule in the "new departure" which was begun in his term of office, and still retain their positions in the institution.

Walter Quincy Scott, D.D., the present principal of the academy, assumed the station in 1885. He is a native of Dayton, Ohio, a graduate of Lafayette College in 1869, and had been the president of the Ohio State University before his appointment to this position.

In the one hundred and five years of its existence, the Phillips Exeter Academy has, as might be expected, made a prodigious growth, in point of means, and numbers and extent and character of instruction. For the first twenty years the average number of students was less than forty, and at the close of Dr. Abbot's connection, did not exceed seventy. It is now nearly five times the latter number. The endowment given by the founder, large as it was for the time, has been increased almost tenfold, in part by wise management, but chiefly by additional gifts from various benefactors. The average age of the pupils has increased by at least two years within the last half century, and in the extent and thoroughness of the work accomplished, the advance has been fully commensurate with the progress of the institution in the other respects mentioned.

The original endowment of Dr. Phillips has been since supplemented by various benefactions.

John T. Gilman of Exeter gave, in 1794, two and one-quarter acres of land, which constitute a great part of the inclosure in which the present academy buildings stand.

Nicholas Gilman of Exeter bequeathed, in 1814, one thousand dollars, the income to be expended for instruction in sacred music.

John Langdon Sibley of Cambridge, Massachusetts, began, in 1862, a series of gifts, amounting in all to more than forty thousand dollars, the income to be expended for the support of students of poverty and merit.

In 1870 the academy building was burned to the ground, and subscriptions were raised to the amount of nearly fifty thousand dollars to replace it. The chief contributor was William Phillips of Boston, Massachusetts, who gave ten thousand dollars.

Jeremiah Kingman of Barrington, in 1873, bequeathed the residue of his estate, amounting to above thirty-six thousand dollars, the income to be appropriated to the support of indigent and meritorious students.

Woodbridge Odlin of Exeter left by his will, in 1875, twenty thousand dollars to endow a professorship of English.

In 1877 and 1879 a gentleman, who preferred that his name should not be known, made gifts to the amount of ten thousand dollars.

In 1878 and 1880 Henry Winkley of Philadelphia made donations amounting to ten thousand dollars.

John C. Phillips of Boston gave twenty-five thousand dollars in 1884.

Francis P. Hurd, son of the Rev. Dr. Isaac Hurd, bequeathed, the same year, fifty thousand dollars.

Francis E. Parker of Boston made a residuary bequest in 1886, which yielded about one hundred and ten thousand dollars.

The last five gifts were unrestricted, and are applicable to the general purposes of the academy.

In addition to the foregoing principal donations, four scholar-

Charles Burroughs, in 1868, of the value of one thousand dollars.

George Bancroft, in 1870, of the value of two thousand dollars.

Samuel Hale, in 1872, of the value of two thousand dollars.

Nathaniel Gordon, in 1872, of the value of two thousand dollars.

To-day the Phillips Exeter Academy has a faculty of ten instructors, pupils to the number of three hundred and twenty and upwards, representing nearly every State and Territory in the Union, and divided between a classical and an English course of instruction of four years each; property, including lands and school buildings, to the amount of nearly six hundred thousand dollars; chapel, recitation rooms, dormitory, gymnasium and in process of construction a laboratory, — all fitted with the best modern improvements.

And these advantages are not for the rich alone; they are equally within the reach of any young man who has the ability and determination to obtain an education. Good conduct and diligence are the only requisites. The payment of tuition is remitted in all cases where students are in needy circumstances, and twenty-four scholarships are annually distributed among the pupils, who are applicants, according to proficiency and general merit. Four of the scholarships, the Bancroft, Gordon, Hale and Burroughs, are worth in money from seventy to one hundred and forty dollars each. The others — foundation scholarships as they are termed — yield between one and two dollars per week during the school year. The rooms in Abbot Hall are assigned to students of restricted means, at a trifling rent, and accommodate about fifty. In the same hall there are commons for the board of a somewhat larger number, at simply the cost price. A young man who obtains a foundation scholarship, therefore, needs little more to defray his expenses. About one-third of the whole number of students receive free tuition.

No distinctions have ever been made in the academy by reason of pecuniary condition. The poorest lad is as free to carry away the honors, and is as much respected if he is deserving of respect, as the *millionnaire*. Indeed, some of the most venerated names on the list of *alumni* are those of men who received aid from the foundation, which alone enabled them to accomplish their education, and who were proud in after years to attribute their success in life thereto.

The present faculty of the Phillips Academy is as follows:

Walter Quincy Scott, D. D., Principal, and Odlin Professor of English.
George A. Wentworth, A. M., Professor of Mathematics.
Bradbury L. Cilley, A. M., Professor of Ancient Languages.
Oscar Faulhaber, Ph. D., Professor of French and German.
James A. Tufts, A. B., Professor of English in the Classical Department.
George L. Kittredge, A. B., Professor of Latin.
Clarence Getchell, A. B., Instructor in Physics and Chemistry.
Carlton B. Stetson, A. M., Instructor in Latin and English.
Albertus T. Dudley, A. B., Director of the Gymnasium.
William A. Francis, A. M., Instructor in Mathematics.

The board of trustees consists of the following : George S. Hale, Boston, President; Charles H. Bell; Walter Q. Scott, *ex-officio;* Charles F. Dunbar, Cambridge; John T. Perry; Francis O. French, New York; and there is one vacancy.

THE FEMALE ACADEMY.

The Exeter newspapers of the earlier part of the century show repeated advertisements of private schools for " young misses." They met with so much patronage that it naturally occurred to the people that a permanent seminary for the instruction of females would be desirable. In 1826 a charter was obtained from the State Legislature, to incorporate the Exeter Female Academy. It went into operation soon afterwards, and the upper story of the building on Centre street, in which was the vestry of the First church, was secured for the accommodation of the school. The first teacher is believed to have been Miss Julia A. Perry, who was a pupil of the celebrated educator, Miss Z. Grant. Miss Perry remained at the head of the academy until 1834, when she was succeeded by Miss Elizabeth Dow, daughter of Jeremiah Dow of Exeter. She continued in charge of the academy for two years, it is believed. Her successor was Isaac Foster, A. M., a native of Andover, Massachusetts, and a graduate of Dartmouth College, in the class of 1828. He also served two years, from 1834 to the spring of 1836, when Miss Emily S. Colcord, of South Berwick, Maine, a lady who is remembered as possessed of peculiar qualifications for the charge of such an institution, became the principal of the academy. Her term of service extended over a period of seven years. Miss Elizabeth A. Chadwick, a daughter of Colonel Peter Chadwick of Exeter, was the next principal teacher for four years, and in the spring of 1849 gave place to Miss Sarah J. P. Toppan, daughter of the Hon. Edmund Toppan of Hampton. She held the position two years at least. Miss Harriet Russell, daughter of Dr. Richard Russell of Somersworth, is believed to have been the next in the order of preceptresses. Her stay was probably not longer than two years. Elbridge G. Dalton was at the head of the academy in 1853–4. At that time he had five assistants, and the aggregate number of pupils for the year was one hundred and sixty-six. The course of instruction extended over a period of five years, and Latin, modern languages, instrumental music, designing and landscape drawing, and other accomplishments were taught. The trustees at that time were the Rev. Isaac Hurd, Dr. David W. Gorham, Hon. Amos Tuck and Joseph Tilton, Esq. It is supposed that Mr. Dalton retained the direction of the academy until in 1858 he assumed the same position in the High school.

Miss Mary A. Bell, daughter of the Hon. James Bell of Exeter, next had the principalship of the Female Academy, probably for four years, when she was succeeded by Miss Amanda C. Morris of Somersworth, daughter of Captain John Morris. John Foster, a graduate of Dartmouth College in 1858, was the last principal of the Female Academy. He had the charge of it through the summer and autumn of 1864, and then gave it up. It was never revived. The splendid gift of William Robinson for the education of the girls of Exeter became known the next spring, and the Female Academy was superseded.

CHAPTER XV.

THE PRESS.

As there is no more efficient educational agency than the printing press, a chapter upon what it has accomplished in Exeter cannot be out of place in this division of our history.

The first printer who practised his art in the town was Robert Luist Fowle, a nephew of that Daniel Fowle who introduced printing in the province at Portsmouth in 1756. The uncle and nephew were partners there for a time before the latter came to Exeter, which was apparently before 1775. It is intimated that a difference in their political opinions was a moving cause of their separation, Daniel favoring the views of the "liberty-boys," while Robert inclined towards the conservatives. If so, they made a poor choice of abiding places, for while there was a strong ministerial party under the wing of the royal governor at Portsmouth, Exeter, almost to a man, stood up for the liberties of the country.

Robert Fowle, though a poor enough printer, is said to have done some work for the royal government, and afterwards, in 1775, for the new *régime*. He had enough of the Vicar of Bray in his composition, to appear, at least, to be true to the ruling powers, whoever they might be.

THE EARLIEST NEWSPAPER.

In 1776 he began to publish a newspaper in Exeter, called *The New Hampshire Gazette or Exeter Morning Chronicle*. It was sufficiently patriotic in tone, of course, for nothing else would have been tolerated. He was discreet enough to gain the confidence of the leading men in the popular movement, so that he was at length employed in the delicate and confidential business of printing the bills of credit for the State.

It was not long before counterfeits were discovered, of these, and of the similar paper currency of other States, and suspicion arose, from various circumstances, that Fowle was concerned in issuing the spurious bills. The Committee of Safety at once ordered him to be committed to the jail in Exeter. He had the effrontery then to propose to the committee that in case they would screen him from punishment, he would confess what he knew in reference to the offence. If he had done this from principle, in order that justice might be vindicated, it would have been pardonable, if not commendable, but his subsequent conduct forbids such a construction of his motives. The committee took him at his word, and he made disclosures of his furnishing the types to one or more tories, from which to print the fraudulent paper money. In return for his revelations the authorities were to allow him his liberty on bail. Whether it was that no one cared to be his surety is not known, but he remained in jail until he took "leg bail," and escaped to the British lines. This was about the first of August, 1777. The Committee of Safety wrote to the committee in Boston to ask their aid in arresting him; but he was beyond their reach.

In 1778 the Legislature of the State proscribed him with many other loyalists who had fled, and ordered his property confiscated; but probably he had little left to confiscate, if his complaint afterwards made of the pillaging of his effects had any foundation in fact.

He did not make his appearance again in Exeter for a number of years, nor until peace was established. He was then a pensioner, as was said, of the English government as a loyalist who had suffered loss of property for his principles. He married the widow of his brother Zechariah Fowle, and apparently kept a small shop for the sale of English goods in the town. An advertisement of his in *The American Herald of Liberty*, August 13, 1793, requests all indebted to him for newspapers, advertisements, blanks, etc., in the years 1776 and 1777, to make immediate payment; and notifies those persons who "plundered him of his printing office, books of account, papers, book-shop, etc., in 1777, to make satisfaction, or they will be called upon before the Court of the United States." After living in Exeter a few years, he removed to Brentwood, and there died in 1802.

There is a tradition that the "forms," from which the unauthorized bills of credit were printed in 1777, were some years afterwards found, concealed under a barn. They were probably some of those which Fowle acknowledged that he furnished to the tories of the time, who took off impressions from them, to which they forged the signatures. It was one of the methods of injuring and discrediting the government in the Revolutionary War, as is well known, to counterfeit its currency.

Robert Fowle kept up the publication of his newspaper until his arrest in 1777. The number for January 7, in that year, contained an account of Washington's victory at Trenton, and a notice by Joseph Stacy, jail keeper, of the escape of three prisoners "lately brought from New York as enemies to American liberty."

He was succeeded in the printing business in Exeter by his brother Zechariah. The latter must have had something of an establishment, for he continued to issue a newspaper, and in 1780 put forth an edition of the laws of the State in a folio volume of one hundred and eighty pages, with various continuations. Zechariah was an undoubted whig, and does not appear to have lost the confidence of his party by the defection of his brother. How long he continued his paper is uncertain; but certainly into 1781, and not improbably a couple of years longer.

It had the same title as the paper contemporaneously issued at Portsmouth, *The New Hampshire Gazette*. The Exeter journal, from the beginning, exhibited no publisher's name, and was sufficiently like its Portsmouth namesake to be mistaken for it except for the imprint at the bottom of the last page — "printed at Exeter."

The political tone of this gazette may be gathered from one or two specimens of its contents. In the number for May 28, 1781, is this item of military intelligence:

"FISHKILL, May 17. A party of ours under Colonel Green were surprised by the enemy about sunrise. Major Flagg was murdered in his bed; the colonel badly wounded. They attempted to carry him off, but finding he could not march so fast as their fears obliged them, they inhumanly murdered him. Blush, Britain, at the horrid relation!"

In a subsequent number, which contained an account of General Arnold's expedition in Virginia, were these lines, which are more remarkable for their force than for poetical grace:

> Oh Benedict, thy name recorded shall stand
> On shame's black roll and stink through all the land,
> In memory fixed so deep that time in vain

Zechariah Fowle died near the close of the war.

A newspaper is said to have been established in Exeter in June, 1784, and to have been discontinued in the succeeding December. Its title was *The Exeter Chronicle*, and its publishers were John Melcher and George J. Osborne. They were inhabitants of Portsmouth, but whether either of them lived in Exeter while this short lived venture lasted, is not known.

The next printer who is known to have set up an office in the town was Henry Ranlet. He began business in 1785, and about July in that year commenced the publication of a weekly paper called *The American Herald of Liberty*, which was continued under different names, and by various publishers until 1797. One remark may be made respecting all these early journals, that they are uniformly destitute of local intelligence, and are usually made up of articles extracted from other papers, of a few political essays, and of advertisements, which last are the most interesting of all their contents.

Ranlet was a more skilful printer than either of his predecessors, and the list of his publications is remarkable in number and in variety. Besides his newspaper he printed many books, partly on his own account and partly for publishers in Boston and Worcester, Massachusetts, and in Portsmouth. He was one of the earliest of country printers to supply his office with the types for musical characters, and issued as many as ten or twelve volumes of collections of vocal and instrumental music. He closed his industrious and respectable life in 1807.

On the principle, perhaps, that "competition is the soul of business," another printing office was opened about the year 1790 in Exeter by John Lamson, who had been a partner of Ranlet in 1787. Mr. Lamson took for his associate Thomas Odiorne, a son of Dea. Thomas Odiorne, and a graduate from Dartmouth College in 1791. He possessed literary taste and ability but had no practical acquaintance with the business of a printer. Their connection was of short duration. Mr. Odiorne's name appears alone in the imprint of a few volumes, in point of typography very tastefully executed for the time. He was an author of two or three poetical works, one of which, entitled *The Progress of Refinement*, was published in Exeter.

THE FIRST NEW TESTAMENT PRINTED IN THE STATE.

In 1794 William Stearns and Samuel Winslow brought out a

partially bound an edition of two thousand copies of the New Testament, the first ever issued in New Hampshire. New Ipswich has claimed the honor of having the first press in the State to put forth any part of the Scriptures, but Dover had preceded it by an edition in 1803, and Exeter was seven years in advance of that. Nearly the whole edition was unfortunately consumed by a fire in the printing office, so that it is almost impossible to find a copy at this day.

The *American Herald of Liberty*, which was begun by Henry Ranlet, and underwent repeated changes of title, to *The New Hampshire Gazette* in 1791; *The New Hampshire Gazetteer* in 1792; *The Weekly Visitor or Exeter Gazette* in 1795, and *The Herald of Liberty or Exeter Gazette* in 1796, was published successively by the printers already named, Lamson, Lamson & Odiorne, Samuel Winslow and Stearns & Winslow.

SAMPLES OF EARLY JOURNALISM.

One or two extracts from the paper may be amusing. The first is an advertisement of a lost mare:

Perdited or furated on an inauspicious nocturnal hour subsequent to the day lately authoritatively devoted to humiliation and penitence from the fœnilian dome of the hyposcriptoratid, a leucophœated quadruped, of the jumentean order, equestrian genus, feminine gender, capitally fuscated, asterically marked in cinciput, in stature according to equisonic admeasurement fourteen and a half clenched fists, in the quindecimal year of existence, tollutates with celerity, succussates with agility a course concitated, is elegantly graceful, and all in the superlative degree. Whoever from the preceding iconism, by percontation, deambulation, perscuitation or otherwise, shall give intelligence of the nonpareil, and will apport or communicate the same to me, shall become reciprocal of a remuneration adequate to the emolument from

JOHN HOPKINSON.

April 18, 1788.

This effusion must probably have been the production of some mischievous student of Dr. Phillips's new academy, as Mr. Hopkinson was a worthy tradesman, who was about as likely to have written one of Cicero's orations as to have produced such a farrago of turgid bombast.

Another passage from the paper of February 22, 1788, was in relation to the convention then sitting to ratify the proposed Federal Constitution.

Yesterday the honorable Convention concluded their debates on the several sections of the Constitution, and it is supposed it will be canvassed upon general principles previous to the all important question. In their debates has been the greatest candor, a desire for information on the important subject appears to have been the object of the members composing that honorable body, and from their desire to promote the great interest of the community, we hope the most salutary determinations.

> The all important moment is at hand
>   When we the fate of millions must decide,
> Freedom and peace will soon pervade the land,
>   Or Anarch stretch his horrid pinions wide.

From this extract it is not difficult to infer the political leaning of the paper.

The journal, entitled *The Freeman's Oracle or New Hampshire Advertiser*, was commenced in the town about August 1, 1786, presumably by Lamson and Ranlet who conducted it in 1788. It bore the imprint of John Lamson alone in 1789, and did not survive that year.

In 1797 Henry Ranlet established a paper entitled *The Political Banquet and Farmer's Feast*. *The Exeter Federal Miscellany* was established about December 1, 1798, and the former paper was probably merged in the latter, which, thus fortified, was certainly continued to October, 1799, and perhaps longer.

No complete files of any of these early Exeter journals, which were all weekly publications, are known to exist, and it is from a few scattering copies that the foregoing information has been chiefly derived. It will be seen, however, that from 1774, or earlier, when Robert L. Fowle first set up his press in Exeter, to the end of the century, the town was probably always supplied with one or more printers, and for nearly all the time with a like number of newspapers.

As has been stated, Mr. Ranlet lived and continued his printing business until 1807. During the last part of his life he had as a partner, Charles Norris, a practical printer, who kept up the business after Mr. Ranlet's death until 1832. A part of that time he had partners. John Sawyer was one, and Ephraim C. Beals another; and Mr. Norris was for some time connected with the publishing firm of E. Little & Co. of Newburyport, Massachusetts, for which he did a considerable amount of printing. The *chef d'œuvre* of his press was Hoole's translation of Tasso's *Jerusalem Delivered*, published in 1819 in two octavo volumes. It is a really beautiful specimen of Exeter typography.

It is not known that the town could boast a newspaper between 1800 and 1810, but on May 21, of the latter year, Ephraim C. Beals began the publication of *The Constitutionalist*, a weekly journal of fair dimensions. In February, 1811, Mr. Beals transferred the paper to Charles Norris & Co., and at the expiration of the first year it came to a stop, probably for lack of support; but Mr. Beals recommenced it June 23, 1812, and it survived, with two other changes of proprietors, till June, 1814. It has been said that James Thom, a young lawyer, afterwards of Derry, had the editorial charge of the paper, but it is pretty evident that he could have given little time to it, for in respect to original matter and local news, it was but scarcely in advance of its predecessors of the last century. In March, 1813, Joseph G. Folsom became its publisher and editor, but gave it up in the following June on account of ill health, when Nathaniel Boardman took it up and carried it to its end. The period of the war of 1812 was characterized by great bitterness of political feeling and by very unpleasant personalities in journalism, and *The Constitutionalist* was not entirely free from them.

It was two years after the termination of *The Constitutionalist*, before another paper arose. It was started by Henry A. Ranlet, October 2, 1816, under the name of *The Watchman*. Two months later it went into the hands of Nathaniel Boardman, and its title was changed to the *Exeter Watchman*. But newspaper property in the town was not very permanent in those days, and November 9, 1819, George Lamson became the proprietor, and added to it the second title of *Agricultural Repository;* and to complete the round of metamorphoses, Samuel T. Moses became the publisher February 6, 1821, and gave it the designation of *The Northern Republican*. Mr. Moses was a practical printer, and his name appears upon the title page of several publications at about this date. *The Northern Republican* was continued only to the fortieth number.

John J. Williams, a native of Exeter, and a trained printer, began business in 1818, in the office which had been occupied by Henry A. Ranlet, then lately deceased. His brother, Benjamin J. Williams, was a bookbinder; and a short time afterwards they united, under the firm of J. and B. Williams, in the printing and publishing business, to which they subsequently added that of stereotyping. Their establishment grew to be large and profitable, and for upwards of twenty years issued a great variety of works, for the most part new editions of those which were already favorites of the public. Some of them were books of sterling value, and put forth in handsome style; perhaps a greater number were novels and tales issued in 24mo volumes and usually in boards on roan bindings. These had a great sale, and included many of the works of Scott, Bulwer, Marryat and others.

George Lamson was a native of the town, who had a collegiate education and studied the profession of the law. For a few years he was engaged in the publication of legal works in Exeter, and then removed to the city of New York, where he died.

Francis Grant began life as a bookbinder, but was afterwards the proprietor of a small printing office and became a bookseller and publisher. As such his name and appearance were familiar to the students of the academy for half a century and more. He published that very useful little work, called *A Book for New Hampshire Children, in Familiar Letters from a Father*, written by Hosea Hildreth, which ran through five editions. Mr. Grant commenced the issue of *The Rockingham Gazette*, a weekly newspaper, September 21, 1824. The editor was Oliver W. B. Peabody. The paper was a decided improvement upon all that had preceded it, but the profession of journalism was yet in its infancy. The *Gazette* came to a close in October, 1827, when its subscription list was transferred to *The Portsmouth Journal*.

Within the next three years two abortive attempts were made to establish journals in the town, one by Joseph Y. James, February 12, 1829, whose experiment was called *The Hive*, but apparently lacked the industry of the bee or the sweetness of the honey, for it came to an end in 1830; and the other by Michael H. Barton, the "2d. mo. 12th. 1830" whose venture was issued in duodecimo form, eight pages in a number, and named *Something New*. This publication was designed to introduce a perfect alphabet and a reformed orthography; a scheme which has employed the attention of many ingenious men. Mr. Barton's plan, whatever it was, was not of sufficient interest to make his publication a success, for it probably never got beyond the first number.

THE NEWS LETTER.

At length, however, a permanent newspaper was established by John S. Sleeper, May 31, 1831, in *The Exeter News Letter*. Mr. Sleeper, though not a native of the town, was the son and grandson of residents, and passed his childhood in Exeter. Being of an active, adventurous disposition, he went early to sea, and by his ability and intelligence rose to the command of a merchant vessel. For twenty-two years he followed the profession, and then undertook the launching and management of a newspaper. In this he was equally successful. He held an easy and graceful pen, and knew well the kind of matters in which the public are interested. He edited and published *The Exeter News Letter* for two years, and then sought a wider field, first in the growing town of Lowell, and afterwards in Boston, Massachusetts, where he founded, and for twenty years conducted, to great popularity and success, *The Boston Mercantile Journal.*

John C. Gerrish, who was familiar with the printing office, succeeded to the control of *The News Letter*, and fortunately engaged for his editor John Kelly, a college graduate and a lawyer by profession, possessed of much literary taste and a pleasant vein of humor that enabled him to give attractiveness to the driest subject. He was a thorough antiquary, and prepared for the columns of the paper a series of historical and genealogical "Collectanea," which were the fruits of much study and research, and have been of value and assistance to many investigators of family history since. Mr. Kelly for nearly twenty years retained the editorial charge of the paper, though the proprietorship was in the meantime transferred to Messrs. Smith, Hall & Clarke, all of them skilled printers.

The Rev. Dr. Levi W. Leonard subsequently edited *The News Letter*, and, at a later date, Charles Marseilles became the proprietor. It afterwards went into the hands of William B. Morrill, who managed it for several years, and is now the property of John Templeton, a graduate of the printing office, and not without experience in writing for the press. *The News Letter* has been repeatedly enlarged in dimensions, and now contains nearly twice the amount of reading matter that it had in the beginning.

The firm of Smith, Hall & Clarke was composed of Oliver Smith, Samuel Hall and Samuel B. Clarke, all straightforward, successful business men. Mr. Hall is the only survivor, and has for some years retired from active occupation. Thomas D. Treadwell, who was employed for many years as a printer in the establishment of J. and B. Williams, and afterwards in the office of *The News Letter*, has recently died, at an advanced age.

But we have not yet done with the Exeter newspapers. On the second of April, 1835, was begun *The Christian Journal*, a fortnightly publication, by the Executive Committee of the Eastern Christian Publishing Association. Elijah Shaw was the editor, and J. C. Gerrish, the printer. There was also an "editorial council" of three, chosen yearly. At the beginning of the fifth year the title of the paper was altered to *The Christian Herald and Journal;* at the beginning of the sixth, it was abbreviated to *The Christian Herald*, and the paper was issued weekly. It was next removed to Newburyport, Massachusetts, and was published there afterwards.

The first number of *The Granite State Democrat*, a weekly paper, appeared in January, 1840. James Shrigley was publisher, and Joseph L. Beckett, printer. Mr. Shrigley was a minister of the Universalist denomination, and Mr. Beckett was a native of Exeter, who had served his time in a printing office, and was long employed by the proprietors of *The Boston Post*. He was a genial soul, with a good deal of humor. This paper, like so many others, changed hands repeatedly. In 1842 it was conducted by Ferdinand Ellis, Jr., and afterwards by William Young. In January, 1843, Samuel C. Baldwin became the proprietor, but, by reason of the failure of his health, it was discontinued March 9, 1843. A subsequent effort to revive it proved unsuccessful.

In 1841 no less than three attempts were made to establish new journals in the town. The first was in February, when a prospectus was issued of a semi-monthly, to be called *The Rose and Thorn*, but it is supposed that no sufficient encouragement was offered. In June appeared the first number of *The Granite Pillar and New Hampshire Temperance Advocate*, to be continued monthly by Abraham R. Brown under the editorship of Joseph Fullonton, but it was short-lived. The last literary venture of the year was a semi-monthly, called *The Factory Girl and Lady's Garland*. It appeared November 1, J. L. Beckett being the publisher. It, or its successors, continued to be issued in Exeter for about six years it is believed. In 1842 it was known as *The Factory Girl* simply, and was conducted by C. C. Dearborn; and in 1843 as *The Factory Girl's Garland*, by A. R. Brown. In 1845 and 1846, it was much enlarged and entitled *The Weekly Messenger, Literary Wreath and Factory Girl's Garland*. Later it was removed to Lawrence, Massachusetts, by J. L. Beckett.

A weekly sheet, called *The Squamscot Fountain*, and devoted to the cause of temperance, was begun in 1843 by Samuel Webster and J. P. Clough. It also underwent a change of title and of

In 1846 was begun a paper called *The Factory Girl's Album and Operatives' Advocate*, by Charles C. Dearborn, as publisher, and William P. Moulton, as printer. At first it was issued weekly, and afterwards, semi-monthly, and was enlarged; but it was continued only a little more than a year.

January 1, 1853, a single number of a projected weekly, of a religious and literary character, to be styled *The Olive Leaf*, appeared under the editorship of R. O. Williams, by Currier & Co., proprietors, but it never reached a second number.

About the year 1857, Thomas J. Whittem, who had established *The American Ballot*, a weekly paper dedicated to the interests of the American party, at Portsmouth, about three years prior to that time, transferred it to Exeter, and continued to publish it there until its discontinuance in 1865.

THE GAZETTE, AND PRESENT PUBLICATIONS.

The Exeter Gazette was founded in 1876 by James D. P. Wingate and A. P. Dunton. Three years afterwards, J. H. Shaw purchased the interest of Mr. Dunton. In 1883 Mr. Wingate became, as he still is, the sole proprietor. An experiment was made, a few years since, of issuing a daily paper from the same office, but the general circulation of the metropolitan journals is fatal to ventures of that kind in the smaller towns. *The Daily Gazette* struggled against fate for six months, when it succumbed.

The Weekly Protest was established by Andrew J. Hoyt in 1880, an organ of the Greenback party.

The Exonian, published by the students of the Phillips Academy, was begun in 1878; and *The Phillips Exeter Literary Monthly*, a magazine in octavo form, in May, 1886.

The present periodical publications of the town are *The News Letter*, *The Gazette*, *The Protest* and *The Exonian*, all weekly, and *The Literary Monthly*.

CONTRIBUTORS TO THE PRESS.

Exeter has had its share of authors, though none very voluminous. No attempt will be made here to give a complete or exact bibliographical account of their productions; but a list of such writers as are recalled is subjoined, with the titles, or some brief description of the character of their works. The letter *n.* after a name stands for native, and *r.* for resident of the town.

Rev. John Emery Abbot, *n.* Sermons; and Memoir by Henry Ware, Jr., 1829.

Rev. John W. Adams, *r.* Sermons, 1884 and 1885.

Joseph L. Beckett, *n.* Directory and History of Exeter, etc., 1872.

Charles H. Bell, *r.* John Wheelwright, 1876. History of Phillips Exeter Academy, 1883.

Rev. John N. Brown, *r.* Emily and other poems, 1840.

Rev. Ebenezer L. Boyd, *r.* Thanksgiving Discourse, 1813.

James Burley, *n.* Company Discipline, 1820.

Rev. Jacob Chapman, *r.* Genealogy of the Folsom Family, 1882. Genealogy of the Philbrick Family, 1887.

Rev. Jonathan Cole, *r.* One or more sermons.

Charles Denis Rusoe D'Eres, *r.* Memoirs, 1800.

This person, a Canadian, claimed to have been a captive among a tribe of Indians with an unpronounceable name, for eleven years. His story is generally regarded as apochryphal, and the chief merit of the book is its rarity.

Rev. Ferdinand Ellis, *r.* Election Sermon, 1826, and other sermons.

Rev. Joy H. Fairchild, *r.* Autobiography and Remarkable Incidents, 1855.

A perfect sheaf of pamphlets were issued in relation to the offence imputed to him, and containing reports of the various investigations and trials to which he was subjected.

Jeremiah Fellowes, *n.* Reminiscences, moral poems and translations, 1824.

Charles L. Folsom, *n.* Oration before Handel Society of Dartmouth College, 1821.

Henry F. French, *r.* Treatise on farm drainage.

Dr. Selah Gridley, *r.* A volume of poems.

Rev. James Haughton, *r.* One or more sermons.

Rev. Hosea Hildreth, *r.* Discourse before Washington Benevolent Society, 1813. Two discourses to townsmen, 1824. Book for New Hampshire Children, 1839, 5th ed.

Joseph G. Hoyt, *r.* Miscellaneous writings and reviews, 1863.

Mary W. Janvrin, *n.* Peace, or the Stolen Will, etc.

Rev. Henry Jewell, *r.* Dedication Sermon, 1846.

Caroline E. Kelly, *n.* Grace Hale, and other juvenile works.

John Kelly, *r.* Historical communications to various publications.

Alexander H. Lawrence, *n.* Examination of Hume's Argument Against Miracles, 1845.

Rev. John C. Learned, *r.* Obituary Sermon on L. W. Leonard, D. D., etc.

Rev. Orpheus T. Lanphear, *r.* One or more sermons.

Rev. Charles Lowe, *n.* Sermons and various religious writings.

Rev. Benjamin F. McDaniel, *r.* One or more sermons.

Rev. Elias Nason, *r.* Sermons and other tracts.

Rev. Alfred C. Nickerson, *r.* Sermons, 1887.

Thomas Odiorne, *n.* The Progress of Refinement, 1794, etc.

Rev. John Odlin, *r.* Sermons, 1725, etc.

[Woodbridge Odlin], *n.* Review of Result of Council, 1842.

Amos A. Parker, *r.* A Trip to the West and Texas, 1836.

Rev. Samuel P. Parker, *r.* One or more sermons.

Oliver W. B. Peabody, *n.* Poem on bi-centennial of New Hampshire, 1823. Address before Peace Society, 1830, etc.

William B. O. Peabody, *n.* Sermons; and Memoir by his brother, 1849.

Robert F. Pennell, *r.* The Latin subjunctive, etc.

John T. Perry, *n.* Sixteen Saviors or One? 1879. The Credibility of History, etc.

Dr. William Perry, *r.* Address in behalf of Insane Hospital, 1834.

Rev. William F. Rowland, *r.* 'Election sermons 1796 and 1809, etc.

John S. Sleeper, *r.* Tales of the Ocean, 1842. Salt Water Bubbles, etc.

Jeremiah Smith, *r.* Eulogy on Washington, 1800. Bi-centennial discourse, 1838. Judicial opinions, etc.

William Smith, *n.* Remarks on Toleration Act of 1819, 1823. Remarks on the assassination of Julius Cæsar, 1827.

Rev. George E. Street, *r.* Memorial discourse on Hon. Amos Tuck, 1880, etc.

John Templeton, *n.* Hand Book of Exeter, 1883.

Dr. Samuel Tenney, *r.* Papers in various historical and scientific publications.

Tabitha Tenney, *n.* Female Quixotism, or the Adventures of Dorcasina Sheldon, 3 vols., 1841, 5th ed. Domestic Cookery, 1808

Oliver Welch, r. Arithmetic, 1812, several eds.

George A. Wentworth, r. Series of text books in mathematics.

Rev. John Wheelwright, r. Fast day sermon, 1637. Mercurius Americanus, 1645.

Charles E. L. Wingate, n. History of the Wingate Family, 1886.

This enumeration does not include several authors who were born, or lived for some time, in the town, but whose literary work cannot with reasonable probability be assigned to the period of their residence there. Such were Lewis Cass, n., Henry A. S. Dearborn, n., Timothy Farrar, r., Rev. Roswell D. Hitchcock, r., William Ladd, n., Charles Folsom, n., Dudley Leavitt, n., and others.

INDUSTRIAL.

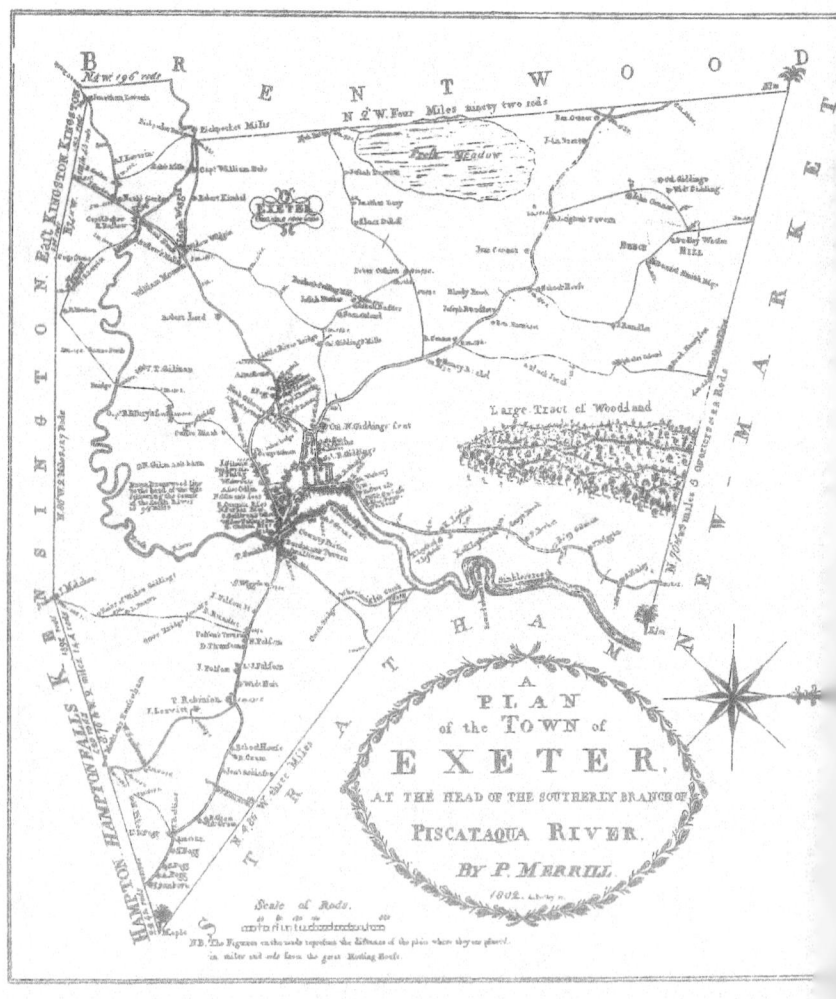

CHAPTER XVI.

MILLS AND MANUFACTURES.

The falls in the rivers were undoubtedly among the inducements which determined the location of the settlement of Exeter. Their immediate value as fishing places was no more fully recognized than their prospective importance as sources of water power for turning the wheels of mills.

The Exeter river afforded, in addition to and above the main falls at the head of tide water, at least five valuable mill sites within the original limits of the town; and Little river, which empties into it, two, if not more, of less magnitude. Lamprey river also had large falls near its mouth, and lesser ones at other points of its course, while the Pascassic,* a branch of the Lamprey, furnished water power which was afterwards utilized for two mills, at least.

The first mill in the town was for grinding grain, and was built by Thomas Wilson at the foot of the main falls on the easterly side of the island now reached by String bridge, near where a similar mill stands to this day. That part of the stream which runs in the channel on the eastern side of the island was known as Wilson's creek. The mill site and the island, on which Wilson also erected his house, were granted to him by the town, probably in the very first season of their occupation, and before any formal records that we know of were kept. The evidence of this is found in depositions taken in the year 1651. Edmund Littlefield and Griffin Montague testified that "the inhabitants of the town of Exeter did give and grant unto Thomas Wilson free liberty to draw as much water from the higher falls as should sufficiently serve his turn at all times for his own use, either by digging through the rocks or by damming the falls; and further the town did freely give and grant unto Thomas Wilson that island that his house stands upon; only did reserve so much liberty for landing

---

* This name, we learn from Jenness, was early spelt Pascassock. It has been modernized without improvement, into Piscassic.

their canoes and laying of fish." And John Compton and Robert Read testified that the town granted "to Thomas Wilson that creek or water course at the higher fall at Exeter to dig and draw that water he should stand in need of at any time without any limitation; and also gave the little island by the falls on which his house and mill standeth." The "higher" fall refers, of course, to that farthest down the river and next to tide water; higher in altitude but lower in location.

Mr. Wilson naturally lost no time in improving his privilege by the erection of a mill, and we find that the town passed an order November 2, 1640, regulating "the miller's toll." He died in 1643, and his widow afterwards married John Legat; but the mill went into the hands of his son, Humphrey Wilson, who had the charge of it for many years after.

Up to the year 1647 we have no account of any saw-mill being built in Exeter. Pipe staves and other kinds of small lumber manufactured before that time, were in all probability riven or split out from the logs. The square timber was hewn with the axe, and the boards needed for home use were sawn in "pits," which were excavations in the ground, of the depth of six or seven feet. The log to be cut up was laid across the mouth of the cavity, and the long, two-handled saw was used by two men, one standing in the pit beneath the log, and the "top sawyer" mounted above it.

An ordinance of the town forbade the digging of saw-pits in places where they were liable to prove dangerous to man or beast.

THE FIRST SAW-MILL.

But in the year 1647 the town took a great step forward. An arrangement was made for the immediate construction of saw-mills, which would give a greatly increased value to the abundant timber.

Edward Gilman, of Welsh lineage, emigrated from Hingham in Norfolk, England, to this country, with five children, in the year 1638, and settled in Hingham, Massachusetts. His eldest son, Edward, thirty years of age, married, and a man of property and enterprise, came to Exeter in 1647 and proposed to become an inhabitant, upon certain conditions. The occasion was esteemed so important that an agreement in writing was entered into between him and the townsmen and principal inhabitants, of the tenor following:

4 November 1647. The agreement of the inhabitants of the town of Exeter.

Imprimis, That we do accept of Edward Gilman the younger to be a townsman amongst us, and do give and grant him liberty to set up a saw mill or mills in any river or within the liberty of Exeter, and to have the privilege of the river for the use of the mills, and of the pines for sawing, or masts or any other timber for sawing, to have the privilege of it within the liberty of Exeter.

2ly. The aforesaid Edward Gilman does engage himself to come and live as a townsman amongst them, and to setup a saw-mill by the last of March next ensuing, if he come, or at the furthest by the last of August next ensuing.

3ly. The said Gilman does engage himself to let the townsmen have what boards they stand in need of for their own use in the town, at three shillings a hundred, and what two-inch planks they shall need for flooring at the same price, and to take country pay at price current, if the mill shall saw it.

4ly. The said Gilman does engage himself that what masts he makes use of, to give them as much as if he sawed them into boards, and to a load haul ten hundred in every 3,000 to the town.

5ly. Its agreed than Anthony Stanell [Stanyan] shall have liberty to put in a quarter part for a saw-mill provided he do make good his proportion or quarter part in every respect of charges as a partner, so that the work be not hindered by him; if he do, to forfeit his share to the aforesaid Gilman and to pay what damages he shall sustain by it. For the true and sure performance of the same we do bind ourselves in a forty pounds sterling. In witness whereunto we have set our hands.

        WILLIAM MOORE, townsman,   EDWARD GILMAN.
        SAMUEL GREENFIELD,*
        NATHANIEL BOULTER,
        BALTHAZAR WILLIX,
        EDWARD HILTON.

Mr. Gilman at once took up his residence in the town and became a leading citizen. His father, Edward Gilman, Sr., and his two brothers, John and Moses, followed him to Exeter within the next five years, and his brother-in-law, John Folsom, in about twelve years. Edward Gilman, Jr., completed and put in operation a saw-mill, according to his agreement, in the spring or summer of 1648. It was on the west side of the river upon the upper fall near the present Great bridge; and before June, 1650, he erected another saw-mill on the opposite side of the river. It is not known that Anthony Stanyan availed himself of the privilege reserved to him in the agreement with the town, of becoming a partner in the mills.

Encouraged by this example, a number of the more enterprising inhabitants made application to the town for mill sites. On April 22, 1649, Nathaniel Drake, Abraham Drake, Henry Roby and Thomas King, were empowered by the town to set up a saw-mill at Little river "with liberty of felling timber on the commons for the said mill, provided they come not for timber on the hither side of the river towards Mr. Gilman his saw-mill, whereby he may be damnified for want of timber." The terms of the grant were the same as those allowed to Edward Gilman, Jr., in respect to his mill. The locality referred to was probably that where the Little river crosses the road to Brentwood, which some of the sentimental young people of a former generation denominated the "vale of Ovoca."

On the same April 22, 1649, liberty to set up a saw-mill was given to Edward Hilton, James Wall, John and Robert Smart and Thomas Biggs, on Pascassic river; and to George Barlow, Nicholas Listen,* Francis Swain, Nicholas Swain and John Warren, at the falls at Lamprey river "a little above the wigwams." The terms in each case were the same as those allowed to Edward Gilman, Jr. Both these localities were probably in the present town of Newmarket.

That it might be distinctly understood that no person should encroach upon the privileges already ceded to Mr. Gilman, it was ordered by the town, June 10, 1650, "that there shall not be liberty granted unto any man to set up any saw-mill at Exeter falls upon the town's ground to hinder Edward Gilman of his former grant of his two saw-mills at the falls, or timber for any other saw-mills near to the said falls."

It appears that another saw-mill was about this time erected on the east side of the river, probably at the foot of the falls nearest tide water, and on land of Humphrey Wilson. This was owned in common by Wilson, James Wall and the Rev. Samuel Dudley. And on the second of January, 1650-1, it was agreed between them and the town that the former two should pay for the lumber two shillings per thousand for the oak and pine boards and plank they should take off the commons and saw; but Mr. Dudley was to "go free without payment for his third."

This exemption was, of course, made in consideration of the ministerial office and services of Mr. Dudley, but it did not pass

---

* This man's name was often written Lissen or Leeson, as it was probably pronounced. It is believed that he came to Exeter from Salem, Massachusetts, where his name was spelt as

unchallenged. Henry Roby and John Gilman dissented from the vote. No doubt they believed that Mr. Dudley was sufficiently compensated by the provision already made for him by the town. Perhaps, too, they discerned, what the records plainly indicate to us, that Mr. Dudley was a keen man of business, and abundantly capable of taking care of himself without having any distinctions made in his favor. But it was a courageous thing, in those days, when the ecclesiastical office was hedged about with so much dignity and authority, for a layman to put his name on record in opposition to a motion for the benefit of his minister.

The fathers of Exeter, however, were never timid or backward in the expression of their opinions, and rarely withheld them out of deference to the views of those who differed from them.

For more than a century the books of the town show the names of dissentients from the majority, oftentimes only one or two in number, on most of the vexed questions of municipal policy.

PICKPOCKET FALLS GRANTED.

Another privilege for a saw-mill was given by the town, on April 20, 1652, to the Rev. Samuel Dudley and John Legat and their heirs and assigns forever, at the second or third fall above the town on the fresh river, as they might prefer, with the right to take timber for their mill from the commons there, upon the terms of paying the town five pounds a year so long as the mill should be employed in sawing, and of supplying the inhabitants for their own use boards at three shillings a hundred, if taken from the mill. They chose what in all probability was then known as the second fall above the town, embracing the present Paper mill fall and Pickpocket fall. These are near together, and not being then defined by dams, might well enough have been counted as one fall. The name of Pickpocket was very early given to the mills there built. Its origin is uncertain. It is probably a corruption of the designation given by the Indians to the locality; though there are not wanting those who derive it from the supposed unprofitableness of some of the business undertakings there.

On May 10, 1652, an agreement was proposed between the town and Edward Gilman, Jr., that he and his assigns should thenceforth pay to the town for the use of what timber his two saw-mills should cut, ten pounds a year, in lieu of half a hundred of boards on every two thousand sawn, as was originally stipulated. Whether it was absolutely concluded, the record fails to state.

On the same day Edward Gilman, Sr., Edward Gilman, Jr., Edward Colcord and Humphrey Wilson had granted to them by the town liberty to set up a saw-mill at the lower falls in Lamprey river by the bridge, and to take timber on the common land there for their mill, on the payment of five pounds a year to the town, after the mill should be built. This site was within the limits of the present town of Newmarket.

On the same tenth of May, 1652, Thomas King had from the town liberty for a saw-mill on the great fresh river below the grant to Mr. Dudley and John Legat at the foot of the fall, and timber for the same on the commons, he and his assigns paying to the town five pounds a year therefor, and furnishing boards for the town's use, at three shillings a hundred. This was the first fall above the town, and has been known from that time to the present as King's fall, from the original grantee.

On the same day Thomas Pettit, Nicholas Listen, Thomas Cornish, John Warren and Francis Swain received from the town a privilege for a saw-mill at Lamprey river "on the next great fall above the fall that some of them have already taken possession of, paying five pounds a year for the privilege, beginning presently after next Michaelmas." This fall was in the present town of Newmarket.

GRANT OF CRAWLEY'S FALLS.

On May 20, 1652, the town granted to Robert Seward and Thomas Crawley liberty to erect a saw-mill on the great fresh river on the next fall above Mr. Dudley's and Mr. Legat's (provided it does not prejudice their or other former grants) and timber on the commons there for it, they to pay the town five pounds a year therefor. This site, which is now in the town of Brentwood, has never lost its name of "Crawley's falls," given it from that of the second of the original grantees.

In the multiplicity of these grants it was obviously necessary that the town's interest should not be neglected, and on the eighth of July, 1652, the inhabitants appointed a committee consisting of Edward Colcord, John Legat and Thomas Biggs to call to account the owners of saw-mills and to make demand for such boards or plank as were due to the town, and upon non-payment to take a legal course for the recovery of the same; and on February 15, 1653-4, their authority was extended to "the present year coming." The duties of this committee were so congenial to the inclination of its chairman, that we cannot help thinking that he must have been instrumental in its appointment. To be "in the law" was the normal condition of Edward Colcord.

On November 6, 1653, the town conferred upon Edward Hilton "in regard that he had been at charge in setting up a saw-mill, to enjoy for himself and his heirs forever, a quarter of a mile below his mill with the land and timber belonging thereunto, and also above his mill a mile and a quarter with the land and timber belonging thereunto. This land and timber is to lie square; only on this side of Pascassic river to come about a stone's cast." The mill referred to is supposed to have been on the Pascassic, and together with the land granted, to have been within the present town of South Newmarket.

In 1653, Edward Gilman, Jr., the principal mill owner of the town, made a voyage to England to procure improved mill gearing, and never returned, having been lost at sea on his passage. His younger brother, John Gilman, succeeded him in his business and in a great part of his property, and was quite competent to fill his place. He survived Edward more than fifty years, and became one of the most useful and distinguished citizens of the place.

Lumbering being then the chief money producing industry in the town, the mill owners were very naturally called upon to pay their dues in cash towards the support of the minister. At a town meeting held April 28, 1656, it was agreed that "for maintaining the public ordinances the saw-mills belonging to the town should be rated as follows: the old mill upon the fall, seven pounds; Humphrey [Wilson's] mill at seven pounds; the new mill of John Gilman at six pounds; Mr. Hilton's mill at five pounds." The natural inference from this is that the other mill sites which had been granted, were not yet profitably occupied. It was also provided that "when the ministry faileth, the old covenant should be in force: to wit, from the old and the new mill, half a hundred upon two thousand; and from the Humphrey [Wilson] mill, eighteen pence upon a thousand, and plank, two shillings upon a thousand."

On May 11, 1657, the town make a grant to Edward Hilton, Jr., of fifty acres of pine swamp adjoining his father's lot, "for his sole use for the mill that he intends to set up on the east side opposite the new mill, upon the falls of Exeter, with liberty to set up said mill, for which he is to pay five pounds annually; upon the proviso that he is not to prejudice the new mill any way in respect of water. If John Gilman and the rest be willing that he should fell timber upon the common, then this grant is to be relinquished; but in case he keeps this grant, he is to make no use of timber upon the common."

On June 8, 1657, it was ordered "that all the pines upon the commons from this time forward shall be reserved for the use of the saw-mills already set up, or that have been granted and shall be set up, except that there is liberty for masts, fence building and canoes; and if, at any time, there shall be any particular grants of lands made to any, yet the owners of saw-mills shall have liberty to carry off the pine timber, except before excepted."

On the twenty-fifth of April, 1664, the town directed that Captain John Clark's mill should pay "five pounds annually to the public ministry, though there be something dubious within the grant, at such times that it shall not be improved." The meaning of the latter expressions quoted seems to be itself "something dubious." The mill referred to must have been that on Little river, afterwards known as Gordon's, and still later as Giddings's and Rowland's. The site was originally granted, April 22, 1649, to the Drakes, Roby and Thomas King, the last of whom, on June 28, 1654, "resigned up his grant of a saw-mill formerly granted to him," which was evidently this one, because he continued to hold and enjoy the other privilege given him on the great river.

In 1653 Edward Gilman, Jr., being on the eve of sailing for Europe, conveyed to his brother Moses one-fourth of a saw-mill "now a building on little fresh river, on the western side thereof," — evidently the mill in question. Apparently, he must have purchased a share of the rights of the original grantees. Captain John Clark, who was an old lumberman with whom both the Gilmans had previously had dealings, probably acquired the mill by purchase afterwards. It is repeatedly referred to in the later records of the town as Captain or Major Clark's mill.

Strict faith appears to have been kept by the town with the owners of mills erected in conformity with its grants. In the numerous donations of land to individuals, subsequently made within the territory whose trees were assigned to the mills, a proviso was always inserted that the pine timber, except masts, etc., should not pass with the soil because it was appurtenant to the mills.

The original grist-mill of Thomas, afterwards of Humphrey Wilson, served for a number of years to grind all the grain of the inhabitants, but at length John Gilman thought it expedient to build another at the main falls. This he probably did by the desire of the inhabitants.

On the twenty-fifth of October, 1670, Nicholas Listen and John Robinson were chosen by the town to go and forewarn Humphrey Wilson not to set his dam over the highway upon the upland near to John Gilman's grist-mill.

What reply Humphrey Wilson made to this "forewarning" is not known, but, perhaps, not a perfectly satisfactory one, for on the very next day the town voted, "that whereas there had been formerly, to their understanding, a privilege of water, and a liberty of a creek granted to Humphrey Wilson upon condition that he should supply the town's use in respect of grinding their corn, and the town since finding, especially of late, by experience, to their great loss and damage, that they have not been answered to their expectation, the town do hereby grant to John Gilman the privilege of the water, so that the saw-mills or any other mill or mills or any other ways by stopping of gates that may hinder his grist-mill, shall be at liberty, for the use of the grist-mill to answer the town for grinding their corn; upon which consideration the said John Gilman do promise upon all occasions to supply the town in grinding their corn, except more than ordinary providence hinder."

On March 3, 1673, it was ordered "that those who have felled any pine trees have liberty to take them away within a year; after which any of those to whom mills appertain, may take them away for the use of their mills; but hereafter, when those who fell pine trees shall not carry them away within three months, they shall be forfeited to any one who takes them away for the use of the owner of one of the mills."

It was also ordered "that whoever shall fell any pine tree (except for canoes, masts [or] building), and shall not improve it and bring it to the use of the mills to which the privilege of the timber is granted, for every tree so felled shall forfeit ten shillings to the town."

The principal mill sites having been thus disposed of, the town had little occasion to take action concerning them afterwards, except in the two instances to be mentioned.

On September 9, 1701, the town granted "to Robert Coffin, his heirs and assigns, all the right the town hath or had in Lowd's falls at Lamprey river, with all the privileges of the flats twenty rods below said falls, said Coffin not to hinder any transportation of timber down said river;" in consideration whereof said Coffin bound himself to pay five pounds yearly to the town or ministry by way of rate, so long as any mill should stand upon said fall on the side next to Exeter. This site was in the present town of Newmarket.

And on the first Monday of April, 1709, the town voted to give "all the right the town have in the stream and island to Captain John Gilman, where the said Gilman's corn-mill now stands, with privilege for a bridge to go on to the island; and the abovesaid John Gilman doth oblige himself to grind the inhabitants' corn when wanted, for two quarts in every bushel."

None of the several mill sites mentioned were improved, so far as has been learned, for any other purposes than for grinding grain and sawing lumber, until the needs of the country during and subsequent to the War of the Revolution impelled men to employ the water power in the manufacture of other indispensable articles.

PICKPOCKET.

The mill site and privilege ceded by the town in 1652 to the Rev. Samuel Dudley and John Legat, embraced, as has already been explained, the fall which has from very early times borne the above unprepossessing name. The first use to which it was put was to drive a saw-mill, and probably it has never since been without one, or more. The Pickpocket mill was a well known locality, both to white men and to Indians. The latter were only too intimately acquainted with it, for in their raids upon the frontier settlements they visited it repeatedly in pursuit of victims or captives.

When Brentwood was set off from Exeter in 1742 the main river was made the boundary between the two towns, for the distance of about half a mile. The Pickpocket fall was in that part of the river, so that one-half of it belonged in each town. There have been mills there on each side of the river, since; but the chief manufactories have been on the Brentwood side.

One of the earliest attempts in this part of the country to manufacture cotton cloth was initiated there, by a company composed mostly of inhabitants of Exeter. They were incorporated by act of the Legislature of the State in 1809, under the name of the Exeter Cotton Manufacturing Company.

They erected a factory containing eight thousand spindles, and for a time employed Samuel Chamberlain as their agent. He had a store at the main village, in which he offered for sale, in any quantity, "yarn and cotton bats," the products of the mill. Joseph Hyde then acted as the resident superintendent. Of course the business was conducted on a small scale, and in a primitive fashion, and probably brought little profit to the original investors, but the company continued to prosecute it for twenty years, and about 1820 a card factory was added to the original works, and an iron furnace for casting machinery.

Not far from the year 1830 Captain Nathaniel Gilman, Jr., purchased the control of the property, and continued the manufacture, with John Rogers as agent. In 1840 he sold it to John Perkins, and a few years later the factory met the fate to which all such establishments are liable, and was consumed by fire.

It was afterwards rebuilt, and adapted to the manufacture of paper. Willard Russell, Jacob Colcord, Joshua Getchell, and a Boston stock company of which Isaac Bradford was agent, successively occupied it, for the latter use.

The manufacture of wooden boxes, in connection with a saw-mill, is carried on there, at the present time.

THE PAPER-MILLS.

The fall in the Exeter river next above King's fall has for more than a century past been improved, and most of the time as the site of paper-mills, as well as of a grist-mill.

The first paper-mill was begun in 1777 or soon after, by Richard Jordan, a practical manufacturer, who came from Milton, Massachusetts. He purchased this site and water power for the purpose, from Joseph Leavitt, 3d, and others. His first experiments were seemingly not entirely successful, but we learn from a newspaper of the time that in September, 1785, the mill had undergone a thorough repair and was nearly finished. In 1787 Jordan sold the paper-mill, power and implements to Eliphalet Hale, who in 1795 conveyed them to William Hale. They both continued the production of paper, the latter until after the year 1806; and the property next passed into the hands of Stephen or Gideon Lamson who in 1813 conveyed it to Enoch Wiswall and John Hunting of Watertown, Massachusetts. They retained it but a couple of years, and in 1815 transferred it to Thomas Wiswall of Newton, Massachusetts. He removed to Exeter, and took into partnership Isaac Flagg, and the firm of Wiswall and Flagg continued the manufacture of paper there with success, until the death of the senior partner in 1836. Three years before, in February, 1833, the mill had been burned, but was rebuilt the same season, with improved apparatus. After the decease of Thomas Wiswall, Mr. Flagg took one of his heirs, Otis Wiswall, into partnership, and they continued the manufacture under the firm of Flagg and Wiswall. Still later, the three sons of Mr. Flagg, Isaac, Jr., Joseph and Samuel C. Flagg, succeeded to the property, and prosecuted the business until the year 1870, when the mill was again reduced to ashes, and was not replaced. The privilege is now owned by the Hon. Nathaniel Gordon.

THE POWDER-MILLS.

Every reader of history will recall the dismay of Washington when he discovered, not long after he assumed the command of the American army at Cambridge in 1775, their destitute condition in the all important article of gun-powder; as well as the sagacity with which he concealed the appalling fact, and reached out, far and near, to supply the deficiency. But still, the scarcity and need of powder in the earlier stage of the war was apparent to all, and stimulated patriotic ingenuity to attempt its manufacture. It was undertaken for the first time in New Hampshire, in Exeter. Colonel Samuel Hobart, a native of Groton, Massachusetts, and a former resident of Hollis, had served as paymaster to the New Hampshire troops about Boston in 1775, and removed in 1776 to Exeter, and there, probably with the assistance of Colonel Samuel Folsom, who was allowed to borrow of the State on his bond three hundred pounds for the purpose, purchased from Samuel Quimby the mills and water privilege at King's falls, and constructed a powder-mill. It was a difficult undertaking, but Hobart was a man not easily discouraged, and soon succeeded in putting his machinery into good working order. The mill commenced operations about the middle of August, 1776. The following description of it appeared in a contemporary newspaper under date of August 24:

A powder-mill erected in this town by Colonel Samuel Hobart, who, for his expedition, merits thanks from the public, having employed a number of the best hands in the country, and is now agoing, and is an improvement upon the former plans of powder-mills; said to be preferable to those before built in New England. Forty-four pestles are carried by one shaft, standing in rows on each side thereof. Besides the mill, within the aforesaid time, has been completed a building for pulverizing and purifying the saltpetre for one part, and on the other, a room for drying the powder. All the works have been contrived and carried on under the inspection of the ingenious Mr. C., late of Boston, and is capable of manufacturing 2400 weight of powder in a week. The Committee of Safety sitting in this town, in company with several other gentlemen, visited the powder-mill on Thursday evening, when it was going in all its parts, performed by water, viz., pounding, grinding, sifting and graining. They were well pleased therewith, fired a number of muskets and pistols charged with the powder taken from the drying room, and judged it in every respect equal to any imported from Europe.

The manufacture of powder was continued by Colonel Hobart for some time, perhaps throughout the war. In 1777 he had a contract with the State to supply the troops therewith. It is marvellous that with the poor materials at command the manufacture was so successful. There was no supply of sulphur or saltpetre in the country, and the State encouraged their production by offering prices in the nature of bounties, for each, of domestic manufacture. The saltpetre was largely procured by leaching the soil taken from beneath old barns and stables; — to such straits were our fathers reduced to obtain the means to defend their liberties.

After the war was over, Colonel Hobart put his mills to a different use. The old method of manufacturing "wrought" nails was by shaping and heading each one separately by hand without the aid of machinery. This was a slow and laborious process, and necessarily very expensive. So valuable were the products, as appears by the inventory of the property of a deceased person, about half a century earlier, that the stock of nails belonging to his estate was actually counted, and the number of them set down at nine hundred and one. The estate was divided amicably among several heirs, and some wonder has been expressed how they disposed of the odd nail.

The art of cutting or slitting iron into nail rods by machinery had recently been invented, and Colonel Hobart fitted his mills for that work. We learn from the *Freeman's Oracle* of September 27, 1785, that "the furnace and slitting-mill some time past undertaken by Colonel Hobart at King's falls, in this town, were last week completed, and visited by the judges of the Superior Court then sitting."

Ten years after this Colonel Hobart sold his land, mills and water rights, including the iron works or forge at King's falls, to Joshua Barstow, who continued to occupy the chief part of them for the same purposes, it is believed, until his death about 1824.

In 1814 Barstow conveyed a small part of the land with one-fourth of the water power to Charles C. Barstow, gunsmith, who set up the manufacture of small fire-arms there, to a limited extent. This, it is presumed, lasted but a few years. After Joshua Barstow's decease the property was occupied by Benjamin Hoit. It then included a large wooden mill, which is said to have been first designed for the manufacture of cotton cloth. Hoit used it for the production of coarse yarns and cotton batting. From his possession the establishment passed into that of Nathaniel Gordon, and subsequently, about 1830, was purchased by Benjamin R. Perkins. The same kind of manufactures were kept up by both the last named proprietors.

About 1838 Mr. Perkins sold the property to Oliver M. Whipple of Lowell, Massachusetts. He established powder-mills upon it, under an act of incorporation, by the name of the King's Mills Powder Company. Alvin White was the superintendent of the works, and at a later period, James F. Huntington. The latter was a man of wonderful coolness and daring. On one occasion the roof of one of the buildings, in which was stored a large quantity of powder, took fire. Ninety-nine men in a hundred would have left it to its fate, but Huntington braved the terrible risk, mounted the roof and poured on water until he extinguished the flames.

Before that time, however, more than one of the mills had been blown up. On the evening of August 25, 1840, about a quarter past nine, the people for miles around were startled by an explosion of a large quantity of powder at the mills, which shook the very ground. Fortunately no one was injured, as all the workmen had gone to their homes. But it is said that the violence of the explosion was so great that it actually emptied the water out from the canal into the adjacent highway.

Another similar accident happened on the seventeenth of May, 1843, when a single building, containing about one hundred and fifty pounds of powder, was destroyed. One of the workmen who was in the building was literally blown to pieces, and fragments of his body were caught and hung in the branches of a neighboring tree.

The powder manufacture ceased some time after 1850, and the old cotton-mill on the falls was burned and the dam carried away. In 1855 the property was purchased by William M. Hunnewell, who repaired the dam and moved a large mill building upon the premises, and fitted it up for the manufacture of hubs, spokes and shingles. This he carried on, besides a grist and saw-mill, until the year 1867, when he conveyed the whole to the Exeter Manufacturing Company, who are still the owners.

"THE FALLS OF THE SQUAMSCOT."

At the principal falls in the village of Exeter there are, and long have been, two dams, twenty or thirty rods apart, known as the upper and lower, with reference to their position on the stream. At the lower dam the river is divided by an island into two channels. There were constructed on these falls, in the following order, first, Thomas Wilson's grist-mill; then Edward Gilman's two saw-mills, one on the eastern and the other on the western side of the river; then Humphrey Wilson's saw-mill, on the eastern side; and lastly, John Gilman's grist-mill on the western side of the island. Some of them changed ownership many times, and others were added in after years; but it was long before a mill was built there for any different use. At length, however, mills for a variety of other purposes sprang up.

When Washington visited the place in 1789 he recorded in his diary that "in the town are considerable falls which supply several grist-mills, two oil-mills, a slitting-mill and snuff-mill."

The oil-mills were for expressing linseed oil from flaxseed; the slitting-mills for cutting nail rods.

In 1795, Dr. Samuel Tenney, in his account of Exeter, stated that the dams over the falls "afforded seats for four double geared corn-mills, four saw-mills, two oil-mills and one fulling-mill."

From Phinehas Merrill's plan of the village in 1802 we learn that there were then, at the upper dam, Ebenezer Clifford's grist and saw-mills and York's grist and saw-mills on the western side; and D. Clark's grist-mill and fulling-mill, S. Wiggin's oil-mill, and S. Folsom's nail factory on the eastern side. On the lower dam were S. Brooks's grist-mill on the western side, and S. Gilman's saw-mill and J. Smith's oil-mill on the eastern.

Merrill's Gazetteer informs us that in 1817 the fulling-mill, the two oil-mills, the saw and grist-mills were still there, and that a woollen factory had been added, which was on the west side of the upper dam. This was a building of considerable size, erected by Nicholas Gilman in 1803 to contain carding and other machinery.

After his death it was owned for some years by Colonel Nathaniel Gilman, and used for the manufacture of satinet cloths, under the management of his sons Nicholas and Daniel. The old woollen-mill, as it was termed, was subsequently occupied by Captain James Derby as a machine shop, and then by Woodbridge Odlin as a storehouse. Between 1845 and 1850 it was burned.

In the latter part of 1824 Dr. William Perry completed a mill situated on the east side of the upper dam, for the manufacture of starch from potatoes. He was induced to undertake this enterprise by a series of experiments which convinced him that British gum, which was used by the cotton manufacturers as a sizing for their cloth, was nothing but charred starch. Moreover, it was imported and expensive. Dr. Perry succeeded in making starch which was highly commended, and furnished the cotton-mills in Lowell, at a lower price, with a perfect substitute for British gum. His mill was burned to the ground March 3, 1827, but he rebuilt it at once. Again it was burned in 1830, and the energetic doctor had it in operation again in three weeks' time. He used from thirty to forty thousand bushels of potatoes annually. At length, some enterprising and not too scrupulous person contrived to discover in a clandestine way the secrets of the business, which gave rise to competition and rendered it less remunerative, and after a time the doctor abandoned it, and the mill was turned to other uses.

EXETER MANUFACTURING COMPANY.

About the year 1827 the design was formed to utilize, for the purpose of cotton manufacture, the water power of the upper falls in the village of Exeter, which was then owned in fractions by several persons, and employed for various objects. Two companies were formed for the purpose. Benjamin Abbott, John T. Gilman, Nathaniel Gilman, John Rogers, William Perry, George Gardner and their associates were incorporated by the Legislature in June, 1827, as the Exeter Mill and Water Power Company; and Nathaniel Gilman, John T. Gilman, Bradbury Cilley, Stephen Hanson, John Rogers, Nathaniel Gilman, 3d, Paine Wingate and their associates as the Exeter Manufacturing Company.

The former corporation purchased the control of the water power, and conveyed to the Manufacturing Company a sufficient part of it to operate five thousand spindles. The Manufacturing Company erected a brick mill of suitable capacity, and commenced the manufacture of cotton sheetings therein in the year 1830. The building agent was Stephen Hanson of Dover; the first president was John Houston, and the clerk and manufacturing agent was John Lowe, Jr.

The plan of two corporations being afterwards found cumbrous and unnecessary, the Mill and Water Power Company, by authority of an act of the Legislature, in 1861 conveyed all their property and franchises to the Manufacturing Company.

The Exeter Manufacturing Company have also acquired all the water rights at the lower dam, so that they are now the owners of the entire available power on the river between the Paper mill fall and tide water.

In the year 1876 that company erected a new mill, adjoining the old one, thereby substantially doubling their manufacturing capacity. By reason of the lowering of the river in the summer months, it became necessary, also, to provide the establishment with auxiliary steam power.

In December, 1887, the upper two stories of the old mill were consumed by fire, but the damage was repaired and new machinery put in and set in operation in about two months. The modern protections against fire, with which the building was provided, no doubt prevented a more extended conflagration.

The management of the company is efficient, and in accord with the improved methods of the times. The goods they manufacture have always maintained the highest standing in the market.

Since the year 1864 Hervey Kent has been the treasurer and agent.

The other officers of the company are Eben Dale, president; Eben Dale, Hervey Kent, Thomas Appleton, John W. Farwell and William J. Dale, Jr., directors.

OTHER WATER-MILLS.

Above the fall in the Little river, which has been mentioned, are two others within the township of Exeter. The one nearest the village was improved almost a century ago, in operating Barker's fulling-mill. Upon the other, further up the stream, near the line of Brentwood, has been erected a saw-mill. The water power of each is somewhat limited.

We have it upon the authority of a gentleman of veracity, some years since deceased, that there was, in former times, a saw-mill carried by the water of Kimming's brook. The brook is fed by springs, and flowed originally through a forest, so that it is easy to believe that its volume of water was once much greater than it now is.

Below the main falls of the river, and on the western side, more than half a century ago, was built a tide-mill for grinding bark for tanning purposes, by John Rogers and Joseph Furnald. The building is still standing, though it is a number of years since it was employed for its original use.

CHAPTER XVII.

BUSINESS AND TRADE.

As has already been stated, the main reliance of the inhabitants, in the early times, for the means of support, was upon the growth of the forest. And lumbering continued to be their chief occupation for upwards of a hundred years, and until the soil was well nigh stripped of its finest timber. It was a pernicious employment for the moral and material welfare of the community. The traders indeed found it profitable. They bought the timber and paid for it in merchandise, then rafted the logs down the river, or had them cut up in the mills into small lumber, which they sent off in coasters, realizing large profits from either transaction. But the lumbermen themselves worked hard, fared hard, and were too apt to drink hard. Agriculture, which should have been their principal dependence, was neglected. The owners of farms that might have been made profitable, failed to raise products enough for their own subsistence, and lived upon Virginia corn and pork, which they bought from the traders. Their great ambition was to keep up their teams of working oxen to haul their lumber to market. At night they gathered in the numerous taverns and spent the hours in drinking and coarse merriment. They were poor in the midst of plenty, and destitute of all wholesome ambition.

It is not easy to estimate the quantity of timber which was carried away from the town while the process of deforesting was going on. Some vague idea of it may, perhaps, be formed from the dealings of a single person. In 1754 Colonel John Phillips, then a principal trader in Exeter, sold to Colonel Warner of Portsmouth, one hundred and twenty-five thousand four hundred twenty-seven feet of boards and lumber; in 1757, nearly the same quantity, and in 1759, one hundred and fifty-nine thousand eight hundred eighty-six feet.

After the peace of 1763 things changed for the better. The cultivation of the soil was seen to be indispensable; the owners of lands turned to farming for their support, and thrift and prosperity gradually took the place of imprudence and poverty.

SHIP-BUILDING.

From a very early period the various kinds of craft to navigate the river, the great highway, from the light canoe to the sturdy gundalow, were constructed in Exeter. From those it was an easy transition to build vessels for sailing along the coasts, and for ocean voyages. As early as 1651 Edward Gilman, Jr., had upon the stocks a vessel of about fifty tons burden. In the returns of the custom-house in Portsmouth for three months in the year 1692, two clearances from Exeter for Boston are found; one of the sloop "Endeavor" of Exeter, twenty tons burden, plantation built, having on board six thousand of pipe staves, and four hundred feet of pine planks; the other of the sloop "Elizabeth" of Exeter, of twenty tons, Francis Lyford, commander, plantation built, having on board one thousand feet of boards, four thousand staves, fourteen thousand of treenails, fifteen hundred feet of pine planks and joist. Within the same period, the arrival of the same sloop "Endeavor" is noted, from Hampton, laden with hay. This shows one of the little rounds of the coasting trade. The vessel took to Boston manufactured lumber sold from Exeter; then probably returned as far as Hampton with merchandise, the proceeds of the sale, which was there exchanged for hay, an absolute necessity to the lumbermen of Exeter, who, as yet, had not mowing land enough to subsist their hard worked teams through the long winters.

As time went on, the building of larger vessels became an important and profitable industry in Exeter. The river was of sufficient depth to allow the passage of a ship of four or five hundred tons, and few so large were required for the commerce of the earlier part of the last century. Most of the voyages to the West Indies and across the Atlantic were made in vessels of not more than one-half that tonnage, and those were the routes most common and most profitable to the New England merchants. Some of the vessels launched from the Exeter ship-yards remained the property of the builders, and were employed in commerce between that place and foreign or domestic ports, but more were contracted for by Portsmouth merchants, or sold in England or elsewhere.

So lucrative had this branch of manufactures become, that shortly after the middle of the last century several gentlemen of energy and means were attracted to the town to engage in it. Between 1750 and 1760, John Montgomery, a partner of Joshua Wentworth of Portsmouth, came to Exeter and set up in the business of ship-building and trade in lumber. A little later, Enoch Poor of Andover moved into town, and engaged in the same calling. Charles Rundlett and Zebulon Giddinge were also among the ship-builders of that day.

In 1761 the partnership of Gilman, Folsom & Gilman was formed, which dealt extensively in lumber and built many vessels. Their trade with the ports of the West Indies and with London was more considerable than that of any other concern in the town. The fifteen or twenty years before the Revolution were the golden period of ship-building in Exeter. As many as twenty-two vessels, great and small, it is said, have been upon the stocks there in a single season; and from eight to ten was the usual annual product.

The water side must have presented a busy scene in those times. From the lower falls down as far as meeting-house hill on the west side of the river, ship and lumber-yards stretched almost continuously between the stores and wharves. On the streets, a little way back, were blacksmith shops, where the roar of the forge and the ringing blows of the hammer were heard from morning till night, making a fitting accompaniment to the sounds of the shipwright's adze and the calker's mallet which arose from the hulls propped up on the ways, waiting the hour when they should take their plunge into the element for which they were destined. Wages were good, and money was abundant. From the lumberman who furnished the framework to the nice joiner who wrought the elaborate finish of the cabin, all concerned in the business enjoyed their increased shares of comforts and luxuries, and devoutly drank to the standing toast, — success to ship-building.

But the War of the Revolution put a stop to all this activity. Capitalists would not risk their money in building vessels which could not sail from our ports without the risk of capture by the king's armed cruisers, and the blacksmiths and ship carpenters who were thrown out of employment enlisted in the military service or entered privateers. Still, a few vessels were kept in use. In 1776 Captain Eliphalet Ladd was permitted by the Legislature to make a voyage to two or three West India ports, on condition that he should bring back, if procurable, certain military stores for the use of the State.

After the war was over, ship-building was resumed, but not to the same extent as before. Colonel James Hackett was employed in it, as were also Joseph Swasey, Gideon Lamson, Daniel Conner and others.

On the fourth of July, 1793, we are informed by a newspaper of the time, "the field pieces in the town fired salutes in honor of the day, and were answered from the Indiaman now on the stocks, being beautifully decorated with French and American colors." In his sketch of Exeter, in 1795, Dr. Samuel Tenney stated that four or five vessels of various burdens were then annually built in the town, and about the same number were employed in foreign trade. Among the deaths recorded in an Exeter paper dated August 20, 1799, is that of Mr. Nathaniel Cotton, aged twenty-three, "on board schooner *Amity* of this port."

The ship-building interest gradually decreased in the town, after the coming in of the present century, though the manufacture of sail-cloth and twine and many blacksmiths' shops are remembered by our oldest citizens. One who recently deceased, used to describe a large vessel of probably five hundred tons that he saw on the stocks, the bowsprit of which projected beyond the fronts of the adjacent buildings, into Water street, between Spring and Centre streets. A vessel of that size had so great a draft of water that it had to be buoyed up by empty hogsheads in order to pass down the river at ordinary tide.

The second war with England, and the measures which preceded it, put a final period to the building of ships in Exeter. For a generation the occupation which had formerly been so prosperous fell entirely into disuse. But in the year 1836, a schooner of from one to two hundred tons was set upon the stocks on the river near meeting-house hill, and launched, fully rigged. The enterprising builder was Nathan Moulton of Hampton Falls. She took in a cargo of potatoes, and sailed, it is believed, for Philadelphia. With that effort, it is feared that ship-building in Exeter breathed its last.

The river has long ceased to be the great thoroughfare for supplying the town with necessaries from abroad. The railroads, by the inducements of greater rapidity and cheapness, have appropriated nine-tenths of that kind of transportation. But many heavy and bulky articles still come up the river from Portsmouth by the old conveyance of "Furnald's packet." The navigation of the channel had become so obstructed, some years ago, by rocks and shoals, that it was found necessary to petition Congress for an appropriation for its improvement. It was granted and wisely expended. Coasters now bring cargoes of coal directly to the wharves without transshipment. But the days of the old-time activity on the river will never be repeated, unless there should be a reversion, in the carriage of merchandise, to the earlier methods.

POTTERY.

The potter's art, one of the earliest inventions of man, must have been practised in Exeter near the middle of the last century. Nathaniel Libbee, who died about 1756, was described in a deed of the time as "potter." Jabez Dodge was established in business as a manufacturer of earthen-ware in 1794, and advertised for an apprentice in June, of that year. From that time to the present, the business has been maintained. Among those concerned in it were Samuel Dodge, William Philbrick, Oliver Osborne, Samuel Leavitt, Asa D. Lamson and F. H. Lamson. The ware produced was generally of the brown kind, for household use, although the present proprietor has an ambition to give a more artistic character to his work. Mr. Osborne for many years manufactured what were called portable furnaces of earthen-ware, which answered well the wants of the housewife, and had a large sale.

DUCK MANUFACTORY.

About the year 1790 Thomas Odiorne began in Exeter the manufacture of duck or sail cloth, the first in the State. His factory was on the present Green street, then called Carpenter's lane, probably from the fact that it had been largely occupied by ship carpenters. The only power employed was that of human muscles. The State Legislature encouraged the work by paying a bounty of seven shillings on each bolt of duck produced. Eight spinners of warp, and about the same number of weavers, were employed in the mill, and the weft was spun in private families. After a few years the establishment passed into the hands of four young men who prosecuted the business for a time, when it was discontinued.

SADDLERY AND CARRIAGES.

The manufacture of saddlery was early, and for a long time one of the principal and lucrative industries of the town. It was asserted, at the close of the last century, that a greater quantity of saddlery was made in Exeter than in any other place north of Philadelphia.

The first light carriage used in the town, according to tradition, was introduced by the Rev. Daniel Rogers, about the year 1754. It was of two wheels, and without a top, much like what, in later times, was termed a gig. It was then called a "chair."* Before that time Mr. Rogers always rode to his meetings on horseback. A few years afterwards, Brigadier Peter Gilman brought into town the first fall-back chaise with a square top. Chaise, carriage and harness making became subsequently a very considerable business in Exeter, for a long period, extending from the latter part of the last century down to near the present time. It is still carried on, but not to the same extent as formerly.

Among the most considerable past and present manufacturers of carriages in the town may be mentioned J. Coffin Smith, James and William Odlin, John Lamson, Daniel Williams, George Smith, Woodbridge Odlin, Robert and Henry Shute, William and Joel Lane, Benjamin Brown, John Dodge, Daniel and James F. Melcher, Lewis Mitchell, Oliver W. Smith, Head and Jewell, William L. Gooch, E. G. and J. G. Robinson, J. C. Safford, J. M. Clark and A. J. Fogg.

HATS; WOOL; LEATHER.

Hat making was an important trade in Exeter, a century ago, when it was conducted in comparatively small establishments and before the aid of steam had been called in to expedite the work and multiply the products. The family of Leavitts are said to have been engaged, for two or three generations, in this branch of industry. Connected with it, of course, was the traffic in furs and skins. This latter, in process of time, exceeded the other part of the business in amount and consequence. Theodore Moses and Abner Merrill were two prominent men of the town, who owed much of their success to this trade. John F. Moses, a son of the former, and Jeremiah L., Joseph and Benjamin L. Merrill, sons of the latter, became afterwards dealers in wool on a large scale, and accumulated much property from it. William Lane, Woodbridge Odlin and Luke Julian were also very prosperous wool merchants. At the present time Henry C. Moses, son of John F. Moses, and George N. Julian, son of Luke Julian, resident in Exeter, are each engaged in similar business in Boston.

Another employment which flourished for some time in the town, was that of tanning and currying leather. Academy street, long ago, received its unsavory alias of "Tan lane" from being the headquarters of this industry. Edmund Pearson is one of the earliest remembered tanners, and his son, Nathaniel, succeeded him. Jeremiah Dow, Jeremiah Robinson and Retire H. Parker were among the principal men afterwards concerned in the business, in the same street. The decline of that interest closed one after another of the establishments, and the burning of John F. Moses's morocco factory a few years since removed the last vestige of the trade, once so actively and profitably pursued in that locality.

The manufacture of boots and shoes for a while occupied a good number of hands in Exeter. Stephen L. Gordon, Jeremiah L. Robinson and others met with variable degrees of success in the business, but it never took a very firm root in the town, in those days. Of late it has been revived, with vastly improved facilities and machinery. The Exeter Boot and Shoe Company have added within a few years a new and productive industry to the town, and are reaping an assured success from their enterprise.

James Derby, an energetic machinist, started several undertakings in Exeter, about half a century since, none of which, however, proved permanent. At one time he was concerned with others in book publishing. They proposed to issue the Bible with Scott's commentaries, in six or eight large volumes; but having completed the New Testament in two volumes, they went no farther. He set in operation machine works, at two several times, the last between 1840 and 1850, in the brick shops on South street. Several other citizens were interested with him, there, in the manufacture of steam and gas pipes, the first establishment for the purpose in New England, as was alleged. It was subsequently disposed of to J. B. Richardson and S. T. Sanborn. Some wooden buildings used in the fabrication of the pipe having been destroyed by fire, the proprietors transferred the business to Boston.

The brick machine shop was then occupied for a time as a brewery, in which J. M. Lovering and I. S. Brown were interested, but the undertaking proved unsuccessful. It has been used since that time for the building of carriages.

The Exeter Machine Works is the name of a company which has existed in the town for almost a generation. Its buildings, which also include an iron foundry, are situated near the railroad station. The chief manufactures are steam engines, sectional boilers, shafting, machinery, etc., and a specialty is made of steam heating apparatus. The work of the company is widely and favorably known. The present officers are, Charles U. Bell, president; William Burlingame, treasurer; C. U. Bell, A. G. Dewey, W. Burlingame and J. K. Burlingame, directors.

The Brass Works of E. Folsom & Co. have been in operation about twenty years. The firm manufacture brass and iron fittings, pipes and the like, for steam, water and gas. Their buildings are near those of the Machine Works, and their business has always been thoroughly well conducted. The partners are Eben Folsom, Josiah J. Folsom and J. F. Wiggin.

The Exeter Gas Light Company, mentioned in a former chapter, was chartered in 1854. Their works are situated at the corner of Green and Water streets. The officers are F. H. Odiorne, president, Austin M. Copp, treasurer, and Arthur F. Cooper, superintendent.

The Exeter Water Works have their reservoirs and pumping apparatus on Portsmouth avenue, and a stand pipe on Prospect hill. The officers are Edwin G. Eastman, president, Elbert Wheeler, treasurer, and Charles H. Johnson, collector.

There are other companies and business establishments in the town, worthy of mention, as the Rockingham Machine Company, turning out machines for burnishing the heels of boots and shoes, the Tile Drain Manufactory of George W. Wiggin, and the Exeter Coal Company, of which George W. Clark is agent. It is not the purpose of this work, however, to furnish a business guide or directory.

THE EARLIER MERCHANTS.

Exeter, being at the head of tide water and of navigation, secured early an important trade with the towns farther inland. This it has never entirely lost, though the springing up of new centres of business and the substitution of improved modes of transportation of merchandise, have tempted the more distant places to carry their traffic elsewhere.

Several of the early merchants have been named in the account of ship-building. Indeed, every one engaged in that business dealt also in the commodities which his workmen required, and furnished them with necessaries as part of their wages.

HISTORY OF EXETER. 343

In the earlier days, not far from the middle of the last century, Colonel Daniel Gilman, Samuel Gilman, Zebulon Giddinge, Dr. John Giddinge and John Phillips were among the other principal merchants; then followed William Elliot, Peter and Eliphalet Coffin, John Emery, Joseph Lamson, Jr., and Ward C. Dean. Eliphalet Ladd began to trade about the beginning of the Revolution, and was enterprising and very successful.

At a later date, John T. Gilman, Joseph S. Gilman, Gilman and Moses, Gideon Lamson and Simon Wiggin were among the leading men in business, and still later, John Gardner, Daniel Ranlet, Elliot and James, Josiah Gilman Smith, Charles Conner, Nathaniel Weeks, S. B. Stevens, William H. Clark, Thomas Lovering, Thomas Conner, and Joseph T. Porter of the firm of Porter and Thyng.

These, of course, are but a few, and perhaps not all the most important, of the many who have been engaged in mercantile pursuits in the town. The list, however, includes persons whose business lives extend over the period of more than a century, and down to a date within the memory of the present generation. It would be impracticable to attempt more, here.

One business house is exceptional in its hereditary character. Ward Clark Dean commenced trade on Water street about the year 1770. His son-in-law, John Gardner, entered his store as his clerk soon after the year 1800, and continued with him until Mr. Dean retired in 1823. Mr. Gardner then succeeded him in the business with his son, George Gardner, as his partner; George Gardner continued the business in 1848, with John P. P. Kelly as his partner, until 1857, when John E. Gardner, the great-grandson of the founder of the business, became partner of Mr. Kelly, and has so remained up to this time.

It ought also to be remembered, to the credit of our fathers, that women were not debarred, in the olden time, from their natural right to engage in merchandise. The widow of the Rev. Nicholas Gilman, near the middle of the last century, kept a shop, as well as managed a considerable landed estate; and a daughter of Ward Clark Dean, a generation or more later, was a rival of her father in trade, and is said to have been by no means unsuccessful in enticing away his customers.

BANKS.

The old Exeter Bank was chartered in 1803. Before that time

from a bank in Portsmouth, of which Oliver Peabody, and afterwards John T. Gilman, was the president.

The Exeter Bank had originally a capital of two hundred thousand dollars. Jeremiah Smith was the president, and Nathaniel Rogers the first cashier. Afterwards, John Rogers succeeded to the post of cashier; and about 1830 Samuel D. Bell, for about five years; and then Timothy Farrar, who continued in it until the charter of the bank expired by limitation; it having been renewed in 1824 for the term of twenty years.

The Exeter Bank was kept in a building of one story at the corner of Centre and Water streets, afterwards occupied for a number of years by the Atlantic and Rockingham Fire Insurance Companies. The bank had quite a history. In its earlier days the cashier had occasion once to be absent from his post, and requested Mr. L., one of the directors, to take his place. That gentleman, very obligingly consented, though entirely inexperienced in the duties. This was before the time when country banks had arrangements with banks in the city to redeem their circulation, and when they were liable to be called upon at any time to pay a considerable amount of their own bills in other money. So the cashier left in the drawer a sufficient sum to meet such a demand.

While the temporary cashier was in control, a person entered the bank and presented a draft for two hundred dollars and upwards for payment, and received for it four bills, supposed by Mr. L. to be for fifty dollars, but in reality for five hundred dollars each, and the balance in smaller currency. The receiver took away the money, but soon after returned and asked Mr. L. if the bank rectified mistakes. "No, sir," said the quasi cashier, "after a man has taken his money and gone out, no mistakes are corrected." The customer departed.

When the cashier returned home and reckoned up the day's business, he found his cash eighteen hundred dollars short. He interrogated his substitute, who told him about the transaction mentioned. "Where did you get the fifty dollar bills from?" inquired the cashier. The partition was pointed out. "Those," said the cashier, "are bills for five hundred dollars." The other was astounded, and said he did not know that there were any of that denomination.

The bank called upon the person who had thus been overpaid, to refund the money. But he refused, probably salving his conscience with the answer made him at the time, that "no mistakes were corrected." The bank brought a suit against him to compel restoration. The matter was bitterly contested, for the defendant had influential friends. In the end the bank recovered back the amount of the overpayment. But a little episode at the trial is worth relating. The jury were sent out into their room to deliberate upon the case just at nightfall. It was found that there was a wide difference of opinion among them. So they fell to arguing the matter. One of their number, a small tradesman, who was used to going to bed early, grew drowsy, and quietly lay down upon a bench in a dark corner and went to sleep. His absence was not noticed by the others, and they continued to discuss the questions in the case till well towards morning. The arguments advanced by those who favored the defendant were one by one overthrown and abandoned, and at length it appeared that there was no one who would not acquiesce in a verdict for the bank. A ballot was then taken, when it appeared that only eleven had voted. The sleeper was roused. The foreman explained the question to him. "Well," said he, "I am in favor of giving the defendant a verdict." The foreman answered, that there were others of the jury who were at first of the same opinion, but after fully considering the case they had one after another changed their minds, and were now all in favor of the plaintiff. "Well," said the accommodating juror, "if you gentlemen have been discussing this matter all night, and have all agreed for the plaintiff, you may put me down for the plaintiff too."

The old Exeter Bank was doubtless extremely well managed, for its time. But a modern cracksman would laugh to scorn its protections against plunder. Its locks were primitive, with keys that were large enough for weapons of offence. Now-a-days they would not stand an hour against a burglar. But in 1828 the art of breaking banks was in its infancy. And when a gang of thieves from Rhode Island robbed the Exeter Bank, as they did in that year, they found it necessary to take at least two or three weeks to make the necessary preparations. It is a wonder that their purpose was not discovered. They had one or two huts or haunts in the neighboring woods where they remained and prepared their false keys by day, and at night came into the village and tested their work, in the locks of the bank. At length they succeeded in entering the stone vault, and took therefrom about thirty thousand dollars in bills, and some hard money, with which they made off. The story of the detection of the guilty parties is a long one, and much of the ingenuity displayed in the process, does not appear in the published report of the trial. A quantity of the money was found hidden under a stone wall. The stolen bills that they passed were a chief means of fastening the crime upon the robbers; and it is said that some incrusted silver coin which Ebenezer Clifford had brought up in his diving-bell from a wrecked ship at the bottom of the ocean, and deposited in the bank, furnished another clue. It is sufficient to say that the depredators were discovered, and brought to trial, and after a full hearing sentenced to imprisonment, and the greater part of the stolen property was recovered.

The Exeter Savings Bank was incorporated in 1828, and managed in connection with the Exeter Bank. John Houston was the first president and Samuel D. Bell, treasurer. Afterwards William Perry was chosen president, and Timothy Farrar, treasurer. The business of the Savings Bank was in 1842 wound up and closed, but in 1851 it was revived, and carried on in the building of the Granite State Bank. Woodbridge Odlin was chosen president and Samuel H. Stevens, treasurer, who was afterwards succeeded by N. Appleton Shute. Upon the flight of the latter in 1873, after having embezzled a great part of the funds, the Savings Bank went into the hands of a receiver, and the residue of its assets were distributed ratably among the depositors.

The second bank of discount in the town was incorporated in 1830, and styled the Granite Bank. Its capital was two hundred thousand dollars. John Harvey was the president until about 1844, when James Bell was chosen. James Burley was the cashier. It continued in business until 1851 and was then rechartered under the name of the Granite State Bank, and the capital was reduced one-half. Moses Sanborn was then made president, and Samuel H. Stevens, cashier. Joseph T. Gilman afterwards became president, and N. Appleton Shute, cashier. After Mr. Gilman's death in 1862, Abner Merrill was elected president, and held the office until 1877, the bank in the meantime having been organized under the national laws. Mr. Merrill was succeeded in the office of president by his three sons, in turn, Jeremiah L. Merrill, Benjamin L. Merrill and Charles A. Merrill. In January, 1873, the cashier, N. Appleton Shute, became a defaulter to a large amount and fled the country. The deficit was made up by the stockholders and the bank kept on, Warren F. Putnam being chosen cashier.

HISTORY OF EXETER. 347

After the decease of Dr. Charles A. Merrill, Benjamin F. Folsom was chosen president, and subsequently Charles E. Byington was elected cashier in place of W. F. Putnam. They still hold their offices. The directors of the Granite State National Bank are Benjamin F. Folsom, Eben Folsom, John E. Gardner, Warren F. Putnam and Amos C. Chase; and there is one vacancy.

In 1868 the Union Five Cents Savings Bank was incorporated, and opened with Joshua Getchell as president and Joseph S. Parsons as treasurer. The successive presidents since have been William B. Morrill, Charles Burley, William P. Moulton and W. H. C. Follansby; the treasurers, Frank P. Cram and Sarah C. Clark.

After the Exeter Savings Bank went into the receiver's hands in 1873, the Squamscot Savings Bank was incorporated. Its first president was Obadiah Duston, who was followed by Joseph Janvrin. George B. Webster is now the president, Francis Hilliard, treasurer, and William H. Belknap, cashier.

INSURANCE COMPANIES.

Fifty years ago, when mutual insurance was in vogue, Exeter was quite a centre for that business. In 1832 was incorporated the Rockingham Mutual Fire Insurance Company, of which Nathaniel Gilman, Jr., was made president, John T. Burnham, secretary, and James Burley, treasurer. In 1837 John Harvey was chosen president, and in 1838, Timothy Farrar. In 1839 there was a change of directors, attended with some feeling, but the president and secretary remained in office, with John Sullivan as treasurer. In 1843 James Burley was elected president, Isaac L. Folsom, secretary, and Jeremiah Dearborn, treasurer. This board of officers continued till about 1852, when Moses Sanborn became president, William P. Moulton, secretary, and John Tyrrell, treasurer. Five years afterwards, John S. Wells was chosen to the presidency, and Joseph C. Hilliard to the treasurership, William P. Moulton remaining secretary. The company had been very successful, and issued policies on a large amount of property.

The Atlantic Mutual Fire Insurance Company was chartered in 1847. Its business must have been limited prior to 1856, when we find that it was managed by the same executive officers as the Rockingham. This continued to be the case for several years. Charles Conner succeeded John S. Wells as president of both companies about 1863, and remained with W. P. Moulton and J. C. Hilliard as officers of the Rockingham until about 1866, when its affairs were wound up. The business of the Atlantic was carried on with Charles Conner as president, and Joseph S. Parsons as secretary and treasurer, until about 1871, when that company, too, succumbed to the growing preference for insurance in stock companies.

The Rockingham Farmers' Mutual Fire Insurance Company was incorporated in 1833. For some years little was heard of it, but in 1856 William Conner was its president, William P. Moulton, the secretary, and Joseph C. Hilliard, treasurer. John S. Wells succeeded Mr. Conner as president, and was succeeded by Charles Conner. Then William Conner was again chosen president, and held the office until his decease a year or two since. Charles E. Lane was secretary and treasurer a few years, and then George W. Wiggin was elected, about 1866, to those offices, and held them till 1874. The present officers are George B. Webster, president, and Henry A. Shute, secretary and treasurer. As its name imports, this company confines its insurance to farm buildings, or equivalent risks. It is now the oldest company in the town.

In 1885 the insurance of property in New Hampshire against fire, was mostly in stock companies existing out of the State. On account of a law enacted by the Legislature in that year, they, by a concerted action, determined to take no more risks in New Hampshire. It became necessary, therefore, that other means of insurance should be provided at home, and without delay.

The Exeter Mutual Fire Insurance Company was the first new company organized in the State to meet the new condition of things. It was put in operation under the general law of the State on the fifteenth day of October, 1886. Charles H. Bell was chosen president, and Arthur B. Fuller, secretary and treasurer. In 1887 Mr. Fuller resigned his offices, and George W. Weston was elected in his place. This and the Rockingham Farmers' are the only insurance companies now in the town.

BIOGRAPHICAL.

CHAPTER XVIII.

JUDGES AND LAWYERS.

JOHN GILMAN, the second son of Edward Gilman, Sr., born in England January 10, 1624, came to Exeter before 1650, and immediately became a prominent citizen. From the first he was concerned with his brother Edward in mills and lumber. After Edward was lost at sea in 1653, he inherited much of the latter's property, and took his place in developing the resources of the town. He was chosen selectman more than one-half the years between 1650 and 1680; was repeatedly elected commissioner to end small causes; and appointed upon committees to care for the town's interests. He had several handsome grants of land from the town, and a special right of a grist-mill. In the two years before New Hampshire was emancipated from the Massachusetts government he held the office of associate (judge) of the old Norfolk county court.

In 1680 Mr. Gilman was made a councillor of the newly erected province of New Hampshire, and in 1682 a judge of the Court of Pleas; but in 1683 he was by Governor Cranfield relieved of both offices. It is needless to say that his reputation in the province did not suffer by reason of his removal. In 1693 he was chosen by his townsmen a delegate to the Assembly, and was made Speaker of the House, and again chosen in 1697.

He married, June 30, 1657, Elizabeth, daughter of James Treworgy (from which came the popular Christian name of Trueworthy), and had six sons and ten daughters, and very numerous descendants. He built the "log house" opposite the Great bridge, which is still standing. He died July 24, 1708.

Robert Wadleigh was accepted as an inhabitant of Exeter September 26, 1676, at which time he probably removed there with his family. He was then a man of mature years, and had five sons, some of them tending towards manhood. He had lived in Wells, Maine, more than twenty years before, and in 1666 purchased a considerable tract of land at a place since known as Wadleigh's falls on Lamprey river in the present town of Lee, one-half of which he conveyed to Nicholas Listen. There Mr. Wadleigh lived until he came to Exeter. He soon became known to the people of Exeter, and was chosen to responsible positions. In 1680 he was a deputy to the General Assembly, of which he acted as clerk. In 1681 the inhabitants made him a grant of two hundred acres of land, and the next year his tax was the highest in the town.

A year afterwards he was sued by an agent of Mason, probably for the possession of some of his lands, and by exceptional good fortune won the verdict of the jury. His antagonist took an appeal to the king, upon which Wadleigh determined to go himself to England to look after his interests. He had a further reason for so doing, in the fact that his three sons were at that time under condemnation for taking part in "Gove's rebellion" against Governor Cranfield's tyrannical administration. The impression which Wadleigh made upon the Privy Council must have been favorable, for he was, after his return, appointed a justice of the peace and councillor of the province, doubtless on their recommendation.

Mr. Wadleigh continued to receive marks of the confidence of his townsmen, and of the provincial authorities. In 1692 he was appointed one of the justices of the Court of Common Pleas, and, a year afterwards, a judge of the Superior Court. This position he continued to fill until 1697. He died in Exeter not far from the year 1700. His descendants are somewhat numerous, and the name is still kept up in the town and vicinity.

Kinsley Hall was a son of Ralph Hall, one of the signers of the Combination, and was born in Exeter in 1652. He was a captain in the militia, an office then of no small repute, and served the town in various capacities, which denote the popular appreciation of his ability and intelligence. He was one of the selectmen for some years, moderator, and deputy to the General Assembly in 1694 and 1695. He was also a councillor of the province, appointed in 1698, and a judge of the Superior Court from 1697 to 1698, and again from 1698 to 1699. He married Elizabeth, daughter of the Rev. Samuel Dudley, and, after her decease, a second wife, and had several children, by whom the name has been preserved in the town until very recently. Judge Hall died in 1736.

Peter Coffin was born in Devonshire, England, in 1630 or 1631. He came to this country young, and removed to Dover before 1650. There he became a merchant, and was interested with Major Richard Waldron in a trucking house for dealing with the Indians. He was a lieutenant in service in Philip's Indian war, and was elected while in Dover to various town offices, and received some of the minor judicial appointments. He was quite successful in the accumulation of property. In 1689 when the garrisons at Dover were attacked by the savages and Major Waldron was killed, Mr. Coffin's house was entered, and the Indians compelled him to scatter among them handfuls of silver money, of which they found a bag full, that they might scramble for it.

He fortunately escaped from their hands. Shortly afterwards his house and buildings were burned, and he removed to Exeter in 1690, and was received an inhabitant by a vote of the town, and land was granted him for a wharf. He immediately engaged in business there, and was selected by the town to serve on important committees, and twice chosen moderator. In 1692 he was appointed a councillor of the province, and in 1697 Chief Justice of the Superior Court. This position he held for a year, and until a change of governors. In 1699 he was commissioned an associate justice of the same court, and continued in office until 1712.

He died March 21, 1715, and this obituary notice was published in *The Boston News Letter* of March 25:

On Monday the 21st current, died at Exeter the honorable Peter Coffin, Esq., in the 85th year of his age, who was late judge of his Majesty's Superior Court of judicature, and first member of his Majesty's Council of this province, a gentleman very serviceable both in Church and State.

He left five sons and four daughters. His son Robert, born in 1667, resided in Exeter, and married Joanna, daughter of John Gilman, and widow of Henry Dyer. He died in 1710 without issue. His son Tristram also lived in Exeter and had four children, of whom two, daughters, married Bartholomew and Benjamin, sons of Jonathan Thing.

Richard Hilton was a son of Captain William Hilton and grandson of Edward Hilton, and lived in that part of Exeter which is now South Newmarket. He served as one of the selectmen for seven years, between 1693 and 1715, and was a judge of the

Superior Court in 1698 and 1699. Little is known of him besides, except that he married his cousin Ann, daughter of Edward Hilton, Jr.

Nicholas Gilman was a son of Councillor John Gilman, and was born in Exeter December 26, 1678. He was a farmer and merchant. He lived in Exeter village on the south side of Front street, on the spot where the late John Williams built his brick house, afterwards occupied by Isaac Flagg. In 1729 he was commissioned a justice of the Court of Common Pleas, and held his seat on that bench for about a year, when he resigned in order to give his whole time to his private business. But in 1732, on receiving the appointment of judge of the Superior Court, he accepted it and performed the duties until 1740, and then retired to private life. He died in 1741, leaving children, several of whom occupied distinguished positions. He was a man of large property, and the owner of several slaves.

Samuel Gilman was a son of the foregoing, and was born in Exeter May 1, 1698. He was twice married and had children, who all died before him. He had an ample estate, and lived in the house on the south side of Water street, afterwards the home of Judge Oliver Peabody. He kept a public house there for a number of years, was a colonel in the militia, and was appointed to the bench of the Superior Court the same year that his father left it. He discharged his judicial duties for seven years. All accounts agree in representing him to be a man of the highest character, universally respected and esteemed. He lived to the age of eighty-six.

None of the above-named judges of the highest provincial court were educated as lawyers. And the custom of appointing to that responsible position men of sound sense, business knowledge and uprightness, without regard to their legal knowledge, was continued for many years after this time, mainly, it is supposed, for the want of enough suitable men educated to the profession. But, for the purposes of the time, the appointments were quite satisfactory.

The first trained lawyer in Exeter was Nicholas Perryman. He was born in England December 24, 1692, but emigrated quite young, after the death of his parents, and appeared in Exeter between 1710 and 1720. Where he received his education is not known, but that it was not neglected is apparent from the fact that he was employed as master of the grammar or classical school from 1716 to 1718. With whom he pursued his legal studies does not appear. But as early as 1730 he seems to have been fully engaged in the practice of the law. He was repeatedly employed by the town in suits, and in contested matters in the Assembly. He was the chief conveyancer of the inhabitants, and his work was neatly executed and correctly expressed, so far as it has been observed. He married Joanna, daughter of Stephen Dudley, and granddaughter of the Rev. Samuel Dudley, by whom he had four children, all of whom he outlived except one daughter, who married Noah Emery. He died in Exeter August 9, 1757.

Noah Emery was a son of a lawyer of the same name, and was born in Kittery, Maine, December 22, 1725. He must have come to Exeter before his maturity, for he married Joanna, the daughter of Nicholas Perryman, March 20, 1745, she then being but fourteen years of age and he under twenty. He studied his profession with his father-in-law, and probably was associated with him in business during the latter part of his life. The amount of purely legal business at that time must have been small, and it is likely that they added to it trade or other sources of profit. But Mr. Emery doubtless had his fair share of such professional employment as there was.

When the Revolution broke out he took sides warmly with the patriotic party, and was chosen a delegate to the Provincial Congress, of which he also served as clerk. He was prominent enough to be appointed upon some of the most important committees in that body and in the House of Representatives, into which it resolved itself.

In 1776 Mr. Emery was commissioned clerk of the Court of Common Pleas, and held the office until his death in 1787. He left five sons and four daughters. His son of the same name succeeded him in the clerkship.

William Parker was a son of Judge William Parker of Portsmouth, where he was born in 1731. He was a graduate of Harvard College in 1751, and after being employed as a teacher for a while, studied law with his father, and commenced practice in Exeter in 1765. He was able, well read and possessed of no small store of ready wit, but was afflicted with an unconquerable diffidence which prevented him from taking part in oral trials, so that his employment was chiefly confined to office work. But he stood high in the estimation of the community, who bestowed upon him a fair share of remunerative business.

When the Revolution swept away the old *régime* in the State, his father was removed from the office of Register of Probate, and the son, who was identified with the popular movement, was appointed in his place, and was continued in the post until his death in 1813, on which his son John J. Parker was chosen register and remained so through his life until 1831. Thus three generations of this family held the office continuously for near a century.

In 1790 Mr. Parker was commissioned judge of the Court of Common Pleas, and retained the position till 1807 when he was more than seventy-five years of age. The new constitution, adopted after his appointment, declared that the commissions of judges should be void when they reached the age of seventy, but it was an open question whether that provision applied to cases like his. The Legislature settled the question by passing an address for his removal; not because of any dissatisfaction, however, with him or his official conduct. He died, universally esteemed and respected, at the age of eighty-one.

John Pickering, a lawyer of eminence, afterwards Chief Justice of the State, and judge of the District Court of the United States, resided in Exeter for one or two years during the Revolution. Whether he came with the intention of making the place his permanent home, or to be in a more congenial atmosphere during the contest between the provinces and the mother country, is a matter of conjecture. He was taxed as a citizen in 1778, and the same year was chosen by the town a delegate to the convention to revise the constitution of the State. Though Mr. Pickering was known as a friend to the liberties of his country, he appears to have been a little timid in taking steps that might compromise him with the loyal party. In 1774 he was chosen by the Provincial Congress a delegate to the Continental Congress. He publicly declined the honor, upon the plea that the court was coming on, and his engagements to his clients would not permit him to be absent. John Sullivan was elected in his place, who, in thanking the convention, remarked, with a sly glance at Pickering, that he, too, had his court engagements, but he regarded his duties to his clients as of small moment in comparison to his higher duties to his country in that time of trial. The impression was general that Pickering's patriotism was of rather a faint-hearted kind.

Oliver Peabody was the son of a man of the same name, and was born in Andover, Massachusetts, September 2, 1753. He graduated from Harvard College in 1773; studied law in the office of the distinguished Theophilus Parsons, and began practice in Exeter about the year 1778. He was a careful and diligent student, and a faithful and punctual practitioner. His business capacity was appreciated by the community, and his personal qualities, his amiable disposition and courtesy of manner gave him much popularity. A great part of his life was passed in public stations. From 1789, for several years, he was annually chosen treasurer of the county; and in 1790 he was elected State senator, but resigned his seat to accept the appointment of Judge of Probate. After holding that position three years, he was again elected to the State Senate two successive years, in the latter of which he presided over that body. He again resigned the senatorship on being chosen treasurer of the State, which he continued to be for nearly ten years. The next year he was made sheriff of the county, and held that post five years. Again elected to the State Senate, he was appointed judge of the Court of Common Pleas, and remained upon the bench until the re-organization of the judiciary of the State in 1816.

In addition to all these, he held other positions of trust of comparatively private character. Yet Judge Peabody was no office seeker. He had pressed upon him other and more important positions, any of which, in all probability, he might have obtained had he consented to be a candidate, but declined them. He was fond of social and domestic life, and had no desire for anything that would separate him from that.

He died in Exeter August 3, 1831. He was the father of the two distinguished twin brothers, Oliver W. B. and William B. O. Peabody, and of the wife of Alexander H. Everett.

Nathaniel Parker was a son of Judge William Parker, then of East Kingston and afterwards of Exeter, and was born October 22, 1760. He obtained his education in the excellent schools of Exeter, studied law in his father's office, and began practice in the town before 1790. He, like his father, had little aptitude or inclination for the forensic side of his profession, though he probably had a sufficiency of legal knowledge. He was chosen clerk of the State Senate in 1803 and the following year, and representative from Exeter from 1805 to 1809 inclusive. In some of the latter years he was also Deputy Secretary of State, and in 1809 was chosen Secretary. His death occurred in Exeter April 2, 1812, and he left no descendants.

George Sullivan was a son of General John Sullivan of the Revolution, and was born in Durham August 29, 1771. He obtained his education at the Phillips Exeter Academy and at Harvard College, and took his degree in 1790. He read law in his father's office, and settled in practice in Exeter in 1793 or 1794. He was a good student, well fitted for professional work, and of fine personal presence, and soon secured an ample clientele. He was sent as representative to the State Legislature in 1805, and made so good an impression there that the Executive conferred upon him the appointment of Attorney General of the State, which he held for two years. In 1811 he was elected to the Congress of the United States for one term, and in 1814 and 1815 was a member of the State Senate. In the latter year he was a second time appointed Attorney General of the State and continued in the faithful and satisfactory discharge of the duties of the post for twenty years, when he resigned it upon the passage of a law which, though increasing the salary, forbade the occupant of that office to practise in civil causes. Mr. Sullivan's civil engagements were too important and lucrative to be sacrificed even for the sake of an office to which he was so peculiarly adapted.

Mr. Sullivan was an honorable, high minded lawyer, and had none of that petty sharpness which would take advantage of every trifling slip of an adversary. He was essentially an orator, and spared no pains to perfect himself in the art of eloquence. His voice was musical, and he trained it with care. His gesticulation was graceful, his language was well chosen, and his sentences were beautifully rounded. His addresses to the jury were models of argument, persuasion and appeal, and were extremely effective.

While in point of technical legal knowledge, and in the power to deal with abstract principles, Mr. Sullivan was confessedly not the equal of some of his competitors, yet in his own chosen field there was no one of them who surpassed him. He ranked among the first advocates in the State, and measured himself with the leaders of the bar, without losing by the comparison.

He belonged to a family noted in the law, and in which the attorney-generalship might almost be said to be hereditary, as his father held it before him and his son after him. The united terms of service of the three generations in the positions of public prosecutor, as attorney general or county solicitor, must have exceeded fifty years.

Mr. Sullivan died in Exeter April 14, 1838. He was twice married. Two of his sons followed his own profession, John, of Exeter, and James who, after practising a few years in Pembroke and Concord, removed to Michigan where he passed the residue of his life.

Moses Hodgdon, a native of Dover, who began practice there in 1801, came to Exeter and lived in the town from about 1811 to 1813, when he returned to Dover, and continued to reside there afterwards till his death. He had the reputation of being a sound and careful lawyer.

Solon Stevens was born in Charlestown October 3, 1778, the son of Samuel Stevens, and the grandson of the Phineas Stevens who defended the fort at "Number Four" from the assaults of the Indians, about the middle of the last century.

He was a graduate of Dartmouth College in 1798. After studying law with Benjamin West and John C. Chamberlain, he was admitted to the bar, and came to Exeter to settle, about the year 1801. He remained, probably, seven years, and then removed to Boston. But there his health failed him, and he went back to his early home, to die, at the age of thirty years.

Jeremiah Smith was for forty years one of the foremost citizens of Exeter. A native of Peterborough, he attended the schools of the town, and was early noted for his mental acumen and aptitude to learn. In 1777 he entered Harvard College, and at the same time enlisted in the army for two months in a company raised to oppose the advance of General Burgoyne. He fought valiantly at Bennington, and was slightly wounded, but declared afterwards that the music of bullets had no charms in his ears. After two years in Harvard he finished his collegiate course in Queen's (now Rutgers's) College in New Jersey. For three or four years afterwards he was engaged in teaching, at the same time reading law. When he presented himself before the Hillsborough bar for admission, it was objected that he had no counsellor's certificate that he had spent the proper time in study. Smith rode all the succeeding night to Salem, Massachusetts, and back, and produced the proper certificate the next morning, but the president of the bar declined to call another meeting to consider his application, on the ground that there was not time during the term.

The Scotch-Irish blood of the young applicant, who now saw that he was being trifled with, was instantly up, and he applied to the court for his admission, at the same time stating the treatment that he had received from the bar. The judges ordered that he should be admitted, much to the disgust of the lawyers, who did their best to make it unpleasant for him. Smith wrote to a friend that "it was devilish hard to be refused admittance to *bad* company!" However, he had his revenge. When the next court met without his name appearing on the docket, two of the lawyers, Baruch Chase and Nathaniel Green, to annoy him, asked if they should pass his list of entries to the clerk. He thanked them and wrote and handed them the following:

> Common sense v. Baruch Chase.
> Common honesty v. Nathaniel Green.

They troubled him no more; nor, to do them justice, did the rest, when they discovered how thoroughly qualified he was for his profession. Business rapidly flowed in upon him, and he was soon one of the leading lawyers of his section.

After three years' service in the State Legislature he was, in 1790, elected a member of the Congress of the United States, and afterwards was thrice re-elected. While in Congress, he made the acquaintance of many of the most eminent men of the country, with some of whom he remained on terms of intimacy ever after.

He resigned his seat in 1797 to accept the appointment of District Attorney of the United States, and, the same year, came to Exeter to reside. He was already married. For the next three years he labored assiduously in his profession, attending the courts in at least four counties. In 1800 he received the appointment of Judge of Probate for the county of Rockingham. A treatise upon probate law which, with characteristic diligence he drew up at that time, has since been published, in great part, and shows his thoroughness, learning and judicious application of principles. In February, 1801, he was commissioned by President Adams, then just about to go out of office, a judge of the United States Circuit Court. He prepared himself for his new functions by careful study, and until the law was repealed, by which the court was established, performed his duties with fidelity. When he was thus relieved from that office, he was at once appointed Chief Justice of the Superior Court of New Hampshire. The salary attached to the place was so inadequate that he could not, in justice to himself and his young family, accept the appointment. But the Legislature twice raised the salary in order to retain his services.

He filled the office with consummate ability and learning until date for the governorship of the State. He was elected, but the position was not at all to his liking, and he felt no regret when he found that he was not re-elected. In 1813 he was again commissioned Chief Justice of the Superior Court, and presided there until the change in the judicial system in 1816. For a few years after this he engaged in legal practice, and about 1820 retired from the profession.

He was not entirely relieved from the cares of business afterwards, as he was the president of the Exeter bank and the treasurer of the Phillips Exeter Academy. But he gave most of his time to his family and friends, and to reading and writing. He was never idle. He enjoyed society, and was a great talker among congenial companions. Once, when he had passed an evening in the company of Judge Theophilus Parsons and others, where he had furnished the lion's share of the conversation, he was late at breakfast the next morning. One of the gentlemen inquired where he was. "Oh," said Parsons, "he is in bed, resting that —— tongue of his."

Many anecdotes are told of his ready wit among his townsmen. It was once proposed in the town meeting to construct a new fence around the burying ground, which the judge considered unnecessary. "What use is there, Mr. Moderator," said he, "in going to the expense of a new fence about such a place? Those who are outside of it have no desire to go in, and those who are inside *cannot* get out!"

One of the most marked traits of Judge Smith was his uniform cheerfulness. He had his disappointments and trials in life, some of them of a serious character. But he bore them without repining or bitterness. He was always found the same.

He was certainly one of the ablest men, and most learned lawyers that New Hampshire has produced. Long after his death a volume of his legal decisions was for the first time published, edited by his son, who bears his name, and has also occupied a seat upon the supreme bench of the State. Their great value was universally acknowledged by the members of the profession, and one distinguished judge expressed regret that they had not been published much earlier, as they would have saved the people of the State a great sum of money in litigating questions which had long ago been so satisfactorily decided by him.

Judge Smith died in Dover September 21, 1842.

James Thom was a son of Dr. Isaac Thom of Londonderry, where he was born August 14, 1785. He graduated at Dartmouth College at the age of twenty, studied law under the direction of George Sullivan in Exeter, and after his admission in 1808, set up an office there. He was bright and popular, and had one accomplishment better appreciated in his time than in ours — he sang a good song. In the war of 1812 he was in command of a company of militia which was ordered to Portsmouth for the defence of the sea-coast for a brief tour of duty. He used to tell ludicrous stories afterwards of his military service. "There came once an alarm that the British were landing at Rye," he said, "and all my company were instantly taken sick, and I the worst of all." However, there was no real occasion to try their mettle against the enemy.

After seven years' life in Exeter, Mr. Thom removed to Derry, where he passed the remainder of his days in the practice of his profession, and a part of the time as the cashier of a bank.

Joseph Tilton came to Exeter to engage in the practice of the law in 1809. He had been admitted eight years before, which time he divided between Wakefield and Rochester. He was a native of East Kingston. He has been described as a "business lawyer," as he rarely took any prominent part in trials in court. But he was a sound and well read counsellor who acquired a respectable practice, and enjoyed the friendship and respect of his eminent contemporaries in the profession, Mason and Webster, Sullivan and Bartlett, and particularly of Chief Justice Richardson, who enjoyed Mr. Tilton's humorous stories and conversation, and admired that quality so much more appreciated by the bench than by the bar, his invariable promptness and readiness for trial when his cases came in order. "Mr. Tilton is *always* ready," was the judge's testimony.

The good things said that set the table in a roar, often fall flat when they come to be committed to paper. But lawyers, at least, will see the point of one of Mr. Tilton's sayings. A coach full of members of the bar were on their way from Portsmouth to Exeter. One of them remarked upon the beauty of a farm by the roadside, and wished he were the owner of it. "I'll tell you how you can get half of it," said Tilton. "Bring a suit for the whole, and refer it out of court. The referees will be sure to give you half!"

Mr. Tilton was a member of the Legislature from Exeter for nine years from 1814 to 1823, and though he made little noise in the political world, was really a power there. He had the entire confidence of his townsmen and of those who knew him best, and administered the trusts that fell upon him with uprightness and fidelity.

He married Nancy, the daughter of Colonel Samuel Folsom, and lived in the house in which she was born. He died, without leaving descendants, March 28, 1856, at the age of eighty-two years.

Jotham Lawrence was a descendant of one of the early residents of Exeter. His father lived in Epping, where he was born February 7, 1777. He was educated at the Phillips Exeter Academy, and studied his profession with George Sullivan. Admitted a counsellor of the Superior Court in 1805, he had probably been in practice in the inferior courts for two years before. He began business in his native town, but in 1809 removed his residence to Exeter, which was thenceforth his home.

Mr. Lawrence was not distinguished as an advocate, but had his fair share of the business of a general character, such as fell to the lot of most country lawyers. There were a few distinguished men in his day who were leaders of the bar, and argued nearly all the causes. They rode the circuits into the different counties, with the judges. This was a survival of the English fashion, which has now entirely disappeared in New Hampshire. The other members of the profession drew writs and deeds and other instruments, and aired their eloquence only in the inferior tribunals.

Mr. Lawrence took no special interest in political affairs though he was a member of the Legislature from Exeter in 1831, and afterwards held the office of Bank Commissioner. In his later years, and before a regular Police Court was established in the town, he was the Justice before whom the complaints for criminal offences were usually brought.

He was twice married and had three sons and several daughters. One of his sons, Alexander H. Lawrence, was a lawyer of eminence in Washington, D. C.

Mr. Lawrence died in Exeter November 6, 1863.

Stephen Peabody practised law about two years in Exeter, from 1811 to 1813. He was a native of Milford, and after quitting Exeter returned there to live. He was a lawyer of excellent standing and a man highly respected.

Jeremiah Fellowes, born in Exeter May 1, 1791, and a son of Ephraim Fellowes, was educated at the Phillips Exeter Academy and Bowdoin College, graduating at the age of nineteen. He was fonder of poetry than mathematics in college, or than Blackstone when he was a student at law afterwards. He went through the usual course of study in George Sullivan's office, and began practice in 1813. He still devoted much of his attention to literature, and in 1824 published a volume of his metrical productions, entitled *Reminiscences, Moral Poems and Translations*. Before he reached middle life, however, his mental powers lost their balance, and it became necessary for him to enter an asylum for the insane. He never recovered, but remained there till his death in 1865.

George Lamson, who has already been referred to in the chapter on the Press, was a son of Gideon Lamson of Exeter, and was born in 1794. After a course of preparation at the academy in the town, he passed through Bowdoin College, and studied for the bar with George Sullivan. Though he opened a law office, he was apparently chiefly interested in the printing office. He became the publisher of *The Exeter Watchman* in 1819, and began the issue of law books. In 1823 he gave up his legal business and removed to New York city where he undertook the business of a bookseller, but with little success. He died there August 4, 1826. He has been described as "a good scholar, an insatiable reader, and a ready writer." He had many and warm friends who mourned his untimely death.

William Smith opened his law office in Exeter in 1820. A son of Hon. Jeremiah Smith, he was born in Exeter August 31, 1799, and graduated from Harvard College in 1817. He studied his profession with his father.

He was bright, able and popular. Brought up among the principal people in the place, and in the midst of abundance, he lacked but the spur of necessity to bring out his best powers and to enable him to take his stand among the very foremost. At the age of twenty-two his townsmen elected him to the State Legislature, and returned him the two following years. He was appointed a colonel upon the staff of the governor, and received repeated invitations to deliver addresses before literary and other societies, which he accepted, and for which he received high encomiums.

He developed a taste, also, which is not common among the young, for historical and antiquarian studies. The past of his native town he investigated with special interest, and ransacked records, interrogated the old inhabitants, and gathered from all sources a large mass of historical information in reference to it. His purpose was to prepare and publish a history of Exeter, and it is unfortunate that he did not live to complete it. His labors in this direction, however, were not wasted. His father used the materials which he collected, for the foundation of the excellent bi-centennial address which he delivered in 1838; and the same memoranda have been of very great service to the present writer.

Mr. Smith did enough in the law to show that he was capable of attaining eminence. But he never realized the need of exertion, and never settled down to steady, hard work. He was generous and careless in regard to money, and in other ways was unbusinesslike, and caused anxiety to his friends. But he was always loved and esteemed; his foibles were regarded as venial, and a splendid future appeared to be before him.

At this point his career was interrupted by failing health. In the spring of 1828 he had a severe attack of lung fever, which left him with a cough and other indications of pulmonary feebleness. He never recovered from it. The next season he did not rally, and he then determined to try the effect of a milder climate. He passed the winter of 1829-30 in Mississippi, among friends living there. But the hoped for relief never came. He died March 29, 1830, unmarried.

Another of Exeter's brilliant young lawyers was Oliver W. B. Peabody, son of Judge Oliver Peabody, born July 9, 1799. He graduated from Harvard College in 1816, and from the Harvard Law School six years later, having been a teacher in the interim a part of the time. He was a diligent student, a thorough scholar and a well read lawyer, and his native abilities were of the first order. The highest expectations were naturally formed of his success in his profession. But he was formed for the pursuits of literature, and not for the contests of the forum. His commencement part at college was a poem. After he was admitted to the bar he was the editor of an Exeter newspaper, *The Rockingham Gazette*. He wrote and delivered numerous addresses and poems on public occasions, one of which, a poem on the two hundredth anniversary of the settlement of New Hampshire, was specially admired. The last eight years of Mr. Peabody's professional life, he was annually elected to the Legislature, where he made his mark as an accomplished scholar and law-maker. In 1830 he removed to Boston, Massachusetts, not with the design of prosecuting his profession, so much as to find a wider field for the occupation of his pen. He assisted his brother-in-law, Alexander H. Everett, in conducting *The North American Review*, and for some time had the editorial charge of *The Boston Daily Advertiser*. In 1835 he was chosen a representative from Boston in the General Court, and received the next year the appointment of Register of Probate. He held the office six years, during which he found time for much literary work. Jefferson College, in Louisiana, then offered him the chair of English Literature. He accepted it for a short time, hoping that his health, which was delicate, might be benefited by a change to a milder climate. In this he was disappointed, and returned to the North and began the study of divinity with an eye to the Unitarian pulpit. He read with his brother William, who was a settled clergyman in Springfield, Massachusetts.

In 1845 he was installed over a society in Burlington, Vermont, where he spent the short residue of his life in the enjoyment of the love and honor of all who knew him. He died there July 5, 1848.

John Sullivan belonged to a family of lawyers. His father and grandfather were such, his brother and two of his own sons, to say nothing of his granduncle, also, and several of *his* descendants. They had some inherited qualities which fitted them for the profession, especially the power of addressing juries in a peculiarly persuasive and effective manner. The oratory of John Sullivan so much resembled that of his father, that Ichabod Bartlett, who knew them both well, said that if he heard the voice of the former where he could not see him, he should think it was the father come back again.

John Sullivan was educated in the Phillips Academy in Exeter, and read law with his father. He never lived elsewhere than in his native town. He was admitted to the bar about 1825, and soon had to measure himself with the promising young lawyers at that time living in the town. He was able and high spirited, and the competition did him good. In 1828 he was commissioned solicitor of the county, and thus gained an opportunity to show his capacity in the department of criminal law, which was always to his liking. The stately march of the precedents pleased his ear, and his habits of accuracy were gratified by the strict technicalities. Moreover, his *forte* was the marshalling of evidence and

For ten years he performed the duties of the solicitorship, and then received the appointment of Judge of Probate. That office he held for the same period of time, and then was commissioned Attorney General of the State, which he continued to be, by successive appointments, to the close of his life.

Of this important office his administration was worthy of all praise. Diligent, faithful and accurate, he rarely made even the slightest mistake, and his uprightness and honor secured him from any suspicion of wrong or impropriety. He was singularly judicious in dealing with his cases. Instead of becoming by familiarity callous to the feelings and fate of the culprits brought under his official notice, he made broad distinctions between the hardened offenders and the unfortunate victims of folly or imprudence, and treated the latter in a way creditable to his humanity. More than one offender who had fallen into bad company, but had not become vicious, have had reason to thank Attorney General Sullivan for saving them from the stigma and contamination of a long term of imprisonment, and for the opportunity to retrieve their past errors.

Though by nature of a quick temper, he was courteous in his treatment of all men, unless he had reason to believe that some slight or unfairness was intended. *Then* his anger blazed up. But in the court-room, where forensic blows were given and taken fairly, he fought out his battles manfully, and bore no malice. And when he was cut down by death, November 17, 1862, the unanimous verdict of the profession pronounced him a model attorney general.

Another of the promising young lawyers of Exeter, who was taken away in his early prime, was Samuel T. Gilman, a son of Colonel Nathaniel Gilman, born May 7, 1801; died January 23, 1835. He graduated from Harvard College at eighteen, with a high rank for scholarship, and after a year's service as Assistant in the Phillips Exeter Academy, pursued the study of the law under Jeremiah Smith, and began practice in his native village about 1823. His talents were superior, and he had the gift of popularity. He was elected representative to the State Legislature, and appointed to deliver a Fourth of July address in Exeter; and scarcely a young man of his generation gave promise of a brighter future. But the indications of pulmonary disease made their appearance, and though everything was done to arrest the fatal malady, it was all in vain. Before he reached the age

For some five or six years Samuel D. Bell, afterwards Chief Justice of the Superior Court, lived in Exeter. He was invited there from Chester, where he first practised, by Judge Jeremiah Smith, who was pleased with the manner in which Mr. Bell, who was solicitor of the county, conducted the prosecution against the robbers of the old Exeter bank in 1828. The Judge was president of the bank, and offered Mr. Bell the post of cashier, upon the expectation, probably, that he would be able to combine with it a certain amount of the practice of the law. But that was undoubtedly found not to be feasible, and after holding the office until about 1835, Mr. Bell removed from the town, for the purpose of pursuing his profession elsewhere.

James Bell came to Exeter in 1831, from Gilmanton, where he had originally begun practice, after having graduated from Bowdoin College, and studied his profession with his brother, Samuel D. Bell, and at the Law School in Litchfield, Connecticut. He was thoroughly equipped for the position of a leading lawyer. Modest and unassuming by nature he never lost the perfect command of his powers, and contended for every right of his clients with the most pertinacious. His temper was under perfect control, and he treated all with the respect which their conduct allowed. He was quick in his perceptions, but his logical faculties were never hurried out of their sound, deliberate conclusions. His acquired were fully equal to his natural powers. By careful study and reflection he had made himself a master of the learning of his profession. Of the affairs of every day life, agriculture, business, mechanics and trade, he had a competent knowledge that stood him in good stead in his varied professional engagements. He had thoroughly trained himself for the duties of his calling, and no surprise daunted him; no exigency found him unprepared. Added to this he possessed a ready tact, to present always the equitable side of his cause, and had the weight of an upright private character, which never fails to tell, for counsel and client.

Mr. Bell was not long in acquiring a wide and valuable practice. He accomplished his work rapidly, and was capable of much continuous application. Before the sessions of the courts he prepared his causes with care and system. There was then no rest for him until the "previous proclamation" at the end of the term. His engagements for several years embraced nearly every contested cause of importance on the dockets of his own county and many on those of other counties. After listening to the judge's charge to the jury in one trial, he packed up his papers, and moved across the bar to open the next cause to another jury; and so on in a great proportion of the cases till the final adjournment of the court.

Such work, though he apparently went through it with ease, was of course wearing, and at length resulted in a disease that insidiously sapped the foundations of his life. In 1846 he received the offer of the post of Agent of the Lake Manufacturing Company, which would be less confining in its duties, while it was much in the line of his profession. He accepted it and removed from Exeter to Gilford.

In that year he had been elected a member of the Legislature from Exeter. In 1850 he was sent from his new home a delegate to revise the Constitution of the State. In 1853, and the two following years, he was the candidate of his party for governor of the State, but his party was in the minority. But then came a change in the political complexion of the State, and in 1855 he was elected by the Legislature a senator of the United States for six years. He took his seat, but he felt that his days were numbered. The disease that had long lurked in his system increased in violence, and he died at his home in Gilford May 26, 1857.

He left daughters and sons, one of whom followed his father's profession.

John Kelly did not come to live in Exeter until 1831, twenty-three years after he had been admitted to the bar, and when his legal practice was substantially over. He was born in Warner March 6, 1786, the son of the Rev. William Kelly, and received his bachelor's degree from Dartmouth College in 1804. He pursued his legal studies in the office of Jeremiah H. Woodman, and began practice in Henniker, but soon removed to Northwood. There he continued to reside and to attend to the business of his profession until his removal to Exeter, with the exception of the year 1814, which he spent in Concord in the editorial charge of *The Concord Gazette.* From Northwood he was sent in 1826 and 1827 a representative to the State Legislature.

In 1831 Mr. Kelly received the appointment of Register of Probate, which necessitated his residence in Exeter. He held the office till 1842, at which time he was chosen treasurer of the Phillips Exeter Academy, and remained in that post up to the year 1855. In 1833 he became editor of *The Exeter News Letter*, after the departure of its founder, John S. Sleeper. Under his oversight the paper lost none of the valuable features imparted to it by its former conductor, but took on others derived from its new editor. A vein of pleasantry ran through its articles, which entertained the readers, and often enabled the writer to exert a useful influence on subjects where didactics would have repelled.

But it was the historical and antiquarian information which, as has heretofore been stated, Mr. Kelly contributed to the columns of the paper that especially gave it a wider circulation and repute. His Collectanea have been mentioned in a former chapter.

Mr. Kelly was an original member of the New Hampshire Historical Society, and served as its recording secretary for a number of years. To the valuable historical Collections edited by Farmer and Moore he contributed a carefully prepared series of sketches of the early clergy of New Hampshire. After his removal to Exeter he was again chosen a representative in the Legislature in 1845; in 1847 and 1848 a member of the Executive Council; and in 1850 a delegate to the convention to revise the State Constitution.

He married Susan Hilton "the belle of Northwood," a descendant of Edward Hilton, and had several children; among them one son, John P. P. Kelly, and a daughter, the wife of the late Joseph L. Cilley of Exeter.

Timothy Farrar, a son of a distinguished judge of the same name, a graduate of Dartmouth College, who had practised law in Portsmouth and Hanover, and had been a judge of the Court of Common Pleas for some years, came to Exeter in 1836, to take the office of cashier of the Exeter Bank, which he held till the expiration of its charter in 1844, when he removed to Boston which was ever after his home.

Amos Tuck, a native of Parsonsfield, Maine, in 1810, and a graduate of Dartmouth College in 1835, came to Exeter in 1838 from Hampton where he had been teaching an academy and studying law. He entered the office of James Bell and completed his preparatory studies there, so that in December of the same year he was admitted to the bar, and became the partner of Mr. Bell. They remained together eight years, until the senior partner removed to Gilford. Their practice was extensive, and their trials of contested causes were particularly numerous and successful. Mr. Tuck was diligent, sagacious and faithful to the interest of clients, and soon won the reputation of an able and trustworthy lawyer.

Though bred a democrat in politics, he early showed his disapprobation of the position of his party upon the slavery question, and was among the earliest, in company with John P. Hale, to take his stand against it. He employed all his energies and influence to strengthen the Free Soil party, which united in 1847 with the Whig party to elect him a representative in the Congress of the United States. He served there six years, with marked ability and credit.

In 1847 he associated himself with the late William W. Stickney in the practice of his profession. Their partnership, which commanded a large and profitable business, continued about ten years. For two or three years, subsequently, he had for his partner in practice, his son-in-law, Francis O. French, now of New York city.

In 1856 he was a member of the convention in Philadelphia which founded the Republican party, and served upon the committee which reported its platform of principles; and in 1860 he was a delegate to the Chicago Convention which nominated Abraham Lincoln for the presidency. In 1861 he was appointed by the governor of the State to attend what was called the "Peace Convention," which attempted in vain to avert the threatened sectional conflict. In that body he reported the Declaration of the Northern members, of the concessions they were willing to make for the preservation of peace.

Mr. Tuck was appointed by President Lincoln, with whom he had enjoyed an acquaintance while in Congress, naval officer of the port of Boston, a post of importance and value. This he held by a re-appointment until 1865 when he was removed by President Johnson. He was afterwards for some years employed by the Atlantic and Pacific railroad to take charge of the sales of lands of that corporation, and took up his residence for the time in St. Louis. He was, later, engaged in various enterprises, which carried him much away from Exeter, but gave him agreeable and gainful occupation. Twice also he visited Europe, and travelled there somewhat extensively.

He was always much interested in the cause of education. For nearly thirty years he was a trustee of the Phillips Exeter Academy, and for about ten years of Dartmouth College. When the town of Exeter received the noble donation of William Robinson for the foundation of a female seminary, Mr. Tuck took great interest in the shaping and location of the institution; was the author of the constitution adopted by the town, and a trustee, and the first president of the board.

Mr. Tuck's life was an active and honorable one. His public career reflected much credit upon his ability and judgment. He had a high ambition, and was endowed with the qualities of a leader of men. His separation from his original party was based on grounds which were as creditable to his sense of right as to his political sagacity. His administration of the several positions of honor or trust that were conferred upon him was able and faithful. He was an astute man of business and accumulated a large estate, but was liberal in contributing to public objects and in private charity.

He was twice married, and had by his first wife, the daughter of David Nudd of Hampton, three children who survived him: Mrs. Frye of Boston, Ellen, wife of Francis O. French, and Edward Tuck, both of New York city.

Henry F. French lived in Exeter about eighteen years, from 1841 to 1859. He was a son of Daniel French, a lawyer in Chester, where he was born in 1813; and after an academic education, studied law with his father and at the Harvard Law School, and was admitted to practice in 1835. He was appointed solicitor of the county in 1838 and retained the office for ten years. In 1848 he received the appointment of bank commissioner which he held for four years. In 1855 he was commissioned a judge of the State Court of Common Pleas, and remained upon that bench until the court was abolished in 1859. These several offices he filled with ability and credit and to the general satisfaction.

He removed in 1859 to Massachusetts, where he was assistant district attorney for the county of Suffolk from 1862 to 1865, and then accepted the presidency of the Massachusetts Agricultural College, which he resigned after little more than a year's service, and returned to practice in Boston. In 1876 he was appointed second assistant secretary of the United States Treasury, and removed to Washington where he remained in the discharge of his duties until the accession of President Cleveland, when he retired to his farm in Concord, Massachusetts, and died there November 29, 1885.

Judge French was a ready, keen and thoroughly equipped lawyer. He had studied his profession diligently, and could bring to the front his knowledge and his best powers at a moment's notice. His habits of business were methodical, and nothing was neglected. While he was upon the bench he never left any cases or questions at loose ends; when the term was over the entire business, so far as he could control it, was done.

He was an agreeable companion, and kept on pleasant terms with all. He was also a man of marked public spirit. In Exeter he was interested in the streets and sidewalks and school-houses, in the laying out of the new cemetery, in the planting of shade trees, and in all that pertained to the improvement and beautifying of the place.

The judge was fond of husbandry, and read and wrote much on that subject. As the representative of an Agricultural Association he visited England to examine the improvements made by the great proprietors there in the cultivation of their lands, and after his return he published a volume on *Farm Drainage*.

Though the greater part of his active life was passed away from Exeter, he retained many warm friends there who were interested in his welfare and mourned his loss.

John S. Wells passed in Exeter the last fourteen years of his life. He was born in Durham in 1803, and was a grandnephew of General John Sullivan of the Revolution. In his youth he learned the trade of a cabinet-maker, but by his own exertions obtained an education and prepared himself for his profession. His first practice was in Guildhall, Vermont, from which place he removed after about eight years to Lancaster, New Hampshire, where he acquired a large practice, and held the office of county solicitor during two terms. He was also elected to the Legislature from Lancaster three years, the last of which he was chosen Speaker of the House.

He came to Exeter in 1846. The recent departure of James Bell from the county made an excellent opening in the town for a leading lawyer, and his political opinions also helped him to clients. In a very little while his docket became a large one, and his time was fully employed. In 1847 he received the appointment of attorney general, but he probably felt that he could not afford to surrender his private practice for the office. In 1851 he was elected to a seat in the State Senate, and was re-elected the following year. He presided over that body both years. In January, 1855, he was appointed by the governor a senator of the United States to fill out the unexpired term of Moses Norris, and held his seat until the succeeding fourth of March. Two years before, he had been a candidate before the Legislature for the same honor, but missed it by a few votes. In 1856 and 1857 he was the candidate of his party for governor of the State, but the political revolution of 1854 left him in the minority.

Mr. Wells was highly successful in his profession. He was a keen business man, and believed that the laborer is worthy of his hire.

Though not what would be called particularly studious in his habits, yet he had a considerable library, and consulted it not a little in his business. His legal learning was more than respectable, and he was capable of a good deal of continuous work. But he was fonder of trials at *nisi prius* than of any other professional employment, for there his peculiar qualities were at their best. He had a fine person, and a winning address. His voice was like that of his kindred Sullivans, sweet and well modulated. He had fluency of speech, and a knowledge of the weaknesses of human nature, which enabled him to address himself to the vulnerable side of the jury with much effect.

His domestic life was a chief source of enjoyment to him. He married early, and was the father of five children, three of whom outlived him. He was a fond parent, and felt the deepest interest in the welfare and happiness of his family. He died in Exeter of a lingering disease August 1, 1860.

William W. Stickney removed to Exeter from Newmarket in 1847. He was no stranger, as he had practised law in the county for near twenty years before. He was born in Enfield, graduated from Dartmouth College in 1823, and was admitted an attorney three years afterwards. Before he came to Exeter he had been three years a member of the State Legislature, and was again elected one year from Exeter. In 1849 he was appointed United States attorney for the district of New Hampshire, and served until the coming in of President Pierce. In 1857 he was made judge of probate for the county, and performed the duties of that office with entire acceptance until he reached the constitutional limit of seventy years of age. He was also for many years a director of the Granite State Bank and of the Manchester and Lawrence Railroad, and president of the Exeter Machine Works. Judge Stickney's qualities were rather solid than brilliant. He was a diligent, methodical, careful practitioner, who neglected no business entrusted to him. In the course of his long professional life, he is said to have missed attending but a single term of the courts, and that was by reason of illness. His reputation for integrity was never questioned, and he had the confidence and respect of all. His preparation of his causes for trial was most thorough, and he argued them to the jury and to the court with earnestness and force. His example can be cited to young men entering upon the legal profession as in all respects worthy of imitation.

He died March 19, 1888, at the advanced age of eighty-six years.

Alva Wood was a native of Georgetown, Massachusetts, and was born August 18, 1821. He received his education in the schools of that place and at Pembroke Academy. His law studies he pursued in the office of Bell and Tuck in Exeter, was admitted to practice about 1847, and immediately opened his office in the town. He had the art of making acquaintances easily, and soon became known as an active, working lawyer. His business increased as time went on, until few of the practitioners in the county could show so heavy a docket as his. He was persistent and spared no pains to carry out his plans, and succeeded in some instances where a less determined person would have failed. He was liberal in his practice, and by his uniform good nature and obliging disposition preserved friendly relations with all, even those who represented the most adverse interests. The legal profession was to him at once his occupation and his pride, and he valued his successes in it above all else. Politics he cared little for in comparison, though he maintained his fealty to his party.

For a year before his death his powers had obviously been failing, but it was not generally suspected that he was near his end, so that the news of his sudden decease February 17, 1878, was a great shock to his townsmen and friends. Enemies he had few or none, for he never allowed the friction of forensic contests to rouse any permanent ill feeling in his breast. His wife was a daughter of John C. Gerrish, and she, with a son and two daughters, survived him.

The life of George C. Peavey, several years of which were passed in Exeter, was a remarkable one. An injury to his spine, caused by an accident, resulted in almost total inability to walk, and such sensitiveness of his eyes to the light, that he was practically almost blind. He was compelled to pass most of his time in a reclining position, with a bandage over his eyes. Most men would have despaired of performing any business under such circumstances. Not so he. He had studied law, and he entered vigorously into practice. He found somebody to read to him and to write for him. He lay upon his lounge in the office and in court, but he could talk, and he had the command of all needed faculties.

After remaining ten years or upwards in Exeter he went to Strafford, was married to a devoted wife, who was not only eyes but hands and feet to him ever afterwards. With her aid he carried on not only a large law practice, but four country stores besides, and extensive dealings in lumber. Nearly twenty years afterwards some favorable features in his malady encouraged him again to remove to Exeter, but he found that he could not continue there without a recurrence of his worst symptoms, and he returned to Strafford, where he died May 5, 1876, at the age of sixty-one years.

Other names, besides those mentioned, are found upon the roll of practitioners of the law in Exeter. Joseph Bell purposed making the place his home and staid there a short time in 1812 before he began his successful career in Haverhill. Thomas Rice appears to have been there in 1817 and Abram Smith in 1829, but of them we learn nothing. Gilman Marston came in 1840, and a brief sketch of him will be found in the chapter on the War for the Union. David A. Gregg, who had practised in Derry, came to Exeter in 1842, to take the office of Register of Probate. He died in Derry in 1866. Melburn F. Eldridge had an office in the town two or three years between 1840 and 1850, and then took his departure, it is believed, to Nashua. E. Frank Tucke, a native of Kensington, a graduate of Dartmouth College in 1843, and a man of many winning qualities, began business in the place about three years afterwards, but died in 1857 at the early age of thirty-five years. J. Hamilton Shapley, a native of Portsmouth and for a number of years a lawyer there, filled the offices of Register of Deeds and Register of Probate, in Exeter, and continued in practice there for a time, but has now retired from the active pursuit of his profession. Nathaniel Gordon, a native of the town and a graduate of Dartmouth College in 1842, practised law for a number of years after 1850, and then quitted it for what he found to be more profitable occupation. Horace C. Bacon studied law with John S. Wells and was his partner from about 1852 to 1856, and then removed to Epping and afterwards to Lawrence, Massachusetts. Nathaniel G. Perry, a native of the town and a graduate of Harvard College, had barely entered into practice when a disease of the lungs cut short his career. Charles H. Bell came to the place from Somersworth in 1854, and practised law about fourteen years, ten of which he was solicitor of the county, and then retired. John W. Clark kept an office in Exeter from about 1857 to 1868, and went to Washington, D. C., to accept a position in one of the departments. Moses N. Collins has already been noticed in one of the military chapters. Samuel H. Stevens, who had practised law in Bristol, became cashier of the Granite State Bank in Exeter in 1856, and remained a few years, but afterwards fixed his residence in Concord, where he died in 1876. Samuel M. Wilcox, a former practitioner in Orford and in Francestown, entered into partnership with John S. Wells about 1859, and after his decease continued in practice in the town a few years, and then removed to Washington, D. C. Francis O. French was a partner of Amos Tuck two or three years after 1860, and then became a banker, first in Boston and afterwards in New York. Benjamin F. Ayer removed from Chicago, Illinois, to Exeter in 1862, but after a brief stay returned again. Hendrick D. Batchelder practised law in the town a few years about 1860, and then went to Poughkeepsie, New York. John J. Bell, who had resided in Maine, came to Exeter about 1865, and after practising his profession about ten years and accepting the office of Judge of the Police Court, retired. Andrew Wiggin opened an office in the town about 1865 and after a few years removed to Boston. Joseph F. Wiggin, a native of Exeter, entered practice between 1860 and 1870, and for a few years held the office of Judge of Probate. For some time past he has had an office in Boston, but retained a connection with some lawyer in Exeter. S. Dana Wingate was admitted an attorney about 1867, and did a considerable probate and pension business, but died shortly after. Charles U. Bell began practice in Exeter about 1868, and after about five years went to Lawrence, Massachusetts. B. Marvin Fernald was a partner of Joseph F. Wiggin for a time, and is now in Boston. P. Webster Locke, L. G. Hoyt and Fred S. Hatch each passed from one to three or four years in Exeter, and have gone elsewhere.

The present lawyers in practice in the town are Gilman Marston, J. Warren Towle, Thomas Leavitt, Albert C. Buzell, Edwin G. Eastman, Charles H. Knight, Arthur O. Fuller, Henry A. Shute and E. W. Ford.

CHAPTER XIX.

MEDICAL MEN.

The number of physicians of education in the country two centuries ago was very small. Exeter had none that we know of. Walter Barefoote, so far as is recollected, was the only one in the province. But it is not to be supposed that there was an entire absence of practitioners of the healing art. There were always those who had a certain skill in nursing and administering to the relief of the sick, even if they did not claim the ambitious title of doctors. Barbers practised venesection. Clergymen frequently studied medicine in addition to divinity, as did Dr. John Phillips, that they might minister to bodies as well as to minds diseased.

But it was not until one-quarter of the seventeenth century had passed, that a regular physician was established in Exeter. It was, perhaps, an era in the history of the town. The doctor was a man of consequence in the early times, second only to the minister. His dress indicated the importance of his profession. His cocked hat and full bottomed wig and his indispensable cane were awe-inspiring, to say nothing of his saddle bags stuffed with strange and nauseating medicaments which he dispensed with profusion to his patients.

The mistakes of the early doctors, if they made any, in prescribing internal remedies, are long buried out of remembrance. But some accounts of the manner of their treatment of external injuries have been preserved. One of those worthies is said to have replaced and bound on, *upside down*, a toe which had been cut from a patient's foot, and it grew so. Another put bandages around the hands of a child which had been badly burned, confining the fingers together, so that they adhered to each other and could not be separated.

Exeter's first physician, so far as can be discovered, was Dr. Thomas Deane. He was a native of Boston, Massachusetts, born November 28, 1694, and a son of Thomas Deane. The family moved to Hampton while the son was a young man, and this, perhaps, led him to Exeter. There in 1718 he married Deborah, daughter of the Rev. John Clark, and afterwards made his home. Where and to what extent he prepared himself for his profession is not known, but he began practice, without doubt, no long time after his marriage. He lived in Exeter till his death in 1768. He was once or twice chosen to the office of selectman, but his preference seemed to be for military position. He was a captain and afterwards major in the militia, and upon the books of the town, where every man's rank was scrupulously given him, his professional was usually supplanted by his military title.

Dr. Deane was one of the proprietors of the town of Gilmanton and took an active part in building up the second church and parish in Exeter, which is the more noticeable as his wife was a stepdaughter of the Rev. John Odlin, the minister of the old parish. No evidence of his professional skill has come down to us, but he was not without books. One which belonged to him—*The Art of Chirurgery*—is still preserved, in the possession of John Ward Dean of Boston, a descendant.

Dr. Deane is said to have lived on the east side of the river in a house next to that afterwards occupied by Dr. Nathaniel Peabody. He had three wives and eleven children.

We learn from the diary of the Rev. Nicholas Gilman that on returning from Cambridge to Exeter greatly indisposed, July 10, 1725, he "applied himself" to Dr. Sargent. It is not known that this was an Exeter practitioner. It is probable that he was of Hampton or Salisbury, Massachusetts, where there were families of the name.

The next Exeter physician in the order of time, so far as has been ascertained, was Dr. Josiah Gilman, a son of Judge Nicholas Gilman. He was born in Exeter February 25, 1710, and died January 1, 1793. In 1731 he married Abigail, daughter of Captain Eliphalet Coffin. Where he studied his profession we do not know; quite probably, however, with Dr. Deane. Dr. Gilman was a medical practitioner in the town for probably half a century, and seems to have satisfied the people. In that time he saw several competitors enter the field, but apparently they did not crowd him out.

He was a man of considerable education, with good business capacity. He subscribed for a copy of *Prince's Chronology*, shortly after reaching his majority, and was clerk of the Proprietors of Gilmanton more than thirty years, as well as the draftsman of a plan of that town. He was the father of ten children.

Dudley Odlin was born September 22, 1711, a son of the Rev. John Odlin of Exeter. He was a practitioner of medicine, and so far as is known, was never married. He built the large gambrel roofed house on Front street, afterwards occupied by Colonel Nathaniel Gilman. He died at the age of thirty-six, and by his will gave the house to his nephew Dr. John Odlin.

Robert Gilman was a son of Colonel John, and a brother of Brigadier Peter Gilman. He was born June 2, 1710, and was bred a physician. His wife, by whom he had three children, was Priscilla Bartlett. The most that can be learned of Dr. Robert Gilman is that he volunteered to go as a surgeon in the expedition against Louisburg in 1745, and was wounded in the leg by a piece of shell, on account of which the Assembly of the province made him an allowance. His wife had died in 1743, and it is probable that he did not survive his injury many years.

Dr. Eliphalet Hale appears to be the next Exeter physician in chronological order. He was a son of Nathan Hale of Newbury, Massachusetts, where he was born in 1714. He was in practice in Exeter before 1750, and died at the age of fifty years. His first wife was Elizabeth Jackson, and his son Eliphalet was for a time a manufacturer of paper at the mill in Exeter. His second wife was a daughter of Colonel John Dennet, and after her husband's death she married Dr. John Phillips.

John Giddinge was a native of Exeter, born September 11, 1728, and a son of Zebulon Giddinge. He became a physician, and was also engaged in mercantile business. At the age of twenty-three he married Mehetabel, eldest daughter of Brigadier Peter Gilman. Dr. Giddinge was a man of prominence. He was elected selectman several years, and a representative just before and during the early years of the Revolution. He commanded a company of those who marched from Exeter to Portsmouth to support, if necessary, the party of General Sullivan and Langdon in the raid upon Fort William and Mary in Portsmouth harbor, in December, 1774, and was one of the most active and trusted supporters of the patriotic cause in the Legislature. In 1775 he was nominated for the important appointment of delegate to the Continental Congress, but modestly withdrew his name. His death occurred, it is believed, about the year 1785.

John Odlin was a son of the Rev. Elisha Odlin, and was born in Exeter September 4, 1732. He studied medicine, very probably, with his uncle, Dr. Dudley Odlin, and practised for above twenty years in Exeter. He married Mary, daughter of Joshua Wilson, and had three children. In 1782 he sold his house in Exeter and removed to Concord where he lived afterwards.

Nathaniel Gilman was a son of Colonel Daniel Gilman and was born in Exeter about the year 1740. He was a practising physician. His wife was a Treadwell of Portsmouth. They had three children, one of whom, Nathaniel Waldron Gilman, was a merchant in the town, and died in 1854. Dr. Gilman was in practice before the Revolution and probably died about 1782.

Caleb G. Adams was born in Exeter January 8, 1752. He became a physician, and practised in the town. He married, December 8, 1774, Mary, daughter of Nathaniel Folsom of Portsmouth, and granddaughter of General Nathaniel Folsom of Exeter. In 1775 he was appointed surgeon of Colonel Enoch Poor's third New Hampshire regiment, but did not remain in the service beyond that year. He died probably in 1783, leaving a widow and two children. His widow married Governor John T. Gilman.

John Lamson was a native of Exeter, and born about 1736. He received a medical education, and was at the age of twenty-one appointed surgeon's mate in the New Hampshire regiment raised for actual service under the command of Colonel Nathaniel Meserve. Two hundred men of the regiment were ordered to Fort William Henry at Lake George, under the command of Lieutenant Colonel John Goffe, and Dr. Lamson accompanied them. His adventures after the surrender of the garrison to Montcalm, have been described on page 236 of this history. After his return home, though he served in another military expedition, he spent most of the residue of his life in the practice of medicine and surgery in Exeter. He died in November, 1774.

It seems that during his captivity in Canada he manifested qualities that won the regard of the savages among whom he lived. The year after his decease a party of them visited Exeter and made inquiry for him, supposing he was still living. On being informed of his death, they all sat down and maintained profound silence for a season, that being their mode of manifesting their respect and sorrow for the departed.

Dr. Joseph Tilton was born at Hampton Falls September 26, 1744. He received his early education in the town schools there, and it was necessarily somewhat scanty. At sixteen years of age he began the study of medicine and surgery with Dr. Ammi R. Cutter of Portsmouth, a physician of note, and remained with him for five years. Being then fitted to commence practice he married the daughter of John Shackford of Portsmouth, and in 1767 settled in Exeter. There were then three other physicians in the place, and the opening was not a promising one. But he persevered, and as the fashion of the time was, opened an apothecary's shop, and offered his services as a physician and surgeon. His industry and fidelity were in a few years rewarded by a good share of practice, which extended into no less than thirteen towns, and was exceedingly laborious, as he had no means of travelling except on horseback.

During the Revolutionary War he was absent from home as the surgeon of a privateer for one or two cruises. With this exception he continued his practice in Exeter for above sixty years. In early life his constitution was slender, but he strengthened it by his active habits, his temperance in eating and abstinence from ardent spirits, so that in his later years he enjoyed uninterrupted health.

He lived for sixty-eight years in the house still standing on the north side of Water street, nearly opposite the foot of Spring street, and died in January, 1838. He left no male descendants.

Dr. Samuel Tenney was a native of Byfield, Massachusetts, born November 27, 1748. He was educated under Master Moody at Dummer Academy, and at Harvard College, in the class of 1772. He studied medicine with Dr. Kittredge of Andover. He came to Exeter early in 1775 to settle, but on the breaking out of the Revolution determined to enter the army. He mounted his horse and rode to the vicinity of Boston, arriving just in season to assist in relieving the wounded at the battle of Bunker Hill. He served through the war as surgeon; one year as assistant to Dr. Eustis in a Massachusetts regiment, and afterwards in the Rhode Island line. He was present at the surrender of Burgoyne and of Cornwallis. He volunteered for the defence of Red Bank on the Delaware, himself using a musket in emergency; and dressed the wounds of Count Donop who was mortally hurt in the assault upon that work. The Count delivered to him his pocket-book for safe keeping,—remarking that he looked like an honest man.

At the close of the war Dr. Tenney returned to Exeter where he married and resided for the residue of his life, though he did not resume professional practice. The tradition is that he had some trouble about a case of dislocation of the shoulder which he undertook to reduce, and abandoned the profession in disgust.

He was fond of scientific studies, and had a strong inclination towards political life. He was a member of the convention for forming the Constitution of New Hampshire in 1791; in 1793 he received the appointment of Judge of Probate for Rockingham county, which he held until 1800 when he was elected a member of Congress. He served there for three terms. His death occurred in 1816.

Dr. Tenney was a member of several literary, historical and scientific societies and contributed articles to their publications. For the American Academy of Arts and Sciences he wrote an account of the mineral waters of Saratoga, and a theory of prismatic colors; for the Massachusetts Historical Society a historical and topographical account of Exeter, and a notice of the dark day, May 19, 1780; and for the Massachusetts Agricultural Society a much approved treatise on orcharding. He also prepared valuable political essays for the newspapers, particularly in favor of the Federal Constitution, in 1788.

He was a man of fine presence, and of much dignity. His domestic and social relations were of the happiest character. He was universally esteemed and respected, and in his death, his townsmen felt that they had met with no ordinary loss.

Dr. Tenney's wife was Tabitha, daughter of Samuel Gilman, a highly accomplished lady. She was the author of two or more published works, the chief of which was *Female Quixotism* which had much popularity in its time, and went through several editions.

Dr. Nathaniel Peabody was born in Topsfield, Massachusetts, March 1, 1741. He never attended school a day but derived his early education from his father who was an eminent physician. He studied and practised medicine with him from twelve to eighteen years of age and till his father's death. When he was twenty he settled in Plaistow, now Atkinson, and obtained an extensive practice as a physician. At thirty years of age he was commissioned by the royal governor, a justice of the peace and quorum. In 1774 he was appointed a lieutenant colonel in the militia. He espoused with ardor the cause of his country, and took part in the raid upon Fort William and Mary in Portsmouth harbor in December of that year.

In the earlier years of the Revolution he was a leading member of the Legislature, and of the Committee of Safety. In 1778 he was appointed adjutant general of the militia of the State, and served as such that year in Rhode Island. In 1779 he was elected a delegate to the Continental Congress. After his return home he was for several years a member of the State Legislature, and major general of the militia.

He was one of the chief founders of the New Hampshire Medical Society, and received from Dartmouth College the honorary degree of Master of Arts. Doctor or, as he was commonly styled, General Peabody was fond of display, and probably injured his property by indulging in it, and in the later years of his life his affairs became deranged, and he was arrested by his creditors for debt, and committed to jail in Exeter. Thus it happened that he became a resident of the town for about twenty years. He enjoyed the privilege of the prison limits, and was not actually confined, but lived in a house on the eastern side of the river, not far from the Great bridge. But he was restricted to certain bounds, which he could not pass without involving his sureties in heavy liability. The limits, however, allowed him the freedom of the greater part of the village.

He continued to practise his profession, to some extent, through life, and was esteemed a physician of skill and learning.

Dr. Peabody in his best days had the confidence and respect of the prominent men among whom he moved. But pecuniary embarrassments exposed him to the charge of dishonorable dealings, and his manners were not such as to render him an agreeable companion. He was cynical in his notions, and having himself great powers of endurance, he had little patience with others who complained. He had probably acquired the rough habits and expressions of the camp, also, and employed them without much discrimination. He is said to have been a man of wit, and to have had his softer side; but, apparently, he did not often present it to others.

He was undoubtedly a man of much ability, and if he had paid less attention to public affairs and more to his own, might have acquired fortune and a life of ease. His patriotism and services for his country entitle him to our gratitude, and his foibles may well be consigned to oblivion. He died in Exeter, June 27, 1823.

William Parker, Jr., is supposed to have been a son of Judge William Parker of Exeter, and was born near the middle of the last century. Little is learned of his early history, but he was in November, 1776, sufficiently versed in the knowledge of his profession to be considered worthy of the responsible appointment of surgeon in the second regiment of the New Hampshire line in the Revolutionary army. He served through the following year, and was at Ticonderoga when that post was evacuated upon being invested by General Burgoyne, and at the affair of Hubbardton, where his regiment lost so heavily. His service in the field ended apparently with that campaign. He then resumed his medical practice in Exeter. He must have been a physician of some standing, for he was called to prescribe for a lady visiting in the family of Benjamin Abbot, the principal of the academy, about 1796, the lady being very ill with an unknown disease. It proved to be the yellow fever. Dr. Parker contracted it from his patient and died of it.

Nathan North came to Exeter to practise medicine in the latter part of the last century, and remained about twenty years. He is represented as a man of sense and ability, with a competent knowledge of his profession, and became the attending physician of the principal families of the town. But he was not proof against the prevailing convivial fashions of the time, and at length fell into habits of inebriety, which, of course, seriously interfered with his practice. In the year 1815 Dr. North removed from the town, and is said to have abandoned his pernicious habits, and maintained a high standing in his profession afterwards.

William Perry was a son of Nathan Perry of Norton, Massachusetts, and was born December 20, 1788. He prepared himself for college in part at an academy, of which his brother Gardner was then principal, at Ballston, New York, and entered Union College, but at the close of his freshman year migrated to Harvard College, where he took his degree in 1811. While an undergraduate, in 1808 he made a trip down the Hudson river in Fulton's first steamboat, the "Clermont." He studied medicine with Dr. James Thacher of Plymouth, and afterwards in Boston under the instruction of Drs. John Gorham and John Warren. By the latter he was recommended to a few gentlemen of Exeter who had applied to him to advise them of some promising young physician to settle in the town. He accordingly opened his office there in 1814. His progress at first was obstructed by the resident medical men who were naturally jealous of a young competitor; but before long his professional learning and correct habits with his industry and ability opened his way to a wide practice, which he retained even to old age. It reached to the remotest parts of the county and sometimes beyond it. It was, of course, very laborious, and not what would in these times be called lucrative. But it was sufficient for his needs, and enabled him to live as he desired, to educate his family, and to realize a handsome competency.

Dr. Perry was of an inquiring and inventive bent; and was not content to follow outgrown methods. He contrived new appliances for the treatment of injuries, and devised new remedies for disease, and gained much reputation thereby. He was one of the earliest of the medical men of the State to agitate the project of establishing an Asylum for the Insane, which has since been accomplished in so admirable a manner. In 1835, after delivering a course of lectures before the students of the Bowdoin Medical College, he was offered a professorship there, but declined it.

An account of his enterprise in the manufacture of potato starch, has already been given in a former chapter.

For much more than half a century Dr. Perry was the principal physician and surgeon, not only in the town, but in the section. In all difficult cases which arose in the neighboring places, he was the natural consulting authority. In surgical operations, especially, his experience was large, and his opinion was of the greatest weight. He was often called into court, to give testimony as an expert in important causes. He was decided in his opinions, but he based them on authorities and the soundest reasoning. Cross examination never shook his testimony, but rather brought out fresh support for his views.

He was a conscientious and positive man. He strove always to discern the right course, and then pursued it unswervingly. He tolerated no temporizing, and still less anything approaching to a compromise of principle. People always knew where to find him. He was sometimes involved in differences with others, but he marched straight on, and in the end won the respect of even his antagonists, for his honesty and uprightness. He lived to the age of ninety-six years.

An old age like Dr. Perry's was something to be desired. Free from nearly all the infirmities incident to advanced life, his memory and judgment for the most part unclouded, in the midst of relatives and friends, and of a community who valued and respected him, he passed his later years in serenity and peace. He was gratified by the respect and consideration everywhere shown him. At the last two presidential elections his fellow citizens of the town with one accord refrained from voting, until he cast the first ballot. On his later birthdays his old patients and friends called on him to wish him health and happiness, and to present him tokens of their love and good will. And when his long life was brought to a close, the community, as one man, sincerely mourned the loss of him who had so long been a faithful and valued leading character in the town.

David W. Gorham was a son of Nathaniel Gorham, Jr., and was born in Canandaigua, New York, in the year 1800. He obtained his education at the Phillips Exeter Academy and at Harvard College, from which he graduated in 1821. He chose the profession of medicine, and established himself in practice in Exeter, and there remained until his death in 1873. He was a careful and reliable physician, and acquired an extensive practice, and few medical men commanded the confidence of their patients more completely than he. He was an excellent man of business, liberal, but exact, and the impersonation of promptness. In 1844, on the decease of Dr. Abbot, he was chosen a trustee of the Phillips Exeter Academy, and continued in the discharge of the duties to the time of his decease. His services in that capacity were of the highest value. He was assiduous in looking after the interests of the institution, in every way. His accurate business habits and sound judgment were always a source of strength to the management. When the old academy building was burned in 1871, it was largely through his exertions and influence that it was replaced by the present beautiful and appropriate structure.

He was one of the most important members and a principal supporter of the Unitarian Society. He served annually as one of the executive committee, and voluntarily took upon himself the undesirable duties of treasurer and collector. His uniform patience, good temper and excellent system enabled him to keep the financial affairs of the society in a sound condition, and thus a chief source of variance and difficulty was avoided. The minister's salary was never a day in arrear, during his term of office. His death was a heavy blow to the institutions to which he had been so helpful, and a serious loss to the community, where he was highly esteemed. Dr. Gorham married early in his professional life, Elizabeth P., daughter of Dr. Benjamin Abbot. He survived her death only about two months. Of their three children, two outlived him, Dr. William H. Gorham, who divides his time between Exeter and Boston, and Mary, wife of George C. Sawyer of Utica, New York.

Samuel B. Swett was a native of Boston, a son of Colonel Samuel and grandson of Dr. John Barnard Swett of Newburyport, Massachusetts, a distinguished physician. He obtained his medical education in New York and Paris, and came to Exeter about 1840. He had a large practice in that and the adjoining towns for upwards of twenty years, and then removed to Jamaica Plain, Massachusetts, where he still resides.

William G. Perry, a son of Dr. William Perry, graduated from Dartmouth College in 1842 and after completing his medical course in this country, studied a year in France. He has been in practice in the town since about the year 1846.

In addition to the medical practitioners named, there have been many others who lived for longer or shorter periods in the town. Dr. Josiah Rollins, a native of Exeter, appears to have practised between 1750 and 1778. Dr. Selah Gridley was a resident of the town for some years before his death in 1826, though it is believed that he did little in his profession. Dr. Thomas O. Folsom, a native of the place, died in 1827, shortly after he received his degree of M. D. Dr. Abraham D. Dearborn, a son of Freese Dearborn, practised in the town a few years about the year 1840, as did also Dr. Thomas Flanders and Dr. Blodgett. Dr. Charles Warren passed more or less time in Exeter for a number of years, attending to patients. Dr. George W. Gale had at one time a considerable practice. Dr. Franklin Lane, a son of Joel Lane, began his medical life in Exeter, and at the same time was editor of *The Exeter News Letter*. He afterwards removed to Baltimore, Maryland, where he still lives.

Dr. George G. Odiorne, also a native of the town, commenced practice there, but afterwards went to the West. Dr. Ezra Bartlett was a number of years a practitioner in the town, and removed to Taunton, Massachusetts, where he now is. Dr. E. P. Cummings established himself in the town as a homœopath, a little time prior to the war, and then was employed in the naval service, and died in Newburyport, Massachusetts. Dr. Samuel Perham for some years passed a great part of his time in Exeter in treating certain classes of disease. Dr. Albert Carroll practised a few years in the place, but is now deceased. Dr. Charles C. Odlin, a son of Joseph Odlin, was born in the town, and pursued his profession there for several years with success, and is now located in Melrose, Massachusetts.

Dr. Joseph M. Patch was one of the earliest medical men in Exeter to give his chief attention to dentistry which he did from 1838 to 1849. Dr. William L. Johnson afterwards practised as a dentist for something near twenty years, in the town, and then removed to Boston. He was succeeded in that branch of the profession by Drs. W. D. Vinal, Mark W. Pray, Charles H. Gerrish, J. E. S. Pray and A. T. Severance. The last three are still in practice.

The physicians now in general practice in Exeter are Drs. William G. Perry, Robert Mason, Lafayette Chesley, Edward Otis, A. H. Varney, Walter Tuttle and W. B. Mack.

CHAPTER XX.

FAMILIES AND INDIVIDUALS.

There are several Exeter families which settled early in the town, and are still represented there by descendants. Some of them have been more numerous, and some more conspicuous than others. A part of them have already been referred to in these pages, and others will hereafter be. The limited extent of the work forbids extended notices of many individuals.

The Dudley family in the town dates from 1650. The Rev. Samuel Dudley had no less than eighteen sons and daughters, most of whom lived to be married. They became connected with the Hiltons, the Gilmans, the Leavitts, the Lyfords, the Halls and other families, and their descendants in the vicinity are very numerous. The Christian names of Dudley and Wintbrop, still widely used, indicate how extensive are the relationships of the family. Several prominent members of the family are mentioned in various connections elsewhere in this work. A fact was stated in an earlier chapter which showed the Rev. Samuel Dudley's interest in improving the breed of neat stock in the town. Since that was printed, it has come to the knowledge of the writer that the same taste has been inherited by his descendants. To this day the Dudleys are said to be peculiarly fond of fine cattle. And it is not too much to say that other qualities, which gave repute to the earlier holders of the name, have also been transmitted to their progeny.

Of this family, one member, Judge John Dudley, merits particular notice. Born in Exeter April 9, 1725, he was brought up in the household of Colonel Daniel Gilman. Though deficient in education he engaged in trade with success, and became one of the foremost men of his day in the province. He removed to Raymond in 1766, was a representative in the Legislature and Speaker of the House, a member of the Committee of Safety, and in 1784 was appointed to the bench of the Superior Court, and performed the duties of the position for twelve years. His native sound understanding, sagacity and impartiality enabled him to acquit himself as a Judge to the acceptance of the bar no less than of the people at large.

The Folsom family is among the foremost in numbers. John Folsom, who emigrated from England to this country, came to Exeter between 1650 and 1660, and served the latter year as well as in 1668 as selectman of the town. His son John was a selectman in 1691 and a representative in the provincial Assembly in 1688, 1694 and 1695. It was he who refused to attempt to collect by distress the illegal taxes levied by Governor Cranfield and his Council. Other members of the family held office in the town from time to time afterwards, but it was two of the great-grandsons of the early settler who attained the highest distinction.

Nathaniel Folsom, the son of Jonathan and Anna (Ladd) Folsom, was born in 1726. At the age of twenty-nine he commanded a company of the New Hampshire regiment in the expedition against Crown Point, and distinguished himself, as has been related on a previous page. He was appointed by the royal governor a colonel of militia, but took the popular side when the division came between the colonies and the mother country. He was a member of the Continental Congress in 1774 and was elected to the same body three times afterwards. He took part in the movement to strip Fort William and Mary of its armament in 1774, and in 1775 was honored with the responsible appointment of Major General of all the New Hampshire militia, and retained it through the war. Drafts from the various regiments were often called into active service, and his duties were important and sometimes arduous, but he performed them with exemplary fidelity.

General Folsom was also a member of the Committee of Safety, a Councillor, and a Judge of the Inferior Court. His time during the Revolution was almost constantly devoted to the public service in various capacities, and perhaps no one of the men of the time enjoyed a greater measure of the reliance of the people than he. Among his last public duties was that of presiding temporarily over the convention for framing a new Constitution of the State in 1783.

This able man and true patriot died May 26, 1790.

Samuel Folsom, his brother, was less conspicuous, but stood high in the confidence of the community. He was an innkeeper, and his house was on the corner of Court square and Water street, and is now occupied by Dr. George W. Dearborn. It was there that Washington partook of a collation on his visit to the town in 1789. Samuel Folsom was the lieutenant colonel of the Exeter Cadets, under Colonel John Phillips.

Charles Folsom, of a later generation, was a graduate of Harvard College in 1813, and was afterwards tutor and instructor in Italian. For several years he was chaplain and teacher of mathematics in the United States navy, and had among his pupils David G. Farragut, afterwards the distinguished Admiral, who never forgot his obligations to Mr. Folsom, but, years afterwards, presented him with a magnificent silver vase suitably inscribed, in testimony of his gratitude. His classical scholarship was thorough and exact, and he died with the respect of all who knew him.

The Leavitt family was one of the earliest in the town. Samuel Leavitt was one of the selectmen in 1675, 1691 and 1696, and was a representative in the Assembly in 1685, and three subsequent years.

Moses Leavitt, his brother, was selectman in 1682, and three years besides; representative in 1693 and three other years, and moderator seven years. Descendants of theirs have from time to time held town offices since. Dudley Leavitt, the well known compiler of the almanacs, derived his descent from the same family.

The Thing family dates also far back in the history of the town. Jonathan Thing, the first comer, was a selectman in 1658 and seven years afterwards, town clerk in 1689, and representative in 1693. Samuel and Bartholomew, his sons, held the same offices for even longer periods, and the service of the latter did not end till 1737. They were among the leading men of the town for a long period.

The Conner family was also an early one, and has produced in several generations men of prominence. Benjamin Conner was one of the shrewdest political managers of his time, and represented the town in the Legislature thirteen years in succession. Daniel Conner, who is remembered by many, was a man of energy and large dealings; and William and Charles, sons of Nathaniel Conner, a noted builder, occupied positions of trust; to say nothing of the living.

The Lyford family is another of those who have long clung to Exeter. They have not been ambitious for public employment, but they have led respectable, useful lives. Some of the earlier members of the family followed the sea, but most of them have settled independently upon their farms. The late Gideon C. Lyford was at one time largely engaged in trade, and always sustained the character of an upright, honorable dealer.

The ancestor of the Gordon family appeared in Exeter within the first half century after its settlement. He had a mill upon the Little river. His descendants occupied lands in the southwestern part of the town, and were generally farmers, except one or two who had the control of mills at King's falls. One, of a later generation, George William Gordon, was appointed consul at Rio Janeiro, and was afterwards postmaster of Boston. Nathaniel Gordon, a present resident of the town, was a lawyer by profession, and has been president of the State Senate.

The family of Robinsons has been somewhat conspicuous in the town. Ephraim Robinson was for a long series of years in town offices, and was apparently one of those square, uncompromising men whom any town is fortunate to entrust its interests to. Caleb Robinson rose to the rank of major in the continental service in the Revolution, and Noah Robinson to that of captain. William Robinson, the founder of the Female Seminary, was of the same blood, as was Jeremiah L. Robinson, who for a number of years was one of the active business men of the place.

The Smiths, of whom there were two or three different families in the earlier times, and perhaps more later, included several members of prominence. Theophilus Smith was a name which came to the front for two or three generations. It would, however, require careful investigation to trace out the different branches of the earlier Exeter families of the name. Judge Jeremiah Smith was not connected with either. He was of Scotch-Irish descent.

The Odlin family, though not so extensive as some of those mentioned, has been a noted one in the town. The two generations of ministers, and their descendants among the influential business men a great part of the time since, have done much for Exeter's advancement. William, James and Woodbridge Odlin are well remembered. The last was the founder of the chair of English in the Phillips Academy.

The families of Barker, Colcord and Dolloff have been long settled in Exeter, and those of Kimball, Shute and several others for a somewhat less time. Their members have been, generally, good citizens and reputable men. Want of space forbids a more extended notice of them.

Of the many individuals outside of the families spoken of, who have attained more or less prominence, brief sketches are here given of a few, of whom little or no mention has yet been made. There could be many more added, if the dimensions of the volume permitted.

Jonathan Cass was a native of Exeter, born about 1750. He was a blacksmith by trade. At the beginning of the Revolution he enlisted in the army, and served through the war, coming out at the close with a captain's commission. He then resumed his business in the town and remained for several years, when he re-entered the military service, emigrated to Ohio and attained the rank of major. He had several children born in Exeter, one of whom was the distinguished Lewis Cass, who used afterwards to pay occasional visits to the place of his nativity. The house in which he was born was upon the east side of Cross, now called Cass street.

Enoch Poor was born in Andover, Massachusetts, and distinguished himself in his early manhood by making a run-a-way match with his wife. He was an enterprising ship-builder and merchant in Exeter when the War of the Revolution broke out. All eyes were turned to him, as one of the natural leaders. He was resolute, brave, and accustomed to command. Appointed colonel of the third New Hampshire regiment in the continental line, he justified by his conduct the most favorable expectations that were formed of his military talents. Lafayette chose him in 1780 after his appointment as brigadier-general, to lead a brigade in his corps of Light Infantry. His death occurred that year in New Jersey. The accounts of the time attributed it to bilious fever, but recent investigations point to a duel with a brother officer, as the cause. In the army the "point of honor," as it was termed, led to many fatal meetings between those who should have turned their weapons only against the common enemy. General Poor was highly esteemed by Washington and by Lafayette. Nearly fifty years after his death the latter visited Concord, New Hampshire, and partook of a collation there as the nation's guest. On being called on for a toast he gave " the memory of Light Infantry Poor and Yorktown Scammell;" a graceful compliment to the State which sent those Revolutionary heroes into the service of the country.

Colonel John Rogers was one of the most enterprising and influential men of his day in Exeter. A few of the principal people used to govern the place then. They nominated officers, determined what improvements were necessary, and arranged all the town business; and the majority of the voters fell in with their plans without objection. Of these leaders Colonel Rogers was for many years the ruling spirit.

He was a son of Judge Nathaniel Rogers, and was born July 2, 1787, at Newmarket. He received his education at the Phillips Exeter Academy, and was appointed in 1808 cashier of the old Exeter Bank, and so continued for twenty-two years. He was also the colonel of the fourth regiment of militia. For fourteen years from 1817 he was chairman of the board of selectmen. He was interested in the manufacturing companies, in tanning, in morocco dressing, and, indeed, in almost too many of the movements for the improvement of business in the town.

Colonel Rogers was a large, fine looking man, of courteous manners, and was exceedingly popular. He was three times married, his first two wives being daughters of Colonel Nathaniel Gilman, and his last a daughter of Rev. Jacob Cram. He died in July, 1837, leaving a widow and six children, two of whom are still living, Frances, the widow of John Chadwick of Exeter, and Jacob Rogers of Lowell, Massachusetts.

James Burley was born in the town in 1784, and was a prominent character for many years. He early manifested a great aptitude for military exercises. For a long time he commanded a uniformed company, was colonel of the fourth regiment of militia, and published a work on military tactics in 1820. For some years he was the landlord of the hotel nearly opposite the First church, and afterwards was chosen cashier of the Granite Bank, an office which he held to the time of his death, in 1850. He was a man of prompt and resolute character, and was highly respected for his integrity and honor. He held repeatedly the office of moderator and selectman. He was twice married, and his sons and step-son were among the early residents in Chicago, Illinois.

Samuel Hatch was long a prominent figure in the political affairs of the town. He was a cabinet-maker and dealt in furniture. A Democrat of positive faith, he lived in the days when his party opposed granting to railroads the right of way over private lands. He was thoroughly honest and of no small ability. He was once chosen representative to the Legislature, though a majority of the voters belonged to the opposite political party; and was twice a member of the State Senate. He had several sons, who were well educated, but none of them settled in Exeter. One of them, Daniel G. Hatch, was a judge in Kentucky.

Seth Walker was born in Portsmouth August 29, 1756. Early in the Revolution he joined the army, and was at the siege of Boston. He afterwards entered a privateer and was captured by a British man-of-war. He retired from the service with the rank of captain, and afterwards had the command of a regiment of militia. Early in the present century he was elected Register of Deeds for the county of Rockingham and took up his residence in Exeter. In those days when they found a good officer they kept him; and Colonel Walker held the Registership nearly thirty years, without opposition. He, and his daughters, who assisted him in his office, filled a great succession of volumes with their clerkly chirography, and Colonel Walker became known throughout all the county. His conduct in his official as well as in his private capacity was above reproach. A year or two before his decease he removed to Derry, where one of his daughters resided.

Joseph Pearson was a son of Jethro Pearson, an officer in the old French war, and was born in Exeter. He was well educated, and in 1786 received the appointment of Secretary of the State. He was a fine penman, and performed his duties so satisfactorily that he retained his office for twenty years. He then returned to Exeter to pass the remainder of his life. His house was on Water street, at the summit of meeting-house hill, which on that account was sometimes known as Secretary's hill.

Waddy V. Cobbs was a native of Virginia, enlisted in the United States army, and so distinguished himself in the wars with the Indians in the South, that he was promoted to a commission. In the latter part of 1814 he was in command of a company, and was ordered to New Orleans, and arrived there on the ninth day of January, 1815, just one day too late to take part in the famous battle. He continued in the service until he reached the rank of major, and then was retired from active service by reason of paralysis of his lower limbs. He then came to Exeter, where his wife's relatives were, and there lived until his death January 1, 1847, at the age of fifty-nine. His wife survived him more than thirty years, and was very efficient in charitable and benevolent undertakings. During the Rebellion she was at the head of the ladies' organization for the relief of the soldiers, and perhaps no one in the town did more than she to supply the volunteers in camp and hospital with necessaries and comforts.

John C. Long was a native of Portsmouth, and a grandson of Pierse Long, a gallant Revolutionary officer, and a member of the old Congress. His father was for many years a shipmaster. He entered the United States navy in 1812 as a midshipman. Only four months afterwards he was on the frigate "Constitution" when she captured the "Java." It was a trying introduction to his new profession for a youngster of sixteen, but he never repented of the choice he had made. He remained in the service more than fifty-one years. In this time he was intrusted with every variety of duty, afloat and ashore, and in all situations acquitted himself with success and honor. One of the most unpleasant of his employments was the transportation of Louis Kossuth and his followers to this country on board the steam frigate "Mississippi." The Hungarian exile so entirely mistook the purpose of our government in offering him a conveyance on a national vessel, that he insisted on making an inflammatory address from the ship to the red republicans in the harbor of Marseilles. The captain firmly forbade conduct so certain to embroil us with a friendly power. The result was that Kossuth withdrew from the vessel. Captain Long was fully sustained by the government.

In 1857 Captain Long was promoted to the command of the Pacific squadron, and became commodore. A severe accident which he met with on board his flagship the "Merrimac," almost incapacitated him for active duty. But he served out his term of two years, and then returned to his home in Exeter. In 1861 he was placed upon the retired list, and died September 2, 1865.

As an officer, Commodore Long was distinguished for professional knowledge, fidelity to duty and a high sense of honor. He exacted from his subordinates no more than he was willing to perform himself.

In his social relations he was unassuming, kindly and generous. His manners were marked by the high bred ease and courtesy of the old school. He was emphatically a good man. The poor had in him a liberal and constant friend. And when he quitted the earth he left no enemy behind.

The colored population of Exeter has always been more considerable, proportionally, than that of other country towns in New Hampshire. In colonial times the wealthier inhabitants held slaves, whose descendants remained domesticated in the place, and intermarried with others, so that their numbers have been well kept up. Several of them fought for their liberties in the War of the Revolution. One of these was Oxford Tash, who died October 14, 1810, at the age of about sixty. He had probably been brought up a servant in the family of Colonel Thomas Tash of Newmarket, and perhaps was freed as a reward for his military service. He was wounded in action, but with a high sense of honor refused to apply for a pension so long as he was able to support himself.

He left descendants, and his son, Charles G. Tash, is well remembered. He was of excellent manners, and high spirited like his father. He became enamored of a white girl and wished to marry her, but her friends were unwilling that she should become his wife. He brooded over it until his reason became unsettled. One evening he called to see her, and as she bade him good night he discharged a pistol at her loaded with two bullets, which severely wounded her, and with another pistol inflicted a wound upon himself. There is little doubt that his design was to put an end to the lives of both. But both recovered. Tash was tried for the offence and found guilty of an assault with intent to kill, but was respited by the court on the ground of unsoundness of mind.

Tobias Cutler, a Revolutionary pensioner, died in Exeter in September, 1834, at the age of seventy-six. He was born in Rindge and was a slave of Colonel Enoch Hale. In 1781 he enlisted in the continental army with the consent of his master who engaged to free him at the age of twenty-one years. The town of Rindge thereupon agreed that he should be received and deemed a free inhabitant, upon his manumission by his master. After the war he came to live in Exeter. He left descendants who are still living in the town.

Another colored Revolutionary pensioner was Jude Hall who died in August, 1827, at the age of eighty. He was a man of powerful physique, and it is said that the parts of his ribs which are usually cartilaginous were of solid bone, so that his vital organs were inclosed in a sort of osseous case. He lived on the old road to Kensington, near the line of that town. He was the chief witness of the government in the trial of John Blaisdell for the homicide of John Wadleigh, and was charged by the counsel with a disposition to " stretch the truth," but not, however, with perjury.

A very remarkable family of colored preachers originated in Exeter, of the name of Paul. The Rev. Nathaniel Paul who had been in the ministry twenty-one years died in Albany September 10, 1839, at the age of forty-six, having, it was said, been the means of much good. He had two older brothers who were also Baptist ministers,— Thomas, the eldest, who died in Boston, and Benjamin of New York city.

One of the centenarians of Exeter was a man of African descent, Corydon, who is said to have been once a slave of Dr. John Phillips. He died in 1818 at the age of one hundred years.

The older inhabitants recall many "characters" among the colored population, London Daly, Prince Light and others. The last named was a favorite leader among them. Harry Manjoy, sometimes called Emery, is well remembered. He was brought to Exeter by Noah Emery, a shipmaster, not from Africa, probably, but from some foreign port where he was offered for sale. He claimed to have been a prince in his native country. He lived with Captain Emery until the latter's death, and afterwards supported himself by his labor. He was industrious and respectable, and lived to a good old age.

At the southern extremity of what is now Elliott street, formerly a mere lane, lived a colored man named Whitfield, whose wife was quite a superior woman, belonging to the Paul family already mentioned. Their son, Joseph M. Whitfield, went to Buffalo, New York, and there followed the business of a barber. He was a man of some education and of decided talent, and was the author of poems, generally on the subject of slavery, which attracted much notice. A number of his friends united in publishing a volume of his metrical productions, in 1858. They certainly will compare favorably with those of three out of four of the collections of verse issued in the country.

MISCELLANEOUS.

CHAPTER XXI.

HOMICIDES; BURIAL-PLACES; THE "WHITE CAPS."

SINCE the settlement of Exeter by white men, its annals have been stained by only four known cases of homicide. The earliest and latest were the most painful, the victim in each case being a woman.

Balthazar Willix was a man of more than ordinary education, and came to Exeter about the year 1644. He had married, the preceding year, Mary, the widow of Thomas Hawksworth, as we are informed, and she was probably the unfortunate person who was the subject of the tragedy about to be related.

In the month of May or June, 1648, she went by water from Exeter to Oyster river in Dover, to dispose of some cattle. She seems to have been a woman of business capacity, and it may be that her husband, who was apparently a foreigner, thought her more likely to be successful in her dealings than himself. Robert Hethersay or Hersey, rowed her to Dover in his canoe, and engaged also to return with her in the same conveyance, when her business was accomplished.

She sold the cattle, and received payment partly in corn, and the residue, three pounds, in money. Then she proceeded to the landing at Oyster river, to meet and return with Hersey, but he was not to be found. He must have gone off with his canoe without waiting for her, for what cause we know not.

What then befell the poor woman can only be conjectured. Whether she attempted to return home by land or employed some person to transport her in a boat is not known. The fact that she had with her what was then a considerable sum of money was undoubtedly known. It proved a temptation to some unscrupulous person so powerful that it cost the unhappy creature her life. Her dead body was afterwards found in the river, bearing marks of brutal violence.

Her husband was shocked, and naturally indignant with Hersey whose negligence he regarded as the cause of the terrible calamity, and who, to exculpate himself had apparently made insinuations against the character of the murdered woman. In the heat of his anger and distress Willix brought two actions at law against him, one for failure to perform his contract of re-conveying the woman to her home, and the other for defamation, in "raising an evil report" about her. The unhappy man, perhaps, hoped by ventilating the whole matter in a court of justice, to vindicate the character of his dead wife. But he appears to have been better advised, before the session of the court, and never summoned Hersey to answer to the suits, and they were dropped.

Nothing further has been learned respecting the case, and the ruffian who perpetrated the shameful deed was apparently never brought to justice. Willix quitted Exeter the following year, and removed to Salisbury, Massachusetts, and died there in March, 1651.

MURDER OF JOHNSON.

Almost a century and a half passed by, before Exeter lost another inhabitant by criminal violence. The second homicide was committed in the autumn of 1794. The name of the victim was Johnson, and his slayer was his own son. They lived on the eastern side of the river, near the old jail. The father was somewhat given to drink, but not quarrelsome. The son, Jack Johnson, followed the sea, was short and thick in figure, and resented any allusion to his "duck legs." He did not get on well with his father, and had been heard to threaten him that he would "come up with him" soon.

One evening the father and son were at the barn of Mr. Grant, a neighbor, at a husking party. Old Mr. Johnson was somewhat intoxicated, and very talkative, and staid till after the others were all gone; then he took his departure. That was the last time he was seen alive. The next morning he was missed at his home, and his son Jack went about ostensibly in search of him. He first made inquiries at Hackett's ship-yard, across the river, where Joseph Swasey was building a vessel. He said to him and the workmen present, "I believe some of you have killed my father." "What's that you say, Jack," replied Mr. Swasey, "you know none of us would hurt your father — not near as soon as you would."

Jack next went to Mr. Grant's, and said to the family, "I believe you have my father hid in your cellar." They bade him go down and see. He did so, and made a great show of peering behind the tubs and barrels.

His conduct excited the suspicions of the neighbors, but they did not know enough to take any decided steps against him. Meantime a new vessel was going down the river to Portsmouth, and Jack got on board to go in her. At night she lay about a mile below the town, and he went on shore. In the middle of the night he returned to the vessel and crawled into the bunk with Mr. Swasey, in a state of great fright and perturbation.

At Portsmouth he shipped with Captain (Nathaniel?) Boardman for a voyage to sea. But there was no rest for him anywhere. The consciousness of crime so pursued him that he was impelled to confess all the circumstances of it to the captain, and then threw himself overboard into the sea and perished.

It appears that he lay in wait for his father's coming forth from Grant's, and struck him down with an axe. He dragged the body to Clark's barn which stood alone in a field, and buried it in the cellar. Afterwards, on the night when he was on his way to Portsmouth, in the vessel, he disinterred the body and cast it into the river. It was on his return from this errand that he manifested such agitation and fear.

Under the circumstances, no legal investigation was thought necessary, and the wretched story of this parricide and suicide does not appear upon our criminal records, but has come down to us only by imperfect tradition.

HOMICIDE OF JOHN WADLEIGH.

On the evening of the eighteenth of February, 1822, John Wadleigh of Exeter received injuries which resulted in his death the next morning. His home was on the old road to Kensington, and some forty rods or more from the line of that town. Wadleigh and John Blaisdell of Kensington left Exeter village at about half past five o'clock in the evening, to return to their homes. It was a dark and stormy night, and the walking was very slippery. Though they were sober when they started, Wadleigh had in his pocket a bottle of rum. He carried with him an axe, and Blaisdell had a rough, heavy axe handle.

Three hours afterwards the two appeared at the house of Jude Hall, a colored man, less than two miles from the place from which they took their departure, and Blaisdell applied to Hall to help him to lead Wadleigh in, saying that he was drunk, and "had been fighting with a sleigh." He said that Wadleigh would have died if he had not taken him up, and that he had led him from the Cove bridge. In fact he had taken him directly past his (Wadleigh's) own house, to Hall's which was thirty or forty rods beyond. Blaisdell in explanation of this circumstance said he would not have carried Wadleigh into his own house for ten dollars, implying that it would have excited suspicion that he had inflicted the injury from which Wadleigh was suffering.

Blaisdell and Hall helped Wadleigh, who was covered with blood, and almost insensible from the effect of a fracture and depression of the skull at the temple, to his own house, where Blaisdell remained but ten minutes, excusing himself from staying longer by saying that he must go home to take care of his cattle. Hall staid through the night until Wadleigh breathed his last.

The next morning a party went to Blaisdell's house to arrest him on the charge of murder, and found that he had disappeared. They followed him, by his tracks in the snow, for many miles through the woods, and by cross roads, through Kensington and the adjoining towns, and at length apprehended him in Exeter near the border of Epping.

On the trial which took place in the succeeding September, these facts were shown, as well as the following: The two men were seen by two different parties not far from the Cove bridge, on the evening when Wadleigh received his hurt. The first party consisted of Robinson and Smith, and they were going in a sleigh towards Exeter. They inquired of the two men, who were standing beside the road, how far it was to Wedgewood's, and were answered by one of them — not by Wadleigh. The other party were Brown and Cheney, the former in a sleigh and the other walking beside it. They were going in the direction of Kensington, away from Exeter. They passed the two men standing beside the road near the Cove bridge, one of whom said to Brown, "Take this man aboard, he is drunk and has been fighting with a sleigh," and stating that it was John Wadleigh. Brown, who knew Wadleigh, said, "Come John, get in, I am going by your house and will carry you home." Wadleigh gave no answer to that nor to a second invitation of the same purport, but was observed to breathe very heavily. Brown then said to his companion, "He don't seem to care about getting in, and I will go along, if you will take care of him." The other replied that he would do so, and Brown and Cheney went on.

Near the Cove bridge and about four feet outside of the travelled path of the road was found the next day a great pool of blood, " as if a hog had been killed there." The axe and the axe handle which the two men carried were found near, in the snow, and the former on the other side of the fence. A physician testified that the fracture of Wadleigh's skull could hardly have occurred from a fall on the ice, nor from contact with the runner of a sleigh, but appeared to have been caused by a blow from some blunt, square-cornered instrument. There was also slight evidence that Blaisdell harbored a grudge against Wadleigh.

The case was argued with great ability by Ichabod Bartlett for the prisoner, and by Attorney General George Sullivan for the prosecution, and the charge to the jury was given by Mr. Justice Levi Woodbury. The jury, after an hour's deliberation, returned into court with a verdict of "guilty of manslaughter," and the prisoner was sentenced to confinement in the State prison for the term of three years.

MURDER OF MRS. FERGUSON.

Bradbury Ferguson, a native of Sandwich, was living in Exeter in 1840, employed as a journeyman hatter. His home was in the western skirt of the village, on the north side of the road leading to Kingston. His wife's maiden name was Eliza Ann Frothingham, and she was a native of Portsmouth. They had six children, the eldest but twelve years of age.

On the first day of October of that year, Ferguson had been at the regimental muster at Epping, where he performed military duty. He returned home in the evening intoxicated to the point of being morose and quarrelsome. He soon drove his wife to the house of a neighbor for protection. He followed her, and insisted on her being given up to him, and used violence to the neighbor who attempted to interfere in her behalf. The police were sent for, and arrived between ten and eleven o'clock. Mrs. Ferguson returned to her home while they were there. She complained to them that she had been abused by her husband then and at other times. He denied the charge and called on her to "show the wounds." After a good deal of conversation, Ferguson was induced to promise that he would be quiet and not abuse his wife any more that night; but he declared that in the morning "he would give her a divorce, for he would not live with her any more."

The poor wife at length consented to pass the night in the house with him, but with evident forebodings. In the night the children were awakened by the discharge of a gun. They ran into their mother's room, and found her lying on the floor, and their father standing beside her. They asked him what he had done, and he answered that he had shot her. The wounded woman desired her husband to lay her upon the bed, and he did so. He then inquired of her where his best clothes were. She told him. He collected them together. Then he looked at the wound upon his wife's body, and remarked that she would not live. One of his little boys inquired what he shot his mother for. He answered that she provoked him to it. He gave his gun, with which he did the deed, to his eldest son, and told him he might go and call in the neighbors; and then gathering up his bundle of clothing he left the house and went away on foot.

The unfortunate woman lived but a short time after his departure, and gave no account of the circumstances of the shooting. Ferguson was arrested four days afterwards, in Sandwich. He was indicted and tried for murder at the Court of Common Pleas in Portsmouth in the following February. He was ably defended, but his guilt was manifest, and the jury rendered a verdict of guilty of murder of the second degree; on which he was sentenced to imprisonment for life. He died in the State prison several years ago.

BURIAL-PLACES.

In the two hundred and fifty years of Exeter's history, five successive places have been used for the general burial of the dead. The earliest was on the northwestern slope of meeting-house hill, near the site of the first unpretending house of worship. This was probably in use for the first two generations. No doubt some rude stones were originally set up to mark the spots where the bodies lay, and the ground was held sacred for a time. The Rev. Mr. Dudley was permitted by the town to enclose it, and to pasture his cattle upon its herbage, provided he should not attempt to cultivate it or break its surface. But for a long time past no traces of memorial stones have been visible there, and all feeling of sanctity about the spot has vanished.

The next place of sepulture, in the order of time, was a beautiful knoll on the west side of the salt river, near the present gas works. So far as can be gathered from the remaining tombstones, its use extended from the latter part of the seventeenth to the early part of the eighteenth century. It has been sometimes called the "Thing burying ground," perhaps because several of the inscriptions still legible upon the head-stones commemorate persons of that name. There are, however, an equal number bearing the names of early members of the family of Ladd, and those have been enclosed by a neat and durable fence, erected in 1850 by Alexander Ladd, a descendant. Only a part of the original contents of this burial-place is now marked by mounds or monuments. Within the memory of living men the graves extended on both sides of the elevation, to the lower ground beyond, but no traces of them are now perceptible. All the mortuary inscriptions remaining in 1864 were copied by the Rev. Elias Nason, and published in the sixteenth volume of *The New England Historical and Genealogical Register*. One of the monuments, from which the inscription plate has been removed, is thought on probable evidence to be that of the Rev. Samuel Dudley. This place of burial became disused when in 1696 the new meeting-house was erected "on the hill between the great fort and Nat. Folsom's barn," the site of the present First church. The yard surrounding the meeting-house was then devoted, after the English fashion, to burials. For a long period, most of the dead, except in the remoter districts, were interred there. There rest the remains of two or three of the clergymen, and of a great number of those who were the pillars of the religious and civil society, in their day and generation. The church-yard was originally much more capacious than it now is, and has been repeatedly curtailed by the widening of the street and of the sidewalk in front of it. It remained in use for probably almost a hundred years, and must have been overcrowded at last.

Early in the present century, on the sole authority of a few of the leading men of the town, all the tomb and head stones were removed from the yard, or levelled to the ground and covered with earth, so that in a little time the enclosure was overgrown with turf, and all marks of the tenants beneath were substantially obliterated.

On what grounds this apparent act of vandalism was justified, we cannot imagine. Yet it is clear that it met the approval of the majority of the people, or it could not have been accomplished, at least without the most strenuous opposition. But it is not learned that the least objection was made. It must be supposed that weighty reasons were in existence for so extraordinary a step, which we cannot appreciate. The loss which it caused to the antiquary and the investigator of family history, is well nigh irreparable.

About the year 1742 Colonel John Gilman devised to the town a tract of land for a burial-place, upon the condition which was seasonably complied with that it should be fenced within three years. It is situated upon the north side of Front street, west of the railroad, and extends across to Winter street. It thus became the fourth public burying-yard of the town, and continued in use about a century. The remains of the Rev. Daniel Rogers, of John Taylor Gilman, of Jeremiah Smith and of many other distinguished citizens there repose. The opening of the new cemetery in 1844 nearly put an end to burials in this inclosure, and naturally it fell into neglect. It became overgrown with weeds and bushes, and was in sad need of an Old Mortality to prevent further dilapidations. One of the citizens, unwilling that it should share the fate of its predecessors, recently took steps that resulted in the appropriation by the town of a sum of money for the restoration and improvement of the burying-place, so that its lease of existence is prolonged for a season.

This fourth burying-ground having been filled, past further service, several gentlemen of the town in 1843 conceived the plan of establishing a private cemetery which could be increased in extent as occasion might require, and would be permanent and not liable to be abandoned and neglected. For this purpose they organized under the statutes of the State a company incorporated as the Exeter Cemetery Association. Dr. D. W. Gorham, Amos Tuck, Henry F. French, James Burley and Charles C. P. Moses were the principal promoters of the scheme.

They procured a lot of land and laid it out for the purpose. The lots found purchasers readily, and the cemetery has now been in use for more than forty years. It is situated somewhat too near the village, perhaps, but the successive enlargements which have increased its dimensions to thirty acres or more, have all been in the opposite direction. It is well planted with trees and shrubs, and is an attractive spot. Much good taste has been manifested in the fitting and ornaments of the lots, and in the monuments erected upon them. The late William P. Moulton was at his decease president of the Association, Charles Burley is the treasurer, and William H. Belknap the secretary.

In addition to the public burial-places enumerated, another situated in the southwestern part of the town, near Great hill, should be mentioned. It is for local use, and its age has not been ascertained.

There are also several private or family burying-yards in different parts of the town. Two of them are near the main village, on the east side of the river, and have been used chiefly, if not wholly, by the families of Leavitt and Folsom respectively.

THE " WHITE CAPS."

A natural transition from the subjects of the earlier part of this chapter, murders and church-yards, would be to ghostly apparitions and the diabolical pranks of witches, if there were any such to relate. But in the times when the great witchcraft delusion, two centuries ago, subverted the religion and the common sense of the people of other neighboring places, Exeter maintained its equipoise. A town of so much antiquity might, perhaps, be expected to have its old time traditions, at least, of visitations from the unseen world, but none such have been heard of. Not a haunted house is known to the oldest inhabitant. Nearly everything that can be said to verge on the supernatural, is modern. A story is indeed told of the re-appearance of an elderly gentleman after his decease, for the purpose of warning his youthful widow that she must follow him within a year, which she did. But the story is only a single generation old, and has excited curiosity rather than awe.

One house, in which a servant girl accidentally inflicted a fatal wound upon herself with a pistol, is said to have been avoided since by her countrywomen, but it was never asserted that her spirit walked there. Another house was for a time the scene of some strange and inexplicable freaks of self-propelling articles of furniture, and the like; but it never received a bad name on that account.

Towards the close of the last century, however, an occurrence took place in the town, which denoted, at least, that the belief in the existence of supernatural agencies was common. Indeed we know, from various sources, that at that time, and much later, the mass of the people hardly questioned the existence of witches, or the appearance and interposition in human affairs of disembodied spirits. This credulity was often taken advantage of by the mischievous to cause affright, and by the mercenary to extort money. Unprincipled impostors are known to have travelled the country to work upon the hopes and fears of those whom they could influence by pretending to magical powers, in order to swindle them out of their property.

One such sharper, a perfect Dousterswivel in the art of imposture, was named Rainsford Rogers. He was a native of Connecticut, but lived also in Massachusetts and in New York. Though illiterate he was once a school teacher. He pretended to a deep knowledge of chemistry, and claimed that he possessed the power to raise, or to lay, spirits, good and evil, at his pleasure. He began his career of operating on the superstitious belief of people, at Morristown, New Jersey, in 1788. There he succeeded in defrauding his followers out of a large sum of money, by the pretence that he could secure for them a concealed treasure, through the agency of the spirits. Then he absconded. The story of his methods of deluding his dupes is told at large in a little volume entitled *The Morristown Ghost*, published soon after the occurrence.

The same person, with sometimes a different name, was said to have depleted the pockets of the people in several of the Southern States, afterwards, by similar means. In 1797, he appeared in Adams county, Pennsylvania, under the alias of Rice Williams. There, with a confederate or two, he repeated his tricks upon confiding persons, and succeeded in making off with a considerable sum.

It was not far from that time that he came to Exeter, bearing his true name of Rainsford Rogers, which had, perhaps, not acquired so bad an odor in New England as in some other quarters. In a short time he formed the acquaintance of a number of persons whom he judged to be suitable for his purpose. They were, of course, men of substance, able to furnish the money which he was planning to transfer to his own pocket, and sufficiently credulous to put entire faith in his representations. When he had enlisted a dozen or more, after fully sounding them, he broached to them his project. He informed them that he had reason to believe that a subterranean treasure of great value existed in the neighborhood, which, by his magical skill and with proper means and aid, he could discover and appropriate for their common benefit. He secretly visited several localities for the purpose of "prospecting," and at meetings of his followers, reported his discoveries. So skilful was he in stimulating their greed, and so plausible in explaining every successive step of his operations, that they never dreamed of any trick or dishonesty, but followed all his directions to the letter.

He repeatedly conducted them on dark nights to out-of-the-way places, to dig in the swamps with spades and other implements, and kept them at work, sometimes, it is said, for hours, in delving for the hidden prize. He instructed them that on those expeditions it was essential that they should wear white caps — a circumstance which afterwards gave the name to the company. On one of the nocturnal excursions there appeared before the eyes of the awe-stricken diggers a figure all in white, representing a spirit, which uttered some words which were not well understood. One of the "white caps," anxious to lose nothing of the weighty communication, responded — "a little louder, Mr. Ghost; I'm rather hard of hearing!"

But dig as diligently as they might, they reached no treasure. After a time Rogers disclosed what he declared to be the reason of their want of success. The golden deposit was there, beyond question; but they needed one thing more to enable them to find and grasp it. That was a particular kind of divining-rod. It must be made of dear materials, but it was infallibly sure of doing the business. It could not be obtained this side of Philadelphia, and would cost several hundred dollars. But if they would contribute the necessary sum, he would at once proceed to Philadelphia, purchase the needful implement and then return and introduce them to a golden hoard that would reimburse them a hundred-fold for their advances.

It is a marvel that the faith of his adherents was not shaken by so transparent a device, but he had tutored them so adroitly that their cupidity got the better of their caution and common sense. The deluded company raised the money required, and delivered it to the sharper, who mounted his horse, with a saddle and bridle borrowed from one of his dupes, and rode off — to parts unknown, never to return.

It was but a little time after his departure before the whole affair was made public. The white caps had not held their clandestine meetings unobserved. Each midnight rendezvous, each delving excursion in the swamps, had been watched, and all their credulity and imbecility were revealed. The worthy but superstitious persons who had been seduced into this ridiculous position, became heartily ashamed of themselves, and prayed that their folly might never be mentioned. But the joke was too good to be kept in silence, and many a sly allusion to their white head-gear made their ears tingle for years after. The deaf man who required the ghost to "speak a little louder" never heard the last of his unfortunate speech.

The names of most of the sufferers by this imposture have been preserved, but as their conduct was weak rather than culpable, to publish them could serve only to gratify an idle curiosity, and might cause pain to the feelings of their descendants.

Possibly the exposure of this fraud may have had a beneficial effect upon succeeding generations. The belief in the supernatural does not appear to have misled any to similar acts of credulity in later years. Digging for hidden treasure has never been attempted in the town, since the memorable experience of the "white caps."

CHAPTER XXII.

THINGS NEW AND OLD.

The town of Exeter is noted for its fine ornamental trees. In the early years of the century the Lombardy poplars in trim rows mounted guard around the principal edifices, but they did not take kindly to the northern climate. The stately sycamores were next introduced, but those, too, drooped, and disappeared. Maples and elms supplied their places, and thrive in the congenial soil, giving refreshing shade and adding beauty to the village.

The elms are not all of recent growth. Some of them can boast a life more than double that usually assigned to man.

The oldest elm in Exeter is probably that which stands in front of the house of the late Isaac Flagg on Front street. A hundred and fifty-eight years ago the residence of Judge Nicholas Gilman was there. His son, the Rev. Nicholas Gilman, afterwards of Durham, on the third of April, 1730, according to his diary, "set out elms before father Gilman's house." The father died in 1741 and his son followed him in 1748. How long the house stood we know not, but the elms lived on and survived them all.

One of them had a narrow escape from destruction in the early part of the present century. The axe was already laid at its root, when Colonel Nathaniel Gilman, who loved a fine tree, interposed. "What are you going to cut that elm down for?" he inquired of the occupant. "For firewood." "Let the tree stand," said the colonel, "and I'll give you a load of firewood." The offer was accepted and the doom of the tree was averted for the time.

When Deacon John Williams purchased the lot, about 1828, two of the elms were standing in the prime of their beauty, and he was very proud of them. "I gave five hundred dollars for the lot," said he, "and I would not take that sum for the trees." But since then one of them has succumbed to the ravages of time, and has disappeared. The other is still standing, and has been stayed by iron bolts, where the branches diverge from the trunk. It has now seen more than a hundred and sixty summers and winters. Eight generations may have enjoyed its shade, from Judge Nicholas Gilman to his great-great-great-grandson who is now living.

The old tree is a living link that binds us to the distant past. Long may it continue to lift on high its venerable crown.

A notice of a few of the old houses in Exeter and of their occupants, will not be out of place here. The distinctive names given them are those by which they have been popularly known. The first is

THE CLIFFORD HOUSE.

The oldest house in the town is undoubtedly that on the northerly corner of Water and Clifford streets, now owned by Manly W. Darling. It was built by Councillor John Gilman. He was living in it in 1676, and there is ground for the belief that it dates back to 1658. It was constructed of square logs, the upper story projected a foot or more beyond the lower, and the windows were scarcely more than loop-holes. It was thus completely adapted for the defence of its inmates against the attacks of the savages, and is known as a "garrison house."

The original structure was small, and constitutes the main body of the present house. No doubt additions must have been soon made to it, for the first occupant had sixteen children, all but four of whom lived to maturity. The wing which protrudes towards the street was a much later appendage.

In this wooden castle lived Councillor Gilman till his death in 1708. His son, Colonel John Gilman, succeeded him in the ownership of the house. He was then about thirty-two years of age, with a wife and three or four children. He was active and energetic, and acquired property and influence. In 1719 and 1720 he was licensed by the provincial Assembly to keep a place of public entertainment in "his log house by the bridge." Colonel Gilman was the father of eleven children, and died in 1740.

His eldest son was Peter, born in 1703, and married seven days after reaching the age of twenty-one. His father, realizing that no house is large enough for two generations, then proceeded to build himself another dwelling near by, to which he presently removed; and in 1732 executed to Peter a deed of gift of the old mansion.

Peter's family would not be considered a small one in these degenerate days. He had seven daughters, but it was doubtless a sore trial to him that he had no son to inherit the house that his grandfather built, so as to "keep it in the name." Peter Gilman was a man of note, in civil and military life. He was Speaker of the House of Assembly and a councillor of the province, and rose to the rank of brigadier general in the militia, through his exploits in the French and Indian wars. He was much esteemed by his townsmen. It is related that on one occasion a press-gang came from Portsmouth to Exeter to seize men to serve in his majesty's navy, but the brigadier warned the party that any whom they might capture would surely be rescued before they reached Stratham, and they desisted. When the separation between the mother country and her American colonies was impending, the brigadier felt bound by the oaths of allegiance he had taken to Britain, to set his face against all disloyal proceedings. If he had been less respected by his neighbors, he would have been tabooed, or perhaps maltreated, by the " high sons of liberty ;" but no insult was offered to him.

He was a man of strong religious feelings, and a great admirer of the evangelist Whitefield. An amusing story has been preserved of his being so deeply affected by a discourse of the great preacher that he fairly rolled on the ground, in an agony of penitence. Of course when the schism took place in the First society in 1743, the brigadier went off into the new church, and became one of its chief supporters.

It was during Peter Gilman's occupation of the house that the front wing was added to it. It was probably built in 1772 or 1773, while he was a councillor. John Wentworth was then the governor, young, popular and fond of show and ceremony. His Exeter councillor, the first in the place since the century came in, was desirous of showing him due honor, on occasion of his visiting the town. The low-storied rooms of the old house seemed hardly suitable for the reception of the highest dignitary of the province. The brigadier, therefore, had this addition made to it, of two stories, so as to lodge the governor, and perhaps to furnish a chamber for the meeting of the council also. The whole was finished inside with panelled work, in the elaborate style of the joinery of the time.

As the brigadier left no son to succeed him in the homestead, the place after his death in 1788 went into the possession of Ebenezer Clifford, who removed from Kensington to Exeter about that time. He was an ingenious mechanic, and studied architecture and made scientific experiments outside of his regular calling.

He manufactured a diving bell, with which he brought up from the bottom of the sea valuable property from one or more wrecked vessels. A relic of the old diving bell is still extant. It is the wooden duck which now serves as a weather vane upon the rear wing of the old house. This was the float by means of which the diver in the water below, was enabled to communicate his wants to his assistant in a boat at the surface.

While Mr. Clifford was master of the house he had for a boarder a lad who was destined at a later day to become the pride and boast of two States, that of his birth, education, and professional training, and that of his matured powers and later life. Daniel Webster came to Exeter to attend the Phillips Academy in 1796, and was an inmate of Mr. Clifford's family for several months. He had lived in a frontier settlement without instruction in the minor graces of life, and was habitually guilty of some breach of etiquette at the table, which Mr. Clifford was desirous of correcting. But knowing that young Webster was diffident and sensitive he was reluctant to hurt his feelings by pointing out the fault directly. Trusting to the youth's quick sightedness to make the proper application, he one day reproved his apprentice, who in the homely fashion of the time sat at table with the family, for committing the self-same fault which he had observed in Webster.

He did not overrate the latter's discernment. Never again did he give cause for criticism on that account.

THE DEAN HOUSE.

On the site of the present town-house, formerly stood a handsome dwelling with a gambrel roof, which dated from about the year 1724. It was erected by Nathaniel Gilman, or by his father Judge Nicholas Gilman for him. He, according to tradition, was commonly known as "Gentleman Nat," probably on account of his nicety of dress or manners. He was a man of property and lived handsomely, but died at an early age, leaving a widow and one or more children. The eldest of these, John Phillips would have afterwards taken to wife, but she preferred another. He therefore wooed and won her mother, the widow, in despite of a slight disparity in their ages, she being forty-one while he was but twenty-seven. But she was well dowered. It is highly probable that they occupied the house after their marriage, but this is not positively asserted. At a later date Mr. Phillips erected for himself a house on the north side of Water street near by, and there lived with his second wife, until his death.

Joseph Gilman resided in the earlier habitation, afterwards, through the Revolution, and until his emigration in 1788, to the Ohio country, which in those days was a greater undertaking than it now is to cross the continent. He had obtained a thorough business training in Boston, and returned to Exeter in 1761 to become a partner in the firm of Gilman, Folsom & Gilman, which was largely engaged in commerce and trade. He was then a widower, but in 1763 married again, and probably at that time set up his establishment in the house. He made a singular discovery there. In the middle of the structure was a large stack of chimneys. Between the flues was a secret repository, left perhaps for the purpose of concealment of property or persons, and in it he found deer-skin pouch filled with old French crowns. The history of the deposit he could never learn, but suspected that some former occupant had bestowed his stock of specie in this secret storehouse, when he was about departing on some hazardous errand, to the Indian or French wars, and never returned, nor revealed the secret to others.

During the Revolution the house was the place of meeting of the Committee of Safety of the State, of which Mr. Gilman was a member, and a resort of the Whigs, of the town and elsewhere. The second Mrs. Gilman was a superior and highly accomplished woman. To some of the young French officers who were in the American army it was a great boon to visit Exeter and converse with a lady who understood their language so thoroughly, and was accustomed to the elegancies of life. The Gilmans had no lack of distinguished visitors. One of them was Samuel Adams. It was in the darkest hours of the Revolution. His spirits were depressed, and not even Mrs. Gilman's sprightly talk could rouse him to cheerfulness. He walked the room and wrung his hands. "Oh God," he cried, "must we give it up!" His ailment was one which nothing but a military success could relieve.

Not many years after Mr. Gilman left Exeter, John Gardner came there to live. He married Deborah, daughter of Ward Clark Dean, and occupied the house that Mr. Gilman quitted. Mr. Gardner was a native of Boston, and became a merchant. Of a confiding disposition, he suffered himself to become responsible for others, until he failed in business. His creditors pocketed their percentage and reconciled themselves to a loss in which there was nothing dishonorable. But he did not. He never rested until he was able to repay to every creditor the full amount of his claim, with interest. Mr. Gardner is remembered by the older citizens, as a man of pleasant address, and remarkable even after he had long passed his threescore years and ten, for his cheerfulness and buoyancy of spirits.

Somewhere about the year 1820, probably, Mr. Gardner built the house on Court square now occupied by his grandchildren, and removed into it. His father-in-law, Ward C. Dean, then came into the occupation of the old habitation, and resided there until his decease in 1828; after which his widow lived there till her death in 1843. In 1855 the land on which the house stood was purchased by the town, and the present town-house was erected there. The old building was razeed by cutting away one of its stories, and removed to Franklin street, where it now remains.

THE LADD HOUSE.

On a little elevation a few rods south of Water street is the residence of John T. Perry. It has an old time look, never having been modernized without, so that no one can see it without feeling that it has a history. It consists of two sections, of different dates, the earlier of which was built by Nathaniel Ladd in 1721 or soon after. It was of brick, which is now covered with wood, to correspond with the portion which was added later.

The Ladd family is an old one in the town. We have already mentioned one of the name who sounded the trumpet in Gove's rebellion against Governor Cranfield, and was afterwards slain in an expedition against the Eastern Indians. There were other notable characters in the family. Simeon Ladd, who came upon the stage at least three generations afterwards, was keeper of the jail. He was something of a wag, and the president of a society of choice spirits called the "Nip Club," who used to assemble at one of the taverns on regular evenings for convivial purposes. He perhaps inherited a tendency to eccentricity from his father, who is said to have long kept a ready made coffin in his house to meet an emergency, and who invented a pair of wings which he fondly believed would enable him to cleave the air like a bird, until he tried the experiment from an upper window.

Eliphalet Ladd was born in 1744, and while young developed much aptitude for business. He was a shipmaster and merchant during the Revolutionary contest, and made at least one voyage in the war time to the West Indies, from which he returned after an absence of sixty days, with a cargo of rum, molasses, etc. His vessel was several times chased by English men-of-war. He also built several ships, one of which was among the largest ever launched in Exeter, and was called the *Archelaus*. She was of about five hundred tons, and was nearly three years in building. Captain Ladd's energy and pluck were rewarded by the acquisition of a competency. In 1792 he removed to Portsmouth.

His son, William Ladd, born in Exeter in 1778, and a graduate of Harvard College, was well known as the " apostle of peace."

The Nathaniel Ladd who built the house which is under notice had two sons, to whom he conveyed it, and who probably occupied it until 1747 when it was bought by Colonel Daniel Gilman. His son Nicholas then moved into it. This was " Treasurer " Nicholas Gilman who was afterwards distinguished as the financier of New Hampshire in the Revolution. He had three sons, John Taylor, afterwards governor of the State many years, Nicholas, an officer of the Revolution and a senator of the United States, and Nathaniel who was State senator and treasurer. The father was a man of much business and many cares. He was a devoted Whig, notwithstanding he was a particular friend of the royal governor, who would have sacrificed much if he could have secured Mr. Gilman's support to the British cause. In his capacity of treasurer of the State he had his office in this house, and there, no doubt, he affixed his handsome signature to the paper bills of credit to which the State and the country were obliged to resort, to carry on the war. The treasurer lived to thankfully witness the termination of hostilities and the virtual establishment of the independence of his country, and died April 7, 1783.

His eldest son, John Taylor Gilman, next owned and occupied the mansion, and it was during his tenancy, no doubt, that the narrow street upon which it is situated received the designation of "Governor's lane." About the year 1815 he removed to the dwelling on the south side of Front street, which was afterwards his home, and the old house came into the occupation of Colonel Peter Chadwick, a native of Deerfield, it is believed. He long held the office of Clerk of the Courts. An honorable, high minded gentleman, he was much respected, and is pleasantly remembered by the older residents. He died in 1847, but his family resided in the house for many years after.

The old mansion at length came into the possession of the present owner, a descendant of Treasurer Gilman, who appreciates it, and has improved and adorned it without sacrificing its antique character. It is a remarkable coincidence that Mr. Perry moved into the dwelling in April, 1883, just one hundred years to a day after the death of his great-grandfather there.

THE ROWLAND HOUSE.

The square edifice on the northwest corner of Park and Summer streets, which is surmounted by a hipped roof with overhanging eaves, was erected quite early in the last century and was occupied for two or three generations by families of the name of Giddinge. Zebulon Giddinge was married in 1724 at the age of twenty-one, and probably lived in the house from that time to his death in 1789. He was chosen representative to the Assembly nine years, and clerk of the town thirty-nine. He was an innkeeper, and his house stood by the road over which all the lumbermen hauled their logs to the river side. Naturally, he did a large business in dispensing liquid refreshments. It was at his house that the participants in the mast-tree riot in 1734 assembled to put on their disguise of Natick Indians, and perhaps to prime themselves for their illegal undertaking. At a much later date meetings used to be held there for a more creditable purpose ; — for consultations on the irritating course of the British Parliament towards the colonists, and how best to unite the whole people in measures of resistance.

Dr. John Giddinge was a son of Zebulon, as was also Colonel Eliphalet, who continued to live in the house after his father's death. The colonel was engaged in ship-building and lumbering. He had a son Nathaniel who, while quite young, exhibited superior talents for business. His father naturally encouraged him and pushed him forward. He was popular and was early appointed a colonel of the fourth regiment of militia, a rank which conferred distinction, but cost no small amount of time and expense to meet the expectations of the officers of his command. His father built for him the stately house on the plains, which was subsequently occupied by Jeremiah Smith, and after him by Joseph L. Cilley. But the young man was a fast liver, and died before he reached middle age.

Eliphalet Giddinge survived until 1830, and his successor in the paternal residence was the Rev. William F. Rowland, who was his son-in-law. Mr. Rowland had resigned the pastorship of the First church in 1828, and was never again settled over a society. He died in 1843, and his children continued to live in the house until the death of the last surviving daughter in 1886. The house is now the property of Dr. Charles H. Gerrish.

THE ODIORNE HOUSE.

On the corner opposite to the house just described is another which for more than fifty years past has been occupied by Mrs. Bickford, and was built about 1737 by Major John Gilman, whose losses at Fort William Henry are recorded on pages 236 and 237. It has the gambrel roof characteristic of its time, and is a fine specimen of colonial architecture. Major Gilman spent the residue of his life in it. He was the owner of a slave whose three sons were the colored preachers of the name of Paul, referred to in a former chapter.

Major Gilman had twelve children, the eldest of whom became the wife of Deacon Thomas Odiorne who lived in the house after the death of its first owner, until his own death in 1819. The deacon was a worthy, patriotic citizen and had the respect of all. His widow survived him about ten years. Not long after her decease, the house came near being the scene of a double tragedy. It was in one of its rooms that Charles G. Tash, as has already been related, attempted to take the life of Sally Moore, a white girl, and of himself, but fortunately failed to inflict a fatal hurt upon either.

THE HILDRETH HOUSE.

Upon the triangular lot at the intersection of Front and Linden streets is a large dwelling which evidently belongs to two periods. The easterly portion of it is the older, and was built about the year 1730 by Daniel, son of Judge Nicholas Gilman. Twenty-five years afterwards he was commissioned colonel of the militia, and, according to tradition, then enlarged his house with the western addition, in order to receive as a guest Governor Benning Wentworth, who was about to pay a visit to Exeter. Colonel Daniel Gilman was a large farmer and trader, and employed as a servant John Dudley, afterwards judge of the Superior Court, who owed to his employer the encouragement and assistance that enabled him to develop his native powers and attain his high position. The Rev. George Whitefield had in Colonel Gilman a stanch friend and admirer. When he visited Exeter for the last time, and preached there his final sermon, on the twenty-ninth of September, 1770, it is recorded that he "dined with Captain [Col.] Gilman." Whitefield commenced his service in the forenoon of that day in the church of the Second parish, but as it was found altogether insufficient to accommodate the throng who assembled to hear him, he was obliged to preach outside. In order to avoid the shining of the sun in his face he crossed the street, and mounted upon a board laid upon a couple of hogsheads, from which he addressed his congregation. In the afternoon he rode with the Rev. Mr. Parsons to Newburyport. But he had long overtaxed his strength, and his hours were numbered. The next morning he breathed his last.

Colonel Gilman died suddenly in church, of apoplexy, in 1780. His son, Dr. Nathaniel Gilman, succeeded to the ownership of the house, but survived his father a few years only. The house then passed through several hands into the possession of the Rev. Hosea Hildreth, who resided in it during his stay in Exeter.

It is now occupied by two families, those of Mrs. Samuel Tilton and of the Rev. Noah Hooper.

THE PEABODY HOUSE.

The house on the south side of Water street now owned by Warren F. Putnam was erected by Samuel Gilman, who moved into it November 3, 1725, and lived there during the succeeding sixty years. He was an innkeeper, a colonel and a judge. In 1734 he entertained the party sent by Surveyor General David Dunbar from Portsmouth to Exeter to discover what mast trees had been illegally felled, when the stalwart woodsmen broke in upon them and gave them entertainment of a very different nature.

After the death of the worthy builder, the habitation was purchased by Oliver Peabody, and he with his interesting family lived there till 1831. Jeremiah Dow, a tanner, and a man of much force of character, succeeded to the occupancy of the house. Since his time the property has had several owners, and has undergone such transformations that it is difficult now to realize that the house has seen a hundred and sixty-three years.

THE GILMAN HOUSE.

The large gambrel roofed house on Front street nearly opposite the Baptist church is above one hundred and fifty years old, and was erected by Dr. Dudley, son of the Rev. John Odlin. Dying in middle life he devised it to his kinsman Dr. John Odlin. After occupying it twenty years or more, the latter transferred his residence to Concord, and sold the house to Colonel Nathaniel Gilman. His home it was until his death. It was truly the abode of plenty and good cheer. The colonel was a public spirited citizen, interested in trade, in manufactures and in agriculture, and with a large acquaintance in the State. His wife was the impersonation of hospitality. Their children were numerous, and popular. They literally kept open house. On public occasions, especially, their rooms and table overflowed with guests.

Colonel Gilman died in 1847, and the house was, afterwards, the home of his widow, and of his youngest son Joseph T. Gilman, until his decease in 1862. His widow married Charles H. Bell, and they now occupy the house.

THE TILTON HOUSE.

On the southeast corner of Water street and Court square, is a house which enjoys the distinction of having once sheltered the Father of his country. It was built by Colonel Samuel Folsom, in 1770 or the following year, to replace a former house which had been burned, on the same spot. The account of Washington's visit to Exeter in 1789 is given on a previous page. Colonel Folsom died the year following, and his family continued to reside there. One of his daughters was afterwards married to Joseph Tilton, an Exeter lawyer, who lived in the house until his decease in 1872. It is now owned by Dr. George W. Dearborn.

There are other houses in the town of perhaps equal antiquity with those named, but space is wanting to describe them. The Peavey house on the Newmarket road is one of the most ancient and curious; the Colcord house on the plains is covered with plank for the purpose of defence, and has been styled a half garrison house; the Leavitt house on the corner of Front and Winter streets is very early, and contains a good deal of panelling. Unfortunately for the lover of antiquity many of the older dwellings have been so much modernized that their real age can hardly be detected.

STATISTICS; SOCIETIES; LOCALITIES.

The town of Exeter is situated in the southeastern part of

ingham. It is nine miles from the sea, and fifty miles almost northerly from Boston, with which it is connected by the Boston and Maine Railroad opened in 1840. It is a half shire town, and is the seat of the county offices, of the clerk of the Judicial Courts, the Registry of Deeds, and of Probate. They contain the records of the entire province up to the year 1771, when it was divided into counties, and of the county of Rockingham since that date. Two terms of the Supreme Judicial Court are held in the town annually, and a term of the Court of Probate monthly.

The census shows that the population has about doubled, since the beginning of the century. In 1800 it was 1727; in 1820, 2114; in 1850, 3274; in 1880, 3569. The assessed value of the taxable property in 1887 was $3,197,884.

The public buildings of the town are a town-house containing a county court-room, another used for the public library and other purposes, eight houses of public worship, the buildings of the Phillips Exeter Academy, the Robinson Female Seminary and the High School, and Opera House, the county record offices and the jail.

Three weekly newspapers are published in the town, besides a weekly paper and monthly journal issued by the students of the Academy during term time.

The *Washington Lodge* of F. and A. Masons was established in the town early in the century, and was discontinued some years after, but was revived about 1820 under the name of the *Phoenix Lodge*. This was kept up ten or twelve years.

Star in the East Lodge No. 59 was instituted in 1857, and has furnished the following officers of the Grand Lodge: Charles H. Bell and John J. Bell, Grand Masters; Charles G. Conner, Samuel M. Wilcox, Jeremiah D. Parker and Joseph S. Parsons, Deputy Grand Masters. The present chief officers of Star in the East Lodge are, George N. Cross, *W. M.*, Joseph E. Knight, *S. W.*, Edmund E. Freeman, *J. W.*, William F. Rundlett, *Sec.*, and William H. C. Follansby, *Tr.*

St. Albans Royal Arch Chapter was constituted in 1869. Its present chief officers are Charles G. Conner, *H. P.*, John P. P. Kelly, *K.*, Winthrop N. Dow, *S.*, George W. Weston, *Sec.*, Robert C. Thomson, *Tr.*

Sagamore Lodge No. 9, I. O. O. F., was established in 1845. It became dormant in 1864, but was revived in 1873. It has furnished one Grand Master of the Grand Lodge, James W.

Odlin. The present chief officers of Sagamore Lodge are S. Abbott Lawrence, *N. G.*, Charles L. Palmer, *V. G.*, G. W. Wetherell, *Sec.*, John P. Elkins, *Tr.*

Swamscot Lodge No. 2, K. of P., was instituted April 6, 1870. Its present chief officers are F. E. Rollins, *C. C.*, Adolphus Smart, *V. C.*, J. Warren Tilton, *K. of R. & S.*, John S. Hayes, *M. of E.*

Moses N. Collins Post No. 26, G. A. R., was established in 1870. Its chief officers are A. J. Gilman, *Com.*, B. F. Rowe, *S. V. C.*, G. L. Stokell, *J. V. C.*, G. W. Gadd, *Adj't*, Lewis E. Gove, *Q. M.*

Jady Hill is the eminence rising from the east bank of salt river, just below the village. From the earliest times it has been called by that name. The derivation of it cannot be learned. Some have fancied it was a corruption of *shady* hill, but for no better reason than the resemblance of the words.

Bride Hill is an elevation on the Hampton road about three miles from the Great bridge, and is in fact just over the line in the town of Hampton. A romantic story of the marriage of a pair of lovers in the olden time under the "bridal elm," a symmetrical tree on the side of the hill, is told, but not verified. The hill has long borne the name.

Ass Brook, which crosses the road to Hampton about two miles east from the village, has been so styled from the very earliest times, but from what circumstance is unknown. The claim that it was originally Ash brook is unsupported by early documents.

Wheelwright's Creek, which crosses the road to Stratham, within a mile from the village, received its name from the founder of Exeter.

Powell's Point is a projection of the east bank into the salt river between Wheelwright's creek and the village. Its name came from Robert Powell, an early settler.

The Roundabout is a bend in the salt river, a couple of miles below the village, in the shape of a horse-shoe.

The Oak Lands is the name affixed to a large tract of woodland containing many oaks, in the northern part of the town.

Beech Hill is an elevation in the northwestern part of the town, about four miles from the village.

Bloody Brook crosses the road to Epping about two and a half miles from the village. Its name is probably derived from the dark color of the bed of the stream.

Fresh Meadow is the name given to a tract of low land adjoining the Brentwood line about midway between its two extremities.

The Mast Swamp Road leads from the western part of the town towards Epping.

Great Hill is a commanding eminence at the point where the corners of the townships of Exeter, East Kingston and Brentwood come together.

Rocky Hill is on the road to Hampton, about three-fourths of a mile from the Great bridge.

Tower Hill is an ascent on the east side of the river nearest the Great bridge.

Town Hill is in the village, near the intersection of Main and Water streets.

The Plains is the name given to the level stretch of land in the northwestern part of the village.

Other names of localities, that have not become obsolete in Exeter and in the towns which once belonged to it, have been heretofore referred to. There were, however, in the earlier times places whose designations were then familiar as household words, but have long been disused and forgotten. Who now can tell where was the Nursery, the Temple, or the Patent land,—places doubtless well known a century ago? Probably no man living.

Does not this render it likely that other things, well understood by the fathers, have since their time perished from memory, and should it not make us distrustful of passing upon their conduct, judgments liable to be based upon inadequate knowledge?

APPENDIX.

APPENDIX I.

THE INDIAN DEED OF 1629 TO WHEELWRIGHT & ALS.

WHEREAS wee the Sagamores of Penacook, Pentucket, Squamsquot & Nuchawanick are Inclined to have ye English Inhabitt amongst us, as they are amongst our Countrymen in the Massachucets bay, by wch means wee hope in time to be strengthned against our Enemyes the Tarratens who yearly doth us Damage: Likewise being Perswaided y^t itt will bee for the good of us and our Posterety &c^t. To that end have att a generall meeting (att Squamsquot on Piscataqua River) wee the afores^d Sagamores wth a universall Consent of our subjects doe Covenant and agree wth the English as followeth: Now Know all men by these Presents that wee Passaconaway Sagamore of Penacook, Runawitt Sagamore of Pentucket, wahangnonawitt Sagamore of Squamscott, and Rowls Sagamore of Newchawanick, for a Compitent Valuation in goods allready Received in Coats, Shurts & victualls, and alsoe for ye Considerations afores^d doe (according to ye Limits and bounds hereafter granted) give, grant, bargaine, sell, Release Rattafie and Confirme, unto John Whelewright of ye Massachucets baye Late of England, A minister of ye Gospel, Augustin Story, Thom^s Wite, Wm Wentworth and Thom^s Levitt, all of ye Massachucetts baye in New England, to them their heires and Assignes forever, all that part of ye maine Land bounded by the River of Piscataqua and the River of Merrimack, that is to say, to begin att Newchewanack ffalls in Piscataqua River afores^d, and soe Doune s^d River to the sea, and soe alongst the sea shore to merrimack River, and soe up along s^d River to the falls att Pentucett afores^d, and from s^d Pentucett ffalls upon a Northwest Line twenty English miles into the woods, and from thence to Run upon a Streight line North East & South West till meete wth the maine Rivers that Runs down to Pentucket falls & Newchewanack ffalls, and ye s^d Rivers to be the bounds of the s^d Lands from the thwart Line or head Line to ye afores^d ffalls, and ye maine Channell of each River from Pentucket

& Newchewanack ffalls to the maine sea to bee the side bounds, and the maine Sea betweene Piscataqua River And Merrimack River to be the Lower bounds, and the thwart or head Line that runs from River to river to be y[e] uper bound; Togeather wth all Ilands wth in s[d] bounds, as alsoe the Iles of Sholes soe Called by the English togeather wth all Proffitts, Advantages and Appurtenances whatsoever to the s[d] tract of Land belonging or in any wayes appertaineing; Reserveing to our Selves Liberty of makeing use of our old Planting Land, as alsoe ffree Liberty of Hunting, ffishing and fowling; and itt is Likewise wth these Proviseos ffollowing viz[t].

First, that y[e] s[d] John Wheelewright shall wth in ten years after the date hereof sett Doun wth a Company of English and begin a Plantation att Squamscott ffalls In Piscataqua River afores[d].

Secondly, that what other Inhabitants shall Come & Live on s[d] Tract of Land Amongst them from Time to Time and att all times shall have and Enjoye the same benefitts as the s[d] Whelewright afores[d].

Thirdly, that If att any time there be a numb[r] of People amongst them that have a mind to begin a new Plantation that they be Encouraged soe to doe, and that noe Plantation Exceede in Lands above ten English miles Squaire, or such a Proportion as amounts to ten miles Squaire.

Fourthly, that y[e] afores[d] granted Lands are to be Divided into Tounshipps as People Increase and appeare to Inhabitt them, and that noe Lands shall be granted to any p[r]ticular p[r]son but what shall be for a Township, and what Lands w[th]in a Township is granted to any Perticular Persons to be by vote of y[e] major part of y[e] Enhabitants Legally and ord[r]ly settled in s[d] Township.

Fifthly for manageing and Regulateing, and to avoide Contentions amongst them, they are to be under the Goverment of the Collony of the Massachusetts (their neighbours) and to observe their Laws and ord[rs] untill they have a settled Goverment Amongst themselves.

Sixthly wee the afores[d] Sagamores and our Subjects are to have free Liberty (w[th]in the afores[d] granted tract of Land) of ffishing, fowling, hunting & Planting &c.

Sevently and Lastly every Township w[th]in the aforesaid Limits or tract of Land that hereafter shall be settled shall Paye to Passaconaway our Cheife Sagamore that now is, & to his successors forever, If Lawfully Demanded one Coate of Trucking Cloath a year & every yeare for an Acknowlegment, and also shall Paye to Mr John Whelewright afores^d his heires and successors forever, If Lawfully Demanded, two bushills of Indian Corne a yeare for and in consideration of said Whelewright's great Paines & Care as alsoe for ye Charges he have been att to obtain this one grant for himselfe and those aforementioned, and the Inhabitants that shall hereafter settle In Townships on ye aforesaid granted Premises: And wee the afores^d Sagamores, Passaconaway Sagamore of Penecook, Runawitt Sagamore of Pentucet, Wahangnonawitt Sagamore of Squaamscott and Rowls Sagamore of Newchewanack doe by these Presents Rattafie and Confirme all ye afore granted and bargained Premises and Tract of Land afores^d (excepting & Reserving as afore Excepted & Reserved & the Proviseos afores^d fullfilled) wth all the meadow and Marsh grounds therein. Togeather wth all the mines Mineralls of what Kind or Nature soever, with all the Woods Timber and Timber Trees, Ponds, Rivers, Lakes, runs of Water or Water Courses thereunto belonging, with all the ffreedome of ffishinge, ffowlinge, and Hunting as ourselves with all other benefitts, Proffitts, Privledges and Appurtenances whatsoever thereunto, of all and any Part of the said Tract off Land belonging or in any wayes Appertaineinge, unto him the said John Whelewright, Augustin Storer Thomas Wite, William Wentworth and Thomas Levitt and their heires forever as afores^d. To have and to hold ye same As their owne Proper Right and Interest, without the Least Disturbance Mollestation or Troble of us, our heires, Execcutors, and Administrators, to and with the said John Whelewright Augustin Storer Thomas Wite William Wentworth and Thomas Levitt their heires Execcutors, Administrators and assignes and other the English that shall Inhabitt there And their heires and assignes forever, shall Warrant Mainetaine and Defend. In Wittnes whereof wee have Hereunto sett our hands and seales the Seventeenth day of May 1629 And in the fiifth yeare of King Charles his Reigne over England &c^t.

Signed Sealed & Delivered
    In Presents off us.

WADARGASCOM mark   PASSACONAWAY mark
MISTONOBITE mark   RUNAWIT mark
JOHN OLDHAM   WAHANGNOWNAWIT mark

SAM^{LL} SHARPE   ROWLS   mark *

Memorand^m ; on ye Seventeenth day of maye one thousand six hundred twenty & nine, In the ffifth year of the Reigne of our Sovereigne Lord Charles King of England, Scotland ffrance & Ireland, Defend^r of ye ffaith &c^t. Wahangnownawit Sagamore of Squamscot in Piscataqua River, did in behalfe of himselfe and the other Sagamores aforementioned then Present, Deliv^r Quiett & Peaceable Possession of all ye Lands mentioned in the w^thin writen Deed, unto the w^thin named John Whelewright for the ends w^thin mentioned in Presents of us Walter Nele Governer Geo. Vaughan ffacktor and ambros Gibins Trader for ye Company of Laconia, Richd Vines Governer and Rich^d bonithan Assistant of ye Plantation of Sawco, Thom^s Wiggin agent and Edward hilton Steward of the Plantation of Hiltons Point, and was signed sealed & Delivered In our Presents.

In Wittness whereof we have hereunto sett our hands the day & yeare above Written.

      Rich^D Vines Walter Neale
      Rich^D Bonithon Geo. Vaughan
      Thon^s Wiggin Ambrose Gibbins
      Edward^r Hilton

Entered and Recorded According to the originall the 20th may 1714.

         Pr. W^M. Vaughan Record^r.

---

* The marks or totems of the Indians are affixed to their names as follows: Passaconaway, a man with extended arms; Runawit, a deer's antlers; Wahangnownawit, a bow and arrow; Rowls, a one-armed man. What the marks of the two Indian witnesses, Wadargascom and Mistonobite, are intended to represent, it is not easy to say.

APPENDIX II.

TRANSCRIPTS OF THE EXETER RECORDS, 1639 TO 1644.

CERTAINE ord^{rs} made at the Co^{te} houlden in Exeter the 4th day of the first weake in the 10th Month, 1639.

Imprimis. That M^r. Edward Hilton his vpland ground is bounded in Breadth from the Creeke next from his house towards Exeter on the one side & a Certaine point of Land ov^r against Captaine Wiggins his howse between the Mash and the vpland that his bounds one the oth^r side and it is to extend into the maine the same distance in Length as it is in Breadth, and that he shall have all the meadowes wch hee formerly ocupied from his howse to the mouth of Lamprell River.

2^d Lye. That all the Meadowes wch belonge vnto the Toune of Exeter, leying betweene the Townes and mr. Hilton's howse, as Likewise the Meadowes from Lamprell River vnto the head of the little Baye shall be equally devided into fouer parts whereof the 4th p^{te} shall be devided by lott to such of the inhabitants of the Towne of Exeter as have noe Cattle or fower Goats, and the profitt of the haye w^{ch} [now] growes thereupon shall bee devided amongst them wch have the [three] oth^r pt^s ontill such tyme as they have Cattle of there owne or [till] they sell the Grounds to those that have Cattles.

3^d Lye. That the three oth^r pt^s shall bee equally devided amongst those that have Cattle, to each head of Cattle

there pportion to bee devided to each of them by [lott] wch devisions are to bee made betwixt this and the next Co^{te}.

[4]th Lye. That all the inhabitants of the Towne of Exeter shall have their vpland lotts for planting laid out by the Riv^r bettweene Stony Creeke and the Creeke on this side Mr. Hiltons, according to the num^r of ye psons and Cattle, in equall p portion wch p portion is to be devided to them by lott, except such psons as live one the oth^r side the Riv^r, and Will. Hilton and Goodm. Smart who are to have the lotts one the oth^r side the Riv^r where

the Toune shall bee thought most Convenient, By o^r Rul^r Needam and Mr. Starre deputeis to this purpose.

5th Lye. That whosoever shall Carry themselves disorderly vnreverently in the Co^te Towards the Magistrates or in y^r p^rsence shall bee lyable to such a Censer as the Co^te shall thinke meete.

A Division of the vplands From the Cone against Rocky poynt to the Creeke next on this Side Mr. Hiltons.

1. Imp^r. Mr. Stanjon 27 acers 135 poole, one end butting vpon the river Eastward & the other end running vp into the majne six scoore poole in Length.
2. Mr. Grosse 28 acres 140 poole butting as afforesayd.
3. Goodman Walker 4 acers 20 poole butting as aforesayd.
4. Goodman Mower 22 acers 110 poole butting as aforesayd.
5. Thomas Louett 4 acers 20 poole butting as aforesayd.
6. William Wentford 4 acers 20 poole butting as aforesayd.
7. Goodman Coole 12 acers 60 poole butting as aforesayd.
8. Edward Rishworth 4 acers 20 poole butting as aforesayd.
9. Robert Smyth 6 acers 30 poole butting as aforesayd.
10. Goodman Littlefejld 4 acers 20 poole butting as aforesayd.
11. Goodman Winborne 7 acers & 40 poole butting as abouesayd.
12. Jeremiah Blackwell 4 acers 20 poole butting as aforesayd.
13. George Raborne 4 acers 20 poole butting as aforesayd.
14. Goodman Dearborne 10 acers 50 poole butting as aforesayd.
15. Mr. Needum 12 acers 60 poole butting as aforesayd.
16. Goodman Elkine 4 acers 20 poole butting as aforesayd.
17. Goodman Crame 8 acers 40 poole butting as aforesayd.
18. Goodman Littlefejld 21 acers butting as aforesayd.
19. Thomas Weight 6 acers 30 poole butting as aforesayd.
20. Jams Wall 10 acers 90 poole butting as aforesayd.
21. Mr. Pormott 14 acers 70 poole butting as aforesayd.
22. William Wardell 10 acers 50 poole butting as aforesayd.
23. Goodman Compton 12 acers 60 poole butting as aforesayd.
24. Thomas Wardell 12 acers 60 poole butting as aforesayd.
25. Goodman Pettit 6 acers 30 poole butting as aforesayd.
26. Goodman Willix 4 acers 20 poole butting as aforesayd.
27. Goodman Bulgar 4 acers 20 poole butting as aforesayd.
28. Mr. Morris 33 acers butting as aforesayd.
29. Mr. Wheelewright 80 acers butting as aforesayd.
30. Robert Read 9 acers & 50 poole butting as aforesayd.
31. Abner

32. Mr. Storr 20 acers 100⁶ poole butting as aforesayd.
33. Griffine Mountegue 10 acers 50 poole butting as aforesayd, bought by Mr. Edward Hillton of Thomas Croly.

Thomas ✕ Crolys marke, witnes Richard Bullgar.

Noate here a great mistake, in this Record viz. euery akeer herein mensioned stands but for halfe an aker as atests

Rob. Booth,
Sept. 26, 1670.

A note how the marshes were diuided in the First diussion next the Towne, the quantity being 14 acers.

1. Imp^r to Goodman Smart one acre & 26 poole bee it more or lesse.
2. To Goodman Coole ½ acre & 13 poole bee it more or lesse.
3. To o^r pastor 8 acers 2 quarters bee it more or lesse.
4. To Goodman Mountegue 1 acre 26 poole bee it more or lesse.
5. To Mr. Storr 2 acers 3 quarters bee it more or lesse.

Theire is also diuided 14 acres to ye Sayd partys at Lamprome Riuer & the Same p portion to each party as aboue Sayd.

In the Second Diuission 19 acers on this sid Mr. Hiltons is diuided & six acers on Lamprone Riuer, as Followeth,

1. Imp^r to James Walls one acre & 54 poole bee it more or lesse & halfe an acree at Lamprone riuer.
2. To Mr. Morris 7 acres bee it more or lesse & 2.acres 40 poole at L: Riuer.
3. To Goodm : Willson 3 acres 28 poole bee it mor or lesse & 1 acre a Lamp : Riuer.
4. To Mr. Grosse 6 acers & 50 poole be it more or lesse & 2 acres a Lam : Riuer.

In the Third Diuission 18 acres on this side Mr. Hilton's & six acers at Lamprone Riuer diuided & giuen as before as followeth.

1. Imp^r. to William Hilton 2 acres & 40 poole be it more or lesse & 120 poole at Lamprone Riuer.
2. To William Mower 2 acres & 40 poole bee it more or lesse & 120 pool L : Riv :
3. To John Compton 12 acrs be it more or lesse & 120 poole at Lamp : riuer.
4. To William Wardell 120 poole bee it more or less & 120 poole at Lamp : Riuer.
5. To Mr. Stanjon 8 acers more or lesse & 2 acers & halfe at Lamp : riuer.

6. To Mr. Needum 3 acers bee it more or lesse & 1 acre at Lamp: Riuer.

In the 4th Diuission 19 acres on this side Mr. Hiltons & 14 acers at Lamp: Riuer diuided & given to them that haue noe cattle, & to euery man an equall p portion wch comes to euery one an acer & an halfe.

Theire is a small parcell about 2 acers of marsh bee it more or lesse wch was giuen to William Winborne that lyeth betwixt Mr. Needums march & theire marsh wch had noe cattle betwixt this & Mr. Hilton's.

1. It was agreed by the Inhabitants in the yer 1639 upon the 18th day of the 11th month that Isack Grosse, Rular, Agustin Store and Anthony Stanyon shall haue ye Ordring of all towne affaiers according to god.

Orders made by the Co^{te} held at Exeter the 6 day of the 12 Mo. 1639.

That noe man shall sett fier vpon the wood to the destroying of the feed for the Cattle, or to the doing of any oth^r hurt vnd^r paine of payeing the damage that shall insue thereby, after the midle of the 2 month.

That every man shall fall such trees as are in his lott being offencive to any oth^r. And if aft^r due warninge any shall refuse, to pay halfe a Crowne for every tree that is soe offensive.

That every action that is tryed the pty that is Cast in it shall pay to the Jury foure shillings.

Orders made by the Co^{te} held at Exeter the 6 day of the 1 moth (1639-40.)

That noe wines or Strong watter shal be Sould by retaile to the English but by thomas Wardle.

It is ordered that whosoeuer shall dige a saw pitt & shall not fill it or Cover it, shal be liable to pay the damage that shall com to man or beast thereby.

It is ordered that all the Swine that is not cared doune the riuer by the 4 day of the 2 month, the owners shall be liable to pay the damage that shall befall any thereby.

That all grounds, woods & such preuiliges as appertaine to the towne, such inhabitans as haue their lotts small or great in the bounds of the toune shal be liable to pay such comon Charges as the towne shal be at, according to theire proportion of ground, Catles, or other preuilidges they doe injoye in ye towne, whither

It is furder ordered that euerie man that is an inhabitant of the Toune shall haue free libirtie to trade with the Indians in any thinge exsepte it be powder, shot, or any warelike weapons, or Sacke or other Stronge watters, according to the former order ; and as for prizes of what Corne there shal be traided with them shall not exceed foure Shillings the bushell.

6. It is here recorded that Anthonie Stanyon hath satisfied the Cort Conserneing the offence giuen by hime to ou^r Ruler Nedham.

It is inacted for a law constituted & made & consented vnto by the whole assemblye at the Cort Sollomly meet togeather in Exeter this 9 day of the 2 moneth Ano. 1640.

That if any person or persons shall plot or practise eyther by Combination or otherwise the betrayeing of his Contrie or any prinsipall part thereof into the hands of anye forrainge state, Spanish Duch or french, Contrarye to the Allegiance we p fesse & owe to ou^r Dread Souveraigne lord kinge Charles his heires & successors, it being his majesties pleasuer to ptect vs his loyall Subjicts, Shal be punished with death, if anye person or persons shall plot or practise Trecherge, treson or rebellion, or shall reuile his majestie the lords anoynted Contrarye to the Allegiance we professe and owe to our dread Souveraine lord kinge Charles his heires & successors (ut supra) shal be punished with death.

Numb. 16
Exo. 22. 28
1 Kings, 2, 8, 9, 44.

An Order about purchesing howse lots.

3. It was Ordered by the Inhabetants in the yere 1640 in the 11th day of the 2^d month that none Inhabetant nor farinar shall purchese aney howse lots of aney but thay shall bulde an habetation or dweling house vpon it with in the space of six months next folowing aney such purchese, & whosoeuer shall kepe lots in thar hand aboue six months vnbult one or haue seurall howse lots in there hands shall pay such charges vpon eurey loot as shall a Rise in the towne Rates and whosoeuer shall sell house or howse lots before they haue tendred the saile tharof to the townsmen, that ded of saile is voyd, if the town shall giue as good a prise as he that formerly bought it.

4. It was Agreed vpon and ordred by the Inhabetants of Exetar in the yer 1640, in the first day of the 8th month that none

shall fell aney timbar within halfe a mile of the towne, except it be vpon thar particular lots without it be for buldinge or fencing vpon the pennaltie of 5ˢ for eurey tree so felld.

5. It was Agreed vpon and Ordred the day & yere next aboue writen that none but such as are Inhabetants and town dwelars shall haue libertie to fell or sawe aney timber thar Oake or pine or aney othar, but they shall be liable to an equal fine a Cording to the proporshon so feled or sawn.

It is ordered and Agreed vppon by the inhabitanc of the Towne of Exeter that noone shall fell Aney Oke timber wᵗʰ in halfe A mile of Aney part of the Towne, Except it be vppon there pticular lott or for building or fenceing, vppon the penialltie of [each tree] five shillings.

Its ordered by the Inhabitance of the Towne at A [meeting] whoseuer shall Absent themselves from Towne [meeting] after] due warning shall for [each] offence forfeit

Orders mayd by the Cort at Exeter houlden the secund day moth 9ᵗʰ, 1640.

Impʳ yᵗ Edward Rishwoorth is chosen by order of Cort to be Secritery to the Cort to looke to the booke & to enter all such actions are brought, and to have 12ᵈ layd downe at the entring euery action.

2 ly. Its likewise agreed vpon yᵗ the lands yᵗ are layd outt according to the former order, both for theire butting, bounding & p portion, are now confirmed & ratifyd in the cort Rowles.

3 ly. It is a lawe mayd yᵗ if either pson or psons shall by any means draw sids, to make comuotions or seditions in these oʳ Jurisdictions, hee shall pay tenn pounds & stand liable to the further Censure of the Court.

4 ly. Its agreed vpon that the Milner shall take for his wast & towle 5ᵈ of meale, & wᵗ euer is wanting more is to be mayd good by him, & hee to stand lyable to the Corts censure vpon Just & sufficient testimony of the same.

5 ly. Its agreed that all pitts & hooles are to bee filled up & trees remoued, wᶜʰ ly neare the way, within a fortintts tyme or else they are to pay 10ˢ & bee lyable to the Censure of the Court.

6 ly. That all Creeks are free, only hee yᵗ maks a ware therein is to haue in the first place the benefitt of it in Fishing tyme & soe others may sett a ware either aboue or below & enjoy the same liberty.

It is agreed upon by the Inhabitants of Exeter that euery man shall Fence the next spring a generall fence euery man an equall p portion according to the quality of ground lyng within the fence by the middle of the secund moenth wch will bee 1641, and w^t damage can bee mayd [to] appear for the want of a sufficient Fence hee y^t ows it is to make it good, & if the sayd Fence bee not sett vp at the day appoynted euery day after hee y^t is behind hand herein shall pay Five Shillings a day.

Orders mayd & agreed vpon at Exeter, houlden this 3^d day, moenth 12th 1640.

Its agreed vpon y^t Mr. William Hilton is to enjoy those two marshes in Oyster River wch formerly he hath had possession of & still are in his possession & the other marsh wch Mr. Gibbies doth wrongfully detayne from him with the rest of those marshes wch formerly hee hath mayd use of soe fare forth as they may bee for the publique good of this plantation, And soe much of the vpland (adjoining) to them as shall bee thought conueiyent by the neighbores of Oyster Riuer, wch are belonging to this body.

It is further agreed vpon y^t vpon o^r former agrement euery one shall fence his p portion of ground & if any refuse, whoseuer will fence it shall haue the use of it till they bee fully satisfyd, if it bee ould ground, & if it bee new hee shall have it for his payens.

where As it was formerly agreed vpon in generall y^t all the Toune should generally fence & w^n they come to fence prticularly others should doe as much for them in fencing as they did for y^r outsids wch vpon farther consideration is not thought equall yrfore now it is agreed y^t w^n wee come to fence in particular y^t it must bee putt to the consideration of two indifereit men w^t y^r fence is worth by those wch fenced the out side, is to bee mayd good unto them again by such as [the land] appertains two.

Its likewise agreed that whosoeuer buyes the Indean ground by way of purchase is to tender it first to the towne before they are to make p per vse of it in prticular to themselves.

Orders mayd by the Court at Exeter, moenth First, day the 12th 1640 [1641.]

Imp^r. whereas the highwayes by vertue of a forme^r order were to bee in breadth 3 pole at the least, yet notwithstanding they are straytned in diuerse places, wee doe therefore here againe order that they should bee rectifyd & mayd the full breadth as aforesayd betwixt this & the middle of the secund moenth wch shall be in the yeare of o^r Lord 1642, & alsoe such ground as is taken in contary to order, to bee rectifyd within the sayd tyme.

Orders mayd by the Court at Exeter d: 30: m: First, 1641.

Its agreed vpon y^t all the Swine aboue ½ a yeare ould and vpwards are to bee sent downe into the great bay by the 10th day of secund moenth, & w^t Swine are found in the towne after ye tyme aboue y^t age, w^t hurt they doe in a sufficient Fence, there owners are to make it good.

Its further agreed y^t according to former orders y^t all are to have y^r fences finished of y^r home lotts by the middle of y^o next moenth, or otherwise to stand to ye perill y^t may ensue.

Its agreed that none but inhabitants of the towne shall plant w hin the townes libertys w hout there consent.

Whereas the freemen of Exeter haue mayd choyce of Mr. Richard Bulgar to be Leefetenant of ye band of Souldgers in Exeter, & prsented to ye court houlden at Exeter d: 30: m: First 1641, I the ruler of the sayd plantation doe ratify & confirme ye sayd choyse & doe further grant y^t the sayd Mr. Richard Bulgar shall bee enstauled & confirmed Leeftenant by the freemen ye next trayning day.

NICHOLAS NEEDHAM.

Whereas the freemen of Exeter haue mayd choyse of Thomas Wardell to bee Sargiant of the band of Souldgers in Exeter, & pr sented to ye Court houlden at Exeter d: 30: moenth First 1641, I the Ruler of the sayd plantation do confirme the sayd choyse & d(oe further) grant y^t the sayd Thomas Wardell shall be enstaled by the
the next trayning day.

NICHOLAS NEEDUM.

An order mayd by the (Court at) Exeter, d: 10th. m: 4th 1641.

Its ordered y^t Goodman   shall allow the Indeans one bushell of corne for y^r labor &   wch was spent by y^m in replaynting of y^t corne of y^{rs} wch was spoyld by his corne (swine?) & hee to make vp y^r lose at haruest, according as y^t corne may bee judged worse then there corne wch was nev^r hurt.

An order mayd at the Court at Exeter the last day of June 1641, it is agreed vpon that thar shall be none accusations deulged or spread abroud of aney parsone or parsons but what thare be proued by the mouth of to or three witneses for they that shall so doe shall be liable to the Court Sensur, this is not in poynt of damidegs   trespas but in point of slanders in a mans good name.

It was Agreed vpon and ordred by the Inhabetants of Exetar in the yere 1641 (-42) in the 14th day of the 11th month, that no farenars shall worke within the limmets of our towne, to be paid out of timbar or pipstaues for thar worke, nor to hindar any any of the Inhabtants from Imployment prouided that the Inhabetants Can or will doe that worke as Cheap and sufishent as the farinar, but if thay will not, then are the Inhabetants free to bringe in Farenars.

Vpon the great complaint of the great distruction & spoyle of timbar about the towne of Exetar it was Agreed and ordred by the Inhabetants in yt 14th day of the 11th month that all such of ye Inhabetants that haue felled aney timbar for pipstaues or boults before this Ordar wos made, shall haue one yers time to worke it vp, Except it be such as had timbar lieing vnwrought vp a yere, and such are alowed but 6 months to worke vp such timbar, and if aney timbar belonging to these men shall be found vpon the Common vnwrought vp aftar the 6 months then it shall be forfit and at the townsmens disposing and the Common to be Clered of all timbar which was felled for pipstaues or boults euery 6 months, except they be in pipstaues or boults, vpon the pennaltie of the forfetur tharof.

Cort at Exeter, mth. 5, d : 10th 1642.

The Censure of the Court against Thomas Weight for [contemptuous carriages] & speeches against both ye Court & the magestrate wch hee is to bee fined 20s & to pay all Court charges besids, & his liberty to bee taken away as hee is a freeman.

Its agreed yt all maner of cattle are to haue keepers a days & are to bee looke to of nights & kept vp, if any damage come by any answerable satisfaction mst be mayd.

Att the Court houldne att Exeter the 20th of the 8th moneth 1642.

Mr. Needham resines vp his offise of being Ruler, and by the choyce and Approbation of the boddey of the Towne, mr. Thomas Wilson is Established Ruler.

John Legat is Chousene by the Court to be secritere to the Court to keepe the booke, and to enter all such Actiones as are brought and to haue 12s layede downe att the enterey of euerey Action.

Att the Courte houldene att Exeter the 7th Day of the 9th mo. 1642.

Our honored Ruler mr. Thomas Willson doth give his Approbation and confermes All thouse howlesome lawes and orders wch are here Recorded wch ware made in the time that mr. Needam was Ruler.

It is ordred by the Court houldne att Exeter the 6th day of the third m° 1643, That m^r Thomas Rashley shall haue giuene vnto him for A house lott that peece of land wch lyeth betweene Grifing Mountegue his lott and Mr Stanyon his Creeke, Conteyneing 14 or 16 Akers be more or lese, only excepteing 2 Akers and A halfe for A loot for Grifing Mountegue next to the creeke.

It is farther ordred by the Court Above named that Thomas Wardall, William Winborne, Samuell Walker and Robert Reade shall haue libertey and Athoretey to searche [in] the howse or howses of Aney p son or p sones wi [thin our] Jurisdictiones, And to take into theire Custodey [and make] sale of Aney such Corne as they shall find in ther [houses] which is more then the ptie or pties shall have ne [ed] of for theire one Families till haruist next, prouided th [at] the pties Above named make good pay for the sd Co [rne] and as good A pryce as it is ginerally sould for in [the Riuore, and theis pties to dispoose of such Corne so [taken] by them vnto such poore people as stands most in n [eed.] of it for the best pay they Can Make, and att the f [irst] price wch the pties Aboue named bye it att.

It is Ordred by voate at a towne meetinge houlden at Exetar ye 21th of Agust 1643 that aney Inhabetant of the towne of Exetar which shall finde vndar 20 Ackars of marsh shall Injoye the same as his owne foreuer by vertew of this ordar but if he or thay shall finde above 20 Ackars then it is at ye towns disposall, prouided that he or thay which finde ye march of aboue 20 Ackars shall haue a duble portion out of it.

At the Court houldne the 5th of the 7th mo. (43.)

Christey Lawson binds himselfe in the som of Ten pounds starling vnto the countrey to Answere A presentment brought Against him for extortion by William Coale, Tho. Weight, James Wall, William Wentworth, and Tho. Petet, and this to be Answerd by him att the next Court wch shall be houlden for Exeter, either heere or else whare.

William Coale, Thomas Weight, James Wall Willm Went{oh} and Tho. Petet do bind themselues in the som of 50{s} the peece to be payd to the Countrey, In Case they do not follow the p{r}sentment brought Against Christey Lawson by them for extortion, the next Court houldne for Exeter heere or elsewhare.

Corne spoyled by swine, it is ordred that James Wall shall haue Alowd him 3 bushells of Corne, George Rabone 3 bushells, Tho. Weight 1 bushell and halfe, George barlow 1 bushell to be payde by John Bursley for leaveing opne A cart gapp or by whome he Can prove hath left it opne, or hath bine the Cause of the leaueing it opne.

It is ordred that William Coale, Tho. weit and Tho. Wardall shall pay vnto Samll Walker, Hen. Robay and Tho. Petet either of them A peck of Corne for harme dune vnto them by swine.

It is ordred that Tho. Biggs shall pay vnto Grifing Mountegu for taking Away his oure 2^s 6^d and charges or a new owre and the Court charges.

It is farther ordred att the Court houlden the 5th of the 7th mo. 1643, that Tho. Biggs shall pay vnto the Sagamoure for takeing Away his Net and parting of it 5^s.

It is farther ordred that Tho. Bigs shall be whipt 6 strips for takeing Away a sith of Captanie Wigons and other petey lasones.

It is ordred that Christoy Lawson shall speedely puide A fyle for Willm Wentwoth, and Willm Wentwoth to pay 7^s for it.

It is ordred that Will. Coale and Rob. Smith shall ouersee the fences About the Towne and giue warning to them whose fences Are defectiue, and If they be not Amended the owners there of to pay for what hurt is done through those fences.

3^d 19 day (44.)

Its agreed that the tounsmen shall pocure a bridg ouar lamprill Riuar.

Its left to the 3 townsmen to purches mr. Whelwrights howse with all lands belonging thervnto for the towne.

It is agred that all dogs shall be Clogd and [sid lind] in ye day and tid vp in the night, and if aney dogs shall be found trespasing in the lots they that shall find them may showt them or folow them to the howse to which that dog doth belong and Charg 5^s vpon the onar of that dog or bitch which shall be leued by ordar from the townsmen & halfe the fine to faul to towne and halfe to the partie that takes that dog, and the trespas to be judged by tow men and the trespas to be paid for.

Samuell Grenfel Chosen to kepe the a sufishent ordenarey and draw wine and strong waters and trad with the Indans, and Sargant Wardall hath libartie to draw of his wine that is in his hands or Samuel grenfeld to take his wine of his hands.

when we Coul a generall meting, men to haue 3 days warning.

[It]s agred that the trained bands minds should be knowne and if thay would   hands to be pocured to the Genrall Court for the Restablishing leftenant Richard Bullgar in his formar ofis and Sargant Wardall pocure the like libartie and both to be sent to the Court.

the 17 day of y° 4th month 44.

its agred that at a towne meting in Exetar that the marsh that wos promist to Anthoney Stanyon by seuen of the Brethren as far as in them lay shall be giuen to mr. Whelwright his aiers and sucksesors for euer, allso that Anthoney Stanyon is to haue as much in anothar deriction as will ansor to the shars of 6 brethren and himselfe as Conuenient, if not in qualitie then it is to be in quantitie, this grant to Mr. Whelwright is with these Condishons that he doth Com amongst us againe, if not it is to be still in the towns hands, and Anthoney Stanyon is to be satisfied by y° toune for his charges that he is out.

It is ordered at this Toune meeting that every man shall kepe vp his cattell every night in some yard or Pen vpon the penalty of 12ᵈ a peece every night, excepting working cattell, & if any mans cattell trespass they are to pay the damages besides the fine, the 17 of y° 4th M. 1644.

17 day 4 mo. 44.

Its ordred that thar shall be a Heyway downe to the marches without side of grifen mountegs lot, Right downe to the Riuor.

It is agred that that fence which Runs by the broke which Runs betwen Humfrey Willsens house and Mr. Whelwrights shall be set vpon to be set vp within 2 dayes aftar the date of this ordar, and if it shall be neglected then thay whos fensing shall be downe aftar this weke shall pay 10ˢ the Rood for eurey weke tell it shall be set vp.

It is agred that 4 dayes shall be set apart to mend the heywayes to begine one the 4th day of the weke Com a seuen night and to be at thar labors from 6 and leue at 12 and Rest tell 2 and worke tell 6 a clock, and such as shall be absent from the worke at the ours aboue writen shall be fined 5ˢ for euery day, and thay that haue tems shall worke them vpon the penalltie of 20ˢ for euery day

Ordred voted and granted at a town metinge by a goynt Consent that Christepher Iason hath a grant to set a weare in the Riuar of Exetar y° 28th of the 4th mo. 1644, to him and his Aiers foreuer vpon the Condishons as foloweth, first that y° Inhabetants of y° towne of Exetar shall be supplyed with Alewifes to fish thar ground euery yere before aney othars at 3° par thousand, and whot Alewifes are taken shall be equally deuided according as y° Inhabetants shall agre, and if thar be no fish taken then Christepher to be fre from aney damiedges to y° towne, and whot fish the Inhabetants shall buy of ye said Christepor he y° said Chrisephor doth binde himselfe to take such pay for it as y° towne afords, to be paid once in six months, and In case the said Christepor or his sucksesors shall heraftar tendar y° saile of y° weare that then he shall in y° first place tendar it to y° towne for Countrey pay, and we y° Inhabetants do Retaine our liberties to fish in y° fawls or elce whar in y° Riuar, but not to set vp aney othar ware so as to forstall that ware which Christopher is to set vp, and y° said Christepher is to make flud gats so that barkes botes and Canows may Com to the towne, in witnes her vnto we do set to our hands for vs and our sucksesars Interchangably for euer y° day and yere aboue writen.

In y° behalfe of y° towne

RICHARD BULLGAR
SAMUEL ┼ GRENFELDS   marke.
CHRISTOPHER LAWSON.

It is ordered that none but seteled inhabitantes shall make use of woode or common, nor that noe inhabytant shall inploy anny Aboute wod worke, but of the setteled inhabitants.

APPENDIX III.

BICENTENNIAL ADDRESS OF HON. JEREMIAH SMITH.

A FEW PASSAGES, FOR THE MOST PART BIOGRAPHICAL, ARE OMITTED AS THE INFORMATION THEY CONTAIN IS GIVEN IN THE EARLY PART OF THIS VOLUME.

WE need not be told, that our ancestors were not so rich; that they were laborious, industrious and economical; that they belonged to the middle class of society in their native country, embracing, however, none of the lowest of that class, who had neither the wish nor the ability to emigrate.

It will be my endeavor to vindicate the religious character of the first settlers, and that of their leader, in an especial manner, under the cruel persecution he underwent. Persecutors are much in the habit of giving false characters of the men they persecute, as if that would palliate, which only aggravates the injury. The civil fathers of Massachusetts, and the reverend elders, must have had hard hearts, if, when they beheld the little band,—thirty or forty families,—collecting their wives and children, their cattle, their furniture and their scanty stores, for the wilderness of Swamscot, they felt no pity for the sufferers. Albeit these men were not of the melting mood, they must have shed tears at the piteous sight. It was but a journey of three or four days, but in prospect it was dreary enough. There was a small settlement at Lynn, older ones at Salem and Ipswich, and a plantation just begun at Newbury; but all between was a thick, dark forest, and the path little better than marked trees. We are told that about this time a person lost his way in the *woods*, between Salem and Lynn, and wandered about several days before he reached a settlement. Two years before, the famous Hooker, with his little colony of one hundred souls, who settled Hartford, were a whole week performing their journey, encumbered as our little colony was. I need not say, that, after three or four days' journey ours reached Swamscot Falls greatly fatigued. Here they found no friends to bid them welcome. This was the most painful circumstance of all.

Several weeks must have been spent in preparing log huts to shelter them from the weather. But the toils of our emigrants were but just beginning. Their views were merely agricultural, to till the ground for a subsistence; and we must remember it was the hard and plain tillage of a common, not of an exuberant soil. The settlements at Portsmouth and Dover were made by traders, factors and fishermen, who hoped to carry on a profitable traffic with the natives and foreigners, and to enrich themselves from the sea, not the land. Mason and Gorges aimed at still greater things. Their connections at Court, and their influence with the Great Council of Plymouth, obtained grants of large tracts; to Gorges, Maine, and to Mason, New Hampshire. These lands they intended to parcel out to others at a small quit-rent. They were to be cultivated by tenants, while the proprietors were to be clothed with the *jura regalia;* with all the trappings of little monarchs. Experience soon taught them the fallibility and the futility of all such schemes. They expended large sums in putting the machine in motion, and died in debt. Neither they nor their posterity ever realized a tenth part of the sums they expended. Our lands are not rich enough to support *landlord* and *tenant.* The cultivator must have all the produce, and little enough, too. The views of some projectors were still more romantic. They flattered themselves with immense wealth from the discovery here of rich mines of the precious metals; such as the adventurers in our southern hemisphere had in fact realized.

The little band we have conducted to this place, in point of condition, intelligence and education, will compare well with the first settlers of Massachusetts, if we except a very few of superior family, wealth and education, who took the lead in that enterprise. Perhaps there never was a greater equality in the rank, condition, education and circumstances of the planters of a new colony; none rich, and none without the means of obtaining the necessaries of life; none highly educated, and none without the education common to the same rank in the mother country at the time.

Among our settlers there were no merchants, or manufacturers, or persons skilled in the arts of trade. They were from the agricultural districts of England; of course not ignorant of the art of husbandry, as then practised in that country; but they could hardly be aware how little their knowledge would avail them here. The soil was different from that of Lincolnshire and Norfolk; and there the tillage was of lands long cultivated; here a wilderness was to be subdued and turned into a fruitful field, a new science to them. No doubt their scanty portion of implements of agriculture was ill adapted to their wants; and a supply was not at that day, as now, a matter of easy acquisition. They must have suffered, too, for want of animals. Cattle of all kinds were scarce and dear. The new plantations in Massachusetts could spare none, at any price.

It seems Captain Mason had sent over, a few years before, a large number of cattle of the best breeds, imported from Denmark. He died about two years before, and his servants had possessed themselves of his effects. Probably from these men our settlers were able to obtain a partial supply. But, after all, the prospect was gloomy; gloomy as the dark forests in the midst of which they had seated themselves. What now, think ye, supported the drooping spirits of our emigrants? If ever there was a people thrown entirely upon their own resources, few and scanty as those resources were, we have them here. They were beyond the bounds of Massachusetts; strangers to the people of Dover and Portsmouth; every way strangers. There was no congeniality between them. Massachusetts had driven them out. To whom shall they go? Happily, they belonged to that class of men who find no difficulty in answering the question. They had just been condemned as enemies of God and his religion; but this unjust sentence of their fellow mortals could not deprive them of what they valued above all earthly good — their religious principles and belief; and to these they looked for support.

The bulk of mankind, you know, adopt the religious opinions in which they were born and educated, without examination and without inquiry; and what is so adopted makes but a feeble impression on the mind. But it was not so with the Puritans who settled New England, any more than with the first converts to Christianity; they heard gladly, but did not yield *implicit* faith. "Are these things so?" They inquired, reasoned and compared, and were reasoned with; their convictions, therefore, were strong. They could not fail to produce fruits. They had the faith that overcomes the world and all wordly things.

The Author of nature has implanted in the heart of man a strong attachment to the land of his birth; to parents, children, kindred; to the scenes of his early youth, and even to the graves of his ancestors. Yet all these will he forsake when his conscience calls for the sacrifice. So thought and so acted the Puritans who settled New England. The rulers of their native land, and the church in which they were nurtured and fed, like an unnatural step-mother, as in their anger they called her, cast them out for non-conformity to a few idle ceremonies she was pleased to enjoin. They could not in conscience obey. They had persuaded themselves that this gaudy worship was popish and idolatrous, and therefore to be resisted at all hazards; and so believing, they *left*, such of them as were not *driven* away, their native land, and came to this wilderness.

The settlers of Exeter belonged to this sect of Christians. When they joined themselves to their brethren of Massachusetts, they had the hope that they had reached the termination of all their sufferings for conscience's sake. And was this an unreasonable hope? In this New World, what should hinder their enjoying in brotherly love and Christian fellowship the pure, simple worship of God, unmixed with popish superstitions; accountable for their Christian faith and religious observances, not to the infallible head of the popish or the never-erring head of the English churches, but to the unerring head of the true church, Christ himself. This was the Puritan doctrine in England. And they were mistaken. Their teacher in theology, it was believed, had assigned an undue proportion to the covenant of grace in the economy of salvation, and in politics they were also found in error. They wished to continue Vane in the chair of government, whereas the majority, as it proved at the next election, preferred his rival. *Both questions* were *alike* settled by major vote. Where was now the right of *private* judgment *in matters of religion*, where conscience is so deeply concerned? For these offences (for *in minorities* they are offences), they must now pass once more through the fiery furnace of persecution. This second death was far more painful than the first. It was upon grounds far less intelligible than the first. It was upon a difference of opinion in *abstruse points in theology*.

When persecution visits a country, it is their boldest as well as their best men who become its victims. When all other earthly hopes fail, they abandon their firesides and their altars, that they may keep their consciences. It is the weak and timid minds who remain at home. They meanly crouch beneath the rod of the oppressor, afraid to exercise their reasoning powers. They find it safest to conceal their religious opinions, and seek security in hypocrisy. Who fled from France on the revocation of the Edict of Nantes, one hundred and fifty years ago? The choicest spirits of that gallant nation; the men of the greatest intellectual and moral strength. They enriched the neighboring nations. Our population in America gained moral and intellectual strength by this foolish as well as wicked measure of Louis XIV. To this cause we are indebted for our Bowdoins, our Dexters, our Jays, DeLanceys, Boudinots, Hugers. Who were the men driven from England by the bloody Mary and her no less cruel sister? The Puritans: men of whom the world was not worthy. The effect of persecution for opinions, is to set people to thinking and reasoning. It improves the intellectual and moral powers — gives added strength and firmness of purpose. But I am afraid it hardens the heart; for how often do we find the persecuted, on a change of circumstances, themselves acting the wicked part of persecutors? And so it was in New England in her early days.

Before the arrival of his friends, Mr. Wheelwright had purchased from the Sagamore of Piscataqua a large tract of land, — upwards of five hundred thousand acres. There is no pretence that the men of Exeter acquired any *legal title* by this purchase. Neither Wheelwright, nor any of the other grantees named in the deed, ever asserted any exclusive right in himself. The town *acted as the proprietors*. I would not be understood to adopt Sir Edmund Andros's language, "that such deeds were no better than the scratch of a bear's paw."

The first settlers at the time had no mode of obtaining a legal title. The Council of Plymouth had been dissolved a short time before, and Mason, to whom they had granted, was dead; and his devisees were infants, and no claim was made in their behalf for thirty years; and then they waked up, not to benefit themselves, but to vex and disquiet the peaceable inhabitants who, though destitute of a legal, had, nevertheless, the most equitable of all titles: — purchase from the natural owners; *long possession*, without any adverse claim; *the defence* of the settlement against the savages and the French; and the cultivation and settlement of a part of the country, whereby the value of the rest was greatly enhanced. In truth, they paid the full value and more, and could with a clear conscience hold the lands they claimed, against the world.

I cannot learn that our Indians ever complained, or afterwards set up any title to the lands sold to Wheelwright. The transaction between Wheelwright and the sagamore was a sufficient license to settle and occupy, and was highly creditable to his liberality, prudence and care of his flock. But our ancestors could not only find no one to sell them the lands they possessed, but they could find no person to govern them. As English-born subjects, they knew they could not throw off their allegiance to the Crown. But the Crown had no representative in New England. Massachusetts governed itself, and so, in fact, did all the other settlements. From necessity, therefore, this handful of men were compelled to resort to original principles. That the weak might be protected against the strong, and the good against the bad, they seem at first, by mere verbal agreement, to have instituted government.

At the close of the first year, on the fourth of July, 1639, they solemnly subscribed a written instrument, or constitution, which they called a Combination. With an acknowledgment of some sort of dependence on the Crown, they adopted the English *Christian laws, as they understood them,*—doubtless intending in this truly democratic government, to reject, *in toto*, all that regarded the hierarchy and church establishment, which they deemed popish and anti-Christian, and altogether unsuitable to a settlement like ours. In this opinion they were far more correct than the tyrant Governor Cranfield, half a century afterwards, who instituted a criminal prosecution against Mr. Moody, the minister of Portsmouth, for disobedience to that system, in refusing to administer the sacrament, according to the rites of the English Church, to himself and his unworthy associates. Mr. Moody withstood the little tyrant to his fall, and suffered imprisonment for a long time in the common jail.

John Wheelwright of Lincolnshire was born in the latter end of the reign of Elizabeth. His ancestors, no doubt, were of respectable standing in society, for he inherited a considerable real estate, which he disposed of by his last will. His parents had the good sense to bestow a portion of their wealth in giving their son a learned education. He had bright parts, and in youth was remarkable for the boldness, zeal and firmness of mind he displayed on all occasions. He was educated for the ministry, but embracing the Puritan sentiments, he necessarily incurred the censure of the Church for non-conformity. Laud was then

Archbishop of Canterbury, and determined to enforce the strictest observance of the ceremonies. We are not informed of the particular in which Wheelwright failed. Cotton's was, not kneeling at the sacrament.

Laud was a learned and probably a sincere man; but, like many other good men, he indulged an excessive fondness for the pageantry and splendor of public worship; for the minutiæ and exterior parts of religion. He was, at the same time, the most active member of the High Commission Court — a tribunal with which many of our early and distinguished clergy had occasion to be well acquainted. When the great and undefined power of this Court was wielded by a determined High Churchman, no Puritan could exercise his ministry within its reach, and its jurisdiction was co-extensive with the kingdom itself. The learned, mild and catholic Cotton could not elude its pursuivants. He was obliged to fly his country like a felon. Mr. Wheelwright came to Boston about three years after Cotton.

* * * * * * *

Every thing went on prosperously as could be desired, in the new settlement. A church was gathered, and Mr. Wheelwright, of course, was the pastor. Moderate grants of land were made to him. He had no other compensation for his services and advances. His knowledge and superior talents must have been extremely useful in the infant plantation. Our early records show a strong and grateful sense of the obligation on the part of the town. For a short time he deemed himself safe from his persecutors; but Massachusetts *in that day* had a politic head and *a long arm*, and Mr. Wheelwright was obliged to remove, and the four New Hampshire towns submitted to Massachusetts, — Exeter the last. This was in 1643.

Wheelwright, just before his removal, obtained of Sir Ferdinando Gorges a grant of a considerable tract in Wells. In the deed he is styled "Pastor of the Church in Exeter." He remained in Wells about three years.

His next remove was to Hampton. That people greatly desired his ministerial services. He remained eight or nine years at Hampton, and then returned to England, where he renewed his acquaintance with his old classmate, Oliver Cromwell, and with his old friend, Sir Henry Vane. Both these distinguished men, though at odds with each other, were friendly to Wheelwright. This was near the close of Cromwell's eventful life. Wheelwright is said to have been a favorite with the Protector. While in England he probably resided chiefly on his estate in Lincolnshire, one hundred and thirty miles north of London.

At the Restoration, in 1660, he returned, and was soon settled in Salisbury, in our vicinity, as the successor of their first minister, Mr. W. Worcester. Here he closed a long and busy life, being reputed a sound, orthodox, profitable and approved minister of the gospel. He died November, 1679 — the oldest minister in New England — about eighty-five years of age.

From his family proceeded all the Wheelwrights in Massachusetts, Maine and New Hampshire. Many of his descendants have been respectable in character and property. His son, grandson and great-grandson have been councillors. Thus it pleased heaven to bestow on him the blessing of long life, and a numerous and honorable progeny.

I have gone into the history of Mr. Wheelwright's persecution and sufferings, not for the purpose of condemning the errors and wrongs of the government of that day, but to vindicate the character of our founder. We have an interest in his good name, and he who robs him of that, robs us. I entertain no doubt that, speaking in general terms, the elders and magistrates of Massachusetts were good men, and thought themselves justified in their treatment of Wheelwright and his friends. Without a minute and careful examination of this case we can have no just conception of the early settlers, their bigotry, superstition and intolerance. It arose in some measure from their peculiar situation; and no transaction of the early day can be understood without a minute attention to these traits in their character. To omit these, in giving a history of that time, would be like enacting Shakespeare's Hamlet, leaving out the character of the Prince of Denmark.

Religion at that day entered into every thing; the magistrates were elected, and the government administered, according to the *particular religious* views of the majority. Both clergy and laity were made worse by the union, just as they themselves believed to be the case in the country whence they came. Many of the writers of these times were unfriendly to Wheelwright and Vane; yet even they are obliged to admit that Wheelwright was famous for learning, ability, piety and zeal, and that his moral character was entirely free from spot or blemish.

The amiable Elliot says, Mr. Wheelwright's conduct "in New Hampshire discovered an ambitious turn — a desire to be chief."

Sullivan, in his history of Maine, adds to the ambition, of being the first man in Exeter in 1638, that of mingling in the quarrels of Dover with the redoubtable Underhill, Larkham and Knolles, "as *they pretended* about religion, but in fact for *the chair of the Dover government.*"

The Exeter men are supposed to have taken sides with their chief, in *these ambitious* schemes of rule. I have spared no pains to make myself acquainted with the written memorials of Exeter, and all other records and information within my reach, and I venture to say nothing can be further from the truth. This account of the early times here, to compare small things with great, is just about as fabulous as the early history of Rome.

A short time after Wheelwright's removal to Maine, on his application, his sentence of banishment was repealed. Some writers say he made an open confession of his errors. The letters are preserved, and speak for themselves. He expressed his sorrow for the part he had taken in the controversy, and his grief at the censorious speeches he had made, and his unchristian temper in the sharp contentions of that day. I have no doubt of the sincerity of all this. His personal attendance was dispensed with. Hubbard's remark is no doubt correct, — "and so if the Court have *over done* in passing the sentence, it might *in part* help to balance the account, that they were so ready to grant him a release."

. . . .

Among the persons who united their fortunes to ours during the first century (for I must confine myself for obvious reasons chiefly to that period), and whose names are still "familiar to our ears as household words," — the men who bore the heat and burden of the day, and to whom this day must be devoted; — among these men we find the names of Gilman, Folsom, Hilton, Colcord, Thing, Gordon, Magoon, Conner, Robinson, Pearson, Lawrence, King, Odiorne, Lamson, Tilton, Philbrick, Poor, Perryman, Emery and many others. The descendants of these respectable men still dwell among us. Time would fail me even briefly to mention the good things our records abundantly testify concerning them; — how acceptably they filled the municipal and public offices conferred upon them. But I cannot deny myself the pleasure of a brief notice of two or three.

It is no disparagement to any other family here, to say that in numbers, and every thing that constitutes respectability, the

Gilmans stood at the head. The father, Edward, had come to Hingham, and was admitted a freeman of Massachusetts about the time of our first settlement. He soon removed to Ipswich, and near the close of his life followed his three sons to Exeter, where he died. The sons, Edward, Moses and John, were all sensible, moral, industrious and enterprising, and very soon made themselves acquainted with the best methods of advancing a new settlement in the wilderness. Edward, the son, came first, and was very much engaged in setting up mills, — *useful* at all times, and indispensably so at this early stage of our affairs. He came soon after Wheelwright's removal, and seems quite early to have taken the lead in our town affairs, and to have shared largely, as long as he lived, the confidence of his fellow townsmen. I need scarcely add that he was public-spirited. To obtain improved machinery and mill-gear, he took a voyage to England in 1653, and was lost at sea. Of Moses, we hear less; he left a numerous progeny.

The town and province records, together with those of Massachusetts, would enable us to trace the life of John, the youngest son, at considerable length; but I must be brief. He came here a short time before Edward sailed;—married a respectable woman, and had sixteen children, twelve or thirteen of whom married and left issue. Among his sons were John and Nicholas. The latter had seven sons, one of whom was Daniel, born in 1702, the father of Nicholas who was the first treasurer of our State. This Nicholas filled the most responsible offices, and was the father of the late John Taylor, who, when a young man, was recalled from Congress to succeed his late father in the treasurer's office, early in 1783. I need not enumerate the offices this son filled with so much credit to himself and honor to the State, and double honor to his native town. He was eleven years successively governor, and afterwards three years, making a longer period than that filled by any other person. Probably the same thing may be said at the next *centennial;* and I am sure no man in private or public life ever left a fairer reputation behind him, for firmness, integrity and independence.

The second son, Nicholas, you all know. He entered the Revolutionary army early in the war, and had a full share of its sufferings and its glory to the close. In 1786 he was appointed a member of the old Congress; and, excepting a short period when he was a senator in the State Legislature, and presided over that body, he was a member of the House of Representatives and of the Senate of the United States until his death in 1814. He was also a member of the convention which formed the Constitution of the United States. His integrity and patriotism in all these highly honorable and responsible offices was never questioned for a moment.

But I must not suffer myself to be diverted from the ancestor, by the eminent characters and services of the great-great-grandsons of one branch of his numerous descendants. If that ancestor, one hundred and fifty years ago, could have been indulged with prophetic vision of the future, and could have beheld the various branches of his descendants, filling the highest offices in public life in his beloved and free country, it would surely have yielded him a pleasure than which there is none greater; it would have cheered his old age to the very verge of a most active, long and useful life.

The records of our town show the first John, during the latter half of our connection with Massachusetts, as the first among our able and respectable men. Accordingly, when disconnected, in the latter end of the reign of Charles II., and New Hampshire became a separate province under the immediate government of the Crown, John Gilman was selected to fill the office of councillor. The chief executive and legislative power was vested in that body. He had the honor to be suspended from that body by Governor Cranfield. The measure was honorable to Mr. Gilman, and excited no surprise in the public mind, or his own. When the courts and juries were packed, why should the Council, the supreme judiciary, escape? He died in 1708.

From his son descended the late Brigadier Gilman, whom some of you must well remember. In his day he was among the first men of our country; successively representative, speaker, at the head of the militia, and a member of the Supreme Executive Council, appointed by the Crown.

It would take too much of our precious time to enumerate all the names of this respectable family who have been able and useful ministers of the gospel, members of the Council, and judges in our highest courts of law, all of whom derived their descent from this single stem, and connected in various ways with the first families of the country. I will only add, that the Gilmans at all times, under the provincial, colonial and State governments, have been unwavering in their patriotism and love of country.

The Folsoms, a distinguished family, came early to us; probably they were settled awhile at Hingham, where they acted a distinguished part in a memorable dispute in that place. They have filled no small space in our annals. The late General Folsom was a most zealous patriot of the Revolution, and a member of the old Congress. In the French war of 1755, he distinguished himself as an officer under General Johnson, at the capture of the Baron Dieskau, near Lake George.

But one of the most celebrated names in our annals is that of HILTON. Edward Hilton is justly called the father of New Hampshire. He came from London, and settled in Dover in the spring of 1623. Here he resided from fifteen to twenty years, and then removed to Exeter. He died in 1671, leaving a large estate. His son Edward married the granddaughter of Governors Winthrop and Dudley. His son Winthrop, the fruit of that marriage, was better educated than most young men of the day, and was early introduced into public life. He was distinguished as a soldier,— "among the most *fearless of the brave*, the most adventurous of the daring." He was, of course, much in service, for he lived in stirring and troublous times, in the reigns of William and Anne. His uncle, the second Governor Dudley, was then governor of Massachusetts and New Hampshire, and had great confidence in him. Hilton was particularly obnoxious to the Indians, having been successful in many encounters with them. "His *sharp black eye* and his *long bright gun*" struck terror into the hearts of the savages. They long watched for an opportunity to cut him off on his plantation at the Newfields. He was largely concerned in the masting business; and in 1710, while so employed in that part of Exeter now Epping, his party was suddenly surprised, and Colonel Hilton fell at the first fire. He was then under forty, and a mandamus councillor, and died universally lamented. He was, indeed, an honest and brave man.

We have seen that Exeter was an independent State from the settlement till 1643. There was no connection between the four towns then, and for sixty years after, composing the whole State. Our records were then well kept, and the votes and orders well penned, perhaps with as much correctness as at this day. From these we are able to derive some information concerning the sentiments, temper, views and condition of the people. Their laws and regulations were few,—such only as their peculiar circumstances required.

The besetting sin of this day is, to multiply statutes; many of which are a dead letter, and some worse. It is many times the hardest task imposed on our judges, to find out their meaning. In making the attempt, we often find reason to believe that the makers did not understand their own meaning. The Combination was no doubt from Wheelwright's pen, and compares well with similar compositions before and since. It is the only act of incorporation our town has ever had. We are a self-created body politic.

We cannot now determine how many of our inhabitants were church members, certainly all were not. All who owned the soil participated in the government. The attempt to exclude all but church members is visionary and impracticable. It cannot last long, and generally the society is not a quiet one while it does last. The Massachusetts government of church members was in fact an aristocracy. With us the legislative power was conveniently exercised by the people. The executive and prudential functions were vested in a Ruler, with two assistants. The Ruler and the people were mutually bound by oaths in the form prescribed. Treason and sedition were punished with death. Texts of scripture were added to this law, which show the respect of the framers for the Jewish polity; a worse model, and one less adapted to their circumstances and condition, they could hardly have chosen. Our law makers had a most exalted opinion of the dignity of rulers. Nothing could exceed their zeal to preserve, pure and untarnished, their good name. Insolence to magistrates and contempt of authority were never suffered to escape severe punishment. As they are the mirrors in which the majesty of the people is beheld, this evinced the great respect the people had for themselves.

Our notions are quite different; we treat our rulers as if they were usurpers, and chose themselves instead of being the work of our own hands. They are the *butt*,—the target at which every man may safely thrust his poisoned arrows. Whether this tends to make them high-minded and faithful to us and our interests, I will not pretend to say. If they are, it is at a considerable sacrifice; for it has been observed that few men leave office with the same purity of character and reputation they enter upon it. What is the equivalent they receive for this? Calumny and slander of individuals were also made highly penal. Such prosecutions were, of course, frequent.

There were laws, also, for the protection of the few Indians that seem to have remained a short time among us. Trade with them in arms, ammunition and strong waters was strictly forbidden. If any purchase was made from the Indians, it belonged to the town, if they chose to have it. This was politic, and tended to prevent fraud. Town meetings were the subject of regulations, and all the voters required, under a penalty, to attend. Regulations were made for the organization of the militia,—the appointment of officers was, in the train band, subject to the approbation of the ruler. Laws also were made for the assessment and collection of taxes; and various and minute regulations respecting animals of all kinds. Even dogs did not escape their notice. The same may be said of fishing, and lumber, and laws were enacted to prevent waste and destruction of timber. There was a forecast on this subject hardly to have been expected in the midst of so great abundance. The highways and bridges came in for their share of attention. There was a law against setting fire to the woods; and, what we should hardly have expected, a law requiring trees overhanging the adjoining owner's land to be cut down, or lopped. And there was also a law, copied I believe from that of Massachusetts, about digging pits and leaving them open. The sale of wine and strong waters was subject to license. A few orders were also made regulating trials and judicial proceedings, and, as far as we can now judge, justice was impartially administered. A society more homogeneous in its elements, more affectionate and correct in morals, can hardly be imagined; and without these no new settlement can be made. Weston's company at Weymouth, and Morton's at Mount Wollaston, sufficiently establish the fact. The latter was for a while called the Merry Mount. Its appropriate name soon became that of Mount Misery.

As a mere physical being, man must be governed as animals are — by others; generally by force. As a moral being, he must be instructed in morals, and that can hardly be without religion. Our Constitution treats of them as existing only in union. A few settlers, unaccustomed to the ownership of wild lands, might be expected to err in the management and disposition of a large tract. They seem to have been troubled with no doubts about their title; and, in fact, never were disturbed. The same number of *the people* of 1835-6-7 would have made shipwreck at once. The whole territory would have been granted *out* in the first year. Here, more than one hundred years were occupied in the disposition of the lands. Every man had his share as he needed it. There was no speculation. Liberal grants were made to the mill owners, and a small rent reserved for the support of the ministry, while the timber lasted.

In May, 1643, there was a great scarcity of corn through the land, and it was severely felt here. Authority was given by the town to four of the most respectable inhabitants to search the houses, and where more was found than *they should judge necessary for the use of the family*, they were to take it at the usual price, and dispose of it among the poor for such pay as *they* could make. The measure was arbitrary, but justified by the occasion. If the laws and regulations of that day were not the best possible, I have no doubt they were much better than those framed by the Solomon of the age for his colonies.

Whatever may have been the case as regards Dover and Portsmouth, it does not appear that this settlement could not have continued many years in their independent state. They were the last to yield to Massachusetts, and seem never to have been favorites. The connection lasted thirty-six years, and the dissolution was not occasioned by any dissatisfaction on the part of the New Hampshire towns. A new county was created, called Norfolk, of which Exeter and Hampton were parts; Salisbury the shire town. The separation was in 1679, — twelve years before the disgraceful tragedy of 1691-2 was enacted. We thus narrowly escaped the shame and guilt of the prosecutions for witchcraft.

A very brief account will now be attempted of the ecclesiastical affairs of the town — chiefly of the first century. The church established here by Mr. Wheelwright was composed of men doubly tried in the fiery furnace of persecution. They suffered on his as well as on their own account. They came here because he came, and on his third banishment many removed with him. Indeed, the church was broken up — how short lived! — the first church established in New Hampshire! But I trust religion did not depart. Our settlers were religious men — Puritans. They could say, as Massachusetts did in that "transcript (as they called it) of loyal hearts to *the best of kings*," as they called Charles II., "We could not live without the public worship of God, without human mixture, and without a sinful yoke of conformities." They could not live without a preached gospel. They were small in number, and by no means in affluent circumstances, but they had lands to bestow. With these, and the lumber they sent to market,

A number of the inhabitants *early* expressed the desire to settle the aged Mr. Bachellor, lately dismissed at Hampton for irregular conduct; but the town took no part in the matter, and the friends of the measure luckily were unable to satisfy the civil authority in Massachusetts, without whose consent no church could be formed. The magistrate must be satisfied of their fitness for a church estate, and of the qualifications of the minister best adapted to their wants.

In May, 1646, Mr. Nathaniel Norcross was invited to settle here. This man was a *university* scholar. He declined, and probably soon returned to England. A year or two afterwards it was agreed to invite Mr. Tompson of Braintree, and the committee were instructed to consult with the Elders of Boston, Charlestown and Roxbury.

. . . .

Mr. Emerson of Rowley was soon after called. He declined. These failures,—doubtless blessings in disguise,—did not discourage our people. The committee, probably by the advice of the Elders they were required to consult, directed their course to Mr. Samuel Dudley, the eldest son of Governor Thomas Dudley. The son was born in England about 1606, and came to this country with his father in 1630. He was educated in England, but probably not at either of the Universities. It is not certain he was designed for the ministry. He had resided in Boston, Cambridge and Roxbury; probably teaching school, and perhaps occasionally preaching. He was admitted a freeman in 1640. He had served at one time as a lieutenant under Underhill. About 1633 he married Mary, the daughter of Governor Winthrop, who had followed her father hither. By her he had three sons and a daughter. As early as 1641 he removed to Salisbury, where his wife died. The daughter was afterwards married to Edward Hilton of Exeter, and Winthrop Hilton was the fruit of this marriage. We thus see the origin of the Christian names of Winthrop and Dudley, common in this vicinity. Mr. Dudley married a second and third wife, and had fifteen children. He represented Salisbury in the General Court in 1644. His youngest daughter was married to Kinsley Hall.

The old historian Johnson, in his *Wonder-Working Providence*, is of opinion that it is not easy to purge out the sour leaven of Antinomianism and familistical opinions, yet thinks that hard labor and industry, and he might have added poor living, has some tendency that way. Our society had taken a pretty strong dose of this harsh medicine. But if any should happen to remain, it was a politic step to choose for minister the son and son-in-law of such influential men as Dudley and Winthrop. The choice of Mr. Dudley was unanimous, in May, 1650. He could not regularly be ordained till a church was formed. In the meantime he was to do the duty of a minister, and was to have the house and lands, purchased of Mr. Wheelwright, as a parsonage, and forty pounds sterling a year. For such improvements as he should make he was to be compensated on his leaving, either by death, or "by some *more than ordinary call* of God other ways." The ordinary call guarded against was, no doubt, an invitation from a richer society with the offer of a higher salary. The salary was to be paid half yearly in corn and English commodities, at current price. Various modifications of the contract were afterwards made. The salary was, no doubt, inadequate even in that day, but it appears from the records that liberal grants of lands were made from time to time to Mr. Dudley and his numerous family. He was, doubtless, soon after ordained, and the connection a happy one. His learning and gifts seem to have satisfied his people, and it was not the fashion of that day to starve the minister to enrich the flock.

Mr. Dudley was well acquainted with the business of civil life; and as the town were wholly destitute at that time, and for nearly a century after, of that great blessing, a lawyer, Mr. Dudley's services were in demand; and the records and papers I have seen furnish abundant evidence that they were skilfully as well as usefully performed. He was, it would seem, a catholic, liberal and tolerant man — which was no small improvement on the *old stock.* His father was a violent persecutor of all who differed from him in their religious opinions, and one of the bitterest enemies, among the laity, of our Wheelwright, whom his son succeeded. He viewed toleration as among the seven deadly sins, and when he came to die I suppose he found no sin of this sort to trouble his conscience.

In 1656 Mr. Dudley was invited to settle in Portsmouth, at a salary (the money part) double that of Exeter. He seems at one time to have listened favorably to the proposal. Probably a new arrangement of his first contract prevented. Mr. Dudley died the tenth of February, 1683, at the age of seventy-seven.

On various occasions Mr. Dudley was honored with marks of confidence by the General Court of Massachusetts; and it gives me unfeigned pleasure to mention an act of kindness and confidence done to him by *his own people*. It appears from the records, that soon after his settlement a commissioner was appointed to vindicate, at the expense of the town, "the credit and reputation of Mr. Dudley against the speeches and *calumniations* of a certain person" (I believe a Hampton man). Mr. Dudley made the proper return for this kindness. In 1665, when we incurred the displeasure of Massachusetts, in consequence of a report that *some Exeter men* had signed a petition to the Royal Commissioner sent out by Charles II., which was supposed to reflect on the General Court, Mr. Dudley at once stepped forward and vindicated the men of Exeter, declaring them to be "*clever fellows*, and incapable of any such baseness."

The first house of public worship, of which we have any mention in our records, was built in 1650, and was *twenty feet square*. There was afterwards a gallery and lean-to added. It stood on the left-hand side of the road leading to Newmarket, in the northerly part of the present village, near to which Mr. Wheelwright lived. I am sorry the Norfolk records show it was not kept, small as it was, "in a proper state for Christians to worship in." This our disgrace is a matter of record.

Mr. John Clarke succeeded Mr. Dudley in 1698. He was much esteemed and beloved. He married the granddaughter of the celebrated Mr. Woodbridge, the first minister of Andover, and the great-granddaughter of the first Governor Dudley. Mr. Clarke died in 1705, greatly lamented, at the early age of thirty-five. One of his sons, Ward Clarke, was afterwards minister of Kingston. From one of his daughters was descended our late respected townsman, Ward Clarke Deane.

Mr. John Odlin was the successor of Mr. Clarke, and was settled in 1706. He married the widow of his predecessor, by whom, and a second wife, he left a numerous issue, one of whom, Woodbridge, became his colleague in 1743. The father died in 1754, at the age of seventy-two. The son married a daughter of Brigadier Gilman, and died in 1776, at the age of fifty-seven.

The new parish was formed about the time of the second Odlin's settlement. Their first minister was Daniel Rogers, a descendant in the seventh degree through a line of ministers of the gospel, except one, from the Rev. John Rogers, Prelate of St. Paul's, and Reader in Divinity, who was burnt at Smithfield in 1555, the first martyr of the bloody Mary's reign. Mr. Daniel Rogers was settled in 1748, and died in December, 1785, aged seventy-eight.

From this period our church history is fresh in the recollection of you all. In 1695 or 1696, the second-meeting house was erected on the spot where this house now stands. It is stated in the records as on the hill between the great fort and Nathaniel Folsom's barn. In 1728 the third house was erected on or near the site of the second. This house had double galleries, as most of you remember. A steeple and bell were added in 1739, and a new bell in 1762. The steeple was blown down in 1775, and rebuilt soon after.

Newmarket was set off in 1727, Epping and Brentwood in 1741, and Poplin from the latter in 1764.

An account of the early settlement of Exeter would be miserably deficient, without some notice of the sufferings of its inhabitants from Indian hostilities and depredations. The Indians, at and near Swamscot Falls, seem to have been few in number, and less savage in character than most others, and especially the Eastern tribes. The improvements of such as remained, after the settlement by the white men, were secured to them till they voluntarily made sale to our people, and they were fully protected in their persons and property. In 1643 great fears were entertained that the Indians in Rhode Island, Connecticut and other places were uniting in a conspiracy to expel the new comers from their country. They did not like us on trial quite so well as they had expected. This alarm occasioned the union of the New England colonies, which lasted till 1680. There continued to be, at intervals, fresh alarms, and much apprehension of open hostilities. Some depredations were *actually* committed on Connecticut river and other distant places. It excited, also, much apprehension in our quarter, that the New Hampshire Indians, about 1672, quitted their settlements here, and sat down on the Hudson, near Troy, in the neighborhood of fiercer tribes. These alarms were not without foundation, for, in 1675, thirty-seven years after the settlement here, King Philip's War began.

The scene was more than one hundred miles from us; but savages, you know, have swift feet,—and on every breeze was borne the war-whoop and it required little aid from the imagination to see the glittering tomahawk raised to strike the blow. Forty houses were consumed in Groton and murders committed in Chelmsford, and nearer still in Berwick, York, Winter Harbor, etc. But Exeter escaped actual hostilities till 1690. I have drawn a circle round our village as a centre, thirty-five miles in diameter. The number of killed and captives, within this circle, during a period of forty years, exceeded seven hundred. The actual sufferings of Exeter were in six years, between 1690 and 1710, when the much lamented Winthrop Hilton fell. The killed and captives were between thirty and forty. It is to be remembered, too, that our population was, from a variety of causes, then extremely small. Our settlement had advanced slowly. Among the names of the killed, as appears from our records, were Ephraim Folsom, Sr., and Goodman Robinson. The loss to the country of Colonel Hilton was irreparable. Berwick, Durham, Haverhill and Dover suffered the most. Unfortunately they and *we* lay directly in the track between the Eastern and Western Indians, who were constantly uniting with each other for mischief, and separating for safety;— always on the march.

You can conceive, or rather, you cannot conceive, the misery this dreadful state of things inflicted on our small plantation. We had three garrisons, the principal one was near this spot. Our people lived in continual fear of the savage enemy. Their home was in the garrison, and their cultivated fields became the fields of battle and of blood. There can be no true happiness where we do not sleep quietly in our own habitations, whether they be log huts or palaces. A garrison is, at best, but a miserable substitute; and who can sleep with the sword of Damocles suspended over his head by a brittle hair, ready to break at any moment?

The effect of this state of things on husbandry must have soon become manifest. There was but little cultivation in places remote from the garrisons. The planter, who is obliged to carry his musket with his hoe and axe, will soon find a diminished crop. Implements of husbandry and arms to defend our lives, do not go well together. War and population are in an inverse ratio to each other.

I must be allowed here to say, that our government in those days seems to deserve little credit for the management of their Indian affairs. The French seem to have understood the Indian character much better. It is no reproach to the Protestant religion that the Catholic is better adapted to the savage tribes. They understand it better than Calvinism.

On the subject of our husbandry and population, there are other things beside Indian hostilities to be considered. The uncertainty in our land titles had a most powerful and bad effect. Our first planters had nothing in their character in common with speculators or squatters. They had too much religion and morality for either; but they could not be insensible all the time to the claim of the Masons, and that it was regarded at home as the only legal title. This hung over them like an incubus, and retarded settlements and improvements of all kinds. Perhaps, too, we must allow something for bad government, till a short time before our separation from Great Britain.

At the end of the first century, the population of New Hampshire did not exceed ten thousand, and ours was the smallest of the four towns. We had but twenty qualified voters for the choice of representatives, as fixed by the Council in 1680. Exeter, in its ancient limits, in 1830 contained 7330 inhabitants.

I have left myself no room to speak on many subjects belonging to the occasion, connected as it is with the anniversary of our national independence. I must pass over, altogether, every thing that concerns the trade and business of our early days, — the manners, customs, dress, furniture, houses, style of living, of our early inhabitants; even of their early uniform and steady love of popular liberty and free institutions.

I could state from our records the votes and proceedings, showing how we were gradually prepared for the bold measure of fourth of July, 1776, — how hearty and unanimous we were in our obedience to the measures *recommended* by our wise men, though injurious to our particular interests; — such as the non-importation and non-consumption of articles before deemed necessaries of life; — how we preferred to put off the citizen, and put on the soldier; — how cheerfully we bore the dangers and hardships of the war, contracting heavy debts to raise men and supplies for the army.

If we were not foremost, there were none before us in our zeal for the early declaration and steady maintenance of the independence of our country. And when, at the close of the contest, and under an unexampled pressure of burthens, others were heard to murmur and complain, we were among those who quietly and peaceably submitted to the rule of law. Instead of joining in the clamor for paper money and tender laws, we remonstrated against them.

All these things, and many more of the kind, are they not written in the books of our records? which, if time permitted,

I would gladly recite to you on this occasion. In what regards schools and education, we have at all times aimed, as in all things else, at the useful rather than the showy.

. . . .

The public service of the day is now drawing to a close. We have spent the last hour sitting in judgment on our ancestors and predecessors, and we have found much to commend and little to condemn. I hope their shades now look down upon us and smile their approbation of the doings of the day. What will be the judgment of our posterity pronounced one hundred years hence upon us and our deeds?

This meeting is now adjourned, to meet here fourth of July, 1938. If the progress of the future shall keep pace with the past, the meeting will then be holden in a temple,— I hope a Christian one,— more lofty and spacious than this, as much more as this exceeds the first Exeter church of twenty feet square. The glory of the second temple will, doubtless, exceed that of the first; but the real greatness of a people depends little on the grandeur of their temples, or on the glory of external things, but on the culture of the mind, and the purity and graces of the heart.

We have this day passed the dividing line between ancestor and posterity, and must, henceforth, take our places with the people of the third century. Why then should not we rejoice, if the impartial judgment of the next centennial should award the prize of superior learning, more cultivated mind, and better taste in the fine arts, to the third century.

Let us, then, in this our new character, do all we can, that the superiority shall then be equally manifest in religion, virtue and moral worth.

GENEALOGICAL.

FAMILY REGISTERS.

FROM THE EXETER RECORDS.

Benjamin Abbot, b. Andover, Mass., 17 Sept. 1762, md. 1 Nov. 1791 Hannah Tracy Emery, b. Exeter 7 March 1771.
Their child, John Emery, b. 6 Aug. 1793.
Mrs. Hannah Tracy Abbot d. 6 Dec. 1793.
Benjamin Abbot md. (2d) 1 May 1798 Mary Perkins, b. Boston 24 May 1769.
Their children, Mary Perkins, b. 14 Feb. 1799; d. 23 June 1802.
    Elizabeth, b. 14 Nov. 1801.
    Charles Benjamin, b. 19 Jan. 1805.

Caleb G. Adams, b. 8 Jan. 1752, md. 8 Dec. 1774 Mary Folsom, dau. of Nathaniel Folsom, b. 25 Aug. 1751.
Their children, Dolly, b 7 Jan. 1776; d. 21 Jan. 1810.
    Nathaniel Folsom, b. 19 March 1782.

Samuel and Elizabeth Adams.
Their children, William Parker, b. Exeter 10 Oct. 1784; d. 18 Feb. 1827.
    Sarah, b. Durham 21 Nov. 1785; d. 22 Sept. 1842.
    Samuel Winborn, b. Durham 31 Oct. 1787; d. 1 Jan. 1831.
    Eliza, b. Durham 7 July 1789; d. Portsmouth 4 Aug. 1802.
    Jeremiah Parker, b. Durham 16 May 1791; d. Exeter 30 June 1822.
    Mary Sewall, b. Durham 21 Dec. 1794; d. Exeter 1 June 1817.
    Anna Matilda, b. Durham 30 June 1796.
    Catharine P., b. Durham 31 Aug. 1798; d. Exeter 4 March 1804.
    John, b. Portsmouth 21 Nov. 1800; d. Portsmouth, 17 May 1802.
    Nathaniel Sheafe, b. Exeter 28 Nov. 1802; d. Exeter 14 Sept. 1849.

Col. Samuel Adams d. Portsmouth of yellow fever 2 Aug. 1802.
Mrs. Elizabeth Adams d. Boston 23 March 1845.

Nathaniel Bartlett, Elizabeth Dennet; md. 23 Oct. 1739.
   Their children, Elizabeth, b. 7 Feb. 1741.
        Dorothy, b. 19 April 1742; d. April 1804 [wife of Eliphalet Hale].
        Mary, b. 17 Jan. 1743–4.
        Nathaniel, b. 9 Dec. 1745.
        Catharine, b. 21 Jan. 1748.
        Mary, b. 22 Oct. 1749.
        Priscilla, b. 16 June 1751.

John Bean.
   His children, John, b. 15 Aug. 1661; d. 18 May 1666.
        Daniel, b. 23 March 1662–3.
        Samuel, b. 23 March 1665–6.
        John, b. 13 Oct. 1668.
        Margaret, b. 27 Oct. 1670.
        James, b. 17 Dec. 1672.
        Jeremy, b. 20 April 1675.
        Elizabeth, b. 24 Sept. 1678.

Shackford Sewards Bennet, Mehitable Giddinge; md. 18 Dec. 1788.
   Their child, Charles, b. 20 March 1790.

Amos Blanchard's children b. in Exeter.
        Maria, b. 23 Jan. 1805.
        Luther, b. 12 March 1807.

Joseph Boardman, Lydia Gilman; md. 16 Sept. 1823.
   Their children, Lucy Maria, b. 29 July 1824.
        Juliana G., b. 6 Feb. 1827.
   Mrs. Lydia L. Boardman, wife of Joseph Boardman, d. 2 Feb. 1832.

Thomas Bond md. 23 May 1762 Mary Giddinge, dau. of Zebulon and Deborah Giddinge.
   Their children, Deborah, b. 2 July 1764.
        Abigail, b. 18 Dec. 1765.
        Mary, b. 10 May 1768.
   Widow Mary Bond d. 28 June 1790, in her 56th year.

Francis Bowden, son of Michael Bowden of Lynn, md. 18 Feb. 1734–5 Elizabeth Webster of Exeter, dau. of Thomas and Deborah Webster.
   Their children, Deborah, b. 7 Dec. 1735.
        Rebecca, b. 28 Sept. 1740.

Samuel Brooks, son of Samuel Brooks of Medford, md. 27 June 1751 Elizabeth Pike, dau. of William and Judith Pike, late of Exeter, said William being son of Joseph Pike, late of Barnstaple, Eng.
Their children, Oliver Pike, b. 16 Feb. 1751-2; d. 8 June 1755.
Samuel, b. 23 Oct. 1753; d. Natchez 1818.
Joseph, b. 17 April 1755; d. 1 Aug. 1775.
Elizabeth. b. 17 Jan. 1760; d. 19 Feb. 1760.
Elizabeth, b. 3 Dec. 1761.
William, b. 20 Jan. 1764.
Mary, b. 23 Dec. 1767.
Mrs. Elizabeth Brooks d. 7 March 1794.
Samuel Brooks md. (2d) Tirzah James, dau. of Dudley James.
Their children, Oliver, b. 9 Aug. 1796.
James Emery, b. 28 July 1799.
Elizabeth, b. 27 June 1801.
Samuel Brooks d. March 1807.
Mrs. Tirzah Brooks d. Philadelphia 25 Jan. 1831, aged 76.

Samuel Brooks, Jr., son of Samuel and Elizabeth Brooks, md. 14 Dec. 1779 Mary Giddinge, dau. of John and Mehitable Giddinge.
Their children, Dolly, b. 25 June 1781.
Betsey, b. 1 April 1783.

Isaiah S. Brown, b. Hampton Falls, md. 1 April 1842 Elizabeth Ann Fuller.
Their children, William H., b. 6 Feb. 1843; d. 16 Sept. 1843.
Abby J., b. 10 March 1844.

John Burley.
His children, Mary, b. 19 Oct. 1715.
John, b. 8 Dec. 1717.
Jacob, b. 23 Jan. 1720.

James Burleigh of Ipswich md. 14 Feb. 1780 Susanna Swasey of Exeter.
Their children, James, b. 7 Sept. 1784.
Susanna, b. 15 Feb. 1789.
Rufus, b. 21 March 1791; d. 26 March 1809.
William, b. 24 April 1794; d. 24 Aug. 1844.
Selina, b. 17 Dec. 1796.
Harriet, b. 14 July 1798.
James Burleigh d. very suddenly 3 April 1812.

Lieut. Jonathan Cass md. 20 Dec. 1781 Mary Gilman, dau. of Theophilus and Deborah Gilman.
Their children, Lewis, b. 9 Oct. 1827.
Deborah Webster, b. 16 April 1784.
George, b. 25 Jan. 1786; d. 1873.
Charles Lee, b, 15 Aug. 1787; d. Ohio 4 Jan. 1842.

Polly, b. 12 Aug. 1788.
John Jay, b. 28 Feb. 1791; d. 29 April 1792.

Samuel Chamberlain, son of John, of Charlestown, md. 30 Sept. 1783 Mary Tilton of Exeter.
Their children, Samuel Phillips, b. 24 Jan. 1786; d. Portsmouth 8 Feb. 1822.
Mary Parker, b. 15 Feb. 1788; d. 10 March 1817 [wife of Rev. Mr. Perry of Bradford].
Jacob Tilton, b. 6 Aug. 1791; d. at sea.
William Frederick Rowland, b. 29 April 1797.
Elizabeth Dorothy, b. 3 Jan. 1800.
Margaret Tilton, b. 4 Dec. 1801; d. 20 Jan. 1821.
Frances Groves, b. 23 April 1804.
Julia Ann, b. 4 Nov. 1806.
Edward Groves, b. 14 Nov. 1808.
Henry Phillips, b. 4 Sept. 1811.
Mrs. Mary Chamberlain d. 22 April 1826.

Frederick Charlton (Carlton), son of Theodore Charlton and Deborah, was b. 7 Oct. 1764; d. 2 Feb. 1766.

John Clark.
His children, Solomon, b. 19 Feb. 1672.
Ichabod, b. 25 Dec. 1674.
Mary, b. 18 June, 1678.

The Rev. John Clark, minister of Exeter, md. 19 June 1694 Elizabeth Woodbridge, dau. of Rev. Benjamin Woodbridge.
Their children, Benjamin, b. June 1695.
Nathaniel, b. 19 Dec. 1697.
Deborah, b. 3 Nov. 1699.
Ward, b. 12 Dec. 1703.
The Rev. John Clark d. 25 July 1705, aged 35.

Samuel B. Clarke, Philena F. Robinson; md. 27 Jan. 1847.
Their children, Frank Bartlett, b. 23 Nov. 1847.
Elizabeth F., b. 11 Jan. 1849.

William Henry Clark, son of Moses Clark and grandson of Dea. Moses Clark, md. 16 Feb. 1825 Sarah Hilton, dau. of Col. Richard Hilton of Newmarket.
Their children, Charles Edwin, b. 22 Nov. 1825.
William A., b. 30 Sept. 1827.
John M., b. 4 Jan. 1830.
George W., b. 27 Jan. 1832.
Edward H., b. 31 March 1834.
Martha J., b. 27 Jan. 1837.

Sarah E., b, 28 March 1840.
James A., b. 23 March 1843.

Eliphalet Coffin md. 11 Feb. 1710 Judith Noyes, widow of Parker Noyes and dau. of James Coffin of Newbury.
  Their children, Abigail, b. 13 Nov. 1711.
      Peter, b. 8 Dec. 1713.
      Judith, b. 22 Dec. 1717.
      Eliphalet, b. 5 Nov. 1719; d. 3 May 1722.
      Deborah, b. 11 Feb. 1720–1; d. 25 Sept. 1721.
  Capt. Eliphalet Coffin d. 16 Aug. 1736.

Jeremiah Connor, Anne Gove; md. 3 July 1696.
  Their children, Jeremiah, b. 18 April 1697; d. April 1722.
      Jonathan, b. 5 Dec. 1699.
      Philip, b. 3 March 1701–2.
      Samuel, b. 3 May 1704.
      Hannah, b. 20 Sept. 1706.
      Anne, b. 30 March 1709.
      Benjamin, b. 7 Sept. 1711.
Anne, wife of Jeremiah Connor, d. 12 Feb. 1722–3.

Cornelius Connor.
  His child, Moses, b. 6 Dec. 1707.

Jonathan Connor, son of Jeremiah and Ann Connor, b. 5 Dec. 1699, md. 23 Jan. 1723–4 Mehitabel, dau. of John and Mehitabel Thing; b. 19 July 1706.
  Their children, Anne, b. 15 Sept. 1724.
      Mehitabel, b. 5 Dec. 1726; d. 30 Aug. 1736.
      Jeremiah, b. 8 Feb. 1730–1.
      Jonathan, b. 14 Oct. 1737.
      Anne, b. 10 Dec. 1739.
      Mehitabel, b. 27 July 1742.
      John Thing, b. 16 July 1745.

Philip Connor, Maria Dudley; md. 14 May 1729.
  Their children, Maria, b. 22 Sept. 1731.
      Philip, b. 25 Sept. 1733.
      Joseph, b. 16 Feb. 1735.
      Joshua, b. 18 Aug. 1743.

Samuel Connor, b. 3 May 1704, md. 26 May 1726 Sarah Gilman, b. 18 Dec. 1708.
  Their children, Maria, b. 12 May 1728.
      Anna, b. 2 Nov. 1730; d. 22 Aug. 1742.
      Samuel, b. 2 April 1733.

Jeremiah, b. 18 Nov. 1736.
Joshua, b. 2 Aug. 1738; d. 16 Aug. 1742.
Sarah, b. 5 Dec. 1741; d. 22 Aug. 1742.
Eliphalet, b. 14 Aug. 1743.
Joseph, b. 7 Aug. 1746.
Mary, b. 3 Oct. 1750.

Benjamin Conner, Abigail Bartlett; md. 25 June 1734.
Their children, Abigail, b. 4 Feb. 1736.
Jeremiah, b. 26 March 1739.
Nathaniel, b. 8 April 1742.
Abigail, b. 31 May 1744.
Anne, b. 18 March 1746.
Benjamin, b. 28 March 1748.
Mary, b. 25 Jan. 1750.
Joseph Bartlett, b. 15 Oct. 1752.
Benjamin Conner md. (2d) Mary Leavitt, widow of Jeremiah Leavitt.
Their children, Huldah, b. 4 Dec. 1760.
Ephraim, b. 5 Feb. 1763.
Nathaniel, b.

Benjamin Conner d. 18 Oct. 1811, aged 101 yrs. 1 mo.
Mrs. Mary Conner d. 20 March 1820, aged 93 yrs. 6 mos.

Jeremiah Conner, son of Jonathan and Mehitable Conner, md. 1 Sept. 1754 Hannah Sanborn, dau. of Jabal and Abiah Sanborn,
Their children, Mary, b. 30 May 1755.
Dudley, b. 29 Nov. 1756.

Jonathan Conner, Jr., Mary Jewett; md. 10 March 1765.
Their children, Jesse, b. 18 Dec. 1765; d. Parsonsfield, Me., 8 Jan. 1841.
Elizabeth, b. 14 Aug. 1770; d. 25 Sept. 1770.
Daniel, b. 17 Aug. 1771; d. 23 Sept. 1863.
Nathaniel, b. 16 Oct. 1773; d. 5 July 1849.
Jedediah, b. 20 Oct. 1775; d. 28 Jan. 1838.
Mary, b. 11 Jan. 1778.
Jonathan, b. 29 April 1780; d. 7 Sept. 1780.
Eunice, b. 24 May 1782; d. 22 July 1867.
Mrs. Mary Conner, wife of Jonathan, d. 25 Nov. 1816.
Jonathan Conner d. 13 Nov. 1820, aged 83.

Nathaniel Conner and Tirzah (Lyford) Conner.
Their children, Charles, b. 17 May 1798; d. 29 July 1804.
Mary Ann, b. 17 Feb. 1800.
Oliver W., b. 25 Oct. 1801; d. 17 April 1840.
John L., b. 16 Aug. 1803; d. 24 Jan. 1847.
Charles, b. 30 Nov. 1805.

William, b. 23 Feb. 1808.
Jewett, b. 21 March 1810; d. 27 July 1810.
Thomas, b. 12 Aug. 1812.
Alfred, b. 12 Aug. 1814.
Freeman, b. 11 May 1816; d. 1 Jan. 1817.
Nathaniel, b. 13 May 1818; d. 24 Sept. 1818.
Mrs. Tirzah Conner d. 28 July 1828, aged 53 yrs. 4 mos.
Nathaniel Conner md. (2d) Mrs. Elizabeth Palmer 22 Jan. 1833.
Their child, Freeman, b. 22 March 1836.
Nathaniel Conner d. 5 July 1849, aged 76 years.

Charles Conner, b. 30 Nov. 1805, md 27 Aug: 1832 Mary Taylor Gilman, b. 26 May 1806.
Their children, Charles Gilman, b. 6 July 1833.
Edward Joseph, b. 11 Aug. 1835; d. 15 Aug. 1868.
Elizabeth Gilman, b. 13 Jan. 1838; d. 5 Sept. 1838.
William Thomas, b. 14 Feb. 1840; d. 1 Aug. 1841.
Daniel Gilman, b. 21 Jan. 1842.
Mary Elizabeth, b. 24 Aug. 1845.

Joseph Cram, son of Benjamin and Martha Cram, md. 7 June 1780 Ann Brown, dau. of Nathan and Ann Brown of Hampton Falls.
Their children, Benjamin, b. 10 March 1781.
Jacob, b. 9 Jan. 1783.
Anne, b. 8 March 1787.
Sarah, b. 18 Aug. 1790.

Robert Cross of Portland md. 5 Oct. 1807 Caroline Tilton, dau. of Dr. Joseph Tilton.
Their child, Caroline Matilda, b. 5 Aug. 1808; d. 16 Dec. 1808.

Isaac Currier md. 10 April 1760 Elizabeth Robinson, dau. of Ephraim and Mary Robinson.
Their children, Isaac, b. 10 Nov. 1760.
Ephraim, b. 9 Sept. 1762.

Rufus E. Cutler, son of Tobias Cutler, b. 2 March 1797, md. 12 March 1825 Anna Cilley, b. 2 Oct. 1796.
Their children, Sarah A., b. 22 June 1827; d. 6 May 1836.
Harriet F., b. 26 Feb. 1828.
Rufus E., b. 10 March 1830.
John G., b. 10 May 1832.
Eliza A. C., b. 4 Sept. 1834.

William B. Dana and Margaret Ann Dana.
Their child, Elizabeth Ann, b. 13 Aug. 1827.

William Davis and Elizabeth Davis.
   Their children, William Putnam, b. 11 Sept. 1823.
         Abigail Bartlett, b. 25 May 1825.

Dr. Thomas Dean md. 2 Oct. 1718 Deborah Clark, dau. of Rev. John Clark.
   Their children, John, b. 5 Sept. 1719.
         Jane, b. 20 June 1721.
         Thomas, b. 23 Dec. 1723.
         Elizabeth, b. 28 Dec. 1725.
         Deborah, b. 15 June 1728; d. 6 Sept. 1735.
         Mary, b. 17 July 1731.
         Abigail, b.

Col. John Dennet of Portsmouth md. 3 Feb. 1798 Elizabeth Lamson, dau. of Dr. John Lamson of Exeter.
   Their children, Elizabeth, b. 4 Feb. 1799.
         John Sherburne, b. 25 June 1800.

Jabez Dodge, son of Benjamin Dodge of Beverly, b. 15 Jan. 1747, md. 15 Aug. 1771 Lydia Philbrick, dau. of Benjamin Philbrick.
   Their children, Hannah, b. 22 Aug. 1772; d. 7 April 1787.
         Benjamin, b. 1 May 1774.
         Joseph, b. 9 May 1776.
         Jabez, b. 10 June 1778; d. 28 Jan. 1803.
         Lydia, b. 31 Dec. 1780; d. 7 Aug. 1847.
         Samuel, b. 26 Feb. 1783.
         Elizabeth, b. 28 April 1785.
         Hannah, b. 4 Aug. 1787; d. 28 Dec. 1787.
         Anne, b. 16 May 1789.
         John, b. 30 Nov. 1791; d. 31 Jan. 1865.
         Isaac, b. 13 April 1794.
   Mr. Jabez Dodge d. 11 April 1806.

John Dodge, b. Exeter 30 Nov. 1791, md. 1 Sept. 1816 Lydia Gerrish, b. Portsmouth 20 Aug. 1793.
   Their children, Caroline G., b. 11 July 1817; d. 24 July 1842.
         Frances M., b. 22 Sept. 1819.
         Lydia, b. 4 Jan. 1822.
         Harriet, b. 10 May 1824.
         Sarah E., b. 5 June 1827.
         Alexander, b. 16 Feb. 1830; d. 27 Oct. 1830.
         Elizabeth Hurd, b. 18 Dec. 1834; d. 8 April 1836.

Christian Dolhoof (Dolloff).
   His children, Mary, b. 17 Sept. 1667.
         John, b. 17 Feb. 1668–9.
         James, b. 25 Dec. 1670.

HISTORY OF EXETER.

Richard Dolloff.
   His children, Sarah, b. 10 Jan. 1702.
         Margaret, b. 18 March 1704.
         Abigail, b. 26 Feb. 1706.
         John, b. 20 April 1708.
         Jonathan, b. 17 Oct. 1710.

Samuel Dolloff.
   His children, Samuel, b. 1 Feb. 1703.
         Elizabeth, b. 1 March 1706.

Abner Dolloff and Miriam Dolloff.
   Their children, Mercy, b. 6 Dec. 1752, N. S.
         Richard, b. 2 Jan. 1755.
         David, b. 19 Jan. 1757.
         Phineas, b. 11 April 1759.

Jeremiah Dow, b. Salem, N. H., 9 April 1773, md. 27 Nov. 1797 Hannah Parker, b. Bradford, Mass., 18 Oct. 1776.
   Their children, Ednah Parker, b. 18 Jan. 1799.
         Retire Parker, b. 10 March 1801.
         Jeremiah, b. 5 Feb. 1803.
         Elizabeth, b. 11 Sept. 1806.
         Hannah Parker, b. 1 Nov. 1808.
         Mary Frances, b.
Jeremiah Dow d. 13 Oct. 1847.

Stephen Dudley, Sarah Gilman; md. 24 Dec. 1684.
   Their children, Samuel, b. 19 Dec. 1685.
         Stephen, b. 10 March 1687-8.
         James, b. 11 June 1690.
         John, b. 4 Oct. 1692.
         Nicholas, b. 27 Aug. 1694.
         Joanna, b. 3 May 1697.
         Treworthy, b.

Samuel Dudley, Hannah Colcord; md. 24 Nov. 1709.
   Their children, John, b. 22 June 1711.
         Samuel, b. 9 Feb. 1713-14.
         Hannah, b. 9 April 1716.
         Samuel, b. 26 Aug. 1718.

Joseph Dudley, Merriah Gilman; md. 26 Nov. 1724.
   Their child, Sarah, b. 25 Sept. 1725; d. 30 Aug. 1742.

Ezra S. Durgin of Greenland md. 7 Dec. 1837 Ruth Stevenson of Saco, Me.
   Their children, Mary E., b. Exeter 7 Nov. 1839.
         William E., b. Exeter 1 Oct. 1841.

Albert A., b. Exeter 13 June 1844; d. 19 Jan. 1845.
Ednah J., b. Exeter 10 Dec. 1845.

Eleazer Elkins.
His children, John, b. 3 Dec. 1674.
Samuel, b. 27 June 1677.

Epes Ellery, b. Gloucester, Mass., 29 Oct. 1769, md. 11 Sept. 1794 Anna Odell, b. 27 Feb. 1771; moved to Exeter in the year 1800.
Their children, Anna Mary, b. Gloucester 24 March 1796.
Epes, b. Gloucester 26 March 1800.
James, b. Exeter 26 June 1803.
George, b. Exeter 29 July 1804.
David Haraden, b. Exeter 11 Sept. 1805.
Nathaniel, b. Exeter 18 Jan. 1807.
William Parsons, b. Exeter 1 Dec. 1809.
Edward Turner, b. Exeter 16 June 1812; d. 11 March 1813.

Noah Emery, b. 10 Nov. 1748, md. 5 Dec. 1771 Jane Hale.
Their children, Mary, b. 24 Sept. 1772; d. 20 Sept. 1856.
Elizabeth, b. 15 Oct. 1774.
Nicholas, b. 4 Sept. 1776.
John, b. 29 Oct. 1780.
Noah, b. 30 Dec. 1782; d. at sea 1813.
Jane, b. 19 Oct. 1788; d. 19 June 1802.
Betsy Phillips, b. 15 Aug. 1794.

Noah Emery d. 6 Jan. 1817.
Mrs. Jane Emery d. 19 June 1813.

Jonathan Flood, Mary Foy; md.
Their children, Joseph, b. 15 Aug. 1768.
William, b. 2 Oct. 1773.

Mary Foulsam, dau. of Samuel Foulsam, b. 27 Sept. 1664.

John Foulsam d. 27 Dec. 1681.
Abigail Foulsam, dau. of John Foulsam, b. 23 Dec. 1676.

Samuel Foulsam, son of Nathaniel Foulsam, b. 18 Aug. 1679.

Peter Foulsam, Catherine Gilman; md.
Their children, Susanna, b. 27 Sept. 1704.
Elizabeth, b. 20 March 1706–7.
John, b. 14 March 1708–9.
James, b. 16 Oct. 1711.
Peter, b. 27 July 1714.
Catherine, b. 24 Jan. 1716–17.

Richard Calley and Catherine, Relict of Peter Folsom, md.

Daniel Folsom.
His children, Daniel, b. 27 Aug. 1739.
Ann, b. 2 April 1741.

Josiah Folsom, Martha Gold; md. May 1754.
   Their children, Jemima, b. 7 March 1755.
                  Martha, b. 7 Dec. 1756.
                  Mary, b. 17 March 1763.
                  Josiah, b. 1 June 1765.
                  Dudley, b. 15 Dec. 1767.
                  John, b. 26 June 1770.
                  Deborah, b. 12 May 1772.
Josiah Folsom, b. 25 Sept. 1725; d. 27 July 1820.

James Folsom, Elizabeth Webster; md. Dec. 1763.
   Their children, James, b. 12 Aug. 1765.
                  Elizabeth, b. 5 March 1767.
                  Thomas, b. 11 May 1769.
                  Nathaniel, b. 2 April 1771.
                  Peter, b. 22 Feb. 1775; d. June 1817.
                  Polly, b. 12 July 1776.
                  John, b. 5 Nov. 1779.

Samuel Folsom, Elizabeth Emery; md. 30 April 1780.
   Their children, Anne, b. 4 Feb. 1781.
                  Samuel, b. 7 June 1783.
                  Betsy, b. 26 March 1785.
                  Joanna, b. 25 June 1787.
Samuel Folsom d. 22 May 1790.
Mrs. Elizabeth Folsom d. Sept. 1805.

James Folsom, b. 22 July 1756, md. 2 Dec. 1784 Mary Folsom, b. 17 March 1763.
   Their children, James, b. 24 Nov. 1785.
                  Josiah, b. 2 March 1787.
                  Mary, b. 13 Feb. 1789.
                  Lydia B., b. 30 April 1791.
                  Martha N., b. 23 July 1793.
                  Sarah R., b. 12 Aug. 1795.
                  Frances, b. 12 Feb. 1798.
                  Peter G., b. 1 Nov. 1799.
                  Nancy Y., b. 16 March 1802.
                  Nicholas D., b. 10 June 1805.
                  Lavina, b. 30 March 1808.

James Folsom, Sarah Gilman; md.
   Their children, Sophia, b. 26 Feb. 1787.
                  Joseph Gilman, b. 7 Dec. 1788; d. Sept. 1813.
                  Sarah, b. 1 Nov. 1790.
                  Henry, b. 5 Oct. 1792.
                  Charles, b. 24 Dec. 1794.
                  Anne, b. 12 Feb. 1797.

Mary Gilman, b. July 1799.
William, b. 12 July 1803.
Mrs. Sarah Folsom d. 11 July 1805.

Josiah Folsom, b. 2 March 1787, md. 11 Oct. 1812 Mary Woodruff, b.
Feb. 1783.
Their child, Mary W., b. 9 Oct. 1813.
Mrs. Mary Folsom d. 22 March 1814.
Josiah Folsom md. 22 May 1825 Mary James, b. 12 Jan. 1798.
Their children, Elizabeth S., b. 14 May 1826.
Josiah J., b. 1 Aug. 1827.
Ebenezer, b. 25 Oct. 1828.
Mary, wife of Josiah, d. 12 April 1847.

Henry F. French md. Chester 9 Oct. 1838 Anne Richardson, dau. of Ch.
Jus. William M. Richardson.
Their children, Harriette Van Mater, b. Chester 29 Sept. 1839.
William Merchant Richardson, b. Exeter 1 Oct. 1843.
Sarah Flagg, b. Exeter 14 Aug. 1846.
Daniel Chester, b. Exeter 20 April 1850.
Mrs Anne R. French d. Exeter 29 Aug. 1856.

John George, Elizabeth Towle; md. 24 Sept. 1734.
Their children, Sarah, b. 16 Oct. 1736.
Josiah, b. 19 Sept. 1738.
John, b. 23 March 1739–40.
Olive, b. 27 Feb. 1741–2.

Zebulon Giddinge md. 12 Oct. 1724 Deborah Webster, dau. of Thomas
Webster.
Their children, Pernal, b. 28 Sept. 1725.
John, b. 11 Sept. 1728.
Abigail, b. 30 Oct. 1729; md. 10 Sept. 1756 Philip, son
of John Babson.
Zebulon, b. 7 Feb. 1732–3; d. 9 March 1759.
Mary, b. 23 Oct. 1734.
Eliphalet, b. 17 Sept. 1736.
George, b. 17 July 1738.
Nathaniel, b. 26 Dec. 1744.
Deborah, b. 2 Feb. 1746–7.
Mrs. Deborah Giddinge d. 2 Feb. 1767, aged 64 yrs. 2 mos. 22 days.
Zebulon Giddinge md. (2d) 8 May 1773 Mrs. Joanna Cottle, widow of
Joseph Cottle of Newburyport. She d. 21 July 1773, aged 62 yrs. 5 mos.
Zebulon Giddinge d. 30 May 1789, aged 86 yrs. 20 days.

John Giddinge, Mehetabel Gilman; md. 20 Nov. 1751.
Their children, Mary, b. 13 July 1752.

Dorothy, b. 15 Oct. 1758.
Mehetabel, b. 1 Feb. 1764.
Deborah, b. 30 May 1770.

Zebulon Giddinge, son of Zebulon and Deborah Giddinge, md. 30 May 1754 Lydia Robinson, dau. of Ephraim and Mary Robinson.
Their children, Lydia, b. 14 Aug. 1755.
Deborah, b. 22 Dec. 1756.
Zebulon, b. 14 Oct. 1758.
Zebulon Giddinge d. at Cape Cod 9 March 1759, aged 26 yrs. 19 days.
Mrs. Lydia Giddinge md. (2d) 4 May 1761 Samuel Gilman, and d. Dec. 1791. [Gilman Genealogy says 4 July 1778.]

Eliphalet Giddinge, Anne Lovering; md. 18 Dec. 1760.
Their children, Zebulon, b. 26 Sept. 1761; d. March 1769.
Nathaniel, b. 6 Feb. 1765; d. March 1803.
Pernal, b. 23 Sept. 1768; d. Dec. 1768.
Joseph, b. 11 July 1770 ; d. 10 Sept. 1770.
Eliphalet, b. 12 July 1773; d. 19 Aug. 1773.
Anne, b. 15 Feb. 1775; d. 15 Aug. 1776.
Lucretia, b. 10 Dec. 1776; d. 13 May 1777.
Anne, b. 22 Oct. 1779; d. June 1811 [the wife of Rev. W. F. Rowland].
Mrs. Anne Giddinge d. 7 March 1809 in the 70th year of her age.
Eliphalet Giddinge md. (2d) 16 Feb. 1812 widow Ann Lyford.
Ann Giddinge, 2d wife of Eliphalet Giddinge, d. 12 Aug. 1818.
Col. Eliphalet Giddinge d. 30 June 1830, aged 94 yrs.

Nathaniel Giddinge, son of Zebulon and Deborah Giddinge, md. 6 Jan. 1769 Mary Elwell, dau. of Zebulon and Lucy Elwell.
Their children, Abigail, b. 17 Oct. 1769; d. June 1776.
Lucy, b. 22 Feb. 1774.
Nathaniel, b. 17 April 1784.

Nathaniel Giddinge, son of Eliphalet Giddinge, md. Anne Folsom, dau. of Gen. Nathaniel Folsom.
Their children, Eliphalet, b. 13 Dec. 1783.
Dolly, b. 9 Jan. 1785.
Polly, b. 15 Aug. 1786.
Harriet Amelia, b. 25 Feb. 1789.
Nathaniel, b. 1 Aug. 1791; d. June 1814 at Newburyport, unmd.
Mrs. Anne Giddinge d. 27 April 1794, aged 32 yrs. 8 mos. 27 days.

Nathaniel Giddinge md. (2d) 6 Nov. 1794 widow Peggy Warren.
Their children, Ann Elizabeth, b. 20 Feb. 1796.
Joseph, b. 9 Feb. 1798; d. 15 Aug. 1798.

John Gilman, Elizabeth Treworthy; md. 30 June 1657.
  Their children, Mary, b. 10 Sept. 1658.
        James, b. 6 Feb. 1659-60.
        Elizabeth, b. 16 Aug. 1661.
        John, b. 6 Oct. 1663.
        Catherine, b. 17 March 1664-5; d. 2 Sept. 1684.
        Sarah, b. 25 Feb. 1666-7.
        Lydia, b. 12 Dec. 1668.
        Samuel, b. 30 March 1671; d. Aug. 1691.
        Nicholas, b. 26 Dec. 1672.
        Abigail, b. 3 Nov. 1674.
        John, b. 19 Jan. 1676-7.
        Deborah and Joanna (twins), b. 30 April 1679; Deborah
          d. 30 Sept. 1680; Joanna d. 24 Dec. 1720.
        Joseph, b. 28 Oct. 1680.
        Alice, b. 23 May 1683.
        Catherine, b. 27 Nov. 1684.
  Mrs. Elizabeth Gilman, wife of John Gilman, d. 8. Sept. 1719.
  John Gilman d. 24 July 1708.
  Joanna, dau. of John and Elizabeth Gilman, was twice md., first to Capt. Robert Coffin, son of Peter Coffin, then to Henry Dyer.

Moses Gilman.
  His children, Jeremy, b. 31 Aug. 1660.
        Elizabeth, b. 19 April 1663.
        James, b. 31 May 1665.
        John, b. 7 June 1668.
  Byley Dudley and Elizabeth Gilman md. 25 Oct. 1682.

Edward Gilman.
  His children, Edward, b. 20 Oct. 1675.
        Antipas, b. 2 Feb. 1677; d. the 27th.
        Maverick, b. 11 April 1681.

Nicholas Gilman, Sarah Clark; md. 10 June 1697.
  Their children, Samuel, b. 1 May 1698.
        John, b. 24 Dec. 1699.
        Daniel, b. 28 June 1702.
        Nathaniel, b. 2 March 1704.
        Nicholas, b. 18 Jan. 1707-8.
        Josiah, b. 25 Feb. 1709-10.
        Sarah, b. 25 June 1712.
        Treworthy, b. 15 Oct. 1714.
        Elizabeth, b. 5 Nov. 1717.
        Joanna, b. 14 July 1720.

John Gilman, Elizabeth Coffin; md. 5 June 1698.
  Their children, Joanna, b. 20 Sept. 1700.

HISTORY OF EXETER. 17

        Elizabeth, b. 5 Feb. 1701–2.
        Peter, b. 6 Feb. 1704–5.
        Abigail, b. 19 Aug. 1707.
        Robert, b. 2 June 1710.
        John, b. 5 Oct. 1712.
        Joanna, b. 27 Oct. 1715.
Elizabeth, wife of John Gilman, d. 10 July 1720.

Samuel Gilman, Abigail Lord; md. 2 Sept. 1719.
  Their children, Samuel, b. 20 May 1720.
        Nicholas, b. 6 Oct. 1722.
        Robert, b. 30 Aug. 1724.
        Sarah, b. 1 Dec. 1725; d. 8 Dec. 1725.
        Abigail, b. 8 April 1727; d. 4 Aug. 1729.
        Daniel, b. 30 Jan. 1728; d. Nov. 1728.
        John, b. 24 May 1730; d. 24 Sept. 1735.

John Gilman, Mary Thing; md. 8 Nov. 1720.
  Their children, John, b. 23 Dec. 1721; d. March 1721–2.
        John, b. March 1722–3; d. April 1723.
John Gilman d. 6 Dec. 1722.

Peter Gilman md. 8 Dec. 1724 Mary Gilman, Relict of John Gilman.

Daniel Gilman, Mary Lord; md. 2 Sept. 1724.
  Their children, Mary, b. 12 Nov. 1725.
        John, b. 17 Sept. 1727.
        Daniel, b. 18 Nov. 1729.
        Nicholas, b. 21 Oct. 1731.
        Sommersby, b. 1733.
Mary Gilman, wife of Daniel, d. 22 March 1735–6.

John Gilman, Elizabeth Hale; md. 29 Dec. 1720.
  Their children, Nicholas, b. 20 Jan. 1721–2.
        Samuel, b. 20 April 1723.
        Sarah, b. 23 July 1724.
        Nathaniel, b. 18 June 1726.

Nicholas Gilman, Mary Thing; md. 22 Oct. 1730.
  Their children, Bartholomew, b. 26 Aug. 1731.
        Nicholas, b. 13 June 1733.
        Tristram, b. 24 Nov. 1735.
        Joseph, b. 5 May 1738.
        Josiah, b. 2 Sept. 1740; d. 8 Feb. 1801.
        John, b. 10 May 1742; d. 8 June 1752.
Mrs. Mary Gilman, wife of Nicholas, d. 22 Feb. 1789, aged 76 yrs. 1 mo. 9 days.

Daniel Gilman, Abigail Sayer; md. 23 Sept. 1736.
Their child, Abigail, b. 21 Sept. 1738.

Nathaniel Gilman, Sarah Emery; md. 16 Sept. 1725.
Their children, Tabitha, b. 21 July 1726.
Sarah, b. 14 Feb. 1727–8; d. July 1729.
Nathaniel, b. 9 April 1730.
Sarah, b. 5 Sept. 1733; d. 6 Jan. 1735–6.
Elizabeth, b. 14 Dec. 1735; d. 1 Jan. 1735–6.
Joanna, b. 23 Aug. 1737.

Treworthy Gilman, Susanna Lowe; md. 17 June 1736.
Their child, Treworthy, b. 23 May 1738.

Josiah Gilman, Abigail Coffin; md. 2 Dec. 1731.
Their children, Abigail, b. 12 Aug. 1732; d. 17 Jan. 1797.
Eliphalet, b. 22 March 1734; d. 29 Sept. 1735.
Peter, b. 14 March 1735–6.
Judith, b. 11 Jan. 1737–8; d. Nov. 1815.
Josiah Gilman d. 1 Jan. 1793.

Joshua Gilman, Meriah Hersey; md. Nov. 1702.
Their children, Mariah, b. 2 Oct. 1704.
Sarah, b. 20 Dec. 1708.
Hannah, b. 14 Sept. 1712.
Joshua, b. 2 Feb. 1716.

Andrew Gilman, Joanna Thing; md. 27 Jan. 1714–5.
Their children, Abigail, b. 19 April 1717.
Jeremiah, b. 3 June 1719.
Joanna, b. 6 Dec. 1721.
Deborah, b. 28 Jan. 1723–4.
Mary, b. 31 Aug. 1727.
Joanna Gilman, wife of Andrew, d. 16 Nov. 1727.

Andrew Gilman, Bridget Hilton; md. 3 April 1729.
Their children, Winthrop, b. 14 Feb. 1730–1.
Elizabeth, b. 30 Nov. 1732.
Anna, b. 23 Oct. 1734.
Andrew, b. 28 Oct. 1736; d. 28 Jan. 1736–7.
Bridget Gilman, wife of Andrew, d. 10 Nov. 1736.

Jonathan Gilman, Jr., Elizabeth Sanburn; md. 12 May 1737.
Their children, Elizabeth, b. 19 Aug. 1741.
Hannah, b. 8 Dec. 1742.

Nathaniel Gilman, b. 10 Nov. 1759, md. 29 Dec. 1785 Abigail Odlin.
Their children, Frances, b. 11 Sept. 1787; d. 7 April 1821.
Abigail, b. 10 Dec. 1789.

HISTORY OF EXETER. 19

        Nathaniel, b. 13 Nov. 1793.
        Ann, b. 10 Aug. 1796; d. 2 Jan. 1827.
  Mrs. Abigail Gilman d. 10 Aug. 1796.
Nathaniel Gilman md. (2d) 13 Dec. 1796 Dorothy Folsom of Portsmouth.
  Their children, Nicholas, b. 2 Sept. 1799; d. 23 Jan. 1840.
        Samuel T., b. 17 May 1801; d. 23 Jan. 1835.
        Daniel, b. 28 June 1804; d. 4 Dec. 1841.
        John T., b. 9 May 1806.
        Charles E., b. 12 Feb. 1808; d. 23 Jan. 1840.
        Mary O., b. 9 March 1810.
        Joseph T., b. 12 Oct. 1811.

Samuel Gilman, b. 15 March 1752, md. 30 May 1774 Sarah Hall.
  Their child, Josiah H., b. 15 Aug. 1775; d. 24 Dec. 1775.
  Mrs. Sarah Gilman d. 18 Jan. 1776.

Samuel Gilman, Martha Kinsman; md. 16 Sept. 1779.
  Their children, Samuel, b. 1 July 1780; d. 28 Aug. 1781.
        Samuel K., b. 31 Jan. 1782; d. 1 Oct. 1795.
        Jonathan, b. 27 April 1784; d. 7 June 1809.
        Martha, b. 20 Feb. 1786; d. 22 Feb. 1786.
        John K., b. 14 Aug. 1787.
        Martha, b. 21 Feb. 1789.
        Lydia, b. 11 May 1791; d. 2 Feb. 1832.
        Hannah, b. 15 May 1794.
        Samuel K., b. 2 May 1796.
  Mrs. Martha Gilman d. 19 Oct. 1809.
  Samuel Gilman d. 29 Aug. 1838.

Samuel Gilman, Jr., Lydia Giddinge; md. 4 May 1761.
  Their children, Tabitha, b. 7 April 1762; d. 2 May 1837.
        Frederick, b. 28 Jan. 1764; d. 1798.
        Elizabeth, b. Jan. 1765; d. May 1766.
        Robert, b. May 1768; d. Nov. 1769.
        Peter, b. 9 Feb. 1771; d. in France.
        Arthur, b. 28 Oct. 1773.
        Henry, b. 30 Aug. 1777.
  Samuel Gilman, Jr., d. July 1778.

Jonathan Gilman, Elizabeth Leavit; md. 16 Jan. 1723–4.
  Their children, Alice, b. 15 April 1725.
        Elizabeth, b. 5 June 1727.
        Robert Briscoe, b. 21 June 1729.
        Alice, b. 11 July 1731.
        Jonathan, b. 18 May 1733.
        Hannah, b. 29 Dec. 1734.

Mary, b, 7 May 1737.
John, b. 28 Nov. 1738.
Robert Briscoe, b. 27 Nov. 1740.
Hannah, b. 20 Nov. 1743.
Dorothy, b. 18 July 1746.

Josiah Gilman, Sarah Gilman; md. 30 Nov. 1763.
  Their children, John Phillips, b. 7 Nov. 1764.
                Sarah, b. 8 July 1766.
                Mary, b. 10 May 1768.
                Elizabeth, b. 11 June 1770.
                Bartholomew, b. 9 Nov. 1772.
                Tabitha, b. 13 Aug. 1775; d. 11 Oct. 1777.
                Anne, b. 9 Sept. 1777; d. Aug. 1823.
                Rebecca, b. 29 Sept. 1780; d. 21 Oct. 1815.
                Catherine, b. 3 Sept. 1782.
                Charlotte, b. 17 July 1785.
  Sarah Gilman, wife of Josiah, d. 26 July 1785.

Joseph Gilman, Rebecca Ives; md. 21 Sept. 1763.
  Their children, Robert Hale, b. 6 Dec. 1764.
                Benjamin Ives, b. 29 July 1766.

Thomas Gilman, Elizabeth Rogers; md. 31 Dec. 1772.
  Their children, Whittingham, b. 30 Nov. 1773.
                Thomas, b. 25 Aug. 1775.
                John, b. 4 Dec. 1777.
                Nathaniel Clark, b. 20 Dec. 1779.
                Henry, b. 28 Aug. 1782.
                Elizabeth, b. 5 May 1786.
                Abigail Bromfield, b. 14 Feb. 1789.
Thomas Gilman was b. 15 June 1747.
Elizabeth Rogers, b. 22 Feb. 1754.
Mrs. Gilman d. 8 Feb. 1791.

Samuel Gilman, Mary Blodget; md. 30 Nov. 1780.
  Their child, Elizabeth Blodget, b. 16 Dec. 1781.

John Ward Gilman, b. 9 May 1741, md. 3 Dec. 1767 Hannah Emery, b. 24 June 1745.
  Their children, Stephen, b. 27 Aug. 1768; d. 9 Oct. 1849.
                Ward, b. 18 Dec. 1769; d. 14 Dec. 1821.
                Jane, b. 14 Sept. 1771; d. 3 April 1778.
                Allen, b. 16 July 1773.
                Deborah Harris, b. 26 May 1775; d. July 1864.
                John, b. 8 April 1777; d. 11 April 1777.
                Hannah, b. 6 May 1778.
                Jane, b. 23 July 1780.

John, b. 15 Aug. 1782; d. 10 Sept. 1822.
Samuel, b. 4 Jan. 1785.
Joseph, b. 4 March 1789; d. 18 Aug. 1805.
Elizabeth, b. 29 May 1791.
Mrs. Hannah Gilman d. 22 June 1802.
John W. Gilman d. 16 June 1823.

Joseph S. Gilman, Elizabeth Odlin; md.
Their children, Elizabeth Ann Taylor, b. 5 July 1797; d. 9 Jan. 1882.
Mary Taylor, b. 26 May 1806; d. 13 July 1877.
Joseph S. Gilman d. 26 Sept. 1826.
Elizabeth Gilman d. 1 April 1840.

Eliphalet Gilman, Sarah Conner; md. 10 May 1778.
Their children, Sally b. 17 Aug. 1779.
Harriot, b. 8 June 1783.
Patty, b. 15 April 1786.
Eliphalet, b. 19 May 1788.
Betsey, b. 13 Dec. 1789.
Dorothy Bartlett, b. 11 May 1792.
Mrs. Sarah Gilman d. 1796.
Eliphalet Gilman d. 24 Nov. 1822.

John Phillips Gilman, Elizabeth Hanson; md. 7 Dec. 1788.
Their children, Sarah, b. 4 May 1790.
Elizabeth, b. 20 June 1794.
Mary Ann, b. 4 Aug. 1797.

Benjamin Clark Gilman, Mary Thing Gilman; md. 24 June 1788.
Their children, Phillips, b. 8 April 1789; d. 1836.
Clarissa, b. 14 Nov. 1790.
Charles William, b. 10 Feb. 1793.
William Charles, b. 2 May 1795.
Serena, b. 10 Sept. 1797.
Samuel Frederick, b. 2 Dec. 1799; d. 5 Dec. 1816.
Arthur Frederick, b. 23 Dec. 1801.
Rufus King, b. 18 March 1804; d. 8 Feb. 1828.
Mrs. Mary Thing Gilman d. 7 Dec. 1841.

Nicholas Gilman, Sarah Hudson Mellen; md. 8 Sept. 1823.
Their children, Augustus Henry, b. 9 Aug. 1824.
Henry Augustus, b. 9 Aug. 1824; d. 25 Aug. 1824.
Sarah Almira, b. 29 Aug. 1827.

Alexander Gordon, said to be Scotch soldier of Charles II., taken prisoner by Parliamentarians, sent to America 1651, md. 1663 Mary Listen, dau. of Nicholas Listen of Exeter.

Their children, Elizabeth, b. 23 Feb. 1664.
　　　　　　　Nicholas, b. 23 March 1665-6.
　　　　　　　Mary, b. 22 May 1668.
　　　　　　　John, b. 26 Oct. 1670.
　　　　　　　James, b. 22 July 1673.
　　　　　　　Alexander, b. 1 Dec. 1675.
　　　　　　　Thomas, b. 1678.
　　　　　　　Daniel, b. 1682.
Alexander Gordon, Sr., d. Exeter 1697.

Thomas Gordon, son of Alexander Gordon, md. 22 Nov. 1699 Elizabeth Harriman of Haverhill, Mass.
Their children, Timothy, b. 19 Aug. 1700; d. in infancy.
　　　　　　　Thomas, b. 24 Aug. 1701.
　　　　　　　Diana, b. 26 Jan. 1703.
　　　　　　　Daniel, b. 1 Dec. 1704.
　　　　　　　Abigail, b. 28 May 1707.
　　　　　　　Benoni, b. 1709.
　　　　　　　Timothy, b. 22 March 1716.
　　　　　　　James, b.
　　　　　　　Hannah, b.
　　　　　　　Nathaniel, b. 25 March 1728.
　　　　　　　Benjamin, b.
Thomas Gordon, Sr., d. 1762.

Timothy Gordon, son of Thomas Gordon, md. 1748 Maria Stockbridge of Stratham.
Their children, Abraham, b.
　　　　　　　Mary, b. 22 Oct. 1753.
　　　　　　　Hannah, b. 4 Dec. 1756.
　　　　　　　Timothy, b. 30 Dec. 1757.
　　　　　　　Maria, b.
　　　　　　　Elisha, b. 11 April 1763.
　　　　　　　Emma, b.
　　　　　　　John, b.
Timothy Gordon, Sr., d. 1796.

Timothy Gordon, son of Timothy Gordon and a Revolutionary soldier, md. 23 Jan. 1782 Lydia Whitmore of Newbury, Mass.
Their children, William, b. 17 May 1783.
　　　　　　　Lydia, b. 11 Dec. 1785.
　　　　　　　John S., b. 23 Dec. 1786.
　　　　　　　Charles, b. 5 Sept. 1788.
　　　　　　　Nathaniel, b. 7 Dec. 1792.
　　　　　　　Timothy, b. 10 March 1795.
　　　　　　　Ebenezer, b. 28 Feb. 1797.
　　　　　　　Harriet, b. 4 Aug. 1804.
Timothy Gordon d., a pensioner of the United States, 1836.

Nathaniel Gordon, son of Thomas Gordon, md. 1756 Elizabeth Smith of
Exeter.
Their children, Elizabeth, b. 19 Feb. 1758.
Nathaniel, b. 1760.
John, b. 19 June 1765.
Mary, b. 23 April 1774.
Nathaniel Gordon, Sr., d. 24 March 1789.

Nathaniel Gordon, son of Nathaniel Gordon, Sr., md. 14 Nov. 1790 Sarah
Shepard, dau. of Rev. Samuel Shepard of Brentwood.
Their children, Frances, b. 22 Sept. 1793.
Sophia, b. 6 April 1795.
Two others d. in infancy.
Nathaniel Gordon md. (2d) 30 Aug. 1808 Mary Robinson.
Their child, Mary Elizabeth, b. 22 Aug. 1809.
Nathaniel Gordon d. 30 Dec. 1815.

John Gordon, b. 19 June 1765, md. 8 Aug. 1790 Mary Batchelder of Kingston, b. 4 Jan. 1764.
Their children, Nathaniel Batchelder, b. 2 March 1791.
John T., b. 27 Oct. 1792.
Stephen Leavitt, b. 25 April 1795.
George William, b. 8 Feb. 1801.

John S. Gordon, son of 2d Timothy Gordon of Newbury, Mass., md. 11
March 1814 Frances Gordon, dau. of 2d Nathaniel Gordon.
Their children, Frances Sarah, b. 7 Feb. 1815.
Sarah Frances, b. 2 July 1817.
Nathaniel, b. 26 Nov. 1820.
Mary D., b. 24 Dec. 1827.
John S. Gordon d. 1845.

Nathaniel Gordon, son of John S. Gordon, md. 26 Dec. 1853 Alcina Eveline Sanborn, dau. of Moses Sanborn of Kingston.
Their children, Moses Sanborn, b. 14 Dec. 1854.
John Thomas, b. 4 May 1857; d. in infancy.
Nathaniel, b. 24 March 1859.
Frances Eveline, b. 29 March 1861.
Mary Alcina Elizabeth, b. 7 March 1864.
Mrs. Alcina Gordon d. 14 April 1864.
Nathaniel Gordon md. (2d) 4 June 1868 George Anne Lowe, dau. of John
Lowe, Jr., and Sarah Anne (Simes) Lowe.

James Gordon, son of Jonathan Gordon, b. 5 July 1725, md. Elizabeth Gilman, dau. of Cartee Gilman, b. 14 April 1727.
Their child, William, b. 13 March 1753.

Mrs. Elizabeth Gordon d. and James Gordon md. (2d) Elizabeth Dolloff, dau. of Samuel Dolloff, b. 6 Feb. 1728.
Their children, Joseph, b. 25 Aug. 1759.
Esther, b. 24 March 1764.
Lydia, b. 1 Nov. 1766.

Benjamin Gordon, b. 20 Sept. 1798, md. 27 April 1823 Frances Folsom, b. 12 Feb. 1798.
Their children, Calvin Folsom, b. 3 Feb. 1824.
Frances Mary, b. 17 June 1827.
Benjamin Franklin, b. 8 May 1830.
Lydia Ann, b. 2 April 1833.

Francis Grant, son of James and Betsey Grant, md. 2 Nov. 1822 Mary W. Carleton, dau. of Theodore and Mary Carleton.
Their children, Daniel Francis, b. 13 Feb. 1824.
Betsey, b. 15 April 1825; d. 12 March 1856.
Charles, b. 26 March 1827.
Mary Frances, b. 27 March 1829.
Mrs. Mary W. Grant d. 13 June 1831.
Francis Grant md. (2d) 3 May 1832 Abby J. Pike, dau. of Elias Pike of Newburyport.
Their children, George Augustus b. 28 Oct. 1833; d. 3 Nov. 1846.
Ann Burley, b. 24 Nov. 1835; d. 27 May 1858.
Abby Jane, b. 1 Dec. 1839.
William, b. 15 Sept. 1841; d. 13 Aug. 1854.
James Henry, b. 20 Nov. 1843; d. 10 Sept. 1847.
Elias Pike, b. 21 Aug. 1848; d. 18 Sept. 1848.
Mrs. Abby J. Grant d. 25 Oct. 1848, aged 41 yrs. 8 mos.

Josiah Hall md. 10 May 1719 Mrs. Hannah Light, widow of John Light.
Their children, Kinsley, b. 11 Nov. 1720.
Josiah, b. 21 Oct. 1721.
Dudley, b. 20 Jan. 1722–3.
Samuel, b. 20 April 1724.
Abigail, b. 20 June 1726.
Paul, b. 18 April 1728.
Josiah Hall, Sr., d. 16 Oct. 1729.

Kinsley Hall, Jr., and Mary Hall.
Their children, Henry Ranlet, b. 20 July 1812.
Catharine Norris, b. 10 July 1814.
Charles Edward, b. 14 June 1816.
Henry R.
Benjamin E.

John Harris md. Mary Hall, dau. of Capt. Kinsley Hall, b. 18 Aug. 1678.
Their child, Mary, b. 25 July 1707; md. Herbert Waters.
Mrs. Mary Harris d. 2 March 1707–8.

Samuel Hatch of Wells, Mass., b. 14 July 1774, md. 14 May 1797 Mary
Gilman, b. 2 April 1777.
Their children, Daniel G., b. 3 Aug. 1798.
    Samuel, b. 19 May 1800; d. 26 Oct. 1801.
    Samuel, b. 9 Dec. 1802.
    Joseph W., b. 29 Sept. 1804; d. 20 Feb. 1822.
    William, b. 27 July 1806.
    Johnston, b. 17 July 1808; d. 7 April 1809.
    Johnston, b. 14 July 1810.
    Charles H., b. 14 July 1812; d. 21 June 1825.
    Mary Ann, b. 19 April 1815; d. 22 Feb. 1828.
    Edward W. b. 16 Aug. 1818.

C. W. Hervey, b. Newburyport, Mass., md. 9 Nov. 1836 Eliza H. Lunt, b. Portsmouth.
Their children, Francis H., b. 20 Feb. 1838.
    Charles W., b. 10 Dec. 1839; d. 8 Oct. 1846.
    Louis P., b. 18 April 1848.

John Holland, Bethiah Magoon; md. 1 Jan. 1730-1.
Their children, Annis, b. 5 Oct. 1731.
    John, b. 14 June 1733.
    Mary, b. 8 July 1735.
    Robert, b. 5 Jan. 1737-8.
    Martha, b. 25 Dec. 1739.
    Bethiah, b. 25 March 1742.

Daniel Holman and Hannah Holman.
Their children, Daniel, b. 3 April 1715.
    Hannah, b. 3 April 1715.

Francis James.
His children, Kinsley, b. 19 Feb. 1708-9.
    Dudley, b. 5 Nov. 1713.
    Francis, b. 16 Feb. 1714-5.

Kinsley James md. 5 Nov. 1735 Mary Hilton, dau. of Dudley and Mercy Hliton, b. 22 Oct. 1709.
Their children, Elizabeth, b. 15 Sept. 1736; d. 27 July 1737.
    Mary, b. 10 Dec. 1737.
    Lois, b. 30 Sept. 1739; md. Theophilus Lyford, and (2d) Gideon Colcord.
    Kinsley.
    Ann, md. Thomas Lyford, and (2d) Col. Eliphalet Giddings.

Dudley James, son of Francis and Elizabeth James, md. 5 March 1740-1 Mary Light, dau. of John and Hannah Light.
Their children, Abigail, b. 8 June 1742.
    Dudley Hall, b. 8 Sept. 1744; d. 8 May 1765.

Dudley James, Tirzah Emery; md. 12 July 1753.
Their children, Tirzah, Caleb, b. 15 May 1755.
    Joshua, b. 31 Aug. 1757; d. 4 Oct. 1825.
    Mary, b. 2 Dec. 1759.
Mrs. Tirzah James d. 2 Dec. 1759.
Dudley James d. 24 Feb. 1776, aged 62 yrs. 3 mos. 19 days.

Samuel Jones md. Mary Lunt, dau. of Henry Lunt of Newbury.
Their children, Henry, b. 7 July 1731.
    Abigail, b. 3 Oct. 1733.
    Susannah, b. 22 June 1739.

Joel Judkins, Mary Bean; md. 1674.
Their children, Job, b. 25 Jan. 1674–5.
    Sarah, Hannah, b. 13 Nov. 1678. (?)
    Mary, b. 7 Nov. 1678. (?)

John Kimball, Abigail Lyford; md. 14 Feb. 1722–3.
Their children, Judith, b. 11 June 1724.
    Abigail, b. 18 Aug. 1726.
    John, b. 20 July 1728; d. 1 July 1738.
    Joseph, b. 29 Jan. 1730–1.
    Lydia, b. 4 Oct. 1733.
    Thomas, b. 10 March 1735–6.
Mrs. Abigail Kimball d. 12 Feb. 1737–8.
John Kimball md. (2d) 18 Sept. 1740 Sarah Wilson, dau. of Dea. Thomas Wilson.
Their children, Sarah, b. 24 Aug. 1741.
    John, b. 25 Nov. 1742.
    Noah, b. 31 May 1744.
    Olive, b. 12 July 1746.
    Nathaniel, b. 16 Oct. 1747.
    Moses, b. 13 May 1749.
    Caleb, b. 16 July 1750.
    Thomas, b. 7 Feb. 1751–2.
    Jesse, b. 16 Nov. 1753.

Thomas Kimball, Elinor Dudley; md. 25 Sept. 1746.
Their children, Elinor, b. 10 June 1747.
    Dudley, b. 13 March 1748–9.

John Kimball, b. 1 Jan. 1771, md. 8 Sept. 1825 Sarah Hodgkins, b. 7 Dec. 1792.
Their children, Mehetabel Ann, b. 12 Sept. 1826.
    John Henry, b. 8 Dec. 1827.
    Mary Abigail, Samuel Ney, b. 31 May 1831.
    Robert Porter, b. 18 Oct. 1833.

Mrs. Sarah Kimball d. 9 Aug. 1848.
John Kimball d. 29 Oct. 1849.

Nathaniel Ladd, Elizabeth Gilman; md. 1678.
Their children, Nathaniel, b. 6 April 1679.
    Elizabeth, b. 6 Jan. 1680.
    Mary, b. 28 Dec. 1682.
    Lydia, b. 27 Dec. 1684.
    Daniel, b. 18 March 1686-7.
    John, b. 6 July 1689.
    Anna, b. 25 Dec. 1691.
Nathaniel Ladd was mortally wounded in a fight with the Indians at Macquoit, and d. 11 Aug. 1691.

Eliphalet Ladd, son of Josiah Ladd, b. 10 June 1744, md. 14 May 1772 Abigail Hill, dau. of Elisha Hill of Berwick, b. 7 Sept. 1750.
Their children, Sally, b. 6 July 1774; d. 12 Oct. 1798 [wife of Rev. W. F. Rowland].
    Betsey, b. 12 Aug. 1776; d. Portsmouth 18 Nov. 1821 [wife of Capt. Samuel Chauncy].
    William, b. 10 May 1778; d. Portsmouth 1841.
    Henry, b. 30 April 1780; d. Portsmouth 1842.
    Charlotte, b. 9 April 1782.
    John Alexander, b. 9 May 1784.
    Caroline, b. 4 May 1786
    Sophia, b. 12 Feb. 1788.

Joseph Lamson md. 7 Sept. 1747 Pernal Giddinge, dau. of Zebulon Giddinge.
Mrs. Pernal Lamson d. 21 Feb. 1809, aged 83 yrs. 5 mos.

Benjamin Lamson, b. 11 Nov. 1740, md. 14 March 1765 Martha Dennis, b. 27 Aug. 1735, and removed from Ipswich.
Their children, Stephen, b. 24 Jan. 1766.
    Thomas Dennis, b. 27 April 1767; drowned 17 July 1784.
    Sarah, b. 24 Dec. 1768.
    Joseph, b. 11 Jan. 1771.
    Martha, Lydia, b. 8 June 1773; Martha d. 16 Feb. 1788; Lydia d. 7 Nov. 1790.
    Eunice, b. 4 Dec. 1775; d. 14 Sept. 1777.
    Clarissa, b. 29 Aug. 1780; d. 11 March 1824 [wife of George Sullivan].
Benjamin Lamson d. Concord July 1817.

Joseph Lamson, Jr., md. 29 April 1769 Rachel Sanborn of Hampton Falls.
Their children, Joseph, b. 8 Nov. 1770; d. 1793.
    Mehetable, b. 6 Oct. 1773.
    Polly, b. 9 Aug. 1775; d. 28 July 1792.
    Caleb, b. 29 June 1778.

Asa, b. 7 Jan. 1783.
John, b. 8 Dec. 1785.

Stephen Lamson, son of Benjamin Lamson, b. 24 Jan. 1766, md. 22 Aug. 1793 Lucy Kendall of Ipswich, Mass., b. 4 Oct. 1774.
Their children, Lydia, b. 24 May 1794.
Ephraim Kendall, b. 4 Jan. 1797.
Susannah Kendall, b. 26 June 1801.
Lucy, b. 2 Nov. 1805.
Ruth Kendall, b. 14 Aug. 1808.
Elizabeth Phillips, b. 7 May 1810.

Jotham Lawrence of Epping md. 21 Feb. 1803 Deborah Robinson of Exeter.
Their child, William F., b. 22 March 1804.
Mrs. Deborah Lawrence d. 1 April 1804.
Jotham Lawrence md. (2d) 25 Dec. 1810 Caroline Conner.
Their children, Alexander H. b. 18 June 1812.
Caroline F. b. 18 April 1815.
Fitz Henry, b. 20 June 1817.
Ellen C., b. 25 May 1819.
Samuel C., b. 24 July 1823.
Elizabeth D. C., b. 24 Aug. 1825.
Sarah C., b. 20 Nov. 1828.
Lydia L., b. 28 July 1831.

Samuel Leavitt.
His children, John, b. 2 July 1665.
Mary, b. 13 Jan. 1666-7.
Elizabeth, b. 9 Jan. 1668.
Hannah, b. 15 Aug. 1669.
Samuel, b. 25 Dec. 1671.
Jeremy, b. 6 April 1673.

Moses Leavitt, Dorothy Dudley; md. 26 Oct. 1681.

James Leavitt, Alice Gilman; md. Nov. 1702.
Their children, Elizabeth, b. 31 March 1704.
Mary, b. 5 June 1706.
Samuel, b. 14 June 1709; d. 29 June.
Joanna, b. 22 Feb. 1710–11.
Alice, James, b. 14 Aug. 1713.
Sarah, b. 14 Sept. 1715.
Josiah, b. 22 Nov. 1718; d. 25 Dec. 1718.
John, b. 23 May 1720; d. 1 March 1721.
Mrs. Alice Leavitt d. 2 June 1721.

Benjamin Leavitt, Abigail Batchelor; md.
Their children, John Blake, b. 1 April 1782; d. 4 Oct. 1859.

HISTORY OF EXETER. 29

    Jeremiah, b. 9 Jan. 1785; d. 9 Feb. 1827.
    Benjamin Dow, b. 16 April 1787.
    Abigail Thorndike, b. 12 May 1790.
    Mary Fogg, b. 1 July 1792.
    Daniel Sherburne, b. 1 Feb. 1795.
    Hannah Taylor, b. 17 April 1797.
    Frances, b. 9 Oct. 1799.
 Benjamin Leavitt d. 23 Aug. 1826.

John Light md. 8 Nov. 1705 Hannah Lord, dau. of Robert Lord of Ipswich.
 Their children, Abigail, b. about 1 Nov. 1706; d. Jan. 1706–7.
    Hannah, b. 23 Dec. 1707.
    Dorothy, b. 6 Aug. 1709.
    Robert, b. 12 Sept. 1711.
    John, b. 3 Feb. 1713.
    Joseph, b. Feb. 1715; d. March.
    Ebenezer, b. 20 April 1716.
    Mary b. 10 March 1718.

Jonathan Lord, Hannah Light; md. 14 Oct. 1731.

John Lord, son of Thomas Lord of Ipswich, md. 31 Oct. 1712 Abigail Gilman, dau. of Moses and Anne Gilman, b. 24 July 1693.
 Their children, Anne, b. 18 Dec. 1713.
    John, b. 23 Oct. 1716; d. 21 Nov. 1716.
    Mary, b. 16 Jan. 1717; d. 28 Jan. 1717.
    Abiel [dau.], b. 9 March 1719; d. 26 March 1719.
    Robert, b. 23 March 1720; d. April 1720.
    John, b. 1 Aug. 1721; d. 15 Aug. 1721.
    Edmund, b. 22 Sept. 1722; d. Oct. 1722.
    Abigail, b. 15 Jan. 1723–4.
    John, b. 27 March 1725.
    Robert, b. 22 Oct. 1726; d. Sept. 1727.
    Elizabeth, b. 6 Nov. 1727; d. 1 Sept. 1735.
    Jonathan, b. 7 Nov. 1729; d. 22 April 1730.
    Eliphalet, b. 18 Aug. 1731.
    Robert, b. 8 April 1733.
    Samuel, b. 5 May 1735; d. 23 Oct. 1735.
    Elizabeth, b. 22 Jan. 1736–7.

Robert Lord, b. 16 Aug. 1735, md. 20 Oct. 1757 Elizabeth Lougee.
 Their children, Robert, b. 17 Aug. 1758; d. 16 April 1759.
    William, b. 11 Dec. 1760.
    Mary, b. 22 Oct. 1762.
    Hannah, b. 23 Sept. 1765.
    Robert, b. 24 Jan. 1768.
    Betty, b. 27 Sept. 1770.

Daniel Loverain, Mary Sylla; md. 25 Dec. 1724.

Their children, Abigail, b. 15 Dec. 1725.
John, b. 10 Jan. 1726-7.
Mrs Mary Loverain d., and Daniel Loverain md. (2d) Mary Smith.
Their children, Mary, b. 13 April 1729.
Ebenezer, b. 5 April 1731.
Moses, Miriam, b. 1 July 1735.
Hannah, b. 31 March 1738-9.

Benjamin Lovering, Jr., son of Benjamin Lovering, md. Sally Swasey, dau. of Edward Swasey.
Their children, Sally W., b. 4 Feb. 1807.
Elizabeth, b. 11 Aug. 1808.
Benjamin, b. 22 Sept. 1809.
Mary Ann, b. 23 Oct. 1811.
Olivia, b. 9 June 1814.
Caroline, b. Feb. 1817.
Charles E. b. 1819.

Thomas Lyford, Anne Conner; md. 5 Dec. 1728.
Their children, Abigail, b. 6 Aug. 1741.
Thomas, b. 12 May 1743.
Elizabeth, b. 1 June 1745.

Thomas Lyford, Jr., Anne James; md.
Their children, James, b. 14 Feb. 1764; drowned 13 Aug. 1789.
Anne, b. 6 June 1767.
Deborah, b. 3 May 1769.
Molly, b. 13 Feb. 1771.
Abigail, b. 12 Dec. 1772; d. 1870.
Tirzah, b. 31 March 1775; d. 28 July 1828.
John, b. 1 March 1777; d. 1803.
Betty, b. 16 March 1779.
Lois, b. 10 June 1781.
Liberty, b. 6 July 1783.
Thomas, b. 30 Nov. 1786; d. 2 April 1870.
Thomas Lyford d. 27 July 1787, aged 44 yrs. 2 mos.
Mrs. Lyford (afterwards wife of Col. Eliphalet Giddings) d. 12 Aug. 1818.

Henry Magoon and Elizabeth (Listen) Magoon.
Their children, John, b. 21 Oct. 1658.
Alexander, b. 6 Sept. 1661; md. Sarah Blake 7 Dec. 1682.
Mary, b. 9 Aug. 1666.
Mrs. Elizabeth Magoon d. 14 June 1675.

Mark Malloon and Abigail Malloon.
Their children, John, b. July 1732.
Nathaniel, b. 7 April 1733.
Jonathan, b. June 1735.
Josiah, b. July 1737.

Rev. Isaac Mansfield of Exeter md. 9 Nov. 1776 Mary Clap, dau. of Nathaniel Clap of Scituate.
Their children, Theodore, b. 5 May 1778.
     Isaac, b. 6 Dec. 1786.

William Meeds, Mary Dorin ; md.
Their children, William, b. 3 Dec. 1766 ; d. New York 15 Oct. 1782.
     Benjamin, b. 31 Sept. 1768 ; d. Oct. 1815.
     Abigail, b. 23 May 1771 ; d. 20 Sept. 1799.
     Stephen, b. 13 May 1774 ; d. 5 Feb. 1775.
     Stephen, b. 14 May 1776 ; d. May 1800.
     Horatio Gates, b. 4 May 1778 ; d. Dec. 1816.
     Polly, b. 2 July 1781.
     William, b. 8 Dec. 1783.
     John, b. 5 Aug. 1789 ; d. 28 Dec. 1824.
William Meeds, Sr., d. 20 March 1816.
Mrs. Mary Meeds d. 7 Jan. 1827, aged 82 yrs.

Daniel Melcher, b. Portsmouth 15 Jan. 1799, md. 27 April 1823 Nancy Y. Folsom, b. Exeter 16 March 1802.
Their children, Daniel Flagg, b. 22 July 1824.
     James Folsom, b. 1 Aug. 1826.
     Charles Henry, b. 23 Feb. 1829.
     Gershom Flagg, b. 22 May 1831.
     Mary Olivia, b. 27 Sept. 1833.
     William Perry, b. 6 Sept. 1836 ; d. 3 June 1838.
     William P., b. 16 Feb. 1839.
     Ann Elizabeth, b. 30 Oct. 1841.
     Lewis Cass, Edwin Forrest, b. 28 Sept. 1844.

Jeremiah L. Merrill, b. 4 Jan. 1819, md. 29 Nov. 1841 Mary E. Moses, b. 25 June 1813.
Their child, Joseph W., b. 25 March 1843.

Lewis Mitchell, b. Limington, Me., 6 April 1805, md. 11 Nov. 1829 Frances D. Wedgwood, b. 22 Sept. 1807.
Their children, Lewis F., b. 6 May 1831 ; d. 30 Aug. 1839.
     Oriana, b. 8 Feb. 1834.
     Isaac H., b. 2 May 1836 ; d. 21 June 1845.
     Ellen E., b. 4 Nov. 1838.
     Fanny D., b. 8 June 1841.
     Harriet M., b. 1 May 1844.
     Isaac L., b. 26 Aug. 1846.
     Emma E., b. 12 July 1849.
     George W. E., b. 18 Feb. 1853.

Rev. John Moody md. 5 April 1730 Ann Hall, dau. of Capt. Edward Hall.
Their child, Mary, b. 4 March 1730-1.

William Moore and Elizabeth Moore.
 Their children, John, b. 25 Dec. 1789.
  Ann, b. 23 April 1792; d. 21 Sept. 1841.
  Elizabeth, b. 10 Feb. 1795.
  Nicholas G., b. 9 Oct. 1797; d. 18 Oct. 1795. (?)
  Nicholas, b. 30 May 1800; d. Oct. 1825.
  William, b. 27 June 1803; d. 19 May 1843.
  Catharine, b. 16 Feb. 1806.
  Charles, b. 20 Feb. 1810; d. 26 June 1814.

Theodore Moses, b. 20 Sept. 1766, md. Stratham Nov. 1789 Deborah Emery, b. 22 Nov. 1769.
 Their children, Theodore B., b. 15 Nov. 1790.
  John F., b. 10 Sept. 1792.
  Susan T., b. 27 Aug. 1794.
  Samuel T., b. 20 Jan. 1798; d. 26 Oct. 1842.
  G. W., b. 7 Jan. 1800.
  Charles C. P., b. 17 May 1802.
  William P., b. 9 Aug. 1804.
  A. A., b. 2 Oct. 1807.
  A. T., b. 11 Feb. 1810.
  Elizabeth M., b. 25 June 1813.
  Mary E., b.

John F. Moses, Mary Smith Pearson; md. Dec. 1815.
 Their children, James Colman, b. 21 Nov. 1817.
  Deborah, b. 16 Oct. 1819.
  John Lees, b. 9 May 1822.
 Mrs. Mary S. Moses d. 10 Aug. 1844, aged 54 yrs. 2 mos.

Thomas Mudget, Elizabeth Smith; md. 2 May 1723.
 Their children, Sarah, b. 3 March 1725.
  Thomas, b. 11 Nov. 1727.
  Nicholas, b. 1 Jan. 1730–31.

Josiah Nelson, b. 23 Nov. 1758, md. Mary Robinson, b. 9 April 1758.
 Their children, Sally, b. 19 July 1781; d. April 1805.
  John, b. 30 April 1783.
  Polly, b. 4 Aug. 1785; d. Nov. 1801.
  Caroline, b. 7 Oct. 1788; d. 11 Aug. 1837.
  Sophia, b. 31 March 1791; d. 2 March 1819.
  Ann, b. 27 Jan. 1795.
  Josiah, b. 19 July 1797.
  Horatio G., b. 31 March 1800; d. Fayetteville, N. C., 1831.
  Samuel, b. 9 Dec. 1804.
 Josiah Nelson, Sr., drowned in river just below mill, Aug. 1812.
 Widow Mary Nelson d. 1 Nov. 1840, aged 82 yrs.

Nicholas Norris.
His children, Moses, b. 14 Aug. 1670, md. 4 March 1691-2 Ruth Folsom.
Jonathan, b. 5 March 1673.
Abigail, b. 29 Nov. 1675.
Sarah, b. 10 April 1678.
James, b. 16 Nov. 1680.
Elizabeth, b. 4 Sept. 1683.

Dr. Nathan North and Nancy North.
Their children, Alfred, b. 10 March 1807.
Henry, b. 25 July 1811; d. 31 Dec. 1814.
Charles, b. 5 Oct. 1813; d. 25 Sept. 1814.
Dr. North moved from Exeter into Vermont June 1815.

Mark Nutter.
His children, Henry, b. 6 April 1786.
John, b. 25 April 1789.
Mark, b. 25 Oct. 1792.
Mary, b. 24 Aug. 1796.

Joseph Odlin, Harriet A. Downs; md. 8 Sept. 1846.
Their child, Charles Cushing, b. 31 Oct. 1847.

Thomas Odiorne, b. 1 Dec. 1733, md. 31 Jan. 1762 Joanna Gilman, b. 30 Sept. 1739.
Their children, Deborah, b. 11 May 1763; d. 1814.
George, b. 15 Aug. 1764.
Jane, b. 3 March 1766; d. 5 April 1766.
John, b. 21 March 1767; d. 17 May 1824.
Thomas, b. 26 April 1769.
Joanna, b. 6 Feb. 1771.
Ebenezer, b. 7 May 1773; d. 23 Dec. 1817.
Elizabeth, b. 7 Jan. 1775.
Ann, b. 9 Oct. 1778; d. 1830.
Thomas Odiorne d. 28 April 1819. Mrs. Joanna Odiorne d. 5 April 1829.

George Odiorne, b. 15 Aug. 1764, md. 4 Oct. 1787 Dolly Tufts of Newburyport, Mass., b. 22 March 1767.
Their child, Samuel Tufts, b. 27 May 1793.
Mrs. Dolly Odiorne d. 8 Sept. 1793.

John Odiorne, Polly Thayer; md. 6 March 1800.
Their children, Mary Jane, b. 21 Nov. 1800.
Anna Maria, b. 13 Oct. 1802; d. 25 Oct. 1803.
Henry Moore, b. 26 Aug. 1804; d. 14 Sept. 1805.
Joanna, b. 30 Dec. 1806; d. 26 Jan. 1842.
Richard Thayer, b. 14 March 1808; d. 17 Oct. 1808.
Ann Moore T., b. 10 Dec. 1814.

HISTORY OF EXETER.

Rev. John Odlin, Elizabeth Clark; md. 21 Oct. 1706.
  Their children, John, b. 7 Nov. 1707.
         Elisha, b. 16 Nov. 1709.
         Dudley, b. 22 Sept. 1711.
         Samuel, b. 14 Aug. 1714; d. 31 Aug. 1714.
         Woodbridge, b. 28 April 1718.
  Mrs. Elizabeth Odlin d. 6 Dec. 1729.
Rev. John Odlin, Mrs. Elizabeth Briscoe; md. 22 Sept. 1730.

Elisha Odlin, Judith Pike; md. 1 Nov. 1731.
  Their children, John, b. 4 Sept. 1732.
         Winthrop, b. 23 Oct. 1734.
         William, b. 7 Feb. 1737–8.
         Elisha, b. 28 April 1741; d. 8 Dec. 1741.
         Anna, b. 10 Jan. 1743–4.

John Odlin, Jr., Mrs. Alice Leavitt; md. 27 Feb. 1734–5.
  Their children, Elizabeth, b. 7 Feb. 1735–6; d. 16 Feb. 1735–6
         Abigail, b. 11 Feb. 1736–7; d. 12 Aug. 1747.
         Elizabeth, b. 30 April 1739.
         Sarah, b. 14 March 1740–1; d. 3 Sept. 1747.
         Alice, b. 5 Oct. 1743; d. 1814.
         John, b. 27 Dec. 1745; d. 3 Sept. 1747.
         Abigail, b. 28 May 1748; d. Dec. 1816.
         Samuel, b. 18 Dec. 1750.

Rev. Woodbridge Odlin, Mrs. Abigail Strong; md. 23 Oct. 1755.
  Their children, Elizabeth, b. 6 Aug. 1756; d. 21 Aug. 1756.
         Dudley, b. 13 Aug. 1757.
         Woodbridge, b. 26 Sept. 1759.
         Peter, b. 25 March 1762.
         Elizabeth, b. 8 April 1764.
         Abigail, b. 26 Aug. 1766; d. 19 July 1768.
         Abigail, b. 21 Oct. 1768; d. 10 Aug. 1796.
         John, b. 2 Dec. 1770; lost at sea.
         Mary Ann, b. 24 Sept. 1772.

Dudley Odlin, Elizabeth Gilman; md. 14 Feb. 1782.
  Their children, Abigail, b. 5 Feb. 1783.
         Betsy, b. 14 Dec. 1784; d. Oct. 1785.
         Woodbridge, b. 4 June 1786; d. 11 June 1809.
         Peter, b. 25 Dec. 1787.
         Caroline, b. March 1790; d 17 March 1817.

William Odlin, b. 16 Feb. 1767, md. Betsey Leavitt, b. 21 Dec. 1769.
  Their children, James, b. 9 Jan. 1792.
         William, b. 10 Jan. 1793.

Thomas, b. 16 Nov. 1794; d. 5 March 1826.
Joseph and Benjamin (twins), b. 16 Jan. 1797.
Betsey, b. 23 Nov. 1799.
Woodbridge, b. 9 May 1805.
Mary Ann, b. 29 July 1810.

James Odlin, Martha H. Osborne; md. 27 Oct. 1816.
Their children, James William, b. 3 Nov. 1817.
George Osborne, b. 10 Sept. 1819; d. 10 Nov. 1820.
George Osborne, b. 26. Aug. 1823.
Joseph Edwin, b. 20 June 1825.
Martha Jewitt, b. 21 July 1828.

Nathaniel Page md. 21 March 1809 Charlotte Tilton, dau. of Dr. Joseph Tilton, b. 1 June 1779.
Their children, Charlotte Dorothy, b. 20 Sept. 1809.
Joseph Tilton, b. 29 Nov. 1811.
Mrs. Charlotte Page d. 17 Aug. 1813.

William Parker and Elizabeth Parker.
Their children, Nathaniel, b. East Kingston 22 Oct. 1760; d. 2 April 1812.
John J., b. Exeter 17 Nov. 1770; d. 5 Oct. 1831.
Mary Sewall, b. Exeter, 12 Feb. 1772.
Samuel, b. Exeter 16 Aug. 1773.
Hon. William Parker d. 6 June 1813, aged 82 yrs.
Mrs Elizabeth Parker d. 7 Oct. 1816, aged 76 yrs. 6 mos.

Robert Parkes, Dorothy Gilman; md. 6 March 1783.
Their children, Charles, b. 1 April 1784; d. 8 May 1841.
Anne, b. 15 Sept. 1785; d. 6 Feb. 1821.

Thomas Parsons.
His children, Joseph, b. 6 Sept. 1762.
Enoch, b. 16 June 1764.
Stephen, b. 24 April 1766.

Oliver Peabody, Frances Peabody; md.
Their children, Sarah, b. 23 Aug, 1783.
Frances, b. 15 Nov. 1784; d. 17 July 1799.
Lucretia, b. 4 July 1786.
Oliver, b. 11 June 1788; d. 9 Feb. 1793.
William Bourn, b. 14 March 1790; d. 17 Aug. 1790.
Deborah Tasker, b. 30 April 1793; d. 12 May 1798.
Oliver Wm. Bourn, Wm. Bourn Oliver (twins), b. 19 July 1799; Oliver Wm. Bourn d. 5 July 1848.
Edward Bass, b. 19 May 1802; d. 4 June 1830.
Frances Bourn, b. 28 July 1804; d. Sept. 1805.
Oliver Peabody d. 3 Aug. 1831.

Edmund Pearson, son of Jethro Pearson, b. 26 April 1758, md. Dorothy Swasey, dau. of Joseph Swasey, b. 24 Feb. 1760.
Their children, Dorothy, b. 8 June 1780.
    James, b. 24 March 1782; d. at sea.
    William, b. 17 Feb. 1784; d. July 1844.
    Fanny, b. 4 Oct. 1785.
    Edmund, b. 20 June 1787.
    Mary Smith, b. 10 June 1790; d. 10 Aug. 1844.
    Henrietta, b. 4 Dec. 1792.
Mrs. Dorothy Pearson d. 2 Feb. 1820.
Maj. Edmund Pearson d. 23 Jan. 1842.

Nathaniel Pearson, son of Edmund Pearson, b. 11 Sept. 1797, md. 21 Oct. 1821 Caroline Gerrish, dau. of Timothy Gerrish of Portsmouth, b. 8 July 1798.
Their children, Olivia Gerrish, b. 18 Oct. 1822.
    Edmund, b. 18 July 1824.
    Nathaniel, b. 23 June 1826.
    Augustus William, b. 2 April 1830.
Nathaniel Pearson, Sr., d. 5 Feb. 1841.

Nathaniel Pease, Phebe Sanborn; md. 4 Nov. 1725
Their children, Sarah, b. 10 July 1726.
    Samuel, b. 14 Dec. 1727.
    Ann, b. 17 Nov. 1729.
    Abigail, b. 28 Jan. 1731–2.
    Beersheba, b. 16 March 1733–4.
    Phebe, b. 21 Dec. 1735.

William Perry, b. Norton, Mass., 20 Dec. 1788, md. 13 April 1818 Abigail Gilman, b. 10 Dec. 1789.
Their children, Caroline Frances, b. 11 Dec. 1820.
    William Gilman, b. 21 July 1823.
    Abigail Gilman, b. 14 Nov. 1824.
    Nathaniel Gilman, b. 28 Oct. 1826.
    John Taylor, b, 5 April 1832.

Joseph Perkins of Hampton Falls md. 30 Nov. 1825 Elizabeth Odlin of Exeter.
Their children, Joseph William, b. 29 April 1827; d. 24 May 1827.
    Elizabeth Odlin, b. 16 Oct. 1828.
    Woodbridge Odlin, b. 12 June 1831.

Samuel Philbrick, son of Benjamin Philbrick, b. 20 April 1759, md. Hannah Robinson, dau. of John Robinson of Cape Ann, b. 26 Aug. 1763.
Their children, Samuel, b. 12 June 1785.
    Elizabeth, b. 7 Feb. 1787.
    John Robinson, b. 29 Sept. 1789.

HISTORY OF EXETER. 37

    Hannah, b. 22 Sept. 1791.
    Benjamin, b. 3 Dec. 1793.
    Joseph, b. 8 Jan. 1797.
    Mary, b.
    William, b. 24 May 1803.
Mrs. Hannah Philbrick d. 5 Nov. 1810, aged 47.
Samuel Philbrick md. (2d) 17 Nov. 1814 Elizabeth Smith, dau. of Maj. Benjamin Smith.
Samuel Philbrick, Sr., d. 10 March 1840.

John Phillips, son of Rev. Samuel Phillips of Andover, md. Mrs. Sarah Gilman, widow of Nathaniel Gilman.
Mrs. Sarah Phillips d. Oct. 1765.
John Phillips d. 21 April 1795, aged 75 yrs. 3 mos.

William Pike, son of Joseph Pike of Barnstaple in England, md. 29 July 1725 Judith Hilton, dau. of Col. Winthrop Hilton of Exeter.
Their child, Elizabeth, b. 22 May 1726.
William Pike d. 25 Oct. 1726.
Mrs. Judith Pike md. (2d) 1 Nov. 1731 Elisha Odlin, son of Rev. John Odlin.

Rev. James Pike of Somersworth md. 26 Aug. 1730 Sarah Gilman, dau. of Nicholas Gilman.
Their child, Sarah, b. 13 July 1731.

Moses Pike of Hampton Falls md. 6 April 1791 Theodate Sanborn.
 Their children, Abraham Sanborn, b. 5 Dec. 1792.
    Benjamin, b. 16 April 1794.
    Moses Hook, b. 11 March 1796.
    Jonathan, b. 23 Aug. 1798.
    Levi, b. 27 May 1801.
    Arvilla, Adeline, b. 9 July 1803.
    Hannah Hook, b. 23 Oct. 1805.
    John Kimball, b. 6 April 1808.
    Mary Shaw, b. 13 Oct. 1810.
    Ednah Dow, b. 2 July 1813.
    Sarah, b. 3 March 1816.

Abraham S. Pike, son of Moses Pike, b. Dec. 1792, md. 11 Sept. 1817 Elizabeth Walton, dau. of Samuel and Nancy Walton of Salisbury, b. 31 May 1798.
 Their children, Elizabeth Ann, b. 13 April 1818.
    Samuel Walton, b. 8 Feb. 1820.
    Mary Adeline, b. 1 April 1823.

Nathaniel Prescott, Sarah Tuck ; md. 4 Feb. 1741-2.
 Their children, Nathaniel, b. 22 April 1743.

38   HISTORY OF EXETER.

    Sarah, b. 24 Nov. 1745.
    John, b. 16 Dec. 1747.
    Nathaniel, b. 6 Aug. 1750.
    Edward, b. 6 Aug. 1755.

John Purmort of Newcastle, b. 13 July 1715, md. 12 March 1741 Hannah Sinclair of Stratham, b. 25 April 1719.
 Their children, John, b. 11 Oct. 1742.
    Anne, b. 3 Jan. 1746.
    Hannah, b. 1 Aug. 1747.
    Joseph, b. 18 July 1749.
    Richard, b. 16 Feb. 1751.
    Abigail, b. 16 July 1753; d. 7 Aug. 1754.
    Mark, b. 29 May 1755; d. 12 July 1776.
    Mary, Abigail, b. 22 March 1758.
 John Purmort d. 5 Oct. 1758.

Joseph Purmort, b. 18 July 1749, md. 28 Feb. 1775 Mercy Dolloff, b. 6 Dec. 1752.
 Their children, Miriam, b. 25 Dec. 1775.
    Hannah, b. 13 May 1777.
    Abner, b. 13 March 1780.
    John, b. 24 Oct. 1784.
 Mrs. Mercy Purmort d. 31 Oct. 1784.

Jonathan and Mercy Quimby.
 Their children, Sarah, b. 20 Feb. 1732–3.
    James, b. 12 April 1736.
    Jonathan, b. 12 Feb. 1741.

Samuel Randall of Cape Ann, son of Jacob Randall, md. 16 Jan. 1759 Abigail Fafether, dau. of Daniel and Elizabeth Fafether, b. 21 Dec. 1733.
 Their children, Abigail, b. 6 Feb. 1761.
    Susy, b. 7 Aug. 1762.

Jacob Randall, son of Jacob Randall of Portsmouth, md. 5 June 1787 Anna Shute, dau. of Michael Shute of Newmarket, shipwright.
 Their children, Jacob, b. 25 Dec. 1788.
    Sarah, b. 6 Oct. 1790.
 Mrs. Anna Randall d. 28 March 1792.
Jacob Randall md. (2d) 7 Feb. 1793 Rebecca Masters, dau. of Dr. John Masters of Newmarket.
 Their child, Anna, b. 26 May 1794.

Thomas Rawlins.
 His children, Thomas, b. 14 July 1671.
    Moses, b. 14 Oct. 1672.

Joseph, b. 6 May 167–.
Mary, b. 8 May 167–.
Benjamin, b. 6 July 1678.

Joseph Rawlins, son of Joseph and Hannah Rawlins, b. 19 Dec. 1702, md. 7 March 1728 Hannah Redman of Hampton.
Their children, Joshua, b. 4 Oct. 1729.
   Patience, b. 20 Oct. 1732.
   Eliphalet, b. 23 July 1734.
   Joseph, b. 20 Aug. 1737.

Edward M. Robinson, b. Stratham, md. Dover 27 May 1838 Olivia Jacobs, b. Hope, Me.
Their children, Mary O., b. Exeter 7 Jan. 1839.
   Charles E., b. Exeter 3 Jan. 1845.

John Rice md. 1 Jan. 1734–5 Anna Wilson, dau. of Dea. Thomas Wilson.
Their child, John, b. 24 Dec. 1743.

Jonathan Robinson.
His children, John, b. 7 Sept. 1671.
   Sarah, b. 29 Oct. 1673.
   Hester, b. 12 Aug. 1677.
   Elizabeth, b. 6 Sept. 1679.
   Jonathan, b. 9 July 1681.
   David, b. 28 July 1684.
   James, b. 7 Dec. 1686.
   Joseph, b. 1 May 1690.

John Robinson, Elizabeth Folsom; md. 1 Feb. 1725–6.
Their children, Mehitable, b. 27 March 1729; d. 12 April 1731.
   Peter, b. 19 June 1731.
   Elizabeth, b. 5 Nov. 1734.
   John, b. 6 Aug. 1736.
   Mehitable, b. 6 April 1738.
   Catharine, b. 20 June 1742.
   Daniel, b. 14 July 1745.
   Mary, b. 7 Feb. 1748.
   Simeon, b. 18 Dec. 1752.

Ephraim Robinson and Mary Robinson.
Their children, Lydia, b. 16 Nov. 1735.
   Mary, b. 9 Feb. 1737–8.
   Elizabeth, b. 24 May 1740.
   Anne, b. 7 April 1741–2.
   Ephraim, b. 19 April 1744.
   Caleb, b. 22 May 1746.
   Samuel, b. 17 Dec. 1750.
   Lucia, b. 25 June 1757; md. Jonathan Blake and d. 27 Dec. 1808.

40   HISTORY OF EXETER.

Ephraim Robinson, son of Ephraim and Mary Robinson, b. 19 April 1744, md. 22 Jan. 1767 Deborah Giddinge, dau. of Zebulon and Deborah Giddinge, b. 2 Feb. 1747.
Their children, Ephraim b. 16 Oct. 1767.
    Mary, b. 23 Aug. 1770; d. 9 June 1776.
    Zebulon, b. 2 Sept. 1772; d. 17 June 1776.
    Harriet, b. 19 June 1774; d. 14 June 1776.
    Mary, b. 12 Feb. 1777.
    Zebulon, b. 14 Feb. 1780.
    Deborah, b. 26 Jan. 1782; md. Jotham Lawrence.
    Harriet, b. 19 July 1784.
    Elizabeth, b. 7 Oct. 1786.
    William Frederick, b. 11 May 1790; d. 1 Sept. 1798.
Ephraim Robinson d. 10 April 1809, aged 65 yrs.
Mrs. Deborah Robinson d. 2 Aug. 1811, aged 64 yrs.

Benjamin Rogers and Margaret Rogers.
Their children, Susanna, b. 14 May 1746.
    Abigail, b. 5 Nov. 1749.
    Dionysius (dau.), b. 10 May 1752.
    Mary, b. 1 Nov. 1755.

John Rogers, b. Newmarket 2 July 1787, md. 15 Nov. 1810 Frances Gilman, dau. of Nathaniel Gilman, b. 11 Sept. 1787.
Their children, Nathaniel Gilman, b. 25 April 1818.
    John Francis, b. 1 Dec. 1819.
Mrs. Frances Rogers d. 7 April 1821, aged 33 yrs. 7 mos.
Col. John Rogers md. (2d) 8 Sept. 1822 Ann Gilman.
Their children, Frances Gilman, b. 25 Jan. 1824
    Ann Gilman, b. 20 May 1825.
Mrs. Ann Rogers d. 2 Jan. 1827, aged 31 yrs.
Col. John Rogers d. Exeter 22 July 1837, aged 50 yrs.

Samuel Rowe, son of Capt. Enoch Rowe of Kensington, md. 15 May 1802 Olive Rundlett, now of Exeter.
Their children, Olivia, b. 19 Jan. 1803.
    Edward, b. 11 May 1805.
    James Samuel, b. 20 Oct. 1807.
Samuel Rowe d. 23 Sept. 1828, aged 48 yrs.

Capt. Charles Rundlet and Dorothy Rundlet.
Their children, Dorothy, b. 8 March 1743.
    Charles, b. 2 Dec. 1747.
    Daniel, b. 5 Aug. 1749.
    Elizabeth, b. 7 April 1751.
    James, b. 15 Jan. 1752.
    Jonathan, b. 5 Feb. 1757.

Lydia, b. 14 Dec. 1758.
Honor, b. 29 Nov. 1760.
Henry, b. 17 Oct. 1762.
Joseph, b. 13 Sept. 1764; d. 30 May 1841.
Josiah, b. 3 March 1766.

James Rundlet, son of James Rundlet of Exeter, b. 10 June 1744, md. 1 June 1767 Dorothy Stevens of Epping.
Their children, Hannah, b. 20 Feb. 1768.
Dorothy, b. 21 Oct. 1770.
James, b. 8 Dec. 1772.
Edward, b. 25 Nov. 1774.
Olive, b. 7 March 1778; d. 12 April 1778.
Samuel, b. 12 April 1779; d. on ship Warren 3 July 1800.
Olive, b. 27 April 1782.
John, b. 2 Dec. 1787.
Sarah, b. 9 April 1789.
Nathaniel, b. 8 March 1794.
Mrs. Dorothy Rundlet d. 29 Sept. 1795.
James Rundlet md. (2d) 10 Nov. 1796 Sarah Rust.
Their child, Benjamin, b. 8 Sept. 1797; d. 18 Sept. 1797.
James Rundlet d. 28 Dec. 1800.

Dudley Safford, b. 15 Nov. 1776, md. Betsey Gilman, dau. of Bradbury Gilman of Meredith.
Their children, Charles Gilman, b. 17 Nov. 1804.
Benjamin, b. 23 May 1806.
Hannah Gilman, b. 1 Feb. 1807.
Sophia, b. 29 July 1809.
Oliver, b. 21 July 1811.
Frances, b. 19 Feb. 1813.
James Gilman, b. 6 April 1815; d. 21 Dec. 1815.
Sophronia, b 9 Dec. 1816.
Henry, b. 10 Oct. 1819.
Elizabeth Ann, b. 2 July 1822.
Dudley Safford d. 18 July 1822.

William Sanborn of Exeter md. 2 Sept. 1731 Elizabeth Dearborn of Hampton.
Their children, Simon, b. 28 Sept. 1736.
Elizabeth, b. 25 Aug. 1738.
Hannah, b. 30 March 1740.
William, b. 9 Feb. 1741–2.
Henry Dearborn, b. 23 Dec. 1743.
Mary, b. 19 Sept. 1745.
Josiah, b. 19 June 1747.
Sarah, b. 12 May 1749.
Anne, b. 15 Aug. 1751.

Theodate, b. 30 Aug. 1753.
Abigail, b. 3 Oct. 1755.

Josiah Sanborn, Deborah Bowden; md. 8 April 1770.
Their children, Josiah, b. 9 Nov. 1771.
John, b. 21 Sept. 1773.

Edward Sewall.
His children, Sarah, b. 17 Sept. 1676.
Thomas, b. 28 March 1679.
Joseph, b. 28 Dec. 1681.

Benjamin Pearse Sheriff, b. 10 July 1763, md. 12 Aug. 1788 Martha Gilman, b. 14 June 1768.
Their children, Abigail, b. 24 Sept. 1789.
Benjamin D., b. 30 Dec. 1791.
Henry A., b. 25 Oct. 1793.
Charles C., b. 8 Feb. 1795.
Frederick, b. 12 May 1797.
Martha Gilman, b. 10 Sept. 1799.
Sarah, b. 6 March 1803.
John Langdon, b. 18 Nov. 1804.
Susannah, b. 24 Oct. 1806.
John Langdon, b. 16 Aug. 1808.
Mary, b. 16 May 1810.

Henry Shute, b. Newmarket 18 April 1794, md. 27 Feb. 1820 Eliza R. Smith, b. Exeter 7 Feb. 1800.
Their children. Henry Augustus, b. 18 June 1821; d. 18 Dec. 1841.
Ann Eliza, b. 15 Nov. 1824; d. 25 May 1858.
George Smith, b. 2 March 1827.
Sarah Frances, b. 26 May 1831.

John Sinclair.
His children, James, b. 27 July 1660.
Mary, b. 27 June 1663.
Sarah, b. 15 Sept. 1664.

Jonathan Fifield Sleeper md. 20 Nov. 1791 Dorothy Tilton, dau. of Dr. Joseph Tilton, b. 20 April 1770.
Their children, Elizabeth Jewett, b. 28 June 1792.
John S., b. 25 Sept. 1794.
Charles T., b. 24 Aug. 1796; d. 8 March 1818.
Catharine Parker, b. 19 March 1804.
Jonathan Fifield Sleeper d. 16 Dec. 1805, aged 38 yrs.
Mrs. Dorothy Sleeper d. 27 May 1809.

John Sherburne Sleeper, b. 25 Sept. 1794, md. 22 Feb. 1826 Mary Folsom Noble.

Their children, Charles Frederick, b. 27 Dec. 1826.
Ariana Elizabeth Smith, b. 9 July 1829.
John Howard, b. 24 Dec. 1831.

Nicholas Smith.
His children, Nathaniel, b. 9 June 1660.
Nicholas, b. 3 Sept. 1661.
Anne, b. 8 Feb. 1663.
Theophilus, b. 14 Feb. 1667.

Edward Smith, Mary ———; md. 13 Jan. 1668-9.

Jonathan Smith.
His children, Israel, b. 16 Jan. 1670-1.
Jacob, b. 10 Aug. 1673.
Joseph, b. 7 Feb. 1680.
Leah, b. 7 April 1683.
Mehitabel, b. 14 Aug. 1685.

Jonathan Smith, Mary Ames; md. 17 March 1713-4.
Their children, Jonathan, b. 9 Jan. 1714-5.
Mary, b. 21 Feb. 1716-7.
Mrs. Mary Smith d. 21 Dec. 1717.
Jonathan Smith md. (2d) 11 Aug. 1719 Bridget Keniston.
Their children, Abraham, b. 1 June 1720.
Lydia, b. 20 June 1722.
Isaac, b. 22 May 1724.
Elizabeth, Abigail, b. 25 Feb. 1725-6.
Hepzibah, b. 23 July 1727.
Jacob, b. 12 March 1728-9.
Obadiah, b. 26 March 1731.
Deborah, b. 23 Feb. 1732-3.
John Waldron, b. 8 Dec. 1735.
Caleb, b. 4 March 1736-7.
Bridget, b. 16 Feb. 1738-9.
Nathan, b. 7 May 1741.

Nathaniel Smith, son of Nicholas Smith, b. 15 Sept. 1695.
His children, Mary, b. 7 Dec. 1721.
Nathaniel, b. 17 April 1725.
Patience, b. 24 Nov. 1727.
Daniel, b. 13 April 1730.
Elizabeth, b. 24 Feb. 1731-2.
Sarah, b. 1 March 1733-4.
Anna, b. 7 May 1740.

Benjamin Smith md. 24 Jan. 1760 Mary Swasey, both of Exeter.

Their children, Mary, b. 16 Oct. 1760; d. 8 April 1790.
    Joseph, b. 19 July 1763.
    Sarah, b. 15 Dec. 1766.
    Benjamin, b. 21 April 1767; d. 8 April 1790.
    Elizabeth, b. 6 Sept. 1769.
    Sally, b. 6 Dec. 1771; d. 3 July 1787.
    Susanna, b. 8 Jan. 1774.
    John, b. 6 Dec. 1777.
    John, b. 19 Oct. 1778.
    Charlotte, b. 9 April 1780.
Major Benjamin Smith d. 23 June 1811, aged 74 yrs.
Mrs. Mary Smith d. Nov. 1814.

Joseph Smith, Polly Burley; md. 13 Nov. 1786.
Their children, John, b. 10 Oct. 1787.
    Mary, b. 18 Nov. 1792.
    Fanny, b. 2 April 1798.
    Sophia, b. 18 Sept. 1799.

Jeremiah Smith, then of Peterborough, N. H., md. 8 March 1797 Elizabeth Ross of Bladensburgh, Md.
Their children, Ariana Elizabeth, b. 28 Dec. 1797; d. 20 June 1829.
    William, b. 31 Aug. 1799.
    Jeremiah, b. 20 Aug. 1802; drowned 14 Oct. 1808.
Mrs Elizabeth Smith d. 19 June 1827.
Hon. Jeremiah Smith d. Dover 21 Sept. 1842.

Samuel Somerby and Hannah Somerby.
Their children, Mary Ann Montgomery, d. 4 Jan. 1821, aged 5 mos. 11 days.
    George Adolphus, b. 2 Nov. 1821.
Samuel Somerby d. 17 May 1824, aged 42 yrs.

Thomas Sullivan, Frances A. Leavitt; md. 7 Oct. 1836.
Their children, Frances E., b. 18 March 1837.
    Mary H., b. 21 Jan. 1839.
    Charles W., b. 6 July 1841.
    George E., b. 26 Oct. 1843.
    Henry G., b. 18 July 1846.

Richard Wenman Swan, b. New York City, md. 18 Dec. 1845 Katharine Day, b. South Hadley Falls, Mass.
Their children, Mary Hale, b. 24 July 1847.
    Richard H., b. 27 July 1848.

Joseph Swasey, Apphia Morrill; md. 13 Dec. 1735.
Their children, Mary, b. 15 Oct. 1737.
    Joseph, b. 20 May 1743; d. 8 Jan. 1829.

Joseph Swasey, Jr., b. 30 May 1743, md. 10 March 1765 Olive Lamson, b. 6 Sept. 1744.
  Their children, Olive, b. 11 Jan. 1766; d. 16 Oct. 1821, widow of Ep. Dean.
  Joseph, b. 12 Feb. 1768; d. 18 May 1820.
  Nathaniel, b. 26 March 1770; d. Sept. 1840.
  Lucretia, b. 23 Oct. 1772; d. Sept. 1837.
  William, b. 10 March 1778; d. 25 Dec. 1835.
  Susanna, b. 20 July 1780; d. 17 May 1840.
  Lydia, b. 15 Jan. 1783.
  Harriot, b. 28 July 1785.
  Rufus, b. 16 April 1788; d. in Boston 1840.
Mrs. Olive Swasey d. 16 Jan. 1822.
Capt. Joseph Swasey d. 8 Jan. 1829.

Moses Swett and Hannah Swett.
  Their children, Josiah, b. 31 July 1743.
  John, b. 17 Dec. 1748.

Samuel B. Swett, M. D., Mary S. Lowe; md. 4 Sept. 1845.
  Their child, Samuel, b. 16 June 1846.

William Tarbox and Dolly Tarbox.
  Their child, Edwin Hill, b. Exeter 4 Aug. 1819; d. 28 Jan. 1821.

Oxford Tash and Esther Tash.
  Their children, Mary, b. Exeter 14 March 1784; d. 20 July 1819.
  Lucy, b. Exeter 6 April 1786; d. 23 Nov. 1812.
  Susan, b. Exeter 3 July 1788.
  Robert, b. Exeter 3 Sept. 1790.
  Catherine, b. Exeter 25 July 1792.
  Charles G., b. Exeter 9 Dec. 1794; d. 11 June 1864.
  William G., b. Exeter 9 March 1797.
  Member Matilda, b. Exeter 25 July 1799.
Oxford Tash d. 15 Oct. 1810.
Mrs. Esther Tash d. 26 March 1844, aged 87 yrs.

William Taylor.
  His children, Mary, b. 26 Oct. 1667.
  Nathan, b. 5 Feb. 1674.

Jonathan Thing and Joanna Thing.
  Their children, Elizabeth, b. 5 June 1664.
  John, b. 20 Sept. 1665; d. 4 Nov. 1665.
  Samuel, b. 3 June 1667.
  Mercy, b. 6 March 1673.
  Jonathan, b. 21 Sept. 1678.

Capt. Jonathan Thing md. 26 July 1677 Mary Gilman, dau. of Hon. John Gilman, b. 10 Sept. 1658.
Their children, Jonathan, b. 21 Sept. 1678.
John, b. June 1680.
Bartholomew, b. 25 Feb. 1681–2.
Joseph, b. March 1684.
Elizabeth, b.
Benjamin, b. 12 Nov. 1688.
Josiah, b.
Mrs. Mary Thing d. Aug. 1691.
Capt. Jonathan Thing md. (2d) July 1693 Martha Wiggin, widow of Thomas Wiggin and dau. of John Denison of Ipswich.
Their child, Daniel, b. 12 May 1694.
Capt. Jonathan Thing d. 31 Oct. 1694.

Samuel Thing, Abigail Gilman; md. 8 July 1696.
Their children, Joanna, b. 22 June 1697.
Samuel, b. 28 March 1699.
Abigail, b. 1 Dec. 1700.
Elizabeth, b. 19 Dec. 1702.
Sarah, b. 8 Jan. 1704–5.
Lydia, Deborah, b. 14 Feb. 1707–8.
Catharine, b. 19 May 1711.
Josiah, b. 15 Sept. 1713.
John, b. 17 May 1716.
Mary, b. 18 May 1718.
Alice, b. 14 Feb. 1722–3.

Bartholomew Thing md. 7 Dec. 1705 Abigail Coffin, dau. of Tristram Coffin.
Their children, Tristram, b. 26 Oct. 1707; d. 22 June 1709.
Josiah, b. 18 Aug. 1710; d. 5 March 1710–1.
Mrs. Abigail Thing d. 2 May 1711.
Bartholomew Thing md. (2d) 3 April 1712 Mrs. Sarah Kent, widow of John Kent and dau. of Capt. Joseph Little of Newbury.
Their child, Mary, b. 3 Jan. 1712–3.
Bartholomew Thing d. 28 April 1738, aged 57.

Benjamin Thing md. Jan. 1711–2 Pernal Coffin, dau. of Tristram Coffin.
Their children, Coffin, b. Sept. 1713.
Deborah, b. 29 April 1719.
Mrs. Pernal Thing d. 2 June 1725.
Benjamin Thing md. (2d) 21 Oct. 1725 Mrs. Deborah Thing, widow of Samuel Thing.
Their children, Pernal, b. 29 July 1726.
Winthrop, b. 10 Jan. 1727–8.
Mary, b. 24 May 1730.

HISTORY OF EXETER. 47

Anna, b. 18 Oct. 1732.
Samuel, b. 13 Dec. 1735.
Elizabeth, b. 2 Sept. 1740.

Daniel Thing md. 3 March 1717-8 Elizabeth Clark, dau. of Henry Clark of Newbury.
Their children, Elizabeth, b. 13 Aug. 1719; d. 27 Oct. 1719.
Stephen, b. 28 Sept. 1720.
Martha, b. 2 Jan. 1722-3.
Bartholomew, b. 4 Aug. 1725.
Eunice, b. 15 Oct. 1727; d. Oct. 1813.

Samuel Thing, son of Samuel Thing, Esq., md. 26 Dec. 1722 Deborah Hilton, dau. of Col. Winthrop Hilton.
Their child, Samuel, b. 9 Oct. 1723; d. 14 March 1723-4.
Samuel Thing d. Sept. 1723.

Stephen Thing md. 6 July 1768 Mehitable Connor, dau. of Lieut. Jonathan and Mehitable Connor.
Their child, Betsey, b. 5 Jan. 1773.
Stephen Thing d. 20 Sept. aged 70 yrs. 11 mos. 18 days.

John Thompson, Anne Miller; md. 26 Dec. 1750.
Their child, Joseph Miller, b. 12 Nov. 1751.

Daniel Thurston, b. 6 Aug. 1776, md. 4 Aug. 1798 Deborah Folsom, b. 29 April 1778.
Their children, Elizabeth Gilman, b. 6 Nov. 1798; d. 1820.
Mary Jane, b. 3 Sept. 1801; d.
Mary Jane, b. 15 June 1804.

John Tilton, son of Samuel Tilton of Hampton Falls, md. 30 June 1791 Patty Odlin, dau. of Winthrop Odlin of Exeter.
Their children, John Folsom, b. 8 Dec. 1792.
Ebenezer, b. 29 Dec. 1795.
Samuel, b. 28 Nov. 1797.
Winthrop Odlin, b. 7 March 1800.
Amy Folsom, b. 3 May 1802.
William, b. 26 July 1804.
Elizabeth, b. 18 Aug. 1806.
Joseph, b. 22 July 1809.
Sarah Ann, b. 1 Aug. 1813; d. 1814.
Mrs. Patty Tilton d. 7 Sept. 1823.

Dr. Joseph Tilton, b. Hampton Falls 25 Sept. 1744, md. 10 Sept. 1767 Catharine Shackford, b. Portsmouth 12 Oct. 1745.
Their children, Catharine, b. 18 Sept. 1768; md. Nathaniel Parker Nov. 1793.

Dorothy, b. 20 April 1770; md. J. F. Sleeper 20 Nov. 1791.
John Shackford, b. 5 Oct. 1772; lost at sea 26 or 27 Oct. 1810.
Joseph, b. 15 April 1776; d. 13 Sept. 1777.
Charlotte, b. 1 June 1779; md. Nathaniel Page.
Caroline, b. 30 May 1781; md. Robert Cross of Portland.
Mrs. Catharine Tilton d. 19 Jan. 1812.
Dr. Joseph Tilton d. 5 Dec. 1837.

Oliver Towle, b. Hampton 2 March 1783, md. 2 April 1806 Betsey Leavitt, b. Hampton 26 Sept. 1785.
Their children, Oliver, b. 16 Oct. 1806; d. 20 Oct. 1809.
Mary G., b. 24 Dec. 1807.
Oliver, Jr., b. 13 Jan. 1810.
Enoch W., b. 15 June 1811.
Betsey, b. 26 Oct. 1814; d. 2 April 1817.
Angelina, b. 4 June 1816.
Betsey L., b. 22 Nov. 1820.
Amos, b. 23 July 1823.
Adoniram J., b. 26 June 1827.
Emily B., b. 2 June 1829; d. 11 March 1848.

Henry Wadleigh, Elizabeth Ladd; md. 3 Dec. 1693.
Their children, Sarah, b. 3 Sept. 1694.
Abigail, b. 2 Sept. 1696.
Joseph, b. Sept. 1698.
Martha, b. Jan. 1700-1.
Benjamin, b. 1703; d. 1716.
Henry Wadleigh d. 2 Aug. 1732.

Joseph Wadleigh, son of Robert Wadleigh, b. 7 Sept. 1711, md. 5 Jan. 1737-8 Ann Swain.
Their children, Hannah, b. 1 Aug. 1739.
Sarah, b. 29 Nov. 1741.
Joseph, b. 3 Nov. 1743.
Anna, b. 17 Jan. 1745-6.
Rachel, b. 3 Feb. 1747.

Herbert Waters, Mary Harris; md. 13 Nov. 1733.
Their child, Herbert (daughter), b. 8 Aug. 1735.

Humphrey Wilson.
His children, Judith, b. 8 Nov. 1664; d. 3 May 1667.
Elizabeth, b. 11 Jan. 1665.
John, b. 17 July 1667.
Hannah, b. 12 Nov. 1670.
Thomas, b. 20 May 1672.
James, b. 27 Aug. 1673.

Thomas Wilson, Mary Light; md. Oct.
Their children, Humphrey, b. 9 Dec. 1699.
    Rebecca, b. 18 Nov. 1701.
    Anna, b. 18 June 1703.
    John, Thomas, b. 3 Nov. 1704.
    John, b. 7 Jan 1705-6.
    Sarah, b. 26 Sept. 1707.
    Joshua, b. 3 Sept. 1708.
    Sarah, b. 23 Nov. 1709.
    Mary, b. 19 Sept. 1711.
    Jabez, b. 1 June 1712; d. same day.
    Jonathan, b. 4 Sept. 1713.
    Moses, b. 1 May 1715.
    Judith, b. 18 Feb. 1717-8.

Samuel D. Wingate, b. Stratham, md. 8 Feb 1854 Orianna Mitchell.
Their children, James D. P., b 2 April 1855.
    Charles E. L., b. 14 Feb. 1861.

Samuel Winslow, Sarah Johnson; md.
Their children, Samuel, b. Exeter 8 Feb. 1795.
    George, b. Exeter 7 May 1796; drowned 27 Aug. 1812.
    Jonathan, b. Exeter 4 Nov. 1797.

William Woodbridge, b. Glastonbury, Conn., md. 5 April 1785 Elizabeth Brooks, dau. of Samuel Brooks of Exeter.
Their children, Elizabeth, b. 27 June 1786.
    Mary, b. 27 June 1786; d. 6 Aug. 1786.
Mrs. Elizabeth Woodbridge d. 16 Nov. 1787.

Jonathan Young, son of Robert Young, b. 22 Nov. 1712, md. 11 April 1738 Abigail Scribner, dau. of John Scribner, b. 30 March 1717.
Their children, John, b. 1 April 1739.
    Anna, b. 28 June 1741.
    Daniel, b. 17 Sept. 1743.
    Abigail, baptized 12 Oct. 1746.
    Joseph, b. 18 Sept. 1748.
    Benjamin, b. 1 Nov. 1750.
    Sarah, b. 15 Oct. 1752.
    Hannah, b. 18 Oct. 1755.
    Abigail, b. 5 July 1759.

MARRIAGES.

FROM THE EXETER RECORDS.

Edward Arm, Joanna Meloney; 13 Jan. 1782.
Benjamin Abbot, Hannah Tracy Emery; 30 Oct. 1791.
Samuel Agedent, Jerusha Daniels; 10 July 1800.
Moses Atkinson, 3d, Newbury, Charlotte Dutch; 5 June 1808.
Richard Alley, Elizabeth A. Weeks; 21 Oct. 1823.
Obed E. Adams, Dover, Selina Burley; 5 June 1825.
Sween Anderson, Charlestown, Mass., Lydia Barker; June 1830.
Landen Adams, Lowell, Mary F. Leavitt; 27 Nov. 1834.
Monroe Ayer, Haverhill, Hannah M. W. Proal; 9 Oct. 1838.
Francis Bowden, Elizabeth Webster; 18 Feb. 1734-5.
Jonathan Blake, Lucey Robinson.
Samuel Brooks, Jr., Mary Giddinge; 14 Dec. 1779.
Benjamin Bodge, Meribah Hall; 19 Oct. 1780.
Michael Brown, Ruth Allerd; 9 Sept. 1781.
Laurence Batson, Anne Creighton; 1 Nov. 1783.
John Brooks, Elizabeth Mash; 17 April 1785.
Joshua Bangs, Anne B. Folsom; 28 Feb. 1786.
Shackford S. Bennett, Mehitable Giddinge; 18 Dec. 1788.
Noah Barker, Mary Philbrick; 7 Oct. 1789.
Nathaniel Batchelder, Roxbury, Elizabeth Mudget; 25 March 1790.
Joshua Blanchard, Ruhannah Lovering; 14 Jan. 1793.
John Batchelder, Rachel Moore; 14 May 1793.
Joseph Blanchard, Chester, Mrs. Dorothy Folsom; 1 April 1794.
John Bickford, Phebe McCoy; 24 Dec. 1794.
James Bracket, Jr., Quincy, Mass., Elizabeth Odiorne; 7 Oct. 1795.
Benjamin Boardman, Sarah Haven; 30 Nov. 1795.
Samuel Brooks, Tirzah James; 6 Dec. 1795.
Reuben Byram, North Yarmouth, Lois Swasey; 11 Feb. 1808.
Amos Blanchard, Lydia Boardman; 12 March 1809.
Allen Bastow, North Yarmouth, Mary Swasey; 12 Aug. 1810.
James Burley, Charlotte Gilman; June 1811.
Rev. Abraham Burnham, Pembroke, Elizabeth Robinson; 19 Nov. 1816.
James Burley, Mrs. Harriet L. Gale; 17 May 1818.
Abel Brown, East Kingston, Elizabeth P. Dean; 8 June 1818.
John S. Beardslee, Hannah Hayes; 4 June 1820.
Moses P. Bickford, Eunice Burpee; 9 Nov. 1820.
Nathaniel R. Burleigh, Mary Jane Odiorne; 30 June 1823.

Joseph Boardman, Lydia L. Gilman; 16 Sept. 1823.
Dudley Beckett, Mary A. Marsh, North Hampton; 1 Aug. 1828.
Joseph A. Bailey, Dartmouth, Clarissa Clifford; 7 Nov. 1827.
John T. Blake, Kensington, Mary E. Moulton; 1 Feb. 1829.
Andrew Baker, Newmarket, Mary J. Sawyer; Nov. 1832.
Alfred M. Beck, Elizabeth S. Gilman; 29 Oct. 1832.
Josiah Blake, Sophia Smith; 13 Nov. 1832.
Oliver S. Bowley, Pamelia Leathers; 5 Nov. 1833.
Joseph Boardman, Sarah A. Smith; 16 Dec. 1833.
Stephen J. Batchelder, Sarah A. Hale; 14 April 1834.
Thomas H. Bartlett, Nancy L. Hayes; 28 Aug. 1836.
William G. Bragdon, Boston, Mary W. Folsom; 1 Jan. 1837.
Philip Carty, Elizabeth York; 23 Sept. 1668.
Jacob Carter, Abigail Steel; 13 Jan. 1777.
Cæsar Clough, Priscilla Glasgo (negroes); 9 Dec. 1777.
Moses Clark, Deerfield, Anna Loverain; 8 March 1781.
Jonathan Cass, Mary Gilman; 20 Dec. 1781.
Samuel Chamberlain, Mary Tilton; 30 Sept. 1783.
Dudley Cram, Sanbornton, Mary Rundlet; 21 Dec. 1783.
Ephraim Currier, Abigail Hackett; 27 June 1784.
Samuel Colcord, Anne Gilman; 21 April 1785.
Timothy Chamberlain, Esther Moses; 24 Sept. 1786.
Isaac Currier, Sarah Lamson; 21 Nov. 1788.
Tobias Cutler, Dolly Pauls, Stratham; 15 Jan. 1790.
John Caldwell, Polly Gilman; 10 April 1791.
Bradbury Cilley, Nottingham, Martha Poor; 19 Nov. 1792.
Harvey Colcord, Polly Wiggin, Stratham; 20 Oct. 1795.
Joseph Coomes, Stratham, Abigail Godfrey; 9 April 1799.
George Colcord, Joanna Jones; 19 Dec. 1801.
Jedediah Conner, Elizabeth Jenkins; 17 April 1801.
Rev. Jacob Cram, Hampton Falls, Mary Poor; 13 Sept 1804.
Gideon Carter, Hannah Gilman; 22 Sept 1804.
William S. Chase, Deerfield, Nancy Sanborn; 28 Nov. 1805.
Robert Cross, Portland, Caroline Tilton; 5 Oct. 1807.
Samuel Lee Count, Deborah Leavitt; 10 Sept. 1809.
Jedediah Conner, Abigail Gilman; 29 Dec. 1811.
Thomas Colcord, Judith Wiggins; 23 May 1812.
Jacob Carter, Jr., Mrs. Nancy Davis; 4 March 1814.
Andrew Cook, Madbury, Harriet Speed; 1 Dec. 1814.
Benjamin Clark, Nancy Lougee; 22 Oct. 1815.
James Conner, Berwick, Caroline Nelson; 31 Oct. 1815.
Joshua Coffin, Haverhill, Clarissa Dutch; 2 Dec. 1817.
Rufus E. Cutler, Dinah Cilley; 25 March 1823.
Charles Carter, Wakefield, Mandana Safford; 15 June 1822.
John Cook, Martha T. Smart; 2 Jan. 1823.
William H. Clark, Sarah Hilton; 16 Feb. 1825.
William T. Choate, Sarah W. Lovering; 4 Dec. 1825.
Henry Chew, Windham, Nancy J. Whitefield; 10 Nov. 1827.

William Conner, Betsy Lyford; Sept. 1832.
William Cutts, Betsy Swasey; 18 Nov. 1830.
Enoch G. Currier, Newmarket, Jane Hill; March 1830.
Nathaniel Conner, Mrs. Elizabeth Palmer; 22 Jan. 1833.
Samuel Cutler, Portland, Elizabeth D. Gardner; 19 June 1833.
Aretus Chandler, Lydia York, Brentwood; 1 Jan. 1834.
Horatio L. Cowles, Williamsburg, Mass., Sarah A. Gordon; 18 Jan. 1837.
Samuel Colcord, Sophia Norwood; 12 April 1838.
Andrew H. Collins, Kensington, Abigail Brown; 30 Dec. 1838.
Byley Dudley, Elizabeth Gilman; 25 Oct. 1682.
Jonathan Dolhoof, Mary Young; 17 Nov. 1737.
Lemuel Davis, Eleanor Dearing; 20 March 1780.
Lenon Daily, Margaret —— (negroes); 11 March 1781.
Thomas Dean, Lucretia Coffin; 13 April 1781.
Samuel Daniels, Sarah Taylor; 24 Oct. 1781.
Minus Daniels, Elizabeth Taylor; 11 Nov. 1784.
Eliphalet Dean, Olive Swasey; 17 Jan. 1785.
Abner Dolloof, Irene Smith, Brentwood; 22 March 1787.
Cepio Duce, Phillis Folsom; 29 Nov. 1787.
Robert Duce, Lois Straits; 21 June 1790.
Samuel T. Dudley, Abigail Randel; 21 Nov. 1791.
Samuel Densmore, Ossipee, Sally Wallace; Nov. 15, 1792.
John Dennett, Portsmouth, Elizabeth Lamson; 3 Feb. 1798.
Benjamin Dodge, Portland, Abigail Gilman; 16 April 1797.
John Dean, Jr., Anne Boardman; 11 May 1799.
Samuel Dodge, Fanny Pearson; 30 June 1812.
John Daniels, Eunice Kelly; 7 Dec. 1814.
William H. Dickey, Elizabeth Locke; 23 Oct. 1816.
Andrew Dorsey, Nancy G. Duce; 31 Aug. 1817.
William C. Dolloff, Betsy Leavitt; 13 Nov. 1817.
Thomas Dean, Catharine Gilman; 26 Sept. 1824.
Nathaniel Dean, Elizabeth Gilman; 25 June 1826.
Josiah Dudley, Sarah Robinson; 27 Sept. 1827.
Samuel Durant, Susan Daniels; 18 Oct. 1829.
Charles H. Dunbar, Haverhill, Mass., Mary B. Leavitt; March 1830.
Charles H. Daniels, Nancy M. Purington; 8 Nov. 1841.
Joseph Eldridge, Abigail Hall; 8 Oct. 1781.
Richard Emery, Liberty Hale; 14 Nov. 1784.
John Emery, Deborah Webb; 11 Jan. 1802.
Samuel Endicott, Beverly, Mass., Sarah F. Holt; 4 June 1826.
Kimball Eastman, Albany, N. Y., Mary Wentworth; 10 Jan. 1829.
James Foulsam, Elizabeth Thing; 18 June 1735.
Seth Fogg, Elizabeth Marshall; 7 Dec. 1779.
Samuel Folsom, Elizabeth Emery; 30 April 1780.
David Fogg, Katherine Johnson; 8 Nov. 1780.
Theophilus Folsom, Sarah Fogg; 12 Dec. 1780.
Jonathan Folsom, Lydia Folsom; 29 March 1781.
Fortune Fogg, Lucy Hale; 15 July 1781.

Stephen Fogg, Mary Piller ; 2 May 1782.
Stephèn Fogg, Sarah Marsh ; 1 Sept. 1782.
Mark Fifield, Stratham, Deborah Young ; 16 Aug. 1783.
James Folsom, Jr., Mary Folsom ; 2 Dec. 1784.
James Folsom, 4th, Sarah Gilman ; 15 Oct. 1786.
James Folsom, 3d, Sarah Robinson ; 31 Dec. 1786.
Dearborn Fogg, North Hampton, Dorothy Rundlet ; 5 Sept. 1787.
Joseph Flood, Elizabeth Akers ; 17 Aug. 1789.
Robert L. Fowle, Mrs. Sarah Fowle ; 6 Aug. 1789.
Stephen Fogg, Mrs. Elizabeth Grant ; 3 April 1790.
John Fogg, Mary Grant ; 13 Nov. 1791.
James French, Epping, Mehitable Moody, Brentwood ; 27 Jan. 1792.
Stephen Fogg, Jr., Anne Batchelder ; 29 Sept. 1793.
Dudley Folsom, Lucretia Swasey ; 17 Jan. 1796.
Richard Fuller, Elizabeth Fowler ; 5 June 1796.
George Fuller, Jr., Nancy York, Brentwood ; 26 April 1797.
John Folsom, Jr., Newmarket, Anne Odlin ; 22 March 1798.
Nathaniel Folsom, Hallowell, Mary Bond ; 6 Nov. 1800.
David Fuller, Anne Watson, widow ; 13 Nov. 1800.
William Flood, Lydia Carter ; 6 Aug. 1804.
Nathaniel Foster, North Yarmouth, Rebecca Swasey ; 19 Dec. 1804.
William Fuller, Sukey Sleeper ; 31 March 1806.
Jonathan Folsom, Lydia Folsom ; 17 April 1809.
Peter Folsom, Hannah P. Hook ; 17 Aug. 1809.
William Flood, Hannah Moulton ; 18 Dec. 1823.
John Foss, Lucy H. Bailey ; 2 June 1826.
Bradstreet French, Newmarket, Olive Gilman ; 22 May 1831.
Lucius G. Felt, Martha A. Colley ; 4 May 1836.
Abraham Flood, Abigail Dearborn ; May 1829.
Nicholas D. Folsom, Celina Blake ; 10 Oct. 1832.
Benjamin Furbish, Mary Lane ; 16 May 1833.
John Farnham, Jr., Newburyport, Lois D. Jenness ; 24 May 1838.
Joseph B. Flagg, Harriet M. Flanders, Lowell, Mass. ; 15 April 1840.
Joseph H. Ford, Elizabeth Whitcomb ; 7 Sept. 1840.
Peter Gilman, Mary Gilman, wid. of John Gilman ; 8 Dec. 1724.
Nathaniel Gookin, Judith Coffin ; 1 Jan. 1740-1.
Eliphalet Gilman, Sarah Conner ; 10 May 1778.
John Giddinge, Elizabeth Wiggin ; 25 Sept. 1781.
Nathaniel Giddinge, Jr., Mrs. Anne Folsom ; 21 May 1783.
Zebulon Gilman, Jr., Mary Mash ; 4 Oct. 1785.
Nathaniel Gilman, Abigail Odlin ; 29 Dec. 1785.
Benjamin Clark Gilman, Mary Thing Gilman ; 24 June 1788.
James Grant, Betsy Piper ; 15 Feb. 1789.
James Gilman, Patty Gilman ; 25 May 1789.
Joseph Gorden, Dolly Smith ; 31 Oct. 1790.
Noah Gilman, Mahitable Steel ; 1 Jan. 1792.
John Gilman, Dorothy Kimbal ; 30 Jan. 1792.
John Taylor Gilman, Mrs. Mary Adams ; 5 July 1792.

Nathaniel Giddinge, Mrs. Peggy Warren; 6 Nov. 1794.
William Gross, Dolly Leavitt; 16 April 1795.
John Gardner, Boston, Deborah Dean; 11 Dec. 1796.
Joseph Smith Gilman, Mrs. Elizabeth Odlin; 13 Nov. 1796.
James Gilman, Jr., Susanna Mason; 23 Aug. 1800.
Stephen Gale, Newburyport, Harriet Eastham; 31 Aug. 1807.
Jonathan Gilman, Lydia Lougee; 25 Nov. 1807.
Nathaniel Gordon, Mary Robinson; 30 Aug. 1808.
Stephen Grover, Nancy Barns; 31 Jan. 1812.
Eliphalet Giddinge, Mrs. Ann Lyford; 16 Feb. 1812.
Tony Gardner, Newburyport, Mary Paul Cutler; 25 March 1810.
John Gordon, Newbury, Frances Gordon; 1814.
Phillips Gilman, Betsy Gilman; 8 Nov. 1815.
Harrison Gray, Portsmouth, Clarissa Eastham; 26 April 1818.
William Gould, Mary Beckett, Brentwood; 5 July 1819.
Stephen L. Gordon, Rebecca Thayer; 6 July 1819.
James Gilman, Isabel Peavey; 18 Sept. 1825.
Biley Gilman, Harriet Burley; 28 Feb. 1820.
Andrew Gorham, Sarah G. Smith; 11 March 1822.
Charles Gaylord, Mary J. Blake; 10 July 1822.
John Gilman, Hallowell, Me., Sally Becket; 2 Feb. 1823.
Benjamin Gordon, Jr., Frances Folsom; 27 April 1823.
John T. Gordon, Sarah Folsom; 20 Nov. 1823.
Silas Gould, Sarah G. Folsom; 29 June 1823.
James Gilman, 3d, Mary A. Chapman; 4 Jan. 1826.
David W. Gorham, Elizabeth P. Abbott; 3 May 1826.
Theophilus Goodwin, Lois Dutch; 28 May 1826.
John C. Gerrish, Mary G. Folsom; 4 Dec. 1826.
Nehemiah Gilman, Martha J. Gray, Portsmouth; 25 Nov. 1828.
Stephen Goodwin, Mary Floid; 24 June 1831.
Charles C. P. Gale, Martha Walker; April 1832.
Oliver Gordon, Candia, Mary C. Dudley; 21 Nov. 1833.
Nathaniel Gilman, 4th, Betsey F. Batchelder; 26 Dec. 1833.
William F. Gordon, Mary L. Young; 17 Feb. 1834.
Seth Goodwin, Lavina Willey; 22 Oct. 1837.
Esop Hale, Lucy Sinegall (negroes); 3 April 1777.
Pery Hardy, Mehitable Lawrence; 13 Nov. 1777.
Moses Hopkinson, Lucy Calf; 13 May 1781.
Kinsly Hall, Honner Rundlet; 5 Nov. 1781.
Benjamin Hilton, Elizabeth Thurston; 23 March 1783.
Levi Healey, Hampton Falls, Abigail Robinson; 2 Sept. 1784.
Jonathan Hill, Sarah Wiggins; 12 Sept. 1784.
Nathaniel Herrick, Mary Hackett; 17 Dec. 1784.
Thomas Hains, Hannah Lord; 17 March 1785.
Edward Hilton, Jr., Newmarket, Deborah Wiggin; 26 Nov. 1792.
Caleb Hill, Newburyport, Mary Fowler; 19 July 1795.
Ezra Hutchins, Sally Currier; 26 Feb. 1797.
Samuel Hatch, Mary Gilman; 14 May 1797.

Richard Hilton, Newmarket, Patty Leavit; 31 Jan. 1798.
Jonathan Hamilton, Berwick, Mass., Mrs. Charlotte Sweat; 12 April 1801.
Joseph Hoit, Stratham, Betsy Odlin; 26 Nov. 1801.
Jonathan Hale, Coventry, Mrs. Mary Parker; 6 May 1802.
William Hill, Betsy Wyatt; 12 Aug. 1806.
Ezekiel Hook, Lucretia Hill; 1 Oct. 1807.
Cuffe Hoit, Rose Whidden, Greenland; 28 Sept, 1809.
Noyes Hopkinson, Elizabeth R. Eaton; 6 Oct. 1816.
William Hoit, Ellen E. Bacon, Sutton, Mass.; 27 Sept. 1818.
Rev. Isaac Hurd, Elizabeth Emery; 16 March 1819.
George Hanson, Brentwood, Mrs. Elizabeth Leavitt; 3 Dec. 1821.
Purmot Hill, Lydia R. Smith; 13 Feb. 1820.
Jonathan Hunnewell, Mary Parker; 23 March 1820.
Abel F. Hildreth, Londonderry, Ann E. Giddings; 21 Aug. 1820.
Henry Hovey, Mary E. Dolloff; 10 Sept. 1821.
James Hill, Gilford, Elizabeth M. Hall; 13 Sept. 1821.
Joshua M. Haley, Mary Willey; 26 Oct. 1821.
Thomas R. Hopkins, Boston, Anna M. Adams; 3 July 1823.
Samuel Ham, Frances Leavitt; 20 May 1824.
Thomas Hardy, Boston, Sarah R. Folsom; 31 Aug 1826.
Moses Harris, Clementine Rundlet; 18 Oct. 1826.
Joshua Holt, Elizabeth M. J. Emery; 15 May 1827.
Samuel Hodgdon, Joanna Tilton; 25 Oct. 1835.
Jeremiah Hall, Durham, Sarah A. Holt; Jan. 1832.
Charles A. Hartshorn, Boston, Abigail S. Floyd; 21 March 1834.
Charles Henss, Boston, Sarah Folsom; 9 Nov. 1835.
Henry R. Hall, Mary A. Boardman; 7 Oct. 1836.
George Harrington, Martha A. Chapman; 20 April 1841.
Moses Jewett, Martha Hale; 17 Nov. 1737.
Francis James, Abigail Lighton; 27 Jan. 1736-7.
Isaac, belonging to Paul Jewett, Catherine, belonging to Josiah Robinson (negroes); 21 Nov. 1776.
John Judkins, Abigail Swasey; 12 Jan. 1778.
Bradbury Johnson, Rachel Short; 24 Sept. 1786.
John Johnson, Jr., Mary Piper; 14 Jan. 1789.
Daniel S. Jones, Mary Steel; 18 Sept. 1791.
Samuel Jones, Joanna Bond; 22 Nov. 1792.
Pomp Jackson, Susanna Dimond (negroes); 5 April 1794.
Nathaniel Jefferds, Wells, Mass., Mary Folsom; 13 Jan. 1802.
Joseph A. Janvrin, Lydia A. Colcord; 14 Nov. 1822.
James Jones, Ann Rowley, foreigners, 23 Dec. 1821.
Luke Julian, Fitchburg, Abigail T. Moses; Oct. 1832.
Ebenezer James, Hampton, Abigail Robinson; 3 Nov. 1829.
Nathan Jewett, Mrs. Eliza S. Lang; July 1830.
Roger Kelly, Mary Holdridge; 29 Sept. 1681.
Moses Kimball, Pheebe Smart; 14 Feb. 1781.
Casar Knnap, Mimbo Cottle; 13 Dec. 1781.
Peter S. Kimball, Abigail Dean; 6 Jan. 1783.

Dudley Kimball, Anne Folsom ; 21 May 1789.
John Kimball, Wakefield, Mrs. Mary Weeks ; 20 Aug. 1789.
John Kimball, Anne Gilman ; 1 Oct. 1790.
John Kennedy, Lydia Blaisdell ; 25 Jan. 1807.
John Kimball, Mrs. Sarah Hodgkins ; 8 Sept. 1825.
Samuel Kingsbury, Portsmouth, Mary J. Thurston ; 24 Nov. 1825.
John Kennedy, Mary Hart ; 31 Dec. 1826.
Francis Lyford, Rebecca Dudley ; 21 Nov. 1681.
Nicholas Lisson, Jane ——— ; 14 Dec. 1682.
Jonathan Lord, Mrs. Hannah Light ; 14 Oct. 1731.
John Leavitt, Abigail Giles ; June 1735.
Josiah Ladd, Sarah Moss ; 3 Jan. 1737-8.
Elias Ladd, Ann Gilman ; 27 Nov. 1740.
John Lord, Abigail Eliots ; 27 Nov. 1777.
John Light, Sarah Marvel ; 4 Dec. 1777.
Josiah Leavit, Lydia Lawrence ; 6 July 1780.
Joseph Lovring, Elizabeth Creighton ;, 2 Nov. 1780.
Joseph Lougee, Miriam Fog ; 14 Nov. 1780.
Daniel Leavitt, Elizabeth Magoon ; 21 Nov. 1780.
Eliphalet Lord, Abigail Lord ; 2 May 1781.
Jonathan Louge, Nancy Simpson ; 6 Feb. 1783.
Joseph Lamson, 3d, Mehitable Philbrick ; 3 Sept. 1784.
Stephen Leavitt, Brentwood, Elizabeth Gordon ; 30 April 1787.
Simeon Ladd, Deborah Gilman ; 31 Jan. 1789.
Robert Lord, Jr., Mary Davis, Poplin ; 30 Sept. 1789.
Joseph Lamson, 3d, Susanna Folsom ; Jan. 1793.
Isaac Lord, Effingham, Susanna Leavitt ; 4 Feb. 1793.
Robert Lyford, Newmarket, Mary Lyford ; 28 March 1793.
Elisha Logie, Nancy Lord ; 7 Sept. 1794.
James Laine, Stratham, Deborah Folsom ; 23 Nov. 1794.
John Lovering, Apphia Wyatt ; 18 Sept. 1794.
Kinsley Lyford, Elizabeth Scammons, Stratham ; 16 Feb. 1796.
Samuel Lovering, North Hampton, Susanna Taylor, Hampton ; 8 March 1796.
Prince Light, Phillis Currier (negroes) ; 16 March 1800.
Joseph Lamson, Jr., Mary Sewal Parker ; 14 Oct. 1800.
Jotham Lawrence, Epping, Deborah Robinson ; 21 Feb. 1803.
Samuel Leavitt, Abigail Kimball ; 6 March 1803.
Thomas Leighton, Elizabeth Mitchell ; 7 March 1804.
Benjamin Leavitt, Betsy Dodge ; 1 July 1804.
Joseph Lovering, Mrs. Sarah Calef, Kingston ; 24 March 1808.
John Lakeman, Boston, Sally Rundlet ; 12 Nov. 1808.
John Lamson, Nancy Dodge ; 15 Sept. 1811.
William Lane, Abigail Daniels ; 19 Nov. 1815.
John Lougee, Hannah T. Leavitt ; 1817.
Hasket D. Lang, Salem, Mass., Eliza S. Sleeper ; 7 June 1819.
Sargent S. Littlehale, Boston, Edna P. Dow ; 10 June 1819.
Jonathan Larabee, Mary Davis ; 13 Oct. 1819.

Benjamin Leathers, Eliza Fogg ; 4 March 1822.
Edmund Leavitt, Concord, Nancy Reed ; 14 Jan. 1821.
Gideon C. Lyford, Hannah E. Gilman ; 9 Sept. 1821.
Oliver Larkin, Waterville, Me., Mary Gilman ; 5 Nov. 1821.
Charles Ladd, Abigail Hilton ; 19 May 1822.
John Leavitt, Mary S. Taylor ; 3 Nov. 1822.
Heman Ladd, Haverhill, Mass., Hannah Gilman ; 14 May 1823.
Benjamin Leavitt, Sarah E. Stevenson ; 25 April 1833.
Jonathan Leavitt, Angelina Towle ; 30 June 1833.
George W. Leathers, Mrs. Frances Deverson ; 28 Nov. 1833.
Isaac Ladd, Mary James, Kensington ; 15 June 1836.
Joshua A. Lunt, Jerusha H. Young ; Oct. 1830.
Parker Lovejoy, St. Stephens, N. B., Harriet Swasey ; July 1832.
Wm. B. Lowd, Rebecca L. Shaw ; 3 Jan. 1836.
Josiah Lane, Eliza A. Sanborn ; 5 April 1836.
George W. Little, Amesbury, Mary E. Swasey ; 27 Aug. 1836.
Calvin Lovering, Mary J. French ; 5 June 1838.
Benjamin Morss, Mary Gilman ; 2 Jan. 1777.
Samuel Mash, Hannah Bell ; 16 Jan. 1777.
Juba Merrile, Newbury, Hannah Holland (negroes) ; 3 Aug. 1777.
Caleb Michele, Ann Hains ; 13 Nov. 1777.
Francis Mason, Susanna Moses ; 6 June 1779.
Winthrop Merrill, Date Steel ; 1 Sept. 1779.
Joseph Mash, Olley Abuckle ; 17 Dec. 1780.
Zebulon Marsh, Abigail Young ; 27 Sept. 1784.
William Moore, Elizabeth Rundlet ; 2 Dec. 1789.
Ebenezer Melony, Anne Hacket ; 24 Dec. 1797.
John Meader, Elizabeth Gilman ; 1 Jan. 1798.
Simon Magoon, Kingston, Betsey Barstow ; 22 Nov. 1796.
Ebenezer Mingo, Phena Sharp ; 23 Dec. 1796.
James Marston, Packersfield, Mass., Mrs. Elizabeth Giddinge ; 31 Aug. 1799.
Henry Moore, Portsmouth, Ann Odiorne ; 10 Sept. 1804.
William Mace, Stratham, Catharine Swasey ; 29 Jan. 1812.
Samuel Moses, Mary E. Haskell ; 29 March 1812.
Amos Morse, Newbury, Lucretia Dean ; 3 Nov. 1817.
Abner Merrill, Sally W. Leavitt ; 2 July 1816.
John Mead, Olive Lovering ; 31 Dec. 1818.
Henry Menjoy, Abigail Pickering ; 7 March 1819.
Ebenezer L. Moulton, Mary Leavitt ; 27 Oct. 1822.
Daniel Melcher, Nancy Y. Folsom ; 27 April 1823.
Francis Mager, Catharine Thompson (negroes) ; 6 Nov. 1823.
William Moore, Jr., Rachel French ; 11 Aug. 1824.
Sibley Moulton, Lucinda Fogg ; 30 Sept. 1824.
Samuel H. Marsh, Martha B. Davis ; 30 March 1826.
Thomas J. Marsh, Nancy S. Davis ; 30 March 1826.
John Morrison, Mary Sheriff ; 29 Nov. 1827.
Thomas Moulton, Mary Gordon ; 4 June 1828.
Isaac G. Morse, Eunice Crockett ; 21 June 1837.

John Moulton, Lydia Leavitt; Dec. 1829.
Thomas G. Morse, Eliza J. Blanchard; 3 July 1833.
George S. Marden, Eliza A. Pickering; 8 Nov. 1835.
Gilman McNeal, Emeline N. Batchelder; 4 Sept. 1836.
Archelaus Martin, Dinah Barne; 11 March 1837.
Peltiah Moulton, York, Me., Susan H. Card; 22 Dec. 1839.
William P. Moses, Abby K. Leavitt; 14 Nov. 1839.
Theodore Moses, Harmony, Me., Abigail G. Colcord; 19 Jan. 1840.
Joseph H. Morrill, Salisbury, Mass., Olive Greenleaf; 9 April 1840.
Jonathan Nelson, Martha Folsom; 27 April 1777.
Josiah Nelson, Mary Robinson; 6 Dec. 1780.
Eliphalet Norris, Lydia Rundlet; 14 Dec. 1780.
Dudley Nichols, Molly Badger; 2 April 1783.
Mark Nutter, Lydia Nelson; 28 Dec. 1785.
Harvey Nicolle, Hannah Mead; 23 Dec. 1790.
Benjamin Nason, Shapleigh, Me., Hannah Gilman; 17 Aug. 1794.
Charles Norris, Catharine Ranlet; 1 Sept. 1807.
Rev. Ichabod Nicolles, Portland, Dorothea F. Gilman; 1810.
Charles Norris, Teresa Orn; April 1811.
Nathaniel F. Nelson, Gilmanton, Lydia B. Folsom; 28 Feb. 1817.
Dudley Nelson, Gilmanton, Martha N. Folsom; 5 Feb. 1818.
Josiah Nelson, Martha W. Colcord; 31 March 1822.
Rufus Newhall, Betsy Dolloff; 27 Feb. 1825.
Joseph Newman, Mary Steele; 29 Aug. 1827.
Josiah Norton, Deborah Fogg; 15 —— 1836.
Adam Nichols, Gloucester, Mass., Martha B. Folsom; Nov. 1829.
Samuel F. Nelson, Lavina Folsom; 3 Oct. 1832.
Dudley Odlin, Elizabeth Gilman; 14 Feb. 1782.
Woodbridge Odlin, Mary Brooks; 11 Feb. 1789.
William Odlin, Betsey Leavitt; 19 June 1791.
Philip Osgood, Joanna Davis; 17 March 1794.
Samuel T. Odiorne, Philadelphia, Clarissa Gilman; 1 Nov. 1815.
James Odlin, Martha H. Osborne; 27 Oct. 1816.
Woodbridge Odlin, Joanna Odiorne; 4 Feb. 1828.
Oliver W. Osborne, Mary A. Allen, Bradford; 27 April 1837.
Jonathan Perkins, Sarah ——; 20 Dec. 1682.
Jonathan Perkins, Elizabeth Folsom; 1 April 1778.
—— Primus, Cill Clough (negroes); 19 May 1779.
Edmund Pearson, Dorothy Swasey; 26 Oct. 1779.
Samuel Page, Elizabeth Langdon; 18 May 1780.
Robinson Peters, Vilet ——; 4 Sept. 1781.
Oliver Peabody, Frances Bourn; 28 March 1782.
Robert Parkes, Dolly Gilman; 6 March 1783.
Samuel Philbrick, Hannah Robinson; 28 Oct. 1784.
Daniel Philbrick, Susanna Carty; 19 Dec. 1790.
Moses Pike, Hampton Falls, Theodata Sanborn; 6 April 1791.
Nathaniel Parker, Catharine Tilton; 14 Nov. 1793.
Joseph Pearson, Dorothy Giddinge; 5 April 1795.

Stephen Perkins, Rochester, Lydia Smith; 23 Feb. 1796.
Rev. Walter Powers, Gilmanton, Mrs. Elizabeth McClure; 7 Aug. 1805.
Offin B. Palmer, Wakefield, Sally Rogers; 25 Sept. 1805.
William Pearson, Sophia Osborne; 16 April 1807.
Nathaniel Page, Charlotte Tilton; 21 March 1809.
Joseph Plummer, Jr., Newburyport, Ann Cram; 4 Sept. 1809.
John Paul, Martha Gilman; 15 March 1810.
John Pearson, Jr., Newburyport, Harriet P. Carlton; 30 Sept. 1810.
Jacob Paul, Jr., Catherine Wallace; 18 Jan. 1813.
Edmund Pearson, Wells, Mass., Hannah Philbrick; 16 Oct. 1814.
Samuel Philbrick, Elizabeth Smith; 17 Nov. 1814.
John Peavey, Hannah Daniels; 16 Jan. 1816.
Jeremiah Palmer, Elizabeth Moore; 28 Jan. 1816.
Rev. Gardner B. Perry, Bradford, Mass., Maria P. Chamberlain; 22 May 1816.
James Pearson, Susan Swasey; 10 Nov. 1816.
William Perry, Abby Gilman; 8 April 1818.
Nathaniel P. Page, Eastport, Me., Mary A. Robinson; 16 Aug. 1822.
Dennis Poor, Raymond, Mary Lovering; 25 April 1824.
Joseph Perkins, Elizabeth Odlin; 29 Nov. 1825.
James G. Page, Newmarket, Elizabeth Sawyer; 6 Dec. 1827.
Daniel Pearson, Hannah Carter; 5 June 1831.
John W. Pettengill, Olive M. Fellows; 29 Sept. 1833.
Jeremiah J. Peavey, Luella J. Rowe; 3 June 1834.
Benjamin R. Perkins, Mary J. Dolloff; 21 Dec. 1834.
Lewis W. Perkins, Eliza Leavitt; Dec. 1829.
Asher C. Palmer, Boston, Ann R. Folsom; 27 Aug. 1833.
William Philbrick, Sarah Lyford; 29 Aug. 1829.
William Parker, Canajoharie, N. Y., Dolly Blake; 26 April 1834.
Michael Prescott, Mary N. Hill; 14 July 1834.
Samuel Peavey, Sarah Gilman; 30 Oct. 1837.
Lucian M. Pike, Newmarket, Satira D. Wadleigh; 22 June 1840.
Joseph Quince, Martha Gilman; 29 Dec. 1822.
Ephraim Robinson, Mary Shaw; 24 Jan. 1734–5.
James Rundlet, Jane McCluer; 25 Dec. 1777.
John Robinson, Sarah Smith; 9 Jan. 1777.
Francis Roberts, Jane Lovrain; 30 Dec. 1778.
Benjamin Robinson, Huldah Conner; 24 July 1781.
William Robinson, Jane Smith; Sept. 1782.
Daniel Robinson, Abigail Robinson, Sanbornton; 7 March 1785.
Jonathan Rundlet, Anne Johnson; 16 Feb. 1786.
Joseph Rundlet, Priscilla Wilson; 18 March 1787.
Joseph Rundlet, Hannah Dow, Epping; 3 Dec. 1788.
John Robinson, Sanbornton, Lydia Calfe; 2 Jan. 1790.
William Robinson, Mary Leavitt; 12 July 1792.
Zechariah Robinson, Rebecca Hall; 21 Nov. 1793.
James Robinson, Sanbornton, Deborah Dean Lord; 23 Nov. 1793.

James Rundlet, Sally Rust; 12 Nov. 1796.
Josiah Sanborn, Hannah Moulton; 25 Aug. 1681.
Benjamin Shaw, Molly Sanborn; 16 Sept. 1778.
John Shepard, Gilmanton, Elizabeth Gilman; 13 Dec. 1779.
John Smith, Pheebe Thurston; 20 Sept. 1781.
John Sanborn, Anne Sanborn; 29 July 1782.
John Setier, Sarah Rundlet; 24 Sept. 1783.
Benjamin Silsbee, Polly Folsom; 8 Oct. 1786.
Joseph Smith, Polly Burleigh; 13 Nov. 1786.
Lowel Rawlins, Sukey Fogg; 28 Dec. 1802.
Samuel Rowe, Olive Rundlet; 15 May 1802.
Wm. F. Rowland, Ann Giddings; 29 Aug. 1802.
Robert Roberts, Boston, Dorothy Hall; 15 Dec. 1805.
Daniel Rundlet, Sophia Folsom; 6 April 1807.
Henry A. Ranlett, Mary Fellows; 30 March 1817.
Trueworthy Robinson, Jr., Lucy Melcher, Kensington; 30 Oct. 1817.
Thomas S. Robinson, Brentwood, Sophia Gordon; 16 Dec. 1818.
Jeremiah L. Robinson, Irene Fellows; 26 Jan. 1823.
James Robinson, Mary Elliot; 18 Feb. 1827.
Daniel Ranlett, Sarah G. Smith; 18 Nov. 1827.
John Rogers, Martha P. Cram; 20 March 1828.
Samuel Rand, Epping, Mary Willey; 13 April 1829.
William Rowe, Mary A. Philbrick; Nov. 1836.
Lucian B. Robee, Elizabeth Dean; May 1832.
Henry Robinson, Almira Kelly; 14 March 1836.
Jona. Robinson, Jr., Sarah S. Dearborn, North Hampton; 27 Sept. 1837.
Charles H. Robinson, Ann M. Colcord; 16 April 1840.
Levi Rundlett, Irena M. Foye; 4 July 1841.
Thomas Swasey, Elizabeth Folsom; 7 Jan. 1787.
Zadoch Sanborn, Gilmanton, Abigail Tilton; 31 Jan. 1788.
Benjamin Pierce Sheriff, Patty Gilman; 29 Sept. 1788.
Josiah Coffin Smith, Annie Leavitt; 11 July 1789.
John Smith, Jr., Elizabeth Calef; 18 July 1790.
Rev. Jonathan Strong, Braintree, Joanna Odiorne; 3 Nov. 1790.
Joseph Sceavy, Rye, Martha Patten, Candia; 13 June 1790.
Nathaniel Sother, Mrs. Esther Chamberlain; 16 Dec. 1790.
Daniel Smith, Jr., Polly Pickering; 14 Feb. 1791.
Jonathan F. Sleeper, Dorothy Tilton; 18 Nov. 1791.
Titus Sharp, Phena Jacobs (negroes); 29 Dec. 1791.
William Sibley, Gilmanton, Anna Thing, Brentwood; 6 Sept. 1792.
Thomas Stickney, Jr., Concord, Mary Ann Odlin; 7 Nov. 1792.
Josiah Sanborn, Sanbornton, Olive Fogg; 4 Feb. 1794.
Simeon Stevens, Stratham, Ruth Sanborn; 8 May 1794.
Jeremiah Stickney, Portsmouth, Charlotte Odlin; 4 May 1795.
John Steel, Elizabeth Hilton; 2 Nov. 1793.
Dudley Swasey, Danville, Vt., Apphia Loogee; 5 March 1796.
John Sawyer, Lovey Paul (negroes); 13 Jan. 1797.
Robert Steel, Olive Hilton; 4 Sept. 1796.

Josiah Sleeper, Margaret Taylor ; 29 Sept. 1796.
Richard Smith, Jr., Seabrook, Hannah Tucker, Pittsfield ; 20 Dec. 1798.
Timothy Smith, Jr., Sanbornton, Polly Smith, Brentwood ; 7 Jan. 1799.
William Swasey, Mary Robinson ; 7 Aug. 1800.
Greenleaf Seavey, Nancy Parks ; 13 July 1806.
Jacob H. Sanborn, Kingston, Betsey Hoit ; 13 Jan. 1807.
Joseph Smith, Jr., Sally Dutch ; 17 Nov. 1808.
Samuel B. Stevens, Newburyport, Joanna Folsom ; 27 Aug. 1810.
James Smith, Lydia Taylor ; 1810.
Rufus Swasey, Abigail T. Leavitt ; 30 Aug. 1812.
Samuel Somerby, Mary Swasey ; 7 Oct. 1812.
Buswell Stevens, Pembroke, Catharine H. Emery ; 16 May 1814.
Amos Saunders, Salem, Maria Steele ; 22 July 1816.
Robert Shute, Emma Smith ; 5 Oct. 1817.
Benjamin Swasey, Caroline Clark ; 15 Oct. 1818.
Parker Sheldon, Gardiner, Me., Elizabeth W. Conner ; 1 Nov. 1820.
Henry Shute, Eliza R. Smith ; 29 Feb. 1820.
Lewis Smith, Plymouth, N. H., Henrietta Robinson ; 1 Sept. 1822.
James Sanborn, Hannah V. Colcord ; 16 Nov. 1823.
John L. Stokle, Northwood, Mrs. Lydia Gilman ; 12 Feb. 1824.
John Scammon, Stratham, Mary G. Barker ; 1824.
Joseph Safford, Danvers, Mass., Sally R. Folsom ; 10 June 1826.
Josiah G. Smith, Francis A. Eastham ; 18 June 1826.
William O. Smith, Mary G. Towle ; 3 May 1827.
Oliver Smith, Charlotte Rundlett ; 1828.
Timothy F. Shaw, Mrs. Mary Gale ; 27 July 1829.
Jeremiah Sawyer, Susan Sheriff ; Dec. 1832.
William L. Swasey, Mary Gilman ; 10 Nov. 1830.
Lewis F. Shepard, Sarah Dow ; March 1830.
Elihu T. Stevens, Mary A. Odlin ; June 1832.
Nathaniel Shute, Fitchburg, Susan G. Barker ; 1 Oct. 1832.
Thomas Sullivan, Frances A. Leavitt ; 7 Oct. 1836.
John R. Storey, Caroline C. Tilton ; 24 Dec. 1837.
Elijah Tilton, Eunice Lee ; 5 April, 1778.
Ephraim Thursten, Ann Mash ; 11 Jan. 1780.
John Thompson, Anne Wilson, 27 July 1784.
James Thurston, Elizabeth Peabody, Brentwood ; 9 Oct. 1791.
Caleb Thurston, Jr., Mary Gilman ; 17 Nov. 1792.
John Tilton, Patty Odlin ; 30 June 1793.
Moses Thurston, Sarah Moses ; 2 Sept. 1793.
Nathaniel Taylor, Nancy Eastham ; 21 Sept. 1794.
Simeon Tole, Parsonsfield, Betsey More, Stratham ; 25 March 1794.
Richard Thayer, Randolph, Mass., Deborah Odiorne ; 10 Feb. 1799.
John Poor Taylor, Lydia Jones ; 22 July 1799.
Caleb Thurston, Jr., Anne Wiggins ; 31 Aug. 1799.
Joseph Tilton, Rochester, Nancy Folsom ; 13 Jan. 1806.
Dudley Thing, Lydia Swasey ; 28 Aug. 1808.
Dr. Joseph Tilton, Catharine Shackford ; 10 Sept. 1767.

John Tilton, Mary Luey; 6 March 1811.
Abraham Towle, Mary Merrill; 29 Sept. 1816.
William G. Tash, Sally P. Duce; 2 Oct. 1819.
John F. Tilton, Sarah Fogg; 2 Dec. 1819.
Winthrop Tilton, Joanna T. Morse; 4 March 1823.
James Tuttle, Maria Jenks; 5 Feb. 1824.
Laban A. Tyler, Mary Ranlet; 8 April 1824.
Zebulon G Thing, Sarah A. York, Brentwood; 16 Nov. 1830.
Perley Tuck, Kensington, Lavina Safford; 6 Jan. 1828.
Elisha Towle, Kensington, Hannah S. Dolloff; 5 April 1829.
Nathaniel K. Thurston, Bradford, Mass., Sarah A. York; 13 May 1832.
James D. Townsend, Dover, Sarah W. Hook; 21 Sept. 1834.
William Treadwell, Harriet M. Ladd; 9 Sept. 1836.
Joseph Twombly, Shuah Wentworth; 26 Sept. 1837.
David D. Thompson, Mary E. King; 9 Aug. 1840.
Enoch W. Towle, Susannah Perkins; 15 Nov. 1832.
James Underwood, Anna Thurston; 4 Dec. 1777.
Ned R. Underhill, Chester, Abigail Conner; 27 Aug, 1817.
John White, Haverhill, Lydia Gilman; 24 Oct. 1687.
Josiah Weeks, Abigail James; 9 Oct. 1776.
Joseph Wait, Esther Heerd; 3 Feb. 1783.
Cesar Wallace, Katy Duce; 25 March 1783.
Thomas Waters, Portsmouth, Deborah Rundlet; 24 July 1783.
Cato Wallingsford, Margaret Peterson; 26 Feb. 1784.
John Wadleigh, Elizabeth Daniels; 3 March 1784.
Isaac Williams, Elizabeth Jenkins; 16 Aug. 1786.
Nathaniel Weeks, Polly Pottle; 6 May 1787.
Daniel Williams, Nottingham, Polly Jenkins; 17 Oct. 1790.
John Webb, Polly Corney; 27 Feb. 1792.
Abner Wood, Loudon, Dolly Pearson; 18 June 1792.
Simon Wiggin, Joanna Thurston; 15 July 1792.
David Watson, Jr., Lucretia York, Brentwood; 30 March 1793.
Joseph Whitfield, Newburyport, Nancy Pauls, Newburyport (negroes); 12 Dec. 1797.
James Weeks, Elizabeth Marsh; 30 Nov. 1800.
John Walker, Portsmouth, Dolly Adams; 2 Jan. 1802.
William Webb, Polly Odiorne.
Dan Weed, Gloucester, Lucy Rust; 7 Dec. 1807.
Joshua Wiggin, Comfort Wiggin, Newmarket; 20 April 1809.
George Wallace, Dolly Pauls; 1 Feb. 1818.
John Walker, Mary Adjutant; 28 Aug. 1818.
William Wadleigh, Sally Leavitt; 1 Jan. 1817.
John Watson, Newmarket, Betsy Gilman; 9 Jan. 1822.
Benjamin Wiggin, Boston, Mary A. Conner; 2 March 1823.
Nathaniel Weeks, Harriet B. Gilman; 6 Aug. 1820.
Benjamin J. Williams, Maria Thayer; 5 May, 1825.
Richard B. Ward, Catherine F. Moore; 2 June 1826.
Joseph L. White, Mary P. Whitefield, Londonderry; 23 Dec. 1826.

James Weeks, Jr , Sarah Sheriff; 5 Feb. 1827.
Ebenezer Wyatt, Sarah M. Leavitt; 4 Dec. 1828.
Edward W. Warren, Malinda Crosby; 3 Nov. 1829.
Levi Wilson, South Hampton, Eliza A. Fellows; 15 June 1834.
Foster G. Whidden, Celestia W. Gridley; 11 Oct. 1835.
Ebenezer Willis, Mary F. Batchelder; 22 Feb. 1836.
John Williams, Abigail P. Stockbridge; 29 Nov. 1838.
Jonathan B. Wadleigh, Sarah Hicks; 21 Oct. 1838.
Hiram Whittemore, Pembroke, Elizabeth J. Hoyt; 15 Nov. 1838.
Jonathan P. West, Sarah F. Card; 2 Feb. 1840.
Josiah R. West, Esther G. Card; 2 Feb. 1840.
Alvan White, Susan Goodwin; 5 March 1840.
Jonathan Y. York, Sarah Smith, Stratham; 17 Nov. 1785.
John York, Abigail Melcher, Kensington; 18 Dec. 1802.
Joseph Young, Sarah B. Hall; 17 Oct. 1819.
Isaac P. Yeaton, South Berwick, Me., Frances S. Gordon; 15 June, 1835.

BIRTHS.

FROM THE TOWN RECORDS.

Samuel, s. of Hannah Adkinson; 29 March 1766.
Josiah, s. of Jonathan and Susannah Bradley; 20 Sept. 1745.
John, s. of Samuel and Mary Brown; 2 Nov. 1761.
Sarah, d. of Moses and Anne Coffin; 19 Sept. 1733.
Frederick, s. of Theodore and Deborah Charlton (Carleton); 7 Oct. 1764; d. 2 Feb. 1766.
Enoch Coffin March, s. of Peter Chadwick; 13 Sept. 1818.
John, s. of Peter Chadwick; 21 Oct. 1821.
Henry Salter, s. of Andrew and Harriet Cook and grandson of Thomas and Mercy Speed; 18 Jan. 1817.
Ferdinand, s. of Rev. Ferdinand Ellis; 12 March 1819.
Susanna, d. of John and Mary Folsom; 10 May 1718.
Josiah, s. of John and Mary Folsom; 24 July 1725.
Abigail, d. of Daniel and Elizabeth Favor; 21 Dec. 1733.
James, s. of James and Elizabeth Folsom; 27 June 1737.
Charles Lee, s. of Isaac and Frances B. Foster; 2 March 1836.
Mary, d. of Stephen and Molly Gorham; 1 April 1785.
Mary, d. of Dudley and Mercy Hilton; 22 Oct. 1709.
Jane, d. of Dr. Eliphalet and Elizabeth Hale; 9 May 1751.
John, s. of John Kimming; 11 June 1670.
Thomas Dolloff, s. of Martha Kimming; 21 March 1737.
John, s. of Robert Kimball; 1 Jan. 1771; d. 29 Oct. 1849.

Nathaniel, s. of Dudley and Ann Kimball; 12 June 1805.
Samuel Gilman, s. of Heman and Hannah Ladd; 7 Sept. 1825.
William Frederic, s. of Jotham and Deborah Lawrence; 22 March 1804.
Alexander Hamilton, s. of Jotham and Caroline Lawrence; 18 June 1812.
Abigail Lighton; 7 Nov. 1713.
Mary Mann; 4 Sept. 1796.
John Mann, George Mann (twins); 18 May 1799.
Horace Edward, s. of Horace W. and Lydia S. Morse; 4 Aug. 1840.
Serena Maria, d. of Samuel Tufts and Clarissa Odiorne; 8 Sept. 1817.
Jeremiah Dow, s. of Retire H. and Hannah Parker; 4 Oct. 1833.
Charles, Jane, children of Charles Rundlett; 9 May 1676.
Thomas M., s. of James and Jane Rundlett; 26 Nov. 1798.
Abigail, d. of Jonathan Smith; 22 June 1678.
Sarah, d. of Elisha and Lydia Sanborn; 21 Aug. 1734.
Benjamin, s. of Nicholas and Mary Smith; 1 Feb. 1702.
Lydia, d. of Timothy and Abigail Somes; 19 June 1760
John, s. of Timothy and Abigail Somes; 28 Oct. 1763.
Catharine Shackford; 12 Oct. 1745.
Joseph Tilton; 25 Sept. 1744.
George Veasey; 20 Oct. 1665.
William, alias Elijah, s. of Elijah and Lydia Vickery; 17 March 1782.
Mary, d. of Jesse and Patience Worster; 16 March 1747-8.
Elizabeth, d. of Thomas and Susanna Webster; 21 June 1740.

DEATHS, PRIOR TO THE YEAR 1800.

FROM THE TOWN RECORDS.

Deborah Warren, wife of John; 26 June 1668.
George Randol; 15 Feb. 1666-7.
Catharine Hilton, wife of Edward; 29 May 1676.
Antipas Marverick; 2 July 1678.
Eliphalet Coffin; 16 Aug. 1736.
Catharine Shackford, wid. of John; 16 Dec. 1799.
Samuel Thursten; 21 Jan. 1751.
Anna Wadleigh, wife of Jonathan; 8 March 1743-4.
Ralph Hall; 6 June 1671.
Col. Samuel Gilman, s. of Nicholas; 3 Jan. 1785.
Peter Gilman, s. of John; 1 Dec. 1788.

HISTORY OF EXETER. 65

BIRTHS, DEATHS AND MARRIAGES.

FROM THE EARLIEST TOWN RECORDS.

The following is a transcript from the earliest book of records of the town, and is not embodied in the preceding tables.

A record of the births, marriages and deaths of children and others in Exeter as they are brought to the clerk of the writs from the 6th of the first mo. ('48) or ('49.)

1. Joseph Cram the son of John Cram and Lide, aged about 15 years, departed this life, being drouned the 24th of June.
2. At the same time Joseph Duncom servant to Capt. Wiggen was drouned, being in the same canoe with the other.
3. Lidde Cram daughter of John Cram was born the 27th day of July Anno Dom. 1648.

Mary Boulter daughter of Nathaniel and Grace Boulter was born about the middle of May Anº. Dom. 1648.

Hanna Pettet daughter of Thomas and Christian Pettet was born the beginning of February Anno Dom. 1647.

Thomas Roby son of Henry and Ruth Roby was born the f—— day of March Anno Dom. 1645 or '46.

John Roby son of Henry Roby and Ruth was born the 2 day of February An. Dom. 1648.

Mercy Hall daughter of Ralph Hall aged about —— year and a half departed this life in July, 1648.

Hildea Hall daughter of Ralph and Mary Hall was born the 16th of April 1649.

EXETER MARRIAGES, BIRTHS AND DEATHS.

Taken from the records of old Norfolk County by William Smith, Esq., not on the town records.

MARRIAGES.

Nicholas Norris and Sarah Coxe ; 21 Jan. 1664-5.
Edward Smith and Mary Hall ; 1668.
Anthony Stanyan and Ann Partridge ; 1 Jan. 1655-6.
George Veasey and Mary Wiggin ; 23 Jan. 1664.
John Warren and Deborah Wilson ; 21 Oct. 1650.
Humphrey Wilson and Judith Hersey ; 21 Dec. 1665.

BIRTHS.

Mary, d. of John Bean; 18 June 1655.
Henry, s. of John Bean; 5 March 1662.
Mary, d. of Thomas and Mary Cornish; July 1648.
Sarah, d. of Cornelius and Sarah Conner; 23 Aug. 1659.
Lydia, d. of John and Hester Cram; 27 July 1648.
Mary, d. of William Hackett; 2 Dec. 1665.
Mary, d. of Ralph and Mary Hall; 15 Jan. 1647.
Elizabeth, d. of Henry Magoon; 29 Sept. 1670.
George, s. of George Veasey; 20 Oct. 1665.
Edward, s. of George Veasey; 27 April 1667.
A son of Gowen Wilson, b. and d. Nov. 1647.

DEATHS.

Edward Eurin (?); 9 Nov. 1667.
Mary, d. of Ralph and Mary Hall; middle of June 1648.
Edward Veasey; 7 Nov. 1667.

BAPTISMS

OF CHILDREN IN THE FIRST SOCIETY FROM 1743 TO 1763.

The following list is copied from a manuscript record kept by the Rev. Woodbridge Odlin, of all the children baptized by him between the years mentioned. It will be seen at once how small a proportion of the births are recorded upon the books of the town; probably not nearly one-tenth of the whole number. Mr. Odlin's parish embraced only about two-thirds of the families of the town; and children born of parents in the other parish were baptized by their minister. Mr. Odlin's manuscript contained also a number of names already given in the "Family Register," and not repeated here, and a few baptisms of children belonging to other towns where he preached, and those are omitted.

The children were usually baptized at the age of from two days to one month, according to the convenience of the pastor. Sometimes there is an interval of only three or four months between the baptisms of two in the same family. In such cases one was probably considerably older.

HISTORY OF EXETER. 67

Stephen, s. of Benjamin Atkinson; 26 June 1763.
Mary, d. of Benjamin Atkinson; 24 July 1763.
Joshua and Cornelius, sons of Joshua Batchelder deceased; 16 April 1758.
Benjamin, s. of Jeremiah Bean; 26 July 1747.
John, s. of Joshua Bean; 28 June 1747.
Abigail, d. of Nathaniel Bean; 20 March 1747-8.
Deborah, d. of Sarah Bean; 7 Nov. 1749.
Francis, s. of Dudley Beckett; 23 March 1755.
Dudley, s. of Dudley Beckett; 2 Jan. 1757.
Deborah, d. of Dudley Beckett; 6 Jan. 1760.
Sarah, d. of Dudley Beckett; 1 Nov. 1761.
Pernal, d. of Francis Becket; 10 March 1745.
Deborah, d. of Francis Beckett; 10 Dec. 1747.
Betty, d. of John Bellomy; 11 July 1762.
William, s. of Benjamin Boardman; 4 July 1762.
Mercy, d. of John Bond; 2 Feb. 1755.
Jane, d. of John Bond; 24 July 1757.
Jean, d. of John Bond; 10 Dec. 1758.
Susanna, d. of John Bond; 29 June 1760.
John, s. of John Bond; 5 Sept. 1762.
Susanna, d. of John Bowden; 13 Sept. 1747.
Margaret, d. of John Bowden; 18 Nov. 1753.
William Tyler, s. of John Bowden; 5 Oct. 1755.
Michael, s. of John Bowden; 2 March 1760.
Olive, d. of Joshua Brown; 7 Aug. 1748.
Dudley, s. of Samuel Brown; 2 Dec. 1753.
John, d. of Samuel Brown; 16 Nov. 1760.
Elizabeth and John, children of John Bucknal; 14 May 1749.
Elizabeth, d. of James Calfe; 6 Aug. 1749.
Jeremiah and James (twins), sons of James Calfe; 20 Jan. 1751.
Lucy, d. of James Calfe; 31 Oct. 1756.
Lucy, d. of Jeremiah Calfe, Jr.; 6 July 1748.
Mehitable, d. of Jonathan Cauley; 17 March 1754.
Levi, s. of Joseph Chapman; 8 Dec. 1754.
Mary, d. of Josiah Chapman; 29 March 1752.
Tryphena, d. of Pennel Chapman; 5 Nov. 1758.
Abigail, d. of Satchell Clark; 5 Aug. 1750.
Elisabeth, d. of Satchel Clark; 15 Feb. 1756.
Alice, d. of Satchel Clark; 13 Nov. 1757.
Abigail, d. of Satchel Clark; 21 Oct. 1759.
Anne, d. of Thomas Clark; 2 Jan. 1757.
Ebenezer, s. of Ebenezer Colcord, Jr.; 18 Feb. 1753.
Sarah, d. of Benjamin Connor; 20 April 1755.
John and Moses, sons of David Connor; 21 Aug. 1748.
Hannah, d. of Jeremiah Connor; 6 April 1760.
Tristram Sanborn, s. of Jeremiah Connor; 21 Nov. 1762.
Mary, d. of John Connor; 30 Nov. 1755.
Joseph, s. of Joseph Connor; 14 Aug. 1758.

Jacob, s. of Jonathan Cram; 13 March 1763.
Martha, d. of George Creighton; 20 March 1747-8.
George, s. of George Creighton; 10 June 1750.
Robert Light, s. of Thomas Creighton; 8 March 1761.
Thomas, s. of Thomas Creighton; 12 Sept. 1762.
Isaac, s. of Isaac Currier; 18 July 1762.
Ephraim, s. of Isaac Currier; 26 Sept. 1762.
Susanna, d. of Minus Daniels; 4 April 1762.
Reuben, s. of Benjamin Darling; 22 July 1762.
John, s. of Lemuel Davis; 30 July 1757.
Ruth, d. of Lemuel Davis; 29 July 1759.
Abigail, d. of Nehemiah Dean; 17 June 1759.
Sarah, d. of Thomas Dolloff; 6 Nov. 1748.
Caleb, s. of Andrew Downer; 11 Aug. 1746.
Mary, d. of John Dudley; 23 Nov. 1746.
Odlin, s. of Capt. Trueworthy Dudley; 14 Feb. 1747-8.
Dorothy, d. of Trueworthy Dudley; 18 Nov. 1759.
Dorothy, d. of Trueworthy Dudley; 5 Sept. 1762.
John, s. of True. Dudley, Jr.; 29 Nov. 1747.
Abigail, d. of George Dutch; 25 March 1744.
Mary, d. of George Dutch; 20 July 1746.
Betty, d. of George Dutch; 29 July 1750.
Samuel, son of George Dutch; 24 Dec. 1752.
John, s. of George Dutch; 14 Sept. 1755.
Sarah, d. of George Dutch; 10 June 1759.
Mary, d. of Jonathan Edgerly; 14 May 1758.
Mary, d. of Jonathan Edgerley; 28 Sept. 1760.
John, s. of Jonathan Edgerley; 18 July 1762.
Noah, s. of Noah Emery; 20 Nov. 1748.
Richard, s. of Noah Emery; 27 June 1756.
Joanna, d. of Noah Emery; 24 Sept. 1758.
Theresia, d. of Noah Emery; 12 April 1761.
Richard, s. of Noah Emery; 7 Nov. 1762.
Samuel, s. of Daniel Favour; 14 April 1749.
Daniel, s. of Daniel Favour; 14 April 1751.
Susanna, d. of Thomas Flanders; 2 June 1745.
Abigail, d. of Thomas Flanders; 19 July 1747.
Joseph, s. of Thomas Flanders; 30 March 1760.
Hannah, d. of David Fogg; 14 Sept. 1755.
David, s. of David Fogg; 5 Feb. 1758.
Molly, d. of David Fogg; 30 March 1760.
Sarah, d. of David Fogg; 6 June 1762.
Sarah, d. of Enoch Fogg; 14 April 1756.
Seth s. of John Fogg; 10 May 1752.
Miriam, d. of John Fogg; 8 May 1757.
Jonathan, s. of John Fogg; 27 Aug. 1759.
John, s. of John Fogg; 11 Oct. 1761.
Meribah, d. of Jonathan Fogg; 29 Aug. 1751.

Meribah, d. of Jonathan Fogg; 19 Aug. 1753.
Samuel, s. of Josiah Fogg; 31 Oct. 1756.
Mary, d. of widow Fogg; 20 July 1755.
Jonathan Kingsbury and Betty, ch. of Daniel Folsom; 28 June 1747.
Abigail, d. of James Folsom; 9 Oct. 1743.
Sarah, d. of John Folsom; 29 April 1750.
Molly, d. of John Folsom; 11 March 1753.
Theophilus, s. of John Folsom; 29 Aug. 1756.
Samuel, s. of John Folsom; 17 June 1759.
James, s. of John Folsom; 25 Dec. 1760.
Elisabeth, d. of John Folsom; 8 Nov. 1761.
Samuel, s. of John Folsom; 18 Sept. 1763.
Eliphalet, s. of John Folsom, Jr.; 28 Feb. 1747-8.
Susanna, d. of John Folsom, Jr.; 24 Dec. 1752.
John, s. of John Folsom, Jr.; 31 Aug. 1755.
Noah, s. of John Folsom, Jr.; 12 Feb. 1758.
Annah, d. of Jonathan Folsom; 23 Oct. 1757.
Samuel Bradley, s. of Josiah Folsom; 28 June 1747.
Martha, d. of Josiah Folsom; 4 June 1758.
Sarah, d. of Josiah, Folsom; 3 Sept. 1758.
Lydia, d. of Josiah Folsom; 16 Sept. 1759.
Sarah, d. of Josiah Folsom; 12 April 1761.
Josiah Gilman, s. of Josiah Folsom; 13 Feb. 1763.
Katherine, d. of Peter Folsom; 8 June 1746.
Anna, d. of Peter Folsom; 6 March 1747-8.
Elisabeth, d. of Peter Folsom; 21 June 1752.
Jonathan, s. of Peter Folsom; 14 July 1754.
James, s. of Peter Folsom; 29 Aug. 1756.
Nicholas, s. of Peter Folsom; 27 May 1759.
Samuel, s. of Peter Folsom; 8 Nov. 1761.
Anna, d. of Samuel Folsom; 16 Dec. 1753.
Anna, d. of Capt. Samuel Folsom; 17 Dec. 1759.
Deborah, d. of Samuel Folsom; 19 Jan. 1763.
Mary, d. of Thomas Folsom; 20 Oct. 1760.
Anna, d. of Trueworthy Folsom; 23 Oct. 1763.
John, s. of John Fox; 1 June 1755.
Nathaniel, s. of John Fox; 31 July 1757.
John, s. of John Furnald; 31 Dec. 1752.
Bartholomew, s. of Daniel Gale; 15 April 1750.
John Cartee, s. of John Gale; 19 Dec. 1762.
Susanna, d. of Susanna Gale; 24 Oct. 1762.
Josiah, s. of Josiah George; 22 Feb. 1761.
Elisabeth, d. of Josiah George; 6 Dec. 1761.
Jean, d. of Andrew Gerrish; 16 Nov. 1760.
Jonathan, s. of Antipas Gilman; 9 Sept. 1753.
Dudley, s. of Antipas Gilman; 16 Nov. 1755.
Betty, d. of Antipas Gilman; 24 Dec. 1757.
Alice, d. of Antipas Gilman; 10 Dec. 1758.

Lydia, d. of Antipas Gilman; 29 Nov. 1761.
William, s. of Biley Gilman; 17 Dec. 1752.
Biley, s. of Biley Gilman; 13 Oct. 1754.
Hannah, d. of Biley Gilman; 7 Nov. 1756.
Molly, d. of Biley Gilman; 2 Dec. 1759.
Ezekiel, s. of Bradstreet Gilman; 11 Nov. 1750.
Dudley, s. of Bradstreet Gilman; 11 Jan. 1756.
Chase, s. of Bradstreet Gilman; 19 Feb. 1758.
Comfort, d. of Bradstreet Gilman; 16 March 1760.
Bradstreet, s. of Bradstreet Gilman; 31 Oct. 1762.
Sarah, d. of Caleb Gilman, Jr.; 9 March 1755.
Cartee, s. of Caleb Gilman; 12 Feb. 1758.
Mary, d. of Caleb Gilman; 22 Feb. 1761.
Abigail, d. of Cartee Gilman; 3 Oct. 1762.
Dolly, d. of Daniel Gilman (Cartee's son); 9 Oct. 1748.
David, s. of David Gilman; 25 May 1746.
Mary, d. of David Gilman; 4 Sept. 1748.
Samuel Folsom, s. of David Gilman; 25 Nov. 1750.
Elisabeth, d. of David Gilman; 9 Dec. 1753.
William, s. of David Gilman; 10 July 1757.
Betty, d. of David Gilman; 19 Aug. 1759.
Lydia, d. of Israel Gilman; 28 June 1747.
Ezekiel, s. of Jeremiah Gilman; 24 Sept. 1758.
John, s. of John Gilman, 4th; 14 Feb. 1747-8.
Mehitable, d. of John Gilman, 4th; 10 May 1752.
Dorothy, d. of John Gilman; 8 Aug. 1756.
John, s. of Jonathan Gilman; 13 Sept. 1747.
Samuel, s. of Josiah Gilman; 17 Jan. 1759.
Elisabeth, d. of Josiah Gilman; 24 Aug. 1760.
Jonathan, s. of Josiah Gilman, Jr.; 13 Dec. 1761.
Mary, d. of widow Mary Gilman; 17 Sept. 1760.
Jonathan, s. of Moses Gilman; 14 Jan. 1759.
Abigail, d. of Nathaniel Gilman; 10 Dec. 1747.
Mary, d. of Nehemiah Gilman's widow; 29 Nov. 1758.
Tristram and Sarah, twin children of Peter Gilman, Jr.; 1 Nov. 1745.
Nathaniel, s. of Peter Gilman; 20 Aug. 1749.
Peter, s. of Peter Gilman; 6 Oct. 1754.
Nabby, d. of Peter Gilman; 21 Nov. 1756.
Zebulon, s. of Peter Gilman; 24 Sept. 1758.
Lydia, d. of Peter Gilman; 19 July 1761.
Simon, s. of Simon Gilman; 29 June 1755.
Nathaniel, s. of Theo. Gilman; 3 Feb. 1751.
Nathaniel, s. of Theo. Gilman; 20 May 1753.
Deborah, d. of Theo. Gilman; 13 April 1755.
Eliphalet, s. of Theophilus Gilman; 13 Feb. 1757.
Molly, d. of Theophilus Gilman; 12 Aug. 1759.
Patty, d. of Theophilus Gilman; 6 Sept. 1761.
Elisabeth, d. of Theophilus Gilman; 11 Sept. 1763.

Rebecca, d. of Benjamin Gordon; 22 March 1745.
Benjamin, s. of Benjamin Gordon; 14 April 1755.
Benjamin, s. of Benjamin Gordon; 23 Jan. 1757.
Josiah, s. of Benjamin Gordon; 2 July 1758.
Simeon, s. of Benjamin Gordon; 31 May 1761.
Esther, d. of James Gordon; 28 March 1762.
Jacob, s. of John Gordon; 10 Oct. 1756.
Nathaniel, s. of Nathaniel Gordon; 6 April 1760.
Mary, d. of Nicholas Gordon; 26 July 1747.
Abraham, son of Timothy Gordon; 10 July 1748.
Mary, d. of Daniel Grant; 8 April 1744.
Paul Hall, s. of Daniel Grant; 13 Nov. 1748.
Daniel, s. of Daniel Grant; 17 Jan. 1759.
Anna, d. of Wilson Graves; 23 Dec. 1748.
Jean, d. of Eliphalet Hale; 12 May 1751.
Elisabeth, d. of Dr. Eliphalet Hale; 21 March 1756.
William, s. of Dr. Eliphalet Hale; 9 July 1758.
Susanna, d. of Samuel Haley; 2 Feb. 1755.
Esther, d. of Thomas Haley; 15 July 1744.
Benjamin, s. of Thomas Haley; 17 May 1747.
Sarah, d. of Thomas Haley; 7 Nov. 1756.
Samuel, s. of Thomas Haley; 17 June 1759.
Josiah, s. of Samuel Hall; 22 Dec. 1751.
Edward, s. of Samuel Hall; 25 Feb. 1753.
Sarah, d. of Samuel Hall; 23 June 1754.
Jonathan, s. of John Hopkinson; 23 Oct. 1748.
Moses, s. of —— Hopkinson; 17 March 1754.
Daniel, s. of Joseph Hoyt; 20 Jan. 1751.
Jemima, d. of Joseph Hoyt; 11 April 1756.
Elizabeth, d. of Joseph Hoyt; 20 Oct. 1760.
Benjamin, s. of William Hoyt; 14 July 1754.
William, s. of William Hoyt; 8 June 1755.
Sarah, d. of William Hoyt; 10 July 1757.
Richard, s. of William Hoyt; 25 Nov. 1759.
Nicholas Smith, s. of William Hoyt; 26 Sept. 1762.
Josiah, s. of Kinsley James; 13 Feb. 1745.
Jonathan, s. of Thomas Jennes; 5 June 1757.
Bathsheba, d. of John Judkins; 7 Sept. 1746.
Abigail, d. of John Judkins; 12 Oct. 1755.
Bartimeus, s. of Jonathan Judkins; 30 July 1749.
Hannah, d. of Amos Kimball; 23 June 1754.
Elisabeth, d. of Amos Kimball; 15 Feb. 1756.
Anna, d. of Amos Kimball; 15 Oct. 1758.
Abigail, d. of Samuel Hall; 2 May 1756.
Nathaniel Bartlett, s. of Samuel Hall; 11 Dec. 1757.
Meribah, d. of Samuel Hall; 3 June 1759.
Kinsley, s. of Samuel Hall; 12 Oct. 1760.
Elisabeth, d. of Samuel Hall; 5 Dec. 1762.

Anna, d. of Biley Hardy; 30 Nov. 1746.
Judith, d. of Biley Hardy; 9 Oct. 1748.
Sarah, d. of Dudley Hardy; 27 April 1746.
Mary, d. of Dudley Hardy; 8 May 1748.
Theophilus, s. of Dudley Hardy; 27 April 1755.
Samuel, s. of Samuel Harper; 31 Jan. 1747–8.
William, s. of Samuel Harper; 14 June 1752.
John Scribner, s. of Samuel Harper; 4 May 1755.
Benjamin, s. of Andrew Hilton; 25 April 1762.
John, s. of Jeremiah Hilton; 27 June 1756.
William, s. of Jeremiah Hilton; 12 Nov. 1758.
Love and Sarah, ds. of widow Hilton; 10 Nov. 1754.
Caleb and Mary, ch. of Jacob Hobbs; 26 Feb. 1747–8.
Amos, s. of Amos Kimball; 12 Oct. 1760.
Abigail, d. of Benjamin Kimball; 28 Oct. 1750.
Mehitable, d. of Benjamin Kimball; 7 July 1754.
Caleb, s. of Benjamin Kimball; 9 July 1758.
Trueworthy, s. of John Kimball, Jr.; 27 Sept. 1761.
Peter Sanborn, s. of Joseph Kimball; 3 Aug. 1760.
Mary, d. of Nathaniel Kimball; 23 Nov. 1760.
Sarah, d. of Nathaniel Kimball; 22 May 1763.
Nathaniel, s. of Thomas Kimball, Jr.; 27 May 1753.
Elisabeth, d. of Thomas Kimball, Jr.; 2 March 1755.
Nathaniel, s. of Daniel Ladd; 9 March 1745–6.
Nabby, d. of Edward Ladd; 23 July 1749.
Joseph, s. of Edward Ladd, Jr.; 30 Jan. 1763.
Anna, d. of Elias Ladd; 30 Sept. 1744.
Peter, s. of Samuel Lamson; 30 Aug. 1752.
Katharine, d. of Samuel Lamson; 3 June 1759.
Peter, s. of Samuel Lamson; 31 May 1761.
Gideon, s. of William Lamson; 28 June 1747.
Mary, d. of Daniel Lary, Jr.; 21 Dec. 1746.
Jonathan, s. of Daniel Lary, Jr.; 4 Sept. 1748.
Abigail, d. of Samuel Lary; 29 June 1746.
Dolly, d. of Samuel Lary; 3 July 1748.
Sarah and Mercy, daughters of Joseph Lawrence; 26 June 1753.
Molly, d, of Emerson Leavitt; 9 March 1755.
Jeremiah, s. of Jeremiah Leavitt; 12 Feb. 1748–9.
Mary, d. of Jeremiah Leavitt; 21 March 1756.
Susanna, d. of John Leavitt; 5 Sept. 1756.
Josiah, s. of John Leavitt; 29 April 1759.
John, s. of John Leavitt, Jr.; 31 Jan. 1762.
Hannah, d. of John Leavitt, Jr.; 9 Oct. 1763.
Dorothy, d. of Jonathan Leavitt; 14 Sept. 1746.
Joseph, s. of Jonathan Leavitt; 29 Feb. 1747–8.
Gideon, s. of Jonathan Leavitt; 26 Nov. 1752.
Hannah, d. of Jonathan Leavitt; 21 April 1754.
Mary, d. of Jonathan Leavitt; 24 Oct. 1756.

Jonathan, s. of Jonathan Leavitt; 3 June 1758.
Ruth, d. of Jonathan Leavitt; 9 Aug. 1761.
Selah and Edward, sons of Joseph Leavitt; 20 June 1759.
Lydia, d. of Joseph Leavitt; 9 Dec. 1759.
Mary, d. of Joseph Leavitt; 29 March 1761.
Dorothy, d. of Joseph Leavitt; 16 Oct. 1763.
Joseph, s. of Nathaniel Leavitt; 30 Nov. 1755.
Lydia, d. of Nathaniel Leavitt; 5 Dec. 1756.
Moses, s. of Nathaniel Leavitt; 9 Dec. 1759.
Abigail, d. of Nehemiah Leavitt; 14 Dec. 1760.
Reuben, s. of Nehemiah Leavitt; 13 March 1763.
Anne, d. of widow Leavitt; 7 Aug. 1757.
Olive, d. of Ebenezer Light; 6 March 1747-8.
Mary, d. of Ebenezer Light; 12 Nov. 1749.
Jonathan, s. of Jonathan Lord; 2 Aug. 1761.
William, s. of Robert Lord, Jr.; 5 July 1761.
Hannah, d. of Edmund Lougee; 1 June 1755.
Betty, d. of Joseph Lougee; 13 March 1747-8.
Joseph, s. of Joseph Lougee; 12 Aug. 1753.
Simeon, s. of Joseph Lougee; 28 Sept. 1755.
John, s. of Joseph Lougee; 9 Jan. 1757.
Nicholas, s. of Joseph Lougee; 2 Sept. 1759.
Nicholas, s. of Joseph Lougee; 15 Aug. 1762.
Mehitable, d. of Moses Lougee; 28 July 1751.
Jonathan Folsom, s. of Moses Lougee; 18 Nov. 1753.
John, s. of Moses Lougee; 14 Sept. 1755.
Noah, s. of Moses Lougee; 24 Sept. 1758.
Moses, s. of Moses Lougee; 27 July 1760.
John, s. of Ebenezer Lovering; 11 April 1762.
Elizabeth, d. of John Lovering; 14 Sept. 1746.
Jonathan, s. of John Lovering; 7 Aug. 1748.
Jean, d. of John Lovering; 21 Sept. 1755.
Anna, d. of John Lovering; Oct. 1758.
Richard, s. of John Lovering; 18 Jan. 1761.
Nathaniel, s. of John Lovering; 11 July 1762.
Mary, d. of John Prescott Lovering; 8 Dec. 1754.
Theophilus, s. of John Prescott Lovering; 21 Nov. 1756.
Penelope, d. of Moses Lovering; 31 Aug. 1760.
Willoughby, s. of Moses Lovering; 31 Jan. 1762.
Osgood, s. of Moses Lovering; 10 April 1763.
Dorothy, d. of Biley Lyford; 7 Sept. 1746.
Alice, d. of Biley Lyford; 3 July 1748.
Alice, d. of Biley Lyford; 28 April 1751.
James Gilman, s. of John Lyford; 24 Aug. 1746.
Dudley, s. of Moses Lyford; 6 Aug. 1749.
Francis, s. of Moses Lyford; 12 May 1751.
Oliver Smith, s. of Moses Lyford; 26 Aug. 1753.
Mehitable, d. of Moses Lyford; 28 Dec. 1755.

Jonathan, s. of Moses Lyford; 26 Feb. 1758.
Kinsley, s. of Theophilus Lyford; 22 June 1759.
Mary, d. of Theophilus Lyford; 5 July 1761.
Benjamin, s. of Thomas Lyford; 16 July 1749.
Dolly, d. of Alexander Magoon; 17 June 1750.
Elizabeth, d. of Alexander Magoon; 3 Dec. 1752.
Jonathan Leavitt, s. of Alexander Magoon; 1 June 1755.
Alexander, s. of Alexander Magoon; 26 March 1758.
Mercy, d. of Alexander Magoon; 4 April 1762.
Edward, s. of Benjamin Magoon, Jr.; 26 Sept. 1756.
Josiah, s. of Benjamin Magoon, Jr.; 25 June 1758.
Benjamin, s. of Benjamin Magoon, Jr.; 17 Aug. 1760.
Sarah, d. of Benjamin Magoon, Jr.; 5 Sept. 1762.
Hannah and Joseph, s. and d. of Joseph Magoon; 18 Sept 1757.
Ephraim, s. of Joseph Magoon; 28 Jan. 1759.
Mary, d. of Samuel Magoon; 16 June 1754.
Hannah, d. of Samuel Magoon; 11 July 1756.
Elisabeth, d. of Samuel Magoon; 9 July 1758.
Maria, d. of Henry Marsh; 7 Sept. 1746.
Anna, d. of Abigail Marshall; 24 April 1758.
Jonathan Thing and Simeon, sons of widow Abigail Marshall; 1 Oct. 1758.
Mercy, d. of Joseph Maylem; 7 Dec. 1746.
Elisabeth, d. of Thomas Moore; 13 Nov. 1753.
Martha, d. of Thomas Moore; 4 June 1759.
Hannah, d. of Thomas Moore; 10 July 1763.
Mary, d. of Thomas Moore, Jr.; 14 Dec. 1760.
Josiah, s. of William Moore; 10 Nov. 1754.
Josiah, s. of Thomas Nealey; 11 Oct. 1747.
Sarah, d. of John Nelson; 29 June 1746.
Olive, d. of John Nelson; 4 Dec. 1748.
Jonathan, s. of John Nelson; 12 May 1751.
Josiah, s. of John Nelson; 9 Sept. 1753.
Trueworthy, s. of John Nelson; 20 June 1756.
Josiah, s. of John Nelson; 10 Dec. 1758.
Anna, d. of John Nelson; 17 May 1761.
Dudley, s. of Nicholas Nichols; 10 Aug. 1755.
John, s. of Nicholas Nichols; 3 Dec. 1757.
Trueworthy, s. of Nicholas Nichols; 9 Sept. 1759.
Sarah, d. of Captain John Odlin; 28 Nov. 1756.
John, s. of Dr. John Odlin; 11 Feb. 1759.
Mary, d. of John Odlin, Jr.; 17 July 1757.
John, s. of John Odlin, Esq.; 21 Oct. 1759.
Hitty, d. of John Patridge; 20 March 1747-8.
Jonathan, s. of John Partridge; 20 May 1750.
John, s. of John Partridge; 23 Dec. 1759.
Jethro, s. of Jethro Pearson; 24 Jan. 1744.
Abigail, d. of Jethro Pearson; 17 May 1747.
John, s. of Jethro Pearson; 19 May 1752.

Edmund, s. of Capt. Jethro Pierson; 30 April 1758.
Taylor, s. of Joseph Pearson; 20 June 1756.
Jonathan, s. of Joseph Pearson; 5 Nov. 1758.
Joseph, s. of Joseph Pearson; 29 March 1761.
Jacob, s. of Anthony Peavey; 26 Jan. 1755.
Anna, d. of Abraham Perkins; 5 Feb. 1759.
Jonathan, s. of Abraham Perkins; 30 Nov. 1760.
Esther, d. of Abraham Perkins; 24 April 1763.
Jonathan, s. of Jonathan Perkins; 23 May 1756.
Joseph, s. of Jonathan Perkins; 28 March 1758.
Anne, d. of Jonathan Perkins; 17 Feb. 1760.
Joseph, s. of Jonathan Perkins; 5 Sept. 1762.
Benjamin, s. of Benjamin Philbrick; 4 Feb. 1749–50.
Lydia, d. of Benjamin Philbrick; 8 March 1752.
Samuel, s. of Benjamin Philbrick; 15 Dec. 1754.
Edward, s. of Benjamin Philbrick; 16 May 1757.
Samuel, s. of Benjamin Philbrick; 22 April 1759.
John, s. of Benjamin Philbrick; 10 May 1761.
Mary, d. of Benjamin Philbrick; 19 June 1763.
Mary, d. of David Philbrick; 11 Jan. 1761.
David, s. of David Philbrick; 21 Feb. 1762.
Henry, s. of Jacob Pike; 12 Nov. 1758.
Abigail, d. of Thomas Piper; 6 Sept. 1761.
Francis, s. of Thomas Piper; 24 Oct. 1762.
Jonathan, s. of Jonathan Porter; 8 May 1763.
Bradstreet, s. of Philemon Prescott; 21 July 1754.
Elisabeth, d. of Philemon Prescott; 11 Sept. 1757.
Mary, d. of Daniel Quimby; 12 April 1747.
Mary, d. of Daniel Robinson; 20 April 1755.
John, s. of Daniel Robinson; 14 Nov. 1756.
Mehitable, d. of Daniel Robinson; 20 Aug. 1758.
Sarah, d. of Daniel Robinson; 25 Nov. 1759.
Daniel, s. of Daniel Robinson; 16 May 1762.
Anne, d. of Ephraim Robinson; 22 Dec. 1754.
Jonathan and David (twins), s. of Josiah Robinson; 10 April 1748.
Dudley, s. of Josiah Robinson; 17 May 1752.
Sarah, d. of Josiah Robinson; 6 Oct. 1754.
Lydia, d. of Josiah Robinson; 5 Sept. 1756.
Trueworthy, s. of Josiah Robinson; 20 Jan. 1760.
Jeremiah, s. of Josiah Robinson; 13 Dec. 1761.
Eliphalet, s. of Eliphalet Rollins; 17 April 1757.
Nathaniel, s. of Eliphalet Rollins; 4 Feb. 1759.
Joshua, s. of Eliphalet Rollins; 17 May 1761.
John, s. of Joseph Rollins; 2 June 1754.
Mary, d. of Joseph Rollins; 7 Sept. 1755.
Huldah, d. of Josiah Rollins; 28 June 1747.
Josiah, s. of Josiah Rollins; 13 Aug. 1749.
Hannah, d. of Josiah Rollins; 29 March 1752.

Anna, d. of Josiah Rollins; 13 Oct. 1754.
Mary, d. of Josiah Rollins; 8 May 1757.
Rhoda, d. of Josiah Rollins; 27 Aug. 1759.
Elisabeth, d. of Josiah Rollins; 26 Sept. 1762.
Jonathan, s. of Charles Rundlett; 16 March 1755.
Olive, d. of James Rundlett; 8 Feb. 1746–7.
Samuel, s. of Satchel Rundlet; 18 March 1753.
Ruth, d. of Satchel Rundlet; 18 June 1756.
Ruth, d. of Satchel Rundlet; 12 June 1757.
Debby, d. of Satchel Rundlet; 5 Oct. 1760.
Benjamin, s. of Benjamin Safford; 2 April 1758.
Joseph, s. of Benjamin Safford; 10 July 1763.
Sarah, d. of Abraham Sanborn; 26 Oct. 1755.
Mary, d. of Abraham Sanborn; 17 July 1757.
Tristram, s. of Abraham Sanborn; 20 March 1763.
John, s. of Elisha Sanborn; 28 June 1747.
Stephen, s. of Phebe Sanborn; 2 Sept. 1750.
Daniel, s. of Edward Scribner; 31 July 1748.
John, s. of Edward Scribner; 18 Sept. 1757.
Anna, d. of John Scribner; 2 Feb. 1755.
Constant, d. of John Scribner; 20 July 1760.
John, s. of John Scribner, Jr., 5 Aug. 1750.
John, s. of Joseph Scribner; 9 Feb. 1755.
Samuel, s. of William Sibley; 2 Jan. 1763.
Benjamin Folsom, s. of James Sinclair; 22 Nov. 1761.
Elisabeth, d. of Richard Sinclair; 25 July 1762.
Ebenezer, s. of Richard Sinclair; 29 Aug. 1762.
Lydia, d. of Benjamin Smith; 30 Dec. 1753.
Betty, d. of Benjamin Smith; 15 Sept. 1757.
Daniel, s. of Ebenezer Smith; 8 May 1763.
Biley, s. of Israel Smith; 14 June 1747.
Eliphalet, s. of Jacob Smith; 18 April 1762.
Elizabeth, d. of Joseph Smith; 31 March 1754.
Sarah, d. of Joseph Smith; 7 Sept. 1755.
Benjamin, s. of Joseph Smith; 31 Oct. 1756.
Lydia, d. of Joseph Smith; 13 Jan. 1760.
Mehitable, d. of Joseph Smith; 22 Nov. 1761.
Biley, s. of Joseph Smith, Jr.; 24 May 1752.
Reuben, s. of Reuben Smith, Jr.; 27 Dec. 1747.
Tabitha, d. of Reuben Smith; 13 Aug. 1749.
Mehitable, d. of Widow Smith; 16 Aug. 1757.
Lydia, d. of Timothy Somes; 22 June 1760.
John, s. of Timothy Somes; 30 Oct. 1763.
Josiah, s. of Henry Steel; 8 March 1746–7.
Joseph, s. of Henry Steel; 9 Oct. 1748.
Joseph, s. of Henry Steel; 20 Jan. 1754.
Anna, d. of Henry Steel; 11 Jan. 1756.
Elisabeth, d. of Henry Steel; 9 April 1758.

Eliphalet, s. of John Steel; 27 Feb. 1757.
Sarah, d. of Edward Stevens; 13 Nov. 1748.
Abigail, d. of Edward Stevens; 8 June 1755.
Patience, d. of Haley Stevens; 8 Feb. 1746–7.
John, s. of Nathaniel Stevens; 29 Sept. 1754.
Ebenezer, s. of John Swazey; 12 Sept. 1756.
Abigail, d. of John Swazey; 14 Jan. 1759.
John, s. of John Swazey; 14 Dec. 1760.
Thomas, s. of John Swazey; 17 April 1763.
Elizabeth, d. of Joseph Swasey; 10 Feb. 1751.
Apphiah, d. of Joseph Swasey; 9 Sept. 1753.
Sarah, d. of Daniel Taylor; 2 Sept. 1759.
Mary, d. of Daniel Taylor; 27 Sept. 1761.
Betty, d. of John Taylor; 21 June 1747.
Dolly, d. of John Taylor; 5 March 1748–9.
Osgood, s. of John Taylor; 4 Aug. 1751.
John, s. of John Taylor; 2 Sept. 1753.
Rebecca, d. of Joseph Taylor, Jr.; 19 Oct. 1755.
Sarah, d. of Coffin Thing; 21 June 1759.
Abigail, d. of Josiah Thing; 21 June 1747.
Abigail, d. of Winthrop Thing; 16 Dec. 1753.
Winthrop, s. of Winthrop Thing; 23 March 1755.
Deborah, d. of Winthrop Thing; 30 Jan. 1757.
Elisabeth, d. of Winthrop Thing; 18 Feb. 1759.
Anna, d. of John Thompson; 16 Jan. 1754.
Mary, d. of John Thompson; 29 Feb. 1756.
Lydia, d. of John Thompson; 9 April 1758.
John, s. of John Thompson; 10 Feb. 1760.
Anna, d. of John Thompson; 6 June 1762.
Ephraim, s. of Ichabod Thurston; 17 June 1753.
James, s. of Ichabod Thurston; 11 April 1756.
Anna, d. of Ichabod Thurston; 11 June 1758.
Martha, d. of Ichabod Thurston; 7 Dec. 1760.
Huldah, d. of Christopher Toppan; 20 Aug. 1749.
John, s. of Christopher Toppan; 17 Nov. 1754.
Samuel, s. of Christopher Toppan; 14 May 1758.
John, s. of Christopher Toppan; 6 July 1760.
Abraham, s. of Christopher Toppan; 13 March 1763.
Peter Gilman, s. of Daniel Tilton; 13 April 1755.
Robert, s. of Daniel Tilton; 27 Feb. 1757.
Elisabeth, d. of Daniel Tilton; 9 March 1760.
Mary, d. of Daniel Tilton; 30 Jan. 1763.
Samuel, s. of Jeremiah Veasey; 5 April 1747.
Sarah, d. of Elijah Vickery; 7 Sept. 1746.
Hannah, d. of Elijah Vickery; 26 Feb. 1748–9.
Nabby, d. of Elijah Vickery; 21 Oct. 1750.
Betty, d. of Elijah Vickery; 17 Nov. 1754.
Samuel, s. of Joshua Vickery; 25 Jan. 1756.

Judith, d. of Joshua Vickery; 19 June 1757.
Elisabeth, d. of Edward Wadleigh; 10 June 1753.
John, s. of Edward Wadleigh; 6 April 1755.
Mary, d. of Edward Wadleigh; 30 July 1757.
Abraham, s. of Edward Wadleigh; 29 April 1759.
Lydia, d. of Edward Wadleigh; 3 Aug. 1760.
Sarah, d. of Edward Wadleigh; 12 Dec. 1762.
Daniel, s. of Daniel Ward; 30 July 1749.
Sarah, d. of Daniel Ward; 10 Nov. 1754.
Nathaniel, s. of Daniel Ward; 18 June 1758.
Benjamin, s. of Daniel Ward; 20 April 1760.
Andrew, s. of Daniel Ward; 8 May 1763.
Winthrop, s. of Winthrop Watson; 5 Nov. 1756.
Winthrop, s. of Winthrop Watson; 25 April 1760.
Dudley, s. of Matthias Weeks; 9 May 1762.
John, s. of Matthias Weeks; 12 Sept. 1762.
Nabby, d. of James Whidden; 19 July 1747.
Joseph, s. of Joseph Wiggin; 19 Dec. 1762.
David, s. of Nathaniel Wiggin; 16 May 1757.
Deborah, d. of Humphrey Wilson; 23 Nov. 1746.
Susanna and Betty, twin ch. of Joshua Wilson; 13 March 1747–8.
Rebecca, d. of Joshua Wilson; 29 Oct. 1749.
John, s of James Young; 14 Feb. 1747–8.
Samuel and Daniel, twin s. of Jonathan Young; 9 Oct. 1743.

PUBLISHMENTS

OF INTENTIONS OF MARRIAGE IN EXETER FROM 1783 TO 1800.

JOSIAH GILMAN, JR., clerk of the town between the above dates, kept a memorandum-book in which he set down all the publishments made during his term of office. The subsequent marriages of the parties appear upon the town records in about one-half of the cases. Of course it is to be presumed that marriages were duly solemnized in all the other cases, with possibly a few exceptions.

The following list is transcribed from Mr. Gilman's memorandum; omitting of course the publishments of parties whose marriages already appear in this work.

Lt. Samuel Adams, Elizabeth Parker; 1 May 1784.
Ezekiel Barstow, Mary Conner; 27 Sept. 1799.
Edmund Batchelder, Mary Lord; 26 Oct. 1799.
John Bean of Poplin, Molly Kimball; 25 March 1786.
Dudley Beckett, Hannah Langley; 25 March 1792.
Francis Becket, Sally Dudley; 2 Oct. 1790.
Azariah Beede of Kingston, Elizabeth Lord; 8 July 1786.
Jacob Blasdel, Elizabeth Sanborn; 17 Dec. 1784.
Robert Bond, Hannah Calfe; 14 Jan. 1792.
Capt. Nathaniel Boardman, Susanna Smith; 18 Jan. 1800.
John Brimhall, Dorothy Richardson of Newmarket; 11 Aug. 1791.
William Brooks, Tabitha Glover of Marblehead; 22 Aug. 1786.
John Burley, Abigail Smith; 19 March 1785.
Jeremiah Calfe of Sanbornton, Mrs. Hannah Creighton; 3 Nov. 1797.
Rev. Thomas Cary of Newbury, Deborah Prince; 16 Aug. 1783.
John Chase of Kensington, Martha Thurston; Nov. 1783.
Thomas Cheswell, Betsey Eastham; 28 Oct. 1787.
Thomas Clark of Nottingham, Mary Colcord; 29 Sept. 1792.
Gideon Colcord of Newmarket, Mrs. Lois Lyford; 19 July 1799.
Benjamin Conner, Jr., Elizabeth Shepard of Brentwood; 16 Oct. 1784.
John Conner, Jr., Nancy Shepard of Brentwood; 16 April 1791.
John Cook, Elizabeth Blasdell; 9 Aug. 1783.
Richard Cross, Lydia Harford; 27 June 1789.

George Curtis, Temperance Dame; 19 April 1783.
Josiah Danford of New Andover, Sarah Judkins; 4 Dec. 1785.
John Daniels, Abigail Taylor; 18 June 1791.
Joseph Daniels, Molly Akers; 30 Oct. 1790.
Nathaniel Davis, Anne Fall of Kingston; 25 Nov. 1797.
Ward Clark Dean, Margaret Wood of Charlestown; 5 Nov. 1796.
Gideon Doe of Parsonsfield, Mrs. Sarah Gilman; 12 July 1799.
Richard Dolloff, Judith Fellows; 12 June 1785.
Richard Dolloff, Jr., Tammy Knowlton of Ipswich; 10 May 1788.
Benjamin Dow, Catharine Robinson; 24 Feb. 1787.
Chandler Dow of Epping, Abigail Robinson; 6 March 1790.
Zebulon Duda of Newmarket, Mary Gilman; 14 July 1796.
Francis B. Eastham, Love Tuck of Kensington; 18 Sept. 1785.
Nehemiah Emery, Mary Henderson; 6 April 1799.
Robert Emery, Eunice Orne of Salem, Mass.; 15 June 1795.
Cato Fiske, Alice Wooso of Brentwood; 17 Nov. 1785.
Abel Fogg, Polly Smith of Stratham; 14 Feb. 1795.
Jonathan Folsom, Sarah Green of Stratham; 2 Oct. 1784.
Josiah Folsom, Jr., Sally Lane of Stratham; 3 Oct. 1795.
Nehemiah Folsom, Elizabeth Taylor of Hampton; 21 May 1791.
Nicholas Folsom, Dorothy Leavitt of Northfield; 27 June 1784.
Simeon Folsom, Mary Leavitt; 18 Jan. 1800.
James Foster of Canterbury, Mrs. Betsey Sanborn; 27 Nov. 1789.
Antipas Gilman, Deborah Duda of Newmarket; 18 March 1796.
Ephraim D. Gilman, Abigail Sanborn of Barnstead; 20 Aug. 1791.
James Gilman, Jr., Betsey Lyford; 12 Dec. 1789.
Joseph Gilman of Gilmanton, Sarah Fogg; 17 Aug. 1798.
Theophilus Gilman, Jr., Lois Lyford; 16 Oct. 1790.
Benjamin Gordon, Lydia Eastman of Kensington; 23 Oct. 1790.
Joseph Gordon, Jr., Sarah Smith of Stratham; 14 Feb. 1789.
William Gordon, Hannah Ladd; March 1784.
Benjamin Graves, Jr., Polly Taylor of Brentwood; 6 Jan. 1792.
James Hackett, Mrs. Elizabeth Hodge of Newmarket; 18 March 1790.
William Hale, Frances Haven of Wakefield; 15 Nov. 1788.
Capt. William Hale, Sally Farley of Newcastle, Me.; 22 Dec. 1799.
Jude Hall, Rhoda Paul; 21 Jan. 1786.
John Hamilton, Mary Eastham; 12 March 1796.
James Hanaford, Mercy Dudley; 31 July 1784.
Joshua Hill, Lucy Chase of Stratham; 18 Sept. 1789.
Edward Hilton, 3d, of Newmarket, Elizabeth Watson; 24 Aug. 1792.
Winthrop Hilton, Hepsibah Dockum; 7 Nov. 1788.
Dudley Bradstreet Hobart, Sophia Dearborn of Pittston, Mass.; 17 Jan. 1790.
Samuel Hobart, Sarah Adams; 16 Oct. 1784.
Stephen Hodgdon of Limerick, Mary Hill; June 1788.
William Hoit, Elizabeth Young Trickey, residents; 23 Feb. 1793.
William Hook of Salisbury, Sarah Watson; 17 May 1794.
Samuel Hopkinson, Hannah Thurston; 25 Feb. 1792.
Capt. Henry Jackson of Boston, Hannah Swett; 14 Sept. 1799.

David Jewett, Polly Shepard of Brentwood; 7 Oct. 1786.
Caleb Johnson of Hampstead, Mary Thurston; 13 Aug. 1785.
John Johnson, Margaret Greenough; 5 Sept. 1789.
Seth Johnson, Jr., of Haverhill, Ruth Graves; 11 June 1791.
Samuel Judkins, Mary Cushing; 5 March 1785.
Daniel Kelly of North Hampton, Polly Nichols; 6 June 1790.
William Kelly, Elizabeth Robinson; 28 June 1788.
Daniel Kimball, Sally Gilman; 17 Jan. 1790.
John Lamson, Sally Townsend of Charlestown; 26 Sept. 1793.
Gilman Leavitt of Brentwood, Lydia Barker; 29 April 1786.
Luke Libbey, Nancy Crocker; 28 Nov. 1784.
Samuel Loud, Sarah Elliott; 2 July 1791.
Joseph Lovering, Eunice Smith of Newbury; 20 Jan. 1798.
Francis Lyford, Mary Gilman (Biley's); 27 Sept. 1783.
James Lyford of Canterbury, Deborah Lyford; 8 Sept. 1792.
John Lyford, Anne Hilton of Kingston; 30 Aug. 1799.
Theodore Lyford, Rachel Colcord of Newmarket; 16 Sept. 1797.
Capt. Henry McClintock of Greenland, Anne Halliburton; 6 July 1799.
Stephen Marsh of Hubbardston, Betsey Webster; 4 Jan. 1788.
John Melcher of Gilmanton, Rebecca Grant; 17 Aug. 1798.
Daniel Williams Merrill, Mary Wilson Trickey, residents; 26 Jan. 1793.
Jonathan Moody of Brentwood, Betsey Haley; 9 Dec. 1787.
William Moody of Newbury, Sarah Kimball; 29 Sept. 1787.
Coffin Moore of Lancaster, Dolly Leavitt; 6 Feb. 1790.
Joseph Moses, Martha Wiggin of Stratham; 25 Jan. 1800.
William Moulton, Molly Page of North Hampton; 24 Oct. 1795.
Nicholas Nicolle, Jr., Catharine Sanborn; 18 Dec. 1785.
John Nichols, Esther Proctor of Kingston; 19 June 1785.
James Norris, Lydia Sherriff; Nov. 1783.
Charles O'Conner, Mary Spenley; 28 May 1785.
George Odiorne, Polly Brackett of Quincy; 12 Nov. 1794.
Samuel Odlin, Polly Groves of Beverly; 4 Feb. 1792.
Jacob Paul, Dorcas Avery of Kingston; 3 Sept. 1791.
Scipio Paul, Sarah Phelp of Pembroke; 17 July 1789.
James Pickering, Rosamond Fabins of Newington; 17 Feb. 1798.
Moses Pierce of South Hampton, Anne Lovering; 8 June 1799.
John Philbrick, Mehitable Lary of Stratham; 20 Sept. 1788.
Jeremiah Prescott of Gilmanton, Polly Swasey; 16 July 1785.
John Prescott, Elizabeth Nicolle; 20 June 1795.
Jacob Randall, Rebecca Masters; 22 Dec. 1792.
Thomas Rankin, Mrs. Esther McKim; March 1784.
Henry Ranlet, Betsey Hall; 20 Jan. 1787.
Caleb Robinson, Jr., Judith Robinson; 18 Feb. 1792.
Jeremiah Robinson, Mary Page of North Hampton; 2 Oct. 1784.
John Robinson, Elizabeth Smith of Stratham; 23 July 1796.
Jonathan Robinson, Mary Rollins; 7 Feb. 1796.
Joseph Robinson, Jr., Sarah Dow of Epping; 9 Dec. 1796.
Daniel Rollins of Sanbornton, Abigail Godfrey; 17 Dec. 1796.

John Rook of Nova Scotia, Elizabeth March ; 26 March 1785.
Rev. William F. Rowland, Sally Ladd of Portsmouth ; 10 June 1793.
David Rundlett of Stratham, Rhoda Robinson ; 11 Aug. 1794.
Josiah Rundlett, Mary Ward ; 10 Aug. 1793.
Samuel Rust, Jr., Betsey Beckett ; 18 March 1795.
Benjamin Safford, Jr., Judith Vickery of Hampton Falls ; 22 April 1786.
Joseph Safford, Betty Towle of Hampton ; 29 Oct. 1791.
Lieut. Abraham Sanborn, Mrs. Mary Parsons of Amesbury ; 31 July 1790.
Edward Sanborn of Epping, Deborah Cushing ; 3 Sept. 1791.
Jeremiah Sanborn of Sanbornton, Theodate Sanborn ; 3 Oct. 1786.
Jesse Sanborn, Sally Stevens of Stratham ; 14 Jan. 1796.
William Sanborn, Anne Lovering of North Hampton ; 18 Jan. 1794.
William Seward of Boston ; Hannah Hackett ; 10 Feb. 1798.
John Shaw, Elizabeth Folsom ; 28 May 1785.
Nathan Shaw of Kensington, Sarah Haines ; 3 Nov. 1787.
Jonathan Shepard, Elizabeth Severance of Kingston ; 1 Dec. 1792.
William Short, Patty Nowell of Newburyport ; 9 Dec. 1787.
Levi Sleeper of Kingston, Elizabeth Lovering ; 1 Feb. 1800.
Caleb Smith, Lydia Gordon ; 12 Dec. 1789.
David Smith, Sally Bennett ; 25 June 1795.
Ebenezer Smith of Gilmanton, Judith Pearson ; 3 Jan. 1789.
John Smith, Hannah Wiggin of Stratham ; 8 March 1794.
Peter Smith of Brentwood, Hannah Sanborn ; 2 Aug. 1783.
Reuben Smith, Elizabeth Wadleigh ; 9 May 1789.
Richard Smith of Pittsfield, Sally Gilman ; 16 July 1785.
Chase Stevens, Hannah Dow ; 29 Dec. 1798.
George Sullivan, Clarissa Lamson ; 7 Sept. 1799.
Ebenezer Swasey, Jr., Mary Lyford ; Jan. 1784.
Joseph Swasey, 3d, Elizabeth Fogg ; 7 Aug. 1790.
Nathaniel Swasey, Mehitable Rowe ; 25 Aug. 1792.
Dr. Samuel Tenney, Tabitha Gilman ; 6 Sept. 1788.
Lieut. Winthrop Thing, Lydia Gilman ; 28 March 1794.
Daniel Thurston of Stratham, Hannah Creighton ; 1 June 1792.
Oliver Thurston, Anstris Cross ; 25 Aug. 1792.
Reuben Thurston, Sarah Cross ; 19 Nov. 1796.
David Tilton of Hampton Falls, Mrs. Mary Merrill ; 11 Jan. 1800.
George Trefetheren, Anne Hilton ; 3 Jan. 1789.
John Wadleigh, Polly Becket ; 25 Dec. 1785.
David Watson, Elizabeth Hook of Chichester ; 21 May 1795.
William Webb, Deborah Nelson ; 30 April 1795.
Benjamin Wentworth of Portsmouth, Abigail Bennett ; 17 May 1795.
Gideon Wiggin, Dorothy Lyford ; 22 July 1797.
Joseph Wiggin, Jr., Mehitable Kimball ; Aug. 1788.
John Wilson of Sandwich, Abigail B. Hopkinson ; 6 Aug. 1791.
Samuel Winslow, Sally Johnson ; 25 July 1794.
Daniel York of Brentwood, Anne Smart ; 17 Sept. 1799.

INDEX

The following is a complete name index to both the historical and genealogical portions of this book, and replaces the partial index which appeared in the original edition. All subject citations in the original index have been incorporated in the current expanded index. Titles such as Capt., Lt., Mr., etc., have been omitted when the person is identified by a given name, but are otherwise retained. The designations Jr. and Sr. have been retained, but the reader is cautioned that they were transitory designations. Women have been indexed under both married and maiden names when possible. Negroes lacking surnames have been placed at the end of the index. Citations to the genealogical section, which has a separate pagination, are designated by the letter "g" after the page number.

ABBOT Benjamin 294 385 387 3g
   50g Charles Benjamin 3g Dr 294
   295 296 Elizabeth 3g Elizabeth
   P 387 Hannah Tracy 3g 50g John
   Emery 312 3g Mary 3g
ABBOTT Benjamin 332 Elizabeth P
   54g Sewall A 270
ABNER 436
ABUCKLE Olley 57g
ACADEMY Phillips Exeter 126
ADAM Rev Mr 241
ADAMS Anna M 55g Anna Matilda 3g
   Caleb G 246 381 3g Catharine
   3g Dolly 3g 62g Ebenezer 287
   Eliza 3g Elizabeth 3g 4g
   Jeremiah Parker 3g John 3g
   John W 207 312 Landen 50g Mary
   381 3g 53g Mary F 50g Mary
   Sewall 3g Mr 177 207 Nathaniel
   Folsom 3g Nathaniel S 103
   Nathaniel Sheafe 3g Obed E 50g
   President 360 Samuel 3g 4g 79g
   Samuel Winborn 3g Sarah 3g 80g
   Selina 50g William Parker 3g
ADDISON Jonas 230
ADJUTANT Mary 62g
ADKINSON Hannah 63g Samuel 63g
ADVENT Society and Pastors 207
AGEDENT Jerusha 50g Samuel 50g
AKERS Elizabeth 53g Joseph 230
   Molly 80g Samuel 141 229
ALLARD Job C 275
ALLEN 10 Henry 274 Mary A 58g
   Samuel 69 V Waldron 10
ALLERD Ruth 50g
ALLEY Elizabeth A 50g Richard
   50g
ALLISON Sam' 242
AMES Daniel 141 Mary 43g
AMHERST General 238
ANDERSON John 274 Lydia 50g Sween
   50g
ANDROS Edmund 68 452
ANGIER Joseph 209
ANTINOMIAN 6
APPLETON Thomas 333
AQUEDUCT 101 103
ARCHIBALD T H 202 203
ARDELL William 138
ARM Edward 50g Joanna 50g
ARNOLD Benedict 303 General 303
   Robert 249
ARRINGDINE Jeremiah 224 226
ASPAMABOUGH 9
ASSOCIATION TEST OF 1776 90
ATKINSON Benjamin 67g Charlotte
   50g Joseph 230 Mary 67g
   Stephen 67g Theodore 75 232
   Moses 3rd 50g
AUSTIN Mr 197 Samuel 197
AUTHORS IN EXETER 311
AVERY Alfred A 271 Dorcas 81g
AYER Benjamin F 377 Hannah M W
   50g Monroe 50g
Ayers Jos 242

BABSON Abigail 14g John 14g
   Philip 287 14g
BACHELDER Benjamin 257 Benjamin
   P 257
BACHELLOR Mr 463
BACHILER Mr 156 Stephen 155
BACON Ellen E 55g Horace C 376
BADGER Molly 58g Moses 287
BAILEY Clarissa 51g Joseph A
   51g Lucy H 53g
BAIRD John 182
BAKER 393 Andrew 51g Mark 64
   Mary J 51g Moses 233
BALDWIN 246 Samuel C 310
BALLOU Hosea 203
BANCROFT George 295 298
   Lieutenant 217
BANGS Anne B 50g Joshua 50g
BANKS 343
BAPTISMS IN FIRST SOCIETY Gen
   66
BAPTIST SOCIETY AND PASTORS 201
BARBER John 59 224 226 John Jr
   141 John Sr 141 Robert 138
   141 222
BAREFOOTE Walter 68 378
BARKER 333 Benjamin 257 Daniel
   246 248 John J D 273 Josiah
   86 93 Lydia 50g 81g Mary 50g
   Mary G 61g Noah 50g Susan G
   61g
BARLOW George 17 21 132 133 320
   445
BARNARD Edward 287
BARNE Dinah 58g
BARNS Nancy 54g
BARROWS John O 192
BARSHAM John 61 285
BARSTOW Betsey 57g Charles C
   330 Ezediel 79g Joshua 329
   330
BARTER Henry 249 251 252 254
BARTHOLOMEW Mr 116
BARTLETT 362 Abigail 8g Catha-
   rine 4g Dorothy 4g Elizabeth
   4g Ezra 388 Ichabod 366 407

John 253 Mary 4g Nancy L 51g
Nathaniel 141 180 4g Nathaniel
Jr 149 Priscilla 380 4g Thomas
H 51g
BARTON Michael H 308
BASTOW Allen 50g Mary 50g
BATCHELDER Anne 53g Benjamin 233
Betsey F 54g Charles W 271 277
Cornelius 67g Edmund 79g
Elizabeth 50g Emeline N 58g
George W 276 Hendrick D 377
John 50g Joshua 67g Mary 23g
Mary F 63g Nathaniel 50g
Rachel 50g Sarah A 51g
Stephen J 51g William 233
BATCHELOR Abigail 28g
BATES George 12 22 Barnabas 201
BATSON Anne 50g Laurence 50g
BEAL James 245 249 251 Josiah 91
BEALS Ephraim C 306 307
BEAN Abigail 67g Benjamin 67g
Daniel 140 219 224 225 4g
Daniel Jr 139 Deborah 67g
Ebenezer 233 Edward 141 228
Elijah 258 Elizabeth 4g Henry
66g James 138 219 4g Jeremiah
219 228 232 67g Jeremiah Jr
141 Jeremiah Sr 141 Jeremy 4g
John 59 119 135 136 137 219
225 226 228 229 4g 66g 67g
79g John Jr 138 141 228 John
Sr 138 141 219 Joshua 67g Margaret 175 4g Mary 26g 66g
Nathaniel 67g Samuel 138 219
224 228 4g Samuel Jr 226
Samuel Sr 141 Sarah 67g
William 141 277
BEARDSLEE Hannah 50g John S 50g
BEARSE Frederick 275
BECK Alfred M 51g Elizabeth S
51g
BECKET Dudley 233 Francis 257
67g 79g Pernal 67g Polly 82g
Sally 54g
BECKETT Betsey 82g Deborah 67g
Dudley 51g 67g 79g Francis
67g J L 310 Joseph L 310 312
Mary 54g Mary A 51g Sarah 67g
BEEDE Azariah 79g
BELCHER 74
BELKNAP 218 William H iv 148 347
411
BELL 375 Charles H iv 152 299
312 348 377 425 426 Charles U
342 377 Hannah 57g James 107
108 151 152 300 346 368 370
373 John 242 John J 111 151
152 377 426 Joseph 376 Lucy
293 Mary A 300 Samuel D 344
346 368 William 249 251
BELLAMY John 80
BELLINGHAM Susanna 32 William
32
BELLOMY Betty 67g John 67g
BELLOWS John 103
BELLS 183 188
BENNET Mehitable 4g Shackford
Sewards 4g
BENNETT Abigail 82g Charles 277
4g Daniel 266 Edward T 268
John H 262 Mehitable 50g
Sally 82g Shackford S 50g
William 246 248
BERRY Woodbury 264
BICENTENNIAL CELEBRATION 106
address Appendix III 448
BICKFORD Daniel 254 Dennis 250
252 Eunice 50g John 115 50g
Moses 257 Moses P 50g Mrs
423 Nathaniel 257 Phebe 50g
BIGGS Thomas 43 44 59 131 132
133 148 320 322 445
BIGS Tho 445
BIRTHS IN EXETER Gen 63
BLACKWELL Jeremiah 22 436
BLAISDELL 406 407 John 398 405
Lydia 56g
BLAKE Abraham P 152 Celina 53g
Dolly 59g John T 51g Jonathan 39g 50g Josiah 257 51g
Lucey 50g Lucia 39g Mary E
51g Mary J 54g Sarah 30g
Sherburne 107 Sophia 51g
BLANCHARD Amos 4g 50g Dorothy
50g Eliza J 58g Joseph 233
50g Joshua 50g Luther 4g
Lydia 50g Maria 4g Ruhannah
50g
BLAND Isabel 29 John 29
BLASDEL Jacob 79g
BLASDELL Elizabeth 79g
BLODGET Mary 20g
BLODGETT Dr 388 Julius C 205
BOARDMAN Anne 52g Benjamin 150
247 50g 67g Joseph 4g 51g
Juliana G 4g Lucy Maria 4g
Lydia 4g 50g Lydia L 4g 51g
Mary A 55g Nathaniel 307 405
79g Sarah 50g Sarah A 51g
William 67g
BODGE Benjamin 50g Meribah 50g
BOLTER Nathaniel 59

BOND Abigail 4g Deborah 4g Jane
   67g Jean 67g Joanna 55g John
   91 67g Mary 4g 53g Mercy 67g
   Robert 79g Susanna 67g Thomas
   4g
BONITHAN Rich[d] 434
BONITHON Rich[d] 434
BOOTH Robert 59 131 437
BOUDINOT 452
BOULTER Grace 65g Mary 65g
   Nathaniel 44 45 131 132 319
   66g
BOUNDS OF EXETER 113 enlargement
   of 117
BOUNDS Richard 139
BOURN Frances 58g
BOURNE Judge 29 34
BOUTON Nathaniel 10
BOWDEN Deborah 4g 42g Elizabeth
   4g 50g Francis 180 4g 50g
   John 67g Margaret 67g Michael
   4g 67g Rebecca 4g Susanna 67g
   William Tyler 67g
BOWDOINS 452
BOWEN Francis 294 Peter 233
BOWLEY A J 277 Albert 268 Albert
   A 268 Benjamin F 266 268 Eben
   S 277 Oliver S 51g Pamelia 51g
BOWLS 10
BOYD Ebenezer L 201 312
BOYES Mathew 113 115
BRACKET Elizabeth 50g James Jr
   50g
BRACKETT Polly 81g
BRADBURY Jabez 228 Jonathan 232
   Thomas 114
BRADFORD Isaac 327
BRADLEY Jonathan 63g Josiah 63g
   Lieutenant 232 Susannah 63g
BRADGON Mary W 51g William G 51g
BRAY Richard 59 135
BRENTWOOD PARISH SET OFF 184
BRICKETT Jonathan 258
BRIDGER John 70 72
BRIDGES 124 125
BRIDGHAM Jacob 233
BRIGHAM Azel P 205 277 Bruce 277
   Ephraim 277 George H 277
   William H B 276
BRIMHALL John 79g
BRISCOE Elizabeth 187 34g Robert
   187
BROADBENT John 264
BRODERICK William 277
BROMFIELD William 59 135
BROOKS Betsey 5g Dolly 5g

Elizabeth 5g 49g 50g James
   Emery 5g John 50g Joseph 246
   5g Mary 5g 50g 58g Oliver
   257 5g Oliver Pike 5g S 331
   Samuel 84 85 86 87 88 93 150
   197 242 287 5g 49g 50g
   Samuel Jr 249 5g 50g Tirzah
   5g 50g William 5g 79g
BROWN 406 407 A R 310 Abby 5g
   Abel 50g Abigail 52g Abraham
   248 Abraham R 310 Alexander
   274 Ann 9g Benjamin 340
   Caleb 230 Dudley 67g Edward
   246 Elizabeth Ann 5g Eliza-
   beth P 50g G W 277 George 274
   George H 277 I S 341 Isaiah
   S 152 5g John 141 230 63g
   67g John A 290 John C 275
   John N 312 John Newton 202
   Jonathan 247 Joseph 198
   Joshua 67g Lawrence 259 Mary
   63g Michael 246 50g Mr 198
   202 Nathan 248 9g Olive 67g
   Ruth 50g Samuel 63g 67g
   Sebastian A 152 William 266
   5g
BRYANT John S 264
BUCKLEY James M 206 Mr 207
BUCKMINSTER Joseph S 294
BUCKNAL Elizabeth 67g John 67g
BUEL Samuel 194
BULGAR Goodman 436 Richard 12
   19 22 42 44 47 148 442
BULLGAR 49 Richard 17 48 131 437
   446 447
BULWER 308
BURBANK Albion 290
BURDETT George 13
BURGOYNE 382 General 248 385
BURIAL PLACES 408
BURLEIGH Giles 141 Harriet 5g
   James 5g Joseph 141 Josiah
   141 Mary Jane 50g Nathaniel
   R 50g Polly 60g Rufus 5g
   Selina 5g Susanna 5g William
   5g
BURLEY Charles 152 347 411
   Charlotte 50g Harriet 54g
   Harriet L 50g Jacob 5g James
   108 141 150 151 258 312 346
   347 395 410 50g John 146 5g
   79g Mary 5g Polly 44g Selina
   50g
BURLINGAME J K 342 William 152
   293 342
BURNHAM Edwin 205 Elizabeth 50g

John T 347 Moraham 50g Thomas
288
BURPEE Eunice 50g
BURROUGHS Charles 298
BURSLEY John 45 59 133 445
BUSSELL George H 267
BUZELL Albert C 377
BYINGTON Charles E 347 Swift 193
BYLES Mather 187
BYLEY Mary 169
BYRAM Lois 50g Reuben 50g

C Mr 329
CABAN Freeman 277 Samuel 264
   William 264
CADETS Exeter 239
CAESAR Julius 313
CALCORD Edward 8 9
CALDWELL Francis M 271 John 51g
   John R 258 Leonard H 271 Polly
   51g
CALEF Elizabeth 60g Jeremiah 141
   Sarah 56g
CALF Lucy 54g
CALFE Elizabeth 67g Hannah 79g
   James 23- 67g Jeremiah 67g
   79g Jeremiah Jr 182 John 248
   Lucy 67g Lydia 59g
CALLEY Catherine 12g Richard 12g
CAMPBELL John 267
CANNON John 202
CANNING John 208
CARD Esther G 63g Sarah F 63g
   Susan H 58g
CARLISLE Jacob 151 152 James 264
CARLETON Albert 257 Edward 113
   Mary 24g Mary W 24g Theodore
   80 86 88 150 24g
CARLTON Harriet P 59g Mr 85 86
   Thomas 246
CARPENTER John H 270
CARR Captain 249 Robert 55
CARRINGTON James 25
CARROLL Albert 388
CARSWELL John K 271
CARTEE (CARTER) Philip 136
CARTEE Daniel 233 John 91 229
   233 Philip 59 65 119 137
CARTER Abigail 51g Charles 51g
   Frederic W 276 Gideon 276 51g
   Gideon Jr 264 Hannah 51g 59g
   Jacob 51g Jacob Jr 51g Lydia
   53g Mandana 51g Nancy 51g
   Nathan F 290 Richard 45 W Ed-
   win 277
CARTWRIGHT George 55

CARTY Elizabeth 51g Philip 51g
   Susanna 58g
CARVER Edward F 264
CARY Thomas 79g
CASS Benjamin 233 250 Charles
   Lee 5g Deborah Webster 5g
   George 5g John Jay 6g Jonath-
   an 98 246 251 394 5g 51g
   Lewis 98 108 294 314 394 5g
   Mary 5g 51g Polly 6g
CATTLE care of the 49
CAULEY Jonathan 67g Mehitable
   67g
CENSUS OF 1775 87
CHABINOCHE Sagamore Thomas 37
CHADWICK Colonel 107 Elizabeth
   A 299 Enoch Coffin 63g
   Frances 395 John 395 63g
   Peter 198 299 421 63g
CHAM (or CANE) Arthur 135
CHAMBERLAIN Edward Groves 6g
   Elizabeth Dorothy 6g Esther
   51g 60g Frances Groves 6g
   Henry Phillips 6g Jacob
   Tilton 6g John 6g John C 359
   Julia Ann 6g Margaret Tilton
   6g Maria P 59g Mary 6g 51g
   Mary Parker 6g Samuel 326 6g
   51g Samuel Phillips 6g
   Timothy 244 51g William
   Frederick Rowland 6g
CHANDLER Aretus 52g John 287
   Lydia 52g
CHANNING Edwin 257 William 257
CHAPLIN Jeremiah 201
CHAPMAN Jacob 312 Joseph 67g
   Josiah 67g Lev 67g Martha A
   55g Mary 67g Mary A 54g
   Pennel 67g Tryphena 67g
CHARLES II 55 56 21g
CHARLTON (CARLETON) Deborah 63g
   Frederick 63g Theodore 63g
CHARLTON (CARLTON) Frederick 6g
CHARLTON Deborah 6g Theodore 6g
CHASE Amos C 347 Baruch 360
   James 259 James W 277 John
   79g John N 203 Lucy 80g
   Nancy 51g William 277
   William S 51g
CHAUNCY Betsey 27g Samuel 27g
CHELSEA William 248 250
CHENEY 406 407
CHESLEY Lafayette 389 Philip 59
   135
CHESWELL Thomas 79g
CHEW Henry 51g Nancy J 51g

CHICKERING John W Jr 199 Mr 200
CHOATE Benjamin 287 Sarah W 51g
    William T 51g
CHR:HELME 18
CHRISTIAN SOCIETY AND PASTORS 204
CHURCH First 12 Re-organized 174
CHURCH Colonel Benjamin 221
CILLEY Anna 9g Bradbury 332 51g
    Bradbury L iv 296 299 Colonel
    249 251 Dinah 51g John K 273
    Joseph 98 Joseph L 370 422
    Jos Jr 242 Martha 51g
CLAP Mary 31g Nathaniel 31g
CLARK 405 Abigail 67g Anna 51g
    Anne 67g Benjamin 6g 51g
    Caroline 61g Charles Edwin 6g
    D 331 Daniel 258 Deborah 379
    6g 10g Edward H 6g Elisabeth
    67g Elizabeth 175 176 177 187
    6g 34g 47g George W 277 342 6g
    Henry 47g Ichabod 6g J M 340
    James 258 James A 7g James 2d
    258 John 7 59 116 136 137 138
    166 171 175 228 258 267 324
    379 6g 10g John M 6g John W
    377 John Jr 61 Jonathan 138
    141 219 Major 324 Martha J 6g
    Mary 6g Moses 245 6g 51g Mr
    171 174 175 176 Mrs 176 Nancy
    51g Nathaniel 176 6g Rev Mr
    174 176 Richard 141 Sarah 6g
    16g 51g Sarah C 347 Sarah E 7g
    Satchell 67g Solomon 141 6g
    Thomas 67g 79g Ward 141 287 6g
    William A 277 6g William H
    343 51g William Henry 6g
CLARKE Elizabeth 6g Frank Bart-
    lett 6g John 465 Mr 309
    Philena 6g Samuel B 309 6g
    Ward 465
CLAY Cassius M 279 George D 271
CLEMENT John 150 205 John W 264
CLEVELAND President 372
CLIFFORD Clarissa 51g David 259
    Ebenezer 190 331 346 417 Mr
    418
CLOUGH Casar 51g Cill 58g
    Ebenezer 228 Ezekiel 268
    George 277 H C 277 J P 310
    Priscilla 51g Thomas 268
    Thomas H 268 Zaccheus 88 Zach
    242
CLOUTMAN Edward 219
COAKLEY Timothy 270
COALE William 444 445
COBBS George S 270 Waddy V 396

COCHRAN James 96
COFFIN 326 Abigail 379 7g 18g
    46g Anne 63g Captain 172 220
    Clarissa 51g Deborah 175 7g
    Eliphalet 80 141 149 180 245
    343 379 7g 64g Elizabeth 174
    16g Enoch 286 James 7g
    Joanna 353 16g Joshua 51g
    Judith 7g 53g Lucretia 52g
    Moses 63g Mr 175 286 Nathan-
    iel 245 Pernal 46g Peter 69
    72 80 86 93 137 138 139 150
    151 170 171 172 173 174 175
    176 177 179 181 183 220 239
    247 249 252 287 343 353 7g
    16g Peter Jr 88 Prime 253
    Robert 138 139 149 174 325
    353 16g Sarah 63g Tristram
    228 353 46g
COGSWELL Joseph G 294
COLBATH Charles W 264
COLCORD 393 425 456 Abigail G
    58g Ann 23 Ann M 60g Anne
    51g Charles E 262 Charles W
    277 Daniel 258 Ebenezer Jr
    67g Edward 23 132 141 322
    323 Emily S 299 Ezra G 264
    George 51g Gideon 25g 79g
    Hannah 11g Hannah V 61g
    Harvey 150 201 51g Jacob 327
    Joanna 51g Jonathan 141
    Judith 51g Lois 25g Lydia A
    55g Martha W 58g Mary 79g
    Polly 51g Rachel 81g Samuel
    51g 52g Sophia 52g Thomas
    51g William H 262
COLE Eunice 23 Isaac 61 Jonath-
    an 209 312 Lucius 268 Mr 209
    William 8 23 44
COLEMAN James 201 Joseph 229
COLLEY Martha A 53g
COLLINS Abigail 52g Andrew H
    52g Lieutenant Colonel 282
    Moses N 152 273 281 377
COLORED POPULATION 395
"COMBINATION" FOR GOVERNMENT 15
COMINGS Abraham 253
COMMON FIELD 133 137 141
COMPTON Goodman 436 John 8 23
    318 437
CONNER 456 Abigail 287 8g 51g
    62g Alfred 150 152 9g Anne
    8g 30g Benjamin 248 392 8g
    Benjamin Jr 152 79g Betsey
    52g Caroline 28g 51g Charles
    148 152 343 347 348 392 8g

9g Charles G 151 152 293 426
Charles Gilman 9g Cornelius
139 141 149 66g Daniel 150 152
338 392 8g Daniel Gilman 9g
Dudley 8g Edward J 277 Edward
Joseph 9g Ephraim 8g Elizabeth
8g 9g 51g 52g Elizabeth W 61g
Elizabeth Gilman 9g Eunice 8g
Freeman 277 9g Hannah 8g Huldah
8g 59g James 51g Jedediah
8g 51g Jeremiah 71 139 144 145
149 181 182 224 225 226 245 8g
Jeremy 138 219 Jeremy Sr 141
Jesse 8g Jewett 150 152 9g
John 277 John L 8g John Jr 79g
Jonathan 141 149 181 229 8g
47g Jonathan Jr 8g Joseph
Bartlett 8g Lyford 151 Mary
8g 79g Mary A 62g Mary Ann 8g
Mary Elizabeth 9g Mary Taylor
9g Mehitable 8g Moses 141
Nathaniel 152 198 392 8g 9g
52g Oliver W 8g Philip 141 181
Samuel 141 180 230 Samuel Jr
235 Sarah 21g 53g 66g Thomas
343 9g Tirzah 8g 9g W 277
William 108 150 152 348 392
9g 52g William Thomas 9g
CONNOR Ann 7g Anna 7g Anne 7g
Benjamin 7g 67g Cornelius 7g
David 67g Eliphalet 8g Hannah
7g 67g Jeremiah 7g 8g 67g
Jeremy 59 137 John Thing 7g
Jonathan 7g Joseph 7g 8g 67g
Joshua 7g 8g Maria 7g Mary 8g
67g Mehitabel 7g Mehitable 47g
Moses 7g 67g Philip 7g Sarah
7g 8g 67g Tristram Sanborn 67g
CONSTITUTION Earliest Written 89
CONVENTIONS Constitutional 95 99
101
COOK Andrew 51g 63g Harriet 51g
63g Henry Salter 63g John 258
51g 63g 79g Martha T 51g Richard
253 254
COOLE Goodman 436 437 William 18
COOMBS Francis 233
COOMES Abigail 51g Joseph 51g
COOPER Arthur F 342 Major 280
COPELAND Lawrence 24
COPP Austin M 342 H B 207
COPYHOLD 73
CORCORAN Frank 268
CORNEY Polly 62g
CORNISH Mary 66g Thomas 59 114
133 134 322 66g

CORNWALLIS 382
CORYDON 399
COTTER Maurice 277
COTTLE Joanna 14g Joseph 14g
Mimbo 55g
COTTON 26 30 454 John 6 67 169
Nathaniel 338 Seaborn 169
COUNT Deborah 51g Samuel Lee
51g
COURT-HOUSE 71 101 106 108
COVEY Jack 230
COWLES Horatio L 52g Sarah A
52g
COWPLAND Lawrence 8
COXE Sarah 65g
CRAM Alanson 275 Ann 9g 59g
Anne 9g Benjamin 91 9g Dudley
51g Esther 24 Frank P
347 Hester 66g Jacob 395 9g
51g 68g John 24 44 132 133
148 65g 66g Jonathan 68g
Joseph 24 150 152 9g 65g
Lidde 65g Lide 65g Lydia 24
66g Martha 9g Martha P 60g
Mary 51g Newton 275 Robert
233 Sarah 9g Wadleigh 232
CRAME Goodman 436 John 18
CRANFIELD 64 65 66 Edward 63
Governor 33 67 351 352 391
420 453 458
CRAWLEY'S FALLS 322
CRAWLEY Phebe 24 Thomas 18 24
131 132 133 322
CREAN Patrick 271
CREIGHTON Anne 50g Elizabeth
56g George 230 68g Hannah
79g 82g James 248 249 252
John 287 Martha 68g Robert
Light 68g Stephen 91 Thomas
233 245 251 68g
CROCKER Nancy 81g
CROCKETT Eunice 57g
CROLY Thomas 437
CROMWELL 55 216 Oliver 5 39 454
CROSBY Malinda 63g
CROSS Anstris 82g Caroline 9g
48g 51g Caroline Matilda 9g
George N 292 293 426 Isaac
61 Richard 79g Robert 9g 48g
51g Sarah 82g
CROWN POINT EXPEDITIONS 233
CROWNINSHIELD Edward 209
CRUMMETT J N 277
CUMMINGS E P 277 388 Horace S
152 Joseph 288
CUNNINGHAM Timothy 227 228

CURRIER Abigail 51g Andrew J 262
    Enoch G 52g Ephraim 9g 51g 68g
    Elizabeth 9g Isaac 9g 51g 68g
    Jane 52g John 246 Phillis 56g
    Sally 54g Sarah 51g
CURTIS Albert O 277 George 80g
CURWIN Mr 177
CUSHING David 61 Deborah 82g Mary
    81g William 246 248 253 254
CUSHMAN Dr 210 George F 210
CUTLER Anna 9g Dinah 51g Dolly
    51g Eliza A C 9g Elizabeth D
    52g Harriet F 9g John G 9g
    Mary Paul 54g Rufus E 9g 51g
    Samuel 52g Sarah A 9g Tobias
    398 9g 51g
CUTTER Ammi R 382
CUTTS Betsy 52g William 52g

DAILEY Joseph 267
DAILY Lenon 52g Margaret 52g
DALE Eben 333 William J Jr 333
DALTON Dorothy 25 Elbridge G 290
    300 Philemon 25 Samuel 117 119
    Timothy 39
DALY London 399
DAME Temperance 80g
DANA Daniel 294 Elizabeth Ann 9g
    Margaret Ann 9g William B 9g
DANFORD Josiah 80g
DANIEL James 61
DANIELS Abigail 56g Charles H 52g
    Elizabeth 52g 62g Eunice 52g
    Hannah 59g Jerusha 50g John
    52g 80g Joseph 80g Minus 52g
    68g Nancy M 52g Samuel 248
    52g Sarah 52g Susan 52g
    Susanna 68g
DARLING Benjamin 68g Manly W 416
    Reuben 68g
DAVIS Abigail Bartlett 10g Andrew
    J 268 Charles H 270 Eleanor
    52g Elizabeth 10g James 228
    Joanna 58g John 45 68g Lemuel
    52g 68g Martha B 57g Mary 56g
    Nancy 51g Nancy S 57g Nathan-
    iel 80g Ruth 68g Samuel 249
    Solomon 258 William 233 10g
    William Putnam 10g
DAY Katharine 44g
DEAN 418 Abigail 10g 55g 68g
    Anne 52g Catharine 52g Daniel
    226 Deborah 419 10g 54g Eli-
    phalet 52g Elizabeth 10g 52g
    60g Elizabeth P 50g Ep 45g
    Jane 10g John 194 251 10g John
    Jr 52g John Ward 379
    Lucretia 52g 57g Mary 10g
    Nathaniel 52g Nehemiah 68g
    Olive 45g 52g Thomas 141 149
    180 181 10g 52g Ward C 251
    252 343 420 Ward Clark 201
    343 419 80g
DEANE Deborah 379 Dr 379 Thomas
    378 Ward Clarke 465
DEARBORN Abigail 53g Abraham
    267 Abram 266 Abraham D 388
    Calvin L 262 Charles C 311
    Dorothy 25 Elizabeth 41g
    Freese 150 388 George 277
    George W iv 392 425 Godfrey
    5 25 132 133 148 Henry 245
    253 Henry A S 314 J F 277
    J S 277 Jacob 257 Jeremiah
    347 Jeremiah F 271 Jonathan
    259 Joseph R 259 Sarah S 60g
    Sophia 80g Warren S 264
DEARBORNE Goodman 436
DEAREBORNE Godfrye 18
DEARING Eleanor 52g
DEATHS IN EXETER Gen 64
DELANCEY 452
DENISON John 46g Martha 46g
DENNET Elizabeth 4g 10g John
    380 10g John Sherburne 10g
DENNETT Elizabeth 52g John 52g
DENNIS Martha 27g
DENSMORE Sally 52g Samuel 52g
DERBY James 332 James 341
D'ERES Charles Denis Rusce 312
DE ROCHEMONT A P 277
DEVERSON Frances 57g
DEWEY A G 342
DEWHURST G W 277 G W Jr 277
    Henry 277
DEXTER Mr 199 Samuel D 199
DEXTERS 452
DICKEY Elizabeth 52g William
    258 William H 52g
DIESKAU Baron 234
DIMOND Susanna 55g
DIX John A 295
DIXON Victor 267
DOCKUM Hepsibah 80g James 254
DODGE Abigail 52g Alexander 10g
    Anne 10g Benjamin 10g 52g
    Betsy 56g Caroline G 10g
    Elizabeth 10g Elizabeth Hurd
    10g Fanny 52g Francis M 10g
    Hannah 10g Harriet 10g Isaac
    10g Jabez 339 10g John 150
    340 10g John E 277 Joseph 10g

Lydia 10g Nancy 56g Samuel
339 10g 52g Sarah E 10g
DOE Gideon 80g Sampson 141
Samuel 141
DOLHOFF (DOLLOFF) Christian 10g
James 10g John 10g Jonathan
52g Mary 10g 52g
DOLLOFF 226 393 Abigail 11g Abner
11g 52g Amos 230 Betsy 52g
58g Christian 59 65 119 136
137 138 David 230 233 11g
Elizabeth 11g 24g Hannah S
62g Irene 52g Jesse 259 Jesse
L 275 John 223 249 11g Jona-
than 11g Joseph 233 246 248
253 Margaret 11g Mary E 55g
Mary J 59g Mercy 11g 38g
Miriam 11g Nicholas 233 Phineas 11g Richard 138 139 141
219 225 248 11g 80g Richard
Jr 80g Samuel 138 141 219 228
11g 24g Samuel Jr 141 Sarah
11g 68g Thomas 91 139 146 224
227 68g William C 52g
DONOP Count 382
DONOVAN Cornelius 264 J 277
DOODY John 268 William 268
DORAN William 181
DORIN Mary 31g
DORSEY Andrew 52g Nancy G 52g
DOW Benjamin 233 80g Chandler
80g Edna P 56g Ednah Parker
11g Elizabeth 299 11g Hannah
11g 59g 82g Hannah Parker 11g
Jeremiah 150 152 198 299 341
424 11g Joseph 109 Mary Fran-
ces 11g Retire Parker 11g
Samuel 277 Sarah 61g 81g W N
194 Winthrop N 152 426
DOWNER Andrew 231 68g Caleb 68g
John 72
DOWNING Charles H 151
DOWNS Harriet A 33g Zephaniah 254
DRAKE Abraham 44 45 59 123 133
320 Nathaniel 59 133 148 320
Simon 248
DRAKES 324
DRISCO Cornelius 141 John 224 227
Teague 59 137
DUCE Cato 245 Cepio 52g Katy 62g
Lois 52g Nancy G 52g Phillis
52g Robert 52g Sally P 62g
DUDA Deborah 80g Philip 225 227
Zebulon 80g
DUDLEY 108 164 464 Abigail 52g
Albertus T 299 Biley 59 135
137 138 141 148 167 169 171
173 219 Byley 175 52g Daniel
W 265 Dorothy 28g 68g Dr 425
Elinor 26g Elizabeth 169 52g
Ephraim 253 254 Family 390
Gilman 233 Governor 459 465
Hannah 11g James 141 224 225
227 230 231 11g Joanna 355
11g John 80 150 200 224 227
390 423 11g 68g John Jr 230
Jonathan 141 228 Joseph 68
141 221 231 11g Josiah 52g
Maria 7g Mary 169 463 68g
Mary C 54g Mercy 80g Merriah
11g Mr 54 158 160 161 162
163 164 165 166 167 168 169
321 322 465 Nicholas 141 11g
Odlin 68g Rebecca 56g Rev Mr
408 Sally 79g Sam 159 Samuel
27 38 49 54 56 59 113 114
119 131 133 134 135 136 137
155 157 158 159 164 166 176
200 219 224 225 227 233 320
321 326 352 355 390 409 463
11g Samuel Jr 70 137 139 141
Samuel Sr 141 Samuel T 52g
Sarah 175 11g 52g Sereno G
265 Stephen 61 224 227 137
355 11g Stephen Jr 139 142
Stephen Sr 142 Theophilus
59 72 135 137 138 149 151
167 173 174 175 176 177
Thomas 159 175 463 Treworthy
11g True Jr 68g Trueworthy
142 145 149 231 233 238 249
251 253 254 68g Winthrop 247
DUDY Philip 138 219
DUFFY John 265
DUNBAR 74 75 Charles F 299
Charles H 52g David 73 424
Mary B 52g
DUNCOM Joseph 65g
DUNN Robert 259
DUNTON A P 311
DUPEE Lewis F 290
DURANT Samuel 52g Susan 52g
DURGIN Albert A 12g Daniel V
277 Ednah J 12g Ezra S 11g
Francis 139 142 Mary E 11g
Ruth 11g William E 277 11g
DUSTON Obadiah 347
DUTCH Abigail 68g Betty 68g
Charlotte 50g Clarissa 51g
George 68g John 68g Lois 54g
Mary 68g Nathaniel 259 Sally
61g Samuel 248 68g Sarah 68g

DWYER Edward 219
DYER Henry 70 353 16g Joanna 353
   16g John Jr 270

EAMES Daniel 224 227
EARLY Ira E 277
EASTHAM Betsey 79g Clarissa 54g
   Edward 248 250 Francis A 61g
   Francis B 80g Harriet 54g Mary
   80g Nancy 61g
EASTMAN 248 Edwin G 293 342 377
   Joseph 290 Kimball 52g Lydia
   80g Mary 52g Samuel 229
EATON Elizabeth R 55g
EDGERLY Jeremiah 258 John 231 68g
   Jonathan 68g Mary 68g Orrin
   259 Samuel 142 Thomas 142
EDWARDS John 254 272
EGAN Charles 208 Father 208
ELDRIDGE Abigail 52g Joseph 52g
   Melburn F 376 Samuel 257
ELIOTS Abigail 56g
ELKINE Goodman 436
ELKINS Eleazer 59 65 137 12g
   Henry 12 17 25 James 268 John
   12g John P 427 Maria 25 Mary
   25 Peter 258 Samuel 139 142
   228 12g
ELLERY Anna 12g Anna Mary 12g
   David Haraden 12g Edward Tur-
   ner 12g Epes 12g George 12g
   James 12g Nathaniel 12g
   William Parsons 12g
ELLIOT 455 Mary 60g William 343
ELLIOTT Daniel W 265 John W 150
   Sarah 81g William 239 249
ELLIS Charlotte 290 Ferdinand
   202 290 312 63g Ferdinand Jr
   310 Rhoda 290
ELLISON Frank 262 Horace 277
ELWELL Lucy 15g Mary 15g Zebulon
   15g
ELWOOD Melvin 274
EMERSON Joseph 158 Mr 463
EMERY 399 456 Betsy Phillips 12g
   Catharine H 61g Deborah 32g
   52g Elizabeth 12g 13g 52g 55g
   Elizabeth M J 55g Hannah 20g
   Hannah Tracy 3g 50g Jane 12g
   Joanna 68g John 86 239 343
   12g 52g Liberty 52g Margaret
   107 Mary 12g Nehemiah 80g
   Nicholas 12g Noah 80 87 89 91
   99 152 247 355 399 12g 68g
   Noah Jr 243 244 Richard 235
   238 52g 68g Robert 80g Sarah

18g Stephen 287 Theresia 68g
   Tirzah 26g
ENDICOTT Samuel 52g Sarah F 52g
EPISCOPAL SOCIETY AND PASTORS
   210
EPPING PARISH SET OFF 184
EURIN Edward 66g
EUSTIS Dr 382
EVAN Stephen 250
EVANS Elizabeth 19 William 247
EVERETT Alexander H 294 357 366
   Edward 294
EXETER 5 10 11 Statistics 425

FABINS Rosamond 81g
FAFETHER Abigail 38g Daniel 38g
   Elizabeth 38g
FAIRCHILD Joy H 192 312
FALL Anne 80g
FAMILIES, early: Dudley 390
   Folsom 391 Leavitt, Thing,
   Conner, Lyford 392 Gordon,
   Robinson, Smith, Odlin, etc.
   393
FAMILY REGISTERS Gen 3
FARLEY Sally 80g
FARMER 370 Simeon 246
FARNHAM John 277 John Jr 53g
   Lois D 53g S C 207
FARNUM James M 268
FARRAGUT David G 392
FARRAR Timothy 107 314 344 346
   347 370
FARWELL John W 333
FAULHABER Oscar 293 299
FAVOR Abigail 63g Daniel 63g
   Elizabeth 63g
FAVOUR Daniel 68g Samuel 68g
FAWKES Guy 79
FELLOWES Ephraim 364 Jeremiah
   312 364
FELLOWS Eliza A 63g Irene 60g
   Judith 80g Mary 60g Olive M
   59g
FELT Lucius G 53g Martha A 53g
FEMALE ACADEMY 299
FERGUSON 408 Bradbury 407
   Ebenezer 248 Eleaser 244 246
   Eliza Ann 407 Henry 210 Mr
   211 Mrs 407
FERNALD B Marvin 377 Orlando M
   290
FERRIN Moses 231
FEVERYEAR John 287
FICUET John 219
FIELD Darby 8 14 18 25

FIELDSEND Joshua 265
FIFIELD Deborah 53g Mark 53g
    William 231
FINN John 265
FIRE ENGINES 101 103 Steam 110
FISH 17 Gabriel 16 25
FISHERY IN RIVERS 47
FISK Martin H 290
FISKE Cato 80g
FLAGG Harriet M 53g Isaac 152
    259 327 354 415 Isaac Jr 328
    Joseph 328 Joseph B 53g Major
    303 Mr 328 Samuel C 328
FLANDERS Abigail 68g Harriet M
    53g John 205 Joseph 68g Moses
    231 Susanna 68g Thomas 388
    68g
FLATS DIVIDED 132
FLETCHER Mr 204 Silas S 204
FLOOD Abigail 53g Abraham 53g
    Charles A W 262 Elizabeth 53g
    Hannah 53g Jonathan 245 247
    249 251 253 254 12g Joseph 12g
    53g Lydia 53g Mary 12g Samuel
    262 William 12g 53g
FLORD Mary 54g
FLOYD Abigail S 55g Captain 217
    David 272
FOG Miriam 56g
FOGG A J 340 Abel 80g Andrew J
    151 152 264 Anne 53g David 93
    95 248 258 52g 68g Dearborn
    53g Deborah 58g Dorothy 53g
    Eliza 57g Elizabeth 52g 53g
    82g Enoch 68g Fortune 52g
    Frederic A 290 Hannah 68g
    John 53g 68g Jonathan 230 68g
    69g Josiah 69g Katherine 52g
    Lucinda 57g Lucy 52g Mary 53g
    69g Meribah 68g 69g Miriam
    68g Molly 68g Olive 60g Sam-
    uel 146 149 69g Sarah 52g 53g
    62g 68g 80g Seth 142 248 52g
    68g Stephen 53g Stephen Jr
    53g Sukey 60g William 288
FOLLANSBY W H C 347 William H C
    426
FOLLSHAM Peter K 58
FOLSOM 108 312 337 411 419 456
    Abigail 12g 69g Abraham 138
    142 181 219 225 227 229 Ann
    12g Ann R 59g Anna 391 69g
    Annah 69g Anne 13g 15g 53g
    56g Anne B 50g Benjamin 142
    182 233 Benjamin F 347 Betsy
    13g Betty 69g C E 277 Captain

234 Celina 53g Charles 314
392 13g Charles H 277
Charles L 312 Daniel 12g 69g
Deborah 13g 47g 56g 69g
Dorothy 19g 50g Dudley 13g
53g E 342 Eben 152 342 347
Ebenezer 219 14g Edward 142
Eliphalet 69g Elisabeth 69g
Elizabeth 13g 39g 52g 58g
60g 63g 69g 82g Elizabeth S
14g Ephraim 59 65 137 149
150 219 224 227 Ephraim Jr
138 139 142 Ephraim Sr 139
142 467 Family 391 Frances
13g 24g 54g General 101 240
459 Hannah P 53g Henry 13g
Isaac L 347 Israel 59 135
146 J D 207 James 251 13g
63g 69g James Jr 53g James
3rd 53g James 4th 258 53g
James W 275 277 Jemima 13g
Jeremiah 142 228 253 Joanna
13g 61g John 53 56 59 65 66
135 138 144 148 151 171 175
180 182 216 224 225 227 229
232 233 319 391 13g 63g 69g
John Jr 59 118 135 136 142
148 167 53g 69g John Sr 116
118 119 123 135 136 138 142
Jonathan 142 181 224 227 230
231 233 249 251 259 391 52g
53g 69g 80g Jonathan Kins-
bury 69g Joseph 231 277
Joseph G 307 Joseph Gilman
13g Joshua 232 Josiah 91 232
13g 14g 63g 69g Josiah Jr
150 80g Josiah 3d 258 Josiah
Gilman 69g Josiah J 150 152
342 14g Katherine 69g Lavina
13g 58g Lucretia 53g Lydia
13g 52g 53g 69g Lydia B 58g
Martha 13g 58g 69g Martha B
58g Martha N 58g Mary 381 3g
13g 14g 53g 55g 63g 69g Mary
G 54g Mary Gilman 14g Mary W
14g 51g Molly 69g Mr 207
Nancy 363 61g Nancy Y 13g
31g 57g Nathaniel 59 65 80
81 83 84 86 87 92 93 95 135
151 152 172 232 233 241 242
381 391 409 466 3g 13g 15g
53g Nathaniel Jr 227 233
Nehemiah 150 80g Nichols 69g
80g Nicholas D 13g 53g Noah
69g Peter 57 59 65 116 119
135 136 137 149 167 171 219

258 289 12g 13g 53g 69g Peter
Jr 70 138 142 Peter Sr 139
Peter G 13g Phillis 52g Polly
13g 60g Ruth 33g S 256 331
Sally R 61g Samuel 59 80 81 82
86 93 95 100 135 136 150 235
238 239 242 252 328 363 391
392 425 13g 52g 69g Samuel
Bradley 69g Sarah 13g 14g 52g
53g 54g 55g 69g Sarah G 54g
Sarah R 13g 55g Simeon 80g
Sophia 13g 60g Susanna 56g 63g
69g Theophilus 257 52g 69g
Thomas 86 99 150 13g 69g
Thomas O 388 Trueworthy 80
69g William 14g William Jr 142
William Sr 142
FORD E W 377 Elizabeth 53g Joseph
H 53g
FORREST John 231
FORT WILLIAM AND MARY raid upon
240 powder from 241
FOSS Charles H 277 John 150 53g
Lucy H 53g
FOSTER Charles Lee 63g Frances B
63g Franklin H 272 Isaac 299
63g James 80g John 300 Nathaniel 53g Rebecca 53g
FOULSAM Abigail 12g Catherine 12g
Elizabeth 12g 52g James 12g
52g John 12g Mary 12g Nathaniel 12g Peter 12g Samuel 12g
Susanna 12g
FOWLE Daniel 301 Robert L 306 53g
Robert Lewis 301 Robert Luist
96 Sarah 53g Zechariah 302 303
304
FOWLER C J 207 Elizabeth 53g
Mary 54g
FOX Benjamin 233 Edward 233 John
146 69g Nathaniel 69g
FOXCROFT 196 Thomas 196
FOY Mary 12g
FOYE Irena M 60g
FRANCIS William A 299
FREDERIC Charles 274
FREEMAN Edmund E 426
FRENCH Anne 14g Bradstreet 53g
Daniel 372 Daniel Chester 14g
Ellen 372 Francis O 299 371
372 377 Harriette Van Mater
14g Henry F 312 372 410 14g
James 202 53g Joseph 96 Mary
J 57g Mehitable 53g Michael 61
Moses D 272 Olive 53g Rachel

William 149 224 227 William
Merchant Richardson 14g
FROTHINGHAM Eliza Ann 407 John
288
FRYE James 246 Mrs 372
FULLER Anne 53g Arthur B 348
Arthur O 377 David 53g Elizabeth 53g Elizabeth Ann 5g
George Jr 53g George W 277
Jeremiah 258 John G C 268
272 Nancy 53g Richard 53g
Sukey 53g William 258 53g
FULLONTON Joseph 310
FULTON 385
FURBAR William 9
FURBER William 40 115
FURBISH Benjamin 53g Mary 53g
FURNALD George W 150 152 293
J F 277 John 69g Joseph 107
334

GADD G W 427 George W 276
GAINES Major 240
GALE Bartholomew 91 69g Charles
C P 54g Daniel 231 69g
George W 388 George W Jr 277
Harriet 54g Harriet L 50g
John 69g John Cartee 69g
Joseph W 191 Martha 54g Mary
61g Stephen 54g Susanna 69g
GARDENER Peter W 274
GARDNER Deborah 419 54g Elizabeth D 52g George 152 332
343 John 343 419 54g John E
343 347 Mary Paul 54g Mr 420
Peter W 262 Tony 54g
GARLAND George E 275 James H
277 John 59 134 161 Samuel
259
GATES General 253 Joshua C 258
GAY William 76
GAYLORD Charles 54g Mary J 54g
GENERAL COURT 7 13 44 46 48
GEORGE Elisabeth 69g Elizabeth
14g J H 211 John 14g Josiah
14g 69g Michael 249 254
Olive 14g Sarah 14g
GEROULD Gerould Fitz 91
GERRISH Andrew 69g Caroline 36g
Charles H 293 389 423 J C
310 Jean 69g John C 309 375
54g Lydia 10g Mary G 54g
Timothy 36g
GETCHELL Clarence 299 Joshua
151 327 347

GIBBIES (GIBBONS) Mr 130
GIBBINS Ambrose 434
GIBBON Edward 30
GIBONS Ambros 434
GIBSON John 231 John T 290
GIDDINGE 422 Abigail 14g 15g Ann
  15g 54g Ann Elizabeth 15g Anne
  15g 53g Deborah 4g 14g 15g 40g
  Dolly 15g Dorothy 15g 58g Eliphalet 91 93 150 190 235 422
  14g 15g 54g Elizabeth 53g 57g
  George 14g Harriet Amelia 15g
  Joanna 14g John 80 84 86 87
  89 91 149 152 235 240 343 380
  422 5g 14g 53g John Jr 91
  Joseph 15g Lucretia 15g Lucy
  15g Lydia 15g 19g Mary 4g 5g
  14g 15g 50g Mehetabel 380 14g
  15g Mehitable 4g 5g 50g Nathaniel 252 422 14g 15g 53g
  54g Peggy 15g 54g Pernal 14g
  15g 27g Polly 15g Zebulon 73
  75 78 148 149 151 186 188 337
  343 380 422 4g 14g 15g 27g
  40g
GIDDINGS 73 324 Ann 25g 60g Ann E
  55g D^r 242 Edward iv Eliphalet
  251 252 25g 30g George H 264
  John 241 Nathaniel 251 Nathaniel G 150 152 Oliver L 151
GILES Abigail 56g Daniel 142 229
  Joseph 231
GILL George 277 Isaiah W 277 Nathaniel 277
GILLMAN Capt 58 John 58
GILMAN (BILEY'S) Mary 81g
GILMAN 108 337 390 424 456 A J
  427 Abba 258 Abby 59g Abigail
  189 379 16g 17g 18g 19g 29g
  36g 46g 51g 52g 53g 70g Abigail Bromfield 20g Alfred J
  275 Alice 168 174 16g 19g 28g
  69g Allen 20g Andrew 142 144
  223 224 229 18g Ann 19g 40g
  56g Anna 18g Anne 20g 29g 51g
  56g Antipas 235 16g 69g 70g
  80g Arthur 19g Arthur Frederick 21g Augustus Henry 21g
  Bartholomew 80 17g 20g Benjamin 142 Benjamin C 150 Benjamin
  Clark 101 103 21g 53g Benjamin
  Ives 20g Betsey 21g 41g Betsey
  F 54g Betsy 54g 62g Betty 69g
  70g Biley 54g 70g Bradbury
  41g Bradstreet 70g Bridget 18g
  Brigadier 458 465 Caleb 142

149 181 219 233 246 Caleb Jr
70g Cartee 139 181 224 225
227 249 251 252 254 287 23g
70g Carty 142 Catharine 174
52g Catherine 12g 16g 20g
Charles 59 136 Charles E 19g
Charles J 152 Charles
William 21g Charlotte 20g
50g Chase 70g Clarissa 21g
58g Col 242 423 Comfort 70g
Daniel 61 77 80 136 142 180
181 225 227 332 343 381 390
421 423 457 16g 17g 18g 19g
70g David 72 91 138 142 224
227 249 70g David F 268
Deborah 5g 16g 18g 56g 70g
Deborah Harris 20g Dolly 58g
70g Dorothea F 58g Dorothy
19g 20g 35g 53g 70g Dorothy
Bartlett 21g Dr 232 Dudley
69g 70g Edward 49 57 58 66
67 114 116 123 136 138 141
144 145 148 149 158 159 162
163 167 224 227 318 319 331
457 16g Edward Jr 59 132 133
134 142 320 321 322 323 324
336 Edward Sr 59 134 142 319
322 351 Edward H 152 Eliphalet 18g 21g 53g 70g Elisa-
beth 70g Elizabeth 174 175
351 16g 17g 18g 19g 20g 21g
23g 27g 34g 52g 54g 57g 58g
60g Elizabeth Ann Taylor 21g
Elizabeth Blodget 20g Elizabeth S 51g Ephraim D 80g
Ezekiel 77 142 145 149 151
181 229 230 254 289 70g
Frances 18g 40g Frederick
19g Gardiner 277 George 270
Grace 168 Hannah 18g 19g 20g
21g 51g 57g 58g 70g Hannah E
57g Harriet 54g Harriet B
62g Harriot 21g Henry 19g
20g Henry Augustus 21g Isabel 54g Israel 142 145 70g
Jacob 223 James 72 138 142
149 151 185 186 219 231 16g
53g 54g James Jr 142 54g 80g
James 3rd 54g Jane 20g Jeremiah 72 139 142 174 219 223
224 225 227 233 246 18g 70g
Jeremiah Jr 233 Jeremy 61
137 138 16g Joanna 353 16g
17g 18g 33g John 58 59 62 64
66 69 74 115 116 117 118 119
125 134 136 138 139 140 142

145 148 149 151 163 164 165
171 174 175 179 181 219 221
226 228 235 236 237 246 258
289 319 321 323 324 325 326
331 351 353 354 380 410 416
423 457 458 16g 17g 20g 21g
46g 53g 54g 70g John Jr 59 65
135 136 181 221 247 John Sr
135 139 145 John G 152 John K
19g John Nicholas 418 John
Phillips 20g 21g John T 93 95
99 104 126 150 151 152 297
332 343 344 381 19g John Taylor 92 99 243 244 410 421 53g
John W 273 21g John Ward 80 82
243 244 10g Jonathan 140 142
149 180 245 19g 54g 69g 70g
Jonathan Jr 181 18g Joseph 81
84 86 91 142 150 419 16g 17g
20g 21g 80g Joseph S 343 21g
Joseph Smith 54g Joseph T 346
425 19g Joshua 139 142 182
218 228 18g Josiah 80 82 86
93 149 181 194 379 16g 17g 18g
20g 70g Josiah Jr 91 148 152
70g 79g Josiah ter 80 Josiah H
19g Judith 18g Lydia 4g 15g
16g 19g 51g 54g 61g 62g 70g
82g Mahitable 53g Major 231
Mariah 18g Martha 19g 42g 59g
Martha J 54g Mary 5g 16g 17g
18g 20g 25g 46g 51g 53g 54g
57g 61g 70g 80g Mary A 54g
Mary Ann 21g Mary O 19g Mary
Taylor 9g 21g Mary Thing 21g
53g Maverick 142 287 16g
Mehetabel 380 14g Mehitable 70g
Meriah 18g Merriah 11g Molly
70g Morris 228 Moses 59 66
118 119 123 134 135 136 139
148 149 233 319 324 457 16g
29g 70g Moses Jr 61 137 138
142 149 Moses Sr 138 142 171
Mr 66 320 79g Mrs 419 Nabby
70g Nathaniel 97 106 126 142
150 151 152 180 181 182 198
249 287 332 367 380 381 395
415 418 424 425 16g 17g 18g
19g 37g 40g 53g 70g Nathaniel
Jr 108 191 327 347 Nathaniel
3rd 107 152 257 332 Nathaniel
4th 54g Nathaniel Clark 20g
Nathaniel G 151 152 Nathaniel
Waldron 381 Nehemiah 142 54g
70g Nicholas 70 74 80 81 84
86 87 92 98 99 100 120 126 138

139 140 142 149 150 151 174
175 177 178 180 181 185 219
224 226 228 234 240 242 249
251 297 331 332 340 343 354
379 415 416 418 421 423 457
16g 17g 19g 21g 37g 64g
Nicholas Jr 142 181 195 287
Noah 53g Olive 53g Patty 21g
53g 60g 70g Peter 77 78 80
81 82 142 145 149 151 180
181 182 188 189 194 195 234
340 380 416 417 17g 18g 19g
53g 64g 70g Peter Jr 70g
Phillips 257 21g 54g Polly
51g Priscilla 380 Rebecca
20g Robert 230 235 380 17g
19g Robert Briscoe 19g 20g
Robert Hale 20g Rufus King
21g S 331 Sally 21g 54g 81g
82g Samuel 73 76 80 82 84
142 145 149 150 151 180 181
186 194 195 245 251 252 343
354 383 424 15g 16g 17g 20g
21g 64g 70g Samuel Jr 149
19g Samuel 3d 257 Samuel 4th
80 Samuel Folsom 91 70g Samuel Frederick 21g Samuel K
19g Samuel R 259 Samuel T
152 367 19g Sarah 7g 11g 13g
16g 17g 18g 19g 20g 21g 37g
53g 59g 70g 80g Sarah Almira
21g Serena 21g Simon 75 142
246 248 250 252 70g Sommersby 17g Stephen 138 139 219
223 20g Summersbee 235 238
Susanna 18g 54g Tabitha 383
18g 19g 20g 82g Theophilus
84 86 87 149 150 242 5g 70g
Theophilus Jr 80g Thomas 142
20g Treasurer 422 Treworthy
16g 18g Tristram 287 17g 70g
Trueworthy 150 255 Ward 20g
Whittingham 20g William 233
70g William Charles 21g Winthrop 18g Zebulon 91 248 150
70g Zebulon Jr 53g
GLASGO Priscilla 51g
GLEASON William 272
GLIDDEN Andrew 142 227 Benjamin
142 Charles 59 138 219 John
138 139 Jonathan 287 Joseph
142 Nathaniel 142 229 Richard 138 175 Richard Jr 142
Richard Sr 142
GLOVER Tabitha 79g
GLOYD James 331

GODDARD John 61
GODFREY Abigail 51g 81g James 59
   136
GOFFE John 238 381
GOLD Martha 13g
GOOCH William L 340
GOODHUE Joseph 233 Samuel 70
GOODRIDGE Edward 211
GOODWIN David 257 Lavina 54g
   Lois 54g Mary 54g Seth 54g
   Sewall 278 Stephen 54g Susan
   63g Theophilus 152 54g Thomas
   272
GOOKIN Judith 53g Nathaniel 239
   243 244 53g
GORDEN Dolly 53g Joseph 53g
GORDON 324 456 Abigail 22g Abra-
   ham 22g 71g Alcina Eveline
   23g Alexander 59 135 138 142
   218 219 228 21g 22g Alexander
   Sr 219 22g Benjamin 22g 24g
   71g 80g Benjamin Franklin 24g
   Benoni 22g Calvin Folsom 24g
   Charles 22g Daniel 139 142 248
   249 22g Diana 22g Ebenezer 22g
   Elisha 22g Elizabeth 22g 23g
   24g 56g Emma 22g Esther 24g
   71g Family 393 Frances 23g
   24g 54g Frances Eveline 23g
   Frances Mary 24g Frances S 63g
   Frances Sarah 23g George Anne
   23g George William 393 23g
   Hannah 22g Harriet 22g Jacob
   71g James 138 142 219 231 248
   250 71g 22g 23g 24g John 107
   138 150 219 278 71g 22g 23g
   54g John Jr 142 257 John S
   22g 23g John T 150 259 23g 54g
   John Thomas 23g Jonathan 142
   23g 24g 54g 80g Joseph 249 254
   Josiah 246 254 71g Lydia 22g
   24g 82g Lydia Ann 24g Maria
   22g Mary 21g 22g 23g 54g 57g
   71g Mary Alcina Elizabeth 23g
   Mary C 54g Mary D 23g Mary
   Elizabeth 23g Mary L 54g Moses
   Sanborn 23g Nathaniel 86 91 93
   150 152 242 298 328 330 376
   393 22g 23g 54g 71g Nathaniel
   2d 23g Nathaniel Sr 23g Nathaniel B 257 Nathaniel Batchelder 23g Nicholas 70 138
   142 149 179 181 219 22g 71g
   Oliver 54g Paul 272 Rebecca
   54g 71g Robert 231 Sarah 23g
   54g Sarah A 52g Sarah Frances

   23g Simeon 71g Sophia 23g
   60g Stephen L 259 341 54g
   Stephen Leavitt 23g Timothy
   22g 23g 71g Thomas 139 142
   227 22g 23g Thomas Jr 142
   William 249 251 252 254 22g
   23g 80g William F 54g
GORGES 449 Ferdinando 454
   Thomas 28 31
GORHAM Andrew 54g D W 410 David
   W 300 387 54g Elizabeth P
   387 54g John 385 Mary 388
   63g Molly 63g Nathaniel Jr
   387 Sarah G 54g Stephen 63g
   William H 387
GORLY George 219
GORWOOD Charles 74
GOULD Mary 54g Sarah G 54g
   Silas 54g William 54g
GOVE 64 Anne 7g Edward 63 Lewis
   E 427
GOVE'S REBELLION AGAINST CRAN-
   FIELD 63
GOWEN 50
GRAFS (GRAVES) William 138
GRAHAM John 287
GRANT 281 282 Abby J 24g Abby
   Jane 24g Ann Burley 24g
   Betsey 24g Betsy 53g Charles
   148 24g Daniel 91 232 71g
   Daniel Francis 24g Elias
   Pike 24g Elizabeth 53g Fran-
   cis 258 308 24g General 280
   George Augustus 24g James
   107 24g 53g James Henry 24g
   Mary 53g 71g Mary Frances
   24g Mary W 24g Mr 404 405
   Paul Hall 71g Rebecca 81g
   Samuel 274 William 24g Z 299
GRANTS OF LANDS BY TOWN IN 1643
   and 1644 131; in 1645 6 7
   132; in 1648 9 50 133; in
   1651-2 134; in 1654 to 1664
   135; 1665-1678 136; 1681 to
   1693 137; in 1697-8 138;
   1699 to 1706 139; 1706 to
   1724 143; in 1725 141; in
   1740 146
GRAVES Anna 71g Benjamin Jr 80g
   John 142 Ruth 81g William
   219 287 William Jr 142
   William Sr 142 Wilson 71g
GRAY Clarissa 54g Harrison 54g
   Martha J 54g
GREAT BAY 3
GREELEY Peter 75

GREEN Benjamin 233 Colonel 303
   George W 151 Nathaniel 360
   Sarah 80g William 274
GREENFFIELD Samuel 45
GREENFIELD Samuel 47 48 51 59 131
   132 148 319
GREENLEAF Charles 278 Joseph 258
   Matthew N 267 Olive 58g
GREENOUGH Margaret 81g
GREGG David A 376
GREING Patrick 229
GRENFEL Samuell 446
GRENFELDS Samuel 447
GRIDLEY Celestia W 63g Selah 312
   388
GRIST-MILLS 324
GROSS Dolly 54g Isaac 19 26 148
   William 54g
GROSSE Isack 438 Mr 436 437
GROUARD Maria L 293
GROVER Nancy 54g Stephen 54g
GROVES Polly 81g
GROW Isaac 246 249 251
GUSTINE Cecilia F 293

HABORNE 34
HACKET Anne 57g William 59 135
HACKETT 98 404 Abigail 51g Captain 243 245 Colonel 240 Hannah 82g James 239 241 243 244
   251 252 338 80g Mary 54g 66g
   Mr 244 William 66g
HAINES Daniel D 278 Hannah 54g
   Isiah T 262 J H 207 Sarah 82g
   Simeon 249 Thomas 54g
HAINS Ann 57g
HALE Charles E 270 Colonel 249
   251 Dorothy 4g Eliphalet 86
   93 238 327 380 4g 63g 71g
   Elisabeth 71g Elizabeth 380
   17g 63g Enoch 398 Esop 54g
   George S 299 Grace 313 James
   H 257 Jane 12g 63g Jean 71g
   John H 262 John P 371 Jonathan
   55g Liberty 52g Lucy 52g 54g
   Martha 55g Mary 55g Nathan 380
   Robert 287 Samuel 298 Sarah A
   51g William 327 71g 80g
HALEY Benjamin 71g Betsey 81g
   Esther 71g John 258 Joshua M
   55g Mary 55g Samuel 259 71g
   Sarah 71g Susanna 71g Thomas
   142 71g
HALL 223 390 406 Abigail 24g 52g
   71g Ann 31g Benjamin E 24g
   Betsey 81g Catharine Norris
24g Charles Edward 24g
   Dorothy 60g Dudley 24g Edward 75 142 144 149 151 222
   31g 71g Edward F 265 Elisabeth 71g Elizabeth 352 55g
   Hannah 180 24g Henry R 24g
   55g Henry Ranlet 24g Hildea
   26 65g Honner 54g Horace J
   265 Jeremiah 55g John 26 80
   247 John Sr 26 Joseph 60 135
   137 141 142 145 149 222
   Josiah 141 142 148 227 24g
   71g Josiah Sr 24g Jude 398
   405 80g Judge 352 Kinsley 61
   65 136 137 139 142 148 151
   169 173 174 175 218 352 463
   24g 71g Kinsley Jr 24g
   Kinsly 54g Mary 26 24g 65g
   66g Mary A 55g Mercy 26 65g
   Meribah 50g 71g Mr 309
   Nathaniel Bartlett 71g Paul
   142 24g Ralph 4 18 26 45 62
   65 116 118 119 131 133 135
   136 148 151 166 352 64g 65g
   66g Rebecca 59g Samuel 60
   137 151 232 309 24g 71g
   Sarah 19g 71g Sarah A 55g
   Sarah B 63g
HALLIBURTON Anne 81g
HAM Frances 55g Samuel 55g
HAMILTON Charlotte 55g John 80g
   Jonathan 55g
HAMMON Thomas 251
HANAFORD James 80g
HANCOCK John 92
HANNAFORD C H 207
HANSCOM William C 204
HANSON Elizabeth 21g 55g George
   55g Stephen 332
HARDIE Theophilus 246
HARDY Anna 72g Biley 72g Dudley
   72g Judith 72g Mary 72g
   Mehitable 54g Pery 54g Samuel 247 Sarah 72g Sarah R
   55g Theophilus 142 72g
   Thomas 55g
HARFORD Lydia 79g
HARPER John Scribner 72g Samuel
   72g William 247 72g
HARRIMAN Elizabeth 22g
HARRINGTON George 55g Martha A
   55g
HARRIS Caroline E 210 Clementine 55g D C 278 Elijah J
   202 John 24g Mary 48g Moses
   55g Samuel 91 257 Thomas 228

HART John 238 Mary 56g
HARTSHORN Abigail S 55g Charles A 55g
HASKELL Mary E 57g
HATCH Charles H 25g Daniel G 396 25g Edward W 25g Fred S 377 Johnston 25g Joseph W 25g Mary 25g 54g Mary Ann 25g Samuel 152 392 25g 54g W H 206 William 25g
HATHERSAY Robert 131
HATHERSAY (HERSEY) Robert 60
HARTNETT Daniel P 270 J H 278 Michael 278 Thomas 269
HARVEY John 276 346 347
HAUGHTON James 210 312 Mr 210
HAVEN Frances 80g Nathaniel A Sr 294 Sarah 50g
HAVEY Peter 228
HAWKSWORTH Mary 403 Thomas 403
HAYES Daniel F 151 Hannah 50g John S 427 Nancy L 51g
HEAD 340 John M 264 Oren 152 Oren M 262 270
HEALEY Abigail 54g Ira 270 Levi 54g Nathaniel 288
HEATH General 243
HEBBARD Erskine W 265
HEERD Esther 62g
HELME 27 28 Christopher 26 Margaret 27 William 27
HENDERSON Mary 80g Samuel H 270
HENINGER Zephaniah 272
HENNINGER Zephaniah 269
HENSS Charles 55g Sarah 55g
HERITAGE Thomas 273
HERRICK Mary 54g Nathaniel 54g
HERSEY 404 Judith 65g Meriah 18g Peter 230 Robert 132 403
HERVEY C W 25g Charles W 25g Eliza H 25g Frank H 262 25g Louis P 25g S C 278
HETHERSAY Robert 45 403
HICKS James 272 Sarah 63g
HIGHWAYS Repairs of 122 Laying out 123 125
HILDRETH 423 Abel F 55g Ann E 55g Hosea 198 294 295 308 312 424 Mr 198 Richard 295
HILL Abigail 27g Betsy 55g Caleb 54g Captain 70 Elisha 27g Elizabeth M 55g James 55g Jane 52g John B 257 Jonathan 249 252 254 54g Joshua 80g Lucretia 55g Lydia R 55g Mary 54g 80g Mary N 59g Purmot 55g Sarah 54g Theodore 258 Valentine 115 William 55g William B 278
HILLIARD Francis 347 J C 348 Joseph C 152 347 348
HILTON 4 21 108 130 227 390 456 Abigail 57g Andrew 72g Ann 354 Anne 81g 82g Benjamin 142 54g 72g Bridget 18g Captain 217 221 Catharine 64g Colonel 222 223 225 226 459 467 Deborah 47g 54g Dudley 138 139 224 225 227 25g 63g Edward 3 8 20 27 56 114 115 130 134 142 148 157 159 163 173 221 319 320 323 353 370 434 435 437 459 463 64g Edward Jr 135 162 323 354 54g Edward 3rd 80g Elizabeth 54g 60g Jeremiah 72g John 135 246 250 252 254 72g Jonathan 139 224 225 227 Jonathan Jr 142 Jonathan Sr 142 Joseph 142 Judith 37g Love 72g Mary 173 25g 63g Mercy 25g 63g Mr 26 30 37 165 436 438 Olive 60g Patty 55g Rebecca 173 Richard 77 138 139 142 149 171 173 174 176 177 353 6g 55g Samuel 142 Sarah 6g 51g 72g Sobriety 173 Susan 370 William 20 27 68 130 142 149 353 435 437 441 72g Winthrop 138 139 142 149 173 177 221 222 225 463 467 37g 47g 80g
HINDS Ambrose 233 O 206
HINMAN Andrew 288
HITCHCOCK R D 192 Robert S 199 Roswell D 192 314 William D 192
HITHERSEA Thomas 61
HOBART Colonel 329 Dudley Bradstreet 80g Samuel 93 152 328 80g
HOBBS Caleb 72g Jacob 233 72g Mary 72g
HODGDON Alexander 259 Joanna 55g Moses 359 Samuel 55g Samuel S 269 Stephen 80g
HODGE Elizabeth 80g
HODGKINS Sarah 26g 56g
HOIT Benjamin 330 Betsey 61g Betsy 55g Cuffe 55g Ellen E 55g Joseph 55g Rose 55g William 55g 80g
HOITT Ira B 108

HOLDRIDGE Mary 55g
HOLLAND Annie 25g Bethiah 25g
  Hannah 57g John 233 25g Martha
  25g Mary 25g Robert 25g
HOLMAN Daniel 25g Hannah 25g
HOLT Elizabeth M J 55g Joshua 55g
  Sarah A 55g Sarah F 52g
HOMICIDES IN EXETER Mrs Willix
  403 Johnson 404 John Wadleigh
  405 Mrs Ferguson 407
HOOD William Jr 258
HOOK Elizabeth 82g Ezekiel 55g
  Hannah P 53g Lucretia 55g
  Sarah W 62g William 80g
HOOKER 448
HOOLE 306
HOOPER Noah 202 424 Noah Jr 202
HOPKINS Anna M 55g Noyes 258
  Thomas R 55g
HOPKINSON Abigail B 82g Elizabeth
  R 55g John 305 71g Jonathan 91
  250 252 71g Lucy 54g Moses 54g
  71g Noyes 55g Samuel 80g
HORN Armstrong 61 224 227
HORNE Armstrong 219 Strong 219
HOUSE John 267
HOUSES Early: Clifford House 416
  Dean House 418 Ladd House 420
  Rowland House 422 Odiorne
  House Hildreth House 423 Pea-
  body House Gilman House 424
  Tilton House 425
HOUSTON John 333 346
HOVEY Henry 55g Mary E 55g
HOWARD Henry 273 M 207
HOYT Andrew J 152 311 Benjamin
  248 250 251 71g Daniel 71g
  Elizabeth 71g Elizabeth J 63g
  Jemima 71g Joseph 71g Joseph G
  109 151 290 295 312 Joseph J
  258 L G 377 Nicholas Smith 71g
  Richard 71g Samuel 205 Sarah
  71g William 248 250 251 71g
HUBBARD 215 456 Captain 117
  Josiah 117
HUDSON William 30
HUGER 452
HUGHES James 272
HUME 313
HUNNEWELL Jonathan 55g Mary 55g
  William M 330
HUNTING John 327
HUNTINGTON F D 210 James F 330
  William 60 132
HUNTLEY Isaac W 206
HUNTOON John 229 Philip 138

HUNTSON Philip 219
HURD Elizabeth 55g Francis P
  297 Isaac 106 198 297 300
  55g Mr 199 Rev Mr 199
HUSE J H 278
HUSKE John 78
Hutchins Ezra 54g Sally 54g
HUTCHINSON 25 Anne 6 11 Ebenezer
  233 Edward 5 Mary 5 Mrs 7 16
  Samuel 8 28 Susanna 12 28
  William 6 28
HYDE Joseph 327

INDEPENDENCE Earliest Suggestion
  of 87
INDIAN DEEDS OF 1638 8 9, of
  1639 14, Disputed Deed of
  1629 10, Appendix I 431
INDIAN WARS 215
INHABITANTS PRIOR TO 1680 59
INSURANCE COMPANIES 347
IRELAND Asa 245
IRVING James 278
IVES Rebecca 20g

JACKSON Elizabeth 380 Henry 80g
  Pomp 55g Robert 267 Susanna
  55g William 100
JACOBS Olivia 39g Phena 60g
JAMES II, King 68
JAMES 9 215 343 Abigail 25g 55g
  62g Ann 25g Anne 30g Caleb
  26g Dudley 181 5g 25g 26g
  Dudley Hall 25g Ebenezer 55g
  Elizabeth 25g Francis 181
  25g 55g George R 265 Joseph
  Y 308 Joshua 26g Josiah 71g
  Kinsley 182 25g 71g Kinsley
  H 91 248 Lois 25g Mary 14g
  25g 26g 57g Robert 25g Tir-
  zah 5g 26g 50g
JANVRIN Joseph 347 Joseph A 55g
  Joseph E 276 Lydia A 55g
  Mary W 312
JAYS 452
JEFFERDS Mary 55g Nathaniel 55g
JEFFRIES David 86
JENKINS Elizabeth 51g 62g Polly
  62g
JENKS Maria 62g
JENNES Jonathan 71g Thomas 71g
JENNESS 317 Lois D 53g
JEPSON John 250
JEWELL 340 Asa 150 152 Henry
  204 312 Mr 204
JEWETT David 248 81g Eliza S

55g Jedediah 150 152 Martha
55g Mary 8g Moses 55g Nathan
55g
JOHNSON 404 463 Anne 59g Bradbury
55g Caleb 81g Charles H 342
Edmond 60 General 234 459 Jack
404 405 John 81g John Jr 55g
Jonathan 257 Katherine 52g
Mary 55g President 371 Rachel
55g Sally 82g Sarah 49g Seth
Jr 81g William 233 William L
389
JONES Abigail 26g Abner 204 Ann
55g Benjamin 219 224 227 Benjamin Sr 138 139 Daniel S 55g
Harrison 276 Henry 26g James
55g Joanna 51g 55g Lydia 61g
Mary 107 26g 55g Samuel 26g
55g Susannah 26g Thomas 45 60
131 132 133 William 219
JORDAN Richard 327
JOSEPH Jeremiah L 340
JUDGES AND LAWYERS Notices of 349
JUDKIN Joel 287
JUDKINS Abigail 55g 71g Bartimeus
71g Bathsheba 71g Ebenezer 246
Hannah 26g Job 138 139 219 26g
Job Jr 142 Job Sr 142 Joel 60
136 139 146 26g John 218 55g
71g Jonathan 71g Joseph 142
231 Mary 26g Samuel 81g Sarah
26g 80g
JULIAN Abigail T 55g George N 275
340 Luke 340 55g Odlin 340

KAYE Booth 265
KEEFE William 269
KEITH James 273
KELLER David 259
KELLEY Daniel 231 Dany 135 David
G 271 Duny 60 James 250
Patrick 267
KELLY 33 34 Almira 60g Caroline
E 313 Daniel 81g Eunice 52g
John iv 109 152 309 313 369
John P P 343 370 426 Mary 55g
Mr 370 Roger 219 55g Susan 370
William 369 81g
KENDALL Isaac 257 Lucy 28g
KENISTON Bridget 43g
KENNEDY John 56g Lydia 56g Mary
56g
KENNISON Joseph 248
KENNISTON Christopher 146
KENT Hervey 333 John 46g Sarah
46g

KIDD James 60 135 136
KIDDER Hollis C 259 Nathaniel
259
KILHAM Annie M 292
KIMBAL Dorothy 53g
KIMBALL 393 Abigail 26g 55g 56g
72g Amos 71g 72g Ann 64g
Anna 71g Anne 56g Benjamin
91 72g Caleb 142 26g 72g
Charles O 201 Daniel 81g Dud-
ley 26g 56g 64g Elinor 26g
Elisabeth 71g 72g George W
278 Hannah 71g James 278
Jesse 26g John 142 149 150
152 233 250 26g 27g 56g 63g
John Jr 251 72g John H 151
152 John Henry 26g Joseph
26g 72g Judith 26g Lydia 26g
Mary 56g 72g Mary Abigail
26g Mehetabel Ann 26g
Mehitable 72g 82g Molly 79g
Moses 250 251 26g 55g Mr 162
Nathaniel 233 26g 64g 72g
Noah 26g Olive 26g Peter S
55g Peter Sanborn 72g Pheebe
55g Porter 247 Robert 91
Robert Porter 26g 63g Samuel
Ney 26g Sarah 26g 27g 56g
72g 81g Thomas 150 232 26g
Thomas Jr 72g Trueworthy 72g
KIMING John 135 137
KIMMING Benjamin 231 233 John
60 63g Martha 63g Moses 143
219 Thomas Dolloff 63g
KINCAID James 278
KING 456 Mary E 62g Thomas 45
54 60 114 123 126 131 133
134 135 148 157 161 162 320
322 324 William 216 220
KINGMAN Jeremiah 297
KINGSBURY Mary J 56g Samuel 56g
KINSMAN Martha 19g
KITTREDGE Dr 382 George L 299
KNIGHT Adeline A 293 Charles H
377 Joseph E 426
KNNAP Caesar 55g Mimbo 55g
KNOLLES 456
KNOWLTON Tammy 80g
KOSSUTH Louis 397

L. Mr 344
LADD 409 420 Abigail 27g 57g
Alexander 409 Ann 56g Anna
391 27g 72g Betsey 27g Cap-
tain 421 Caroline 27g
Charles 57g Charlotte 27g

230 232 27g 72g Deborah 56g Edward 91 180 72g Edward Jr 72g Elias 56g 72g Eliphalet 93 150 190 241 255 337 343 420 27g Elizabeth 27g 48g Hannah 57g 64g 80g Harriet M 62g Heman 57g 64g Henry 27g Isaac 57g John 224 225 227 237 27g John Alexander 27g Joseph 72g Josiah 182 27g 56g Lydia 27g Mary 27g 57g Nabby 72g Nathaniel 60 64 137 139 143 167 181 217 219 224 225 227 250 420 421 27g 72g Nathaniel Jr 143 Sally 190 27g 82g Samuel Gilman 64g Sarah 56g Simeon 95 Sophia 27g Trueworthy 230 235 238 William 314 421 27g

LAFAYETTE 394
LAFFERTY Edward 267
LAINE Deborah 56g James 56g
LAKEMAN John 56g Sally 56g
LAMBERT Paul 248
LAMPREY Henry 61 Simon N 264
LAMPSON William 181
LAMSON 305 306 456 Asa 28g Asa D 339 Benjamin 252 27g 28g Caleb 27g Clarissa 27g 82g Dr 236 Elizabeth 10g 52g Elizabeth Phillips 28g Ephraim Kendall 28g Eunice 27g F H 339 George 307 308 364 Gideon 93 101 104 150 240 243 249 327 338 343 364 72g John 80 235 238 304 306 340 381 10g 28g 56g 81g Joseph 91 93 288 27g Joseph Jr 343 27g 56g Joseph 3rd 56g Katharine 72g Lucy 28g Lydia 27g 28g Martha 27g Mary Sewal 56g Mehetable 27g Mehitable 56g Nancy 56g Nathaniel 231 Olive 45g Pernal 27g Peter 72g Polly 27g Rachel 27g Rufus 275 Ruth Kendall 28g Samuel 91 246 72g Sarah 27g 51g Stephen 327 27g 28g Susanna 56g Susannah Kendall 28g Thomas Dennis 27g William 72g
LANDS Final Distribution of 145 First Allotment of 19 Appendix II 435 Grants of 130
LANE Abigail 56g Charles E 348 Eliza A 57g Franklin 148 388 George E 148 J B 203 Joel 340 388 Josiah 57g Mary 53g Sally 80g William 107 340 56g
LANG Benjamin 150 Eliza S 55g 56g Hasket D 56g
LANGDON 380 Colonel 240 Elizabeth 58g John 87 251
LANGLEY Hannah 79g
LANPHEAR Orpheus 313 Orpheus T 199
LARABEE Jonathan 56g Mary 56g
LARKHAM 456
LARKIN Mary 57g Oliver 57g
LARY Abigail 72g Cornelius 60 135 137 227 Daniel 227 Daniel Jr 72g Dolly 72g Jonathan 72g Mary 72g Mehitable 81g Samuel 72g Thomas 146 227 231
LASELL Nathaniel 192
LASON Christopher 447
LAWRENCE 456 Alexander H 313 363 28g Alexander Hamilton 64g Carolina 64g Caroline 28g Caroline F 28g David 60 136 151 177 219 242 Deborah 28g 40g 56g 64g Edward 259 Elizabeth D 28g Ellen C 28g Fitz Henry 28g Joseph 224 227 72g Jotham 152 198 363 28g 40g 56g 64g Lydia 56g Lydia L 28g Mary 168 Mehitable 54g Mercy 72g S Abbott 427 Samuel C 28g Sarah 72g Sarah C 28g William F 28g William Frederic 64g
LAWREY Samuel 138
LAWSON Christey 444 445 Christopher 17 28 42 44 47 48 133 148 158 447 Elizabeth 28
LAWYERS 349
LEARNED John C 209 313
LEATHERS Benjamin 57g Eliza 57g Frances 57g George W 57g Pamelia 51g
LEAVIT Elizabeth 19g Josiah 56g Lydia 56g Patty 55g
LEAVITT 340 411 425 Abby K 58g Abigail 28g 56g 73g Abigail T 61g Abigail Thorndike 29g Alice 28g 34g Angelina 57g Anne 73g Annie 60g Augustus J 278 Benjamin 138 246 28g 29g 56g 57g Benjamin Dow 29g Betsey 34g 48g 58g Betsy 52g 56g Charles H 278 Daniel 138 56g Daniel Sherburne 29g Deborah 51g Dolly 54g 81g Dorothy 28g 72g 73g 80g

Dudley 143 314 392 Edmund 57g
Edward 73g 250 Elbridge A 262
Eliza 59g Elizabeth 187 28g
55g 56g Emerson 72g Family
340 Frances 29g 55g Frances A
44g 61g Gideon 72g Gilman 81g
Hannah 28g 72g Hannah T 56g
Hannah Taylor 29g Isaac 107
Isabel 29 James 139 143 149
180 185 219 227 235 28g
Jeremiah 150 8g 29g 72g
Jeremy 60 116 136 28g Joanna
28g John 134 138 143 181 219
228 258 278 28g 56g 57g 72g
John Jr 72g John Blake 28g
John Ward 278 Jonathan 57g
72g 73g Joseph 143 149 229
232 233 245 250 327 72g 73g
Joseph W 278 Joseph Ward 265
Josiah 28g 72g Lydia 58g 73g
Mary 8g 28g 57g 59g 72g 73g
80g Mary B 52g Mary F 50g
Mary Fogg 29g Mary S 57g Molly
72g Moses 60 65 70 137 138
139 143 148 149 151 167 169
172 173 175 176 177 219 248
392 28g 73g Moses Sr 139
Nancy 57g Nathaniel 233 73g
Nathaniel K 152 Nehemiah 139
146 229 73g Reuben 73g Ruth
73g Sally 62g Sally W 57g Samuel 53 60 68 119 123 135 136
138 148 149 151 171 172 173
175 176 177 339 392 28g 56g
Samuel Jr 138 Sarah 28g Sarah
E 57g Sarah M 63g Selah 143
228 73g Stephen 143 56g
Susanna 56g 72g Thomas 4 29
152 377 431 433 Timothy 143
William 246 252 William R 265
LEAVITTS 390
LEAR Tobias 100
LEARY Cornelius 219 224 Daniel
  143 224 225 246 Samuel 143
  Thomas 224
LECHFORD Thomas 19
LEE Eunice 61g
LEESON 320
LEGAT John 40 41 44 45 50 51 52
  60 114 123 131 132 133 134
  148 158 318 321 322 326 443
LEGATE John 159 161 162
LEGISLATION Earliest 21 41
LEIGHTON Elizabeth 56g Joel A 269
  Thomas 56g
LEONARD L W 313 Levi W 309

LEVITT Thomas 18
LIBBEE Nathaniel 339
LIBBEY Luke 253 81g
LIGHT Abigail 29g Captain 230
  Dorothy 29g Ebenezer 230 244
  246 249 250 251 29g 73g
  Hannah 24g 25g 29g 56g John
  69 139 146 227 230 244 246
  251 24g 25g 29g 56g Joseph
  29g Mary 25g 29g 49g 73g
  Olive 73g Phillis 56g Prince
  253 399 56g Robert 149 181
  29g Sarah 56g
LIGHTON Abigail 55g 64g
LIMBOLD Louis 274
LINCOLN Abraham 371 President
  279
LINDE John 216
LISSEN 320
LISSON Jane 56g Nicholas 56g
LISTEN Elizabeth 30g Mary 21g
  Nicholas 114 118 119 133 134
  135 136 148 320 322 325 352
  21g
LISTON Nicholas 60
LITTLE E 306 George W 57g
  Joseph 46g Mary E 57g Patrick 278 Sarah 46g Walter
  257
LITTLEFEJLD Goodman 436
LITTLEFIELD Ann 29 Anthony 29
  Edmond 18 Edmund 29 317 Edward 61 Francis 29 Jane 29
LITTLEHALE Edna P 56g Sargent S
  56g
LIVERMORE Samuel 97
LOCALITIES 426
LOCK Samuel 253 254
LOCKE Elizabeth 52g P Webster
  377 Samuel 249
LOGIE Elisha 56g Nancy 56g
LONG Eben^r 242 John C 397
  Pierse 92 248 397
LONGFELLOW Green 233
LOOGEE Apphia 60g
LORD Abiel 29g Abigail 17g 29g
  56g Anne 29g Betty 29g Deborah Dean 59g Edmund 29g
  Eliphalet 245 250 29g 56g
  Elizabeth 29g 79g Hannah 29g
  54g 56g Isaac 56g John 143
  180 181 272 29g 56g Jonathan
  29g 56g 73g Mary 17g 29g 56g
  79g Nancy 56g Nathan 294
  Robert 91 29g Robert Jr 56g
  73g Samuel 29g Susanna 56g

Thomas 247 29g William 29g
73g
LOUD Benjamin 245 Joel 248 Samuel
81g
LOUETT Thomas 436
LOUGE Jonathan 56g Nancy 56g
LOUGEE Betty 73g Edmund 73g
Elizabeth 29g Hannah 73g
Hannah T 56g John 143 224 225
227 258 56g 73g Jonathan 244
246 Jonathan Folsom 73g Joseph
56g 73g Lydia 54g Mehitable
73g Miriam 56g Moses 231 246
250 251 254 73g Nancy 51g
Nicholas 73g Noah 73g Simeon
73g
LOUIS XIV King 452
LOUISBURG EXPEDITION 230
LOVEJOY Harriet 57g Parker 57g
LOVELL Shubael 201
LOVERAIN Abigail 30g Anna 51g
Daniel 29g 30g Ebenezer 30g
Jannah 30g John 30g Mary 29g
30g Miriam 30g Moses 30g
LOVEREN Benjamin 254 Richard 253
254
LOVERING Anna 73g Anne 15g 81g
82g Apphia 56g Benjamin 30g
Benjamin Jr 30g Calvin 57g
Caroline 30g Charles E 30g
Ebenezer 73g Edmund E 269 Edwin O 150 Elizabeth 30g 73g
82g J M 341 James M 148 151
152 Jean 73g John 56g 73g
John Prescott 73g Jonathan
73g Joseph 246 250 56g 81g
Mary 59g 73g Mary Ann 30g
Mary J 57g Moses 73g Nathaniel
253 73g Olive 57g Olivia 30g
Osgood 73g Penelope 73g Richard 73g Ruhannah 50g Sally
30g Sally W 30g Samuel 225 227
56g Sarah 56g Sarah W 51g
Susanna 56g Theophilus 73g
Thomas 343 Willoughby 73g
LOVEWELL Zaccheus 238
LOVRAIN Jane 59g
LOVRING Elizabeth 56g Joseph 56g
LOWD Rebecca L 57g Wm B 57g
LOWE Charles 313 George Anne 23g
John Jr 333 23g Mary S 45g
Sarah Anne 23g Susanna 18g
LOWELL Moses P 205 Thomas 224 227
LUCY Michael 208
LUEY Mary 62g
LUFKIN Eliza C 293

LUMBERING 51 335
LUNT Eliza H 25g Henry 26g
Jerusha H 57g Joshua A 57g
Mary 26g
LYFORD 390 392 Abigail 26g 30g
Alice 73g Ann 15g 25g 54g
Anne 30g Benjamin 74g Betsey
80g Betsy 52g Betty 30g
Biley 73g Deborah 30g 81g
Dorothy 73g 82g Dudley 73g
Elizabeth 30g 56g Family 392
Francis 138 149 219 336 56g
73g 81g Gideon C 393 57g
Hannah E 57g James 30g 81g
James Gilman 73g John 30g
73g 81g Jonathan 253 74g
Kinsley 56g 74g Liberty 30g
Lois 25g 30g 79g 80g Mary
56g 74g 82g Mehitable 73g
Molly 30g Moses 73g 74g Mrs
30g Oliver Smith 73g Rebecca
56g Robert 56g Sarah 59g
Stephen 143 149 185 Theodore
81g Theophilus 25g 74g
Thomas 91 138 143 25g 30g
74g Thomas Jr 30g Tirzah 8g
30g
LYMAN John D 152 290

MC CLINTOCK Henry 81g
MC CLUER Jane 59g
MC CLURE Elizabeth 59g James
248 251 252
MC COY Phebe 50g
MC CUSIC Ephraim 272
MC DANIEL Benjamin F 209 313 Mr
209 210
MC DONALD Charles 266
MC DONNELL John 208
MC ENERY Thomas 278
MC GINNIS Captain 234
MC GREGORE James 201
MC INTEE James 263 274
MC KEAN John 96
MC KEEN Thomas 224 227
MC KIM Esther 81g William 245
247 248 251
MC MULLEN Patrick 267
MC NARY Daniel 278
MC NEAL D F 278 Emeline N 58g
Gilman 58g
MACE Catharine 57g William 57g
MACK W B 389
MAGER Catharine 57g Francis 57g
MAGOON 456 Alexander 138 143
219 227 30g 74g Benjamin 143

74g Benjamin Jr 74g Bethiah
  25g Betsey 57g Dolly 74g Ed-
  ward 74g Elisabeth 74g Eliza-
  beth 30g 56g 66g 74g Ephraim
  74g Hannah 74g Henry 60 135
  136 137 30g 66g John 226 229
  30g Jonathan Leavitt 74g
  Joseph 74g Josiah 74g Mary
  30g 74g Mercy 74g Samuel 143
  228 246 74g Samuel Jr 250
  Sarah 30g 74g Simon 57g
MALLECK Frank 274
MALLON John M 265
MALLOON Abigail 30g John 30g
  Jonathan 30g Josiah 30g Mark
  30g Nathaniel 30g
MANDE John E 210
MANJOY Harry 399
MANN Asa 199 George 64g John 64g
  Mary 64g Mr 199
MANSFIELD Isaac 189 288 31g Mary
  31g Mr 189 190 Theodore 31g
MANUFACTURERS 341
MARBLE Charles 258
MARCH Captain 217 Elizabeth 82g
  John 173
MARDEN Eliza A 58g George S 58g
MARRIAGES Gen 50
MARRYAT 308
MARSEILLES Charles 309
MARSH Abigail 57g Albert F 269
  Dudley 246 Elizabeth 62g
  Henry 74g James 231 Jeremiah
  W 152 John 143 227 258 Joseph
  245 251 Maria 74g Martha B 57g
  Mary A 51g Nancy S 57g Noah
  252 Samuel 254 Samuel H 57g
  Sarah 53g Stephen 254 81g
  Thomas J 57g Zebulon 245 57g
MARSHALL Abigail 74g Anna 74g
  Capt 242 Christopher 12 30 Ed-
  ward 263 Elizabeth 52g Henry
  181 Jonathan Thing 74g Simeon
  246 248 74g
MARSTON Eliphalet 258 Elizabeth
  57g Ephraim 168 General 280
  Gilman 109 111 152 261 279 280
  281 376 377 James 57g Simon
  248 Thomas 60 131 William S
  265
MARTIN Archelaus 58g Dinah 58g
  Ebenezer 146
MARVEL Sarah 56g
MARY, Queen 452 465
MARSH Ann 61g Elizabeth 50g
  Hannah 57g Joseph 57g Mary 53g

  Olley 57g Samuel 57g
MASON 63 64 362 449 452 Captain
  450 Francis 57g John 30 36
  55 62 65 Nathaniel 228 Robert
  62 67 389 Robert Tufton 55
  64 Susanna 54g 57g
MASONS A 426 F 426
MASRY Edward 218
MASSACHUSETTS JURISDICTION 45
MAST TREES 70 Riot of 1734 72
MASTERS John 38g Rebecca 38g
  81g
MATHER 36 Cotton 217
MATHES 30
MATHEWS Francis 18 30 Thomasine
  30
MATTOON Hubertus 222 Richard
  138 143 145 222
MAVERICK 57 Antipas 64g Samuel
  55 56
MAXWELL Hugh 246
MAYHEW Rev Mr 203
MAYLEM Joseph 74g Mercy 74g Mr
  145
MEAD Hannah 58g John 57g Olive
  57g
MEADER Elizabeth 57g John 57g
  Meserve 258
MEDCALF Alfred 206
MEEDS Abigail 31g Benjamin 31g
  Horatio Gates 31g John 31g
  Mary 31g Polly 31g Stephen
  31g William 31g William Sr
  31g
MEETING-HOUSES 71 160 162 167
  173 179 181 191 194 198
MELCHER Abigail 63g Ann Eliza-
  beth 31g Benjamin 258
  Charles Henry 31g Daniel 148
  340 31g 57g Daniel Flagg 31g
  Edwin Forrest 31g Gershom
  Flagg 31g James F 340 James
  Folsom 31g John 304 81g
  Lewis Cass 31g Lucy 60g Mary
  Olivia 31g Nancy Y 31g 57g
  William P 31g William Perry
  31g
MELLEN Henry O 257 Prentiss 107
  Sarah Hudson 21g
MELLOWS Oliver 32
MELONEY Joanna 50g
MELONY Anne 57g Ebenezer 57g
MELOON Nathaniel 233
MELVIN Michael 271
MENJOY Abigail 57g Henry 57g
MERCHANTS AND TRADES 342

MERRIAM Franklin 202
MERRILE Hannah 57g Juba 57g
MERRILL A 278 Abner 340 346 57g
   Benjamin L 340 346 Charles A
   110 346 347 Daniel Williams
   81g Date 57g Jacob 250
   Jeremiah L 346 31g Joseph W
   152 31g Mary 62g 82g Mary E
   31g Phineas 103 109 331 Sally
   W 57g Winthrop 57g
MERRIMAC RIVER 8 9 13
MESERVE D 219 Nathaniel 235 381
METHODIST SOCIETY AND PASTORS 205
MICHELE Ann 57g Caleb 57g
MIGHILL 223 Samuel 143 222 227
MILLEN C W 207
MILLER Anne 47g James J 272 Louis
   274 William 205 207
MILLS AND MANUFACTURES 317 331
MINGO Ebenezer 57g Phena 57g
MISTONOBITE 433 434
MITCHELL Caleb 244 246 251 Elizabeth 56g Ellen E 31g Emma E
   31g Fanny D 31g Frances D 31g
   George W E 31g Harriet M 31g
   Isaac H 31g Isaac L 31g Lewis
   340 31g Lewis F 31g Oriana
   31g Orianna 49g Samuel 224
MOB Paper Money of 1786 96
MONROE Colonel 235
MONTAGUE Griffin 30 166 317
   Margaret 30
MONTCALM General 235
MONTGOMERY John 337
MOODY Ann 31g Clement 138 219 228
   231 Clement Jr 143 Clement Sr
   143 John 143 229 31g Jonathan
   143 81g Joshua 33 Mary 31g
   Master 382 Mehitable 53g Mr
   453 Philip 229 Samuel 248
   William 223 81g
MOONEY Col 255
MOORE 370 Ann 32g 57g Catharine
   32g Catherine F 62g Charles
   32g Coffin 81g Daniel 267
   Elisabeth 74g Elizabeth 32g
   57g 59g Hannah 74g Henry 57g
   John 32g Josiah 74g Martha 74g
   Mary 74g Nicholas 32g Nicholas
   G 32g Rachel 50g 57g Sally 423
   Thomas 74g Thomas Jr 74g
   William 30 44 45 68 118 119
   131 132 135 136 148 149 151
   164 170 173 175 233 319 32g
   57g 74g William Jr 65 138 57g
MORE Betsey 61g

MOREY William 231
MORGAN Abraham 228 George B 211
   Richard 60 65 135 137 219
   Richard Jr 138 Richard Sr 138
   219 William 61
MORI John 263 274
MORIS Richard 17
MORRILL 233 Apphia 44g Jacob 250
   Joseph H 58g Levi 259 Olive
   58g William B 111 151 152
   309 347 William H 263
MORRIS Amanda C 300 John 270
   272 300 Leonora 12 31 Mr 436
   437 Richard 12 19 31
MORRISON John 288 57g Mary 57g
   William J 265
MORSE Amos 57g Benjamin 91 250
   254 Daniel 250 253 254 Eliza
   J 58g Enoch 250 251 254
   Eunice 57g Horace Edward 64g
   Horace W 64g Isaac G 57g
   Joanna T 62g John W 276
   Lucretia 57g Lydia S 64g
   Thomas G 58g
MORSS Benjamin 57g Mary 57g
MORTON 461
MOSES 343 A A 32g A T 32g Abigail G 58g Abigail T 55g
   Abby K 58g Charles C P 410
   32g Charles O 152 Deborah
   32g Elizabeth M 32g Esther
   51g G W 32g Henry C 152 203
   293 340 Howard M 275 John F
   152 201 203 259 340 32g John
   Lees 32g Joseph 81g Mary E
   31g 32g 57g Mary S 32g Mary
   Smith 32g Samuel 107 57g
   Samuel T 307 32g Sarah 61g
   Susan T 32g Susanna 57g
   Theodore 150 340 32g 58g
   Theodore B 32g William P 32g
   58g
MOSS Sarah 56g
MOULTON Ebenezer L 57g Hannah
   53g 60g John 58g Lucinda 57g
   Lydia 58g Mary 57g Mary E
   51g Nathan 338 Peltiah 58g
   Sibley 57g Susan H 58g
   Thomas 57g W P 348 William
   81g William P 150 311 347
   348 411
MOUNTEGU Grifing 445
MOUNTEGUE Goodman 437 Griffine
   437 Grifing 444
MOWER Goodman 436 William 437
MUDGET Elizabeth 32g 50g John

146 229 Nicholas 32g Sarah
32g Thomas 146 32g
MUGRIDGE William 245
MULLEN Francis 267
MUNJOY John 278
MURPHY Dennis 263 James 278
MURRAY Joseph 267

NASH John 225
NASON Benjamin 58g C P H 278
Elias 192 313 409 Hannah 58g
Paul F 278 Rev Mr 277
NAYLOR J G 202
NEAL Walter 143
NEALE Habertus 91 Walter 434
NEALEY B 278 Benjamin 250 Charles
H 273 278 John Jr 248 Josiah
74g Richard D 273 Thomas 74g
William 250 251 254
NEDHAM Ruler 439
NEEDAM Mr 444
NEEDHAM 28 32 Mr 48 443 Nicholas
9 17 31 40 42 148 442 Nicholas
Ruler 37 Ruler 20 42 436
NEEDOME Nicholas 8
NEEDUM Mr 436 438 Nicholas 442
NELE Walter 434
NELLIGAN Daniel 263
NELSON Ann 32g Anna 74g Caroline
32g 51g Deborah 82g Dudley 58g
Horatio G 32g John 80 32g 74g
Jonathan 58g 74g Josiah 32g
58g 74g Josiah Sr 32g Lavina
58g Lydia 58g Lydia B 58g
Martha 58g Martha N 58g Martha W 58g Mary 32g 58g Nathaniel F 58g Olive 74g Polly 32g
Sally 32g Samuel 32g Samuel F
58g Sarah 74g Sophia 32g Trueworthy 74g
NERO Caesar 235
NEW HAMPSHIRE a Royal Province 62
NEW PARISH 186 Set Off 188 History
of 194
NEW TESTAMENT FIRST PRINTED IN
NEW HAMPSHIRE 304
NEWHALL Betsy 58g Charles 203
Rufus 58g
NEWMAN Joseph 58g Mary 58g
NEWMARKET PARISH SET OFF 178
NEWSPAPERS 301
NICHOLLES Dorothea F 58g
NICHOLLS Richard 55
NICHOLS Adam 58g Dudley 58g 74g
John 246 250 251 74g 81g
Joseph 266 Martha B 58g Molly
58g Nicholas 74g Polly 81g
Trueworthy 74g
NICKERSON Alfred C 210 313
NICOLLE Elizabeth 81g Hannah
58g Harvey 58g Nicholas Jr
81g
NICOLLES Ichabod 58g
NIXON 246
NOBLE John S 259 Mary Folsom
42g
NORCROSS Nathaniel 27 157 463
NORRIS 278 Abigail 33g Benjamin
246 251 Catharine 58g
Charles 306 307 58g Eliphalet
245 250 58g Elizabeth 200
33g James 138 143 200 229
245 250 254 33g 81g Joanna
200 John 143 Jonathan 139
143 228 233 248 250 33g
Joseph 200 Josiah R 150
Lydia 58g Moses 138 139 219
373 33g Moses Jr 143 Moses
Sr 143 Nicholas 60 127 137
139 219 33g 65g Nicholas Sr
143 Ruth 33g Samuel 143 232
246 249 250 254 Sarah 33g
65g Teresa 58g
NORTH Alfred 33g Charles 33g
Henry 33g Nancy 33g Nathan
385 33g
NORTON Deborah 58g Josiah 58g
Mr 157
NORWOOD Sophia 52g
NOTICES OF SETTLERS OF 1638-9
21
NOWELL Patty 82g
NOYES Judith 7g Parker 7g
NUDD David 372 William 276
NUTTER C N 207 Hatevil 156
Henry 33g John 33g Lydia 58g
Mark 33g 58g Mary 33g Mr 157

OATH OF THE ELDERS 18 Of The
People 19
O'BRIEN James 272 John 278 M C
208
O'CONNER Charles 81g
ODELL Anna 12g
ODIORNE 305 423 456 Ann 33g
57g Ann Moore T 33g Anna
Maria 33g Clarissa 58g 64g
Deborah 33g 61g Dolly 33g
Ebenezer 33g Elizabeth 33g
50g F H 342 G G 278 George
150 239 33g 81g George G 388
Henry Moore 33g Jane 33g

Joanna 33g 58g 60g John 33g
Mary Jane 33g 50g Polly 62g
Richard Thayer 33g Samuel T
58g Samuel Tufts 33g 64g
Serena Maria 64g Thomas 80 86
152 242 252 304 313 339 423
33g Widow 107
ODLIN Abigail 189 18g 34g 53g
Alice 34g Anna 34g Anne 53g
Benjamin 35g Betsey 35g 58g
Betsy 34g 55g Caroline 34g
Charles C 388 Charles Cushing
33g Charlotte 60g Dudley 150
152 230 232 288 380 381 34g
58g Elisha 75 148 149 287 381
34g 37g Elizabeth 21g 34g 36g
54g 58g 59g Family 393 George
Osborne 35g Harriet A 33g
James 258 340 393 34g 35g 58g
James W 150 152 427 James
William 35g John 143 151 176
177 181 186 187 238 313 379
380 381 425 465 34g 37g 74g
John Jr 75 149 34g 74g Joseph
258 388 33g 35g Joseph Edwin
35g Judith 34g 37g Martha H
35g 58g Martha Jewitt 35g
Mary 381 58g 74g Mary A 61g
Mary Ann 34g 35g 60g Mr 177
178 183 185 187 188 189 194
66g Patty 47g 61g Peter 34g
Rev Mr 177 186 Samuel 34g 81g
Sarah 34g 74g Thomas 35g
William 91 152 257 340 393 34g
58g Winthrop 80 238 34g 47g
Woodbridge iii 151 152 176 185
186 187 287 297 313 332 340
346 393 34g 35g 58g 66g
OFFICERS Town: Rulers, Assistant
Rulers, Town Clerks, Select-
men 148 Moderators, Represen-
tatives 151
O'HARA Bernard 208
OLDHAM John 433
O'NEAL Patrick 263
ORDWAY Bessie P 293
ORN Teresa 58g
ORNE Eunice 80g
OSBORNE George J 304 Joseph 150
Mary A 58g Martha H 35g 58g
Oliver 339 Oliver W 58g Sophia
59g
OSGOOD Joanna 58g Philip 58g
OTIS Edward 389
OYSTER RIVER 3 5 9 14

PAGE Charles 263 Charlotte 35g
48g 59g Charlotte Dorothy 35g
David 233 235 Elizabeth 58g
59g James G 59g Joseph Til-
ton 35g Mary 81g Mary A 59g
Molly 81g Nathaniel 35g 48g
59g Nathaniel P 59g Samuel
58g
PAINE Harriet E 292
PALFREY John G 294
PALMER Ann R 59g Asher C 59g
Charles L 427 Elizabeth 9g
52g 59g Jeremiah 259 59g
Offin B 59g Sally 59g Simeon
246 248 257
PAPER-MILLS 327
PAPER MONEY 70 93 95
PARKER Amos A 313 Catharine 47g
58g Dolly 59g Dr 385 Elizabeth 35g 79g Francis E 297
Hannah 11g 64g Jeremiah D
426 Jeremiah Dow 64g John J
148 356 35g Mary 55g Mary
Sewal 56g Mary Sewall 35g
Nathan 258 Nathaniel 150 152
288 357 35g 47g 58g Retire H
150 152 341 64g Samuel 35g
Samuel D 294 Samuel P 210
313 Thomas 235 William 86 87
249 252 287 355 357 384 35g
59g William Jr 384
PARKES Anne 35g Charles 35g
Dolly 58g Dorothy 35g Robert
35g 58g
PARKS Charles 259 Joseph 259
Nancy 61g
PARSONS Enoch 35g Joseph 253
287 35g Joseph S 148 347 348
426 Mary 82g Rev Mr 424
Stephen 35g Theophilus 357
361 Thomas 80 35g
PARTRIDGE Ann 35 65g John 74g
Jonathan 74g William 35
PASCATAQUA RIVER 3 7 9 11 57
PASSACONAWAY 431 432 433 434
PASSACONAWAY Sagamore of Pena-
cook 10
PATCH Joseph M 389
PATRIDGE Hitty 74g John 74g
PATTEN John 91 Martha 60g
PATTERSON Alexander 253 254
George 253 254
PAUL 250 423 Benjamin 259 399
Catherine 59g Jacob 81g
Jacob Jr 59g John 59g Lovey
60g Martha 59g Nathaniel 399

Rhoda 80g Scipio 81g Thomas
399
PAULS Dolly 51g 62g Nancy 62g
PAYNE William 113 115
PAYSON J C 278 T K 278
PEABODY 424 Deborah Tasker 35g
　Edward Bass 35g Elizabeth 61g
　Frances 35g 58g Frances Bourn
　35g General 384 Judge 357
　Lucretia 35g Nathaniel 379 383
　Oliver 73 99 104 126 150 151
　152 344 354 356 365 424 35g
　58g Oliver W B 152 308 313
　357 365 Oliver Wm Bourn 35g
　Sarah 35g Stephen 363 William
　288 366 William B O 313 357
　William Bourn 35g Wm Bourn
　Oliver 35g
PEARSON 456 Abigail 74g Augustus
　William 36g Caroline 36g
　Daniel 59g Dole 248 253 Dolly
　62g Dorothy 36g 58g Edmund 150
　341 36g 58g 59g Fanny 36g 52g
　George 136 138 219 Hannah 59g
　Harriet P 59g Henrietta 36g
　Henry H 267 281 James 36g 59g
　Jethro 139 219 228 230 234 396
　36g 74g Jethro Jr 143 Jethro
　Sr 143 John Jr 59g Jonathan
　75g Joseph 287 288 396 58g 75g
　Judith 82g Mary Smith 32g 36g
　Nathaniel 341 36g Nathaniel Sr
　36g Olivia Gerrish 36g Sophia
　59g Susan 59g Taylor 75g
　William 257 36g 59g
PEASE Abigail 36g Ann 36g Beersheba 36g Nathaniel 143 36g Phebe
　36g Samuel 138 222 36g Sarah
　36g
PEASLEE Ebenezer 206
PEAVEY 425 Anthony 75g George C
　375 Hannah 59g Isabel 54g
　Jacob 75g Jeremiah J 59g John
　258 59g Luella J 59g Samuel
　59g Sarah 59g
PECK James J 202
PENNELL Robert F 313
PENNEY William 258
PERHAM Samuel 388
PERKINS Abraham 288 75g Albert C
　296 Albert M 262 282 Anna 75g
　Asa E 278 Benjamin 248 Benjamin
　R 330 59g Eliza 59g Elizabeth
　36g 58g 59g Elizabeth Odlin
　36g Esther 75g Isaac 233 James
　61 John 225 227 327 John Jr 143

John Sr 143 Jonathan 58g 75g
　Joseph 151 36g 59g Joseph
　William 36g Lewis W 150 59g
　Lydia 59g Mary 3g Mary J 59g
　Moses 258 Sarah 58g Solomon
　J 150 Stephen 59g Susannah
　62g Thomas 233 William Jr 143
　William Sr 143 Woodbridge
　Odlin 36g
PERMORT Joseph 250
PERRACHE J Ph 208
PERRY Abigail 36g Abigail Gilman 36g Abby 59g Abraham 246
　Caroline Frances 36g Dr 386
　Gardner 385 Gardner B 59g
　John T iv 299 313 420 John
　Taylor 36g Julia A 299 Maria
　P 59g Mary 6g Mr 422 Nathan
　385 Nathaniel G 152 376
　Nathaniel Gilman 36g Rev Mr
　6g William 152 191 313 332
　346 385 388 389 36g 59g
　William G 388 William Gilman
　36g
PERRYMAN 456 Joanna 355 Nicholas 77 143 185 186 286 287
　354 355
PERSON (PEARSON) George 60
PETERS Robinson 58g Vilet 58g
PETERSON Margaret 62g
PETET Tho 444 445
PETTENGIL Olive M 59g John W
　59g
PETTET Christian 65g Hanna 65g
　Thomas 65g
PETTIGREW Francis 263
PETTINGILL Ephraim 233
PETTIT Christian 32 Goodman 436
　Hannah 32 Joseph 233 Thomas
　18 32 44 52 114 132 133 134
　148 164 322 Thomas Jr 32 60
PHELP Sarah 81g
PHILBRICK 312 456 Benjamin 80
　10g 36g 37g 75g Daniel 58g
　David 75g Edward 75g Elizabeth 36g 37g 59g Ephraim 143
　181 229 Hannah 36g 37g 58g
　59g John 75g 81g John Robinson 36g Joseph 231 37g Lydia
　10g 75g Mary 37g 50g 75g
　Mary A 60g Mehitable 56g
　Samuel 107 36g 37g 58g 59g
　75g Samuel Sr 37g Sarah 59g
　Susanna 58g William 150 339
　37g 59g
PHILIP Chief Sachem of the

the Wampanoags 215 King 353
PHILLIP Dr 305
PHILLIPS EXETER ACADEMY 293
　Notices of Officers and Bene-
　factors 294
PHILLIPS 108 Colonel 239 Dr 293
　297 John 77 80 81 84 99 149
　151 194 239 287 291 293 335
　343 378 380 392 399 37g John C
　297 Samuel 293 37g Sarah 37g
　William 297
PHYSICIANS Notices of 378
PICKERING Abigail 57g Eliza A
　58g James 242 81g John 93 356
　Polly 60g Valentine A 278
PICKPOCKET MILLS 321 326
PIERCE Moses 81g President 374
PIERPONT Jonathan 286
PIERSON Edmund 75g Jethro 75g
PIKE Abby J 24g Abraham Sanborn
　37g Adeline 37g Arvilla 37g
　Benjamin 37g David 263 Ednah
　Dow 37g Elias 24g Elizabeth 5g
　37g Elizabeth Ann 37g Hannah
　Hook 37g Henry 75g Jacob 233
　75g James 37g John Kimball 37g
　Jonathan 37g Joseph 5g 37g
　Judith 5g 34g 37g Levi 37g
　Lucian M 59g Mary Adeline 37g
　Mary Shaw 37g Moses 72 37g
　58g Moses Jr 258 Moses Hook
　37g Robert 114 117 118 119
　143 250 Samuel Walton 37g
　Sarah 37g Satira D 59g
　Theodate 37g 58g William 5g
　37g
PILLER Mary 53g
PIPER Abigail 75g Betsy 53g Fran-
　cis 75g James 233 Mary 55g
　Samuel 72 138 219 Thomas 75g
PLAUSAWA 233
PLUMER William Jr 107
PLUMMER Ann 59g Joseph Jr 59g
POOR OF BOSTON Tax of 85
POOR Support of 105
POOR 456 Col 242 245 247 Dennis
　59g Enoch 80 81 86 87 242 246
　337 381 394 Martha 51g Mary
　51g 59g N P 257
PORMORT Philemon 12 18 32 285
　Susanna 32
PORMOTT Mr 436
PORTER Jonathan 75g Joseph 152
　Joseph T 148 150 343 Nehemiah
　287
POTTER 226

POTTLE Polly 62g Samuel 258
POWDER HOUSE 82 Mills 328
POWELL John 254 Robert 60 135
　138 427 Thomas 227 William
　138 219
POWER John 208
POWERS Elizabeth 59g Walter 59g
PRAY J E S 389 Mark W 389
PRAYER IN TOWN MEETINGS 105
PRESCOTT 246 Abram 257 Brad-
　street 75g Edward 38g Elisa-
　beth 75g George A 276 Jere-
　miah 234 81g John 38g 81g
　Joseph E 265 Mary N 59g
　Michael 59g Nathaniel 37g
　38g Philemon 75g Sarah 37g
　38g Weare 257 William 231
PRESTON Richard 143 228
PRICES Scale of, fixed 94
PRIMUS Cill 58g
PRINCE Deborah 79g
PRINTERS 301
PROAL Hannah M W 50g
PROCTOR Esther 81g George N 293
PROVINCIAL CONGRESS First 84
　Second 87 Fifth 88
PUBLIC LIBRARY 109
PUBLISHMENTS 1783 to 1800 Gen
　79
PULSIFER Samuel 234
PUMMADOCKYON 9 14
PURINGTON Joseph 234 Nancy M
　52g
PURMORT Abigail 38g Abner 38g
　Anne 38g Hannah 38g John 38g
　Joseph 246 38g Mark 38g Mary
　38g Mercy 38g Miriam 38g
　Richard 38g
PUTNAM W F 347 Warren F 346 347
　424

QUAKERS 200
QUEEN ANNE 220
QUIMBY Daniel 75g Eliphalet 231
　James 38g John 143 229 Jona-
　than 38g Mary 75g Mercy 38g
　S E 207 Samuel 91 328 Sarah
　38g
QUINCE Joseph 59g Martha 59g
QUINCY Edward 37
QUINT 33

RABONE George 445
RABORNE George 436
RAND Mary 60g Samuel 60g
RANDALL Abigail 38g Anna 38g

Jacob 38g 81g Rebecca 38g
Samuel 38g Sarah 38g Susy 38g
RANDEL Abigail 52g
RANDLET James 219
RANDOL George 64g
RANKIN Thomas 81g
RANLET 306 Catharine 58g Daniel
    343 Henry 102 259 304 305 306
    81g Henry A 307 Mary 62g
RANLETT Daniel 60g Henry A 60g
    Mary 60g Sarah G 60g
RASHLEIGH Thomas 44 60 131 155
RASHLEY Thomas 444
RAWLINS Benjamin 39g Eliphalet
    39g Hannah 39g Joshua 39g
    Lowel 60g Mary 39g Moses 38g
    Patience 39g Sukey 60g Thomas
    38g
RAWSON Edward 113
READ Deborah 33 Hannah 33
    Rebecca 33 Robert 18 33 318
    436 Samuel 33
READE Robert 444
REARDON Morris 269
REBELLION See "War for the Union"
RECORDS OF TOWN 43 Appendix II
    435
REDFORD William 218
REDMAN Hannah 39g
REED Nancy 57g
REVOLUTIONARY SOLDIERS FROM
    EXETER IN 1775 242 245 in 1776
    247 in 1777 249 in 1778 251 in
    1779 253 in 1780 253 in 1781
    254 Bounties and Supplies to
    255
REYNOLDS Daniel 254 George H 273
    Owen 228 Patrick 272
RICE Anna 39g John 80 149 189 242
    39g Martha F 293 Thomas 376
RICHARDSON Anne 14g Chief Justice
    362 Dorothy 79g J B 341 Phin-
    eas 254 William M 14g
RILEY John Jr 265 Patrick 274
RISHWOORTH Edward 440
RISHWORTH Edward 18 25 33 41 436
ROBEE Elizabeth 60g Lucian B 60g
ROBERTS Dorothy 60g Francis 59g
    George 61 Jane 59g John 146
    228 Robert 60g Thomas 17
ROBERTSON Levi 248
ROBINSON FEMALE SEMINARY 291
ROBINSON 216 406 456 Abigail 54g
    55g 59g 80g Almira 60g Ann M
    60g Anne 39g 75g Benjamin 231
    59g Caleb 239 246 249 251 255
288 393 39g Caleb Jr 81g
Catharine 39g 80g Charles E
39g Charles H 60g Christopher
229 D I 205 206 Daniel 230
39g 59g 75g David 61 137 219
39g 75g Deborah 28g 40g 56g
Deborah Dean 59g Dudley 75g
E G 340 Edward H 39g Elizabeth 9g 39g 40g 50g 81g
Ephraim 78 86 88 148 149 150
152 230 239 242 245 251 393
9g 15g 39g 40g 59g 75g
Ephraim Jr 288 Family 393
George W 278 Goodman 467
Hannah 36g 58g Harriet 40g
Henrietta 61g Henry 60g
Hester 39g Huldah 59g Irene
60g J Jr 107 J G 340 James
242 39g 59g 60g Jane 59g
Jeremiah 150 341 75g 81g
Jeremiah Jr 150 Jeremiah L
341 393 60g John 54 60 75
123 134 135 136 143 145 148
149 163 179 180 325 36g 39g
59g 75g 81g Jonathan 60 65
135 149 167 175 210 227 232
39g 75g 81g Jonathan Jr 143
60g Jonathan Sr 139 143
Joseph 143 39g Joseph Jr 81g
Josiah 86 93 150 152 232 75g
Josiah B 269 Judith 81g
Lucey 50g Lucia 39g Lucy 60g
Lydia 15g 39g 59g 75g Mary
9g 15g 23g 32g 39g 40g 54g
58g 59g 60g 61g 75g Mary A
59g Mary O 39g Mehitable 39g
75g Nathanial 258 Noah 245
249 250 393 Olivia 39g
Pascal L 269 273 Peter 39g
Philena F 6g Rebecca 59g
Rhoda 82g Samuel 258 39g
Sarah 39g 52g 53g 59g 75g
Sarah S 60g Simeon 39g
Sophia 60g Thomas 143 227
Thomas S 60g Trueworthy 150
75g Trueworthy Jr 60g
William 253 257 291 300 371
393 59g William Jr 263
William Frederick 40g Will-
iam H 150 152 Winthrop 259
Zebulon 40g Zechariah 59g
ROBAY Hen 445
ROBY 324 Henry 18 33 44 45 50
    123 131 133 134 148 159 320
    321 65g John 258 65g Ruth
    34 65g Thomas 65g

ROCK Joseph 269
ROE Edward 61
ROGER Anne 196 Mr 196
ROGERS 413 Abigail 40g Ann 40g
    Ann Gilman 40g Benjamin 40g
    Charles W 278 Daniel 78 195
    196 200 340 410 465 Dionysius
    40g Elizabeth 20g Ezekiel 157
    Frances 395 40g Frances Gilman
    40g Jacob 395 John 150 152 196
    197 327 332 334 344 395 465
    40g 60g John Francis 40g Mar-
    garet 40g Martha P 60g Mary
    40g Mr 197 Nathaniel Gilman
    40g Rainsford 412 Rev Mr 195
    Robert 243 Sally 59g Susanna
    40g
ROLLINS 228 229 Aaron 139 228
    Anna 76g Benjamin 138 143 227
    Daniel 81g Eliphalet 254 75g
    Elisabeth 76g F E 427 George
    H 275 Hannah 75g Henry S P 278
    Huldah 75g John 139 75g John
    Jr 143 Jonathan 60 Jos 91
    Joseph 138 219 228 232 75g
    Joshua 75g Josiah 232 388 76g
    75g Josiah Jr 248 Lowell 258
    Mary 75g 76g 81g Meshach 258
    Moses 138 219 245 250 Mrs 229
    Nathaniel 75g Rhoda 76g
    Robert 234 Samuel 143 Thomas
    60 64 116 136 138 218 Thomas
    Jr 138 Thomas Sr 138 139
ROMAN CATHOLIC SOCIETY AND PAST-
    ORS 208
ROOK John 82g
ROSS Elizabeth 44g James 246
ROW John 242
ROWE B F 427 Charles 278 Edward
    40g Enoch 150 250 40g Jacob
    258 James Samuel 40g John 258
    Luella 59g Mary A 60g Mehit-
    able 82g Olive 40g 60g Olivia
    40g Samuel 40g 60g William 60g
    Winthrop 245
ROWELL Ambrose E 265 Joseph S 272
ROWLAND 324 422 Ann 190 60g Anne
    15g Mr 190 423 Sally 190 27g
    Rev Mr 105 107 W F 15g 27g
    William F 73 190 313 422 60g
    82g
ROWLEY Ann 55g Sargent 258
ROWLS 431 433 434
RUGGLES Henry L 271
RUNAWIT 10 434
RUNAWITT 431 433

RUNDLET Anne 59g Benjamin 41g
    Charles 80 139 215 219 40g
    Charles Jr 138 139 Clemen-
    tine 55g Daniel 40g 60g
    Debby 76g Deborah 62g
    Dorothy 40g 41g Edward 41g
    Elizabeth 40g 57g Hannah 41g
    59g Henry 41g Honner 54g
    Honor 41g James 139 40g 41g
    59g 60g Jane 59g John 41g
    Jonathan 40g 59g Joseph 41g
    59g Josiah 41g Lydia 41g 58g
    Mary 51g Nathaniel 41g Olive
    41g 60g Priscilla 59g Ruth
    76g Sally 56g 60g Samuel 76g
    Sarah 41g 60g Satchell 140
    76g Sophia 60g
RUNDLETT 250 Charles 149 337
    64g 76g Charlotte 61g David
    82g Dorothy 53g Frank G 278
    Irene M 60g James 248 251
    257 263 64g 76g Jane 64g
    John 230 259 Jonathan 76g
    Josiah 82g Levi 60g Nathan-
    iel 259 Olive 40g 76g Thomas
    M 64g William F 426
RUOBONE George 17
RUOBONE (RABONE) George 34
RUSSELL Harriet 300 Rev Mr 202
    Richard 300 Willard 327
RUST Lucy 62g Sally 60g Samuel
    257 Samuel Jr 82g Sarah 41g
RYAN William 269 273
RYMES Christopher 239

SADDLERY AND CARRIAGES 339
SAFFORD Benjamin 41g 76g Ben-
    jamin Jr 82g Betsey 41g
    Charles Gilman 41g Dudley
    41g Elizabeth Ann 41g
    Frances 41g Hannah Gilman
    41g Henry 41g J C 340 James
    Gilman 41g Joseph 61g 76g
    82g Joseph Jr 258 Lavina
    62g Mandana 51g Oliver 41g
    Sally R 61g Sophia 41g Soph-
    ronia 41g
SAIL CLOTH Manufacture of 339
SAMPSON Captain 221 John 216
SANBORN A J 278 Abiah 8g Abi-
    gail 42g 60g 80g Abraham 76g
    82g Alcina Eveline 23g An-
    drew 273 Anne 41g 60g Ben-
    jamin R 258 Betsey 61g 80g
    Caleb 252 Catharine 81g
    Daniel 234 Daniel 2nd 152

Deborah 42g Edward 82g Elisha
64g 76g Eliza A 57g Elizabeth
18g 41g 79g Hannah 8g 41g 60g
82g Hannah V 61g Henry Dearborn 41g Jabal 8g Jacob 206
Jacob H 61g James 61g James H
263 Jeremiah 82g Jesse 82g
John 253 42g 60g 76g Josiah
149 231 232 41g 42g 60g Lydia
64g Mary 41g 76g Molly 60g
Moses 346 347 23g Mr 206 Nancy
51g Olive 60g Phebe 36g 76g
Rachel 24g Richard 230 Ruth
60g S T 341 Sarah 41g 64g 76g
Simon 41g Stephen 76g Theodata
58g Theodate 37g 42g 82g Tris-
tram 234 76g William 41g 82g
Zadoch 60g
SARGENT Dr 379
SAUNDERS Amos 61g John 60 113 131
Maria 61g
SAVAGE 26 30 James 10 Mr 39
SAW-MILL PRIVILEGES GRANTED 321
323
SAW-MILLS Taxation of 165
SAWYER Elizabeth 59g Frederic W
275 George C 388 Jeremiah 61g
John 306 60g Joseph B 267
Lovey 60g Mary 388 Mary J 51g
Susan 61g William 258
SAYER Abigail 18g
SCAMMELL Colonel 249
SCAMMON John 61g Mary G 61g
Richard 116 William 149 219
228
SCAMMONS Elizabeth 56g
SCANLAN John 267
SCEAVY Joseph 60g Martha 60g
SCHOOLS OF EXETER 285 Early In-
structors 286 School Districts
289 Grading of 290
SCHUYLER Major 226
SCOTT 308 Walter Quincy 296 299
SCRIBNER 227 Abigail 49g Anna 76g
Constant 76g Daniel 76g Ed-
ward 143 76g John 138 139 225
49g 76g John Jr 143 76g John
Sr 143 Joseph 143 234 76g
Samuel 143 228 231
SCRIGGINS Gideon 258
SCRIVENER John 175
SEAVEY Greenleaf 61g Nancy 61g
SEAWELL Thomas 139
SEBATIS 233
SELDON Robert 234
SEMINARY Robinson Female 291

SENIOR William 266
SENTER Joseph 250
SETIER John 60g Sarah 60g
SEVERANCE A T 389 Elizabeth 82g
John 231
SEWALL Edward 60 136 137 143
42g Henry 67 Jonathan 60
Joseph 42g Sarah 42g Stephen
143 Thomas 42g
SEWARD Robert 34 44 60 322
William 82g
SEWELL Sarah 175
SHACKFORD Catharine 47g 61g 64g
John 382 64g
SHAKESPEARE 455
SHAPLEY J Hamilton 376
SHARP Phena 57g 60g Titus 60g
SHARPE Samll 434
SHAW Benjamin 60g Elijah 205
310 J H 311 John 82g Mary
59g 61g Molly 60g Nathan 82g
Rebecca L 57g Timothy F 61g
SHELDON Dorcasina 313 Elizabeth
W 61g Parker 61g
SHEPARD Elizabeth 60g 79g Isaac
258 John 263 60g Jonathan
82g Lewis F 61g Nancy 79g
Polly 81g Samuel 23g Sarah
23g 61g
SHERIFF Abigail 42g Abraham 234
248 250 Benjamin D 42g Ben-
jamin Pearse 42g Benjamin
Pierce 60g Charles C 42g
Frederick 42g Henry A 42g
John Langdon 42g Martha 42g
Martha Gilman 42g Mary 42g
57g Patty 60g Sarah 42g 63g
Susan 61g Susannah 42g
SHERMAN Isaac 246 288
SHERRIFF Lydia 81g
SHIP-BUILDING 336
SHORT Rachel 55g William 82g
SHORTRIDGE Richard 245
SHRIGLEY James 204 310
SHUTE 393 Ann Eliza 42g Anna
38g Eliza R 42g 61g Emma 61g
George Smith 42g Georgie W
293 Henry 152 340 42g 61g
Henry A 348 377 Henry
Augustus 42g Michael 38g N
Appleton 346 Nathaniel 150
61g Robert 340 61g Sarah
Frances 42g Susan G 61g
SIBLEY Anna 60g John Langdon
297 Samuel 76g William 60g
76g

SILSBEE Benjamin 60g Polly 60g
SIMES Sarah Anne 23g
SIMONS Charles J 271
SIMPSON Nancy 56g
SINCLAIR Benjamin Folsom 76g
    Ebenezer 231 76g Elisabeth 76g
    Hannah 38g James 61 137 138
    139 143 149 224 225 227 247
    42g 76g James Jr 227 John 60
    135 137 139 218 227 42g John
    Jr 143 227 John Sr 143 John A
    276 John T 276 Joseph 143 Mary
    42g Richard 134 76g Samuel 143
    228 231 Sarah 42g
SINEGALL Lucy 54g
SINKLER Deborah 175
SLEEPER Ariana Elizabeth Smith
    43g Catharine Parker 42g
    Charles 278 Charles F 259
    Charles Frederick 43g Charles
    T 42g Dorothy 42g 48g 60g
    Eliza S 56g Elizabeth Jewett
    42g J F 48g John 64 John Howard
    43g John S 148 308 313 370
    42g John Sherburne 42g Jonathan
    F 288 60g Jonathan Fifield
    288 42g Josiah 61g Levi
    82g Margaret 61g Mary Folsom
    42g Sukey 53g William H 278
SLOAN James 250 William 250
"SMALL CAUSES" Commissioners to
    End 51
SMART Abraham 234 Adolphus 427
    Anne 82g Goodman 435 437 John
    20 27 34 45 60 132 143 173 320
    John Jr 60 John Sr 131 Joseph
    143 Martha T 51g Pheebe 55g
    Richard 61 Robert 60 118 119
    134 135 136 143 151 320 Robert
    Jr 61 Robert Sr 149
SMITH 360 406 Abigail 43g 64g 79g
    Abraham 43g Abram 376 Anna 43g
    Anne 43g Annie 60g Ariana
    Elizabeth 44g Benjamin 143 232
    37g 43g 44g 64g 76g Benjamin
    Jr 143 Betty 76g Biley 76g
    Bridget 43g Caleb 43g 82g
    Charles 278 Charlotte 44g 61g
    Daniel 228 43g 76g Daniel Jr
    60g David 91 143 228 82g
    Deborah 43g Dolly 53g Ebenezer
    76g 82g Edward 57 58 60 61 116
    136 137 143 148 167 234 43g
    65g Eliphalet 76g Elias 233
    Elisha 246 251 Eliza R 42g 61g
    Elizabeth 23g 32g 37g 43g 44g
    59g 60g 76g 81g Emma 61g
    Eunice 81g Fanny 44g Francis
    A 61g George 148 150 258 340
    George H 269 Hannah 61g Henrietta
    61g Hepzibah 43g
    Hezekiah 201 Irene 52g Isaac
    43g Israel 139 219 227 234
    42g 76g Ithiel 139 227 J 331
    J Coffin 340 J R 278 Jacob
    139 143 146 218 219 229 233
    43g 76g Jacob Jr 234 Jacob
    3d 234 James 266 61g Jane
    59g Jared P 269 Jeremiah 103
    106 107 126 151 313 344 359
    364 367 368 393 410 422 448
    44g Jeremiah W 276 John 150
    191 220 234 44g 60g 82g John
    Jr 60g John A 276 John Waldron
    43g Jonathan 61 72 139
    143 219 234 43g 64g Joseph
    34 139 173 235 43g 44g 60g
    76g Joseph Jr 61g 76g Josiah
    Coffin 60g Josiah G 258 61g
    Josiah Gilman 343 Judge 106
    361 Leah 43g Lewis 61g Lydia
    43g 59g 61g 76g Lydia R 55g
    Mary 30g 43g 44g 64g 65g
    Mary G 61g Mehitabel 175 43g
    Mehitable 76g Merrick M 269
    Mr 191 309 365 Nathan 43g
    Nathaniel 143 228 43g
    Nicholas 60 119 139 143 148
    219 224 227 43g 64g Obadiah
    43g Oliver 143 182 309 61g
    Oliver W 340 Patience 43g
    Peter 82g Pheebe 60g Polly
    44g 60g 61g 80g Reuben 76g
    82g Reuben Jr 76g Richard
    143 181 224 227 82g Richard
    Jr 61g Rob 445 Robert 18 34
    44 46 51 132 235 Sally 44g
    61g Samuel 146 246 248 252
    Sarah 43g 44g 59g 63g 76g
    80g Sarah A 51g Sarah G 54g
    60g Solomon 233 Solomon Jr
    234 Sophia 44g 51g Susanna
    44g 79g Tabitha 76g Theophilus
    71 80 86 91 138 139
    140 143 149 150 177 180 181
    182 219 393 43g Theophilus
    Jr 143 287 Thomas 234
    Timothy Jr 61g Trueworthy
    246 Widow 76g William iv 234
    258 267 313 364 44g 65g
    William H 262 William O 61g
SMYTH Robert 436

SOCIETIES 426
SOLDIERS First Officers of 42 48
SOMERBY George Adolphus 44g
  Hannah 44g Mary 61g Mary Ann
  Montgomery 44g Samuel 257 44g
  61g
SOMERSBY Elizabeth 176
SOMES Abigail 64g John 64g 76g
  Lydia 64g 76g Timothy 64g 76g
SOTHER Esther 60g Nathaniel 60g
SOULE Dr 296 Gideon L 295
SOWARD Robert 18
SPARKS Jared 294
SPEED Harriet 51g 63g Mercy 63g
  Thomas 138 246 250 251 63g
SPENLEY Mary 81g
SPENLOW Philip 138 219
SQUAMSCOT PATENT 4 Annexed to
  Exeter 120
SQUAMSCOT RIVER 4 12
STACEY Joseph 91
STACY 278 Joseph 303 Mark 219
STAMP ACT Effigies burned 78
STANEAN Anthony 45
STANELL Anthony 319
STANJON Mr 436 437
STANYAN Ann 35 65g Anthony 19 34
  45 51 124 131 132 133 148 319
  65g John 35 Mary 35 Mr 166
STANYON Anthony 446 Anthonie 439
  Anthony 438 Mr 444
STAPLES C H 278 Christopher 273
STARK Colonel 245
STARRE Mr 436
STEARNS 305 Eben Sperry 292
  William 304
STEEL Abigail 51g Anna 76g Date
  57g Eliphalet 77g Elisabeth
  76g Elizabeth 60g Francis 138
  139 146 218 219 Henry 76g
  John 234 247 60g 77g Joseph
  76g Josiah 246 251 76g Mahi-
  table 53g Mary 55g Olive 60g
  Robert 60g
STEELE Maria 61g Mary 58g
STETSON Carlton B 299
STEVEN Edward 146
STEVENS 224 Abigail 77g Buswell
  61g Catharine H 61g Charles W
  278 Chase 82g Chester C 271
  Dorothy 41g Edward 77g Elihu
  T 61g George W 269 H P 204
  Haley 77g Joanna 61g John 77g
  John L 204 Mary A 61g Nathan-
  iel 138 234 77g Patience 77g
  Phineas 359 Ruth 60g S B 343
  Sally 82g Samuel 140 146 223
  359 377 Samuel B 61g Samuel
  H 346 Sarah 77g Simeon 60g
  Solon 359
STEVENSON Ruth 11g Sarah E 57g
STICKNEY Amos 258 Charlotte 60g
  David 278 Jeremiah 60g Mary
  Ann 60g Moses H 274 Thomas
  Jr 60g William W 107 111 152
  371 374
STOCKBRIDGE Abigail P 63g Abram
  231 Maria 22g
STOKELL G L 427
STOKES Rev Mr 206
STOKLE John L 61g Lydia 61g
STONE Daniel W 278 Jacob D 266
  Simon 217
STOODLEY Major 240
STOR Augustine 8
STORE Agustin 438
STORER Augustin 433
STOREY Caroline C 61g John R
  61g
STORR Augustine 9 Mr 437
STORRE Augustine 17 19 20 35
  148 Marie 5 Mary 5 Thomas 5
STORRS George 206
STORY Augustin 431
STRAITS Lois 52g
STREET George E 200 313
STREETS Names 103 107 Lighted
  110 126
STRONG Abigail 189 34g Joanna
  60g Job 189 Jonathan 60g
STUBBS Isaac 246
STUMAN George 274
SULLIVAN 108 456 Attorney
  General 367 Charles W 44g
  Clarissa 27g Daniel 250 254
  Frances A 44g 61g Frances E
  44g General 240 252 255 380
  George 126 152 358 362 363
  407 27g 82g George E 44g
  Henry G 44g Hon Major Gen-
  eral 252 James 359 John 84
  87 97 152 347 356 358 359
  366 373 John Jr 275 Mary H
  44g Mr 359 Patrick W 269
  President 98 Thomas 44g 61g
SWAIN Ann 48g Francis 45 60 132
  134 160 161 320 322 George W
  269 Mr 160 Nicholas 45 60
  132 320 Richard 60 132
SWAMP LAND Clearing of 137
SWAN Katharine 44g Mary Hale
  44g Richard H 44g Richard

Wenman 44g
SWASEY Abigail 55g Abigail T 61g
 Apphia 44g 60g Apphiah 77g
 Benjamin 91 259 61g Betsy 52g
 Caroline 61g Catharine 57g
 Dorothy 36g 58g Dudley 60g
 Ebenezer 250 Ebenezer Jr 82g
 Edward 220 30g Elizabeth 60g
 77g Harriet 57g Harriot 45g
 Henry 258 Joseph 80 91 338 404
 36g 44g 45g Joseph Jr 45g
 Joseph 3d 82g Lois 50g Lu-
 cretia 45g 53g Lydia 45g 61g
 Mary 43g 44g 50g 61g Mary E
 57g Mr 405 Nathaniel 150 45g
 82g Olive 45g 52g Polly 81g
 Rebecca 53g Rufus 45g 61g
 Sally 30g Susan 59g Susanna 5g
 45g Thomas 60g Trueworthy 258
 W C 278 William 45g 61g
 William E 278 William L 61g
SWAZEY Abigail 77g Ebenezer 77g
 John 77g Thomas 77g
SWEAT Charlotte 55g
SWEET Eliphalet 258
SWETT Hannah 45g 80g John 250 45g
 John Barnard 388 Josiah 45g
 Mary S 45g Moses 181 45g Sam-
 uel 388 45g Samuel B 388 45g
 Simeon 205
SYLLA Mary 29g

TANNER George W 273 Jeremiah 263
 Seth 273
TAPPAN David 190 197 James M 278
TARBOX Dolly 45g Edwin Hill 45g
 William 45g
TASH Catherine 45g Charles G 398
 423 45g Esther 45g Lucy 45g
 Mary 45g Member Matilda 45g
 Oxford 398 45g Robert 45g
 Sally P 62g Susan 45g Thomas
 237 248 298 William G 45g 62g
TASSO 306
TAXATION Illegal, of Cranfield,
 Resisted 66
TAYLOR Abigail 80g Benjamin 138
 143 219 227 Betty 77g Brad-
 street 246 250 Daniel 253 77g
 Dolly 77g Edward 221 228
 Elizabeth 52g 80g George A 263
 John 222 234 421 457 77g John
 Poor 61g Joseph 61 135 143 228
 Joseph Jr 77g Josiah W 274
 Lydia 61g Margaret 61g Mary
 45g 77g Mary S 57g Nancy 61g
 Nathan 138 143 219 45g Nath-
 aniel 61g Osgood 77g Polly
 80g Rebecca 77g Sarah 52g
 77g Simon 258 Susanna 56g
 Theophilus K 204 Thomas 134
 William 61 135 138 143 160
 219 45g
TEBBETTS J I 278 Jonathan 271
 L F 278 Warren V B 278
TEDD John 45 61 148
TEMPERANCE ACTION OF TOWN 104
 106 108
TEMPLETON John 152 313
TENNEY Dr 383 Samuel 99 101 104
 126 150 151 313 331 338 382
 82g Tabitha 313 383
THACHER James 385
THAXTER Thomas 218
THAYER Deborah 61g Maria 62g
 Polly 33g Rebecca 59g Richard
 61g
THING 456 Abigail 46g 77g Alice
 46g Anna 47g 60g Bartholomew
 75 139 141 143 148 149 151
 179 180 181 224 227 353 392
 46g 47g Benjamin 71 143 151
 180 181 182 185 353 46g
 Betsey 47g Catharine 46g
 Coffin 46g 77g Daniel 144
 149 181 195 46g 47g Deborah
 46g 47g 77g Dudley 61g Ed-
 Ward 259 Elisabeth 77g
 Elizabeth 45g 46g 47g 52g
 Eunice 47g Family 392 Frederic F 266 George E 266
 George H 263 Joanna 18g 45g
 46g John 138 139 140 224 227
 234 7g 45g 46g John H 266
 Jonathan 61 65 67 68 70 116
 118 119 120 135 136 138 139
 144 148 149 151 167 171 176
 177 218 219 253 353 392 45g
 46g Jonathan Jr 61 116 136
 144 Joseph 91 140 144 149
 181 228 46g Josiah 46g 77g
 Josiah Jr 144 Levi 253 Lydia
 46g 61g Martha 46g 47g Mary
 17g 46g Mehitabel 7g Mehitable 47g Mercy 45g Nathaniel 144 235 246 250 251
 Pernal 46g Peter 231 Samuel
 70 138 140 141 144 148 149
 151 175 177 392 45g 46g 47g
 Sarah 46g 77g Sarah A 62g
 Stephen 91 95 47g Tristram
 46g Winthrop 91 46g 77g 82g

Zebulon G 62g
THOM Isaac 362 James 258 259 307 362
THOMAS 324 John 61
THOMPSON Anna 77g Anne 47g 61g
  Benjamin B 290 Catharine 57g
  David D 62g Ebenezer 92 John
  47g 61g 77g Joseph Miller 47g
  Lydia 77g Mary 77g Mary E 62g
  Matthew 228 Mr 463
THOMSON Robert C 426
THORNTON Mattew 87 92
THURSTEN Ann 61g Ephraim 61g Samuel 64g
THURSTON Abner 144 182 229 249
  250 251 Anna 62g 77g Anne 61g
  Caleb 234 248 Caleb Jr 61g
  Daniel 47g 82g Deborah 47g
  Elizabeth 54g 61g Elizabeth
  Gilman 47g Ephraim 77g Eugene
  273 278 George R 276 Hannah
  80g Ichabod 77g James 150 252
  61g 77g Joanna 62g John 234
  John O 263 Martha 77g 79g Mary
  61g 81g Mary J 56g Mary Jane
  47g Moses 61g Nathaniel K 62g
  Oliver 82g Pheebe 60g Reuben
  82g Sarah 61g Sarah A 62g
THURTON 67 Thomas 66
THYING 343 George E 271
TILTON 456 Abigail 60g Amy Folsom
  47g Caroline 9g 48g 51g Caroline C 61g Catharine 47g 48g
  58g 61g Charlotte 35g 48g 59g
  Daniel 80 86 150 250 77g David
  82g Dorothy 42g 48g 60g Ebenezer 47g Elijah 61g Elisabeth
  77g Elizabeth 47g Eunice 61g
  J Warren 427 Jacob 80 238
  Joanna 55g Joanna T 62g John
  47g 61g 62g John F 62g John
  Folsom 47g John Shackford 48g
  John W 205 Joseph 107 148 198
  287 300 362 381 425 9g 35g
  42g 47g 48g 61g 64g Joseph Jr
  104 152 Mark 259 Mary 6g 51g
  62g 77g Mrs Samuel 424 Nancy
  363 61g Patty 47g 61g Peter
  Gilman 77g Philip 245 Robert
  77g Samuel 205 47g Sarah 62g
  Sarah Ann 47g William 47g
  William P 274 Winthrop 62g
  Winthrop Odlin 47g
TIMBER TREES Respecting Cutting 52 53
TIPPER Bartholomew 62 151

TITCOMB Captain 249
TOLE Betsey 61g Simeon 61g
TOMPSON Rev Mr 28 William 158
TOPPAN Abraham 77g Christopher
  77g Edmund 299 Huldah 77g
  John 77g Samuel 77g Sarah J
  P 299
TOWLE Abraham 258 62g Adoniram
  J 150 48g Amos 48g Angelina
  48g 57g Betsey 48g Betsey L
  48g Betty 82g Charles H 151
  Elisha 62g Elizabeth 14g
  Emily B 48g Enoch W 48g 62g
  Hannah S 62g J Warren 377
  Ludovicus 258 Mary 62g Mary
  G 48g 61g Matthias 234
  Oliver 48g Oliver Jr 48g
  Susannah 62g Charles J 278
TOWN-HOUSE 109
TOWNSEND James D 62g Sally 81g
  Sarah W 62g
TRANSCRIPTS OF EXETER RECORDS
  Appendix II 435
TREADWELL 381 Thomas D 309
  William 62g
TREES Ornamental 415 Oldest Elm 415
TREFETHEREN George 82g
TREWORGY Elizabeth 351 James 351
TREWORTHY Elizabeth 16g
TRICKEY E D 206 Elizabeth Young
  80g Mary Wilson 81g
TUCK 375 Amos 152 300 313 370
  377 410 Edward 372 Ellen 372
  Lavina 62g Love 80g Mr 371
  372 Perley 62g Sarah 37g
TUCKE E Frank 376
TUCKER Hannah 61g
TUFTS Dolly 33g Henry 256 James
  A 299
TURNER Samuel F 274
TUTTLE Charles W 227 James 62g
  James H 266 James S 276
  Mar-a 62g Walter 389
TWILIGHT William H 263
TWOMBLY Joseph 62g Shuah 62g
TYLER Laban A 62g Mary 62g
  Thomas 61 91 257
TYRRELL John 148 347

UNDERHILL 17 456 463 Abigail
  62g Jo 14 John 16 40 Ned R 62g
UNDERWOOD Anna 62g James 62g
UNITARIAN SOCIETY AND PASTORS 208

UNIVERSALIST SOCIETY AND PASTORS
203

VANDUZEE George H 275 John C 275
VANE 451 455 Henry 39 454
VARNEY A H 389
VAUGHAN Geo 434 William 68 434
VEASEY Daniel 259 Edward 66g
  George 139 64g 65g 66g Henry
  278 Jeremiah 230 77g Mary 65g
  Samuel 77g Thomas 139 Wheelock
  G 278
VICKERY Betty 77g Elijah 246 248
  64g 77g Hannah 77g Joshua 77g
  78g Judith 78g 82g Lydia 64g
  Nabby 77g Samuel 77g Sarah 77g
  William 64g
VINAL G A W 278 W D 389
VINES Rich^d 434

WADARGASCOM 433 434
WADE Edward 251
WADLEIGH 144 352 406 407 Abigail
  167 48g Abraham 250 78g Ann
  48g Anna 64g 48g Benjamin 48g
  Captain 174 Edward 78g Elisabeth 78g Elizabeth 48g 62g 82g
  George A 278 Hannah 48g Henry
  138 144 149 175 48g James P
  278 John 37 61 64 137 149 171
  248 250 253 254 398 405 406
  62g 78g 82g John M 151 Joseph
  Jr 230 Jonathan 75 120 138 144
  149 174 179 180 219 64g Jona-
  than Jr 144 Jonathan B 63g
  Joseph 61 64 137 48g Joseph B
  273 Joseph D 150 Lydia 78g
  Martha 48g Mary 78g Philip 288
  Rachel 48g Robert 61 64 68 136
  137 138 151 171 174 351 48g
  Robert Sr 144 Sally 62g Sarah
  168 48g 63g 78g Satira D 59g
  William 152 62g
WAHANGNONAWITT 431 433
WAHANGNOWNAWIT 434
WAINWRIGHT W 278
WAIT Esther 62g Joseph 62g
WALDERNE Richard 117
WALDO Orin P 278
WALDRON 10 John 247 Major 119
  Richard 117 353
WALKER Dolly 62g Goodman 436 Henry
  278 J W 207 John 62g Martha
  54g Mary 62g Samuel 35 44 445
  Samuell 17 444 Seth 396
WALL James 8 18 36 45 50 51 114
  123 124 131 132 133 148 159
  320 436 444 445 Mary 36
WALLACE Catherine 59g Ceesar
  62g Dolly 62g Freeman 278
  George 62g Katy 62g Sally
  52g Spencer 245
WALLES James 18
WALLINGSFORD Cato 62g Margaret
  62g
WALLS James 437
WALSH Canon 208
WALTON Alice 36 Elizabeth 37g
  George 17 36 Nancy 37g Sam-
  uel 37g Shadrach 36 William
  H 278
WANTWORTH William 17
WAR FOR THE UNION 261 Exeter
  Soldiers in 261 277
WAR OF 1812 104 Exeter Soldiers
  in 257
WARBURTON Thomas 266
WARD Andrew 78g Benjamin 78g
  Catherine F 62g Daniel 78g
  Jonas 231 Mary 82g Nathaniel
  197 78g Richard B 62g Sarah
  78g
WARDALL Sargant 446 Thomas 444
  445
WARDELL Alice 37 Benjamin 36
  Eliakim 36 Elizabeth 36
  Martha 36 Meribah 37 Samuel
  36 Thomas 12 18 36 37 42 44
  46 436 442 Uzell 37 Willia
  18 William 12 37 436 437
WARDLE Thomas 438
WARE Henry 294 Henry Jr 312
WARNER Colonel 335
WARREN Charles 388 Deborah 64g
  65g Edward 278 Edward W 63g
  John 61 116 123 133 134 135
  148 162 320 322 385 64g 65g
  Malinda 63g Peggy 15g 54g
  Thomas 61 Thomas Jr 135
WASHINGTON 100 103 328 394
  General 247 George 99
WATER WORKS 110
WATERS Deborah 62g George F 152
  Herbert 24g 48g Mary 24g 48g
  Thomas 62g
WATOHANTOWET 14 25
WATSON Anne 53g Betsy 62g Daniel
  254 David 82g David Jr 62g
  Dudley 91 248 Elizabeth 80g
  Irvin M 266 John 62g Lucretia
  62g Sarah 80g Stephen 253
  Thomas 231 Winthrop 78g

WEARE Meshech 92 287
WEBB Deborah 52g John 62g Polly 62g Samuel 234 William 62g 82g
WEBBER John 258
WEBSTER 362 Benjamin 258 Betsey 81g Daniel 294 418 Deborah 4g 14g Elizabeth 4g 13g 50g 64g George B 347 348 Jacob 254 Nathaniel 144 180 181 Samuel 310 Susanna 64g Thomas 139 140 144 149 181 246 248 249 250 254 4g 14g 64g
WEDGEWOOD John 53 61 226
WEDGWOOD Frances D 31g
WEED Dan 62g Lucy 62g
WEEKS Abigail 62g Augustus H 148 Dudley 78g Elizabeth 62g Elizabeth A 50g H 278 Harriet B 62g Henry A 278 J E G 278 James 62g James Jr 63g Jeremiah S 266 John 254 78g John E G 273 John S 278 Joshua W Jr 270 Josiah 91 62g Mary 56g Matthias 78g Nathaniel 343 62g Nathaniel 2d 278 Polly 62g Sarah 63g
WEHANOWNAWIT 10 14
WEHANOWNOWIT 9 Sagamore of Piskatoquake 8
WEIGHT 39 Thomas 436 443 444 445
WEIT Tho 445
WELCH Oliver 314
WELLS John 231 John S 347 348 373 376 377 Luke 220 Mr 374
WENBOURNE 38 Elizabeth 37 John 37 Willis 18 William 37 44 46
WENTFORD William 436
WENTWORTH Benjamin 82g Benning 423 Elder 38 170 George A 296 299 314 Governor 240 243 John 241 239 417 Joshua 337 Lewis 258 Mary 52g Shuah 62g William 38 169 170 431 433 444 445
WEST Benjamin 359 Esther G 63g Jonathan P 63g Josiah R 63g Sarah 63g William 275
WESTON 461 George W 290 348 426 John P 276
WETHERELL G W 427
WHEELER Elbert 342
WHEELEWRIGHT John 432 436
WHEELWRIGHT 7 8 11 12 13 14 16 21 22 23 24 25 26 27 28 29 30 31 32 33 34 35 36 38 39 40 48 49 108 111 112 116 132 160 172 217 427 431 453 454 455 456 457 460 John 4 5 8 9 10 19 38 131 155 312 314 453 Marie 5 Mary 12 Mr 6 131 155 156 157 158 159 169 452 462 464 465 Mrs 28
WHELEWRIGHT 432 John 17 431 433 434
WHELWRIGHT Mr 445 446
WHIDDEN Celestia W 63g Foster G 63g James 78g Nabby 78g Rose 55g
WHIPPLE Oliver M 330
WHITCOMB Elizabeth 53g
"WHITE CAPS" The 411
WHITE Alvan 63g Alvin 330 John 267 287 62g Joseph L 62g Lydia 62g Mary P 62g Stephen 270 Susan 63g Woodbury C 271
WHITEFIELD 185 417 George 186 196 198 424 Mary P 62g Nancy J 51g
WHITEHOUSE W 278
WHITFIELD Joseph 62g Joseph M 399 Nancy 62g
WHITING Leonard 288 Mr 177
WHITMORE Lydia 22g
WHITRIDGE William 61
WHITTEM Thomas J 311
WHITTEMORE Elizabeth J 63g Hiram 63g
WHITTIER 33
WHITTUM John 234
WIGGEN Capt 65g
WIGGENS Capt 45
WIGGIN Ammi R 150 Andrew 65 149 377 Benjamin 62g Benjamin Jr 258 Bradstreet 149 Comfort 62g David 78g Deborah 54g Elizabeth 53g George W 342 348 Gideon 82g Hannah 82g J F 342 Joanna 62g Jonathan 139 Joseph 78g Joseph Jr 82g Joseph F 377 Joshua 62g Josiah 234 Mark 248 Martha 46g 81g Mary 65g Mary A 62g Nathaniel 78g Polly 51g S 331 Simon 100 149 174 176 177 343 62g Thomas 3 4 13 51 112 116 120 121 136 151 163 175 434 46g William 258
WIGGINS Andrew 218 Anne 61g Captain 130 Captaine 435 Judith 51g Sarah 54g
WIGGONS Capt 45
WIGHT Thomas 17 39 45 132
WIGONS Captanie 445

www.ingramcontent.com/pod-product-compliance
Lightning Source LLC
Chambersburg PA
CBHW071132300426
44113CB00009B/950